Adobe Photoshop Lightroom CC/6

The Missing FAQ

Real Answers to Real Questions asked by Lightroom Users

Victoria Bampton

Lightroom Queen Publishing

Adobe Photoshop Lightroom CC/6—The Missing FAQ

Publication Date 29 May 2015
File Identifier 2015-05-29-PDF

ISBN 978-1-910381-01-4 (eBook Formats)
ISBN 978-1-910381-02-1 (Paperback)

Cover photo - Quilters Vault, Southampton, UK. Built in the late 1200's, this wine vault is the largest of the merchant's vaults beneath Southampton. The photo was shot as 2 images, one exposed for the highlights and one for the shadows, and then merged to HDR using Lightroom CC/6. The resulting file was tone mapped in the Develop module, converted to B&W and a blue tone added using the Split Toning panel.

Acknowledgments

A lot of people have contributed to this project, and although I'd love to thank everyone personally, the acknowledgments would fill up the entire book. There are some people who deserve a special mention though.

I couldn't go without thanking the Lightroom team at Adobe, especially Tom Hogarty, Sharad Mangalick, Jeff Tranberry, Thomas Knoll, Eric Chan, Josh Bury, Simon Chen, Julie Kmoch, Ben Warde, Kelly Castro and Becky Sowada, who have willingly answered my endless questions.

It's been a very long couple of years, rewriting this entire book, and my heartfelt thanks go to Paul McFarlane, who did a great job of editing and proof-reading once again, and who kept me going when I was ready to give up.

Thanks are also due to the team of Lightroom Gurus, who are always happy to discuss, debate and share their experience, especially Jeff Schewe, Martin Evening, Andrew Rodney, Peter Krogh, Ian Lyons, Sean McCormack, John Beardsworth, Lee Jay Fingersh, Mark Sirota, Geoff Walker, Gene McCullagh, George Jardine, Gilles Theophile, Piet Van den Eynde, Jeffrey Friedl, Rikk Flohr, Laura Shoe, Jim Wilde, Jim Michaelsen and the rest of the crew!

I'm also grateful to the members of Lightroom Forums and Adobe Forums, who constantly challenge me with questions, problems to solve, and give me ideas for this book. Special thanks go to our forum members who freely give of their time in supporting others.

And finally I have to thank you, the Reader. Yet again, many of the changes in the book are based on the suggestions and questions that you've sent in. It's your book. The lovely emails I've received, and the reviews you post online, make all the late nights and early mornings worthwhile—so thank you.

Victoria Bampton—Southampton, UK, May 2015

TABLE OF CONTENTS

INTRODUCTION

Adobe® Photoshop® Lightroom™ 1.0 was released on February 19th 2007, after a long public beta period, and it rapidly became a hit. Thousands of users flooded the forums looking for answers to their questions. In the years that have followed, Lightroom has continued to gain popularity, becoming the program of choice for amateur and professional photographers alike.

Google now turns up more than 30,000,000 web pages when you search for the word Lightroom. So when you have a question or you get stuck with one of Lightroom's less intuitive features, where do you look? Do you trawl through thousands of web pages looking for the information you need? Perhaps post on a forum, wait hours for anyone to reply, and hope they give you the right information? From now on, you look right here! *Adobe Photoshop Lightroom CC/6 - The Missing FAQ* is a compilation of the questions most frequently asked - and many not so frequently asked - by real users on forums all over the world.

Unlike many 'how-to' books, this isn't just the theory of how Lightroom is supposed to work, but also the workarounds and solutions for the times when it doesn't behave in the way you'd expect. We're going to concentrate on real-world use, and the information you actually need to know.

I know you're intelligent (after all, you chose to buy this book!), and I'll assume you already have some understanding of computers and digital photography. Unlike the other books, I'm not going to tell you what you 'must' do. I'm going to give you the information you need to make an informed decision about your own workflow so you can get the best out of Lightroom.

Two of my favorite comments about this series of books are "it's like

A MAJOR REWRITE

I've spent the last two years completely rewriting the book, so if you've read previous versions, you'll notice some changes. (All good, I hope!)

Easier for New Users

When I wrote the early FAQ books, they were designed as a reference book for experienced photographers moving over from Adobe Camera Raw in Photoshop and trying to get used to working with a database. Over the years, Lightroom's audience has changed. There's now a wide range of photographers using Lightroom, from those just starting out to others who shot medium format film. As a result, my primary focus with this release is to make the information accessible to less experienced users, without losing any of the advanced geeky detail, so the book's useful to you throughout your whole Lightroom journey.

A Complete Reference

Over the years, the books have grown organically. As new features have been added, I've delved into them in detail for upgraders, but some of the original output modules were missing information for beginners. I've been through the whole program with a fine tooth comb, ensuring that all of the sliders are explained in this release, so you have a complete reference. The main entry for each slider name is in bold to make it easy to spot when you're in a hurry.

Workflow Chapter Order

As the books started out purely as an FAQ, the questions were grouped by module and topic, and you had to skip around the book following the cross-references to find related information. With this release, the chapters follow a typical workflow so most of the related information is grouped together. There are still a few clickable cross-references in the text, but they refer to whole chapters or sections of information that would be redundant if repeated.

Color Print

As with my previous books, I'm still self-publishing, having turned down multiple offers from publishers. This means I have full control over the content, and can offer upgrade discounts and free eBooks, which wouldn't be possible with a large publishing house. A workable solution for color print and distribution has finally become available, so I'm thrilled to be able to release this book in color print. They're still printed on demand in the US and UK, so it's not a glossy paper, but it's a huge step up from the previous black and white print.

Easier to Find

It's a big book, so we've spent many weeks working on a brand new index to make it easy to find the information you need. (And if you go hunting for a word that isn't in there, let me know so I can add it!)

a conversation with a trusted friend" and "it's like having Victoria sit next to you helping." That's my aim - I'm here to help.

THE BOOK FORMAT

Let's just do a quick guided tour so you can get the best out of the book...

The Fast Track for Beginners

Lightroom's a big program these days, and when you're just getting started, it can be overwhelming. Have you heard of the Pareto principle or 80/20 rule? In short, the idea is that 20% of the effort creates 80% of the results. But when you're just starting out, it's hard to know which information you need to understand, so I've done the work for you.

Starting on page 7, the Fast Track weaves its way through the book, giving you the essential information you need to get started. At the end of each Fast Track section is a page reference and clickable link which takes you to the next Fast Track section, so you can either read the book cover to cover, or you can follow the Fast Track to understand the basics, and then dive into the rest of the book to round out your knowledge, or use it as a reference when you have a question.

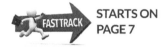

STARTS ON PAGE 7

Workflow Order

If you read the book cover to cover, I'll lead you through a typical workflow. It begins with getting your photos and videos into Lightroom, then viewing them, selecting the best photos, grouping them, adding metadata and filtering the photos. Next, we move on to editing your photos, both in the Develop module and external editors, and then outputting the photos as individual images, emails, publishing them on social media websites or creating slideshows, prints, web galleries and books. Finally, we discuss how to access your photos on multiple computers or mobile devices.

Index

If you're using the book as a reference, you can find the information you need in index at the back of the book. In the eBook formats, you can also use the search facility or bookmarks to find the specific words, and you can add your own bookmarks and notes too.

Appendix

In Appendix A, which is only available in the eBook formats, we explore the pros and cons of the DNG format and other geeky topics such as how to use the DNG Profile Editor and Lens Profile Creator, how to hack the TranslatedStrings.txt file and how to import from other software. Appendix B contains a list of the new features added to each Lightroom release over the years, in case you've skipped a version or two. These lists are also available on my website at http://www.Lrq.me/whatsnew/

Shortcuts

Many controls can be accessed in multiple different ways—buttons in the UI, menu commands, context-sensitive menus and keyboard shortcuts. If I listed every single one, you'd be bored stiff, so I've noted the most frequently used (and most easily remembered) options and listed the shortcuts in the sidebars. You can download the complete keyboard shortcuts list from http://www.Lrq.me/keyboard-shortcuts/

Sidebars

In the sidebars, you'll find additional useful information, links to plug-ins and other add-ons to speed up your workflow.

Links

The links in the eBooks are all clickable. In order to keep the website links current, and make them easy for you to access, I've used my own short-url domain http://www.Lrq.me (that's LRQ.ME) to handle the redirections. There's a full list of links at http://www.Lrq.me/lr6-links

Multiple Formats

You can choose how to you wish to read the book - PDF, ePub, Kindle, Paperback, or all 4! You might want the PDF version on your computer for searching while you work with Lightroom, the Kindle version for reading cover-to-cover while relaxing in the garden, and the paperback for scribbling extra notes. It's up to you.

eBook Images

The ePub or Kindle versions are optimized for viewing on eReaders, and many eReaders also allow you to click on screenshots to see a larger view. If you're viewing on a computer, I'd recommend using

REGISTER YOUR BOOK FOR ADDITIONAL BENEFITS

If you purchased the paperback from Amazon, Barnes&Noble or another retailer, register your copy of this book to download all the eBook formats and get access to updates, as well as gaining access to other member benefits. To learn more, turn to page 576.

the PDF format, because window scaling can make the screenshots difficult to read, and Amazon apply additional compression to images in the Kindle format. I've retained the real page numbers for all page references, so you can easily check them in the paperback edition as well as the eBooks.

Windows or Mac?

It doesn't matter whether you're using the Windows or Mac platform, or even both. Lightroom is cross-platform, and therefore this book will follow the same pattern. The screenshots are mainly of the Mac version because I'm writing on a Mac, but the Windows version is almost identical in functionality, and any significant differences will be explained and illustrated.

Where keyboard shortcuts or other commands differ by platform, both are included. The exception is the shortcut to view a context-sensitive menu, which is right-click on Windows or Ctrl-click on Mac. I'll keep that simple and just refer to right-clicking. If you use a trackpad on a Mac, right-click is a two-finger tap and dragging two fingers up or down the trackpad is the same as scrolling.

TALK TO ME!

This book is based entirely around user feedback, so I'd love to hear the things you like about this book, and anything you feel could be improved. I'm always looking for ways to make this book even better, so if you come across a question that I've missed, something that's not clear, or you just want to tell me how much you love the book, you can email me at members@lightroomqueen.com (start the subject with LRCC/6) or send me a note through the Lightroom CC/6 Premium Email Support page in the Premium Members Area for priority attention (see page 576). I do reply!

If you enjoy the book, posting a review on Amazon or your favorite

---

HELP SHORTCUTS

Lightroom Help Files	F1
Module Help	Ctrl Alt / / Cmd Opt /
Main Module Shortcuts	Ctrl / / Cmd /

online bookstore would make my day, and would help other Lightroom users find it too. Thank you!

Now, where shall we start...?

FAST TRACK INDEX

BEFORE YOU START

If you're anything like me, the first thing you want to do with a new program is dive right in. Who wants to read an instruction manual when you can experiment? If you're nodding in agreement, that's fine, but do yourself a favor and just skim through the Fast Track before you jump in head first.

Lightroom's designed around a database, so it doesn't work in the same way as most other image editing software. You'll save yourself a lot of headaches by understanding the basics!

DESIGNING YOUR WORKFLOW

Before we start using the software itself, let's talk briefly about workflow. It's one of the most popular topics among photographers, but why? What does it actually mean?

The term workflow simply describes a series of steps undertaken in the same order each time. For photographers, this workflow runs from the time of shooting (or even before), through transferring the photos to your computer, sorting and selecting your favorites, editing and retouching them, and then outputting to various formats, whether on screen or in print.

The initial aim for your workflow is consistency. If you do the same thing in the same order every time, you reduce the risk of mistakes. Files won't get lost or accidentally deleted, metadata won't get missed, and you won't end up redoing work that you've already completed **(Figure 2.1)**

There is no perfect workflow for everyone, as everyone's needs are different. The Fast Track sections of this book guide you through a simple workflow, but outside of the Fast Track, we'll also consider other workflow variations and the thought processes behind them, so you can start to build your own ideal workflow. I've also included a diagram of my personal workflow to help get you started. **(Figure 2.2)**

Once you've settled on a good workflow, that isn't the end of the story. You'll likely find that you continue to tweak it, finding slightly more efficient ways of doing things. It'll continue to build with time and experience, as well as with the introduction of new technology. The principles, however, remain the same.

For now, though, let's take a quick overview of the path we'll take...

▽**Figure 2.1** These are the basic workflow elements.

Basic Workflow Elements

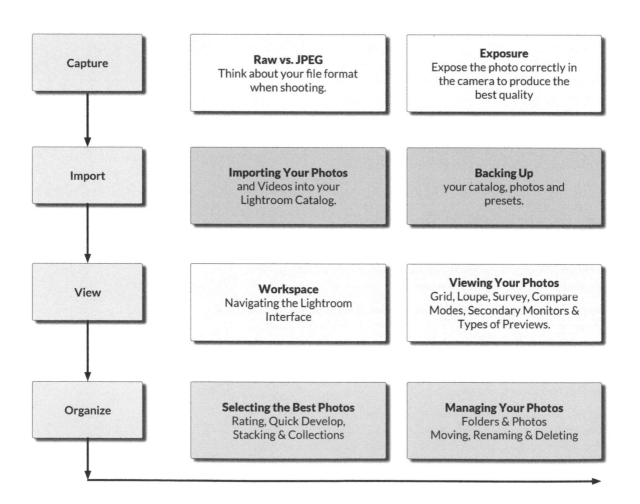

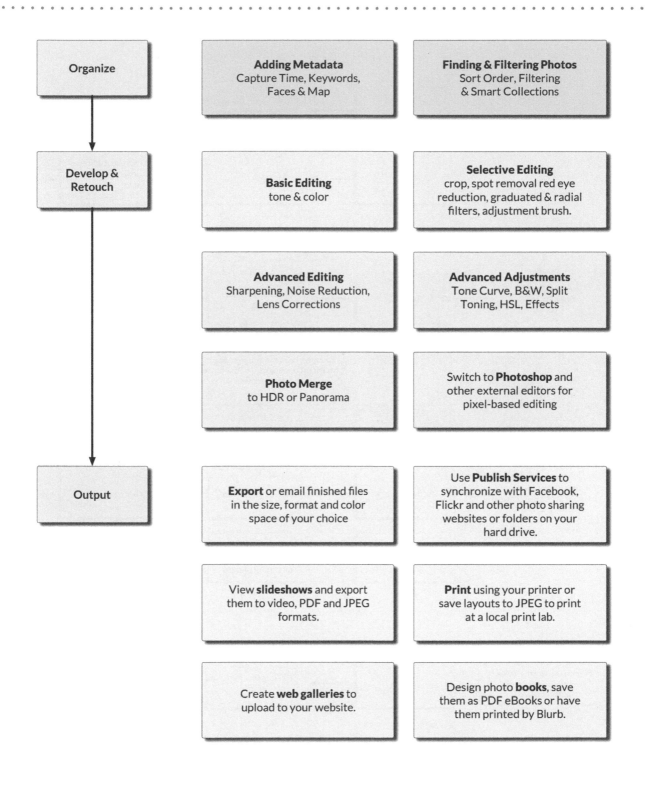

Organize

Adding Metadata
Capture Time, Keywords,
Faces & Map

Finding & Filtering Photos
Sort Order, Filtering
& Smart Collections

**Develop &
Retouch**

Basic Editing
tone & color

Selective Editing
crop, spot removal red eye
reduction, graduated & radial
filters, adjustment brush.

Advanced Editing
Sharpening, Noise Reduction,
Lens Corrections

Advanced Adjustments
Tone Curve, B&W, Split
Toning, HSL, Effects

Photo Merge
to HDR or Panorama

Switch to **Photoshop** and
other external editors for
pixel-based editing

Output

Export or email finished files
in the size, format and color
space of your choice

Use **Publish Services** to
synchronize with Facebook,
Flickr and other photo sharing
websites or folders on your
hard drive.

View **slideshows** and export
them to video, PDF and JPEG
formats.

Print using your printer or
save layouts to JPEG to print
at a local print lab.

Create **web galleries** to
upload to your website.

Design photo **books**, save
them as PDF eBooks or have
them printed by Blurb.

My Personal Workflow

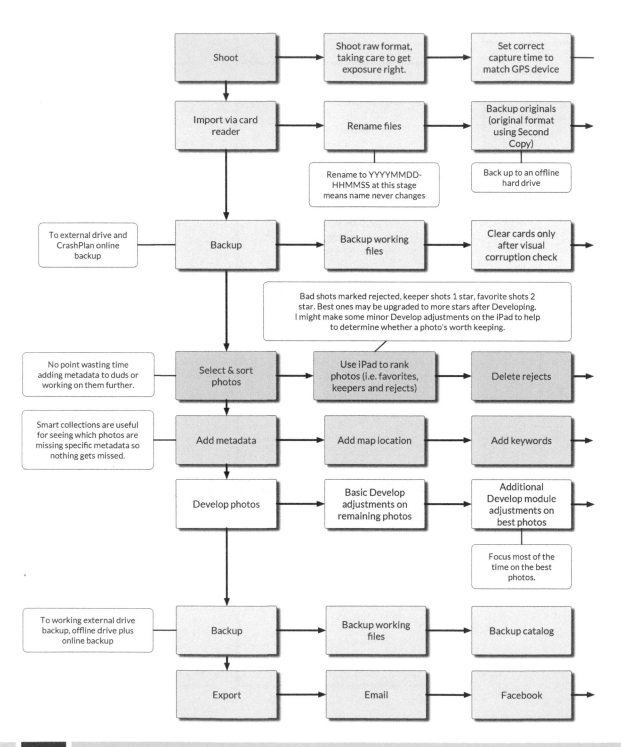

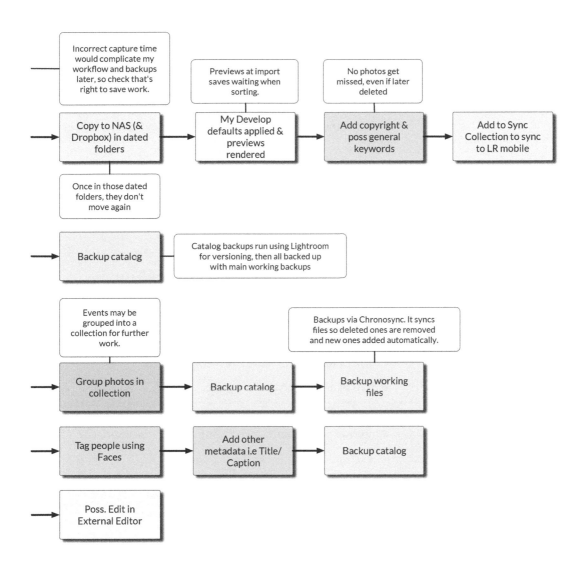

Incorrect capture time would complicate my workflow and backups later, so check that's right to save work.

Previews at import saves waiting when sorting.

No photos get missed, even if later deleted

Copy to NAS (& Dropbox) in dated folders

My Develop defaults applied & previews rendered

Add copyright & poss general keywords

Add to Sync Collection to sync to LR mobile

Once in those dated folders, they don't move again

Backup catalog

Catalog backups run using Lightroom for versioning, then all backed up with main working backups

Events may be grouped into a collection for further work.

Backups via Chronosync. It syncs files so deleted ones are removed and new ones added automatically.

Group photos in collection

Backup catalog

Backup working files

Tag people using Faces

Add other metadata i.e Title/ Caption

Backup catalog

Poss. Edit in External Editor

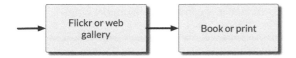

Flickr or web gallery

Book or print

Figure 2.2 This is my personal workflow. Your workflow won't look exactly the same, but it'll share the same principles.

INSTALLING LIGHTROOM

Just in case you haven't installed Lightroom CC/6 yet, we'll briefly run through the installation and upgrade processes, as well as extending Lightroom using plug-ins. If you're already up and running, you can move on to the next chapter starting on page 23.

Lightroom 6 is available as part of the Creative Cloud subscription or as a standard perpetual license. The program itself is essentially the same in either case. It's just the installation and update process that differs.

Minimum System Requirements

The minimum system requirements for installing Lightroom CC/6 are:

Windows

- Intel® Pentium® 4 or AMD Athlon® 64 processor
- DirectX 10–capable or later graphics card
- 64-bit versions of Microsoft® Windows 7 with Service Pack 1 or later
- 2 GB of RAM (4 GB minimum recommended)
- 2 GB of available hard-disk space
- 1024x768 display
- Internet connection required for Internet-based services

SUBSCRIPTION VS. PERPETUAL LICENSE

Subscription	Perpetual License
$10 per month	$149
Free upgrades	$79 upgrade for new releases
Includes Lightroom & Photoshop	Lightroom only
Includes LR Mobile Sync Space	LR Mobile not available
Download only	Download/boxed (updates are downloads)
Some parts (Develop, Map, Mobile Sync) stop working when you stop paying	Continues working indefinitely
New features in dot releases	Bug fixes and new camera/lens support only

Mac

- Multicore Intel® processor with 64-bit support (that's all Intel Macs apart from the original Core Duo)

- Mac OS X 10.8 (Mountain Lion) or later (Mac OS X 10.9 (Mavericks) or later required for GPU support)

- 2 GB of RAM (4 GB minimum recommended)

- 2 GB of available hard-disk space

- 1024x768 display

- Internet connection required for Internet-based services

That is the absolute minimum required in order to actually install Lightroom, but it is likely to 'walk' rather than run on these specs! Lightroom does benefit from higher specification hardware.

GPU support

Many GPU's, from integrated graphics to high end cards, can benefit from the new GPU support in the Develop module, although buggy drivers and underpowered cards may force Lightroom to disable GPU support or cause performance problems. The benefits are most noticeable on high resolution screens, such as 4K and 5K displays.

There is a point of diminishing returns. If you're looking to buy a new graphics card for a Windows machine, a recent generation 2 GB mid-range graphics card is an excellent choice. At the time of writing, these include the AMD R9 2XX series and Nvidia GeForce GTX 700 and 900 series. On a recent Mac, integrated graphics will work great as long as you have enough RAM available, but a discrete graphics card is a better long term investment.

Installing Lightroom

If you want to trial Lightroom CC/6 before purchasing, visit http://www.Lrq.me/cctrial and follow the instructions on screen. The trial uses the Creative Cloud app to manage the installation.

If you have a Creative Cloud subscription, click on the Creative Cloud icon in the System Tray (Windows) / Menubar (Mac) and select the *Apps* tab. Scroll down to Lightroom and press *Install*. **(Figure 2.2)**

If you don't have the Creative Cloud desktop app installed, log in to your account at http://creative.adobe.com and select the *Desktop Apps* from the menu. Find Lightroom and click the *Download* button. It prompts you to install the Creative Cloud desktop app, and then you can follow the previous instructions.

If you've purchased a perpetual license, you can convert the

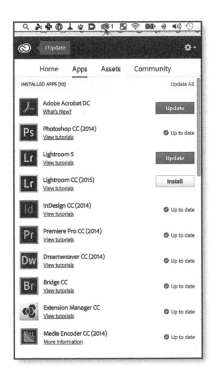

Figure 2.2 The Creative Cloud Desktop app allows you to easily install and update Adobe software.

UPGRADING?

If you're upgrading from a previous Lightroom version, skip to page 17.

LANGUAGES

Lightroom's not just limited to English—it's also available in Chinese Simplified, Chinese Traditional, Dutch, French, German, Italian, Japanese, Korean, Portuguese, Spanish, or Swedish.

To switch to another language, go to *Edit menu* (Windows) / *Lightroom menu* (Mac) > *Preferences > General tab*, select the language you want to use and then restart Lightroom.

Some keyboard shortcuts don't work on international keyboards. In Appendix A starting on page A-22, you'll find instructions for editing the keyboard shortcuts. If that looks a little daunting, there's a plug-in called Keyboard Tamer, which not only allows you to change existing keyboard shortcuts, but can also create some additional keyboard shortcuts. http://www.Lrq.me/armes-kbtamer

Lightroom CC trial to a Lightroom 6 perpetual version by following the instructions here: http://www.Lrq.me/lr6activate

If you don't have the trial installed, a download link is provided with your purchase. This skips the Creative Cloud app and provides a basic installer (a .exe file for Windows or a .pkg file inside a .dmg file for Mac).

Opening Lightroom

On Windows, go to the desktop and double-click on the *Adobe Lightroom* shortcut or single-click on the Adobe Lightroom tile in the Start screen (Windows 8).

On Mac, go to the Launchpad and click on *Adobe Lightroom*, or go to the Applications folder, click on the *Adobe Lightroom* folder and then double-click on the *Adobe Lightroom* app to open the application. Once it's open, right-click on the icon in the dock and select *Options menu > Keep in Dock* if you prefer a dock icon.

Activation

Lightroom CC/6 now requires online activation, and it allows activation on two machines at any time (although you can have it installed on more computers). The activation process runs automatically while installing Lightroom, and all you need to do is remained signed in to your Adobe ID.

You don't need to remain connected to the internet after activation, so even traveling to remote areas isn't a problem. If you have a subscription, Lightroom needs to be able to 'phone home' at least every 99 days. If you have a perpetual license, Lightroom remains activated until you deactivate it.

If you need to switch computers, you can go to *Help menu > Sign Out* to deactivate a computer, but if you forget, don't worry. When you try to activate on a third computer, Lightroom warns that you're already activated on two machines and offers to deactivate them remotely.

Desktop App Usage Information

When you start Lightroom for the first time, it warns you that it'll send some usage information back to Adobe, to help them improve the program. This includes information about your Lightroom usage, but not your photos or other personal information.

If you don't want to share this information with Adobe, go to *Help*

MULTIPLE COMPUTERS

Lightroom's license agreement is cross-platform (both Windows and Mac) and it allows the main user to use Lightroom on two computers, for example, a desktop and a laptop.

Lightroom isn't designed to be used over a network. The Lightroom catalog needs to be stored on a locally attached drive (internal or external), and can only be used by one person at a time. The photos, however, can be stored on a network drive or NAS unit.

There are options for using your catalog on multiple machines, such as between your desktop and laptop. We'll explore the options in the Multiple Computers chapter starting on page 481.

menu > Manage My Account, log in, and select *Desktop App Usage Information* under *Security & Privacy*, then uncheck the checkbox.

Creating Your First Catalog

Once Lightroom's installed, there are very few differences between the Windows and Mac versions, apart from the slightly different appearance. We'll carry on using the Mac version for screenshots, but where there are notable differences, we'll show both. Let's get started...

If you haven't used Lightroom before, it asks where to store the catalog and how to name it. **(Figure 2.3)** This is important, because the catalog contains your Lightroom edits. By default, the catalog is called Lightroom Catalog.lrcat and it's stored in a Lightroom folder in your main Pictures folder.

Next to the catalog, Lightroom creates a Previews folder (Windows) / file (Mac) called Lightroom Catalog Previews.lrdata. The previews folder/file contains a small JPEG preview of all the photos you import so it can grow very large.

If you have plenty of space on your boot drive (usually C:\ on Windows or Macintosh HD on Mac), click *Continue* to select the default location.

DO I HAVE TO USE A CATALOG?

Lightroom always creates a catalog, but you can add the files at their existing location, so it doesn't have to turn your existing workflow upside-down. It's also possible to write some of the settings into the files themselves, or sidecar files for proprietary raw files, using a metadata format called XMP.

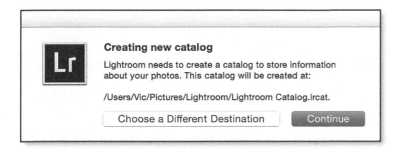

Figure 2.3 Lightroom asks where to store your new Lightroom catalog.

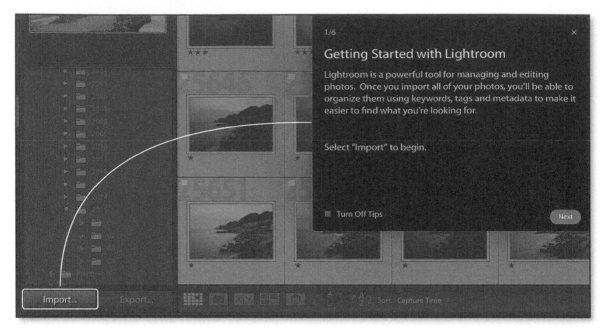

Figure 2.4 Tips appear in the center of the screen.

If your boot drive's low on space or you'd prefer an alternative location for your catalog, click *Choose a Different Destination* and select your chosen folder and catalog name. (The catalog must be stored on an internal or external hard drive, not network storage.)

Either way, make a note of the catalog name and location you choose, as you'll need to ensure these files are backed up.

If you have a subscription or you're running the trial, Lightroom asks whether you want to sync your photos. We'll come back to these options in more detail in the Sync chapter starting on page 565. If in doubt, turn it off for now.

Lightroom's main interface opens with some initial tips in the center of the screen. **(Figure 2.4)** These tips give you a quick guided tour of Lightroom. Press *Next* to view the tips or click anywhere else on the screen to hide them.

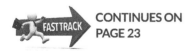

CONTINUES ON PAGE 23

A CLEAN SLATE

If you're just getting started with Lightroom, you may be 'playing,' and then decide to start again with a clean slate for your primary catalog. Rather than deleting everything from the catalog, consider storing that catalog somewhere safe, in case you want to go back to it, and create a new catalog using *File menu > New Catalog*.

If you later decide to delete the original catalog, simply find it in Explorer (Windows) / Finder (Mac) and delete the *.lrcat and * Previews.lrdata files, and any related backups too.

UPGRADING FROM EARLIER VERSIONS

If you're upgrading from a previous version (Lightroom 5 or earlier), you'll need to upgrade your catalogs in addition to upgrading the program. The good news is that's an easy process and any release version catalogs (1-5) can be upgraded to the Lightroom CC/6 catalog format.

How do I install the Lightroom upgrade?

If you have a Creative Cloud subscription, open the Creative Cloud app and click *Install* next to *Adobe Lightroom CC (2015)*.

If you prefer a perpetual license, you'll need to purchase the discounted upgrade license from Adobe's website (it's well hidden, but it is there!) and run the provided installer.

Installing the upgrade doesn't affect your existing Lightroom program installations or update your shortcuts/dock icons. You can choose to uninstall older versions when you're ready.

How do I upgrade my catalog for use in Lightroom CC/6?

Before you open Lightroom CC/6, make sure you have a current catalog backup, just in case something goes wrong. Proper measures have been put in place to avoid disasters, but you can never be too careful.

When you open Lightroom CC/6, it automatically finds your last-used Lightroom catalog and asks for permission to upgrade it. **(Figure 2.5)** This creates a copy of your Lightroom catalog, adds -2 to the end of

BACKWARDS COMPATIBILITY

Once you've upgraded your catalog, you won't be able to open the upgraded catalog in an earlier release. You'll still have your earlier catalog untouched, however if you work on the upgraded copy in Lightroom CC/6, for example, using a trial version, and then decide to go back to Lightroom 5 or earlier, the changes you've made to your photos in version 6 will not show up in your earlier catalog.

Figure 2.5 When you try to open an older Lightroom catalog, Lightroom asks for permission to upgrade it to the current format.

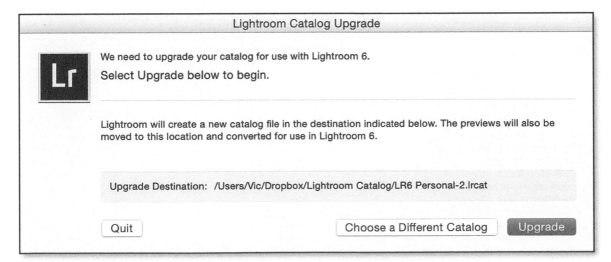

Lightroom Catalog Upgrade

We need to upgrade your catalog for use with Lightroom 6.
Select Upgrade below to begin.

Lightroom will create a new catalog file in the destination indicated below. The previews will also be moved to this location and converted for use in Lightroom 6.

Upgrade Destination: /Users/Vic/Dropbox/Lightroom Catalog/LR6 Personal-2.lrcat

Quit   Choose a Different Catalog   Upgrade

SKIPPED A VERSION

If you're upgrading from Lightroom 4 or earlier, the upgrade process may take a while as it adds additional information to the database, for example, the bit depth and color profile. Note that if the original files are offline, for example, on disconnected external hard drives, then that extra metadata will not be added to the catalog and can't easily be added later.

the catalog name, borrows the previews files from the earlier version, and upgrades the catalog format.

Your original catalog remains untouched, so you may want to move it to your backups folder once the upgrade is complete.

If Lightroom doesn't automatically find your catalog, or you want to upgrade a different one, go to *File menu > Open Catalog.*

DOT RELEASES

Lightroom's usually updated with new camera and lens support on a 3-4 monthly basis. The updates also include bug fixes, particularly in the early dot releases such as 6.1, so it's worth staying current with these updates.

How do I check which version I'm currently running?

To check which version you're running, go to the *Help menu > System Info* and the first line confirms the version and build number. **(Figure 2.6)**

How do I update to a newer Lightroom dot release?

If you have a Creative Cloud subscription, the updates appear automatically in the Creative Cloud system tray/menubar app.

If you have a perpetual license, Lightroom automatically checks for updates on a regular basis, or you can go to *Help menu > Check for Updates* at any time, to see if a new version has been released. Unlike earlier versions, the updates are now a patch installer rather than the whole program, so the downloads are much smaller.

Figure 2.6 The System Info dialog shows your current build number.

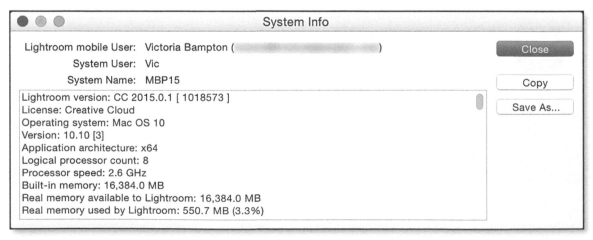

System Info		
Lightroom mobile User: Victoria Bampton ( )		Close
System User: Vic		Copy
System Name: MBP15		Save As...

Lightroom version: CC 2015.0.1 [1018573]
License: Creative Cloud
Operating system: Mac OS 10
Version: 10.10 [3]
Application architecture: x64
Logical processor count: 8
Processor speed: 2.6 GHz
Built-in memory: 16,384.0 MB
Real memory available to Lightroom: 16,384.0 MB
Real memory used by Lightroom: 550.7 MB (3.3%)

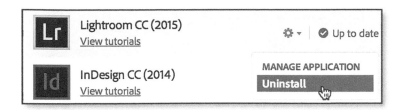

Figure 2.7 To uninstall, click the cog icon in the Creative Cloud app.

How do I uninstall Lightroom?

If you have the Creative Cloud app, the easiest option is to click the cog icon to the right of Adobe Lightroom and select *Uninstall*. **(Figure 2.7)**

Otherwise, on Windows, Lightroom uses a standard uninstaller, so just select *Control Panel > Programs & Features*, select *Adobe Lightroom* and click *Uninstall*.

Mac users are used to just dragging the app to the trash. Don't do that with Lightroom CC/6! That's fine for older versions, but Lightroom CC/6 now requires an uninstaller, and just trashing the app can create a mess. If you can't use the Creative Cloud app to uninstall, navigate to the *Applications folder > Adobe Lightroom* and select *Uninstall Adobe Lightroom* to run the uninstaller.

INSTALLING PLUG-INS

While we're talking about installation, we must also mention plug-ins. Plug-ins allow third-party developers to add additional functionality to Lightroom. They're written in Lua, and the SDK (Software Development Kit) is freely available from: http://www.Lrq.me/sdkdownload

There's a wide variety of plug-ins now available, doing everything from adding a List view to the Library module, to adding borders while exporting photos, to automatically uploading photos to various websites. I've mentioned my favorites in sidebars through the book, but you can find a longer list at http://www.Lrq.me/links/plugins

How do I install a plug-in?

Having downloaded the plug-in of your choice, you need to install it.

1. If the plug-in has a .zip extension, double-click to unzip it, and store it somewhere safe.

2. Go to *File menu > Plug-in Manager* to show the Plug-in Manager dialog. **(Figure 2.8)**

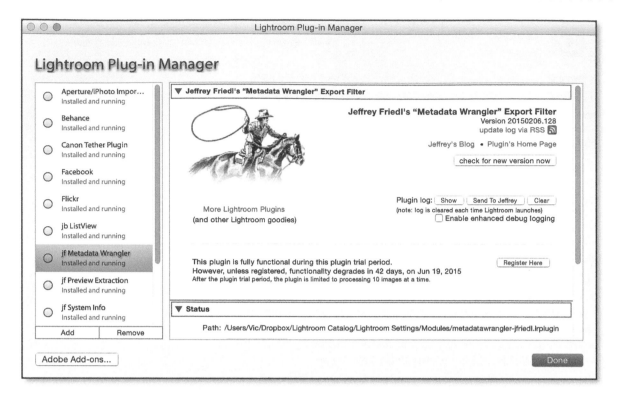

Figure 2.8 Plug-ins are installed and uninstalled using the Plug-in Manager dialog.

3. Click on the *Add* button in the lower-left corner.

4. Navigate to the *.lrplugin* or *.lrdevplugin* folder/file for the plug-in you would like to install. On Windows, you need to select the folder, rather than its contents, whereas .lrplugin files are a single package file on Mac.

5. Some plug-ins have additional instructions, for example, the LR/Mogrify plug-in also needs you to install the Mogrify application. Most developers include full installation instructions.

Where should I store my plug-ins?

It's a good idea to keep all of your plug-ins in one place, to make them easy to find, update, transfer, back up or delete. Creating a *Plug-ins* folder alongside the other presets folders would be an ideal place, and you can find that folder easily by going to *Preferences dialog > Presets tab* and clicking the *Show Lightroom Presets Folder* button.

How do I uninstall a plug-in?

To remove any plug-ins that you've installed by means of the *Add* button, simply select the plug-in in the Plug-in Manager dialog and press the *Remove* button. The *Remove* button isn't available for plug-ins stored in Lightroom's own Modules folder, such as the Tether plug-ins, in case you want to reinstall them later.

How do I use a plug-in?

Once you've installed the plug-in, it's ready to use. The way you access it depends on the individual plug-in, but each developer should provide instructions.

Some plug-ins that export directly to a different destination, such as LR/TreeExporter, show in the pop-up menu at the top of the Export dialog, where it usually says *Hard Drive*. They may also create their own panels in the Export dialog. **(Figure 2.9)**

▼**Figure 2.9** Some Export plug-ins appear in the pop-up at the top of the Export dialog. Other plug-ins create their own section in the bottom left corner of the Export dialog.

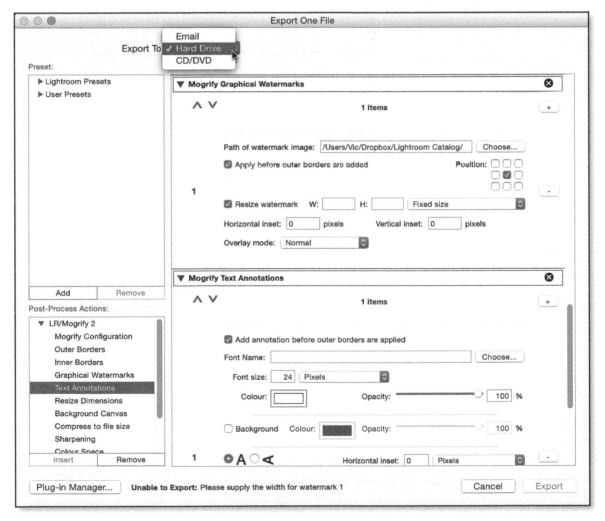

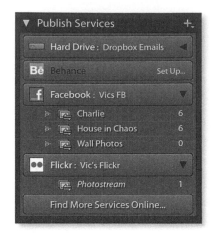

Some plug-ins, such as LR/Mogrify and Metadata Wrangler, appear in the Post-Process Actions section of the Export dialog, below the Export Presets. From there, you can choose which options you want to make available for your current export, for example, on LR/Mogrify, a single border. The plug-in panels that you choose then appear beneath the normal export panels.

Publish Service plug-ins appear in the Publish Services panel, like the built in Facebook and Flickr plug-ins. **(Figure 2.10)**

Most other Export Plug-ins have a menu listing under the *File menu* or *Library menu* in the Plug-in Extras section instead (yes, there are two different menus with the same name!).

Figure 2.10 Plug-ins for Publish Services appear in the Publish Services panel.

PLUG-IN SHORTCUTS

Plug-in Manager	Ctrl Alt Shift , / Cmd Opt Shift ,

Figure 2.11 The splash screen displays when you start Lightroom.

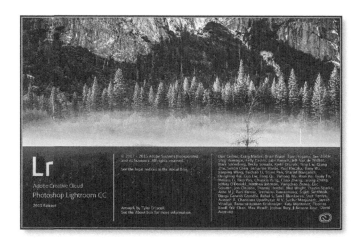

CUSTOM SPLASH SCREEN

The splash screen shows when you start Lightroom, **(Figure 2.11)** but if you'd prefer to display your own photo, create a folder called Splash Screen in the following locations, and put the photo inside.

Windows—C: \ Users \ [your username] \ AppData \ Roaming \ Adobe \ Lightroom \ Splash Screen

Mac—Macintosh HD / Users / [your username] / Library / Application Support / Adobe / Lightroom / Splash Screen

If you add multiple photos to this folder, Lightroom cycles through them.

To turn it off completely, uncheck **Show splash screen during startup** in Lightroom's Preferences dialog.

GETTING PHOTOS & VIDEOS INTO LIGHTROOM

As Lightroom is built around a database, the first thing you need to do is add the information about your photos and videos to this database. This process is called Importing, but don't let that confuse you. Although it's called Importing, the photos don't go 'into' Lightroom. A better word to describe the process might be reference, link, or register.

Importing the photos simply means that the metadata about the photos and videos is added to the database as text records, along with a link to that file on the hard drive and a small JPEG preview. It's like an index of the books in a library. **(Figure 3.1)** The library catalog tells you a little about the book and which shelf it's stored on, and maybe even gives you a preview of the cover, but it doesn't contain the book itself.

While you're importing the photos, Lightroom can copy or move the photos to a new location of your choice, but that's not required—if

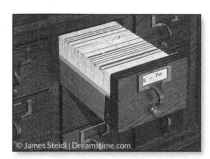

© James Steidl | Dreamstime.com

▲ **Figure 3.1** Like a manual library card catalog, Lightroom keeps track of where your photos and videos are stored, and information about them, but it doesn't contain the photos/videos themselves.

WHAT IS METADATA?

Metadata is often defined as 'data describing data'.

As far as photos are concerned, metadata describes how the photo was taken (camera, shutter speed, aperture, lens, etc.), who took the photo (copyright) and descriptive data about the content of the photo (keywords, caption).

Lightroom also stores all of your Develop edits as metadata, which means that it records your changes as a set of text instructions (i.e. Exposure +0.33, Highlights −30, Shadows +25, etc.) instead of applying them directly to the image data. This means you can edit the photo again later without degrading the image quality.

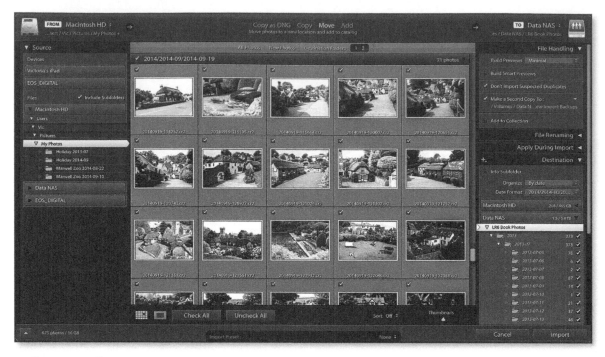

Figure 3.2 Photos are added to Lightroom's catalog using the Import dialog.

IMPORT FROM OTHER PROGRAMS

As a keen photographer, you likely already have a large number of photos stored on your hard drive. Those older photos can also be imported into your Lightroom catalog, either at their current location or while copying/moving them to a new location.

If your photos are already cataloged using other software, for example, Photoshop Elements, Aperture or iPhoto, read Appendix A starting on page A-28 before continuing.

the photos are already safely on your hard drive, Lightroom can reference them at their existing location instead.

Don't worry, importing photos into Lightroom doesn't mean you're locked in to using Lightroom forever. Your photos remain accessible to other software, most of the metadata can be written to the file in a standardized format that other software can understand (excluding Develop settings), and you can export the edited photos to standard image formats. You're in control.

When you initially open the Import dialog **(Figure 3.2)**, it may look a little overwhelming, but don't worry, it's simpler than it looks. There are three main decisions to make: where to find the photos (the source), how to handle the photos (copy/move/add) and if you're copying or moving the photos, where to put them (destination). The rest of the options are, well, optional!

First, we'll step through the basics of getting your photos into Lightroom, and then we'll go back through the individual elements of the Import dialog in more detail. Although we'll mainly refer to importing photos throughout the chapter, the instructions apply to videos too. Let's get started...

Importing Your Photos

1. If you're importing from a memory card, insert your memory card into the card reader or attach the camera to the computer. Card readers usually work more reliably with Lightroom than USB camera connections. By default, the Import dialog displays automatically when inserting a memory card.

   If you're importing from your hard drive, open the Import dialog by going to *File menu > Import Photos and Videos* or by pressing the **Import** button in the lower left corner of the Library module.

2. On the left of the Import dialog is the Source panel, with memory cards at the top and hard drives listed below.

   If you're importing from a memory card, click on its name. If you only have a single device (i.e. card reader, camera or phone) attached, it's selected automatically.

   If you're importing existing photos, navigate to the location of your photos in the lower *Files* section of the Source panel.

   If the photos are stored under a single folder, such as the My Photos folder in **Figure 3.3**, select that folder and check the *Include Subfolders* checkbox. If you have thousands of photos to import, it can help to break the import into smaller chunks, for example, 10,000 at a time.

   If your photos are spread across multiple folders, hold down Ctrl (Windows) / Cmd (Mac) while clicking on each folder, or hold down Shift while clicking on the first and last folder in a series of consecutive folders.

3. Thumbnails start to appear in the central preview area. They make take a while to appear if you have thousands of photos, but you don't need to wait for them to finish appearing before continuing. It's possible to view and check/uncheck photos in the Import dialog, but it's easier to sort through them in the Library module after import.

4. At the top of the Import dialog **(Figure 3.4)**, decide how to handle the files you're importing.

   If you're importing from a memory card, select *Copy, Move* and *Add* are automatically disabled when importing from a memory card.

   If you're importing from a hard drive, you have a choice: do you want to leave the photos where they are, or copy/move them to a new location?

   • To reference the photos at their existing location, select **Add**.

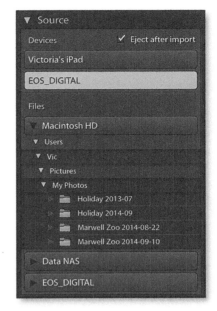

Figure 3.3 Select the memory card or folder of photos in the Source panel.

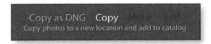

Figure 3.4 Select *Copy* at the top of the dialog to copy the photos to your hard drive, or *Add* to leave them in their current location.

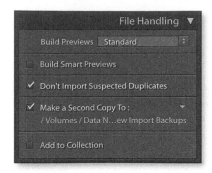

Figure 3.5 In the File Handling panel, choose your preview size and temporary backup location.

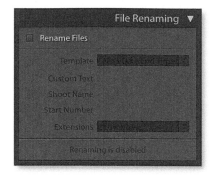

Figure 3.6 In the File Renaming panel, set a new file naming template, or leave it unchecked to retain the camera filename.

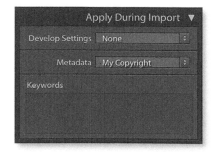

Figure 3.7 In the Apply During Import panel, add your copyright metadata.

This is a good choice if your photos are already arranged in a tidy folder structure that you'd like to keep.

- To let Lightroom move the photos to a new location and automatically reorganize them, select **Move**. This is most useful if your photos are spread across your hard drives in a slightly disorganized fashion.

- To leave the original photos alone and create a copy in the location you choose in the Destination panel, select **Copy**. You'll need twice as much hard drive space if you choose this option, as you'll be duplicating all of your photos, but it leaves your current system intact.

5. On the right-hand side of the Import dialog are a variety of different settings you can apply while importing the photos. We'll use some default settings to get started, and explore the options in more detail later in the chapter.

6. In the File Handling panel **(Figure 3.5)**, set the following:

    - **Build Previews**—*Standard*. If you're importing thousands of photos, select *Embedded & Sidecar* instead. It's quicker initially but stores lower quality previews).

    - **Build Smart Previews**—unchecked.

    - **Don't Import Suspected Duplicates**—checked.

    - **Make a Second Copy**—If you're importing existing photos, leave it unchecked. If you're importing from a memory card, check it then click on the file path and choose a location on another hard drive as a temporary backup.

    - **Add to Collection**—unchecked.

7. In the File Renaming panel **(Figure 3.6)**, if it's available, leave *Rename Photos* unchecked or turn to the File Renaming panel section starting on page 37 to learn more.

8. In the Apply During Import panel **(Figure 3.7)**, set the following:

    - **Develop Settings**—*None*.

    - **Metadata**—*None* or turn to page 42 to learn how to create your copyright metadata preset.

    - **Keywords**—leave it blank.

9. If you've set the import type to *Add*, your work is done—press *Import* and allow Lightroom to register all the selected photos in the catalog.

10. If you've chosen *Move* or *Copy*, you need to choose where to put the photos. By default, Lightroom copies your photos into

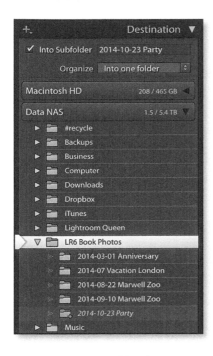

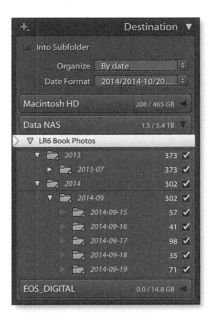

Figure 3.8 When copying from a memory card, you can create a new subfolder to store the photos.

Figure 3.9 Alternatively, you can automatically create a dated folder structure based on the metadata of the selected photos.

the Pictures folder in your user account, but you can choose another hard drive by selecting a folder in the lower half of the Destination panel.

11. Then you need to decide how you're going to organize the photos. The options at the top of the Destination dialog allow you to set the folder structure. As you try different settings, the folders in the lower half of the Destination panel update, so you can test different options to see what will happen. The folders in italic will be created by your import settings.

    To copy/move the photos directly into the folder you've selected, select *Into One Folder* in the **Organize** pop-up.

    To create a subfolder for the photos, check *Into Subfolder*, enter the name of the new subfolder, and select *Into One Folder* in the *Organize* pop-up **(Figure 3.8)**. This is useful when copying photos from a memory card into a manually-created folder structure.

    To create a date-based folder structure automatically, select *By Date* from the *Organize* pop-up and a folder structure from the *Date Format* pop-up. If you're not sure which to select, the YYYY/YYYY-MM/YYYY-MM-DD option is a good default. **(Figure 3.9)** We'll go into more detail in the Destination panel section starting on page 43.

12. Finally, press **Import**.

13. The Import dialog closes and the new photos start to appear

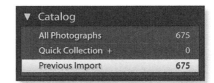

Figure 3.10 The photos are grouped in a special collection called *Previous Import*.

in the Library module. The photos are grouped in a special collection in the Catalog panel called *Current Import* (which then changes to *Previous Import*) **(Figure 3.10)**, and their folders also appear in the Folders panel.

Congratulations, your photos are now cataloged by Lightroom! If you're itching to start using Lightroom, you can now skip on to backing up your photos (page 61) and then viewing them in Lightroom (page 85), and come back to the rest of this chapter later. If you're still with me, let's go back and explore the individual elements of the Import dialog in more detail.

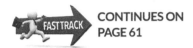

CONTINUES ON PAGE 61

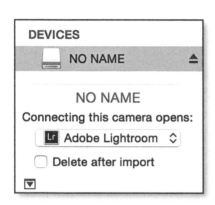

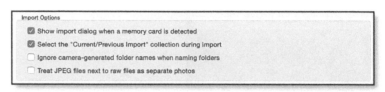

▲ **Figure 3.11** The *Show import dialog when a memory card is detected* checkbox in the *Preferences dialog > General tab* controls whether the Import dialog automatically opens when a device is connected. On Windows it also launches Lightroom if it's closed.

◄ **Figure 3.12** On Mac OS X, Image Capture controls whether Lightroom opens.

AUTOMATICALLY OPENING THE IMPORT DIALOG

There are two different behaviors involved in the Import dialog opening automatically: whether Lightroom opens the Import dialog when the program is already open, and whether the program launches by itself even though it was closed.

To change this auto-open behavior, go to Lightroom's *Preferences dialog > General tab* and check or uncheck ***Show Import dialog when a memory card is detected***. (Figure 3.11)

On Windows, this checkbox controls whether the Import dialog opens automatically when a card is detected, and also whether the program launches from closed (using Windows Auto Play).

On a Mac, the checkbox only controls whether Lightroom opens the Import dialog when the program is already open. To set Lightroom to launch from closed, insert the memory card or plug in the device. Go to the Applications folder, open the Image Capture app, and select the memory card or device on the left-hand side. In the lower left corner, click the arrow, and select Lightroom as the program to automatically open when that device is detected. **(Figure 3.12)**

The same logic applies, not just to card readers and cameras, but also to mobile phones and tablets, USB keys, printers with card readers, and various other devices.

Check the ***Eject after Import*** checkbox to automatically eject the device when the import finishes,

IMPORT IN DETAIL

In Lightroom, there are usually multiple ways to accomplish the same task. For example, to open the Import dialog you can go to *File menu > Import Photos*, press the *Import* button at the bottom of the left panel group in the Library module, or use the keyboard shortcut. (The keyboard shortcuts are listed in sidebar boxes throughout the book.) Lightroom can also open the Import dialog automatically when you insert a memory card.

SOURCE PANEL

When importing photos into Lightroom, you first need to select the source of the photos using the Source panel. **(Figure 3.13)** Remember, at the top of the panel are your devices—cameras, card readers, mobile devices, and so forth—and below that are the hard drives attached to your computer, as well as any mounted network drives. To select a source, simply click on the folder or device of your choice.

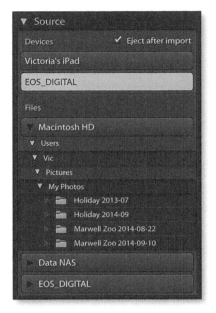

▲ **Figure 3.13** The Source panel on the left of the Import dialog allows you to select the folder or device to import.

Why do the folders keep jumping around when I click on them?

When you click on different folders in the Source panel (and later in the Destination panel too), it can appear to have a mind of its own, with different behavior depending on whether you single-click or double-click, but it's actually a useful feature.

If you navigate around by single-clicking on the folder arrows or folder names, the navigation behaves normally. If you double-click, or if you right-click and choose *Dock Folder* from the context-sensitive menu, you can collapse the folder hierarchy to hide unnecessary folders. **(Figure 3.14)** It makes it easier to navigate through a complex folder hierarchy, especially if it's many levels deep and the panel is too narrow to read the folder names. If you collapse it down too far, just double-click on the parent folder to show the full hierarchy again. **(Figure 3.15)**

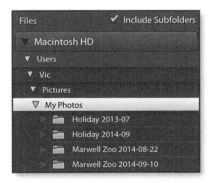

▲ **Figure 3.14** With the My Photos folder docked, the parent folders are hidden.

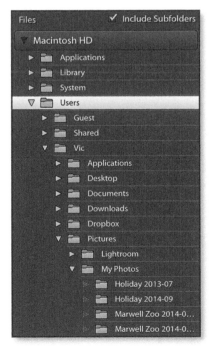

▲ **Figure 3.15** When the folders list is undocked, the folder list can become very long and folder names can be clipped.

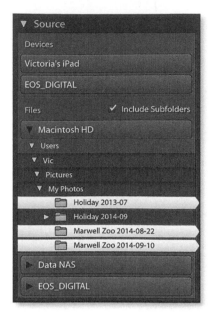

Figure 3.16 You can select multiple folders for import.

Figure 3.17 Click on the top corners of the Import dialog to view a menu of recent sources and to access the operating system dialog.

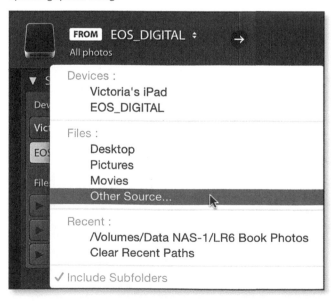

How do I import from multiple folders or memory cards in one go?

If all the photos you want to import are in subfolders under a single parent folder, for example, within a Photos folder, then you can select that parent folder and check the *Include Subfolders* checkbox. All the photos from the subfolders display in the preview area, ready to be imported.

If your photos are spread around multiple folders, hold down Ctrl (Windows) / Cmd (Mac) while clicking on each folder. **(Figure 3.16)** The multiple folders don't even have to be on the same drive as long as they appear in the *Files* section of the Source panel. If the folders are consecutive, hold down Shift while clicking on the first and last folder in a series to select them without having to click on each one.

Multiple selections are limited to folders shown in the *Files* section. You can't import from two separate devices in one go, for instance, two card readers. However if the operating system sees the memory cards as two drives in the lower *Files* part of the Source panel, you can Ctrl-click (Windows) / Cmd-click (Mac) on the folders to import both at once.

Can I use the operating system dialog to navigate to a folder instead of using Lightroom's Source panel?

If you're more comfortable using the operating system dialog to select a folder, click on the large button in the top left corner of the Import dialog. **(Figure 3.17)** (Yes, those corners are large buttons, even though they don't look like it!) The *Other Source* option in that menu displays the operating system dialog. It also lists shortcuts to popular folders such as *Desktop* and *Pictures*, as well as recent sources. When you select a folder using any of these options, the Source panel automatically updates to display that folder.

The top right corner behaves the same way, except it updates the Destination panel.

PREVIEWING AND SELECTING INDIVIDUAL PHOTOS

Having selected the source of the photos, the photo thumbnails start to populate the central preview area. In this grid, you can view the photos and select the ones you want to import.

A photo count displays in the bottom left corner of the dialog, showing how many photos are checked and how much hard drive space they fill. **(Figure 3.18)**

How do I select only certain photos to import?

The checkbox in the corner of the thumbnail controls whether the photo is included in the import. They're all checked by default. The **Check All** and **Uncheck All** buttons below the grid check/uncheck all the photos in one go, or you can click the individual checkboxes to select or deselect specific photos.

To check or uncheck a series of photos, hold down Ctrl (Windows) / Cmd (Mac) while clicking on photos to select non-consecutive photos, or Shift-click on the first and last photo to select a group of consecutive photos. Once you have the photos selected, shown by a lighter gray surround, check or uncheck the checkbox on a single photo to apply that same checkmark setting to all of the selected photos.

Why are some photos unavailable or dimmed in the Import dialog?

You might notice that some of the photos appear dimmed in the Grid. Photos shown with a vignette are unchecked photos, but they can be selected for import by toggling the checkbox. **(Figure 3.19)**

Dimmed photos that don't have a checkbox are unavailable for import, either because they're already in your current Lightroom catalog at that location, or they're already in your catalog at a different location and you have *Don't Import Suspected Duplicates* checked in the File Handling panel.

How do I change the preview size?

On the Toolbar below the grid, to the right, the **Thumbnails** slider adjusts the size of the thumbnails. The thumbnails embedded in the files are usually small and low quality, but there's also a larger JPEG preview embedded in most photos. These larger previews aren't used

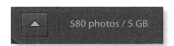

Figure 3.18 A photo count displays in the bottom left corner..

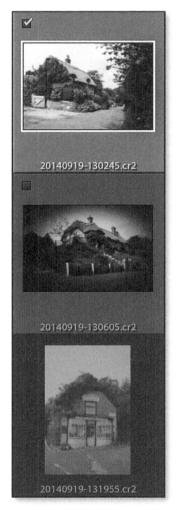

Figure 3.19 Dimmed thumbnails without a checkbox aren't available for import. Thumbnails with a vignette are unchecked and can be imported by checking the box.

Figure 3.20 Below the thumbnails or preview are Grid and Loupe buttons for switching between these views.

Figure 3.21 The Loupe view allows you to see a larger preview of the photo before importing.

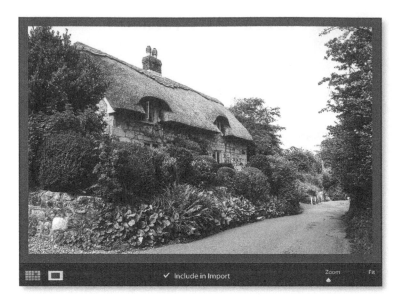

for the Grid view as they're slower to load, but the Loupe view allows you to take advantage of the larger preview.

To show the larger Loupe view of a photo, select any thumbnail and press the Loupe button on the Toolbar **(Figure 3.20)** or double-click on the thumbnail. (If it doesn't work, the file may not include a larger preview, or Lightroom may be having trouble reading it, so go ahead and import the photos and view them in the Library module instead).

Below that Loupe preview is the checkbox to include or exclude the photo from the Import. Press the Grid button on the Toolbar or double-click on the photo to return to Grid view again.

As these previews are embedded in the files, it can be a faster way of doing any initial selections than waiting for Lightroom to build previews. **(Figure 3.21)** However, if you accidentally close the Import dialog before importing, you can lose all the work you've done selecting files, whereas marking photos in the Library module saves as you go along.

Can I change the sort order?

Also on the Toolbar is the **Sort** pop-up **(Figure 3.22)**, which allows you to sort the thumbnails in the Grid.

The options are:

Figure 3.22 At the bottom of the Import dialog grid, you'll find the sort order pop-up and thumbnail size slider.

- **Capture Time** sorts the photos based on their capture time.

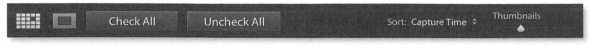

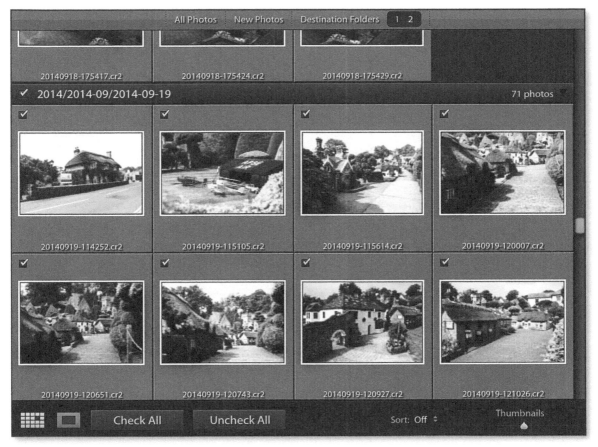

▲ **Figure 3.23** Along the top of the Import dialog grid is a Filter bar. Clicking on Destination Folders divides the thumbnails into groups.

- **Checked State** displays the checked photos first, followed by the unchecked photos.

- **Filename** sorts the photos in alpha-numeric filename order.

- **Media Type** displays the videos first, followed by the photos.

- **Off** disables sorting.

SELECTING SPECIFIC FILE TYPES

You can't filter for specific file types, for example, just the raw files, using Lightroom's Import dialog. One solution is to import all the photos into Lightroom and then filter them using the Library module's Filter bar and remove specific photos. We'll come back to that in the Finding & Filtering Photos chapter starting on page 179.

Alternatively, you can make use of your operating system's sort by file type in Explorer (Windows) / Finder (Mac). Select the files you want to import and drag and drop them onto Lightroom's icon in the Dock (Mac only) or directly on the Grid view in the Library module (Windows or Mac). The Import dialog opens with these specific photos already selected, ready for import.

IMPORT SHORTCUTS

Open Import dialog	Ctrl-Shift-I / Cmd-Shift-I
Grid view	G
Loupe view	E
Move between photos	Left/right arrows
Zoom	Spacebar
Check selected photo	P
Uncheck selected photo	X
Toggle checkbox	`
Auto Advance	Caps Lock
Begin Import	Enter
Cancel / Close Dialog	Escape

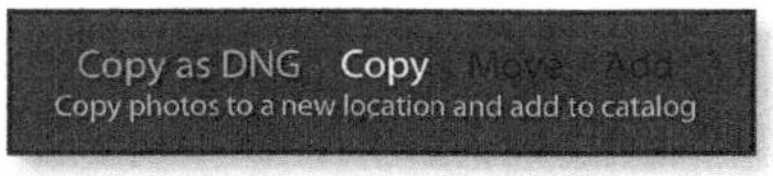

Copy as DNG   **Copy**   Move   Add
Copy photos to a new location and add to catalog

▲ **Figure 3.24** At the top of the Import dialog, choose how to handle the files.

Can I filter the photos?

As well as changing the sort order, you can filter the photos shown in the Grid using the Filter bar above the thumbnails. **(Figure 3.23)**

- *All Photos*—displays all the photos in the selected source.

- *New Photos*—hides any photos that have already been imported and are recognized as duplicates.

- *Destination Folders*—breaks up the grid into sections based on the folder structure you set in the Destination panel, for example, by date. These grid sections can be collapsed by clicking on the triangle on the left, and whole groups of photos can be checked or unchecked using the checkbox on the dividing row.

EXPLORE DNG

DNG, or Digital Negative, is an openly documented raw file format. Some cameras create DNG files natively, and other raw files can also be converted to the DNG format. It's worth understanding the pros and cons so you can make an informed decision. In the Appendix starting on page A-1, we explore all the benefits and disadvantages, as well as how DNG can be integrated into your workflow.

IMPORT METHOD

Having selected the photos, you need to decide how to handle them. While importing, you can copy them, move them, or leave them where they are. **(Figure 3.24)** These options are found at the top of the Import dialog.

- *Copy as DNG* copies the photos to a folder of your choice, and converts the copies of any raw files to DNG format, leaving the originals untouched.

- *Copy* also copies the photos to a folder structure of your choice but it doesn't convert them to DNG format. As it's duplicating the photos, it takes up additional hard drive space, so it's primarily used when copying photos from a memory card or other device, rather than importing existing photos from the hard drive.

- **Move** copies the photos to the folder structure of your choice but it also removes the files from their original location. The *Move* option is particularly useful if you want Lightroom to reorganize your existing photos while importing, as it doesn't take up additional hard drive space.

- **Add** leaves the files in their current folder structure with their existing filenames, and references them, or links to them, in that original location. This is a great option for importing existing photos if you already have an organized filing system. You'll note that the File Renaming and Destination panels on the right are missing, since they don't apply when adding photos without moving them.

FILE HANDLING PANEL

Further file handling options appear in the File Handling panel on the right. **(Figure 3.25)** Using this panel, you choose the size of the previews to be created after importing, how to handle duplicate photos, and whether to copy the photos to a temporary backup location.

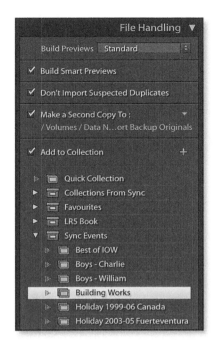

Figure 3.25 The File Handling panel on the right of the Import dialog allows you to set initial preview size, duplicate handling, temporary backups and collection membership.

Why do I have to create previews? Why can't I just look at the photos?

The first option in the File Handling panel is **Build Previews**. All raw processors create their own previews because raw data has to be converted in order to be viewed as an image. Lightroom creates previews of all file types, so that non-destructive edits can be previewed without damaging the original image data. These previews also allow you to view the photos when the original files are offline, for example, when your external drive is disconnected.

What size previews should I build?

There are four preview size options:

- **Minimal**—stores the thumbnail preview embedded in the file. It's a quick option initially, but it's a very small low quality preview, usually with a black edging and about 160px along the long edge, so you then have to wait to for previews to build as you browse. Minimal previews aren't color managed.

- *Embedded & Sidecar*—stores the main preview embedded in the file (approx. 1024px or larger), so it's also quick to import, but gives you something to look at while waiting for Lightroom to build its own previews.

- *Standard*—builds the previews immediately after import, so it takes time initially but it's much quicker when you're viewing the photos.

- *1:1*—builds full size previews. They're slower to build, and take up more space on the hard drive, but they're much quicker when browsing if you need to zoom in to check focus.

There's also a *Build Smart Previews* checkbox. Smart Previews are primarily used for editing the files when the originals are offline, for example, when the original files are on a disconnected external drive. If your original files are always accessible, you can leave this unchecked. We'll come back to Previews & Smart Previews in more detail starting on page 102.

What does *Don't Import Suspected Duplicates* do?

Next in that panel is *Don't Import Suspected Duplicates*. If it's checked, Lightroom matches the photos that you're importing against those that are already in the catalog, to see whether you're trying to import duplicates.

For example, if you forget to reformat the card in the camera before shooting more photos, it recognizes the photos that are already in the catalog and skips them rather than duplicating the files. It's worth leaving checked unless you're intentionally importing duplicate photos.

To be classed as a suspected duplicate, the files must match on the original filename (as it was when imported into Lightroom), the EXIF capture date and time, and the file length (size).

If it doesn't recognize the duplicates, make sure you've inserted the card before opening the Import dialog, as it can be more temperamental if you open the Import dialog first. It also only works if the photos are still in the catalog, so if you've deleted some, they will be reimported from the card. It also won't recognize photos that you've re-saved as an alternative format—only exact duplicates.

What does the *Make a Second Copy* option do?

When using one of the *Copy* or *Move* options, the **Make a Second Copy To** checkbox becomes available in the File Handling panel. This backs up your original files to the location of your choice, in a dated folder called "Imported on [date]". If you choose to rename your files while importing, these backups are renamed to match, but they always remain in their original file format, even if you're converting the working files to DNG while importing.

The Second Copy option is useful as a temporary backup, while the photos make their way into your primary backup system, but it's not a replacement for good primary backups as it doesn't replicate your working folder structure. We'll consider backup systems in the next chapter starting on page 61.

How do I add imported photos to a collection while importing?

While you're importing the photos, you can also add them to a collection. This is particularly useful if you use Lightroom mobile sync, your workflow is designed around collections, or you're importing photos from an event that spans multiple days such as a vacation.

Enable the **Add to Collection** checkbox to display and select your existing collections and collection sets, or click on the + button to create a new collection. You can only add the photos to a single collection while importing, although you can add them to additional collections once the import completes.

FILE RENAMING PANEL

Most cameras use fairly non-descriptive file names such as IMG_5968. The problem with these names is, over the course of time, you'll end up with multiple photos with the same name.

Using the options in the File Renaming panel **(Figure 3.26)**, you can rename your photos while you're importing them. (If your Import dialog is set to *Add*, you won't be able to rename while importing. Either change to one of the *Copy* or *Move* options, or wait until the photos are imported and rename in the Library module.)

FILENAME CHARACTERS

It's sensible to only use standard characters, such as plain letters and numbers, and use underscores (_) or hyphens (-) instead of spaces when you're setting up your filenames, so your filenames will be fully compatible with web browsers and other operating systems without having to be renamed again. Some characters, such as / \ : ! @ # $ % < > , [ ] { } & * ( ) + = may have specific uses in the operating system or Lightroom's database, causing all sorts of trouble, so those are best avoided.

For more information on recommended filename limitations, check http://www.Lrq.me/cv-filenames

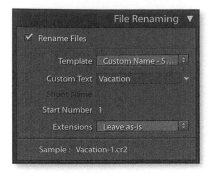

Figure 3.26 The File Renaming panel allows you to rename the photos at the time of import, which means that all versions and backups of the photos will have the same name.

Figure 3.27 Use the Filename Template Editor to build a filename structure of your choice.

Figure 3.28 The Windows version displays the tokens as curly brackets rather than lozenges.

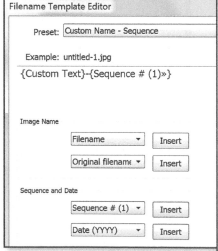

How will you name your photos?

The main thing to consider when naming your files is how you'll make the names unique. If a file doesn't have a unique name, and it's accidentally moved to another folder, other photos could be overwritten.

The date and time works well as a unique file name, for example, YYYYMMDD-HHMMSS (year month day—hour minute second). If you regularly shoot in sub-second bursts or you prefer to keep to the camera file name, YYYYMMDD-original file number (and a camera code if you're shooting with more than one camera) can work well with a low risk of duplication.

Others prefer a sequence number combined with some custom text, for example, *Vacation2015_003.jpg*. Don't add the words *Vacation2015* into the template itself, otherwise you'll have to go back to the Filename Template Editor each time you need to change it. Instead, use the *Custom Text* and *SequenceNumber(001)* tokens, so you can enter *Vacation2015* directly in the Import dialog.

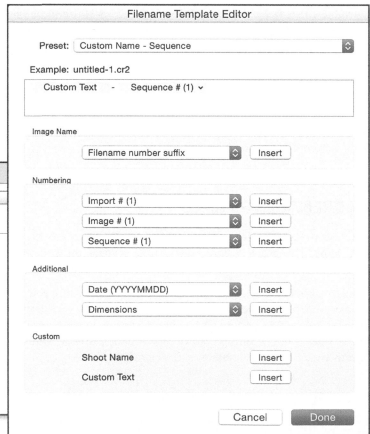

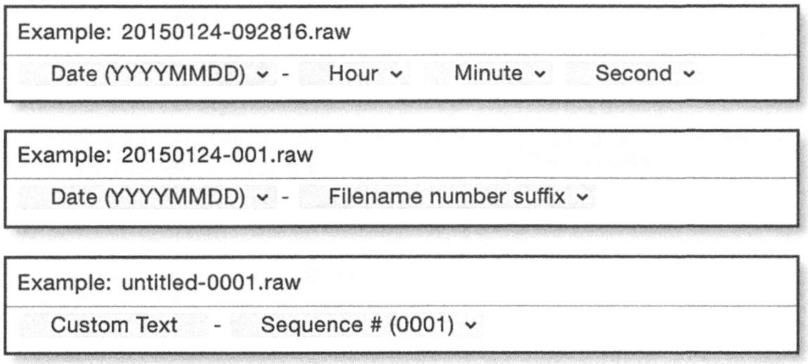

Example: 20150124-092816.raw

Date (YYYYMMDD) ⌄ -   Hour ⌄   Minute ⌄   Second ⌄

Example: 20150124-001.raw

Date (YYYYMMDD) ⌄ -   Filename number suffix ⌄

Example: untitled-0001.raw

Custom Text   -   Sequence # (0001) ⌄

Figure 3.29 These are a few example filename templates.

The first one becomes 20150124-092816.jpg.

The second one becomes 20150124-001.jpg.

The last one becomes London2015-0001.jpg.

You can rename the files at any time, as long as you do it within Lightroom, but doing so while importing means your initial backups will have the same names as the working files. This can be invaluable if you have to restore from import backups.

How do I rename the files while importing?

To rename the files, check the **Rename Files** checkbox and select a template from the pop-up to the right. There's a selection of templates built in to Lightroom, but if you select *Edit* in the **Template** pop-up, you can create your own template using tokens in the Filename Template Editor. **(Figures 3.27, 3.28 & 3.29)**

How do I build a filename template?

1. In the Filename Template Editor, click in the white field and delete the existing tokens. The tokens appear as text in curly brackets on Windows, or blue lozenges on Mac.

   Below the white field is a selection of pop-ups, each containing different types of tokens. There's a huge selection to choose from! The tokens are grouped into pop-ups. The first contains filename tokens (i.e. current filename), then there are 3 pop-ups for numbering tokens (i.e. sequence numbers) with 1 to 5 digits, then date-based tokens (i.e. YYYYMMDD, and metadata-based tokens (i.e. camera model, star ratings, etc.). Finally there are *Insert* buttons for two custom text fields—*Shoot Name* and *Custom Text*.

2. To add a token, click the Insert button next to one of the pop-ups or select a different option from a pop-up.

3. Repeat to add additional tokens.

4. You can type directly into the white field to add punctuation such as hyphens and underscores between tokens. You can also

RENAMING OPTIONS

The available options differ slightly between the Import dialog and the Library module. Import has a *Shoot Name* token, which isn't available in the Library module, but the Library module gains tokens such as *Folder Name, Original Filename, Copy Name*, slightly different sequence number options and additional IPTC metadata. The basic principles remain the same.

▶**Figure 3.30** Lightroom offers a range of numbering systems, including a standard Sequence number which you set in the Import dialog.

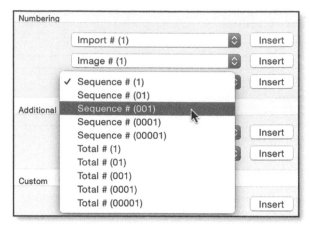

add text such as your initials. Add a custom text field for text that changes regularly, such as the name of the shoot or other descriptive text.

5. Finally, save it as a preset by selecting the Preset pop-up at the top of the dialog and choosing *Save Current Settings as New Preset* and giving it a name.

6. Press *Done* to close the dialog, and check that your new preset is selected in the File Renaming panel.

NUMBER PER DAY OR FOLDER

Lightroom can't automatically restart the numbering for each day (i.e. day3-001.jpg) or remember the last number used in a folder (i.e. start at London-253.jpg). To use that type of numbering system, rename the photos in chunks in the Library module, using the *Sequence #* token and setting a start number manually for each batch.

How do I add additional padding zeros to sequence numbers?

In the Numbering pop-ups, such as Sequence #, you'll note that there are options from (1) to (00001). **(Figure 3.30)** Some programs can have problems sorting in intelligent numerical order, so they sort files as 1, 10, 11... 19, 2, 20, 21. The solution is to add extra padding zeros to set the filenames to 001, 002, and so forth.

To use a padded 3-digit sequence number, select *Sequence # (001)* instead of *Sequence # (1)* from the pop-up menu.

What's the difference between *Import#*, *Image#*, *Sequence#* and *Total#*?

While you're looking at the Numbering pop-ups, you'll notice that there are a number of different types of sequence number available.

*   ***Sequence #*** is the most useful, and the most familiar type of

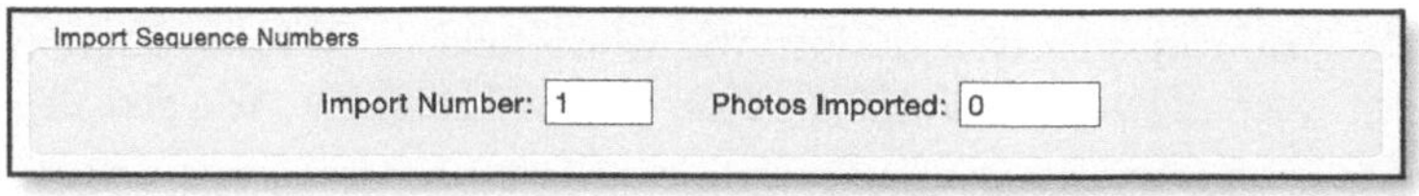

▶**Figure 3.31** In *Catalog Settings > File Handling tab*, you can set the Import Sequence Numbers which are used for the Import # and Image # tokens.

numbering. It's an automatically-increasing number which starts at the number you set in the File Naming panel in the Import dialog or in the Rename Photos dialog in the Library module.

- **Import #** increases with each batch of photos you import. The first time you use the token during import, it's set to 1, then the next time it's 2, etc. It's only available while importing photos.

- **Image #** increases with individual photo you import. The first photo is set to 0, then the next is 1, etc.

Both *Import #* and *Image #* have starting numbers set in *Catalog Settings > File Handling tab*, with **Import Number** used for *Import #* and **Photos Imported** used for *Image #*. **(Figure 3.31)** If you don't use these tokens, the count doesn't increase. Later, when renaming in the Library module, Image # always starts at 1 regardless of the Catalog Settings.

- **Total #** refers to the number of photos it's renaming in one go, so if you're renaming 8 photos, the *Total #* token is replaced with 8. It's only available in Library module Rename Photos dialog.

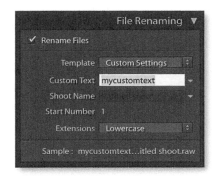

Figure 3.32 If a template includes *Custom Text* or *Shoot Name* tokens, they can be updated in the File Renaming panel.

Where do I enter custom text and start numbers?

After creating your filename template, the availability of the additional fields in the File Renaming panel **(Figure 3.32)** depends on which tokens are used in the selected template.

There are two custom text fields—**Custom Text** and **Shoot Name**—which allow you to add custom text into your filename without returning to the Filename Template Editor each time you want to change the text. The arrow to the right of each field displays recent entries.

Start Number is used with the *Sequence #* token, allowing you to set a starting number of your choice. For example, you may want your numbering to start at 1, or you may want to carry on from a specific number such as 253.

The **Extensions** pop-up sets the case of the file extension (i.e. .jpg, .JPG, etc.). The default is *Leave as-is*, but you can change it to *uppercase* or *lowercase* if you prefer. That choice is personal preference.

At the bottom of the File Renaming panel is the **Sample** filename, which allows you to double check you have the correct template selected.

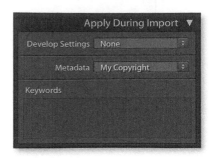

Figure 3.33 The Apply During Import panel allows you to apply initial Develop settings to your photos at import, as well as adding any Metadata or Keywords that will apply to all of the selected photos.

APPLY DURING IMPORT PANEL

Next in line is the Apply During Import panel **(Figure 3.33)**. These options allow you to apply settings to the photos as they're imported—Develop Settings, Metadata or Keywords. The settings apply to all the photos in the current import.

What Develop settings should I apply in the Import dialog?

The **Develop Settings** pop-up allows you to apply a Develop preset to the photos while importing, for example, you may always apply a specific preset to all studio portraits as a starting point. *None* just applies the default settings to new photos but preserves any existing Develop settings stored with the files, so it's the option to choose if you're ever uncertain. Be careful not to confuse *None* with *Lightroom General Presets > Zeroed* which sets every slider back to zero even if there were existing settings.

How do I add copyright metadata to my photos?

Import is the ideal time to apply copyright metadata to ensure that all of your photos include this vital information. To create a metadata preset:

1. Select *New* in the **Metadata** pop-up and the New Metadata Preset dialog appears. **(Figure 3.34)**

2. At the top, enter a name for the preset such as "Copyright Preset".

3. Enter your copyright information below. Only checked fields are saved in the preset.

   In many countries, the copyright notice requires the copyright symbol ©, the year of first publication and then the name of the copyright owner, for example, © 2015 Victoria Bampton. Copyright laws vary by country, so please check your local laws for exact specifications. You may also want to include personal details such as your name, address, website and other contact details.

4. Press the *Create* button to return to the Import dialog, where your new preset is automatically selected.

APPLYING DIFFERENT SETTINGS

You can't apply different settings to different photos in the same import. You could start the first import with selected photos, however doing so runs the risk of missing a photo or two. It's easier to import all the photos in a single process and then add the different settings, or move photos into different folders in the Library module once they've all finished importing. All the settings that are available in the Import dialog, such as Metadata and Develop presets, can also be applied in the Library module.

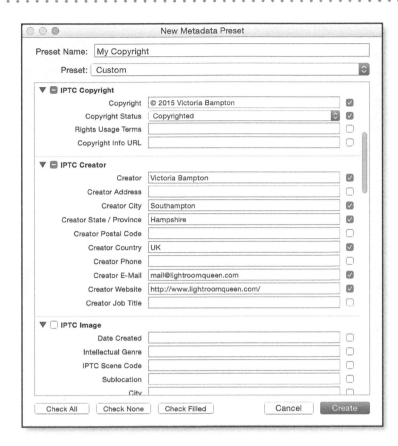

Figure 3.34 Create a Metadata preset to automatically embed your copyright data in every photo.

COPYRIGHT SYMBOL

To add a © symbol in the Copyright field, hold down Alt while typing 0 1 6 9 on the numberpad (Windows), type Ctrl-Alt-C (Windows) / Opt-G (Mac).

Should I apply keywords in the Import dialog?

Keywords can also be applied while importing the photos by typing them in the **Keywords** field, however remember that they're applied to all the photos in the current import, so it's only useful for keywords that apply to everything. Specific keywords are better applied individually in the Library module.

DESTINATION PANEL

Finally, you need to decide where to put the photos (unless you're using *Add* to leave them in their current location) and that's where the Destination panel comes into play. It's worth taking the time to get this right before you start importing, as moving the photos after import is a manual process. We covered the basics in the Fast Track at the beginning of the chapter (starting on page 25), but let's go into a little more detail.

REMOVE EXISTING METADATA

To remove metadata while importing the photos, perhaps because you've entered metadata in other software and want a fresh start, check the applicable fields in a Metadata preset but leave the fields blank. This prevents the metadata being added to Lightroom's catalog. Simply leaving the Apply During Import panel *Keywords* field blank without checking the tick box retains any existing keywords.

Where will you store your photos?

Lightroom doesn't hide your photos away from you. They're kept as normal image files in folders on your hard drive. You can access them using other software, and they don't have to be stored in the same place as the catalog.

By default, Lightroom copies your photos into the Pictures folder in your user account, but you can choose another location, such as another hard drive.

It's best practice to keep the folders of photos under a single parent folder (or one for each drive), rather than scattering them in random locations, because it makes them easy to back up and move. As your collection of photos grows, you may need to expand onto additional hard drives, which isn't a problem for Lightroom.

So where are you going to store your photos? Make that decision before you go any further.

How will you organize your photos into folders?

Once you've decided where to store the photos, you then need to decide how to organize them. There's no right or wrong way of organizing photos on your hard drive, but it's worth spending the time to set up a logical folder structure at the outset.

As far as Lightroom's concerned, your choice of folder structure doesn't make a lot of difference. Folders are just a place to store the photos, and you can use metadata and keywords to organize them. You could just dump them all into a single folder, but that would become unwieldy in time, so some kind of organization helps.

We'll come back to some sample folder structures in a moment, but first let's consider the basic principles behind the best practices.

- **Scalable**—First and foremost, your folder structure must be scalable. You may only have a few thousand photos at the moment, but your filing system needs to be capable of growing with you, without having to go back and change it. Can you add new folders to your system without disturbing existing folders, especially if some of the folders are archived offline?

- **Easy Backup & Restore**—Your folder structure needs to be easy to back up, otherwise you may miss some photos, and it needs to be easy to restore if you ever have a disaster. This is particularly important as your library grows and becomes split over multiple hard drives.

- **Standard characters**—When naming your folders, stick to standard characters—A-Z, 0-9, hyphens (-) and underscores (_)—to

THE DAM BOOK

We could write a whole book on Digital Asset Management, and the pros and cons of various systems, but fortunately, the world-renowned DAM expert Peter Krogh has already done so. If it's a subject that you would like to learn more about, I recommend The DAM Book http://www.Lrq.me/dambook

prevent problems in the future. Although your current operating system may accept other characters, you might decide to move cross-platform one day, leaving you the time-consuming job of renaming all of the folders manually.

- **No duplication**—Each photo should be stored in a single location, plus backups.

- **Consistent**—You should always know where a photo should go without having to think about it. If you have to debate each time, there's a higher chance of making a mistake.

Why use a date-based folder structure?

The simplest option for most people is to use a date-based folder structure. It ticks all of the boxes, and more:

- It's scalable, because you just keep adding new dates to the end.

- It's easy to back up the original photos, even to write-once media like optical discs, because you're adding new photos to the latest folders. (Note that if you save derivative files with the original files, such as those edited in other software, you might still be adding photos to older folders too.)

- It's easy to restore from a good backup. In the event of a disaster, it's even possible to rebuild from files rescued by recovery software, because the capture dates are stored in the file metadata.

- It uses standard characters which are accepted by all operating systems.

- The folders can be nested with days inside of months inside of years, so you don't have a long unwieldy list of folders.

- Lightroom can create the folder structure for you automatically on import, so you don't even have to organize it manually.

Why not organize the photos by topic?

Before you used photo management software, such as Lightroom, you may have organized your photos by subject, so why not carry on doing that? Two reasons: duplication and consistency.

A file can only be in one folder at a time, so if you divide your photos up by topic, how do you decide where a photo should go?

If you have a photo of Mary and Susan, should it go in the *Mary* folder or the *Susan* folder? Perhaps you duplicate in both folders, but then, what happens when you have a larger group of people? Do you

FOLDERS GONE AWOL

If your folders disappear from the Destination panel, click on the + button and select *View : All Folders*. The other option—*Affected folders only*—only displays folders that are receiving new photos, so they only appear when you have photos selected for import.

ASK FOR HELP

There's a friendly group of photographers at http://www. lightroomforums.net/ who will be happy to discuss your proposed folder structure and point out the pros and cons.

FOLDERS PANEL SHORTCUT

In the Library module, right-click on a folder in the Folders panel and select *Import to this Folder* to automatically open the Import dialog and set your Destination folder.

duplicate the photo in all of their folders too, rapidly filling your hard drive and making it difficult to track? And then when you come to make adjustments to that photo, do you have to find it in all of those locations to update those copies too?

Folders work best as storage buckets rather than organizing tools. If you keep one copy of each photo (plus backups!) in a folder, you can then use keywords, collections and other metadata to group and find photos easily. That photo of Mary and Susan may be stored in a *2015* folder, but would show up when you searched for Mary, Susan, or even that it was taken at the beach.

Can I adapt a dated folder structure to suit me?

That's not to say you shouldn't adapt the folder structure to suit your needs.

If you're grouping photos by day or month, you may want to add a descriptive word to the folder name to describe the overall subject, for example, *2015-04-21 Zoo* or or *2015-06_Vacation*. This makes it easy to find the photos in any other file browser too.

A wedding photographer may prefer to use a folder for each wedding within a parent year folder, sorted by name rather than date, for example, *2015/John_Kate_wedding_20150421*.

If you're not shooting thousands of photos a year, you may decide that you don't need a full folder hierarchy with one folder per day. A folder for each year may be plenty, or perhaps one per month.

If you shoot for work as well as pleasure, you may want to have separate dated folder structures for Work vs. Personal. But if you decide to split your system, make sure there are no overlaps where a photo may fit into more than one category.

Alternative filing systems aren't 'wrong' but you'll save yourself a lot of headaches if you follow the basic principles. If you're not using a basic dated structure, make sure you think it through properly, and perhaps discuss it with other experienced digital photographers, in case they can see a pitfall that you've missed.

RENAMING DATED FOLDERS

You can't edit the new folder names in the Import dialog, for example, to add a description after the date. Once the photos have finished importing, you can rename any of the folders by right-clicking on the folder in the Folders panel and selecting *Rename*.

Also, consider how you're going to manage derivatives—retouched masters, and copies exported for other purposes. Are you going to manage these alongside your originals, and if so, how are they going to be backed up and archived?

How do I select a Destination folder?

The Destination panel works just like the Source panel, including single-clicking for standard navigation, double-clicking to dock folders, and the large button in the top right corner which shows recent destination folders and the operating system dialog.

Select your Destination folder by clicking to highlight it. Any folders that Lightroom creates are placed inside your selected folder.

How do I create a new folder?

There are two main ways of creating a new folder. If you click the + button on the Destination panel header, you can use the operating system dialog to create a new folder in the location of your choice.

Alternatively, select a folder in the Destination panel and check the **Into Subfolder** checkbox at the top of the Destination panel. Enter the name of your new subfolder in the field to the right. The new subfolder appears in italic below your selected folder, showing that it will be created by the import process. **(Figure 3.35)**

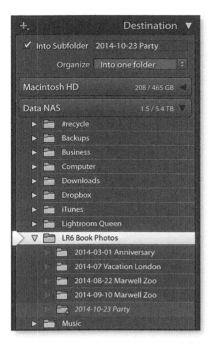

Figure 3.35 Select the Destination folder and preview the results before starting the import.

I've chosen Copy or Move—how do I organize the photos into a folder structure that suits me?

How the photos are organized within your selected folder depends on your **Organize** pop-up selection. You have three choices:

- **By date** gives you a choice of date-based folder structures. It automatically organizes your photos into a tidy folder structure.

- **Into one folder** places the photos in the single folder that you select. It allows you to create your own folder structure manually. For example, a portrait photographer may create a folder for each shoot, or you may choose to create a folder for each family event you attend.

- **By original folders** imports in the same nested hierarchy as their existing structure, but at a new location. This is useful if you're importing existing folders of photos and you wish to keep the existing organization.

Any of these folder structures can also be placed into an existing folder on your hard drive or a new folder.

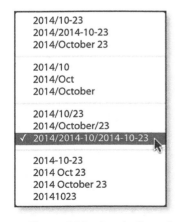

Figure 3.36 A selection of dated folder structures are available in the Date Format pop-up menu.

How do I pick a date structure?

If you select *By date*, the **Date Format** pop-up appears, giving you a choice of difference dated folder structures. **(Figure 3.36)**

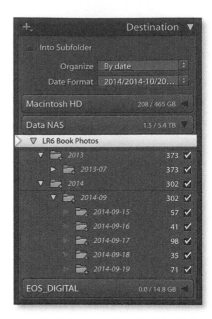

Figure 3.37 Your selected folder structure is previewed in italic. Make sure you check the folder structure is correct before importing the photos.

SORTING DATES

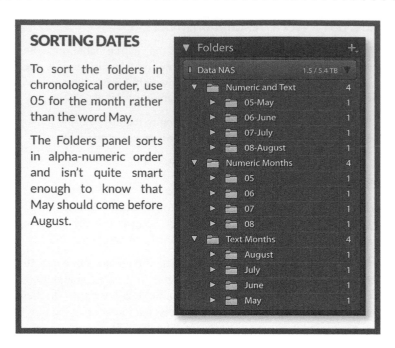

To sort the folders in chronological order, use 05 for the month rather than the word May.

The Folders panel sorts in alpha-numeric order and isn't quite smart enough to know that May should come before August.

The slash (/) creates nested folders so 2014/10/07 creates a folder 07 inside of a folder 10 inside of a folder 2014, not a single folder called 2014/10/07.

If you want a single folder, you need to use a format with hyphens (-) or underscores (_), such as the 2014-10-07 format.

Why are some of the Destination folders in italic?

As you test the different *Organize* and *Date Format* options, watch the folder hierarchy below. The folders shown in italic are folders that don't currently exist, but will be created by the import. **(Figure 3.37)** It's an easy way to check that the folder organization setting that you've chosen is the one that you want.

There's one particular thing to look out for here... nested year folders. If the Destination panel shows a 2014 folder inside another 2014 folder, as shown in **Figure 3.38**, you've selected the wrong Destination folder. Click on the parent folder (*LR6 Book Photos* in this screenshot) and the 2014 month/day folders will slip back into the correct place in the hierarchy. Watch this panel closely to ensure the photos are saved in the correct location.

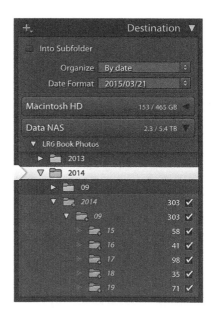

Figure 3.38 In this case, we've selected the wrong folder, resulting in nested 2014 folders. We should have selected the LR6 Book Photos folder.

The 2014 folder has been selected, resulting in the new 2014 folder being nested inside. If you select the LR6 Book Photos folder, then it would work correctly.

To the right of the folder names are numbers and checkmarks. The numbers show how many photos in the current import will be placed in that folder. Two numbers divided by a slash are checked (left) and unchecked (right) photos.

The checkmarks next to the italicized folders select and deselect photos from those folders. They're particularly useful when you're using a dated folder structure, allowing you to select or deselect a whole day or month's photos in one go.

Can Lightroom manage my photos, like iTunes moves my music files?

Lightroom doesn't automatically manage or rearrange your photos once they've been imported. You can move the photos manually by dragging and dropping them into other folders within the Library module, but that could be a big job, so it's better to decide on a sensible filing system at the outset.

Once you've imported the photos, don't tidy up or rename them using Explorer (Windows) / Finder (Mac) or other software, because Lightroom would no longer know where to find them, leaving you the labor-intensive job of relinking the files individually. We'll investigate how do to that in the Missing Files section starting on page 525, but it's easier to prevent than to fix.

SAVING & REUSING IMPORT SETTINGS

Don't worry, having made all these decisions the first time, you can save them to reuse again later. Lightroom remembers your last used settings, but you might need different settings for different uses. For example, you may use different settings when copying from a memory card than you do when importing existing photos. You can save these sets of settings as Import presets.

THE COMPACT IMPORT DIALOG

If you click the arrow in the lower left corner of the Import dialog, it toggles between compact and expanded dialog views. The compact Import dialog allows you to change a few of the settings, such as the Source or Destination folders, and add basic metadata. **(Figure 3.39)** It doesn't read thumbnails of the photos so it's usually quicker, especially on a slow machine or when importing large numbers of photos. The compact Import dialog also displays a quick summary of your other settings, but if you want to change these settings, you need to switch to the expanded Import dialog.

▼ **Figure 3.39** The compact Import dialog only offers a summary of settings. Press the triangle in the lower left corner to switch to the expanded Import dialog

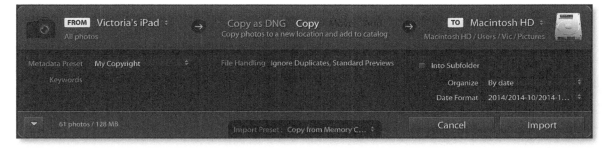

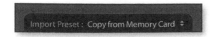

Figure 3.40 Import Presets save the combinations of settings you use regularly.

How do I create Import presets, and what do they include?

The **Import Preset** pop-up is tucked away at the bottom of the Import dialog in both the compact and expanded Import dialog views. **(Figure 3.40)** (See The Compact Import Dialog sidebar) Select your import settings and then choose *Save Current Setting as New Preset* from the pop-up menu and give it a name.

All of the settings in the right-hand panels are included in the presets, along with the *Copy as DNG/Copy/Move/Add* choice. Source panel selections and checked/unchecked thumbnails aren't included in the preset, as these change each time you import.

To use these settings again later, simply select the preset from the *Import Presets* pop-up. You can also update or delete existing presets by selecting the preset, editing it and then selecting *Update* (or *Delete*) from the same pop-up.

AFTER PRESSING IMPORT

Having set up your import preferences, click the *Import* button in the lower right corner of the dialog to start the import. The *Cancel* button closes the dialog without importing any photos.

The import runs as a background task, allowing you to start (or continue) working in Lightroom while it adds the new photos to the catalog. The progress bar displays in the Activity Center in the top left corner of the screen.

Lightroom selects the *Current Import* collection in the Library module's Catalog panel while importing the photos. If you switch to another folder or collection, it then flips back to the same collection (now called *Previous Import*) automatically when the import completes. This can be frustrating if you're trying to work on other photos while the import runs in the background, so there's a **Select the 'Current/Previous Import' collection during import** checkbox in the *Preferences dialog > General tab*. **(Figure 3.41)** It's checked by default,

Figure 3.41 Unchecking the *Select 'Current/Previous Import' collection during import* checkbox stops Lightroom automatically switching views when an import completes.

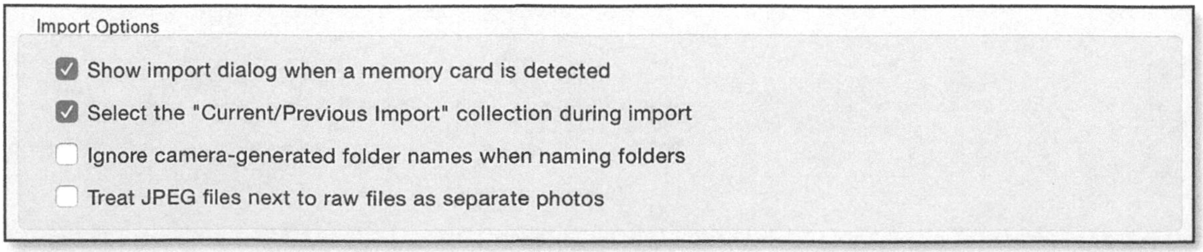

Import Options

☑ Show import dialog when a memory card is detected

☑ Select the "Current/Previous Import" collection during import

☐ Ignore camera-generated folder names when naming folders

☐ Treat JPEG files next to raw files as separate photos

but unchecking it prevents Lightroom from automatically switching view.

Once the import completes and you've built standard-sized or 1:1 previews, visually check the files to ensure that they're not corrupted and your backups are safe before wiping your memory cards.

Some photographers like to delete the files from the memory card using Explorer (Windows) / Finder (Mac), as a reminder that the card's ok to reuse, but it's worth then reformatting the card in the camera. This reduces the risk of corruption.

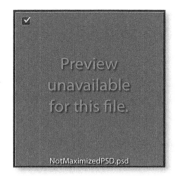

Figure 3.42 If a preview is unavailable, Lightroom displays a gray thumbnail in the Import dialog.

TROUBLESHOOTING IMPORT

We've covered all the controls you need to know about, but there are a few issues that could prevent you importing your photos. To avoid you tripping at the first hurdle, we'll run through the most frequent of these problems and error messages now, and translate them into more helpful terms.

How do I stop the Import dialog hanging?

If the Import dialog simply hangs before displaying any or all of the thumbnails, it's usually caused by having a mobile phone or tablet attached to the computer. It can also be caused by a drive that's slow to respond (perhaps a network drive), or cloud drives that appear as network drives (e.g. JungleDrive). Try detaching all peripherals from your computer and ejecting network drives before attempting to open the Import dialog again, to narrow down the cause of the problem.

Why can't I see my photos in the Import dialog?

Assuming you've correctly selected a source, there are a few reasons why the thumbnails of the photos might not be visible.

If the photo cells are visible, but the thumbnails are gray and say *Preview unavailable for this file* (**Figure 3.42**), there are a few likely reasons:

- The raw file format isn't supported by your Lightroom version.

- The file is corrupt or has the wrong file extension.

- The file doesn't have an embedded preview.

- Lightroom is unable to get the previews from the images. If your camera's connected directly to the computer, a lack of previews

SIDECAR FILES

Sidecar files aren't treated like photos, so you can't view them separately. If you move or rename the primary file (usually a raw file), the sidecar file is moved or renamed too. Sidecar files can be metadata files such as XMP files, audio files such as WAV files, or image files such as the JPEG from a RAW+JPEG pair. If the sidecar is an image file, the filename of the primary file displays as IMG0001.CR2 + JPEG. Sidecar files are also listed in the Metadata panel.

FILE FORMATS

Lightroom can import photos and videos in the following formats:

- Camera raw file formats for supported cameras. You can check whether your camera is supported by the latest version of Lightroom by visiting Adobe's website: http://www.Lrq.me/camerasupport

- Digital Negative (DNG) format

- PSD files set to Maximize Compatibility (8-bit & 16-bit only)

- TIFF (8-bit, 16-bit & 32-bit)

- JPEG

- PNG files

- Some video formats from digital still cameras—AVI, MOV, MP4 and the video files from within AVCHD folders. There's a full list at http://www.Lrq.me/lr5-video

There are a few limitations to be aware of:

- Photos can be no larger than 65,000 pixels along the longest edge, and no more than 512 megapixels (not megabytes)—whichever is smaller. A photo that is 60,000 x 60,000 is under the 65,000 pixel limit, but it still won't import as it's over the 512 megapixel limit. As most cameras range between 8-36 megapixels, that's only likely to become an issue for huge panoramic or poster shots created in Photoshop.

- CMYK, Lab and Grayscale photos can be imported and managed, but editing and exporting them converts them to RGB. This could result in unexpected shifts in files with other color modes, so you may prefer to control the conversion to RGB yourself using Photoshop, and then import the RGB file into Lightroom for further editing.

- PNG files can be imported and managed, but editing in Photoshop or exporting requires conversion to another format (i.e. TIFF/PSD). Transparency shows as white in Lightroom.

- 32-bit HDR files can only be DNG or TIFF format.

- AVCHD format has limited support—Lightroom imports the MTS video clips but not the whole AVCHD folder structure. You'll need to manually copy the AVCHD folder structure from the memory card to your hard drive if you want to retain the additional metadata.

- Sound files (i.e., WAV and MP3) with the same names as imported photos are copied and marked as sidecar files. This means that they're listed in the Metadata panel, and if you move or rename the original file, the sidecar is also updated.

- Files that aren't created by digital cameras, for example, text files that you may have placed alongside the photos, are not be copied to the new location, so always check before formatting the card or drive if you've added extra files.

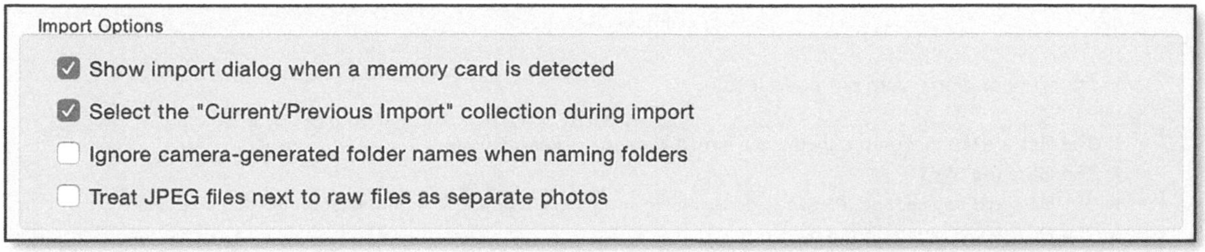

Import Options

☑ Show import dialog when a memory card is detected

☑ Select the "Current/Previous Import" collection during import

☐ Ignore camera-generated folder names when naming folders

☐ Treat JPEG files next to raw files as separate photos

can be a result of problems with the camera driver at the operating system level. You may consider purchasing a card reader, as they're usually quicker, reduce the wear and tear on your camera, and can show previews more reliably.

Figure 3.43 In *Preferences dialog > General tab*, the *Treat JPEG files next to raw files as separate photos* checkbox controls the handling of Raw+JPEG pairs.

- Lightroom simply hasn't finished retrieving all the embedded previews yet.

Regardless of the cause, you can go ahead and press *Import* as normal. Lightroom displays a more descriptive error message if it can't import the photos. We'll discuss some of these errors shortly.

If the photos are completely missing from the Import dialog, there are three main possibilities:

- The photos are in a subfolder inside the selected source, but you've forgotten to check the *Include Subfolders* checkbox.

- The file type isn't supported, for example, Lightroom won't display Word documents. See the File Formats sidebar for a list of supported file types.

- In Lightroom's *Preferences > General tab* is an option to **Treat JPEG files next to raw files as separate photos**. With this option checked, Lightroom displays the JPEG files alongside the raw files, ready for import. If the checkbox is unchecked, the JPEGs are added as sidecars when you import the matching raw file but they're not visible in the Import dialog. **(Figure 3.43)**

What does this error message mean?

If Lightroom can't import the selected files, it displays an error message **(Figure 3.44)** starting with **Some import operations were not performed** followed by the reason:

"Could not copy a file to the requested location."

If Lightroom can't copy or move the photos to their new location, it's usually because the Destination folder is read-only. Try another location with standard folder permissions, such as the desktop, to confirm that permissions are the problem. If it works correctly on the desktop, use the operating system to correct the permissions for

RAW + JPEG FILE FORMATS

If you've imported the raw files already, and you now want to import the JPEGs as separate photos, you can turn off the checkbox and re-import that folder—the raw files are skipped as they already exist in the catalog, and the JPEGs are imported as separate photos. The raw files remain marked as Raw+JPEG, and there isn't an easy way of changing that. Removing them from the catalog and reimporting them resets that label, but if you've made any changes since import, these changes may be lost, so the best solution currently is to close your eyes and ignore them.

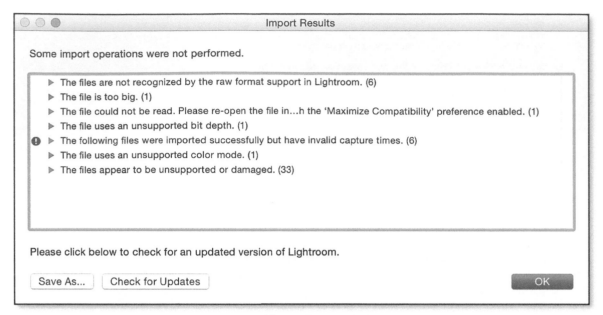

Figure 3.44 If Lightroom can't import your photos, it lists the photos in the Import Results dialog, along with an error message explaining the reason for the failure. Many of these issues can easily be overcome.

that folder. If the permissions appear to be correct already, it may be a parent folder that has the incorrect permissions. (You'll need to Google for instructions on correcting file/folder permissions, as it's an operating system function rather than Lightroom.)

Other possibilities include the drive being nearly full or the drive being formatted using an incompatible format, such as a Mac computer trying to write to an NTFS formatted drive.

"The files could not be read."

When Lightroom says *"The files could not be read,"* it more frequently means that they couldn't be written. Yes, I know that's not very helpful! As with the *"Could not copy a file to the requested location"* error, check the folder permissions for the Destination folder and its parent folders.

Lightroom also shows *"The files could not be read"* error if the memory card or camera is removed while the photos are still copying, or if the photos are deleted from the source folder before the import completes.

"The files already exist in the catalog."

If you're importing a large number of photos and you press the Import button before Lightroom's finished checking the new photos against the catalog, it may get to the end of the import and say *"The files already exist in the catalog."* It simply means that Lightroom didn't need to import them as they're already registered in your catalog at that location. If you search the *All Photographs* collection or look in the folder in the Folders panel, you'll be able to find them.

"The file is from a camera which isn't recognized by the raw format support in Lightroom."

Each time a new camera is released, Adobe has to update Lightroom (and ACR plug-in for Photoshop) to be able to read and convert the raw files. The list of supported cameras can be found at: http://www.Lrq.me/camerasupport

The Lightroom updates are released at 3-4 monthly intervals. Go to *Help menu > Check for Updates* to make sure you're running the latest version. If your brand new camera doesn't appear on the list yet, you can also check to see if Adobe has released an Release Candidate of the next update.

There's one other possibility if Lightroom says *"The file is from a camera which isn't recognized by the raw format support in Lightroom."* If a raw file is corrupted, it may show this error instead of the *"unsupported or damaged"* error.

"The file uses an unsupported color mode."

Lightroom supports RGB, CMYK, Lab and Grayscale color modes. If you try to import a photo in another color mode, for example, Duotone, Lightroom shows the *"unsupported color mode"* error. In this case, you'll need to convert the photo to a supported color mode, or import an RGB copy as a placeholder instead.

"The file is too big."

Lightroom has a file size limit of 65,000 pixels along the longest edge, and up to 512 megapixels, whichever is the smaller. If it tells you that the file is too big, then you're trying to import a photo that's larger than that—perhaps a panoramic photo. If you have any such files that you can't import, create a small version of the photo (i.e. using Photoshop) to import into Lightroom to act as a placeholder.

"The files could not be read. Please reopen the file and save with 'Maximize Compatibility' preference enabled."

Lightroom doesn't understand layers, so if there isn't a composite preview embedded in a layered PSD file, it can't import it and Lightroom displays an error asking you to save the file with *Maximize Compatibility* enabled.

To do so, you'll need to open the PSD files in Photoshop and re-save them. You'll find Photoshop's Preferences dialog under the *Edit menu* (Windows) / *Photoshop menu* (Mac), and in the *File Handling > File Compatibility section*, there's an option to *Maximize Compatibility* with other programs by embedding a composite preview in the file. **(Figure 3.45)** The preference only applies to PSD and PSB format files, as other formats (such as TIFF) embed the composite by default.

▶ **Figure 3.45** Maximize Compatibility in Photoshop saves a composite layer which other applications, including Lightroom, can understand.

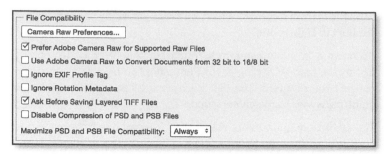

Maximize Compatibility does increase file size, but it ensures that other programs—not just Lightroom—can read the embedded preview even if they can't read the layers. It's safest to set your Photoshop Preferences to *Always*, or simply use TIFF format, which is generally a better choice now anyway.

"The file appears to be unsupported or damaged."

Files that have the wrong file extension, or 32-bit PSD files, can trigger the *"unsupported or damaged"* error message. 32-bit HDR floating point TIFF or DNG files are supported, but not 32-bit PSD's. Most unsupported file formats aren't even shown in the Import dialog, but those are the exceptions.

More frequently, severe file corruption triggers the *"unsupported or damaged"* error message, although files with less significant corruption may import without warning.

SALVAGING CORRUPTED RAW FILES

If you don't have an uncorrupted version, Instant JPEG from RAW may be able to extract a readable embedded JPEG preview from a corrupt raw file. You can learn more at http://www.Lrq.me/instantjpegfromraw

TETHERED SHOOTING & WATCHED FOLDERS

Before we move on to backing up your photos, we should mention one final way of getting photos into Lightroom. Tethered shooting involves connecting your camera directly to the computer. As you shoot, the photos appear on the computer's monitor, rather than having to download them later. Lightroom offers two different options, depending on your requirements.

If you're using one of the supported cameras, you can use the Tethered Capture tool, which allows you to connect your camera to the computer, view your camera settings and trigger the shutter using Lightroom's interface.

If you're shooting wirelessly, for example, using an Eye-Fi card, or other remote capture software, you can use Auto Import to monitor a watched folder instead. Auto Import collects photos from a folder of your choice as they appear and automatically imports them into Lightroom, moving them to a new location in the process.

Which cameras are supported by the built-in Tethered Capture?

The current list of cameras supported for tethering can be found on Adobe's website at: http://www.Lrq.me/tethersupport

Lightroom uses the manufacturer's own SDKs to control the camera, which results in some slight differences between manufacturers. For example, if there's a memory card in the camera, Canon cameras can write to the memory card in addition to the computer hard drive, whereas Nikon cameras only write to the computer hard drive. Waiting for the manufacturer to release an updated SDK can also lead to delays in tethering support for new cameras. Nikon cameras are limited to the list linked above, but due a difference in the SDK's, some unlisted Canon cameras may work. Some Leica cameras are also supported.

How do I set Lightroom up to use Tethered Capture?

To set Lightroom up for tethering:

1. Connect your camera to the computer using your USB or Firewire cable. A few cameras need to be in PC Connection mode, but most need to be in PTP Mode.

2. Go to *File menu > Tethered Capture > Start Tethered Capture* and choose your settings in that dialog: **(Figure 3.46)**

   - Enter a name into the *Session Name* field. This becomes the folder name for the photos.

   - (Optional) Check the *Segment Photos by Shot* checkbox. This subdivides the photos into further subfolders, inside the *Session Name* subfolder. The *Shot Name* can be changed from the main Tethered Capture window while you're shooting.

   - Select a file naming template. The default *Session Name– Sequence* template uses the *Session Name* you've entered at the top of the dialog, followed by a 3 digit sequence number.

3. Select a *Destination* folder. The *Session Name/Shot Name* folder hierarchy is placed inside your selected folder.

4. (Optional) Select your *Metadata Preset* and any keywords to apply to the photos as they're imported.

5. Press OK to display the Tethered Capture window. **(Figure 3.47)** The Tethered Capture window displays the current camera settings, but doesn't allow you to change the settings remotely. You can drag the dialog to another location if it's getting in your way. It floats over the top of Lightroom's

CONVERT TO DNG

For performance reasons, Tethered Shooting doesn't offer the option to convert to DNG while importing. If you prefer the DNG format, once you've completed the shoot, select the files and go to *Library menu > Convert Photos to DNG* to automatically convert the files.

Figure 3.46 The Tethered Capture Settings dialog sets initial import settings including the Destination folder, file renaming and metadata.

Tethered Capture Settings

Session

Session Name: Studio Session

☑ Segment Photos By Shots

Naming

Sample: Studio Session-001.DNG

Template: Session Name - Sequence

Custom Text: Start Number: 1

Destination

Location: /Volumes/Data NAS/LR6 Book Photos   [Choose...]

☑ Add to Collection   [Create Collection]

📁 Quick Collection
📁 Tethered Shoot

Information

Metadata: My Copyright

Keywords:

[Cancel] [OK]

standard window so you can carry on working without closing the Tethered Capture window.

- (Optional) If *Segment Photos by Shot* is enabled, enter a shot name in the Shot Name dialog. To update it for future shots, click on the *Shot Name* field in the Tethered Capture window to show the dialog again.

- (Optional) Select a Develop preset to apply to each photo on import. Certain settings, such as Crop, can't be included in Develop presets, however that doesn't prevent you from applying them automatically. Simply shoot the first photo, apply your crop along with any other Develop settings, and then select the *Same as Previous* option in the Develop presets pop-up menu. Any further tethered shots automatically have those previous settings applied, including the crop.

Figure 3.47 The Tethered Capture window shows the current camera settings and triggers the capture.

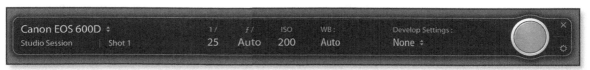

6. Press the shutter button on the camera or the silver button on the dialog to trigger the shutter.

7. When you're finished, close the Tethered Capture window by clicking the X in the top right corner.

How do I set Lightroom up to use a watched folder?

If Lightroom's tethering doesn't support your camera, you need to change the camera settings remotely, or you're shooting wirelessly, you can use other tethering tools such as EOS Utility, Camera Control Pro or Eyefi to capture the photos and drop them into Lightroom's watched folder. Lightroom then collects the files from that watched folder, and moves them to another folder of your choice, importing them into your Lightroom catalog, renaming if you wish, and applying other settings automatically.

To set it up:

1. Go to *File menu > Auto Import Settings*.

2. In the *Watched Folder* section, select an empty folder, perhaps on your desktop. **(Figure 3.48)**

3. Select a destination folder and subfolder to store the photos.

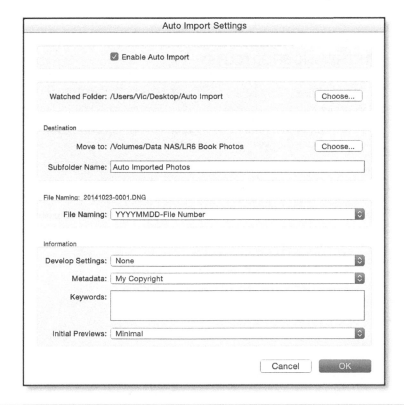

Figure 3.48 You can use alternative tethered capture software to capture your photos, and automatically import the photos into Lightroom using Auto Import.

NO SUBFOLDERS

Make sure your camera's remote capture software (i.e. EOS Utility, Camera Control Pro, Sofortbild) doesn't create a dated subfolder as Lightroom won't look in any subfolders in the watched folder.

4. Select your filename template in the *File Naming* pop-up.

5. Choose any other import options in Auto Import Settings dialog—*Develop Settings, Metadata Preset, Keywords* and *Preview Size.* These are the same as the choices in the main Import dialog.

6. Enable the *Auto Import* checkbox at the top of the dialog or go to *File menu > Auto Import > Enable Auto Import.* The watched folder needs to be empty when you enable Auto Import, and Lightroom needs to remain open.

7. To check you've set it up correctly, copy a file from your hard drive into the watched folder. As soon as the file lands in the folder, it should start the import, and you should see the file vanish from the watched folder. It should then appear in the destination folder and in Lightroom's catalog. If that works, then you've set up Lightroom properly.

8. Switch to your camera's remote capture software and set it to drop the photos into that folder.

9. Finally, connect the camera to the capture software, and ensure it's saving to the right folder. Release the shutter. The file appears in the watched folder, and then Lightroom moves to your destination folder and imports it into your catalog.

TETHERING SHORTCUTS

Hide Tethered Capture Window	Ctrl T / Cmd T
Shrink Tethered Capture Window	Alt-click / Opt-click on close button
New Shot	Ctrl Shift T / Cmd Shift T
Trigger Capture	F12

BACKUP

Before we move on to viewing your photos, it's essential to know how to back up your work. This is one of the shortest chapters in this book, but by far the most important.

There are three main categories of files that you'll want to include in your backups:

- The catalog(s)
- The photos
- The extras, such as presets and templates

We'll work through each in turn. If you already have a reliable backup system, you can skip to the checklist on page 71.

BACK UP YOUR CATALOG

All the work you do in Lightroom is stored as text metadata in your Lightroom catalog. There are four main things that could go wrong with the catalog:

- **User error**—you may accidentally remove photos from the catalog or unintentionally change settings.

- **Hard drive failure**—if your hard drive dies, you'll need to restore your catalog from a backup on another drive.

- **Catalog corruption**—although rare, the database can become corrupted, usually due to hardware errors.

- **Software bugs**—all software has bugs even though it's tested carefully. It's best to err on the safe side!

Most backup software just backs up the latest version, overwriting the previous backup. That's fine if your hard drive dies, but what if you make a mistake and don't spot it for a few days? That's where versioned backups come into their own.

Versioned backups keep multiple copies of a file so you can 'step back in time' to an earlier version. Lightroom's catalog backup tool does this automatically by zipping up a copy of the catalog and using the current date/time as the folder name so you can identify it later.

How do I back up Lightroom's catalog?

By default, Lightroom prompts you to back up the catalog weekly when you quit Lightroom, and it's as simple as pressing the *Back Up* button in this dialog.

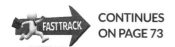

FASTTRACK CONTINUES ON PAGE 73

Let's dive a little deeper into the settings, however, to make sure your catalog backups are safe.

Where are the backups stored?

Unless you change the location, Lightroom saves the catalog backups in a *Backups* subfolder next to the original catalog. This is a fairly logical place, as long as these folders are also backed up to another drive by your primary backup system. However, it won't help if they're your only catalog backups and your hard drive dies.

To change the backup folder:

1. Go to *Edit menu > Catalog Settings* (Windows) / *Lightroom menu > Catalog Settings* (Mac) and select the *General tab*.

2. In the *Back up catalog* pop-up, change the backup frequency to *When Lightroom next exits*.

3. Quit Lightroom so that the Back Up Catalog dialog appears **(Figure 4.1)**.

PHOTOS NOT INCLUDED

Lightroom's catalog backup doesn't include your original image files. It only backs up the catalog containing metadata about the photos. I regularly hear from people who have deleted their original photos, thinking that Lightroom has them backed up, and I don't want to hear that you've fallen into the same trap. We'll investigate photo backup in the next section starting on page 65.

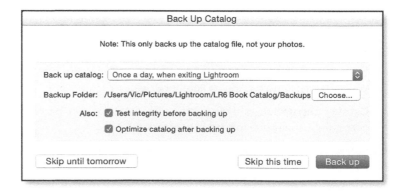

Figure 4.1 When the backup runs, you can change the backup location or frequency.

4. Press *Choose* and navigate to the folder of your choice.

5. Press *Backup* to confirm your choice and run your first backup at the new location.

The backup catalog is compressed into a zip file and placed in a dated subfolder at your chosen location.

Should I turn on *Test integrity* and *Optimize catalog* each time I back up?

Also in the Back Up Catalog dialog, there are two important checkboxes which are worth leaving permanently checked.

- **Test integrity before backing up** checks that the catalog hasn't become corrupted and attempts to repair any problems.

- **Optimize catalog after backing up** tidies up and helps to keep your catalog running smoothly and quickly.

How often should I back up the catalog?

We said that Lightroom prompts you to back up weekly, however if you're working on a large number of photos every day, a week's worth of work is a lot to potentially lose. You can change the backup frequency to prompt you daily, weekly, monthly, or every time Lightroom exits.

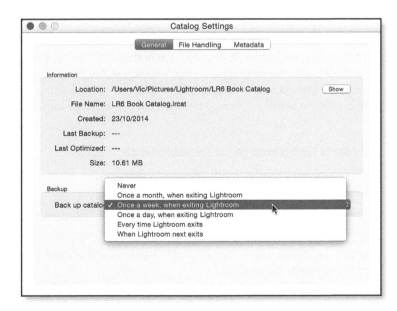

◀ **Figure 4.2** Set your backup frequency in the Catalog Settings dialog.

BACKUP ON DEMAND

If you've done a large amount of work (or moved/renamed files) and your backup isn't scheduled to run for a few days, or you hit skip because you were in a hurry last time you closed Lightroom, you can run an unscheduled backup. Go to *Catalog Settings > General tab* and change the backup frequency to When Lightroom next exits and then quit Lightroom so that the backup can run. When you reopen that catalog, it automatically reverts to your normal backup schedule.

SAVING METADATA WITH THE FILES

As long as you're sensible about backups, then you have nothing to fear from keeping your data in a single catalog. However if you like a belt-and-braces approach to backup, you can also save the metadata to the files in a format called XMP which is stored in the header of JPEG/TIFF/PSD/DNG files and in sidecar files for proprietary raw files. XMP doesn't hold all the information that's stored in the catalog, but as the XMP is stored with the image files, it has been known to save the day on occasion. We'll come back to XMP starting on page 343.

To change the backup frequency:

1. Go to *Edit menu > Catalog Settings* (Windows) / *Lightroom menu > Catalog Settings* (Mac) and select the *General tab*. **(Figure 4.2)**

2. Using the *Back up catalog* pop-up, select the frequency of your choice.

You can also change the frequency in the Backup dialog itself, when a backup runs.

How much work can you afford to lose if the worst happened?

I haven't got time to back up now—can I postpone the backup?

If, on occasion, you don't have time to wait for the backup to run, you can skip the backup. There are two buttons in the Back Up Catalog dialog. **Skip this time** postpones the backup until the next time you close the catalog. **Skip until tomorrow/next week/next month** offers a longer postponement, depending on your selected backup frequency. Don't be tempted to skip it too often, or you could find yourself without a recent backup.

Can I delete the oldest backups?

Lightroom compresses the backups using ZIP compression so they don't take up too much space on your hard drive, but if you're backing up every day, they can start to add up. The backups aren't automatically deleted, but you can go to the Backups folder using Explorer (Windows) / Finder (Mac) and delete older backups yourself.

I'd recommend keeping a couple of older backups in addition to the current ones, for example, 1 year old, 6 months old, 3 months old, 1 month old, plus the most recent 4 or 5 backups. You never know when you might discover a mistake you made a few months ago, and want to retrieve settings for some photos from a much older backup.

Why does Lightroom say it's unable to backup?

If Lightroom says it can't back up your catalog, there are a few possibilities to check:

- Check the backup location—is the drive accessible and does the folder still exist?

- Check the folder permissions for the backup location—do you have read/write permissions?

- Is there enough space on the drive?

If everything looks correct, try changing the backup location to a different folder. If this works, try changing it back to your normal backup location.

BACK UP YOUR PHOTOS

Lightroom's Catalog Backup is just that—a backup of your catalog. Your photos are not stored 'in' Lightroom and Lightroom's Catalog Backup doesn't back up the photos, so we need to consider how you're going to protect your photos from disaster.

There are a few main factors to bear in mind when planning your photo backup system:

- **How many backups?**
  - Backups can fail. For important files such as your original photos, consider keeping 3 copies (1 working plus 2 backups) on 2 different kinds of media (e.g. hard drive and optical), with at least 1 copy at a different location.

- **Are the backups reliable?**
  - Is the backup media (e.g. external hard drive) free from errors? Avoid using old hard drives for your primary backups.

  - Are they easily checked to make sure they don't develop errors over time? If your backup system is a mountain of DVD's, checking whether they still read correctly is a long job!

  - Think about what could go wrong and whether your backups would be protected. This includes hardware errors, software bugs, transfer errors, viruses, hacking, theft, fire, water damage, lightning strike and human error.

  - Is the file transfer validated? Byte-for-byte verification ensures that the files are copied to the backups without introducing corruption.

- **Are the backups protected from user error?**
  - If you accidentally delete a file, could you easily recover it from your backups? For example, RAID1 is not a sufficient backup system as the file is immediately deleted from both drives.

  - Is the backup system automated, or does it rely on you remembering which files you've already copied?

- **Could you easily restore the photos to their working folder structure with the correct filenames?**
  - If the backups are stored in a different folder structure, or

> ### WHERE TO STORE BACKUPS
>
> When considering your backup system, don't limit the backups to attached hard drives, because viruses, theft, computer malfunctions, lightning strikes, floods, and other similar disasters could wipe out all of your backups along with the working files. NAS (network attached storage) units are an option for onsite backups, although they still won't protect you if a disaster affects your house. Online backups, such as Crashplan, are an excellent choice if you have a fast internet connection, or there's always the lower-tech solution of leaving an external hard drive with a friend or family member.

you've renamed the working photos after backing up, you'll have a nightmare trying to restore them.

- How will you keep your primary backups updated with any changes?

- **Will your derivative files (e.g. photos edited in Photoshop) be included?**

  - If you back up to write-once media such as DVD or Blu-Ray, how will you back up the files you've edited in other software or added to the photo folders?

How do I back up my photos?

Every computer system is different, so I can't give you step-by-step instructions on how to back up your photos. Your choices will depend on your workflow, where your photos are stored, how they're organized, and the available backup media, among other things.

If you're not currently backing up your photos, anything is better than nothing. The simplest way to back up your photos is to include them in your main system backups. Windows comes with its own Backup and Restore tool, and Mac OS X includes Time Machine, both of which can back up your computer files to an external drive. For a little more control, you can run dedicated backup software. Ensure that all of your photos are included in the backups, especially if you store them on external drives, as these may be excluded from the default backup settings.

If you're looking for a slightly more flexible option, file synchronization software makes it very easy to keep a mirrored backup on another drive without wrapping your photos up in a proprietary backup format. These can also verify your data during the transfer, as most file corruption happens while copying or moving files between hard drives. Vice Versa and Chronosync are my personal favorites.

FreeFileSync—Windows/Mac—http://www.Lrq.me/freefilesync

Vice Versa—Windows—http://www.Lrq.me/viceversa

Chronosync—Mac—http://www.Lrq.me/chronosync

I back up photos using the Import dialog—isn't that enough?

We mentioned in the Import chapter (page 37) that the *Second Copy* backup in the Import dialog isn't a replacement for a backup system. It simply copies the imported photos into folders called 'Imported on [date]' so it's great as a temporary backup while you ensure the photos have been safely added to your main backups, or even as a write-once backup stored on optical media. It won't, however, replicate your working folder structure, back up any additional photos such as those edited in Photoshop, update photos you've moved or renamed, or remove any photos you've deleted.

Should you ever have to try to restore from these backups, you'd have a very time-consuming job reorganizing all the photos.

Back up the extras

Over the course of time, you'll also gather presets and templates that you've created or downloaded from other websites, so you'll want to back these up too. You can manually copy them from their various locations listed in the checklist on page 71, or set file synchronization software to do it for you.

RESTORING FROM BACKUPS

Now you can relax in the knowledge that your data is protected, but while we're on the subject of backups, let's talk about restoring them. After all, what good is a backup if you don't know how to recover from a disaster?

We'll step through restoring individual backups in this chapter, and restoring everything (after an OS reinstall or moving to a new computer) in the Multiple Computers chapter starting on page 481.

How do I restore a backup of my catalog?

If you're restoring your whole catalog, for example, due to corruption, find your current catalog (*.lrcat file) and rename it, move it or zip it up temporarily.

To restore your backup catalog:

1. Find your most recent backup in your Backups folder. The backups are stored in dated subfolders, with the zip file named to match your catalog name, to make them easy to identify.

2. Double-click on the zip file to open the backup. The *.lrcat file displays next to the zip file.

3. Move the backup *.lrcat file to your normal catalog location, replacing the existing damaged catalog.

4. Double-click on the *.lrcat file to open it.

5. If everything's now working correctly, you can delete the

> **TPG BACKUP**
>
> The TPG Backup plug-in backs up the main Lightroom settings (as long as they're in the standard locations) and manages the number of catalog backups. You can learn more at http://www.Lrq.me/photogeek-backup

> **MOVE IT!**
>
> Don't be tempted to work on your backup catalog without moving it first. It gets confusing when you're working in a backup folder!

previous (corrupted) catalog and you should be ready to continue working. If the catalog opens but is behaving strangely, for example, showing the wrong previews or running slowly, you may also need to rebuild the preview cache. We'll discuss this in the Troubleshooting chapter starting on page 525.

How do I restore part of my backup catalog?

If you only want to restore part of your catalog, there are a few additional steps:

1. Find your most recent backup in your Backups folder. The backups are stored in dated subfolders, with the zip file named to match your catalog name, to make them easy to identify.

2. Double-click on the zip file to open the backup. The *.lrcat file displays next to the zip file.

3. Move the backup *.lrcat file to a temporary location, such as the desktop.

4. Double-click on the *.lrcat file to open it into Lightroom.

5. Find the photos you'd like to transfer to the working catalog.

6. Select them and go to *File menu > Export as Catalog*. Select a temporary location, such as the desktop, and give the exported catalog a name such as "Transfer". Check *Export Selected Photos only* and leave the other checkboxes unchecked.

7. Go to *File menu > Open Recent* and open your normal working catalog.

8. In your main working catalog, go to *File menu > Import from Another Catalog* and direct it to the temporary *Transfer.lrcat*.

9. At the top of the Import from Catalog dialog, check the *All Folders* checkbox.

10. The availability of the options below depends on your reason for restoring the data from the backup catalog. We'll discuss the options in more detail in the Multi-Computer chapter starting on page 481, but these are the most likely options:

    If you're restoring photos you accidentally removed from the catalog, select *Add new photos to catalog without moving* in the *New Photos* section.

    If you're restoring metadata for photos that still exist in the catalog, select *Metadata and develop settings only* from the *Replace* pop-up in the *Changed Existing Photos* section. (To keep

---

SKIPPING EXPORT

If you're familiar with Import from Catalog, you can skip the Export as Catalog in steps 3-6 and select your chosen folders/photos using the Import from Catalog dialog instead. If you're unsure, follow all of the steps.

the current settings as a virtual copy, check the checkbox below too.)

11. Press *Import* to transfer the metadata into your working catalog.

12. Delete the temporary catalog from the desktop.

How do I restore a backup of photos?

If you have good backups, restoring photos is as simple as copying the backup photos to their correct locations.

1. Open your photo backups in an Explorer (Windows) / Finder (Mac) window.

2. Open another Explorer (Windows) / Finder (Mac) window and navigate to your normal working folder structure.

3. Copy the photo backups (whether specific photos or whole folders) back to their correct location in your working folders.

4. Open Lightroom and check that none of the photos are marked as missing. To double-check, go to *Library menu > Find All Missing Photos*. If any photos are missing, copy them from the backups.

That's the simple option, but let's consider a couple of variations that might arise.

You're restoring to a new hard drive.

1. Open your photo backups in an Explorer (Windows) / Finder (Mac) window.

2. Open another Explorer (Windows) / Finder (Mac) window and navigate to your new drive.

3. Copy the photo backups to the new drive, being careful to retain the same folder structure.

4. Open Lightroom. The folders and photos are marked as missing unless you've given the new drive the same drive letter (Windows) / drive name (Mac) as the old one.

5. Turn to the Missing Files instructions starting on page 525 to reconnect Lightroom's records to the new location.

Your backups are out of date, and you've moved/renamed some folders or photos in Lightroom since the backups were created.

(Note that this can be a really time consuming job, so it's worth keeping your backups current!)

1. Open your photo backups in an Explorer (Windows) / Finder (Mac) window.

2. Open another Explorer (Windows) / Finder (Mac) window and navigate to your normal working folder structure.

3. Copy the photo backups (whether specific photos or whole folders) back to their correct location in your working folders.

4. Open Lightroom and survey the damage! The folders and photos you previously moved or renamed are marked as missing, so you need to reconnect these photos manually.

5. Turn to the Missing Files instructions starting on page 525 to reconnect Lightroom's records to the new location of the photos.

How do I restore the extra files such as presets?

Restoring your presets and other files is as simple as copying and pasting them back to the correct locations (listed on page 71) and then restarting Lightroom.

Test it!

The true test of a backup system is how easily you can restore from these backups and continue working in the event of a disaster. If you're reading this before your hard drive dies, prevention is better than cure, so now is an excellent time to make sure you know how to restore your backups in the event of a disaster.

BACKUP CHECKLIST

Ideally you'll be running a full system backup, but as far as Lightroom is concerned, there are a few essentials to ensure you've included. I've listed the default locations, but you may have chosen alternative locations for some items such as the catalog.

- **The catalog(s)**—holds all the information about your photos, including all the work you've done on the photos within Lightroom.

  - Windows Default—C: \ Users \ [your username] \ My Pictures \ Lightroom \ Lightroom Catalog.lrcat

  - Mac Default—Macintosh HD / Users / [your username] / Pictures / Lightroom / Lightroom Catalog.lrcat

  - Go to *Edit menu* (Windows) / *Lightroom menu* (Mac) > *Catalog Settings* to confirm the location of your catalog. Your catalog may have a different name, but they all have *.lrcat as the extension. You may have created more than one catalog.

- **The catalog backups**—just in case your working catalog is corrupted.

  - By default, they're stored in a Backups folder next to the catalog.

- **The previews**—standard and smart previews.

  - These would be rebuilt on demand as long as you have the original photos.

  - If you have available backup space, backing them up would save time rebuilding them, and if you deleted your original photos accidentally, they may be the only copy left.

  - If you run a versioned backup system, which keeps additional copies each time a file changes, you may want to exclude the previews as they change constantly and will rapidly fill your backup hard drives.

  - Previews are stored next to the catalog as folders (Windows) or files (Mac) with a *.lrdata extension.

- **The photos**—in their current folder structure, in case you ever have to restore a backup. You'll want to include your edited files too.

  - Stored in the location of your choice. To locate a specific folder, go to the Folders panel, right-click and select Show in Explorer (Windows) / Show in Finder (Mac).

- **Mobile uploads**—photos uploaded from your mobile phone or tablet using the Lightroom mobile app.

  - Windows—C: \ Users \ [your username] \ My Pictures \ Lightroom \ Mobile Downloads.lrdata

  - Mac—Macintosh HD / Users / [your username] / Pictures / Lightroom / Mobile Downloads.lrdata

  - The Mobile Downloads.lrdata file is always stored in your Pictures folder, regardless of where your catalog and other photos are stored.

- **Presets**—includes Develop presets, Slideshow, Print and Web templates, Metadata presets, Export presets, etc.

  - Windows—C: \ Users \ [your username] \ AppData \ Roaming \ Adobe \ Lightroom \

  - Mac—Macintosh HD / Users / [your username] / Library / Application Support / Adobe / Lightroom /

  - If *Preferences > Presets tab > Store presets with this catalog* is checked, most presets and templates are stored in a Lightroom Settings folder next to your catalog.

- **Default settings and custom camera/lens profiles**—includes Develop default settings and Lens Profile defaults, which are shared with ACR.

  - Windows—C: \ Users \ [your username] \ AppData \ Roaming \ Adobe \ CameraRaw \

  - Mac—Macintosh HD / Users / [your username] / Library / Application Support / Adobe / CameraRaw /

- **Plug-ins**—includes export plug-ins, web galleries and any other extensions that you may have downloaded for Lightroom. Don't forget to keep their serial numbers safe too.

  - Stored in your choice of location. Check File menu > Plug-in Manager for the location of each plug-in.

- **Preferences**—includes last used settings, view options, FTP settings for uploading web galleries, some plug-in settings, etc. The preferences could be rebuilt if necessary, but you may save yourself a little time by backing them up and restoring them.

  - Windows—C: \ Users \ [your username] \ AppData \ Roaming \ Adobe \ Lightroom \ Preferences \ Lightroom 6 Preferences.agprefs

  - Mac—Macintosh HD / Users / [your username] / Library / Preferences / com.adobe.Lightroom6.plist

- **Startup Preferences**—includes the last used catalog path, the recent catalog list, which catalog to load on startup and the catalog upgrade history. The preferences could be rebuilt if necessary, but you may save yourself a little time by backing them up and restoring them.

  - Windows—C: \ Users \ [your username] \ AppData \ Roaming \ Adobe \ Lightroom \ Preferences \ Lightroom 6 Startup Preferences.agprefs

  - Mac—Macintosh HD / Users / [your username] / Library / Application Support / Adobe / Lightroom / Preferences / Lightroom 6 Startup Preferences.agprefs

THE LIGHTROOM WORKSPACE

I t's worth becoming familiar with the whole Lightroom interface as you'll be using different areas in all future tasks, so on the next double page spread, there's a quick guided tour. Flip over to get an overview **(Figure 5.1)**, and then we'll do a deeper dive into the Lightroom workspace.

The highlights are shown on the diagram overleaf are for quick reference, but if they're too small (e.g., on your eReader or tablet), don't worry, as we'll discuss them in detail in the text too.

MAIN WORKSPACE SHORTCUTS

Grid view	G
Loupe view	E
Compare view	C
Survey view	N
Faces view	O
Show/Hide side panels	Tab
Show/Hide all panels	Shift-Tab
Cycle through full screen modes	Shift-F
Show/Hide Toolbar	T
Show/Hide Filter Bar in Grid	\
Undo	Ctrl Z / Cmd Z
Redo	Ctrl Shift Z / Cmd Shift Z
Quit Lightroom	Ctrl Q / Cmd Q

THE LIGHTROOM INTERFACE OVERVIEW

Title Bar

The Title Bar shows the name of the current catalog, along with the standard window buttons. If it goes missing, along with the minimize/maximize/close buttons, press Shift-F once or twice to cancel the Full Screen modes. If the whole interface goes missing, leaving just the photo on screen, press Escape.

Identity Plate & Activity Center

The Identity Plate allows you to add your own branding to your catalogs. When a background task is active, such as building previews, it's replaced by the Activity Center status bars.

Panels

Panels can be opened and closed by clicking on the panel header. If you right-click on the panel header, you can show/hide specific panels.

In that right-click menu, you'll also find Solo Mode, which automatically closes a panel when you open another panel in the same panel group. It's particularly useful when working on a small screen.

Show/Hide Panel Groups

The left and right-hand sides are called panel groups. If you click on the black bars along the outer edges of the screen, you can show/hide the left/right panel groups, as well as the Module Picker and the Filmstrip. Right-clicking on the black bars gives additional options.

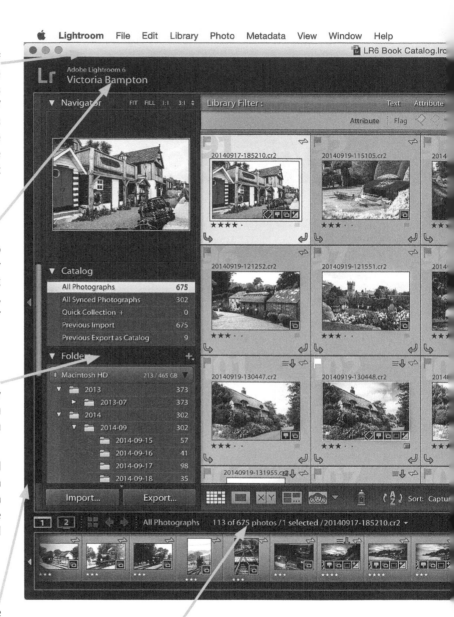

Breadcrumb Bar

The breadcrumb bar at the top of the Filmstrip has controls for the secondary window, as well as information about the selected source folder or collection, the number of photos in the current view and the number of selected photos. If you click on it, there's a list of recent sources for easy access.

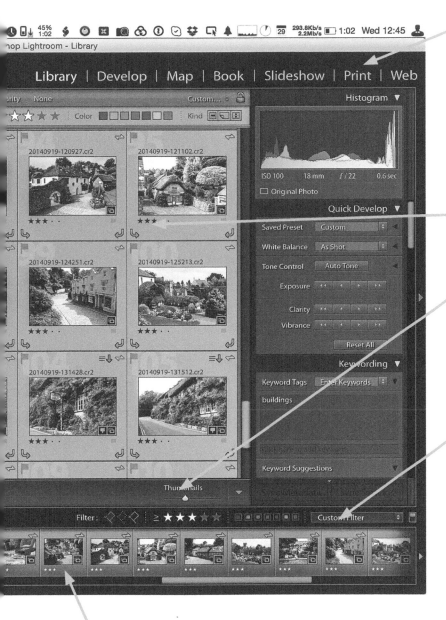

▼ **Figure 5.1** The sections of the workspace for quick reference.

Module Picker

The Module Picker gives you access to the Library, Develop, Map, Book, Slideshow, Print and Web modules. The selected module is highlighted, and you can click on another module name to switch modules. If you right-click on a module name, you can hide modules from view.

Preview Area

The central area of the screen is the Preview Area or main work area.

Toolbar

The Toolbar gives easy access to often used tools. Press T on your keyboard if it goes missing, and click on the arrow at the right-hand end to choose which tools show in the Toolbar.

Filter Bar

When viewing Grid view, the Filter Bar appears above the thumbnails. It allows you to filter the current view to only show photos meeting your chosen criteria. If it goes missing, press the \ key on your keyboard. You can also access frequently used filters by clicking the word Filter on the Filmstrip.

Filmstrip

The Filmstrip is available in all modules and shows the set of photos you're currently viewing. When you select a different photo in the Filmstrip, the main Preview Area is updated too.

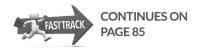

CONTINUES ON PAGE 85

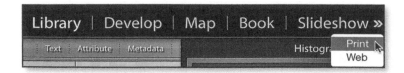

▶ **Figure 5.2** If modules become hidden, right-click on one of the other module names or click on the double arrows at the right hand end of the Module Picker.

THE TOP BAR

Having gained a quick overview, let's work our way round the different elements of the screen in more detail, starting at the top.

Module Picker

Lightroom is divided up into modules. Library is where you manage your photos, Develop is where you process them, Map allows you to add location metadata, and then Book, Slideshow, Print and Web are for displaying your photos in different formats.

In the top-right corner of the Lightroom workspace is the Module Picker where you click to switch modules. **(Figure 5.2)** When you open Lightroom for the first time, the Library module is selected and its name is highlighted in the Module Picker. To switch to a different module, click on its name.

As you'll likely spend most of your time switching between the Library and Develop modules, it's worth learning those keyboard

---

HIDING MODULES

If the Module Picker won't fit because you're working on too small a screen, an arrow appears on the right, allowing access to the other modules. If you don't use a specific module often, for example, you don't print from your netbook, you can right-click on the module name and uncheck to hide it. The hidden module is still accessible from the *Window menu*, and you can show it again at any time by right-clicking on the Module Picker and reselecting the module name in the context-sensitive menu.

If you select a custom Identity Plate, you can also change the font used for the Module Picker to a smaller size or narrower font, allowing them to fit on small screens without hiding any modules.

MODULE SHORTCUTS

Library Module	G/E/C/N or Ctrl Alt 1 / Cmd Opt 1
Develop Module	D or Ctrl Alt 2 / Cmd Opt 2
Map Module	Ctrl Alt 3 / Cmd Opt 3
Book Module	Ctrl Alt 4 / Cmd Opt 4
Slideshow Module	Ctrl Alt 5 / Cmd Opt 5
Print Module	Ctrl Alt 6 / Cmd Opt 6
Web Module	Ctrl Alt 7 / Cmd Opt 7
Go Back to Previous Module	Ctrl Alt up arrow / Cmd Opt up arrow
Go Back	Ctrl Alt left arrow / Cmd Opt left arrow
Go Forward	Ctrl Alt right arrow / Cmd Opt right arrow

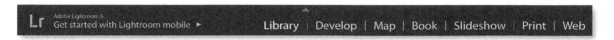

shortcuts—G for Grid view, E for Loupe view, and D to switch to the Develop module. We'll come back to the Library view modes a little later, starting on page 85.

▲ **Figure 5.3** The Identity Plate is to the left of the Module Picker.

Identity Plate

To the left of the Module Picker is the Identity Plate, which allows you to add your own branding to your catalogs. **(Figure 5.3)**

To change the Identity Plate, go to *Edit menu* (Windows) / *Lightroom menu* (Mac) > *Identity Plate Setup*. In the **Identity Plate** pop-up **(Figure 5.4)**, there are three options:

- **Lightroom Mobile** displays your name when you're signed into an Adobe ID, or reminds you to sign in.

- **Lightroom** simply says "Adobe Lightroom 6" or "Adobe Lightroom CC".

- **Personalized** allows you to create your own custom Identity Plate.

   To add your logo, select *Use a graphical identity plate*. Use the *Locate File* button to navigate to your logo, or drag it from Explorer (Windows) / Finder (Mac) into the preview field below.

   To create a text Identity Plate, perhaps using the catalog name, select *Use a styled text identity plate* and type the text of your choice. Select the text and change the font, size and color using the pop-ups below. Different sections of text can have different styling.

▼ **Figure 5.4** You can design your own Identity Plate to brand your catalog.

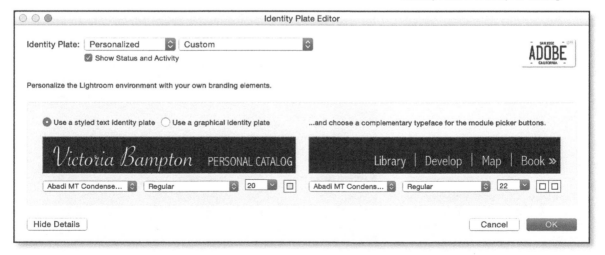

IDENTITY PLATE FORMAT & SIZES

Windows—approx. 48 px high (100% scaling), 74 px high (150% scaling), 99px high (200% scaling) by a maximum of 40% of the window width. JPEG, PNG, GIF, BMP or TIFF format.

Mac—approx. 57 px high or 114 px high (retina), by full window width maximum. JPEG, PNG, GIF, BMP, TIFF, PSD or PDF format.

If the background activity status is enabled (e.g. Sync with Lightroom mobile, Address Lookup, Face Detection), you lose approximately 16px from the height, or double for retina).

PNG format is a good choice, as it retains any transparency.

Larger files can be stored as Identity Plates for use in other modules, but they'll be too big for the Module Picker.

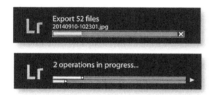

Figure 5.5 The Activity Center shows the progress of current tasks. When more than one task is running, they show as separate lines. The arrow at the end shows more detail for each line

These Identity Plates can also later be used in the Slideshow, Print and Web modules, so you may keep a selection of Identity Plate presets for different uses. To save your settings as a preset, select *Save As* in the second pop-up menu at the top of the dialog and give your Identity Plate a name. The Identity Plates settings are stored in the catalog, so if you have multiple catalogs, you'll need to set them up in each catalog.

Activity Center

When there's an active process running in the background, for example, a large import or previews building, the Identity Plate is temporarily replaced by the Activity Center. **(Figure 5.5)** It shows the progress of any current tasks, and clicking on the X at the end of any of the progress bars cancels the task. Lightroom is multi-threaded, which means it can do lots of tasks at once, so you don't need to wait for it to finish before doing something else. When there are too many tasks to show in one view, for example, more than three exports, it

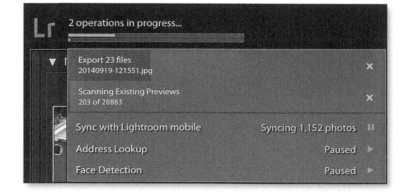

Figure 5.6 Click on the Identity Plate to show the expanded Activity Center which includes additional information and background processes.

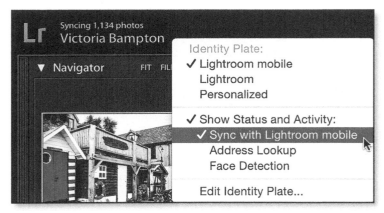

Figure 5.7 Right-click on the Identity Plate to always show background activity for selected tasks.

displays a combined progress bar. Clicking the arrow at the end of the combined progress bar displays each of the individual active tasks in turn.

If you click on the Activity Center, it expands to show more detail on the current tasks, including the name of the file that Lightroom's working on, and in some cases, how many photos are left to complete. **(Figure 5.6)** Clicking the X on the right cancels the selected task.

In the Activity Center you can also control the ongoing tasks that run silently in the background: ***Sync with Lightroom mobile, Address Lookup*** and ***Face Detection***. If these tasks are running in the background and slowing down the computer, you can temporarily pause them using the toggle play/pause button to the right, enabling them again at a time when you don't need to use the computer.

If you right-click on the Identity Plate, you can show these background tasks above the main Identity Plate when they're running. **(Figure 5.7)** By default, *Sync with Lightroom mobile* is enabled but the others are disabled.

Title Bar & Full Screen Modes

Above the Identity Plate and Module Picker is the standard window title bar and menu. If you find these distracting when working with Lightroom, they can be hidden using Lightroom's Full Screen modes. They're all listed under *Window menu > Screen Mode.*

- ***Normal*** window mode allows you to resize or move the window. The title bar along the top of the window shows the name of the

CAN'T ACCESS MENUS

If you can't access the Module Picker and normal menu options, look for a *Cancel* button in the bottom right corner of the window. You may be viewing the Import dialog, which prevents access to the other controls.

If you're not showing the Import dialog, press Shift-F once or twice to exit Full Screen Mode.

Figure 5.8 The Menu bar, Title bar and catalog name.

Menubar   Catalog Name   Titlebar

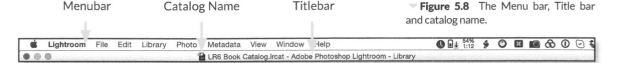

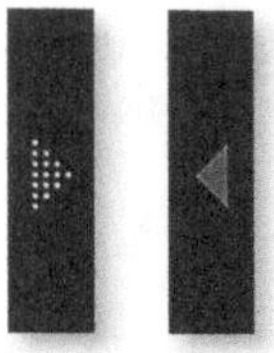

▲ **Figure 5.9** A solid arrow indicates that the panel is locked into position, and an opaque arrow indicates that the panel group is set to automatically show or hide when you float the mouse over that black bar.

current catalog, along with the standard minimize/maximize/close window buttons.

- **Full Screen with Menu Bar** fills the screen but leaves the menu bar showing.

- **Full Screen** hides the menu bar, as well as filling the screen. Floating the mouse right to the top of the screen briefly displays the menu bar.

- **Full Screen Preview** mode hides everything except the photo, allowing you to view it without any distractions. Even the cursor hides if the mouse is stationary. Press the F key to switch to and from the Full Screen Preview mode.

PANELS & PANEL GROUPS

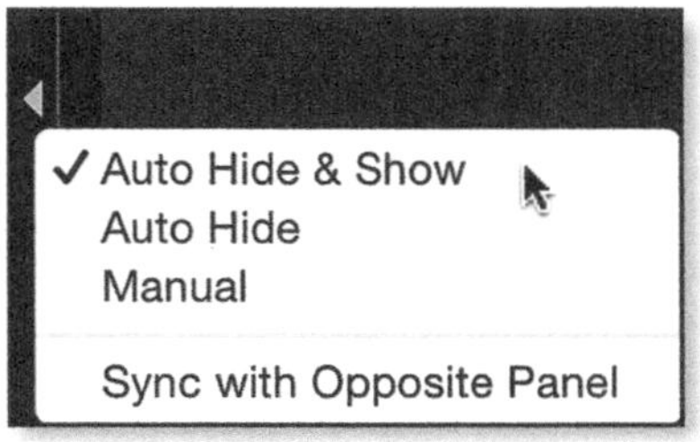

Down the left and right-hand sides of the screen are panel groups, each holding individual panels. The panel group on the left always holds the Navigator or Preview panel and other sources of information—folders, collections, templates, presets, etc. The panels on the right allow you to work with the photos themselves, adding metadata, changing Develop settings, and adjusting settings for books, slideshows, prints and web galleries.

▲ **Figure 5.10** Change the panel show and hide settings by right-clicking on the black bars.

The black bar along the outer edges of the panels controls whether that panel group is showing or hidden. Click on that bar to open or close the panel group. There are matching black bars at the top and bottom of the screen to hide the Module Picker and Filmstrip too. **(Figure 5.9)**

The panel groups are set to **Auto Hide & Auto Show** by default, which means that if you click on the black bar to hide the panel, every time you float the mouse close to the edge, the panels will pop into view. If you right-click on the black bars, you can change the behavior for each panel group, setting it to **Auto Hide** or **Manual**. **(Figure 5.10)** **Sync with Opposite Panel** opens or closes the panel group at the same time as the panel group on the opposite side.

Within the panel groups are individual panels, and they can be opened and closed by clicking on the panel header. If there's a panel you never use, right-click on the panel header and uncheck the panel name in the context-sensitive menu. To bring it back, just check it again or select the panel name under *Window menu > Panels*.

MISSING PANELS

If a panel goes AWOL, don't worry, it's just hidden. Go to *Window menu > Panels* or right-click on any other panel in the group and add a check-mark next to the panel name.

PANEL SHORTCUTS

Expand / Collapse Left Panels	Ctrl Shift 0—9 (panel number) / Cmd Ctrl 0—9 (panel number)
Expand / Collapse Right Panels	Ctrl 0-9 (panel number) / Cmd 0-9 (panel number)
Open/Close All Panels	Ctrl-click /Cmd-click on panel header
Toggle Solo Mode	Alt-click / Opt-click on panel header
Open Additional Panel in Solo Mode	Shift-click on panel header
Show / Hide Side Panels	Tab
Show / Hide All Panels	Shift Tab
Show / Hide Module Picker	F5
Show / Hide Filmstrip	F6
Show Left Panels	F7
Show Right Panels	F8

Solo Mode

In that right-click menu, you'll also find *Solo Mode*, which automatically closes a panel when you open another panel in the same panel group, so you just have one panel open at a time. It's especially useful when working on a small screen, to save scrolling up and down. To open another panel without closing the first one, hold down the Shift key while clicking on the panel header.

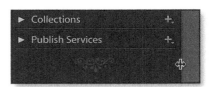

▲ **Figure 5.11** Panel groups can be resized by dragging the inner edge. The Panel End Marks show below the panels.

Panel Preferences

As well as showing/hiding panels, you can adjust the way they're displayed. Dragging the inner edge of the panel groups (or top edge of the Filmstrip), you can make them wider or narrower. This also changes the width of the sliders, making them easier to adjust. (On Mac, hold down the Opt key while dragging the inner edge to stretch beyond their normal limits.) **(Figure 5.11)**

There are additional controls in the *Preferences dialog > Interface tab*, where you can adjust the **Font Size** slightly and add panel **End Marks** to the bottom of each panel group. **(Figure 5.12)** You can create your

▼ **Figure 5.12** Change the Panel End Marks in the Interface tab of the Preferences dialog.

Panels			
End Marks:	Small Flourish ◊	Font Size:	Small (default) ◊

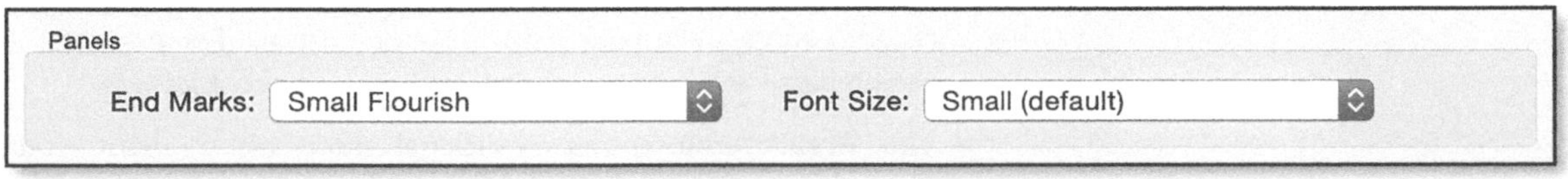

BAD EYESIGHT?

If your eyesight is no longer as good as it used to be, Lightroom's small text and gray-on-gray interface may be difficult to see. In the *Preferences dialog > Interface tab*, you can enlarge the font size slightly, but even the large setting is not very big.

Jeffrey's Configuration Manager (http://www.Lrq.me/friedl-config) offers additional interface tweaks, including changing the font and font size. It's still limited by Lightroom's fixed size elements, such as the lines between folder names, but it can help.

It's not possible to change Lightroom's UI colors, other than the background of the area around the photos, but selecting a bold font increases the contrast between the text and background, making it easier to read.

own panel end marks, for example, you can display your logo or notes such as the meanings of your star ratings and color labels.

To create your own panel end mark, you'll need a pixel editor such as Photoshop or Photoshop Elements. Create a transparent file of up to 250px wide (140px wide generally looks good), type your chosen text or add your logo, and save it as PNG, TIF, PSD or GIF. In the *Preferences dialog > End Marks* pop-up, select *Go to Panel End Marks Folder* and copy your file to that folder. Finally, select your panel end mark name from the pop-up and close the dialog.

THE FILMSTRIP

The bottom panel is called the Filmstrip. It displays thumbnails of the photos in your current view, making them accessible in the other modules. When you select a different photo in the Filmstrip, the main Preview Area is updated too.

To change the size of the thumbnails, drag the top of the Filmstrip to enlarge it or right-click on that edge to view a menu of preset thumbnail sizes.

If you find that the Filmstrip thumbnails become too cluttered with icons, or you like them there for information but don't want them to do anything if you accidentally click, you can select which ones to view using the *Preferences dialog > Interface tab* in the *Filmstrip* section, or by right-clicking and selecting View Options. The square badges automatically disappear when the thumbnails become too small.

Breadcrumb Bar

Along the top of the Filmstrip are other useful tools, including breadcrumb navigation that allows you to retrace your steps. **(Figure 5.13)**

From left to right, they are:

- **Secondary Display controls** allow you to display a second Lightroom window. We'll come back to that in the next chapter starting on page 99.

- **Grid button** gives you quick access to the Grid view from any module.

- **Forward and Back buttons** step backwards and forwards through recent sources, like your web browser buttons. For example, it remembers each time you switch between different folders.

- **The Breadcrumb** shows additional information about your

Secondary Display   Folder/Collection   Recent / Favorite Folders

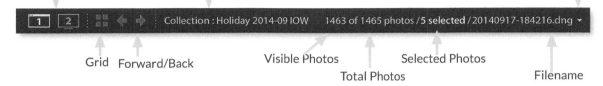

Grid   Forward/Back   Visible Photos   Selected Photos

Total Photos   Filename

current view. It shows whether you're viewing a folder or a collection, the folder or collection name, the number of photos that are currently visible and aren't hidden by a filter or collapsed stack, the total number of photos in that folder/collection, the number of photos selected, and finally the name of the currently selected photo.

Figure 5.13 Breadcrumb Bar

- **Recent & Favorite Folders** are displayed when you click on the breadcrumb, so you can easily skip back to a recent view. It also allows you to add favorite folders/collections that you visit regularly, using the *Add to Favorites* option at the bottom of the menu.

- **Quick Filters** display on the right hand side. They give easy access to basic filtering without having to switch back to Grid view. We'll come back to filtering in the Finding & Filtering chapter (starting on page 179), but to toggle between the compact and expanded views, click the word Filter, and to disable the filters temporarily, toggle the switch on the right. **(Figure 5.14)**

BREADCRUMBS...

Even wondered why it's called a breadcrumb bar? It comes from the story of Hansel & Gretel, where they left a trail of breadcrumbs to retrace their steps. When you click on Lightroom's breadcrumb bar, it shows all of your recent sources.

Preview Area

In the center of the window is the preview area, or main work area, which shows the photo(s) that you're currently working on. In the Library module, this can be Grid, Compare, Survey or People view with multiple photos, or a large Loupe view of the whole photo. We'll come back to these view options in the next chapter starting on page 85. In the Develop module it displays a high quality preview of your photo, and in the other modules the main preview area displays the output layout you're working on, such as book pages, slides, print packages or web gallery previews.

By default, the background surrounding the photo is mid-gray, however you can change it to white, black, or other shades of gray. To change it, go to Lightroom's *Preferences dialog > Interface tab*, or right-click on that gray surround and select an alternative shade from the context-sensitive menu.

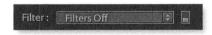

Figure 5.14 The Quick Filters are displayed on the Filmstrip, and if you click the word Filter (above), it opens up to show additional filter options (below).

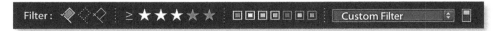

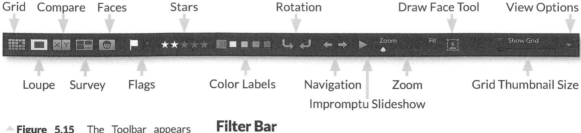

Grid | Compare | Faces | Stars | Rotation | Draw Face Tool | View Options

Loupe | Survey | Flags | Color Labels | Navigation | Zoom | Grid Thumbnail Size

Impromptu Slideshow

⌃ **Figure 5.15** The Toolbar appears below the grid or preview area, and gives you easy access to frequently used tools. This is the Loupe view toolbar.

Filter Bar

When viewing Grid view, the Filter Bar appears above the thumbnails. It allows you to filter the current view to show only photos meeting your chosen criteria. We'll come back to the different filter options and their icons in the Finding & Filtering chapter starting on page 179. If it goes missing, press the \ key on your keyboard. You can also access frequently used filters by clicking the word **Filter** on the Filmstrip.

Toolbar

Beneath the preview area you'll see the Toolbar. If it goes missing, press the T key on your keyboard or select *View menu > Show Toolbar*. **(Figure 5.15)** The options that are available on this Toolbar change depending on your current module or view, and if you click the arrow at the right-hand end, you can choose to show different tools.

Now let's move on to the fun part... viewing your photos!

VIEWING YOUR PHOTOS

You'll browse and manage your photos in the Library module, where there are a number of different view modes.

If you've been exploring, select the Library module in the Module Picker, then go to the Catalog panel in the left panel group and select the *Previous Import* or *All Photographs* collection, or select a folder in the Folders panel, and we'll use these photos to explore the different view modes. **(Figure 6.1)**

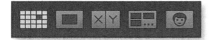

Figure 6.1 The view modes buttons are on the Toolbar. From left to right, they are Grid, Loupe, Compare, Survey and People modes.

VIEWING YOUR PHOTOS IN GRID VIEW

Much of the work you'll do in Lightroom will be in the Grid view, which can be accessed using the Grid icon on the Toolbar, by pressing the G key on your keyboard, or via the *View menu*. **(Figure 6.2)**

Figure 6.2 Enter Grid mode by clicking this button in the Toolbar or by pressing G.

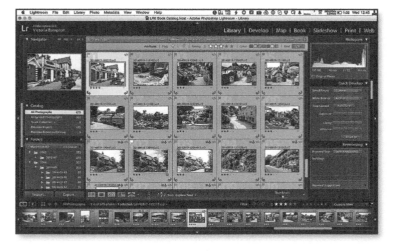

Figure 6.3 Grid view

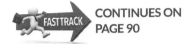

CONTINUES ON PAGE 90

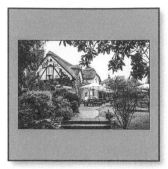

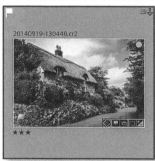

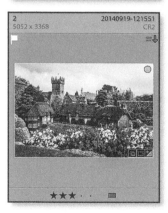

Grid view is a scrolling page of thumbnails **(Figure 6.3)**, and you can change the size of the thumbnails using the slider on the Toolbar. You can drag and drop these thumbnails into a different sort order in the Grid, or drag them onto other folders, collections or keywords to move or copy them. When dragging thumbnails, note that you have to pick them up by the thumbnail itself and not the border surrounding it, otherwise they'll become deselected.

In the Grid View, the thumbnails of the photos are contained within gray cells which hold additional information about the photos. There are three varieties of cell, which you cycle through using the J key or *View menu > Grid View Style*. First is a minimal view showing the thumbnail without any other distractions, then a compact cell view showing the icons and some file information, and finally an expanded cell view showing additional lines of information. **(Figure 6.4)**

Thumbnail Options

If you go to *View menu > View Options*, you can choose the information you want to show on the thumbnail cells. **(Figure 6.5)** The view of the thumbnails updates in the background as you test various

Figure 6.4 The simplest cell style (top) just shows the thumbnail photo. The compact cell (center) and extended cell (bottom) show additional information of your choice.

Figure 6.5 Set the thumbnail options in the View Options dialog.

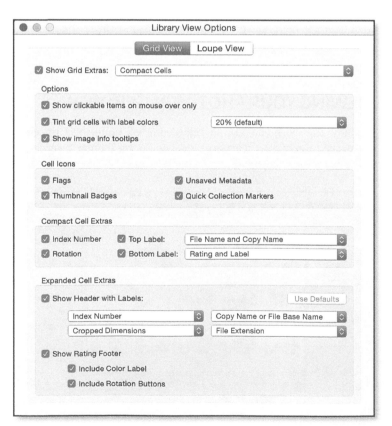

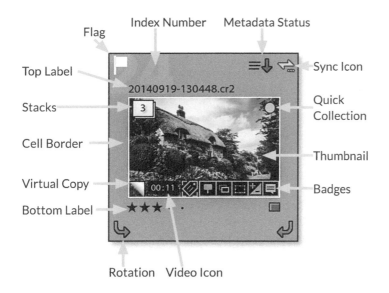

Flag
Index Number   Metadata Status
Top Label
Stacks
Cell Border
Virtual Copy
Bottom Label
Sync Icon
Quick Collection
Thumbnail
Badges
Rotation   Video Icon

Figure 6.6 A wide variety of information can be shown on the thumbnails.

FAST SCROLLING

On the right of the Grid view is a scrollbar which allows you to scroll through the thumbnails. My favorite trick is to Ctrl-click (Windows) / Opt-click (Mac) anywhere on that scrollbar to scroll directly to that point. It's much quicker than having to scroll a line at a time and get dizzy watching the thumbnails pass before you!

combinations of settings, to help you decide which you like best. **(Figure 6.6)**

Thumbnail

In the center, of course, is a thumbnail preview of the photo. When you need to drag a photo, perhaps to another folder or collection, remember to click on the thumbnail itself rather than the cell border surrounding it.

Cell Border

The cell border (or matte) surrounds the thumbnails and holds the extra metadata.

The color of the cell border changes through three different shades of gray, depending on the level of selection, and we'll come back to that in more detail on page 90. Clicking in the cell border deselects all other photos.

If you use color labels (which we'll come to in the Selecting & Grouping the Best Photos chapter starting on page 107), the cell border can be tinted with the label color using *View Options > Tint grid cells with label color.*

Top & Bottom Label

Metadata, such as the filename or capture date, can also be displayed within the cell border, above and below the thumbnail. By default, the top label is turned off and the bottom label displays the star ratings and color labels, but you can select which metadata to display on

HIDDEN PHOTOS

The *All Photographs* collection in the Catalog panel displays all of the photos in the catalog, regardless of where they're stored. If the count on the breadcrumb bar is too low (e.g., 28878 of 28880), some of the photos may be hidden in collapsed stacks or by a filter. *Go to Photo menu > Stacking > Expand All Stacks* and uncheck *Library menu > Enable Filters* to show these hidden files. The same principle applies to other folders and collections.

LIST VIEW

To view a list of your photos and their metadata, try John Beardsworth's List View plug-in from http://www.Lrq.me/beardsworth-listview

each cell using the View Options dialog. Right-clicking on the labels also displays a menu of available options. The Expanded Cells view has additional lines for file information.

Metadata Status

In the top right corner, the metadata status icons keep you informed of the status of the external files, for example, if the original file is missing or corrupted, or the file's metadata doesn't match the catalog records.

Lightroom primarily stores your image metadata in your catalog, but it's possible to store it with the files too. We'll discuss the XMP metadata in more detail starting on page 343. If you choose to write the metadata to the files, enable the *Unsaved Metadata* checkbox in the View Options dialog to display additional status icons.

The meaning of the different icons is shown in the Metadata Status sidebar.

Quick Collection Marker

In the top right corner of the thumbnail is a small circle, which you click to check (gray) or uncheck (transparent). The marker displays as a gray circle when the photo is in the Target Collection (usually the Quick Collection). The Quick Collection is a way of temporarily grouping photos, which we'll discuss in more detail in Selecting & Grouping the Best Photos. If you frequently accidentally hit the circular Quick Collection marker, you can disable it in the View Options dialog.

METADATA STATUS

Lightroom is checking the previews are current, building new previews, or waiting for a better quality thumbnail to load.

The file is missing or is not where Lightroom is expecting, so click the icon to locate the missing file. More on that in the Missing Files section starting on page 525.

The file is missing but a Smart Preview is available.

The file is damaged or cannot be read, likely as a result of file corruption.

Lightroom's catalog has updated metadata which hasn't been written to XMP.

The file has updated metadata which hasn't been read into Lightroom's catalog.

Metadata conflict—both the XMP data in the file and Lightroom's catalog have been changed. Click the icon to choose whether to accept Lightroom's version or the XMP version.

This photo is included in a Sync collection.

Lightroom is waiting to sync this photo.

Badges

The square badges at the bottom of the thumbnails give you additional information about the settings applied to the selected photo, and clicking on them takes you to the related module or panel. They are Keywords, Map Location, Collection Membership (only when not viewing the collection), Crop, Develop Adjustments and Comments (only when viewing a shared collection). **(Figure 6.7)**

Rotation

The rotation icons rotate your photo when you click on them. If **_Show clickable items on mouse over only_** is checked in View Options, the arrows disappear until you float over the photo.

Virtual Copy

A photo can have multiple versions of settings, whether that's metadata or Develop settings. These virtual copies are marked with a turned corner on the thumbnail. We'll come back to virtual copies in the Develop Module Tools chapter on page 311.

Stack

The Stack indicator shows how many photos are grouped together and the double lines on the left and right show the beginning and end of the visible stack. We'll discuss stacking in the Grouping Similar Photos section on page 113.

Flag

The flag state can be unflagged (invisible until you float over it), picked (white flag) or rejected (black flag). Clicking on it toggles between picked and unflagged, and Alt-click (Windows) / Opt-click (Mac) switches to a rejected flag. We'll come back to flagging in the next chapter, starting on page 107. **(Figure 6.8)**

Index Number

The index number counts the number of photos in the current view. For example, if you have 230 photos in your current folder or collection, the first is marked as 1 and the last as 230.

Video Icon

A video thumbnail icon displays the length of the video, and as you move your cursor horizontally across the thumbnail, it scrubs through the video, showing you the content. **(Figure 6.9)**

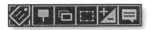

Figure 6.7 On the thumbnails themselves, there are badges with additional information. From left to right, they are keywords, map locations, collection membership, crop, Develop settings and social omments.

Figure 6.8 Photos can be flagged (left), unflagged (center) or rejected (right).

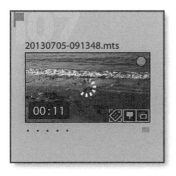

Figure 6.9 Videos have an additional badge showing the length of the clip.

GRID VIEW SHORTCUTS

Go to Grid view	G
Increase Grid Size	= (or +)
Decrease Grid Size	-
Show/Hide Extras	Ctrl Shift H / Cmd Shift H
Show/Hide Badges	Ctrl Alt Shift H / Cmd Opt Shift H
Cycle Grid View Style	J
View Options	Ctrl J / Cmd J

SELECTIONS

When you select multiple photos in Lightroom's Grid view or in the Filmstrip, you'll notice that the cell border displays in three different shades of gray.

Because Lightroom allows you to synchronize settings across multiple photos, there needs to be a way of choosing the source of the settings as well as the target photos, so Lightroom has three different levels of selection (or two levels of selection plus a deselected state, depending on how you look at it). **(Figure 6.10)**

- **Active**—The lightest shade of gray is the active photo. That's the single photo that would be shown in Loupe view or Develop module.

- **Selected**—The mid gray is also selected, but it isn't the active photo.

- **Not Selected**—The darkest shade of gray isn't selected.

Figure 6.10 There are three levels of selection—active (left), selected (center) and not selected (right).

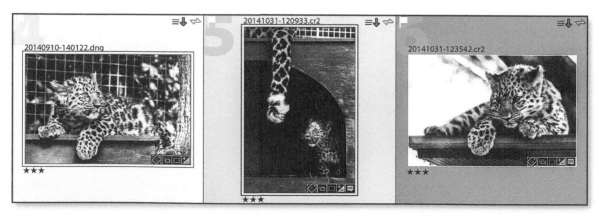

UPDATE MULTIPLE PHOTOS

Most of your actions only apply to the active photo, for example, pressing Delete only usually removes the active photo. To apply a setting to multiple photos, you must select Grid view on the primary window.

This protects you from applying a setting to multiple photos without realizing they're selected (perhaps because the Filmstrip is hidden) and accidentally undoing many hours of work.

With every rule, there are always exceptions. These are the main ones:

If you right-click on the Filmstrip or Secondary Display Grid view, the menu command applies to all selected photos (because you're obviously looking at them at the time!).

A few commands, such as Export and Build Previews, always apply to all selected photos, but they won't do any harm.

You can change the default behavior by enabling *Metadata menu > Auto Sync*. This causes any metadata actions to apply to all selected photos, regardless of the current view mode.

Anything you do in Grid view on the primary monitor, such as adding star ratings or keywords, applies to all the selected photos, whereas other views only affect the active or most-selected photo.

When applying settings, or especially when deleting photos, double check how many photos are selected, otherwise you could accidentally apply a command to all of them.

If you're synchronizing settings across multiple photos, Lightroom takes the settings from the active photo and applies it to the other selected photos.

To select a single photo, you simply click on it. To select non-contiguous photos—ones that aren't grouped together—click the first photo and then hold down the Ctrl key (Windows) / Cmd key (Mac) while clicking on the other photos. To select sequential photos, click on the first photo, but this time hold down the Shift key while you click on the last photo, and the photos in between will also be selected.

There's also a trick to deselecting photos. Clicking on the thumbnail itself retains your current selection and makes that the active photo, leaving the others selected too. But if you click on the cell border surrounding the thumbnail, the other photos are deselected, leaving just that single photo selected.

The thumbnails give you a good overview, but they're a little too small to see the detail in your photos, so Lightroom offers three further view modes—Loupe, Compare and Survey—each with different strengths.

SELECTION SHORTCUTS

Select All	Ctrl A / Cmd A
Select None	Ctrl D or Ctrl Shift A / Cmd D or Cmd Shift A
Select Only Active Photo	Ctrl Shift D / Cmd Shift D
Deselect Active Photo	/
Select Multiple Contiguous Photos	Shift-click on photos
Select Multiple Non-Contiguous Photos	Ctrl-click / Cmd-click on photos
Add previous/next photo to selection	Shift left/right arrow
Select Flagged Photos	Ctrl Alt A / Cmd Opt A
Deselect Unflagged Photos	Ctrl Alt Shift D / Cmd Opt Shift D
Select Rated/Labeled Photo	Ctrl-click / Cmd-click on symbol in Filter bar
Select Previous Photo	Ctrl left arrow / Cmd left arrow
Select Next Photo	Ctrl right arrow / Cmd right arrow

VIEWING YOUR PHOTOS IN LOUPE VIEW

The Loupe view **(Figure 6.12)** displays a larger view of one single photo at a time. To access Loupe view, click the Loupe button on the Toolbar **(Figure 6.11)**, press the E key, or select Loupe in the *View menu*.

You can move from one photo to the next using the left and right arrows on the keyboard, by selecting another photo from the Filmstrip, or by turning on the arrows in the Toolbar.

Figure 6.11 Enter Loupe view by clicking this button in the Toolbar or by pressing E.

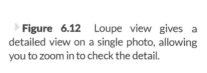

Figure 6.12 Loupe view gives a detailed view on a single photo, allowing you to zoom in to check the detail.

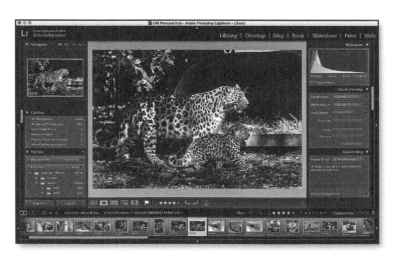

ZOOM SHORTCUTS

Toggle Zoom View	Z
Zoom In	Ctrl Shift = (or +) / Cmd Shift = (or +)
Zoom In Some	Ctrl Shift Alt = (or +) / Cmd Shift Opt = (or +)
Zoom Out	Ctrl Shift—/ Cmd Shift -
Zoom Out Some	Ctrl Shift Alt—/ Cmd Shift Opt -
Lock Zoom Position	Ctrl Shift = / Cmd Shift =

Figure 6.13 The zoom ratios are on top of the Navigator panel.

Zooming In on Photos

To zoom in to check details, press the Z key or Spacebar, or click on the photo. By default, it zooms into 1:1 or 100% view, but there are additional zoom ratios at the top of the Navigator panel. **(Figure 6.13)**

The standard view is the **Fit** view which fits the whole photo within the preview area. **Fill** view fills the entire width or height, hiding some of the photo. **1:1** is a 100% view, and the final option is a pop-up menu which allows you to switch through other zoom ratios. And yes, that last 11:1 option is a *This is Spinal Tap* movie reference!

Lightroom remembers your two most recent zoom settings and toggles between them, so to switch between Fit and 3:1 views, you'd click on *Fit* on the Navigator panel and then *3:1*.

Once you've zoomed in on the photo, the cursor becomes a hand tool and you can click and drag the photo around to view different areas, which is called panning. Alternatively, you can move the selection box on the Navigator preview.

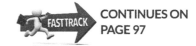

CONTINUES ON PAGE 97

ZOOM RATIOS

Lightroom's zoom ratios are based on the ratio of screen pixels (first number) used to display image pixels (second number). If you're used to working in Photoshop, you might be more comfortable with zoom percentages, so here's how they translate:

1:16 = 6.25% (1 screen : 16 image px)

1:8 = 12.5% (1 screen : 8 image px)

1:4 = 25% (1 screen : 4 image px)

1:3 = 33% (1 screen : 3 image px)

1:2 = 50% (1 screen : 2 image px)

1:1 = 100% (1 screen : 1 image px)

2:1 = 200% (2 screen : 1 image px)

3:1 = 300% (3 screen : 1 image px)

4:1 = 400% (4 screen : 1 image px)

8:1 = 800% (8 screen : 1 image px)

11:1 = 1100% (11 screen : 1 image px)

Figure 6.14 The Info Overlay (top) and Status Overlay (bottom) appear in Loupe view.

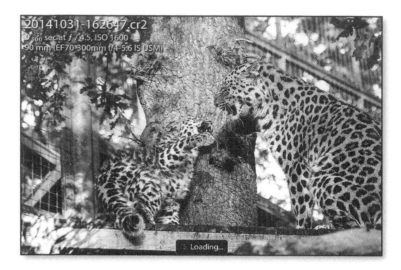

Lightroom remembers the last-used zoom/pan position for each individual photo, and returns to that same position next time you zoom in. If you check *View menu > Lock Zoom Position*, it ignores this saved position and uses the same image area for each photo. This is particularly useful if you're trying to compare the same spot on multiple photos, and you've previously zoomed into different areas on each photo.

Info Overlay

In the top left corner of the Loupe view (or Develop preview) is the Info Overlay, which displays information about the selected photo such as the filename or camera settings used. **(Figure 6.14)** Under *View menu > View Options > Loupe View tab*, you can store two different combinations of information to show in the Info Overlay, and then cycle through them using the I key.

Status Overlay

Whenever you use a keyboard shortcut to apply a setting, a status overlay message appears in the preview area, for example, *Set Rating to 3*.

A similar type of overlay is used in the Loupe or Develop preview when Lightroom is loading or building previews. **(Figure 6.15)** If you find the Loading Overlay distracting, you can turn it off by unchecking **Show message when loading or rendering photos** in the View Options dialog. Personally, I leave it disabled in the Develop module, as you can start working on the photo long before it's finished loading.

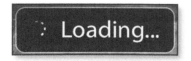

Figure 6.15 The Status Overlay keeps you informed about any changes being applied to the selected photo.

LOUPE & FULL SCREEN SHORTCUTS

Go to Loupe view	E (or Enter/Return from Grid view)
Show/Hide Info Overlay	Ctrl I / Cmd I
Cycle Info Overlay	I
Normal Screen Mode	Ctrl Alt F / Cmd Opt F
Full Screen and Hide Panels	Ctrl Shift F / Cmd Shift F
Full Screen Preview	F
Next Screen Mode	Shift F
Lights Dim	Ctrl Shift L / Cmd Shift L
Cycle Next Light Mode	L
Cycle Previous Light Mode	Shift L
Show Layout Overlay	Ctrl Alt O / Cmd Opt O
Choose Layout Overlay Image	Ctrl Alt Shift O / Cmd Opt Shift O
Layout Overlay Options	Hold Ctrl key / Cmd key
Video Play/Pause	Spacebar

Distraction Free Viewing—Lights Out and Full Screen Preview

While we're on the subject of distractions, let's talk about Lightroom's distraction free view modes. Lights Dimmed and Lights Out dim or black out the interface around the photo, allowing you to focus solely on the selected photos in the preview area. The photos are surrounded by a single white line. To cycle through the Lights Dimmed and Lights Out modes, and then return to normal Lights On mode, press the L key on your keyboard three times. You can adjust the color and dim level in the *Preferences dialog > Interface tab*.

To view a single larger photo in Full Screen Preview mode, press the F key to turn it on and off. Like Lights Out view, Full Screen Preview mode hides everything, displaying just the photo with a plain black background.

Layout Overlay

If you're searching for a photo for a particular purpose—perhaps for a magazine cover or product shots for a catalog—then you may need to preview how the photo will look in its final layout. The Loupe Overlay allows you to preview your photo with an overlaid Grid, movable Guides, and a transparent layout image.

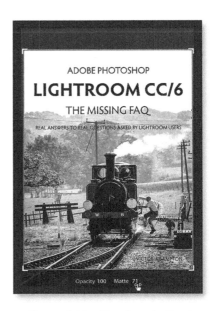

Figure 6.16 The Layout Overlay allows you to preview how your photo will look in the final design.

WHY WON'T MY VIDEO PLAY?

If you're having trouble getting videos to play, there's an excellent Adobe tech note at http://www.Lrq.me/adobe-videotrouble and it's also worth checking that your video format is supported at http://www.Lrq.me/lr6-video

QuickTime is needed for playing certain video formats, so Lightroom may show an error message if it's not installed. If you don't use video at all, or your videos play correctly, you can check the *Don't show again* checkbox and skip the error message. If, however, your videos won't import or play, installing QuickTime may solve the problem. You can click the *Download* button in the error message or go straight to http://www.Lrq.me/quicktime

The Loupe Overlay can be used on any photo in the Library or Develop module, but it's most useful when shooting tethered, allowing you to check that you're keeping the subject positioned correctly within the final frame. To activate the overlay, go to *View menu > Loupe Overlay* and add a checkmark to the *Grid*, *Guides* and/or the *Layout Image*.

If you select Layout Image, it asks you to choose a transparent PNG file. (You can change the overlay file again later by selecting *View menu > Loupe Overlay > Choose Image*.) **(Figure 6.16)**

To adjust any of the overlays, hold down the Ctrl key (Windows) / Cmd key (Mac) to show the controls. When **Grid** is selected, the available options are size and opacity. When **Guides** is selected, holding down the Ctrl key (Windows) / Cmd key (Mac) allows you to drag the crosshairs to move the guides, and double-clicking on the crosshairs resets them to center.

When you have a **Layout Image** selected, there are a few additional options. When the hand tool is showing, dragging the overlay moves it around on the photo. Dragging the corners resizes the overlay. The **Opacity** option affects the opacity of the overlay itself, and **Matte** affects the opacity of the black area surrounding the overlay. The matte works like Lights Out mode, hiding excess picture under a black matte.

Playing Videos in Loupe View

There's one final Loupe view overlay, which only appears when a video is selected. The playback controller overlay has a play/pause button, timeline, timestamp, thumbnail button and editing button. Press the triangular button to play the video. **(Figure 6.17)** We'll come back to basic editing in the Video Editing section starting on page 224.

There are additional view options under *View menu > View Options > Loupe View tab*. **Show frame number when displaying video time** adds the frame number to the minutes:seconds display when the playback

▼**Figure 6.17** The video controls appear when you float the cursor over the video in Loupe view.

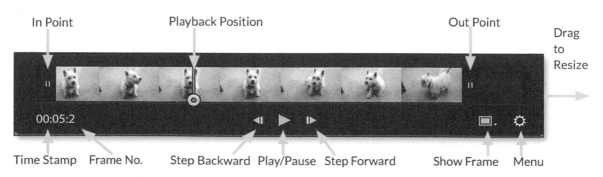

In Point Playback Position Out Point Drag to Resize

00:05:2

Time Stamp Frame No. Step Backward Play/Pause Step Forward Show Frame Menu

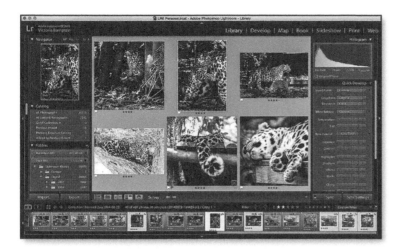

Figure 6.18 Enter Survey mode by clicking this button in the Toolbar or by pressing N.

Figure 6.19 Survey mode allows you to view multiple photos at the same time.

controller is expanded. *Play HD video at draft quality* uses a lower resolution for smoother playback on slower machines.

VIEWING YOUR PHOTOS IN SURVEY VIEW

Survey mode **(Figure 6.19)** allows you to view multiple photos at the same time, so it's particularly useful when you have a series of similar photos to narrow down to your favorites.

Select the photos in Grid or Filmstrip. If they're consecutive photos, click on the first photo, then hold down Shift key and click on the last one. If the photos are scattered, hold down Ctrl (Windows) / Cmd (Mac) while clicking on their thumbnails. Once the photos are selected, press the Survey button on the Toolbar **(Figure 6.18)**, the N key on your keyboard, or go to *View menu > Survey*.

When you hover over a photo, the rating/flag/label icons appear, along with an X icon which removes the photo from the selection and from the Survey view. When you return to Grid view, only the

SURVEY & COMPARE SHORTCUTS

Go to Survey View	N
Go to Compare View	C
Switch Select & Candidate	Down arrow
Mark next photos Select & Candidate	Up arrow
Swap active photo	\

N KEY ORIGIN

Most of the shortcuts use quite logical letters, but there isn't even an N in the word 'survey.' As an interesting piece of trivia, and easier way of remembering the N shortcut, this view was initially called N-Up while it was being developed, which is where the shortcut originated.

Figure 6.20 Enter Compare mode by clicking this button in the Toolbar or by pressing C.

Figure 6.21 Compare mode compares two photos in great detail, so you can choose your favorite before moving onto the next pair.

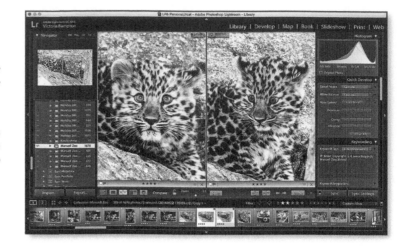

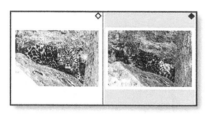

Figure 6.22 When using Compare view, the white diamond is the Select and the black diamond is the Candidate.

WHITE VS. BLACK

I struggle to remember which color diamond is the Select and which is the Candidate, but 'white for good and black for bad' is a handy memory prompt. **(Figure 6.22)**

Figure 6.23 The buttons on the Toolbar switch the Select and Candidate photos.

leftover photos are still selected, so you can mark them using the ranking system of your choice.

VIEWING YOUR PHOTOS IN COMPARE VIEW

Compare view **(Figure 6.20)** is used to compare two similar photos, and unlike Survey view, it allows you to zoom in too. Select two photos and press the Compare button on the Toolbar **(Figure 6.21)**, the C key, or go to *View menu > Compare* to enter Compare mode.

The active photo becomes the Select, shown on the left and marked with a white diamond icon. The other photo becomes the Candidate, shown on the right and marked with a black diamond icon.

The Select on the left is fixed in place, and as you use the left/right arrow keys on your keyboard to step through the photos, the Candidate on the right changes. When you find a photo you like better than the current Select, you can press the XY buttons on the Toolbar to switch them round, making your new favorite photo your new Select. **(Figure 6.23)**

As you upgrade a photo from a Candidate to a Select, the next photo becomes the new Candidate. Imagine you have a series of 5 similar photos, and you want to pick the best one. You start with number 1 as the Select and number 2 as the Candidate. You decide you don't like number 2, so you move to the next photo by pressing the right arrow key. You're now comparing photos 1 and 3, and you decide you like 3 better, so you press the X<Y button to make number 3 the

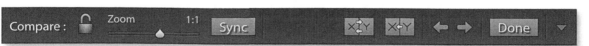

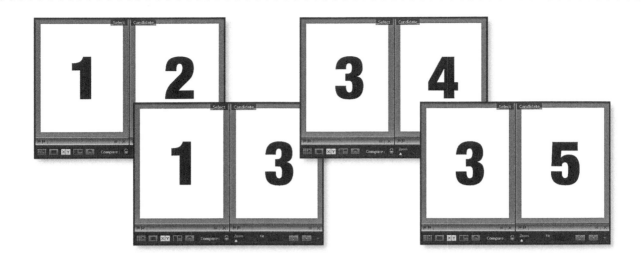

new Select. You compare that against number 4, but you still like 3 better, so you press the right arrow key to compare 3 and 5. In the end, number 3 is your favorite, so you mark it with a star rating. **(Figure 6.24)**

The Zoom Lock icon is particularly useful when checking that all the people in a group photo have their eyes open. If both photos are identically aligned, you can click the lock before zooming, and as you pan around the photo, both photos will pan. If they're not aligned, zoom in first and match up the alignment and then lock the position, so that the positioning follows you as you pan around both photos. With the lock unlocked, they pan and zoom independently.

Figure 6.24 Use the Compare mode to decide on your favorite photo.

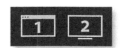

CONTINUES ON PAGE 107

SECONDARY DISPLAY

When many users think of using dual monitors, they think of Photoshop and tear off panels. Lightroom's Secondary Display options don't allow you to tear off panels, but they do allow you to display the photos on a secondary display, whether that's on a second monitor or just another floating window on the same monitor.

The Display controls are on the top left of the Filmstrip. **(Figure 6.25)** A single click on the Secondary Display icon turns that display on or off, and a long click or right-click on each icon shows a context-sensitive menu with the View Options for that display.

The Secondary Display offers a few different view options: **(Figure 6.26)**

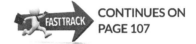

Figure 6.25 The Secondary Display buttons change depending on whether they're set to full screen mode or window mode.

- **Grid** is particularly useful for selecting photos for use in the Map module or one of the output modules.

- **Loupe** displays a large view of the photo currently selected on the main screen.

- **Live Loupe** shows the photo currently under the cursor, and updates live as you float the mouse across different photos on the main screen.

- **Locked Loupe** fixes your chosen photo to the Loupe view, which is useful as a point of comparison or reference photo.

- **Compare** is the usual Compare view, but allows you to select and rearrange the photos in Grid view on the main screen while viewing Compare view on the secondary display.

- **Survey** is the usual Survey view, but allows you to select and rearrange the photos in Grid view on the main screen while viewing Survey view on the secondary display. It's useful for checking consistency when editing a set of photos in Develop.

- **Slideshow** is only available when the Secondary Display is in Full Screen mode, where it runs a slideshow of the current folder or collection, while you carry on working on the main screen. Just be aware that if you switch folder/collection on the main screen, the secondary slideshow will also follow that change.

- **Second Monitor Preview** is useful if your second monitor is facing away from you, for example, facing a client on the opposite side of the table. **(Figure 6.27)** Using the pop-up in the corner of the preview, you can view and control what they see without

▸**Figure 6.26** The Secondary Display Main Window.

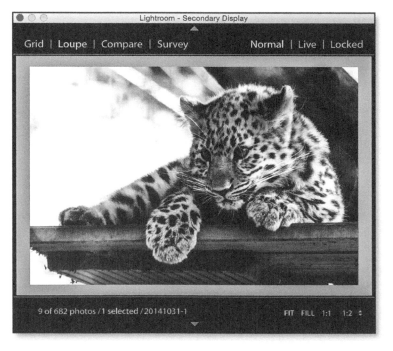

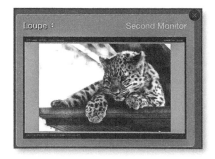

▲**Figure 6.27** The Second Monitor Preview is available when the Secondary Display is set to full screen view.

SECONDARY DISPLAY SHORTCUTS

Show Secondary Display	F11
Full Screen	Shift F11 / Cmd Shift F11
Show Second Monitor Preview	Ctrl Shift F11 / Cmd Shift Opt F11
Grid	Shift G
Loupe—Normal	Shift E
Loupe—Locked	Ctrl Shift Enter / Cmd Shift Return
Compare	Shift C
Survey	Shift N
Slideshow	Ctrl Alt Shift Enter / Cmd Opt Shift Return
Show Filter View	Shift \
Zoom In	Ctrl Shift = (or +) / Cmd Shift = (or +)
Zoom In Some	Ctrl Shift Alt = (or +) / Cmd Shift Opt = (or +)
Zoom Out	Ctrl Shift—/ Cmd Shift -
Zoom Out Some	Ctrl Shift Alt -/ Cmd Shift Opt -
Increase Thumbnail Size	Shift = (or +)
Decrease Thumbnail Size	Shift -

repeatedly running round to the other side of the table. It only works when the Secondary Display is in full screen mode.

Why do shortcuts and menu commands only apply to a single photo even though I have multiple photos selected on the Secondary Display Grid?

Lightroom doesn't know which screen you're looking at when you press a keyboard shortcut or menu command. For that reason, it always assumes that you're looking at the Primary Display (the main Lightroom window). Any shortcuts or menu commands will apply to the photo(s) shown on the Primary Display, unless you have *Metadata menu > Auto Sync* turned on, in which case it will apply to all selected photos.

The exception is the context-sensitive menu command on Grid on the Secondary Display, because if you've just clicked on the Secondary Display, you're obviously looking at it and realize that multiple photos are selected.

RANKING PHOTOS ON TWO SCREENS

If you're using Loupe, Compare or Survey at the same time as the Grid, it's usually better to switch the displays so that the Grid is on the Secondary Display. This is because there's no way of assigning a flag, rating or label to a single photo on the Secondary Display when multiple photos are selected in Grid on the Primary.

PREVIEWS & SMART PREVIEWS

While we're on the subject of viewing photos, we should talk about the previews Lightroom uses to display your photos. Lightroom is a powerful program, offering far more than just basic raw processing, but it can also tax the most powerful of computer systems. Waiting for each photo to load before you can start working can be frustrating, so it's worth spending the time to set up your preferences in a way that will suit your own workflow.

Why are there different kinds of previews?

There are three main types of preview caches, each with their own purpose.

- **Standard Previews**—Lightroom always creates its own previews, regardless of file type. These 'normal' previews allow you to apply Develop changes to the photos without affecting the original image data, and also allow you to view the photos when the originals are offline.

  - *Standard-Sized Previews* are the most frequently used previews. They're used to display the photo in every module except Develop (where they're shown briefly and then replaced with cached raw data). The size of these previews depends on the resolution of your screen, and it's selected in *Catalog Settings > File Handling tab*. For speed, Lightroom stores a range of different size previews, from thumbnails right up to your chosen preview size.

  - *1:1 Previews* are full resolution so they take up more space, but if you want to zoom in on your photos in the Library module, it avoids Lightroom having to build 1:1 previews on the fly, which would slow your browsing experience. If you're concerned about the disc space that they take up, you can choose to have them automatically deleted after 1 day, 7 days, 30 days or Never, or you can discard 1:1 previews on demand by selecting the photos and choosing *Library menu > Previews > Discard 1:1 Previews*.

  - *People Previews* are thumbnails of faces, used in the People/ Person views.

  - Behind the scenes, standard and 1:1 sized Previews are rendered Adobe RGB JPEG files. These standard previews are fast for browsing, but the quality is too low for editing in the Develop module. That's where Smart Previews come in.

- **Smart Previews**—Smart Previews are proxy files that can be used in place of the original files when the original files are offline. They're partially processed raw data (lower resolution Lossy DNG), so they behave like the original raw files when editing in the Develop module. They also help to speed up indexing the image content and mobile sync. We'll come back to Smart Previews in more detail in the Multiple Computers chapter on page 508.

• **Temporary Caches**—Lightroom also uses a selection of temporary caches to improve performance, especially in the Develop module. We'll explore those in the Performance Tips section, starting on page 551.

Choosing the best preview settings for your own browsing habits is essential in keeping Lightroom running smoothly, so let's investigate the most frequent questions.

How do I build previews after importing the photos?

If you haven't built your chosen previews at the time of import, or you want to update the standard previews as you've made Develop changes, select all (or none) of the photos in Grid view and choose *Library menu > Previews > Build Standard-Sized Previews, 1:1 Previews* or *Smart Previews.* **(Figure 6.28)**

If you have no photos selected, or all photos selected, Lightroom builds previews for all the photos in the current view, whether that's a collection, a folder, a filtered view, etc. If you have more than 1 photo selected in Grid mode, it assumes you just want to apply to the selected photos. If you have just 1 photo selected, it asks whether you want to build just that one preview, or previews for all photos in the current view.

How do I check which photos have previews or smart previews?

There isn't an easy way to check whether a photo already has a standard or 1:1 preview, but if you select any of the *Build Preview* commands, Lightroom just builds previews as needed, skipping the photos that already have current previews.

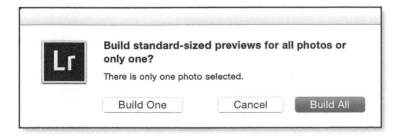

Figure 6.28 When one photo is selected, Lightroom asks whether to build previews for all the photos or just the selected photo.

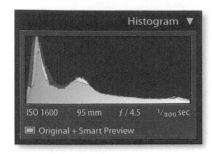

Figure 6.29 File status shows in the Histogram panel.

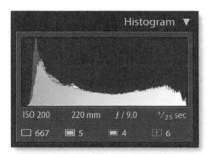

Figure 6.30 When multiple photos are selected, the file status switches to icons.

Smart Previews are a little different, as they're required for offline editing. As with standard previews, the *Build Smart Previews* command skips any existing smart previews, but there's additional status information available too.

Under the Histogram is a file status area. **(Figure 6.29)** When a single photo is selected, it says:

- **Original Photo**—the original is available, but there's no smart preview
- **Original + Smart Preview**—the original is available, but a smart preview is available if the originals go offline
- **Smart Preview**—the original is offline, but a smart preview is available
- **Photo is Missing**—the original is offline and there's no smart preview

If multiple photos are selected, it just displays the icons and photo counts. When more than 1000 photos are selected, a + symbol appears next to the photo counts, showing that it stopped counting for performance reasons. **(Figure 6.30)**

You can also create a Smart Collection for *Has Smart Previews* is True or False, which makes it easy to keep track of which Smart Previews you need to build.

What size and quality should I set for Standard-Sized Previews?

In *Catalog Settings > File Handling tab*, you can set the **Standard Preview Size** and **Preview Quality**. **(Figure 6.31)** (This is a per-catalog setting, so if you use multiple catalogs, you'll need to check each catalog.)

The best size setting depends on your general browsing habits and on your screen resolution. Choosing a size about the width of your screen is a good starting point, and the default *Auto* setting does this automatically. If you always leave the panels open and your hard drive space is very limited, you may prefer a slightly smaller size.

The quality setting is, as with most things, a trade-off. Low quality previews take up less space on disc as they're more compressed, but higher quality previews look better. The default, *Medium*, is a good compromise.

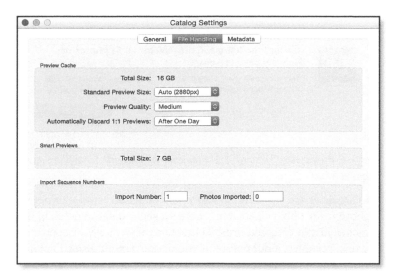

Figure 6.31 Select your preview size in the Catalog Settings dialog.

Where are previews stored?

The previews are stored in a *.lrdata folder (Windows) / package file (Mac) next to your catalog. The name of the folder/file matches the name of their catalog, and you can find them by going to *Edit menu* (Windows) / *Lightroom menu* (Mac) > *Catalog Settings > General tab* and pressing the *Show in Explorer* (Windows) / *Show in Finder* (Mac) button.

The standard previews have *.lrprev extensions and the folder/file name ends in Previews.lrdata. The smart previews have *.dng extensions and folder/filename ends in Smart Previews.

The previews folder is huge—can I delete it?

The previews folders/files can grow very large, especially if you're creating 1:1 previews or smart previews. You can delete any of the previews without permanent damage, but Lightroom will have to rebuild the previews when you next view the photos, and if the files are offline, it will just show gray boxes until the files are next online and the previews can be rebuilt, so deleting the *.lrdata files can be a false economy.

If you find your previews are taking up too much space, consider discarding specific previews rather than deleting the entire preview cache.

How do I delete previews?

You can discard 1:1 and smart previews in the same way as you build them. Simply select the photos in Grid view and choose *Library*

MOVE PREVIEWS

Officially the previews have to be next to the catalog. That said, it's technically possible to move the previews onto another drive using a symbolic link (not a standard alias or shortcut). If you do put the previews on another drive, make sure it's a fast drive, as you'll need good read speeds. And remember, this isn't supported by Adobe or myself!

Figure 6.32 As 1:1 previews take a lot of hard drive space, Lightroom allows you to discard them on demand.

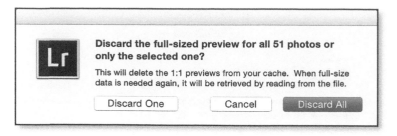

menu > Previews > Discard 1:1 Previews or Discard Smart Previews. **(Figure 6.32)**

The previews are also automatically deleted if you remove or delete a photo from within Lightroom. There's a slight delay in deleting the preview, just in case you press Undo, but they usually disappear at the next relaunch, if not before. If you delete a photo using Explorer (Windows), Finder (Mac), or other software, but it's just marked as missing in Lightroom's catalog, the preview remains until you remove the photo from the catalog.

You can also automatically delete 1:1 previews a set time by selecting **_Automatically Discard 1:1 Previews_** After One Day / After One Week / After 30 Days or Never in the Catalog Settings dialog.

I've discarded 1:1 previews—why hasn't the file/folder size shrunk?

When you discard 1:1 previews, Lightroom only deletes 1:1 previews that are more than twice the size of your Standard-Sized Previews preference. For example, if your Standard-Sized Previews preference is set to 2048 and your 1:1 preview is 3036, Lightroom will keep the 1:1 preview, whereas if your Standard-Sized Previews preference is set to 1024, the 1:1 preview would be deleted.

SELECTING THE BEST PHOTOS

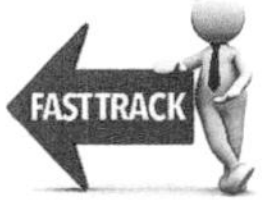

Having imported and viewed your photos, you're ready to start managing them—sorting through them and choosing your favorites, organizing them into groups, adding metadata to describe the photos, and then later going back to find specific photos using various filtering options.

RATING YOUR PHOTOS

Lightroom offers three different ways of ranking your photos.

- **Flags** have three different states—flagged (picked), unflagged and rejected. It's a popular ranking system among Lightroom users, but note that flags can't be written to the files or shared with other software. **(Figure 7.1)**

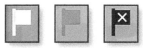

▲ **Figure 7.1** Flags

- **Star Ratings** are used by photographers worldwide, with 5 stars being the best photos. Stars are standardized metadata so they can be understood by other software. Many photographers limit themselves to using 1-3 stars when initially ranking their photos, and leave 4 and 5 stars for the best photos they've ever taken. **(Figure 7.2)**

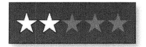

▲ **Figure 7.2** Star Ratings

- **Color Labels** have no specific meaning, so you can decide how to use them. Many use them to mark photos that need further work in other editors, for example, photos that need retouching in Photoshop, sets of photos for merging into HDR, photos to be built into a panorama, etc. **(Figure 7.3)**

There are numerous ways to apply or remove star ratings, color labels and flags including clicking the icons on the thumbnails (or on

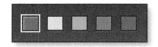

▲ **Figure 7.3** Color Labels

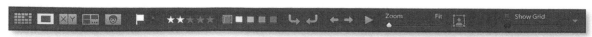

▲**Figure 7.4** The buttons on the Toolbar can be used to set Flags, Stars and Color Labels.

the Toolbar if stars are enabled), selecting them from the *Photo menu* or right-click menu, or using their keyboard shortcuts. **(Figure 7.4)**

On the keyboard, the 0-5 keys apply star ratings, with 1-5 obviously setting 1-5 stars, and 0 clearing your rating. The 6-9 keys apply or remove red, yellow, green and blue color labels. Flags use the P key for Picked or Flagged, U for Unflagged, and X for rejected. The ` key (near the X) toggles between Flagged and Unflagged.

If you're in a decisive mood, turn on Caps Lock, hold down Shift while using these keyboard shortcuts, or enable *Photo menu > Auto Advance*. When you press the keyboard shortcut, Lightroom applies the ranking and automatically advances to the next photo.

How do I rank my photos?

Let's try ranking the photos you've just imported. If you haven't decided which system you prefer yet, use the Reject flag to mark photos to be deleted, and star ratings to grade the quality of the photos.

1. Select the first photo and switch to the Loupe mode using the E key or the Loupe button on the Toolbar.

2. Decide how much you like the photo on screen. Press the X key to mark it for deletion, or the 1, 2 or 3 keys to apply a star rating. If you prefer to use the mouse, click the triangle at the end of the Toolbar and select *Flagging* and *Rating* from the menu to display the icons, then click the icons on the Toolbar to apply your ranking.

3. Use the left/right arrows on the keyboard to move between photos. Keep going until you get to the last photo. Remember, you can change your mind later!

4. If you find a group of similar photos, switch to Compare mode (C key) or Survey mode (N key) to view them together and then mark the best ones from the group.

How do I use color labels?

Color labels are more flexible than star ratings and flags, because they're simple text metadata represented by a color. Add a red label to a photo using the 6 key, then look in the Metadata panel on the right-hand side of the Library module. You'll see the text *"Red"* listed next to the word Label, because the red label is associated with the word *"Red"* by default.

MULTIPASS EDIT

Some people prefer to take multiple passes through the photos when ranking—perhaps marking as reject or 1 star the first time and then going through the 1 star photos again, marking the best ones as 2 stars. You may need to experiment before deciding which workflow suits you best. Workflow examples are shown on the diagram to give you some ideas. **(Figure 7.5)**

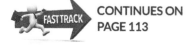

FASTTRACK CONTINUES ON PAGE 113

Workflow—Selecting the Best Photos

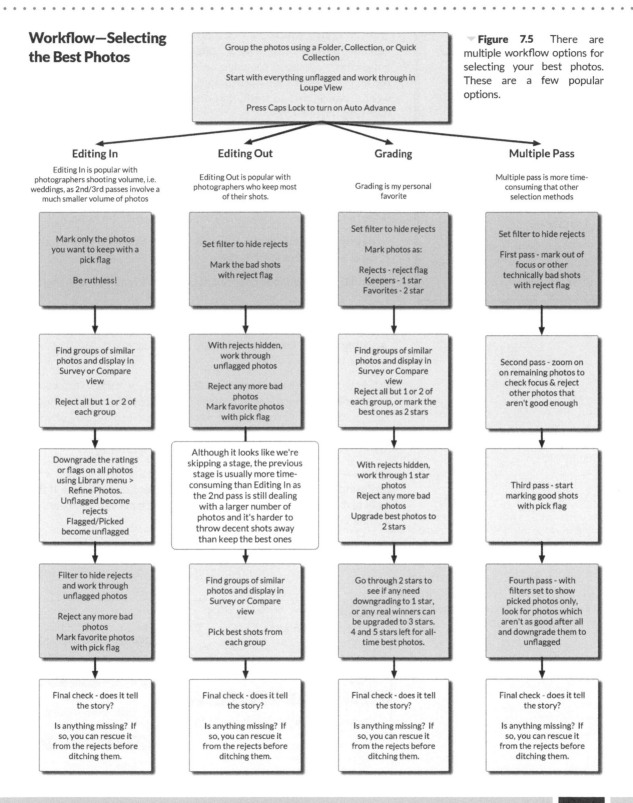

Figure 7.5 There are multiple workflow options for selecting your best photos. These are a few popular options.

Group the photos using a Folder, Collection, or Quick Collection

Start with everything unflagged and work through in Loupe View

Press Caps Lock to turn on Auto Advance

Editing In

Editing In is popular with photographers shooting volume, i.e. weddings, as 2nd/3rd passes involve a much smaller volume of photos

Mark only the photos you want to keep with a pick flag

Be ruthless!

Find groups of similar photos and display in Survey or Compare view

Reject all but 1 or 2 of each group

Downgrade the ratings or flags on all photos using Library menu > Refine Photos. Unflagged become rejects Flagged/Picked become unflagged

Filter to hide rejects and work through unflagged photos

Reject any more bad photos Mark favorite photos with pick flag

Final check - does it tell the story?

Is anything missing? If so, you can rescue it from the rejects before ditching them.

Editing Out

Editing Out is popular with photographers who keep most of their shots.

Set filter to hide rejects

Mark the bad shots with reject flag

With rejects hidden, work through unflagged photos

Reject any more bad photos Mark favorite photos with pick flag

Although it looks like we're skipping a stage, the previous stage is usually more time-consuming than Editing In as the 2nd pass is still dealing with a larger number of photos and it's harder to throw decent shots away than keep the best ones

Find groups of similar photos and display in Survey or Compare view

Pick best shots from each group

Final check - does it tell the story?

Is anything missing? If so, you can rescue it from the rejects before ditching them.

Grading

Grading is my personal favorite

Set filter to hide rejects

Mark photos as:

Rejects - reject flag Keepers - 1 star Favorites - 2 star

Find groups of similar photos and display in Survey or Compare view Reject all but 1 or 2 of each group, or mark the best ones as 2 stars

With rejects hidden, work through 1 star photos Reject any more bad photos Upgrade best photos to 2 stars

Go through 2 stars to see if any need downgrading to 1 star, or any real winners can be upgraded to 3 stars. 4 and 5 stars left for all-time best photos.

Final check - does it tell the story?

Is anything missing? If so, you can rescue it from the rejects before ditching them.

Multiple Pass

Multiple pass is more time-consuming that other selection methods

Set filter to hide rejects

First pass - mark out of focus or other technically bad shots with reject flag

Second pass - zoom on on remaining photos to check focus & reject other photos that aren't good enough

Third pass - start marking good shots with pick flag

Fourth pass - with filters set to show picked photos only, look for photos which aren't as good after all and downgrade them to unflagged

Final check - does it tell the story?

Is anything missing? If so, you can rescue it from the rejects before ditching them.

WHITE COLOR LABELS

If you view the photos in Bridge (having saved the metadata to the files), the color labels may be white, showing that the text labels don't match the current label set. Go to Bridge's *Preferences > Labels section* and change the color names to match Lightroom.

The same principle applies to other software that can display color labels.

You can decide which color is used to represent which text using *Metadata menu > Color Label Set.* **(Figure 7.6)** Preset groups of color assignments are listed, for example, if you select Bridge Default, the red label represents the word *"Select"*, the yellow label represents the word *"Second"*, and so forth. If you select *Edit*, you can create your own sets. **(Figure 7.7)**

I've heard some interesting ideas for using color labels. These are a few of my favorites:

- **what needs to be done to the photos**—HDR/panorama sets, LR/PS retouching needed, finished photos

- **output options**—Facebook, Flickr, web galleries, email, print

- **multiple cameras at the same shoot**—each camera gets its own color, which helps identify them at a glance when developing

- **who took the photo**—particularly useful in a family environment

- **workflow**—to flag/star, to be keyworded, to be developed, to output

- **rating photos**—some people skip flags and stars, and just use color labels

But how do you remember what each color represents? You could repeatedly go back to *Metadata menu > Color Label Set > Edit* to check. You could write them on a post-it note and stick it to the side of your computer. Or you could borrow my trick, and add them as a panel end mark in Lightroom. (See page 81 for details.) **(Figure 7.8)**

You can even create lots of different sets, although that can get a bit confusing as a photo can only have a single color label at a time. If the label text doesn't match a color in the selected label set, it appears as a white label instead.

▷ **Figure 7.6** Sets of color assignments can be saved as Color Label Sets.

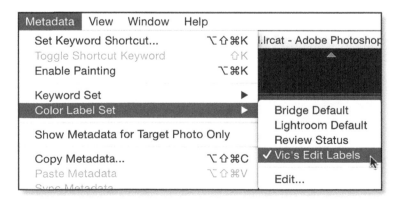

OLD LOCAL FLAGS

In early versions of Lightroom, flags were local to the folder or collection, so a photo could be flagged in one location and rejected in another. Picks and rejects later became a primary rating system for photographers, and local flags caused confusion, so Lightroom was updated to make flags global in version 4.

If you had a photo flagged or rejected in a folder in Lightroom 3 or earlier, that flag is retained when upgrading the catalog. If you also used flags in collections, right-click on the collection to access additional options—***Select Old Contextual Flagged*** and ***Select Old Contextual Rejected***. Selecting each option in turn, you can apply your choice of global flag, color label, star rating, keyword, or any other marker to replace the old local flag.

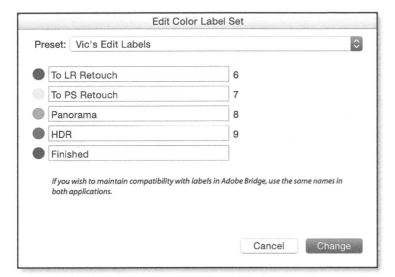

Figure 7.7 You can decide which color is used to represent which text at any one time.

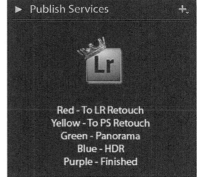

Figure 7.8 Panel end marks are great for reminding you what your color labels mean.

REFINE PHOTOS

If you use Flags, you can select *Library menu > Refine Photos* to downgrade all of the flags at once. This command downgrades the unflagged photos to rejects and flagged photos to unflagged.

It's little-used tool, but it works surprisingly well in a multi-pass workflow. Flag all of the photos you like, then select Refine Photos, so that the photo you didn't flag initially are marked as rejects. Go through the newly unflagged photos again, marking the ones you still like with a flag, and repeat. In the end, only the best photos remain.

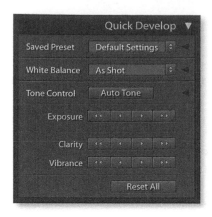

Figure 7.9 Quick Develop is collapsed by default.

RATING SHORTCUTS

Pick flag	P
Unflag	U
Reject flag	X
Toggle Flagged/Unflagged	' (apostrophe)
Increase flag	Ctrl /Cmd down arrow
Decrease flag	Ctrl / Cmd down arrow
Refine Photos	Ctrl Alt R / Cmd Opt R
Increase star rating	]
Decrease star rating	[
0-5 stars	0, 1, 2, 3, 4, 5
Red, yellow, green & blue label	6, 7, 8, 9
Auto-advance	Caps Lock (or hold Shift) while using P, U, X or 0-9

QUICK DEVELOP

While you're sorting through your photos and rating them, you may need to check whether some are worth keeping, for example, under-exposed photos. You could switch to the Develop module to make adjustments, but the Quick Develop panel (on the right in the Library module) offers easy access to the basic adjustments.

At first glance, the panel looks quite limited **(Figure 7.9)**, but if you click the disclosure triangles on the right, it expands to show a wider range of settings **(Figure 7.10)**. Two further adjustments are hiding—if you hold down the Alt (Win) / Opt (Mac) key, the *Clarity* buttons temporarily change to *Sharpening* and the *Vibrance* buttons temporarily change to *Saturation*.

To apply the adjustments to your photos, simply press the buttons. Single arrows make small adjustments and double arrows make larger adjustments. If you hold down the Shift key, the single arrows move in even smaller increments.

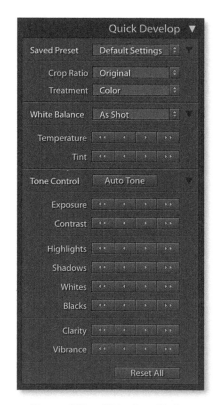

Figure 7.10 Click the Disclosure Triangles to expand the full Quick Develop panel.

If you're viewing in Grid view, it applies to all the selected photos. If you're viewing Loupe, Compare or Survey, it only applies to the selected photo (unless Auto Sync is enabled).

It's also handy for applying Develop corrections to photos you've already edited, as the adjustments are relative to the current settings, but we'll come back to that in the Editing chapters starting on page 193.

GROUPING SIMILAR PHOTOS USING STACKS

As you're sorting through the photos, you may also come across groups of photos that don't mean a lot on their own. For example, groups of photos taken for a panorama or HDR often look awful as individual photos!

Lightroom offers stacking as a way to group photos. You can put your favorite photo on top of the stack and collapse the stack, hiding the other photos to clear some of the visual clutter.

To create a stack, select the photos and go to *Photo menu > Stacking > Group into Stack*, or press Ctrl-G (Windows) / Cmd-G (Mac). The photos automatically collapse into a stack, marked with double lines at the beginning and end. **(Figure 7.11)**

To open the stack, click the white number in the corner. The border surrounding the thumbnails is slightly different when the photos are in an open stack, but it's not always obvious as the thumbnail divide lines don't disappear until the photos are deselected. **(Figure 7.12)**

The photo on the left is the photo that shows when you view a collapsed stack. If the photo that best represents the stack—perhaps the finished panorama or the finished HDR photo—isn't currently at the top of the stack, click on its number to move it to the top of the stack. You can also go to *Photo menu > Stacking > Move to Top of Stack*.

To remove a photo from a stack, you can ungroup the whole stack using *Photo menu > Stacking > Unstack*, or you can drag the single photo out of the stack to a different place in the Grid view, leaving the rest of the stack intact.

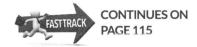

CONTINUES ON PAGE 115

There are a few 'quirks' with Lightroom's stacking that you need to be aware of.

Stacks only work when all the stacked photos are stored in a single folder or collection, so if the stacking options in the *Photo menu* are disabled, you're probably viewing a composite folder view and trying

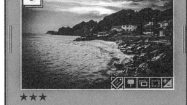

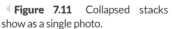

Figure 7.11 Collapsed stacks show as a single photo.

Figure 7.12 When you click on the white rectangle, the stack opens to show the group of photos.

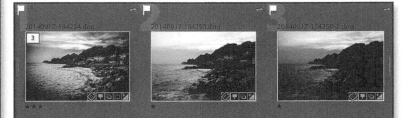

113

STACKING SHORTCUTS

Group into Stack	Ctrl G / Cmd G
Unstack	Ctrl Shift G / Cmd Shift G
Collapse/Expand Stack	S
Move to Top of Stack	Shift S
Move Up in Stack	Shift [
Move Down in Stack	Shift]
Temporarily Expand Stack	Hold down S

to stack photos which are in different folders, or you're viewing a smart collection. To solve it, either select a folder which doesn't have subfolders, deselect *Show Photos in Subfolders* in the *Library menu*, or group the photos in a collection.

Stacks are local to the folder or collection used to create them, so if you stack photos in a folder, they'll still appear as separate photos in their collections, and vice versa.

Also, if a stack is closed, adding metadata (such as keywords) to the stack only applies the metadata to the top photo. There's a trick, however, to make it a little quicker. If you double-click or Shift-click on the stack number, it opens the stack with the stacked photos already selected, so you can go ahead and add the metadata without having to pause to select them.

Finally, filtering doesn't search inside collapsed stacks, but you don't have to open all of the stacks individually. Instead, use the *Photo menu > Expand All Stacks* command to open them all in one go. *Collapse All Stacks*, of course, does the opposite!

SYNC WITH LIGHTROOM MOBILE

If you have a Creative Cloud subscription, you can sync a collection to the cloud so it can be viewed on mobile devices and at http://lightroom. adobe.com Turn to the Sync chapter starting on page 565 for more information.

Figure 7.13 Auto-Stack by Capture Time can automatically stack photos shot in quick succession.

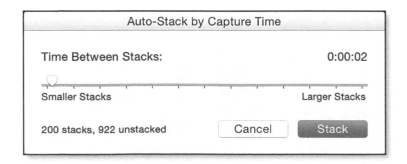

Can I automatically stack sets of photos?

Stacking similar photos manually takes a long time, but Lightroom can automatically stack the photos based on their capture time. For example, you can automatically stack retouched files with their originals or group HDR/panorama sets.

Select the photos and choose *Photo menu > Stacking > Auto-Stack by Capture Time* and choose a 0 second time difference (0:00:00), or a little longer for panorama stacks. The number of stacks at the bottom of the dialog updates as you move the slider, showing how many stacks will be created automatically. **(Figure 7.13)** Once it completes, you may need to tidy up where you've shot in quick succession, but it does most of the work for you.

COLLECTIONS

Collections are another way of grouping photos. They're similar to folders, except the photos don't move on the hard drive. This means the same photo can be in multiple different collections, and the photos in the collections can be stored in various different folders. For example, when you import photos into your catalog, they appear grouped in a *Previous Import* collection in the Catalog panel.

To create a collection, scroll down to the Collections panel, which you'll find in the left panel group in all modules, click the + button at the top and select **Create Collection**. Name the collection, and it appears in the Collections panel. **(Figure 7.14)** When you want to view a different collection of photos, just click on its name.

From the Grid view, select the photos and drag them from the

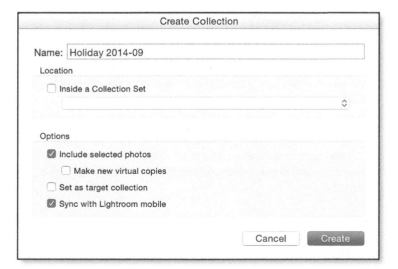

SPLAT DELETE

If you need to delete the photos from the hard drive while viewing a collection, use the wonderfully nicknamed 'splat-delete' or Ctrl-Alt-Shift-Delete (Windows) / Cmd-Opt-Shift-Delete (Mac). It deletes from the hard drive whether you're viewing a folder, collection or even a smart collection, but beware, it also bypasses the warning dialog, so use it with care!

Figure 7.14 To create a Collection, click the + button on the Collections panel and enter the name in the Create Collection dialog.

SMART COLLECTIONS

You can also create Smart Collections, which are saved search criteria, smart folders or rules. We'll come back to these later with the filtering tools on page 190.

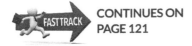

CONTINUES ON PAGE 121

preview area onto the collection. Don't forget to grab the photos by their thumbnails, not the border surrounding them. If you don't like dragging, right-click on the collection and select *Add Selected Photos to this Collection* from the context-sensitive menu instead.

Removing photos from a collection is as simple as hitting the Delete key. When you're viewing a collection, Delete only removes the photo from the collection, rather than from the catalog or hard drive.

That was easy, wasn't it! Collections are more powerful than they look at first glance though, so there's more to explore.

Collections aren't limited to containing photos—they store your chosen sort order, and they can also remember your filtering (depending on your preference setting). Special types of collections store Book, Slideshow, Print or Web module settings too.

As well as creating an empty collection and adding the photos into it, you can first select the photos and then create the collection with *Include Selected Photos* checked in the New Collection dialog.

If you have a whole folder of photos that you'd like to turn into a collection, drag the folder from the Folders panel to the Collections panel. A collection of the same name is created, containing all the photos in the folder. Sadly it doesn't work for a whole hierarchy of folders.

To duplicate a collection, hold down the Ctrl key (Windows) / Opt key (Mac) and drag the collection within the Collections panel. You can either drop it between existing collections (when the blue line appears) or drop it on a collection set. The same shortcut works for smart collections and even whole collection sets.

Figure 7.15 When you click on the Collections badge on the thumbnail, the menu lists all of the standard collections which include that photo.

How do I see which collections a photo belongs to?

If you need to check which collections a photo belongs to, right-click on the photo and choose *Go to Collection*, or click on the Collection badge in the corner of the thumbnail. Lightroom displays a list of collections containing that photo, and clicking on the collection name switches to the collection. **(Figure 7.15)**

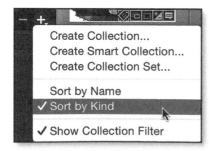

If you're checking a large number of photos, switch to Grid view and hover the cursor over the collections in the Collections panel. All photos belonging to the collection under the cursor temporarily display a thin white border around the thumbnail, making them quick to identify.

Figure 7.16 You can change the collections sot order by clicking the + button on the Collections panel.

How do I organize my collections into sets?

Using the + button on the Collections panel, you can choose whether to sort the Collections panel by name or collection type. **(Figure 7.16)** Changing the sort order works well until you have a large number of collections, at which point collection sets come into their own.

Collection sets allow you to build a hierarchy of collections, just like you would with folders. For example, you may have a collection set called Vacations, and within that set, sets for each of your vacation destinations. These vacation destinations might divide down further into sets for each year that you visited, and then individual collections for the long slideshow of all of your photos from each vacation, the web galleries or sync collections you created to show your friends, the book you created, and the individual pictures you printed. **(Figure 7.17)**

You can also include smart collections inside your collection sets too, so you might have additional smart collections for all the 5 star photos, all the photos of beaches, and so on. We'll come back to smart collections on page 190.

To create a Collection Set, press the + button on the Collections panel and select ***New Collection Set***. Name it, and then drag existing collections onto the set to group them. When you're creating new collections, you can select which set to put them in using the pop-up in the New Collection dialog.

There's a notable difference between collections and collection sets. Collections can only usually contain photos and videos, whereas

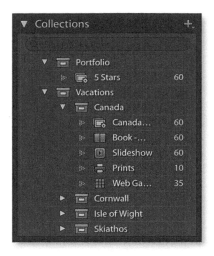

Figure 7.17 Collections can be nested in Collection Sets to keep them organized.

BOOKS, SLIDESHOWS, PRINTS & WEB GALLERIES

In Lightroom 3 and earlier, any collection also automatically stored output module settings, so a standard collection could also remember Slideshow, Print and Web module settings.

In Lightroom 4 and later, this changed. Normal collections no longer store output module settings. Instead, you save individual Book, Slideshow, Print or Web Gallery collections, and they can't contain settings from other modules. Double-clicking on any module-specific (Book, Slideshow, Print or Web) collection takes you directly to that module too.

Although standard collections can't usually contain other collections, there's one exception. If you start with a standard collection, and then create a book, slideshow, print or web gallery, you can store it inside the first collection. This parent collection becomes a composite view of its children, showing all the photos you've used in those books, slideshows, prints and web galleries. If you add a photo to one of its children, it appears in the parent collection. If you remove a photo from the parent collection, it's also removed from any books/slideshows/prints/web galleries nested within.

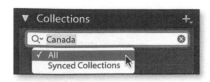

Figure 7.18 Type in the Search bar at the top of the Collections panel to filter the collections.

COLLECTION ICONS

Collection Set

Collection

Book

Slideshow

Print

Web Gallery

Smart Collection

Collection with Comments

collection sets can contain collections or other collection sets but not the photos or videos themselves.

If you have a large number of collections, you can also search for them by name using the search bar at the top of the Collections panel. Type the name of the collection and press Enter to search. If you click on the magnifying glass to the left, you can decide whether to search all collections or just synced collections. Click the X at the end of the search field to clear the search. **(Figure 7.18)**

What are the Quick Collection and Target Collection?

The Catalog panel holds a few more special and temporary collections, for example, *All Photographs* shows all of the photographs in your catalog, *All Synced Photographs* show all of the photos synced to the cloud, and *Previous Import* shows the last set of photos imported into your catalog. Other collections are added temporarily, for example, *Previous Export as Catalog*, *Added by Previous Export*, *Quick Collection* and more.

The **Quick Collection** is a special collection for temporarily holding photos of your choice. If you've added a group of photos to the Quick Collection and then you decide you would like to convert it into a permanent collection, you can right-click on it and select *Save Quick Collection* from the context-sensitive menu. **(Figure 7.19)**

The **Target Collection** isn't a collection in its own right—it's just a shortcut linking to another collection. It's marked by a + symbol next to the collection name. Pressing the shortcut key B or clicking the little circle icon on the thumbnail adds to (or removes the photo from) that Target Collection. By default, the Quick Collection is the Target Collection, but you can change the shortcut to the collection of your choice by right-clicking on your chosen collection and selecting *Set as Target Collection*.

Figure 7.19 The Quick Collection is a temporary collection which is always shown in the Catalog panel. The + next to the name indicates that it's also the Target Collection.

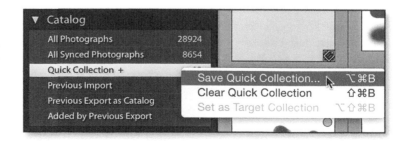

Workflow—Selecting Photos for a Purpose

Figure 7.20 Once you've selected the best photos overall, you may need to select photos for a specific purpose.

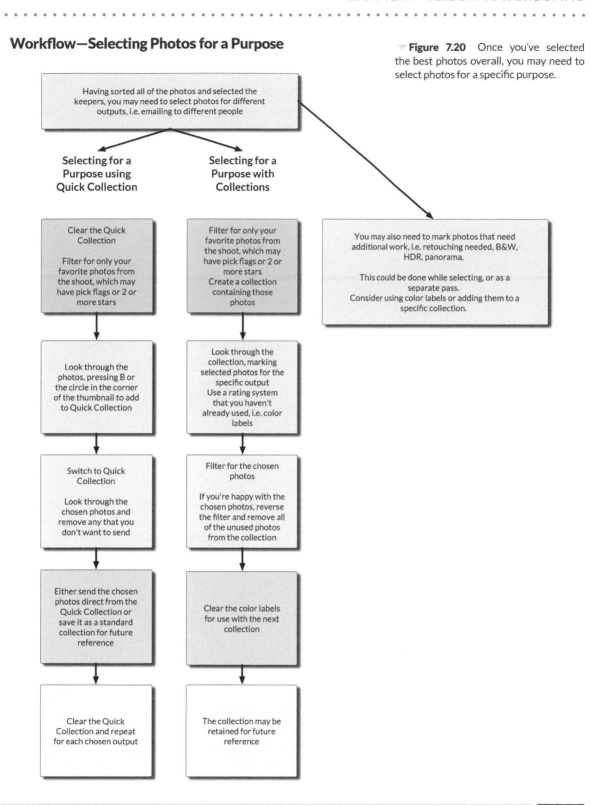

Having sorted all of the photos and selected the keepers, you may need to select photos for different outputs, i.e. emailing to different people

Selecting for a Purpose using Quick Collection

Selecting for a Purpose with Collections

Clear the Quick Collection

Filter for only your favorite photos from the shoot, which may have pick flags or 2 or more stars

Filter for only your favorite photos from the shoot, which may have pick flags or 2 or more stars
Create a collection containing those photos

You may also need to mark photos that need additional work, i.e. retouching needed, B&W, HDR, panorama.

This could be done while selecting, or as a separate pass.
Consider using color labels or adding them to a specific collection.

Look through the photos, pressing B or the circle in the corner of the thumbnail to add to Quick Collection

Look through the collection, marking selected photos for the specific output
Use a rating system that you haven't already used, i.e. color labels

Switch to Quick Collection

Look through the chosen photos and remove any that you don't want to send

Filter for the chosen photos

If you're happy with the chosen photos, reverse the filter and remove all of the unused photos from the collection

Either send the chosen photos direct from the Quick Collection or save it as a standard collection for future reference

Clear the color labels for use with the next collection

Clear the Quick Collection and repeat for each chosen output

The collection may be retained for future reference

COLLECTION SHORTCUTS

New Collection	Ctrl N / Cmd N
Expand All Subcollections	Alt-click / Opt-click on collection disclosure triangle
Add to Quick Collection	B
Add to Quick Collection and Select Next Photo	Shift B
Show Quick Collection	Ctrl B / Cmd B
Save Quick Collection	Ctrl Alt B / Cmd Opt B
Clear Quick Collection	Ctrl Shift B / Cmd Shift B
Set Quick Collection as Target	Ctrl Alt Shift B / Cmd Opt Shift B

MANAGING YOUR PHOTOS

Using a database to catalog photos is a new concept to many Lightroom users, so it's important to understand how the photos in Lightroom relate to the files on your hard drive.

So why have we waited until now to start discussing folders? Folders are primarily storage buckets. Lightroom offers other tools, such as collections and metadata, that are better suited to organizing your photos. (Remember we discussed that in "How should I organize my photos?" on page 44)

You may, however, need to manage files at times, particularly if you start to run out of space on your hard drive. This is primarily done using the Folders panel (on the left in the Library module) and in the Grid view.

MANAGING FOLDERS IN LIGHTROOM AND ON THE HARD DRIVE

The folders listed in the Folders panel are references to folders on your hard drive or optical discs. When you import photos into Lightroom, the folders containing these photos are automatically added to the Folders panel.

Anything you do in Lightroom's Folders panel is reflected on the hard drive. For example, creating or renaming folders in Lightroom does the same on your hard drive. You can drag photos and folders into other folders to reorganize them, just like you would in your file browser.

The reverse doesn't work in the same way—when you rename

or move a file or folder on your hard drive using your file browser, Lightroom simply marks it as missing and leaves you to manually link it back up again. You'll save yourself a lot of time and frustration by only using Lightroom to manage your files once you've imported them.

We'll come back to moving, renaming and deleting the photos themselves in the following pages, but for the moment, let's concentrate on the Folders panel.

How do I set up a folder hierarchy?

If you've imported some photos, one or more folders will be listed in the Folders panel, but it probably won't match your hierarchical folder structure in Explorer (Windows) or Finder (Mac). Only folders that hold imported photos show in the Folders panel.

To make it easier to visualize where the photos are stored on your hard drive, we can display the same hierarchy. This also makes it easier to fix if you run into problems later.

We're going to talk about three levels of folders—top-level folders, parent folders and child folders—so it will help to define these first.

- **Child folders** are folders that are inside another folder.

- **Parent folders** are folders that have other folders inside them.

- **Top-level folders**, otherwise known as root folders, are folders displayed without a parent folder.

Let's start tidying up...

1. Find a top-level folder. In **Figure 8.1**, this is one of the folders starting with 2013.

2. Right-click on this folder and choose **Show Parent Folder**. **(Figure 8.2)** (If this option doesn't appear in the menu, you've

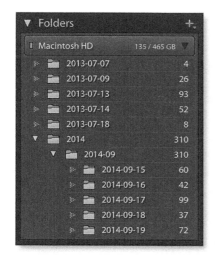

Figure 8.1 The initial view of the Folders panel may not be easy to relate to the folders on the hard drive.

Figure 8.2 Using *Show Parent Folder* to add additional parent folders to the Folders panel view makes it easier to visualize how Lightroom relates to the hard drive.

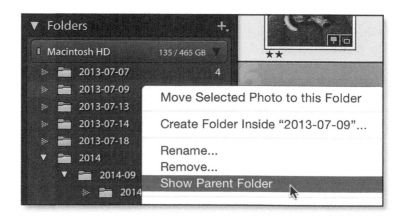

right-clicked on the wrong folder.) This doesn't import new photos. It just adds an additional hierarchy level to your Folders panel, and does a lot more behind the scenes.

3. In some cases, you'll only need to add a single parent folder, but if you have a deep nested hierarchy, you may want to repeat on the new top-level folders until you can visualize the whole tree.

4. In **Figure 8.3**, we're still missing some parent folders, so we right-click on the 2013-07 folder and choose *Show Parent Folder* and then right-click on the 2013 or 2014 folder to show the My Photos folder that contains all of the Lightroom photos. We could go one step further and *Show Parent Folder* on the My Photos folder to show the main Pictures folder too. **(Figure 8.4)**

Once you've finished, you can see a hierarchy of folders that looks

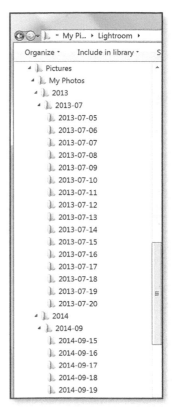

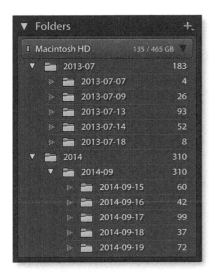

Figure 8.3 In some cases, you'll need to use *Show Parent Folder* on multiple folders.

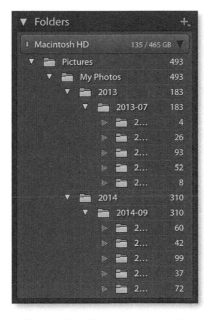

Figure 8.4 The end result of the process is a familiar folder hierarchy.

Figure 8.5 The same folder hierarchy shown in Windows Explorer and Finder. There are more folders here than those showing in Lightroom's folder panel, as some of the folders haven't been imported into Lightroom.

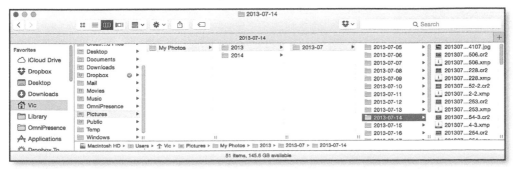

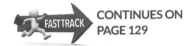

CONTINUES ON
PAGE 129

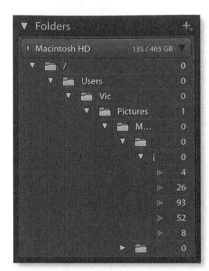

Figure 8.6 If you show too many parent folders, it can be difficult to see the folder names.

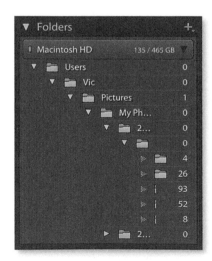

Figure 8.7 Be careful not to hide folders directly containing photos, such as the Pictures folder in this screenshot, as *Hide This Folder* would remove the photo from the catalog too.

much more like the Explorer (Windows) / Finder (Mac) view. **(Figure 8.5)**

How do I hide parent folders?

If you go too far (perhaps showing your username or beyond), you can hide the top-level folder using **Hide This Parent**.

1. First, check whether there are any photos stored directly in the folders you're going to hide, as these photos would be removed from the catalog. To do so, uncheck *Library menu > Show Photos in Subfolders*.

2. In **Figure 8.6**, we see that the / folder, Users folder and Vic folder are empty, but the Pictures folder includes a photo, so we won't remove that one. (If you hide a folder containing imported photos, the photos are removed from the catalog, but it warns you first.)

3. Right-click on the top-level folder (/ in **Figure 8.6** and choose *Hide This Parent*.

4. Select *Hide This Parent* on the Users folder **(Figure 8.7)**, and then on the Vic folder (your folder will have another name, of course!). Once you've finished, your Folders panel looks like **Figure 8.4** again.

5. Once you've finished, you can check *Show Photos in Subfolders* again to put the folder counts back to normal.

That's the basics, but there are more Folder panel tricks and customizations to play with.

How do I switch between a composite folder view and a single folder view?

Now you have a folder hierarchy, Lightroom can show either the photos directly inside the selected folder, or it can show a composite view of all the photos in the selected folder and its subfolders. The folder counts are also affected by that setting, showing either the composite count, or the number of photos directly in each folder.

By default, **Show Photos in Subfolders** is enabled, showing a composite view. In many situations, it's useful to see a composite view of the subfolder contents, but there are a couple of restrictions. You can't apply a custom sort (user order) or stack photos across multiple folders in a composite view.

You can toggle this setting by going to *Library menu > Show Photos in*

Subfolders and checking or unchecking it. You'll find the same option in the Folders panel menu, accessed via the + button.

Can I change the way the folders are displayed?

The Folders panel is divided into Volume Bars for each volume (drive) attached to your computer, whether they're internal or external hard drives, network attached storage, or optical drives.

Each of these Volume Bars can give you additional information about the drive—how many imported photos are on each volume, whether it's online or offline, and how much space is used or available. **(Figure 8.8)** You can choose which information to show by right-clicking on the Volume Bar. **(Figure 8.9)**

Click anywhere on a Volume Bar to expand it to show the folders contained in that drive, or to collapse it to hide the folders.

While you're exploring the Folders panel view options, clicking on the Folders panel + button also gives additional path view options for the root folders. **Figure 8.10** They are *Folder Name Only, Path From Volume,* and *Folder And Path.* They simply display the path of the top level folders in different ways, as you can see from the screenshots in **Figure 8.11**.

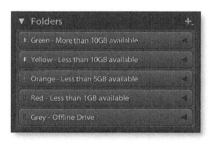

◄ Figure 8.8 The colored rectangle on the left of the Folders panel shows the amount of space available on the drive.

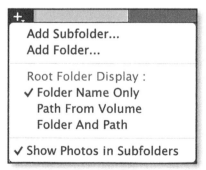

◄ Figure 8.10 Choose the Folder Path display format by clicking on the + button on the Folders panel.

▶ Figure 8.11 The Folder Path can be shown in multiple formats. Folder Name Only, (top) Path From Volume (center), Folder And Path (bottom)

0 PHOTOS!

If you've been used to seeing a composite photo count, it can be confusing if the folder counts suddenly change to 0, but it doesn't necessarily mean that your photos have disappeared. Check *Library menu > Show Photos in Subfolders* to show the composite folder counts.

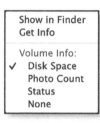

▲ Figure 8.9 You can choose the information shown on a Volume Bar by right-clicking on it.

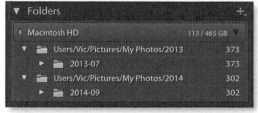

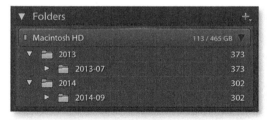

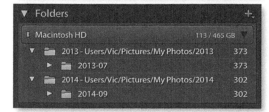

DISCLOSURE TRIANGLES

Next to each folder name is a small triangle, which is officially called a disclosure triangle. You'll also find these triangles used throughout Lightroom's interface. When you click on these triangles, they toggle to show or hide parts of the interface, such as sliders or buttons, or a hierarchy of folders, collections or keywords.

In the case of folders, collections, or keywords, a solid arrow indicates that it's a parent with subfolders/collections/keywords inside. Those marked with dotted arrows don't have any subfolders etc. inside.

To expand or collapse the full hierarchy in one click, Alt-click (Windows) / Opt-click (Mac) on the parent folder's disclosure triangle.

If you're still confused about where to find a folder on your hard drive, just right-click on the folder and select *Show in Explorer* (Windows) / *Show in Finder* (Mac).

MANAGING FOLDERS

Although Lightroom doesn't care how the photos are stored, you may want to reorganize folder structures or move photos to another drive.

Remember, if you start moving folders around in Explorer (Windows) / Finder (Mac) or other file browser software, Lightroom will complain that your folders have gone missing, and leave you to manually relink them.

To avoid that extra work, it's usually simpler to manage the folders within Lightroom.

How do I create a new folder or subfolder?

To create a brand new folder, go to *Library menu > New Folder*, or press the + button on the Folders panel and select **New Folder**. Navigate to the location of your choice.

On Windows, right-click and select *New* then *Folder* and type the name of the folder, then press Enter and select the new folder, then press *Select Folder*.

On a Mac, press the *New Folder* button in the operating system dialog. Give it a name and press *Create*. Your new folder is created on the hard drive and automatically selected in the operating system dialog, so press *Choose* to add it to Lightroom.

If the new folder already exists on the hard drive, but you want to add it to Lightroom, go to *Library menu > New Folder* and navigate to the folder, then press *Select Folder* (Windows) / *Choose* (Mac). If the folder is empty, it's added to the Folders panel. If there are already photos in the folder, Lightroom opens the Import dialog. In this case, you'll need to import at least one photo to add the folder to the Folders panel.

If you're creating a new subfolder, and the parent folder already exists in the Folders panel, it's even easier. Right-click on the parent folder and select **Create Folder Inside** *. Enter the subfolder name and press *Create*. If you have photos selected at the time, you can automatically move them to the new subfolder by checking the *Include Selected Photos* checkbox.

How do I move folders into other folders or drives?

Moving folders into other folders is simply a drag-and-drop operation, just like Explorer (Windows) / Finder (Mac). Select the folders in the Folders panel and drag them onto another folder in the Folders panel. The destination folder is highlighted in blue, showing where the folders will land when you release the mouse.

Selecting a parent folder automatically moves all of its subfolders too. To move multiple separate folders, Ctrl-click (Windows) / Cmd-click (Mac) to select individual folders or Shift-click to select a series of folders, then drag and drop as normal.

If you're moving a large number of photos to a new drive, there's another option which is slightly safer. We'll come back to these instructions in the Moving Lightroom section starting on page 486.

How do I rename folders?

To rename a folder, simply right-click on the folder in the Folders panel and select **Rename**. When you enter the new folder name and press *Save*, it's not only updated in Lightroom but also on the hard drive.

How do I delete folders?

To delete a folder, right-click on the folder in the Folders panel and select **Remove**.

If the folder is empty in Lightroom, it's immediately removed.

If there are photos in the folder, Lightroom requests confirmation because removing the folder will also remove these photos from Lightroom's catalog.

If there are no other files (e.g. text files) left inside the folder, the folder is also deleted from the hard drive.

I've added new photos to one of Lightroom's folders— why don't they show in my catalog?

If you import a folder into Lightroom's catalog and then later add additional photos to that folder using other software, Lightroom won't know about those additional photos until you choose to import them.

If you go back to the Import dialog and import that folder again, Lightroom just imports the new photos, skipping the existing ones. You can also use *Synchronize Folder* to automate the process.

REORGANIZING BY DATE

Lightroom only automatically organizes photos (e.g. into dated folders) while importing. Any reorganization after import has to be done manually by creating, moving, renaming and deleting folders and photos, so it's best to get your folder structure right when importing.

If you do need to manually reorganize the photos into a dated hierarchy after import, the quickest way is to create your new folder structure in the Folders panel. Unless you're shooting thousands of photos each month, one folder per month is usually plenty, and it's quicker to create than individual day folders.

Then select *All Photographs* and use the Metadata Filters (discussed later in the Finding & Filtering Photos chapter starting on page 179) to highlight a day or month of photos at a time and drag them from the Grid view onto their applicable folder.

DON'T SYNCHRONIZE

If your folders or photos are marked as missing (with a question mark on the folders or an exclamation mark in a rectangle on the thumbnail) don't use *Synchronize Folders* to try to fix the problem. If you do so, you may lose the work you've done in Lightroom. Turn to the Missing Files section starting on page 525 instead.

How does the Synchronize Folder command work?

The main purpose of **Synchronize Folder** (also found in the folders right-click menu) is to update Lightroom's catalog with changes made to the folder by other programs, for example, adding or deleting photos or updating the metadata. **(Figure 8.12)**

Synchronize Folder is one of the most misunderstood tools in Lightroom, so let's run through the options carefully...

- **Import new photos** searches the folder and subfolders for any new photos not currently in this catalog and imports them. If you've dropped photos into the folder using other software, it saves you navigating to the folder in the Import dialog.

- **Show Import dialog before importing** displays the photos in the Import dialog, to allow you to adjust the import options prior to import.

- **Remove missing photos from the catalog** checks for photos that have been moved, renamed or deleted from the folder and gives you the option to remove the missing photos from the catalog.

  Be very careful using this option because any metadata for those missing photos, such as Develop settings and ratings would be lost, even if the photos have simply been moved to another location. It doesn't intelligently relink the files. If in doubt, leave this option unchecked.

- **Scan for metadata updates** checks the metadata in the catalog against the file, to see whether you've edited the file in any other programs, such as Bridge.

  If you've only changed the metadata in Lightroom, it doesn't do anything.

  If the metadata has changed in another program, but not

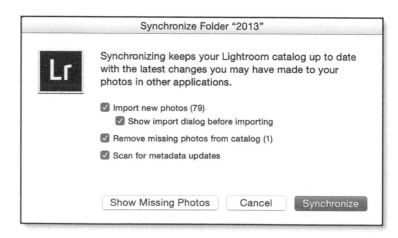

Figure 8.12 Synchronize Folders is powerful, but can cause trouble if you've moved photos outside of Lightroom. Take care to make sure you understand exactly what will happen.

in Lightroom, Lightroom reads the metadata from the file, overwriting Lightroom's settings.

If both Lightroom's catalog and the external file have changed, you'll see a *Metadata Conflict* badge on a thumbnail, and you'll have to click on that icon to choose which set of data to keep—the metadata in your catalog or the metadata in the file.

We'll come back to XMP metadata in more detail on page 343, including the use of the Metadata Conflict dialog.

- The **Show Missing Photos** button searches for photos missing from the folder and creates a temporary collection in the Catalog panel. You can then decide whether to track them down and relink them, or whether to remove these photos from the catalog. If you want to check your entire catalog for missing photos, it's quicker to use the *Library menu > Find Missing Photos* command instead. Once you've finished with the temporary collection, you can right-click on it to remove it.

MANAGING THE INDIVIDUAL PHOTOS

There are one or two more file management tasks you might need, such as deleting, renaming or moving individual photos, rather than whole folders.

Deleting fuzzy photos

Even the best photographers sometimes end up with photos that aren't worth keeping.

It's possible to delete photos while you're sorting through them, simply by pressing the Delete key on your keyboard, but it's quicker to mark them with a Reject flag (X key) and then delete them all in one go.

Photos marked as rejects show in the Grid view as dimmed photos, so it's easy to check that you've marked the right ones. When you're

BE CAREFUL DELETING

If all the photos in your current view are selected, the shades of gray can be difficult to distinguish, leading you to believe that you only have one photo selected. In the Delete confirmation dialog, it states how many photos will be deleted, so it's worth stopping to read that dialog when deleting photos.

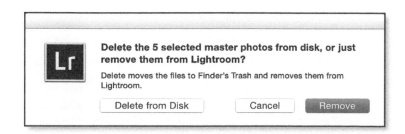

Delete the 5 selected master photos from disk, or just remove them from Lightroom?

Delete moves the files to Finder's Trash and removes them from Lightroom.

Delete from Disk | Cancel | Remove

Figure 8.13 In the Delete dialog, note the difference between *Remove* and *Delete*, and don't forget to check the number of photos that will be deleted.

COMPLEX RENAMING

Lightroom's file naming allows for the creations of complex new filenames, but reusing part of the existing filename is not quite so simple. There's no way, for example, to remove −2 from the end of filenames, unless you can recreate the filename using metadata. It's one reason using a date/time filename is a particularly good choice!

There is a workaround, however, using John Beardsworth's Search Replace Transfer plug-in (http://www.Lrq.me/beardsworth-searchreplace). Taking the −2 scenario as an example, you'd use Search Replace Transfer to copy the filename to any unused IPTC field that Lightroom's renaming dialog can use—perhaps the Headline field. Then you use the plug-in again, this time to remove −2 from the Headline field, and repeat to remove the file extension too. Finally, you'd use Lightroom's main Rename dialog, set to use the Headline token for the new filename. It's not for the faint-hearted, but it does come with excellent instructions.

ready to delete all the rejected photos, go to *Photo menu > Delete Rejected Photos.*

Before Lightroom deletes the photos, it asks whether to *Remove* or *Delete* them. **(Figure 8.13)** Note the difference. **Remove** just removes the reference to the photo from Lightroom's catalog, but the photo remains on the hard drive. **Delete** deletes the photo from your hard drive too (or sends it to the Recycle Bin/Trash if possible).

Before you select either option, double check the number of photos that it says will be deleted, just in case you've accidentally selected photos you want to keep. If you make a mistake with *Remove*, you can immediately use Ctrl-Z (Windows) / Cmd-Z (Mac) to undo it, but that won't work with *Delete*.

How do I rename one or more photos?

We've already learned how to rename photos while Importing them, but you can also rename photos later in the Library module.

To do so, select the photos in Grid view, and then select *Library menu > **Rename**.* The Rename dialog options are almost identical to the Import dialog File Renaming panel, which we used in the Import chapter. **(Figure 8.14)** Select your chosen file naming template or select *Edit* to create your own template using tokens in the Filename Template Editor. Turn back to the File Renaming section of the Import chapter on page 37 if you need a refresher on the file renaming options.

That's great if you want to rename multiple photos, but to rename just a single photo, it's often quicker to open the Metadata panel on the right hand side of the Library module. If you click in the *Filename* field, you can edit the existing filename rather than having to use a template in the full Rename dialog. If you do decide to use a template after all, clicking the little icon at the end of the Filename field takes you directly to the full Rename dialog.

How do I rename photos back to their original filename?

There's another useful rename option which wasn't available in the Import dialog: *Original Filename.* **(Figure 8.15)** If you've renamed

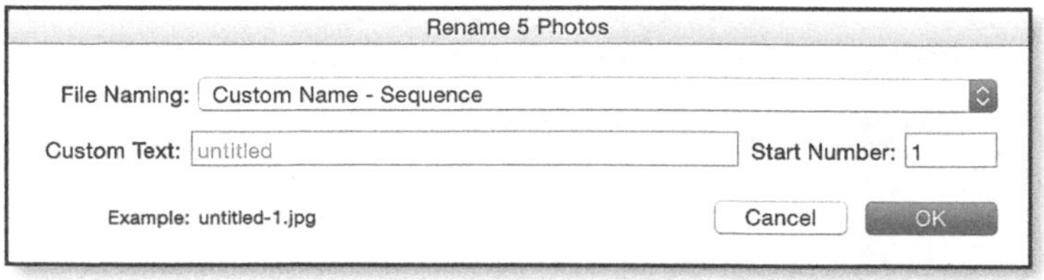

Figure 8.14 You can rename photos in the Library Module using the same templates used in the Import dialog.

Rename 5 Photos		
File Naming:	Custom Name - Sequence	
Custom Text:	untitled	Start Number: 1
Example: untitled-1.jpg	Cancel	OK

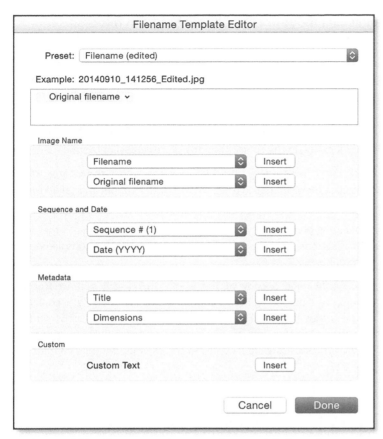

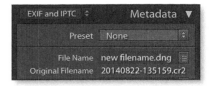

Figure 8.15 *Original Filename* is one of the tokens in the Filename Template Editor.

Figure 8.16 If the original filename is stored in the catalog, you can view it by changing the Metadata panel to *EXIF and IPTC* view.

a photo within Lightroom since you imported it into the current catalog, Lightroom may still have a record of the original filename. That *Original Filename* field would actually be better named *Import Filename*, as it's the name at the time of import, not necessarily the original name at the time of capture. If you want to check whether you have an original filename to revert to, select the *EXIF and IPTC* view at the top of the Metadata panel. **(Figure 8.16)** If the original filename is present in the database, you can go to the Rename dialog and select *Edit* in the pop-up to show the Filename Template Editor. You'll find the *Original Filename* token in the *Image Name* section.

How do I find out where a photo is stored on my hard drive?

If you ever need to find a photo on the hard drive, for example, to open in another program, you can right-click on a single photo and the context-sensitive menu gives you the choice of **Go to Folder in Library**, which selects the folder in the Folders panel, or **Show in Explorer** (Windows) / **Show in Finder** (Mac).

PHOTOS ARE NOT 'IN' LIGHTROOM

Remember, photos are never IN Lightroom. Don't move, rename or delete files or folders using Explorer/Finder or other software after import, as Lightroom won't be able to find them.

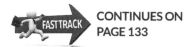

CONTINUES ON PAGE 133

How do I move or copy photos between folders?

Although folders are primarily storage buckets, you may need to move individual photos at times. (Remember, we moved whole folders a little earlier in the chapter on page 127.) It's a simple drag-and-drop.

Select the photos you want to move, then click on the thumbnail of one of the photos (not the surrounding border) and drag it to the new folder location in the Folders panel, before releasing them.

If you don't like to drag and drop, you can select the photos, then right-click on your chosen folder in the Folders panel and select *Move Selected Photos to this Folder* to get the same result.

Duplicating photos isn't quite so simple, because the idea is that you use collections and virtual copies, rather than having multiple copies of the same file.

If you only need a copy of the photo to try out some different Develop settings, or you want to apply different metadata, consider virtual copies instead. They don't create an additional copy on the hard drive, but they behave like separate photos within Lightroom. We'll come back to virtual copies in the Develop module chapter on page 311.

If you do need to create a physical copy on the hard drive, use *File menu > Export*, select the *Export Location* to the folder of your choice, check *Add to This Catalog* if you want to edit the duplicate in Lightroom, and select the *Original* file format setting.

FOLDER & PHOTO MANAGEMENT SHORTCUTS

New Folder	Ctrl Shift N / Cmd Shift N
Expand all subfolders	Alt-click / Opt-click on folder disclosure triangle
Show in Explorer/Finder	Ctrl R / Cmd R
Rename Photo	F2
Delete Photo	Delete
Delete Rejected Photos	Ctrl Delete / Cmd Delete
Remove Photo from Catalog	Alt Delete / Opt Delete
Remove and Trash Photo	Ctrl Alt Shift Delete / Cmd Opt Shift Delete

ADDING METADATA TO YOUR PHOTOS

O nce you've finished selecting your favorite photos, it's time to add metadata to help you find them again later. Sorting through your photos first means you can focus your efforts on the best ones, which are the ones you're likely to want to find again.

First, we'll focus on the Metadata panel, then keywords, tagging people, and finally adding GPS location metadata using the Map module.

ADDING METADATA USING THE METADATA PANEL

The Metadata panel, on the right-hand side of the Library module, allows you to view EXIF metadata added by the camera and add your own IPTC metadata.

TYPES OF METADATA

EXIF data is technical information added by the camera at the time of capture. It includes camera and lens information such as the make and model, and image information such as the capture date/time, shutter speed, aperture, ISO, and pixel dimensions. Apart from the capture date/time, Lightroom doesn't allow you to edit this EXIF data.

IPTC data is added by the photographer to describe the photo, for example, title, caption, keywords and the photographer's name and copyright. There are official definitions for the IPTC fields, and you can view the full IPTC specification at the IPTC website at http://www.iptc.org/ You can add IPTC data to your photos using Lightroom's Metadata panel.

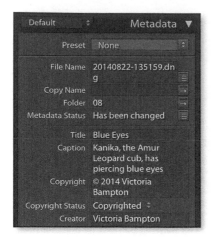

Figure 9.1 Enter your Title, Caption and Copyright in the Metadata panel.

CONTINUES ON PAGE 137

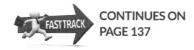

Figure 9.2 The *Sync Metadata* button, at the bottom of the right panel group in Library module, allows you to copy metadata to all the selected photos.

How do I enter metadata for my photos?

Entering metadata in the Metadata panel is as simple as typing in the text fields. **(Figure 9.1)** For example, some photographers like to add descriptive text to the photos, perhaps for use as captions when posting to Flickr or Facebook, or in a slideshow or book.

The *Title* and *Caption* fields do have official IPTC definitions, but many photographers simply use *Title* for a short image title (i.e. Dogs in Snow) and *Caption* for a more descriptive paragraph (i.e. William and Charlie are playing in the snow in the back garden).

You'll also want to add your copyright information and contact details, if you didn't apply them using a preset while importing.

How do I add or change metadata for multiple photos at once?

Adding repetitive metadata would quickly become boring if you had to type that information into the Metadata panel one photo at a time, but there are a few ways to apply it to multiple photos in one go.

We said earlier that actions apply to all selected photos when in Grid view on the primary window, but usually only the selected photo in all other views. That applies in this case too, so the simplest option is to select multiple photos in Grid view (on the primary window) and type your metadata into the Metadata panel. If it doesn't work, make sure that *Metadata menu > Show Metadata for Target Photo Only* is unchecked.

If you prefer to select the photos in the Filmstrip with Compare, Survey or Loupe view on the primary window, or you have Grid on the secondary window, your metadata usually only applies to the active photo (with the lightest gray border). You can override this by enabling *Library menu > Auto Sync*.

AUTO FILL

When you start typing metadata in the Metadata panel, Lightroom offers suggestions based on your recent entries. Click on a suggestion to accept it, or press the up/down arrow keys to select one of the suggestions and then press Enter to confirm.

To view all the available suggestions for a specific metadata field, click on the field label. That context-sensitive menu also allows you to clear the suggestions for that particular field or all fields.

To turn the Auto Fill feature off altogether, go to *Catalog Settings > Metadata tab* and uncheck *Offer suggestions from recently entered values*. There's a *Clear All Suggestion Lists* button in the same location.

When Auto Sync is enabled, your actions apply to all selected photos, so you can type in the Metadata panel and that metadata is applied to all the selected photos. Use it with caution if you work with the Filmstrip hidden, as you may not realize you have multiple photos selected.

Typing directly in the Metadata panel can be slow when working with a large selection of photos, as it updates all of the records each time you move between fields. In these cases, it's quicker to select the photos and press the *Sync Metadata* button (not the *Sync Settings* button) at the bottom of the right panel group. **(Figure 9.2)**

In the Synchronize Metadata dialog **(Figure 9.3)**, enter the details for any fields you want to update. Put a checkmark next to these fields or press the *Check Filled* button at the bottom of the dialog, as only checked fields are updated. Press *Synchronize* when you're finished to apply the metadata to all the selected photos.

Replacing existing metadata, perhaps because you've moved house and need to update the address on your photos, works in exactly the same way. To remove metadata from the selected photos, check the checkboxes in the Synchronize Metadata dialog, but don't type any replacement text.

AUTO SYNC

There are two separate Auto Sync toggle switches—one under the *Library module > Metadata menu* and one under *Develop module > Settings menu*, and they both appear as switches on the *Sync* buttons at the bottom of the right-hand panel groups when multiple photos are selected. The Library switch applies to most metadata actions—assigning keywords, flags, labels, etc.—regardless of which module you're viewing, whereas the Develop switch only applies to Develop changes made in the Develop module.

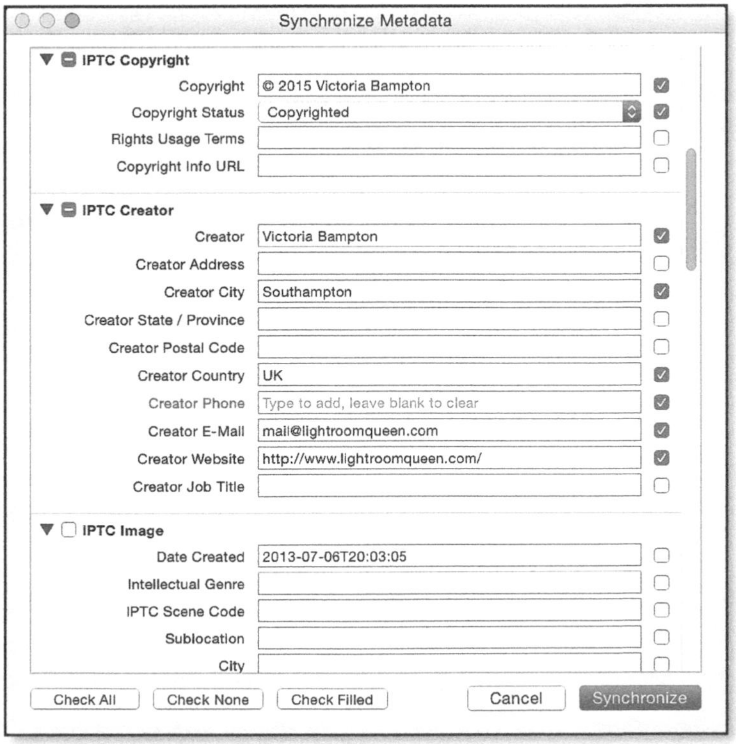

Figure 9.3 The Synchronize Metadata and Edit Metadata Preset dialogs are very similar. Only checked fields will be changed.

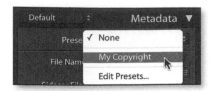

Figure 9.4 Create a Metadata preset for metadata you add regularly, for example, your copyright information.

How do I create and edit a Metadata preset?

If you find you're regularly applying the same metadata, you can save it as a Metadata preset. We used a Metadata Preset to add copyright information while importing the photos (page 42), so we'll quickly recap. At the top of the Metadata panel, choose *Edit Presets* from the *Presets* pop-up. **(Figure 9.4)** The Edit Metadata Presets dialog automatically fills with the metadata from the selected photo, and then you can edit the information that you want to save in the preset. At the top of the dialog, select *Save Current Settings as New Preset* and name the preset before pressing *Done*. Remember, only checked fields are saved in the preset. Leaving fields blank but checked would clear any existing metadata saved in these fields.

If you've created a Metadata preset and want to update it, select *Edit Presets* to open the Edit Metadata Presets dialog. At the top of the dialog, select the preset you want to change, and then edit the metadata below. Finally, select *Update Preset* from the pop-up menu at the top of the dialog. To rename or delete a preset, select it at the top of the same dialog and then return to the pop-up and select *Rename Preset* or *Delete Preset*.

Where's the rest of my metadata?

Most of the available metadata fields are hidden by the default panel view. Using the pop-up menu on the Metadata panel header, select different metadata presets to view the additional metadata fields. The *Default* preset only shows the most frequently-used fields, whereas *EXIF and IPTC* displays most of the available fields.

MYSTERY KEYWORDS

It's easy to accidentally save keywords in a Metadata preset, and then have these keywords mysteriously appear on all imported photos because you're applying the Metadata preset while importing, so it's usually worth excluding keywords from the preset. There's a *Clear All Suggestion Lists* button in the same location.

METADATA PRESETS

To view additional metadata available to Lightroom, or create a custom view preset with information you most often use, try Jeffrey Friedl's Metadata Editor Preset Builder: http://www.Lrq.me/friedl-metadatapresets

---

METADATA SHORTCUTS

Copy (Text)	Ctrl C / Cmd C
Cut (Text)	Ctrl X / Cmd X
Paste (Text)	Ctrl V / Cmd V
Copy Metadata	Ctrl Alt Shift C / Cmd Opt Shift C
Paste Metadata	Ctrl Alt Shift V / Cmd Opt Shift V
Enable Metadata Auto Sync	Ctrl Alt Shift A / Cmd Opt Shift A
Show Spelling and Grammar	Cmd : (colon - Mac only)
Check Spelling	Cmd ; (semi-colon - Mac only)

ADDING NOTES

Some photographers like to add notes to their photos, perhaps noting additional work that they need to do to the photo. Lightroom doesn't offer a notes field for this purpose, but you can use other metadata fields such as the *Workflow Instructions* field, (under the *EXIF & IPTC* view). These fields expand to fit larger quantities of text, and are included when you write to XMP or export the files.

Alternatively, for temporary notes that you don't want to write back to the files, the Big Note plug-in works as a handy scratch pad. http://www.Lrq.me/beardsworth-bignote

How do I change the date format and units of measurement?

The metadata uses units and formats set by the operating system's regional settings. For example, the *Altitude* may display in feet or meters, and dates may display as day/month/year or month/day/year, depending on your locality. To change these settings go to *Control Panel > Region & Language > Additional Settings* (Windows) / *System Preferences > Language & Region > Advanced* (Mac).

What are the symbols at the ends of the fields?

At the end of some metadata fields are action buttons. For example, the button at the end of the filename opens the Rename Photo dialog, the button on the *Capture Time* field filters the photos taken on that date, and the button next to a WAV sidecar plays the audio annotation. Float over the button to display the action as a tooltip. **(Figure 9.5)**

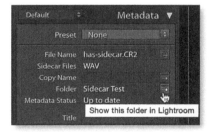

▲ **Figure 9.5** At the end of some metadata fields are buttons. Float the cursor over the button to see what they do.

EDITING THE CAPTURE TIME

We've all done it... you go on vacation abroad, or Daylight Savings Time starts, and you forget to change the time stamp on the camera. It's not a problem though, as Lightroom makes it easy to correct the time stamp.

How do I fix the capture time?

1. Find a photo for which you know the correct time and note the time down—we'll call this the 'known time' photo for the moment.

2. Select all the photos that need the time stamp changed by the

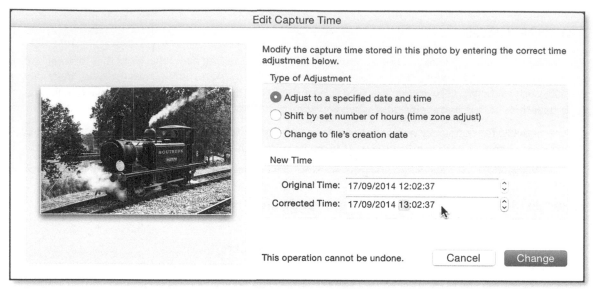

Edit Capture Time

Modify the capture time stored in this photo by entering the correct time adjustment below.

Type of Adjustment

◉ Adjust to a specified date and time

○ Shift by set number of hours (time zone adjust)

○ Change to file's creation date

New Time

Original Time: 17/09/2014 12:02:37

Corrected Time: 17/09/2014 13:02:37

This operation cannot be undone.   Cancel   Change

⬆ **Figure 9.6**   The Edit Capture Time dialog allows you to correct the capture time on a group of photos in one go.

same amount, for example, all those shot on the same vacation with the same camera.

3.   Click on the thumbnail (not the border) of the 'known time' photo that we identified in step 1, making that photo the active (lightest gray) photo without deselecting the other photos.

4.   Go to *Metadata menu* > **Edit Capture Time** to show the Edit Capture Time dialog. If you've selected the photos correctly, the preview photo on the left is your 'known time' photo. **(Figure 9.6)**

5.   If you need to change the time by full hours, you can select *Shift by set number of hours* and enter the time difference, but otherwise, choose the first option, *Adjust to a specified date and time*, as this allows you to change by years, months, days, hours, minutes or seconds.

     If you've selected the *Adjust to a specified date and time option*, enter the correct time—the time you noted down earlier for the 'known-time' photo. You can select each number (hours, minutes, etc.) individually, and change the value either using the arrows or by typing the time of your choice.

6.   Click *Change All* to update all the selected photos.

If you make a mistake, don't panic, the original time stamp is stored in the catalog unless the photo is deleted, and you can return to the original time stamp by selecting the photos and going to *Metadata menu > Revert Capture Time to Original*.

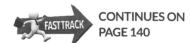

CONTINUES ON PAGE 140

Which Edit Capture Time option should I use?

There are three different options in the Edit Capture Time dialog:

- *Adjust to a specified date and time* adjusts the active (lightest gray) photo to the time you choose, and adjusts all other photos by the same increment. It doesn't set them all to the same date and time. **(Figure 9.7)** This is the most useful option as you can use it to fix incorrect dates, correct capture times that are out by as little as a few seconds, or make half hour time zone adjustments.

- *Shift by set number of hours (time zone adjust)* adjusts by full hours, which is useful when you've only forgotten to adjust the time zone on vacation.

- *Change to file creation date* for each image sets the capture time to the file creation date. This is only usually used on scans that have no capture date, and even then, the file creation date is rarely the date the film photograph was captured.

	Original Time	New Time
Photo 1	08:57:38	09:57:38
Photo 2	12:02:37	13:02:37
Photo 3	16:20:46	17:20:46

◀ **Figure 9.7** Capture Times all move incrementally, rather than setting all the photos to the same time.

How do I sync the times on two or more cameras?

If you're shooting with two cameras, matching the capture times can be even more important, as the *Capture Time* sort order would also be incorrect, muddling up your photos. Of course, synchronizing the time stamps on the cameras before shooting would save you a job, but if you forget, all is not lost.

The principle remains the same as adjusting the time on a single camera, but you need to repeat the process for each camera with the wrong time stamp. It's easiest if you have a fixed point in the day for which you know the correct time and were shooting on all the cameras involved, for example, signing the register at a wedding.

First, separate each camera, so that you're working with one camera's photos at a time. You can do this easily using the Metadata filters, which we'll cover in more detail in the next chapter, starting on page 179. (In short, select *Metadata* from the Filter bar above the grid, select *Camera Model* or *Camera Serial* from the pop-up at the top of a column and then select the model or serial number of the first camera.) Then, using the instructions in the earlier question, change the capture time for these photos. Repeat the process on each additional camera until they all match, then disable the Metadata filter by clicking *None* in the Filter bar.

TIMESTAMPS ON SCANS

Lightroom's Edit Capture Time is designed for digital capture rather than scans, so it won't set all photos to a fixed date and time. John Beardsworth's CaptureTime to Exif plug-in, however, uses Exiftool to add your chosen date to TIFF, PSD, JPEG or DNG files. You can download it from http://www.Lrq.me/beardsworth-capturetimeto-exif

KEYWORDS

It's worth spending a little time adding keywords to help you find specific photos again later, without having to scroll through your whole catalog. Keyword tags are text metadata used to describe the content of the photo.

If you've never keyworded photos before, you may be wondering where to start. There are no hard and fast rules for keywording unless you're shooting for Stock Photography. Assuming you're shooting primarily for yourself, the main rule is simple—use keywords that will help you find the photos again later! For example, they can include:

- **Who** is in the photo (people—we'll come back to Face Recognition in the next section starting on page 151)

- **What** is in the photo (other subjects or objects)

- **Where** the photo was taken (names of locations)

- **Why** the photo was taken (what's happening)

- **When** the photo was taken (time of day, season, event)

- **How** the photo was taken (HDR, tilt-shift, panoramic)

What kind of keywords would you use to describe your photos?

Think about the kinds of keywords you'll use to describe your photos and how you'll organize the keywords before you start applying them to photos. You'll save yourself a lot of time rearranging your keyword list later. It may help to draft your list in a text editor or spreadsheet, or even on a piece of paper. **(Figure 9.8)** While you're doing so, also think about consistency within your keyword list, for example:

- **Grouping**—as with folders and collections, you can use a hierarchical list of keywords instead of a long flat list. A tidy hierarchy is easier to navigate and keeps related items together in the list.

- **Capitalization**—stick to lower case for everything except names of people and places.

- **Quantity**—either use singular or plural, but avoid mixing them. Either have bird, cat and dog or birds, cats and dogs. Where the plural spelling is different, for example, puppy vs. puppies, you can put the other spelling in the *Synonyms* field.

- **Verbs**—stick to a single form, for example, running, playing, jumping rather than run, jumping, play.

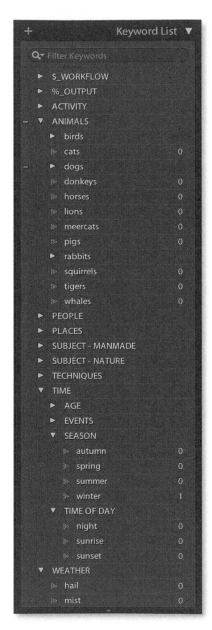

▲ **Figure 9.8** This is a subset of the current keyword list from my personal catalog.

- **Name formats**—consider how you'll handle nicknames or last names for married women. Many use the married name followed by the maiden name (e.g., Mary Married née Maiden), while others choose to put previous names and nicknames in the *Synonyms* field.

Having decided how you'll keyword, you can either start by building your keyword list in the Keyword List panel and then apply these keywords to your photos, or you can start keywording the photos and allow your keyword list to build gradually.

Adding your first keywords

There are multiple ways to add and delete keywords, so we'll just describe one option using the Keywording panel to get you started and then we'll go into more detail.

1. Select the first photo, perhaps in Loupe view so you can see the contents clearly, and go to the Keywording panel in the right panel group in Library module.

2. Click in the keywords field that says *Click here to add keywords.*

3. Type your keywords, separating them with a comma (,). As you start to reuse keywords, Lightroom suggests existing keywords as you type, which helps to avoid creating additional keywords with different spellings.

4. When you've finished, press the Enter key. Your keywords then appear in the *Keywords* field above. If you make a mistake, click in that field and use the Delete/Backspace key to delete the incorrect keyword.

Don't go overboard, especially to start with. If you try to add 30 keywords to every photo you've ever taken, it can become an overwhelming job, so just start with a few significant keywords on your best photos.

That's the basics, but now let's do a deeper dive into keywording.

What's the difference between the Keywording panel and the Keyword List panel?

You'll note that there are two panels for keywording photos—the Keywording panel and the Keyword List panel. The Keywording panel focuses on the keywords applied to the selected photos **(Figure 9.9)**, whereas the Keyword List panel focuses on managing the keywords themselves, organizing them and controlling how they're recorded in

> ### CONTROLLED VOCABULARY
>
> It's possible to download extensive controlled vocabulary keyword lists, covering just about every possible keyword you can imagine, and for Stock Photographers these lists are ideal. Many of the keywords you'll use may not appear on the downloadable lists, as they'll be names of friends, family and local places, but even if you decide to create your own keyword list, you may pick up some good ideas on how to structure your own list. There's a list of the most popular keyword lists at http://www.Lrq.me/links/keywords

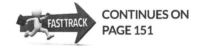

CONTINUES ON PAGE 151

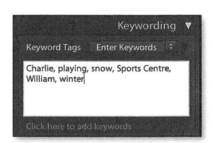

Figure 9.9 You can add keyword tags to your photos by typing them directly into the Keywording panel.

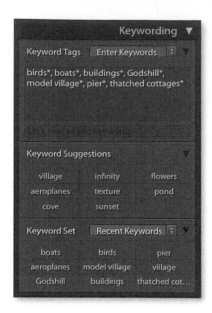

Figure 9.10 You can type keywords directly into the main keyword field in the Keywording panel, or in the small keyword field below.

STOCK PHOTOGRAPHY

To add a large number of keywords for stock agencies, try Tim Armes' Keyword Master plug-in from http://www.Lrq. me/armes-keywordmaster

Note that some stock agencies require keywords in a specific order, however Lightroom always sorts in alphabetical order.

exported files **(Figure 9.10)**. There's overlap in basic functionality, for example, you can create and apply keywords using either panel.

How do I apply keywords to photos?

We said in the Fast Track that there are multiple ways to apply keywords to photos. The main options are:

- **Keywording panel**—In the Keywording panel, type the keywords directly into the main *Keywords* field, divided by commas (as long as the *Keyword Tags* pop-up above is set to *Enter Keywords*), or into the *Click here to add keywords* field below.

  As you start to type, Lightroom offers autofill suggestions from your existing keywords. To select the keyword you want to apply, click on one of these suggestions or use the up/down arrow keys followed by tab, or ignore the suggestion and continue to type.

  You can place a new keyword inside a new or existing keyword by separating them with a pipe character (|), for example, *Places|UK|London|Buckingham Palace*, or a greater than character (>) to type them in the opposite order, for example, *Buckingham Palace > London > UK > Places*.

- **Keyword Suggestions**—The *Keyword Suggestion* buttons intelligently suggest keywords based on your previous keyword combinations and the keywords already assigned to photos nearby. It's smarter than it looks! Clicking on any of those buttons assigns the selected keyword to the photo.

- **Keyword Sets**—Using the pop-up menu in the *Keyword Sets* section, you can create multiple sets of keywords that you tend to apply to a single shoot. For example, you may have sets containing the names of your family members or kinds of animals that are usually found together. To apply the keywords, you can either click on them or use a keyboard shortcut. Hold down Alt (Windows) / Opt (Mac) to see which numerical keys are assigned to each word. (That's why there are only 9 keywords in each set.)

- **Assign an existing keyword in the Keyword List panel**—Click the square to the left of the keyword in the Keyword List panel to add a checkmark.

- **Click and drag to/from the Keyword List panel**—Drag the keyword from the Keyword List panel to the photo or drag the photo to the keyword.

- **Create a new keyword in the Keyword List panel**—If the keyword is new, and therefore doesn't appear in the Keyword List, press the + button on the Keyword List panel. Enter the keyword

PAINTER TOOL

If you like working in Grid view with the mouse (or touchpad, etc.), the Painter tool is a quick way to apply various settings to your photos without having to be too careful about where you click.

The Painter tool **(Figure 9.11)** can be used to assign color labels, ratings, flags, keywords, Metadata presets, settings (Develop presets), rotate photos or add to the Target Collection. It's particularly useful when you have a large number of interspersed photos that need the same settings, for example, a keyword for a particular animal while on safari.

To use it, click the spray can icon in the Grid view Toolbar (press T if you've hidden the Toolbar) to select the Painter tool and pick the setting you want to apply from the pop-up. In this case, you'd select *Keywords* from the pop-up, and enter the keyword(s) in the text field to the right. Multiple keywords can be entered using a comma between each keyword.

Simply click on a thumbnail to apply the setting, or click-and-drag across a series of photos to apply the setting to all the photos the cursor touches.

Any photos that already have that setting applied display a thin white border around the thumbnail, making them easy to spot.

To use the Painter tool to remove a setting, hold down the Alt (Windows) / Opt (Mac) key. The cursor changes to an eraser, then you can click or click-and-drag across the photos to remove the selected setting.

New to Lightroom CC/6 is the Painter Tool Keyword Set pop-up. If you hold down the Shift key while the Painter tool is set to Keywords, a pop-up appears under the cursor. You can then click on any of the keywords to add them to the Painter tool (or remove them) without having to type them into the Keyword field. You can even add an entire Keyword Set in one go by clicking on the *Select All* button. It's a well-hidden feature, but it's useful if you regularly use the Painter tool to apply keywords.

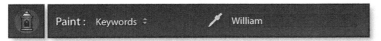

Figure 9.11 The Painter tool is stored on the Toolbar, and the options appear when the tool is selected (left). Hold down Shift to access the Keyword selector (below).

into the Create Keyword Tag dialog and ensure that *Add to selected photos* is checked, then press *Create*. We'll come back to the other options in this dialog a little later.

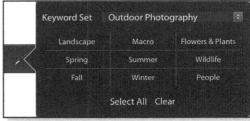

- **Painter Tool**—Use the Painter tool to spray the keywords onto the photos. (See the Painter Tool sidebar)

- **Keyword Shortcut**—To assign a keyword to the keyboard shortcut, right-click on a keyword and choose *Set Keyword Shortcut* then press Shift-K to apply that keyword to selected photos.

- **Face Recognition**—There's also Face Recognition for people keywords, but we'll come back to this in the next section.

KEYWORD CLEANUP

If you've created a tangle of existing keywords in other software, and want to start from scratch, you can clear them automatically at the time of import. Create a Metadata preset with only the *Keywords* field checked, but leave the field empty. This clears any keywords as you import the photos.

Alternatively, once the photos are imported, select them all and delete the contents of the keyword field in the Keywording panel, and then go to *Metadata menu > Purge Unused Keywords* to remove the empty keywords from your Keyword List panel.

To avoid wasting all of the work you've already done, create a keyword called "To Sort" and drag the existing keywords into it. (We'll come back to creating keyword hierarchies shortly.) Then you can build your new keyword list and drag existing keywords into it or filter the photos using their old keywords and assign a new keyword.

How do I edit or remove a keyword?

If you make a mistake, perhaps misspelling the keyword, you can edit it. Simply right-click on the keyword in the Keyword List panel and select *Edit Keyword Tag*, type the correct name and press *Save*. When you rename a keyword, it's automatically updated on all of the tagged photos too.

If you add a keyword to a photo by mistake, you can remove it using either panel. With the photo(s) selected, you can select the keyword in the *Keywords* field in the Keywording panel and press Delete/Backspace to delete the keyword, or you can remove the checkmark against the keyword in the Keyword List panel.

To delete the keyword from the keyword list as well as the tagged photos, select it and press the—button at the top of the Keyword List panel, or right-click and select *Delete*.

How do I create or change the keyword hierarchy?

By default, new keywords are added as a flat list, but you can change them into a hierarchy **(Figure 9.12)**.

You can have multiple levels of parent/child keywords, for example, your *Animal* keyword may be broken down into *Mammal, Reptile, Fish*, etc., with individual species within the sub-categories.

As you drag a keyword onto another keyword, that new parent keyword is highlighted. **(Figure 9.14)** When you release the mouse, the keyword moves inside the new parent keyword, just as you would drag folders onto other folders to make them into subfolders.

If you want to do the opposite and change a child keyword into a top-level keyword, drag and drop the keyword between existing top-level

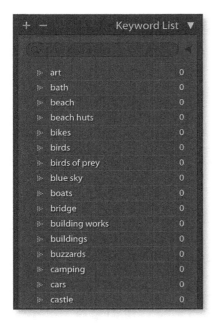

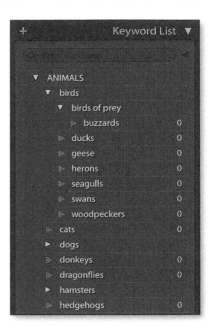

Figure 9.12 Keyword List showing flat list (left) vs hierarchical list (right).

level keywords instead. **(Figure 9.13)** As you drag, a thin blue line appears. Don't worry about dropping it in the right place in the list, as the Keyword List is automatically set to alpha-numeric sort.

Once your hierarchy is underway, you can place new keywords directly into the parent keyword of your choice. You can right-click on the parent keyword and select *Create Keyword Tag inside [keyword]*.

If you want to add a series of child keywords inside the same parent, select ***Put New Keywords Inside this Keyword*** from the right-click menu. Any new keywords are then added to that keyword as child keywords, unless you specifically choose otherwise. The keyword is marked with a small dot next to the keyword name to remind you. To remove it again, right-click on the keyword and uncheck *Put New Keywords Inside this Keyword*.

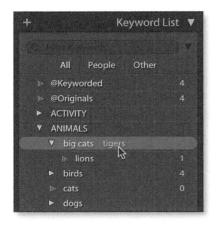

Figure 9.13 To make an existing keyword into the child of another keyword, drag and drop it onto the new parent.

Figure 9.14 To move a child keyword to root level, perhaps to turn a hierarchy into a flat keyword list, drag it to the top of the keyword list and wait for a line to appear.

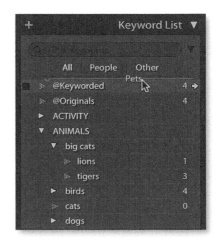

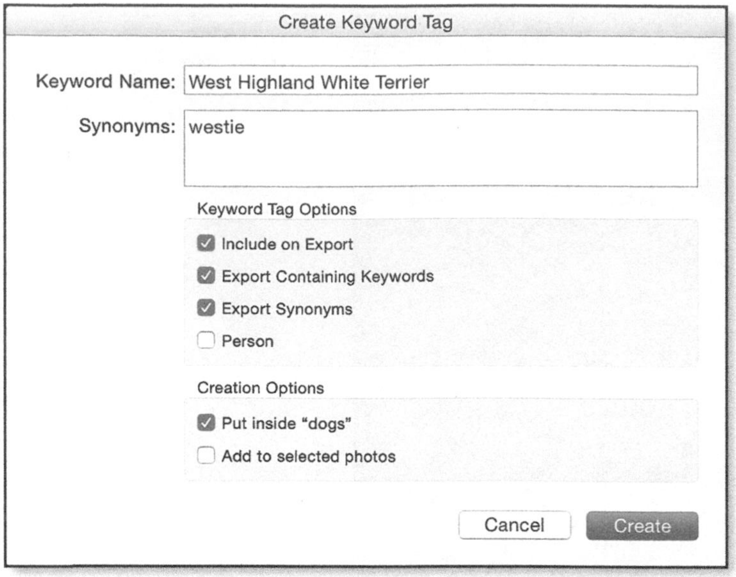

Figure 9.15 You can enter synonyms in the Create Keyword Tag or Edit Keyword Tag dialogs.

Create Keyword Tag

Keyword Name: West Highland White Terrier

Synonyms: westie

Keyword Tag Options

☑ Include on Export

☑ Export Containing Keywords

☑ Export Synonyms

☐ Person

Creation Options

☑ Put inside "dogs"

☐ Add to selected photos

Cancel   Create

Which options should I select when creating or editing a keyword?

In the Create Keyword Tag dialog **(Figure 9.15)**, there are additional options which create a fair amount of confusion. They are *Synonyms, Include on Export, Export Containing Keywords* and *Export Synonyms*. You can also access these options for existing keywords by right-clicking on the keyword in the Keyword List panel and selecting *Edit Keyword Tag.*

The **Synonyms** field allows you to add other words with a similar meaning. For example, you may add the latin name of a plant, or nicknames of family members. Don't go overboard—you don't have to copy the whole thesaurus! These synonyms can be searched using Smart Collections and Text Filters without adding them as separate keywords. The **Export Synonyms** checkbox controls whether these synonyms are included in exported photos.

You might not want all of your keywords included with exported photos, particularly if they include private information, or they're just category heading keywords such as 'Places' or 'People.' They can be excluded by unchecking the **Include on Export** checkbox in the Create/ Edit Keyword Tag dialogs. There's no indicator on the keyword list to show which keywords won't export, but using uppercase characters (PLACES, PEOPLE, etc.) can to help identify them.

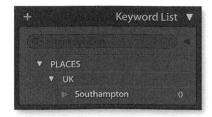

Figure 9.16 This is the keyword hierarchy shown in **Figure 9.17**.

When you assign a keyword to a photo, the parent keywords aren't directly applied, but they can be written to the file when you export the photos. For example, you may have a keyword 'dogs' and inside it you have 'Charlie'. The 'dogs' keyword isn't directly applied to the

Keywords (synonyms in brackets)	PLACES			UK (United Kingdom, Great Britain)			Southampton (Soton)			
Checkboxes	Include on Export	Export Containing Keywords	Export Synonyms	Include on Export	Export Containing Keywords	Export Synonyms	Include on Export	Export Containing Keywords	Export Synonyms	Results
Let's start with everything checked.	Yes	N/A	N/A	Yes	Yes	Yes	Yes	Yes	Yes	PLACES, UK, United Kingdom, Great Britain, Southampton, Soton
We don't want the PLACES category header to export, so we uncheck Include on Export for that keyword.	No	N/A	N/A	Yes	Yes	Yes	Yes	Yes	Yes	UK, United Kingdom, Great Britain, Southampton, Soton
The Export Synonyms checkbox controls whether that keyword's synonyms are included, so if you uncheck Export Synonyms for UK, UK's synonyms are excluded.	No	N/A	N/A	Yes	Yes	No	Yes	Yes	Yes	UK, Southampton, Soton
Export Containing Keywords controls whether the parent keywords are exported or not, but it won't override an unchecked Include on Export.	No	N/A	N/A	Yes	N/A	No	Yes	Yes	Yes	Southampton, Soton

The PLACES checkboxes marked N/A have no effect as the PLACES keyword has no parent keywords or synonyms.

This doesn't do anything as *Include on Export* is unchecked for PLACES.

Unchecking *Export Containing Keywords* for Southampton prevents UK and its synonyms from being included.

photo, but leaving **Export Containing Keywords** checked will include it at export. For simplicity, I'd suggest leaving it checked for all keywords, and then excluding specific parent keywords (i.e. PLACES) by unchecking the *Include on Export* checkbox on the parent keyword.

The interaction between these checkboxes is not as straight forward as you might hope, so I've illustrated it in the table below with a hierarchy of PLACES > UK > Southampton. I've added synonyms too. Southampton has Soton as a synonym, and UK has United Kingdom and Great Britain as synonyms. These are the results of different checkbox combinations: **(Figure 9.16 & 9.17)**

Figure 9.17 The interaction between the different Keyword checkboxes.

How do I see which keywords are applied to my photo?

Still confused about which keywords are applied to your photo? At the top of the Keywording panel is the **Keyword Tags** pop-up.

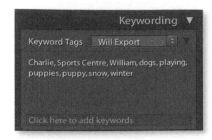

Figure 9.18 The Keywording panel allows you to view the keywords directly assigned to the photo, the keywords that will be exported including synonyms, or the keywords including their parent keywords, as well as entering new keywords.

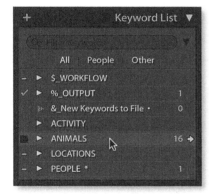

Figure 9.19 Keyword symbols give additional information about the keyword.

- **Enter Keywords** is the normal view. It only displays keywords that are directly applied to the photo. In our example, it simply says Southampton.

- **Keywords & Containing Keywords** shows the keywords directly applied to the photo and its parent keywords. In our example, it says PLACES, UK, Southampton.

- **Will Export** shows all the keywords that will be included in an exported photo. In our example, it displays the results shown in the last column of the table, depending on which checkboxes are checked. **(Figure 9.18)**

If you have multiple photos selected, you may see an asterisk next to some of the keywords in that field. The asterisk indicates that the keyword is applied to some of the selected photos, but not all of them.

What do the symbols in the Keyword List panels mean?

There are a number of symbols displayed in the Keyword List to provide additional information. **(Figure 9.19)** They include:

A **check mark** indicates that all the selected photos have that keyword assigned.

An **empty square** indicates that the keyword isn't currently assigned to the selected photos. It only appears when you hover over the keyword.

A **minus symbol** means that some of the photos you've selected have that keyword assigned, or a child of that keyword. If it's a parent keyword, it can also show that all of your selected photos have some, but not all, of its child keywords assigned.

A **tag** to the left of the keyword shows that it's a People keyword.

A **plus sign** to the right of the keyword means that keyword is currently assigned to the Keyword shortcut or Painter tool.

A **dot** to the right of the keyword means that new keywords will be placed inside the selected keyword.

An **arrow** appears to the right of each keyword when you float over the keyword. It's a shortcut to filter the photos tagged with the selected keyword. We'll come back to filtering on page 179.

How can I keep certain keywords at the top of the list?

The list of keywords is displayed in standard alpha-numeric order, so adding a symbol to the beginning of the name, for example, the @

KEYWORDS TEXT FILE

Lightroom can import and export keywords from/to a text file. **(Figure 9.20)** This means that you can create your keyword list using a plain text editor or spreadsheet and then import it into Lightroom, but be warned, any formatting mistakes may block the import, and it can be a time-consuming job to figure out what's wrong.

If you want to try it, you'll need to save your list as a Tab De-limited .txt file rather than a Comma Separated .csv file. When creating the text file, only use a tab to show a parent-child hi-erarchy, and avoid other characters. Square brackets around a keyword unchecks the *Include on Export* checkbox, and curly brackets denote *Synonyms*. Back in Lightroom, go to *Metadata menu > Import Keywords* and navigate to the file. If it won't im-port, you've probably got some blank lines, extraneous spaces, return feeds, etc., or perhaps a child keyword without a parent.

You can also export the keywords to the text file using *Metadata menu > Export Keywords*. This allows you to view your keywords in a text editor to look for mistakes, and also transfer keyword lists between catalogs. Again, be warned, importing a keyword list from a text file won't remove or edit existing keywords, so you can't use it to tidy up your hierarchy externally.

```
[ACTIVITY]
    eating
    jumping
    playing
    running
    sleeping
[ANIMALS]
    birds
            birds of prey
                buzzards
        ducks
        herons
        seagulls
        swans
    cats
    dogs
        {puppy}
        {puppies}
        Barney
        Charlie
        Maddie
        Nellie
        Rosie
        Tilly
        William
    donkeys
    dragonflies
        {dragonfly}
    fish
    goats
    guinea pigs
    hamsters
        Hercules
    horses
    kangaroos
    lions
    meercats
    pigs
    rabbits
        Rosie
        Smudge
        Wilbur
    seals
    squirrels
    tigers
    wallabies
        {wallaby}
    whales
    wildlife (unknown)
```

symbol, keeps these specific keywords at the top of the keywords list. It's particularly useful for workflow keywords, for example, I always add an @NotKeyworded keyword to all photos as they're imported, and remove it when I've finished keywording. If I get interrupted while applying keywords, any half-done photos might not show in the Without Keywords smart collection, but still appear in my @ NotKeyworded filter.

Is there a quick way of finding a particular keyword in my long list?

If your keyword list becomes lengthy, or keywords are hidden under collapsed parent keywords, it can be difficult to find a specific keyword quickly. Fortunately Adobe thought of this too, and there's a **Keywords Filter** at the top of the Keyword List panel, which instantly filters the keyword list to show matching keywords. **(Figure 9.21)** It's useful if you drop a keyword in the wrong place while making it a parent or child keyword, and then can't find it again. If you click on the magnifying glass to the left, you can choose to search *All* keywords,

▲ **Figure 9.20** Keyword Text File

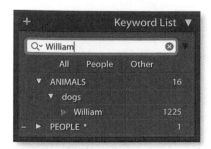

Figure 9.21 Search for a keyword in the list by clicking in the Search field at the top of the Keyword List panel.

Figure 9.22 A text search for *Keywords Are Empty* is a quick way to find all the photos you haven't keyworded yet. Add them to the Quick Collection rather than keywording them in the filtered view, otherwise they'll disappear when you add the first keyword.

People keywords or *Other* keywords. If you select *Show All Keywords Inside Matches*, Lightroom also displays the sub keywords.

If you click the disclosure triangle to the right, Lightroom displays further filtering options to show **All** keywords, **People** keywords or **Other** keywords, but this time without searching for a specific keyword.

Is it possible to display all the photos in a catalog that aren't already keyworded?

If you want to find photos that haven't yet been keyworded, look in the Collections panel. There's a default smart collection called Without Keywords, or you can use a Text filter set to Keywords > Are Empty. **(Figure 9.22)** We'll come back to filtering and smart collections in the next chapter (page 179). If you don't always complete your keywording in one session, you could also use my @ NotKeyworded trick mentioned previously.

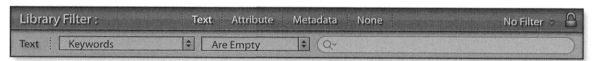

WINDOWS LIMITATIONS

Flat lists of keywords can run into a Windows limitation. There isn't a known limit to the number of keywords you can use, but part of a long flat list may be hidden (or showing but not accessible) in the Keyword List panel. It's possible to work around using the Filter Keywords field at the top of the Keywords panel, but it's far easier to avoid by using a hierarchy instead.

KEYWORD & PAINTER TOOL SHORTCUTS

Go to Add Keywords field	Ctrl K / Cmd K
Change Keywords	Ctrl Shift K / Cmd Shift K
Set Keyword Shortcut	Ctrl Alt Shift K / Cmd Opt Shift K
Toggle Keyword Shortcut	Shift K
Next Keyword Set	Alt 0 / Opt 0
Previous Keyword Set	Alt Shift 0 / Opt Shift 0
Apply Keyword from Set	Alt / Opt & numbers 1-9
Enable Painter Tool	Ctrl Alt K / Cmd Opt K
Remove Painter Tool Setting	Hold Alt / Opt
Show Painter Keyword Sets	Hold Shift
Add Keyword to Painter Tool	Alt Shift / Opt Shift & numbers 1-9

FACES

Face Recognition Technology is new to Lightroom CC/6. It searches your photos for things that look like faces, and displays these faces as a grid, ready for you to identify the people. As you start naming people, Lightroom starts recognizing their facial features and suggesting their names for other faces that look similar, so it's ideal for tagging family and friends.

It gets smarter as you use it. Obviously it's not as smart as you are, and occasionally it identifies trees as people, suggests wrong names **(Figure 9.23)**, and misses incomplete or small faces, but the technology is improving, and even in its current state, it can save many hours of work.

The names are stored as a special type of keyword, so you can search and filter just like normal keywords, but there are a couple of differences. Whereas keywords apply to the whole photo, face recognition tags a specific region of the photo, like Facebook's face tagging. If there are multiple people in a photo, you may remember who's who now, but future generations are sure to appreciate the assistance!

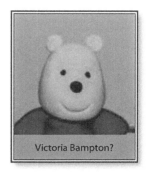

Victoria Bampton?

Figure 9.23 No, that's definitely not me!

Besides being quicker than keywording, confirming name suggestions can be quite funny, when you see some of the ridiculous suggestions. As the faces are all displayed at a similar size in the grid, it's also much quicker to find a specific expression on someone's face when searching.

So if you photograph family and friends, let's take it for a spin.

How to face tag people

1. Select a recent folder or collection containing people you can identify.

2. Open People view using the icon on the Toolbar **(Figure 9.24)** or by pressing the O key (O being round like a face).

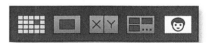

Figure 9.24 Select the People icon in the Toolbar at the bottom.

3. Lightroom asks for permission to index your catalog. The indexing process scans your photos looking for faces and builds thumbnails to display in the People view. **(Figure 9.25)** Select *Only Find Faces As-Needed* for now, and leave the rest for later. If you select *Start Finding Faces in Entire Catalog*, it searches the entire catalog in the background.

Depending on the number of photos in the folder or collection, it may take quite some time and slow down your computer while it works. You can start exploring, but it's less frustrating to wait for this indexing stage to complete before you start tagging. You

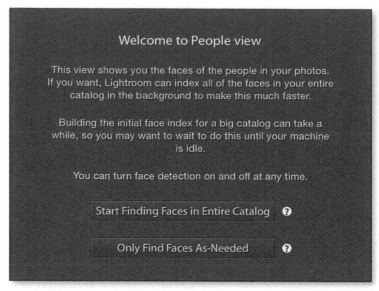

Figure 9.25 Lightroom asks for permission to index your photos.

can check its progress in the Activity Center by clicking on the Identity Plate.

4. While you're waiting for the indexing to complete, think about how you'll name people. The names need to be unique, so *First Name Last Name* (e.g. Victoria Bampton) is an obvious choice.

   If you've previously created keywords for names, select them in the Keyword List panel, right-click and choose *Convert Keywords*

Figure 9.26 If you previously used keywords to identify people, convert them to person keywords.

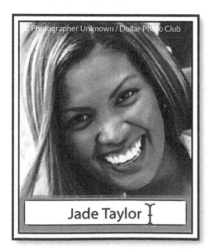

Figure 9.27 Click below the thumbnail to add the person's name.

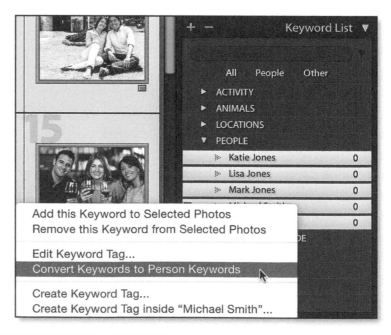

to Person Keywords. This makes the names available for use in the People view. **(Figure 9.26)**

5. Finished indexing? Good!

6. If it's your first time face tagging, click under a face and type the person's name. **(Figure 9.27)** When you add a new name, the person is added to the *Named People* section at the top of the People view. **(Figure 9.28)** Press the Tab key to move to the next photo, or click under the next face, and type the name of the next person and repeat.

   When Lightroom's pretty sure multiple faces are the same person, it stacks them so you can name the entire stack in one go.

7. Try to name one photo of each person who appears regularly in your photos. This gives Lightroom initial information to start suggesting names for the other photos.

Figure 9.28 As you add names, they're aded to the Named People section.

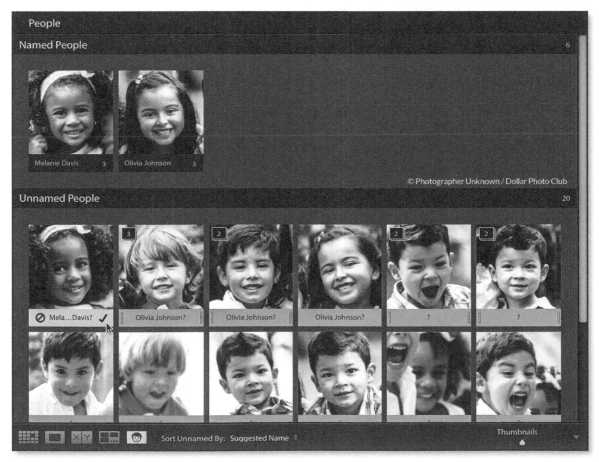

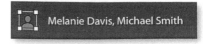

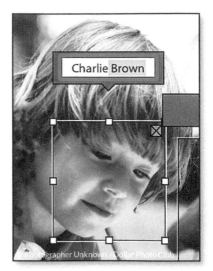

Figure 9.29 Select the Draw Faces tool in the Toolbar.

Figure 9.30 Draw around the face and add a name.

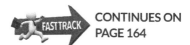

CONTINUES ON PAGE 164

8. Once you've given Lightroom a kick start, it's often quicker to switch to confirming Lightroom's guesses.

   If Lightroom suggests a correct name, click the checkmark in the corner of the photo to confirm it, or hit Shift-Enter.

   If you Ctrl-click (Windows) / Cmd-click (Mac) or Shift-click to select multiple faces, you can confirm them with a single checkmark click. It's quicker than clicking them all individually.

9. Select any photos that aren't people's faces (e.g., trees or animals), or faces that you'll never be able to name (e.g., unknown people in a crowd) and press the Delete key to delete the face region. This doesn't delete the photo itself—just the record of the face region.

10. Clicking the icon to reject a name suggestion just removes the suggestion. If Lightroom suggests an incorrect name or displays a question mark, type the correct name. It's quickest to confirm the most correct guessed names first and then fix the rest.

11. Once the *Unnamed People* section is empty, check the photos for any faces that Lightroom missed, perhaps because they were incomplete.

    Switch to Loupe view and enable the Draw Faces tool in the Toolbar, if it's not already selected. **(Figure 9.29)**

    Start on the first photo and use the right arrow to move through the photos to check for any missed faces.

    If you find a face that Lightroom missed, click and drag a square around the face and type the name in the label above. **(Figure 9.30)**

That's the basics... now let's learn some extra tips and tricks.

How do I index my whole catalog?

If you've experimented with face tagging and decided that you're going to use it, it's worth asking Lightroom to index your entire catalog at a time when you don't need to use the computer (e.g., overnight).

There are pros and cons to indexing the whole catalog. The biggest advantage is it saves you waiting for the indexing process each time you switch to People view for a new folder or collection. The downside is it takes a long time if you have a large number of photos and it may slow your computer down while it's indexing. It also takes up a little extra space in your catalog and previews, but it's only about 2 KB metadata per photo, plus a thumbnail of the face.

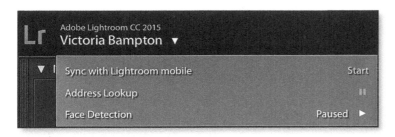

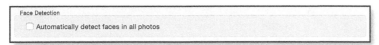

Figure 9.31 In the Activity Center, you can pause or continue background detection of faces.

Figure 9.32 You can also enable/disable indexing in *Catalog Settings > Metadata*.

To start indexing the whole catalog, show the Activity Center by clicking the Identity Plate and click the triangle next to *Face Detection—Paused* label. **(Figure 9.31)** You can also go to *Edit menu* (Windows) / *Lightroom menu* (Mac) > *Catalog Settings > Metadata tab* and check the **Automatically detect faces in all photos** checkbox. **(Figure 9.32)**

Lightroom uses a couple of tricks to speed up the indexing process. If indexing is enabled for the entire catalog when you import new photos, Lightroom uses the embedded preview in the file (1024px or greater) rather than the full resolution data. For photos already in the catalog, Lightroom makes use of any existing Smart Previews as these are quicker to load and provide all the information Lightroom needs.

If neither of these shortcuts are available, then Lightroom uses the original files to build the index. This can be a little slower, depending on the size of the originals and the drive speed. If the originals are offline, they're skipped until the photos are next available.

How do I stop indexing?

If you need to quit Lightroom, the indexing just carries on when you next open Lightroom.

If you need to pause the indexing process, perhaps because the computer's running too slowly and you need to do some other work, click the *Face Detection* pause button in the Activity Center to temporarily pause it, and click again to enable it later.

There isn't a way to disable it completely, but if you leave the indexing turned off for the catalog, never open People view and never select the Draw Face tool in Loupe view, Lightroom won't index the photos.

USING EXISTING KEYWORDS

Converting existing keywords doesn't automatically name all of the faces in the tagged photos because there may be more than one person in each photo. For example, if you have a photo tagged with John and Mary, Lightroom may automatically find their faces but it doesn't know who's who. All is not lost. This information can still help.

If you click the arrow to the right of the keyword, Lightroom filters the photos to only show the photos tagged with that keyword. When you switch back to People view, the *Unnamed People* section will still contain a number of different people (as the photos likely contain other people too), but the percentage of photos of the selected person will be much higher than the unfiltered view, making it easier to tag them all.

How should I organize my people keywords?

In the Keywording section (page 140), we discussed different organizational methods for keywords, so we'll just summarize the main points to consider for your People keywords.

- **Unique Names**—The names must be unique, even if they fall under different parent keywords in your keyword hierarchy.

- **Parent Keyword**—If you decide to keep all of your People keywords together under a parent keyword (such as *PEOPLE*) right-click on the parent keyword and select **Put New Person Keywords Inside This Keyword** to automatically add new people to the group.

  There are some occasions when you might want to leave people keywords in other locations, for example, if you visit a waxworks museum, you might want to nest these people's names under the name of the museum.

- **Family Hierarchies**—You might choose to nest people keywords within a family/surname keyword. This works well for grouping, but you'll still need to use the person's whole name (e.g. *Victoria Bampton* rather than a *Victoria* keyword inside a *Bampton* keyword) as there may be more than one person with the same first name.

- **Consistency**—Like other keywords, keep the formatting consistent. For example, you could use *First Name Last Name* or *Last Name—First Name*. (Note that you can't use a comma to separate *Last Name, First Name* as commas are used to separate keywords.)

- **Previous Names**—Think about how you'll handle maiden names for married women, for example, *First Name Last Name née Maiden Name*.

If you already have keywords for people's names, you can convert them to people keywords. Right-click on the keywords and choose **Convert Keywords to Person Keywords** in the right-click menu. You can convert multiple photos in one go, and it also applies to any child keywords. Be careful, because there isn't a way to batch-convert them back to normal keywords if you select the wrong ones. If you do make a mistake, you must right-click on the keyword, select *Edit Keyword Tag* and uncheck the **Person** checkbox.

This is worth doing at the outset to avoid confusion. For example, if you have a keyword for Victoria (the State) in Australia, and then you type the name Victoria under a face, that Victoria keyword would be converted to a person keyword. That's not much help!

While you're converting the keywords, remember to make sure they're full names and unique, renaming them if necessary. If you have the name Victoria multiple times under different family surname keywords, all of the Victoria faces will end up tagged with the first keyword.

How do I navigate the People view?

The **People** view shows all of the people in the current selected source (e.g. folder, collection, *All Photographs*) and it's split into *Named People* at the top and *Unnamed People* at the bottom. **(Figure 9.33)** When you name a face, it moves from the *Unnamed People* to the *Named People* section.

In the **Named People** section, the name of the person shows below the thumbnail, and the number to the right shows how photos you have tagged with that name. When you hold down the Alt key (Windows) / Opt key (Mac) and float the cursor from left to right (or right to left) over the person's thumbnail, Lightroom scrubs through all of the thumbnails of that person. Unfortunately you can't select which photo to display for each person, because your chosen photo might not be in the current folder or collection. If you double-click on one of the faces, Lightroom switches to *Person View*, which we'll come back to shortly.

In the **Unnamed People** section at the bottom are all of the photos that haven't been identified yet. The label shows Lightroom's best guess, or if it can't guess the name, it just displays a question mark.

Some of the thumbnails may be stacked, shown by a number in the top left corner. **(Figure 9.34)** This means that Lightroom's pretty sure the photos are all the same person.

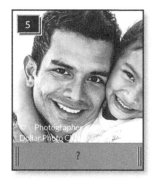

Clicking on the stack number opens and closes the stack. If the face stack's closed, your actions apply to the entire stack (unlike normal stacks) so confirming or typing a name applies to all of the photos in the stack. When a stack's open, your actions only apply to the selected face.

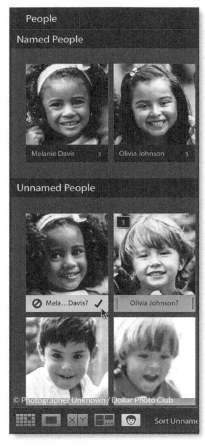

Figure 9.33 When you confirm a face, it moves to the Named People section.

Figure 9.34 When Lightroom's pretty sure the photos are all the same person, it stacks them.

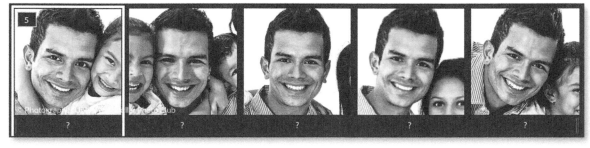

You can quickly look inside the selected stack by holding down the S key (when the text field is inactive) but it's easier just to go ahead and name the stack and check the individual Person view for mistakes later.

Why are the thumbnails unavailable or too dark?

The thumbnails are based on the unedited file, so some may be too dark or light, but there's no way of fixing this at the moment.

They're automatically built at the same time as the indexing process, however if you quit Lightroom before it's finished, it might not have time to build all of the thumbnails. In this case, they'll build as you scroll through the photos (as long as the originals or smart previews are available).

The **Thumbnails** slider on the Toolbar changes the size of the face thumbnails. This makes it much easier to see who's in the photo.

How do I change the sort order?

Also on the Toolbar you'll see the **Sort Unnamed By** pop-up, which changes the sort order in the *Unnamed People* section.

- **Suggested Names** is the default. It sorts all of the suggested names into alphabetical order and puts the ones without guesses at the end.

- **Filmstrip Order** puts them faces in the same order as the photos. It's most useful when naming people in photos taken over a long period of time, as the people progressively age!

- **Stack Size** puts all of the stacks at the beginning, with the largest stacks first. This is handy for getting through the bulk of the photos in one go.

- **Popular Names** puts your most frequently photographed people first. This is useful if you're most concerned with tagging close family and friends and you're not too concerned about people you see less frequently.

How do I add a name to a face?

Like keywording, there are multiple ways to assign a name to a face. They include:

- **Type under Face thumbnail**—The obvious choice is typing the name directly under the photo in the *Unnamed People* section.

The pop-up offers auto complete suggestions from the available People keywords.

- **Confirm suggestion**—If Lightroom suggests the correct name, you can confirm it by clicking the checkmark or using the keyboard shortcut Shift-Enter. **(Figure 9.35)**

- **Drag to Named People**—If the person already appears in the *Named People* section, you can drag the thumbnail and drop it on the correct person.

- **Drag to Keyword List**—If the person's name already exists as a Person keyword, you can drag the thumbnail to the name in the Keyword List panel. This is easiest if you click the disclosure triangle to the right of the Filter Keywords field and then select *People* to only show the People keywords. **(Figure 9.36)**

- **Type on label in Loupe view**—In Loupe view, with the Draw Face tool enabled, you can click in the name label and type the name.

You can also apply your changes to multiple faces in one go, which speeds the process up considerably. Hold down the Ctrl key (Windows) / Cmd key (Mac) while clicking on multiple faces to select them, then name, confirm, reject or delete the faces all in one go. If the faces you want to select are contiguous (not interrupted), click on the first, hold down the Shift key and click on the last to select them.

I made a spelling mistake—how do I fix it?

If you make a spelling mistake, find the person in the *Named People* section and click on the name to correct it. You can also right-click on the name in the Keyword List panel and select *Edit Keyword Tag*.

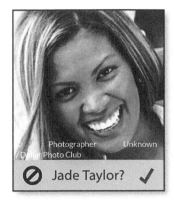

Figure 9.35 You can reject an incorrect suggestion, but it's quicker just to correct it.

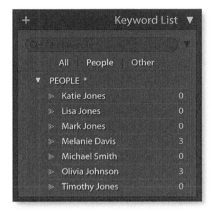

Figure 9.36 You can filter the Keyword List to only show People keywords.

BATCH DELETE

To remove all of the face regions from a single photo, open it in Loupe view, right-click on the photo and select *People > Remove All Face Regions*.

To remove all of the face regions from a larger number of photos—perhaps a series of crowd shots where you don't know anyone—select the photos and add them to the Quick Collection. Switch to the Quick Collection and then open People view. All of the faces will be from the photos in the Quick Collection, so you can easily select all of the faces and press the Delete key to remove them.

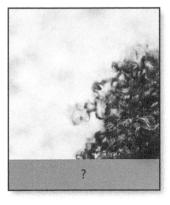

Figure 9.37 Delete regions that aren't people you want to name.

Does rejecting a name suggestion take another guess?

If Lightroom suggests an incorrect name, you can press the icon to reject it, but it's quicker just to replace it with the correct name. Rejecting a name doesn't take another guess, and Lightroom doesn't learn from the photos you reject.

What do I do with people I don't recognize?

If you don't recognize the faces, look in Navigator panel in the top left corner to see whole picture or switch to Loupe view. The context can help to prompt your memory.

If you're still not sure who it is, but you expect to be able to find out (perhaps by asking another friend or family member), either leave them in the *Unnamed People* section, or give them a temporary name. For example, you might call them *Unknown Bampton* or *Victoria Unknown* or even *Unknown Red Jacket Canada*. Using the word Unknown (or something similar) makes it easy to filter to find and name these people later. Be careful to uncheck *Include on Export* in the Edit Keyword Tag dialog for these keywords, as someone marked as *Unknown Big Nose* might be offended!

If don't think you're ever going to name the person, delete the face region by selecting the thumbnail and pressing the Delete key **(Figure 9.37)** If you change your mind, you can draw it back later using the Draw Face tool, but there isn't a way to ask Lightroom to automatically reindex the photo once the regions have been deleted.

How do I access the photos of a single person?

When you double-click on a face in the *Named People* section (or right-click and select *Find Similar Faces*), it takes you to **Person View** and displays only the photos of the selected person in the **Confirmed** section. **(Figure 9.38)**

If you find a face in the *Confirmed* section that has the wrong name, perhaps because it was hidden in a collapsed stack, float over the face to show the label and type the correct name.

In the **Similar** section below, it displays additional photos that may or may not be the same person. The *Similar* section isn't as strict about suggesting faces, so there are a lot more incorrect guesses, but the best guesses are sorted to the top of the section, ready for confirmation. You can't reject suggestions in this section. It's particularly useful to select multiple thumbnails before clicking the checkmark, as the entire *Similar* section refreshes every time you confirm faces.

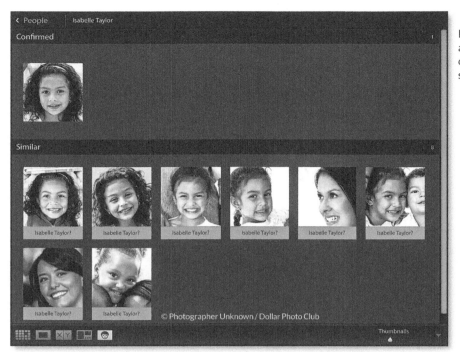

© Photographer Unknown / Dollar Photo Club

Figure 9.38 In the Person view, you can see all of the confirmed faces of a single person and other similar faces.

To switch back to People view, click on the People icon in the Toolbar or on the *People* link in the top left corner of the preview area. If you double-click on a face in *Person* view (or in the *Unnamed Person* section of the *People* view), Lightroom switches to Loupe view with the Draw Face tool enabled.

Why didn't the indexing find all of the faces?

Once you've cleared all of Lightroom's suggestions, you may want to check through the photos to find any extra faces that it missed. Face-on is relatively easy for Lightroom to find, but if it's the side of someone's head, Lightroom needs to be able to see both eyes to recognize it as a face. The faces also need to be big enough, so in a crowd of thousands, you'll be pleased to know it won't ask you to name every face!

How do I draw missing faces on the photo?

If Lightroom has missed some faces, you can use the Draw Face tool to add a face region to the photo. It's automatically selected when you switch to the Loupe view from a People view, or you can click on the icon in the Loupe view Toolbar to enable it. Simply drag a square around the face to add a face region. If you want to be really tidy, hold down the Shift key while dragging to constrain the bounding box

Figure 9.39 Use the Draw Face tool to add any missing faces.

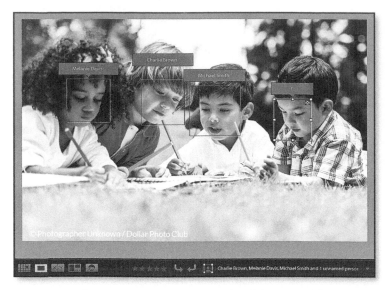

to a square shape. If you draw a rectangle, Lightroom still creates a square thumbnail for the People views. (**Figure 9.39**)

Should I draw round the backs of people's heads?

While you're drawing face regions, you may come across photos of the back of a person's head. You could draw a face region around it. Lightroom won't recognize it as a face if it's missing eyes, so you won't harm the face recognition artificial intelligence, but the back of the head would appear in the Person view, which isn't very helpful. Instead, I'd recommend using the standard keyword tools (e.g., add a checkmark in the Keyword List panel or type the name in the Keywording panel) to tag using a standard keyword. You'll still be able to search and filter on the person's keyword to show all of the photos that include them.

BIRTHDAYS

To take your People information to the next level, try Jeffrey's People Support plug-in. It allows you to enter the date of birth for each of your tagged people, and even tells you how old they were in a particular photo. http://www. Lrq.me/friedl-people

How do I name people in Loupe view?

When you're in Loupe view with the Draw Face tool enabled, the face regions and labels show on the photo. Click on the label to enter or change the name. You can also confirm and reject name suggestions by clicking on the checkmark and reject icon that appear when you float over the label, and delete face regions by clicking the black X in the top right corner of the bounding box.

As a general rule, it's more efficient to do the bulk of the naming in the main People view, but the Loupe is useful for mopping up the ones it misses.

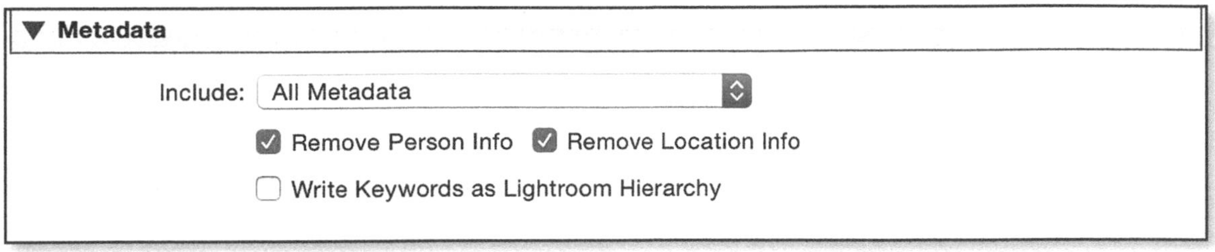

▼ **Metadata**

Include: | All Metadata | ⇕ |

☑ Remove Person Info ☑ Remove Location Info

☐ Write Keywords as Lightroom Hierarchy

How do I keep my people keywords private?

When you come to export the photos, the names are included in the keywords and are also copied to the *Person Shown* IPTC field.

If you want the names to remain private, there's a **Remove Person Info** checkbox in the Metadata section of the Export dialog. You can also selectively excludes names by right-clicking on the keyword in the Keyword List panel, choosing *Edit Keyword Tag* and then unchecking *Include on Export*. **(Figure 9.40)**

▲ **Figure 9.40** To keep people keywords private when exporting photos, check the *Remove Person Info* checkbox.

FACE RECOGNITION SHORTCUTS

People view	O
Confirm suggested name	Shift-Enter

With text field inactive

Navigate through faces	Left/right arrow
Delete face region	Delete
Expand/collapse stack	S
Temporarily expand stack	Hold down S
Show photos inside stack	Hold Alt / Opt while floating over stack
Activate the text field	Shift-S

With text field active

Next photo	Tab
Previous photo	Shift-Tab
Confirm and select next photo	Enter
Delete name	Delete
Stop editing	Escape

MAP LOCATIONS

Lightroom's Map module allows you to sort and manage your photos by location. Some photos, for example, those shot on mobile phones, automatically appear on the map as they include GPS (Global Positioning System) data. If you have a GPS device or smart phone app, Lightroom assists you in linking the tracklog with the photos. But you don't need any high-tech equipment to use the Map module, as Lightroom allows you to assign locations by dragging and dropping the photo directly onto the map.

Map Module Basics

First, we'll add location metadata to some of your photos using the map, and then we'll go into more detail on the other options.

1. Switch to the Map module by selecting *Map* in the Module Picker at the top of the screen, and make sure the Filmstrip is showing at the bottom of the screen. (If it's hidden, click the black bar at the bottom of the screen to unhide it.)

2. Initially the map displays whole world **(Figure 9.41)**, so you'll need to zoom in to the location your photos were shot. The quickest way to zoom in is to hold down the Alt (Windows) / Opt

▼**Figure 9.41** The Map module adds location metadata to your photos.

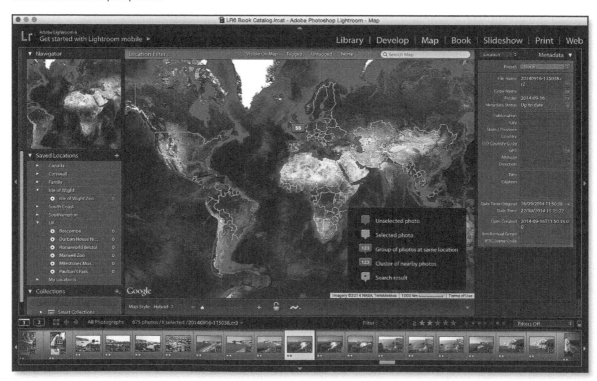

(Mac) key and drag a rectangle on the map, enclosing the area you want to view. **(Figure 9.42)** Once you've zoomed in most of the way, use the slider on the Toolbar to zoom in or out, and click and drag the map to pan around.

3. Using the Filmstrip, select photos shot in the same place and drag them onto the map, releasing them at that location. Lightroom displays a yellow marker where you drop the photos and adds the coordinates to the GPS field in the Metadata panel. If you make a mistake, drag them from the Filmstrip to the correct location. **(Figure 9.43)**

4. At the top of the Map, select *Untagged* to dim the photos you've already tagged and repeat the process until all of the photos are dimmed.

5. To view the photos at a specific location, click on the light or dark orange marker. The photos displayed are limited to those in current folder/collection.

That's the basics, but there's more to learn. Let's start with navigating the map and viewing the photos you've just tagged.

Navigating the Map

The color and style of marker depends on how many photos are tagged at a location, and whether they're selected or not. **(Figure 9.44)**

*   **Photos** are shown with a dark orange marker if they're not selected.

*   **Selected Photos** are shown with a light orange marker.

*   **Groups** of photos shot at the same location are shown using dark orange markers with numbers.

*   **Clusters** are shown using dark orange markers with no arrow. Cluster are groups of photos taken near to each other but not actually at the same location. The photos merge into clusters as you zoom out, and split into their individual markers again as you zoom in.

*   **Search Results** are marked using a light orange marker with a black spot. We'll come back to searching shortly.

When you roll over or select a single tagged photo in the Filmstrip, the marker bounces up and down to help you spot its location on the map. It doesn't work for groups or clusters.

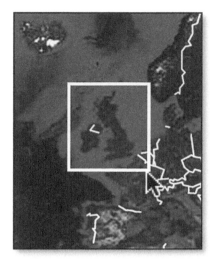

▲ **Figure 9.42** Hold down Alt (Windows) / Opt (Mac) while dragging a rectangle to quickly zoom.

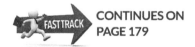

CONTINUES ON PAGE 179

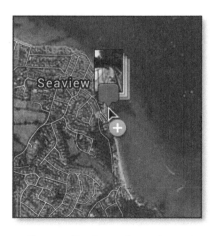

▲ **Figure 9.43** Drag photos from the Filmstrip onto the map.

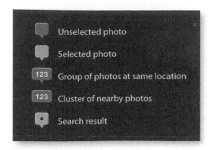

Figure 9.44 The Marker Key explains the meaning of each marker. Close the key by clicking the X in the corner. To bring it back, select *View menu > Show Map Key*.

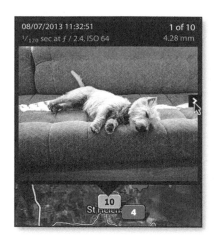

Figure 9.45 When you click on a marker, you can scroll through thumbnails of all the photos taken at that location.

Figure 9.46 The Marker Lock prevents you accidentally moving a location marker.

How do I view the photos attached to each location marker?

When you hover over a marker, a pop-up displays the photos under that pin. **(Figure 9.45)** If it's a group or cluster of photos, click on the left and right arrows or scroll the mouse wheel to scroll through the photos.

When you move away from the marker, the pop-up is automatically dismissed. If you'd like to fix the pop-up so that it remains on screen, click on the selected marker (a yellow one) or double-click on the unselected marker (an orange one). It then stays on screen until you click elsewhere.

How do I avoid accidentally moving a marker?

If you accidentally move a marker, you also change the location data for the photo, so there's a lock icon on the Toolbar to lock the markers in place. **(Figure 9.46)** Assuming you dropped the photos in the right place initially, you'll likely want to leave the markers locked most of the time.

With the markers locked, you can still add new photos to the map, and also change the location of existing photos by dragging them from the Filmstrip to their correct location.

How do I select the map style?

The maps are powered by Google Maps because they offer detailed mapping of most of the planet. By default, Lightroom displays the *Hybrid* style, which is a combination of the *Road Map* and *Satellite* views, but you can select different map styles using the **Map Style** pop-up on the Toolbar. **(Figure 9.47)**

The maximum zoom depth is dependent on the map style—the *Hybrid*, *Road Map* and *Satellite* views offer more detail than the *Terrain* view. It also varies by location, with big cities showing more detail than less built-up areas. This is dependent on the information available from Google.

How do I search for a specific location?

You can zoom in and out and pan around the map until you find the location you're looking for, but it's quicker to search for a specific location. To do so, type the name, a zip or postal code, or coordinates (e.g. 50°44'17" N 1°42'59" W or -33.840663, 151.071579) in the Search Box at the top of the map and hit Enter. **(Figure 9.48)**

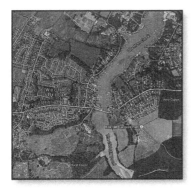
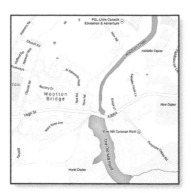
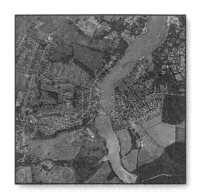
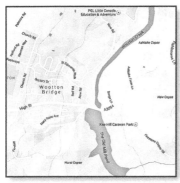
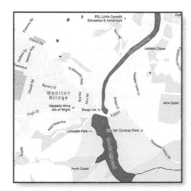
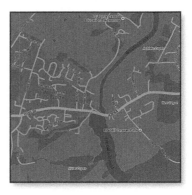

If there are multiple locations that meet your search criteria, Lightroom offers a choice if you search for the same term a second time. **(Figure 9.49)** The search results are weighted using your current map view, so if it doesn't offer the location you're expecting, zoom in to the general geographic region and try again. For example,

▲ **Figure 9.47** There are six different map styles. From top left to bottom right, they are: *Hybrid, Road Map, Satellite, Terrain, Light, Dark*

Location Filter :   Visible On Map   Tagged   Untagged   None   50°44′17″ N 1°42′59″ W ⊗

▲ **Figure 9.48** Use the Search box at the top of the map to search for coordinates or place names.

◀ **Figure 9.49** If multiple locations match your search, Lightroom gives you a choice.

Windsor, Windsor, Windsor and Maidenhead SL4, UK

Windsor, CT, USA

Windsor, CA, USA

Windsor, CO, USA

Windsor, VT, USA

Windsor, NJ, USA

MAP OFFLINE

The Map module requires internet access to be able to view the maps, and Google's terms of service don't allow Adobe to cache this information. If your internet is offline or a firewall is blocking access to Google, it says *We have no imagery here* and then *Map is Offline*. When you reconnect to the internet, the Map module automatically reconnects.

Shanklin, England, United Kingdom

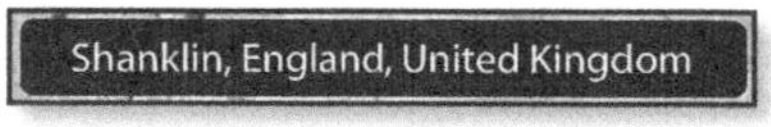

Figure 9.50 Press the I key to show and hide the Location Name overlay.

Figure 9.51 The Map Filter bar allows you to show and hide photos in the Filmstrip based on their geocoding status.

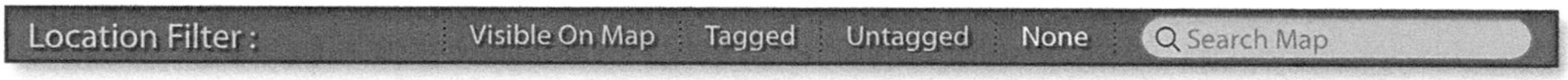

Figure 9.52 The Metadata Filter columns in the Library module allow you to search the location data.

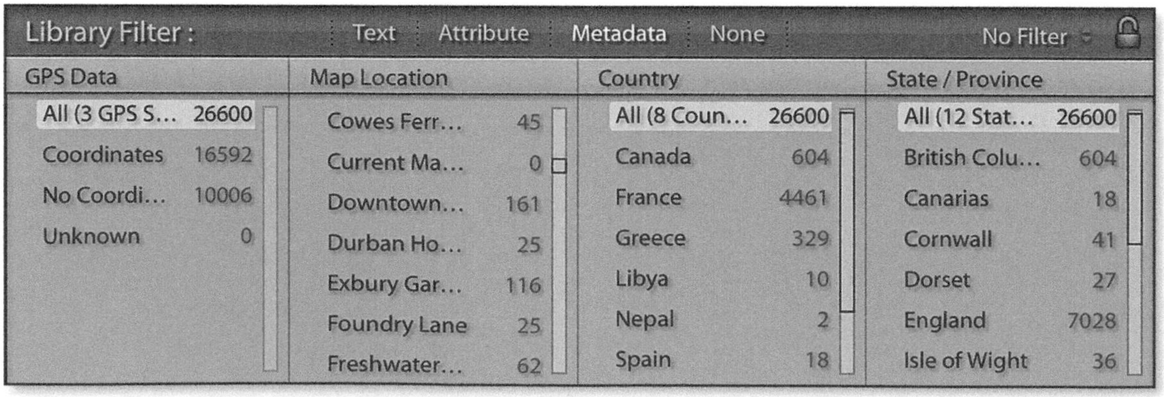

if you are viewing the whole world when searching for *Windsor*, the search results offer a number of places in the United States and Canada. If, however, you zoom into the United Kingdom, the search results change to show Windsor in the UK first.

How do I show or hide the overlays?

In the top right corner of the Map, you'll see an overlay with the name of the current location or search results. **(Figure 9.50)** Like the Info overlay elsewhere, you can press the I key to show and hide it.

How do I use the Map Filter bar?

To the right of the search box is the Map Filter bar, offering three ways of filtering photos in the Filmstrip based on their location data **(Figure 9.51)**. Like the Filter bar in the Library module, press the \ key to show or hide it.

- **Visible On Map** hides photos in the Filmstrip that aren't tagged with the current map location.

- **Tagged** dims the untagged photos, making it easy to spot the tagged ones.

- **Untagged** dims the tagged photos making it easy to spot the ones who haven't been tagged yet.

- **None** clears the filtering.

You can also use the Library module Metadata Filter bar to filter for photos by location, using the Location, City, State/Province and Country IPTC fields or Saved Locations. **(Figure 9.52)** We'll come back to filtering in the next chapter, starting on page 179.

Location Filter : Visible On Map   Tagged   Untagged   None   Q Search Map

Library Filter :   Text   Attribute   Metadata   None   No Filter

GPS Data		Map Location		Country		State / Province	
All (3 GPS S...	26600	Cowes Ferr...	45	All (8 Coun...	26600	All (12 Stat...	26600
Coordinates	16592	Current Ma...	0	Canada	604	British Colu...	604
No Coordi...	10006	Downtown...	161	France	4461	Canarias	18
Unknown	0	Durban Ho...	25	Greece	329	Cornwall	41
		Exbury Gar...	116	Libya	10	Dorset	27
		Foundry Lane	25	Nepal	2	England	7028
		Freshwater...	62	Spain	18	Isle of Wight	36

How do I use Saved Locations?

Many of the photos you take are likely at the same locations—perhaps at home, other places close to home, and favorite vacation destinations. You can save these locations for easy access.

Saved locations are like presets for maps, offering a number of benefits:

- **Shortcuts**—They're shortcuts straight to a location, to save you having to search for it.

- **Photo Count**—The count shows how many photos in the current folder or collection are tagged with this location.

- **Filtering**—You can filter to find photos at saved locations using filters and smart collections.

- **Privacy**—If you mark a saved location as private, you can selectively remove the location information when exporting photos, while retaining location information on other exported photos.

To create a saved location:

1. Navigate to the location on the map.

2. Click the + button on the Saved Locations panel.

3. In the New Location dialog **(Figure 9.53)**, give the location a name and set the radius in *Kilometers, Meters, Miles* or *Feet*. You can adjust the radius and location once the saved location is created.

4. Decide whether to make the location private. If *Private* is checked, any photos taken within the saved location have their location data automatically stripped on export. For example, you may want to mark the area surrounding your home as private,

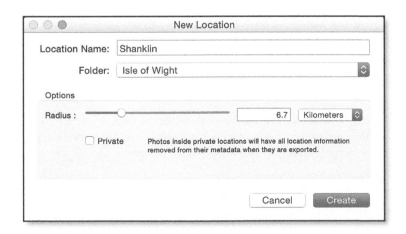

Figure 9.53 Set the options for a saved location in the New Location dialog.

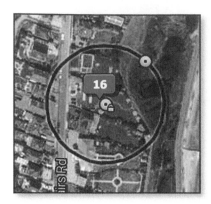

Figure 9.54 Saved Locations show as circles on the map.

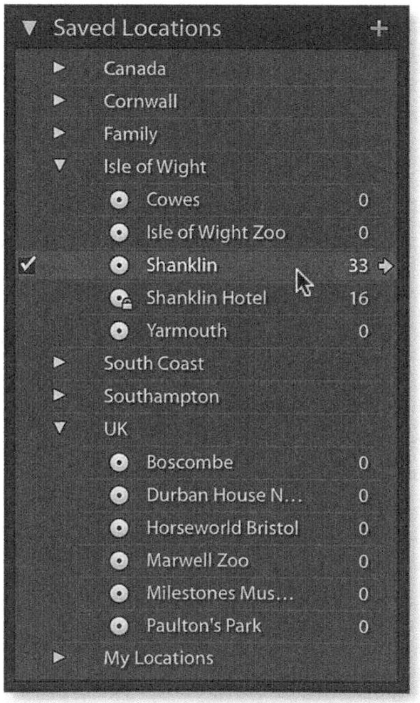

Figure 9.55 The checkmark on the left shows that the selected photo was taken at the Saved Location, and the arrow on the right will take you to that area.

so that photos uploaded to the web are stripped of your home address.

5. Press *Create* to confirm the saved location.

6. The Saved Location appears on the map as a circle—black if it's private, white if it's not. **(Figure 9.54)** If it doesn't show, make sure your location is selected in the Saved Locations panel and press the O key to toggle the overlay (or go to *View menu > Show Saved Location Overlay*).

7. Move the circle to fine tune the location by dragging the dot in the center. The lock icon also indicates that it's a private location.

8. Change the radius of the saved location by dragging the dot on the outer circle to resize the circle.

To rename the location or change the privacy settings, right-click on the saved location in the Saved Locations panel and select *Location Options* to access the Edit Location dialog.

To quickly return to a saved location, click the arrow at the end of the saved location name in the Saved Locations panel, or double-click on its name **(Figure 9.55)**. As you explore the map, you'll also notice that the names of saved locations within the current view light up.

You can have saved locations within other saved locations, for example, you may have a saved location which covers a whole country, and another saved location for a specific town or address.

Adding & Editing Location Metadata Using the Map

We've already covered the basics of adding metadata using the map, but now let's learn some extra tricks.

How do I mark photos on the map?

There are numerous ways to add photos to the map and location metadata to the photo.

- **Drag onto the map**—Simply dragging the photo from the Filmstrip or secondary window and dropping it on the map so a marker appears. This works equally well with multiple selected photos.

- **Right-click on the map**—You can select the photos, right-click on the correct location on the map and select *Add GPS Coordinates to Selected Photos* from the context-sensitive menu.

- **Drag to/from a Saved Location**—Select the photos and drag them onto a location in the Saved Locations panel, or drag the saved location onto the photos in the Filmstrip.

- **Check the Saved Location**—Select the photos and go to the Saved Locations panel. As you float over the locations in that panel, a checkbox appears for each saved location. Click the checkbox to tag the selected photos with the central point of that saved location.

- **Manual Entry**—Select the photos and type (or copy/paste from another photo) the GPS coordinates in the GPS field in the Metadata panel.

- **Sync from another photo**—Select a group of untagged photos, plus a photo that already has coordinates. Click the thumbnail of the tagged photo to make that the active photo, then press the *Sync Metadata* button at the bottom of the right panel group. Check the *GPS* field, leaving the others unchecked, and press *Synchronize* to copy that location to the other photos.

How do I find photos I haven't tagged yet?

If you're working through your entire back catalog and tagging photos with locations, it helps to narrow the photos down to the ones you haven't tagged yet.

The *Untagged* filter at the top of the map is useful, as it helps to identify photos that you haven't geocoded, but it can involve a lot of scrolling as the photos are only dimmed, rather than removed from view.

To hide the tagged photos, switch to the Grid view and select the Metadata Filter bar at the top of the grid. Using a pop-up at the top of a column, select *GPS Data* and then click on *No Coordinates* below. The tagged photos disappear from view. (We'll come back to filtering in more detail on page 179). Switch back to the Map module. As you drag additional photos onto the map, they also disappear from view. It works well as long as you drop them in the right place! If you drop them in the wrong place, press Ctrl-Z (Windows) / Cmd-Z (Mac) to undo and try again.

How do I move a photo or group of photos to a different location?

If you make a mistake when adding location metadata, you can easily move the photos to a new location.

To move photos that you've already added to the map, select them in the Filmstrip and drag them onto a different location, as if you were adding a location for the first time.

SECOND WINDOW

If you have a second screen or a large monitor, use the Grid view on the secondary window and drag the photos onto the map from the grid instead of the Filmstrip. It allows you to see and select more photos.

PREVIOUS METADATA

If you've previously added location information to your photos, perhaps using keywords or IPTC data, you can also use the Library module Metadata Filter bar to find and select groups of photos taken at the same location and drag whole groups of photos onto the map or Saved Locations panel.

MOVING GROUPS

You can't drag group markers—it's a Google Maps API limitation. You can, however, click on the group marker to automatically select the photos, and then drag them from the Filmstrip to the new location, which moves the marker automatically.

If a single marker is in the wrong place, you can also unlock the *Marker Lock* on the Toolbar and drag the single marker to a new location.

How do I delete location information?

To completely remove location information from photos in the Map module, select the photos and go to the *Photo menu*, where you'll find two delete options. **Delete GPS Coordinates** removes the GPS data, removes the photo from the map, and removes any unconfirmed IPTC location data that was automatically added using address lookup. **Delete All Location Metadata** does the same, but also removes any IPTC Location data that you've added yourself. If you have multiple photos selected, a dialog checks whether you want to remove the data from all the photos or only the active photo.

Adding Location Metadata Using Tracklogs

Once you start geocoding your photos, you may want to use a more automated solution, such as a dedicated GPS device. Some GPS devices attach directly to the camera, tagging the photos themselves at the time of shooting, so the photos automatically appear on the map. Other GPS devices create a tracklog, which is a series of GPS locations and timestamps, showing where you were at a specific time. Lightroom then helps you match the tracklog with the photos, showing where the photos were taken.

Which tracklog formats can Lightroom understand?

Lightroom imports GPX files, which is a standard format for the interchange of GPS data, used by many devices. Many devices, or the desktop applications that come with them, can create GPX files. If your device doesn't offer that facility, you can use GPSBabel (http://www.Lrq.me/gpsbabel) to convert the tracklog to a compatible GPX format. Simply select the correct format for the input file, and GPX XML as the output format.

How do I import my tracklog and match it with the photos?

Having a created a tracklog, upload it onto your computer (your device instructions will tell you how to do that) and switch to the Map module.

1. Click the *Tracklog* button on the Toolbar and select *Load Tracklog*.

(Figure 9.56) (All of those options are also found under *Map menu > Tracklog*.)

2. Navigate to your tracklog on the hard drive and click *Choose*.

3. The tracklog is broken up into its individual sections, which are listed in the **Track** pop-up on the Toolbar. **(Figure 9.57)** Select **All Tracks** to see your entire route. The track displays as a blue line on your map. **(Figure 9.58)**

4. Select all the applicable photos in the Filmstrip and click the Tracklog button on the Toolbar, then select **Auto-Tag Photos**. Lightroom checks the photo timestamps against the tracklog timestamps and automatically drop the photos on the map. You may need to apply a timezone offset, which we'll come to shortly.

5. When you're finished, hide the tracks by selecting **Turn Off Tracklog** under the Tracklog button in the Toolbar. To view it again, select *Recent Tracks* from the menu.

How do I apply a timezone offset?

GPX logs, by definition, are time stamped in UTC (Coordinated Universal Time), whereas photos are usually stamped in local time. Rather than changing the photos to match the UTC time, you can apply a timezone offset to the tracklog.

1. Import the tracklog as before, and select the related photos as if you're going to apply the tracklog.

2. Under the *Tracklog* button on the Toolbar, you'll find **Set Time Zone Offset**.

3. Move the slider in the dialog to match the photo times to the tracklog times. **(Figure 9.59)** You don't even need to know what the time difference was, as the times for both the selected photos and tracklog are shown in the dialog, allowing you to match them. The text in the dialog turns black when a likely match is found based on the selected photos, and turns red when the offset is wrong.

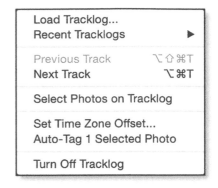

Figure 9.56 The tracklog menu options are found on the Toolbar.

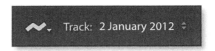

Figure 9.57 Tracks may have multiple sections, which can be selected from the Track pop-up.

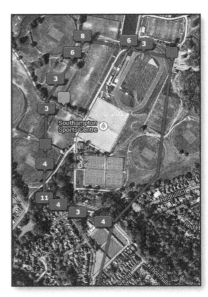

Figure 9.58 The tracklog shows in Lightroom as a blue line, and the photos can be automatically added based on their timestamps.

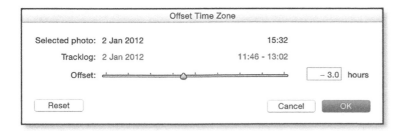

Figure 9.59 Match photos tagged in local time with a UTC tracklog using the Offset Time Zone dialog.

▶ **Figure 9.60** If the timestamps are a few minutes off, you can drop a single photo in the right place on the track and Lightroom will use the relative times to place the other photos.

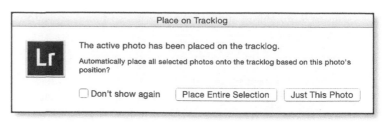

4. Press OK to confirm the time offset. You can then auto-tag the photos.

My camera time doesn't quite match the tracklog—how do I fix it?

If the photos don't land on quite the right spot because your camera timestamp was a few minutes off, there are two ways to fix it.

1. **Fix the photo time stamps** Lightroom allows you to correct the camera timestamp using *Edit Capture Time*. Turn back to the Edit the Capture Time section (page 137) to learn more (and don't forget to correct the time on your camera for future shoots).

2. **Shuffle the photos along the track**—Lightroom allows you to manually move the photos along the track. Select all the photos you want to adjust, either in the Filmstrip or secondary window. Choose a photo for which you know the correct location, and click on its thumbnail to make it the active photo, shown by the lightest gray thumbnail border. Drag this photo from the Filmstrip to the correct position on the blue track line. Lightroom asks whether to adjust all the photos or just that photo. When you allow it to adjust all the photos, it shifts all the photos along the track using their relative timestamps to calculate their correct locations. (**Figure 9.60**)

What is *Address Lookup*?

Address lookup, previously called reverse geocoding, is the process of converting your GPS latitude/longitude data—your map location—into a readable address, which is then entered automatically into the IPTC Location fields. For example, if you drop a photo on Adobe's Headquarters, it would be entered as GPS coordinates of 37°19'52" N 121°53'36" W. From these coordinates Lightroom, in conjunction with Google Map's API, works out the San Jose address details.

TRACKLOG WON'T IMPORT

If your tracklog won't import, check that it's a supported file type. Lightroom only currently supports GPX files natively. If you used GPSBabel to convert the file, try reconverting from the original format, double checking your settings. There's a 10 MB tracklog file size limit on Mac, which could prevent the file from importing, but no equivalent limit on Windows. It may be possible to open the tracklog in a text editor and split it into multiple files, or Jeffrey Friedl's Geocoding plug-in can handle larger tracklogs. http://www.Lrq.me/friedl-geocoding

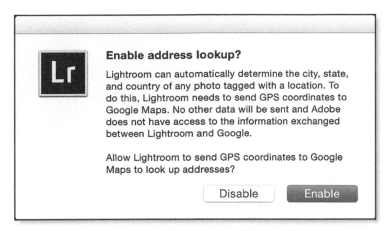

Figure 9.61 As address lookup requires sending the coordinates to Google, Lightroom asks for permission.

Should I turn on address lookup in Catalog Settings?

When you import your first photo with GPS coordinates or drag your first photo onto the map in a new catalog, Lightroom asks for permission to enable address lookup. **(Figure 9.61)** If you decline, you can later enable it (or disable it) using the ***Look up city, state and country of GPS coordinates to provide address suggestions*** checkbox in *Catalog Settings > Metadata tab*, or by clicking the play button next to *Address Lookup* in the Activity Center. **(Figure 9.62)**

This permission is stored for each catalog individually, so you can have different settings for each catalog, and you can disable it again by going to *Catalog Settings > Metadata tab* and unchecking the *Address Lookup* checkboxes.

With address lookup enabled, Lightroom sends the GPS coordinates to Google, so that they can return the address. Only the coordinates are sent, without any personal information, but you must decide whether you're comfortable with this.

You can pause it at any time, perhaps because your bandwidth is limited or costly, by clicking the pause button in the Activity Center.

Will address lookup overwrite my existing location data?

Lightroom only calculates location data if the Location fields (*Sublocation, City, State/Province, Country* or *Country Code*) are all empty. If you've already entered data in any of these fields, the address lookup is skipped.

Figure 9.62 You can disable address lookup in the Catalog Settings dialog.

Address Lookup

☑ Look up city, state and country of GPS coordinates to provide address suggestions

☑ Export address suggestions whenever address fields are empty

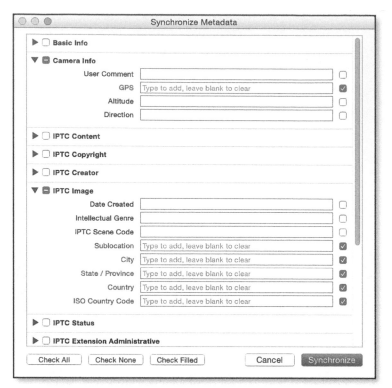

Figure 9.63 To clear manually entered location metadata, check these fields in the Synchronize Metadata dialog but leave the fields blank.

AUTO-POPULATE METADATA

Some have asked whether it's possible to connect certain IPTC fields or keywords with each GPS location, so adding images would automatically populate that data.

At the time of writing, you can't attach keywords or other metadata to a location, apart from the automatic address lookup for the IPTC Location fields. You can use the location data to filter the photos, so that you can manually add keywords or other metadata based on the location.

GOOGLE & YAHOO MAPS

Alt-clicking (Windows) / Opt-clicking (Mac) on the GPS arrow in the Metadata panel opens Google Maps in your default web browser instead of Lightroom's Map module. Ctrl-Alt-clicking (Windows) / Cmd-Opt-clicking (Mac) goes to Yahoo Maps.

If you want to replace manually entered data with reverse geocoded locations, you'll first need to clear the manual data. It's easiest to do as a batch process.

Select the photos in Grid view and press the *Sync Metadata* button at the bottom of the right panel group. Press *Check None* and then check the *Sublocation, City, State/Province, Country* and *ISO Country Code* fields in the IPTC Image section. When you check these fields, the field names go red and the fields say *Type to add, leave blank to clear.* Leave them blank, then press *Synchronize* to remove the data. **(Figure 9.63)**

Why are the Location fields dimmed or italic?

You can view your reverse geocoded location metadata in the Metadata panel. The Location fields are dimmed (and also italicized on Windows) to signify that the location metadata was generated using Google's maps, and may or may not be correct. **(Figure 9.64)** It's not permanent, so if you move the map marker to a new location, this data also updates.

Whether this metadata is included in exported photos depends on the status of the ***Export address suggestions whenever address fields are empty*** checkbox in *Catalog Settings > Metadata tab.* If it's unchecked, only confirmed (white) metadata is included in exported photos. (Note that it only applies to exported files, not writing metadata to XMP in the originals.) Why might you choose not to include Google's guesses? They have been known to be wrong on occasion!

How do I make the lookup data permanent?

If the location metadata is correct, you can commit it by clicking on the field label and then clicking on the menu that appears, or you can edit it manually. **(Figure 9.65)** Once you've done so, the metadata becomes white and no longer updates if you move the photo to a different map location. There isn't a way of committing the location data as a batch process, however.

If it's incorrect, you can type something different in the Location fields. Once you've done so, the metadata becomes white. It's then included when writing to XMP, as if you'd entered it all manually.

Why is address lookup not working?

If you're dropping photos on the map and nothing's appearing in the Metadata panel Location fields, there are a few possibilities to check:

- Go to *Catalog Settings > Metadata tab* and ensure that *Look up city, state and country of GPS coordinates to provide address suggestions* is checked, or click on the Identity Plate to show the Activity Center to check it's not paused. If you've only just turned it on, leave it for a while to catch up or restart Lightroom to trigger the lookups.

- Check that you have internet access and there isn't a firewall preventing Lightroom from accessing Google Maps. If you can navigate around the map in the Map module, that's probably fine.

- Check that you don't already have some user-entered location metadata. If any of the Location fields contain data, the address lookup for that photo is skipped.

- If Google sees the same IP address hit it for more than 100,000 requests per day, it stops sending responses until the next day.

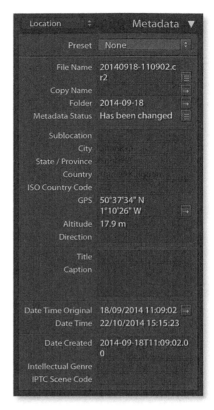

Figure 9.64 Lightroom shows the reverse geocoded data in the Metadata panel.

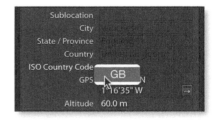

Figure 9.65 The dark grey geocoded locations can be committed by clicking on the field label and clicking on the location in the pop-up menu.

MAP LIMITATIONS

If the Map module has whetted your appetite for geocoding, you may be interested in Jeffrey Friedl's Geocoding plug-in, which offers further options and features including altitude, enhancing Lightroom's own facilities. You can download it from http://www.Lrq.me/friedl-geocoding

MAP SHORTCUTS

Previous Photo	Ctrl / Cmd left arrow
Next Photo	Ctrl / Cmd right arrow
Search	Ctrl F / Cmd F
Previous Track	Ctrl Alt Shift T / Cmd Opt Shift T
Next Track	Ctrl Alt T / Cmd Opt T
Delete GPS Coordinates	Backspace / Delete
Delete All Location Metadata	Ctrl Backspace / Cmd Delete
Show Filter Bar	\
Show Map Info	I
Show Saved Location Overlay	O
Lock Markers	Ctrl K / Cmd K
Zoom In	= (or +)
Zoom Out	-
Zoom to Selection	Alt-drag / Opt-drag rectangle on map
Map Style Hybrid	Ctrl 1 / Cmd 1
Map Style Road Map	Ctrl 2 / Cmd 2
Map Style Satellite	Ctrl 3 / Cmd 3
Map Style Terrain	Ctrl 4 / Cmd 4
Map Style Light	Ctrl 5 / Cmd 5
Map Style Dark	Ctrl 6 / Cmd 6

FINDING & FILTERING YOUR PHOTOS

Being able to add metadata to your photos is great, but the purpose of all this work is to be able to easily locate these photos again at a later date. Using the metadata automatically embedded by the camera, as well as the metadata you've added manually, you can search the database to easily find specific photos.

SORT ORDER

The most basic way of finding your photos is scrolling through the Grid view until you reach the photo you're looking for. If you know the approximate capture date or filename, you can sort the photos into a specific order.

How do I change the sort order?

The **Sort** options are on the Toolbar in Grid view **(Figure 10.1)** or under *View menu > Sort*.

The options are:

- **Capture Time** sorts the photos from oldest to newest. It's the default for most views.

- **Added Order** sorts the photos according to their import time, with the most recent imports first. It's the default for the *Previous/Current Import* collection.

- **Edit Time** sorts the photos according to how recently they were edited, including both Develop and metadata edits.

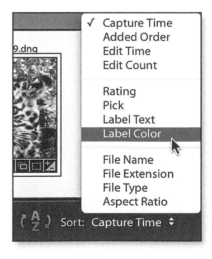

▲ **Figure 10.1** The Sort Order controls are in the Toolbar below the Grid.

NO USER ORDER

User Order isn't available when you're viewing a composite view (a folder with subfolders or a collection set with subcollections) or a smart collection. To solve that, either select a folder with no subfolders, or turn off *Library menu > Show Photos in Subfolders*, so you're only seeing photos directly in the selected folder or collection. If you need a custom sort across multiple folders, group the photos into a collection.

- **Edit Count** sorts the photos according to how frequently you've edited that photo.

- **Rating** groups the photos by their star ratings, with the 5 star photos first.

- **Pick** groups the photos by their flags, with the flagged/picked photos first, then unflagged, then rejected.

- **Label Text** groups the photos alphabetically based on their label text (e.g. Blue, Green, Purple, Red, Yellow)

- **Label Color** groups the photos by their label color (i.e. Red, Yellow, Green, Blue, Purple) regardless of the label text

- **File Name** sorts the photos in alpha-numeric order from A to Z.

- **File Extension** groups the photos by their extension (e.g. *.cr2, *.dng, *.jpg, *.nef, *.psd, *.tiff)

- **File Type** groups the photos by their file type (e.g. Digital Negative Lossless, JPEG, PSD, Raw, TIFF, Video)

- **Aspect Ratio** groups the portrait/vertical photos, then the square photos, then the landscape/horizontal photos, and finally the panoramic photos.

- **User Order** allows you to drag and drop photos into a custom order as long as you're viewing a single folder or collection.

You can reverse the sort order using the **A-Z** button.

You can't change the default sort order, but when you change the sort order for a specific folder, that sort order is automatically selected again the next time you view that folder.

▼ **Figure 10.2** When you drag and drop photos to change the sort order, a black line shows where the photo's going to drop.

How do I drag and drop into a custom sort order?

To drag and drop photos into a custom sort order, or user order, pick up a photo by the thumbnail (not the gray border surrounding it), and drag it to its new location. As you drag the photo, a black line appears between two photos, showing where the photo will drop. **(Figure 10.2)** The sort order popup automatically changes to *User Order*.

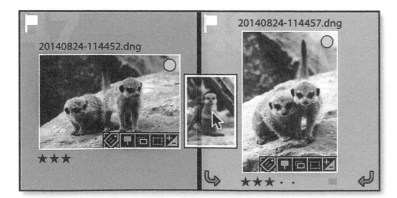

FILTERING YOUR PHOTOS

Scrolling through the photos works well if you only have a small number, but it becomes impractical as your photo library grows. That's where filtering comes in—it hides the photos that don't meet the criteria you choose. For example, you may only want to view the photos with 3 or more stars, or those taken with a specific camera, or even a combination of criteria, such as photos with two specific keywords shot on a particular date.

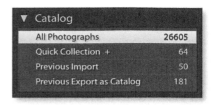

Figure 10.3 To search the whole catalog, select *All Photographs* in the Catalog panel.

How do I filter my photos to show photos fitting certain criteria?

To search your whole catalog, switch to the Library module and select *All Photographs* in the Catalog panel on the left. **(Figure 10.3)** Filters apply to the photos or videos in the current source, so you can limit the search by selecting specific folders or collections in the Folders panel or Collections panel.

The Filter bar is a gray bar at the top of the Grid view. If it's missing, press the \ key or go to *View menu > Show Filter Bar.*

There are three types of filter that can be used separately or together: *Text, Attribute* and *Metadata.* **(Figure 10.4)**

- **Text** filters search the metadata of each photo for the text of your choice. For example, you can search *All Photographs* for a filename (e.g. IMG_5493) to find that photo in your catalog.

- **Attribute** filters search by flag status, star rating, color label, master/virtual copy status and file type (photo vs. video). For example, you can search for the videos with 3 or more stars.

  The main Attribute filters can also be found on the Filmstrip for easy access. If your Filmstrip Filters are collapsed, click on the word *Filter* to show the full range of options.

Figure 10.4 The Text Filters (top), Attribute Filters (center) and Metadata Filters (bottom) can all be combined to drill down through a set of criteria and find the photo you need.

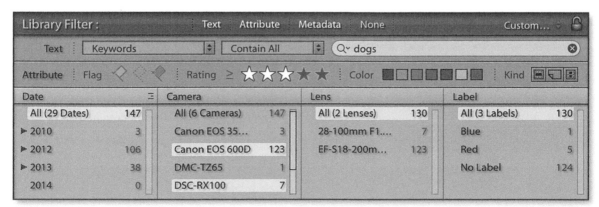

- *Metadata* filters allow you to drill down through a series of criteria to find exactly the photos you're looking for, for example, photos taken of William last Thursday at home using a Sony RX100.

- *None* temporarily disables the filters. If you want to clear them completely, select the *Filters Off* preset on the right of the Filter bar. You can save your own filters using that pop-up menu too.

To view the search options for each filter type, click on the filter label in the Filter bar. To open multiple filter types at the same time, hold down Shift while clicking on the filter labels or set the filter options in the first filter before clicking on another.

Let's try some simple filters before going into more detail.

1. Click on the word *Attribute* and then click on the 3rd star, highlighting it. All the 0, 1 and 2 star photos disappear from view, leaving only the 3, 4 or 5 star photos showing.

2. Click on the 3rd star again, and the other photos reappear.

3. Click on the red square, and only the red labeled photos show.

4. Click the 2nd star, while leaving the red square highlighted. Now the photos with 2 stars or greater and a red label are showing.

5. Click on the word *None* to close to Attribute filters, and then on *Metadata* to open the Metadata filters.

6. In the *Keyword* column, select a keyword of your choice. The other photos disappear from view, leaving only the photos tagged with that keyword.

7. Finally, click on the word *None* to disable the filters, so you're back where you started.

Now let's do a deeper dive to learn more filtering tips and tricks. We'll first look at Attribute filters, as those are most frequently used, then Metadata filters, then Text filters.

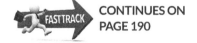

CONTINUES ON PAGE 190

How do I use Attribute filters?

We've already used Attribute filters in this simple example, but there are a couple more tricks to learn.

▼ **Figure 10.5** The Attribute Filters on the Filmstrip are collapsed by default (top), but if you click on the word Filter, the other options will appear (bottom).

The options in the Attribute filter bar or on the Filmstrip Filters are toggle switches **(Figure 10.5)**, so they're highlighted when they're selected, and become a light gray when they're deselected.

The flags from left to right are flagged, unflagged and rejected.

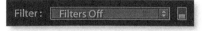

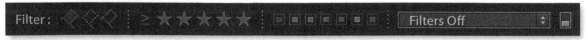

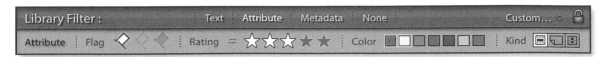

You can combine those, so to hide the rejected photos, click on the flagged and unflagged icons.

The symbol to the left of the stars allow greater control, so you can filter based on:

- ≥ rating is greater than or equal to

- ≤ rating is less than or equal to

- = rating is equal to ()

For example, to display only photos with 0 stars, click on the symbol to the left of the stars and select the = icon, and leave the stars themselves deselected.

To show only photos with selected color labels, click on the colored icons, then click on them again to remove the filer. For example, to show the red and yellow labelled photos, click on the red and yellow boxes.

There are two additional color labels in the filters. The gray square displays photos that don't have a color label. White displays photos with a custom label, where the label name doesn't match a label color in the current Color Label Set.

The final icons are harder to differentiate, but if you float your cursor over the icons, the tooltip shows the button names. The first button shows all normal Master Photos, the second button filters for Virtual Copies and the final button finds Videos. **(Figure 10.6)**

Figure 10.6 You can combine the various attribute filters, for example, show red and yellow labeled master photos with exactly three stars and a flag.

SELECTING PHOTOS BY ATTRIBUTE

If you Ctrl-click (Windows) / Cmd-click (Mac) on the flag, color label or star rating on the main Filter bar or on the Filmstrip, the cursor changes to show that you're selecting rather than filtering, and it selects all the photos in the current view with that flag, label or rating without changing the filtering.

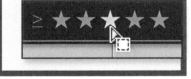

How do I use the Metadata filters?

We briefly used the Metadata filters in the Fast Track to search for a specific keyword, but the tool is far more powerful than that simple search.

The Metadata Filter bar has 4 columns by default, but you can have up to 8. To add and remove columns, click on the button which appears on the right as you float over the column header.

Using the pop-up at the top of each column, you can control which criteria you want to search. **(Figure 10.7)** By default, they're set to *Date*, *Camera*, *Lens* and *Label*, but there's a wide range of options.

Certain columns, such as the date and keyword columns, offer additional options, such as a *Flat* or *Hierarchical* view or *Ascending*

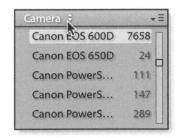

Figure 10.7 Change the Metadata Filter columns by clicking on the pop-up at the top of the column.

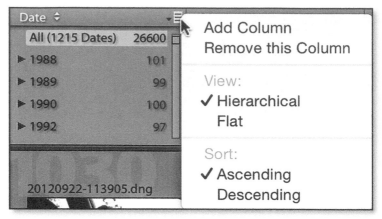

Figure 10.8 Click on the icon at the top right of the column to view the menu.

or *Descending* sort order. Click on the button at the top right of the column to access these options. **(Figure 10.8)**

If you need a bit more vertical space to see a longer list of metadata, drag the bottom edge of the Filter bar to resize it.

How do I view only the photos with the parent keyword directly applied, without seeing the child keywords?

Let's expand the keyword example we used earlier. Imagine you've temporarily applied the parent keyword *Animals* to a group of photos, and now you want to go back and assign the individual child keywords such as *dogs*, *cats* or *mice* instead.

Click the arrow that appears at the right-hand end of the keyword in the Keyword List panel, which is a shortcut to the Metadata filters, or manually select *Animals* in the Keyword column.

By default, the keyword filter is set to **Hierarchical**, so it'll show all of the photos you've already assigned to *dogs*, *cats* and *mice*, as well as the photos you need to work on. That's not much help!

Click the button at the right-hand end of the column header and select the **Flat** view instead. Now the parents keywords are separated from the child keywords, as a long alphabetical list, so you can filter for photos with only the parent keyword *Animals* applied. **(Figure 10.9)**

Can I select multiple options from a single column, creating an OR filter?

But what if you need to find photos that have either a cat or a dog or a mouse? Then you need an OR filter. To do so, hold down Ctrl

---

SLICE & DICE

Like to slice and dice your data? Try these plug-ins:

Lightroom Statistics http://www.Lrq.me/lrstats

Jeffrey Friedl's Data Plot http://www.Lrq.me/friedl-dataplot

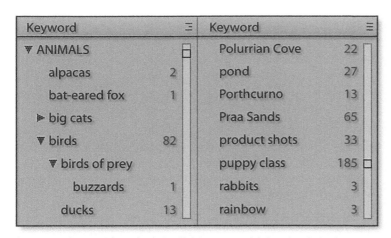

Figure 10.9 Hierarchical (left) and Flat (right) column view.

(Windows) / Cmd (Mac) while clicking on multiple criteria in the same column. (Figure 10.10)

For example, to search for all photos with either a cat, a dog or a mouse, select a single keyword filter column, click on *cats*, then hold down the Ctrl (Windows) / Cmd (Mac) key while clicking on *dogs*, so that they're both selected.

To select a series of keywords, hold down Shift while clicking on the first and last in the series. For example, if your keyword column shows *cats*, *caterpillars*, *chipmunks*, *dogs*, click on *cats* and then shift-click on *dogs* to include *caterpillars* and *chipmunks* in your selection too.

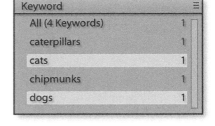

Figure 10.10 Select multiple criteria in the same column to create an OR filter.

How do I select multiple options within the Metadata filter columns, creating an AND filter?

Perhaps you need to do a complex search, drilling down through the catalog to find photos that match multiple criteria, such as photos with both a cat and a dog, taken at a specific location. That's where multiple columns come into their own.

Selecting across multiple columns gives an AND filter, so to search for all photos with both a cat and a dog, select *Keywords* at the top

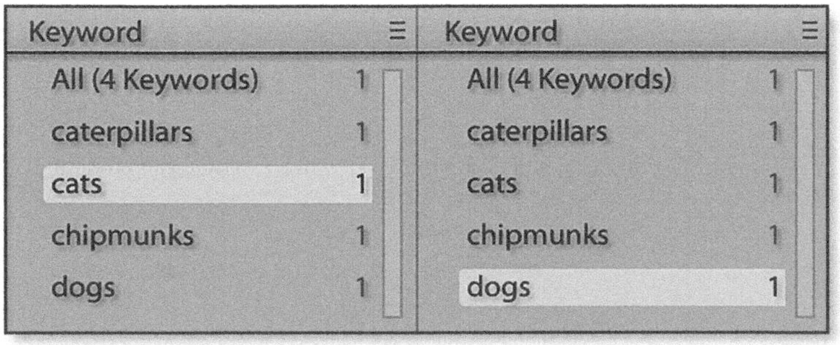

Figure 10.11 Select criteria in multiple columns to create a complex AND filter.

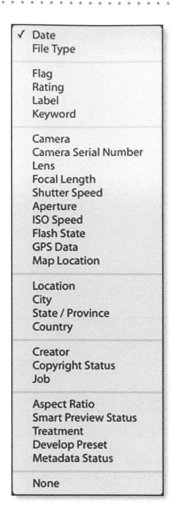

✓ Date
File Type

Flag
Rating
Label
Keyword

Camera
Camera Serial Number
Lens
Focal Length
Shutter Speed
Aperture
ISO Speed
Flash State
GPS Data
Map Location

Location
City
State / Province
Country

Creator
Copyright Status
Job

Aspect Ratio
Smart Preview Status
Treatment
Develop Preset
Metadata Status

None

Figure 10.12 The Metadata Column pop-up offers a wide range of searchable criteria.

Figure 10.13 Multiple types of criteria can be combined to narrow the photos down further.

of two filter columns and select *cats* in one column, and *dogs* in the other. **(Figure 10.11)**

When you select *cats* in the first column, the second column updates to show only the keywords that are also assigned to cat photos, so if *dogs* doesn't appear in the second column, you don't have any photos with both keywords applied.

These multi-column AND filters aren't limited to keywords. You can add additional columns of criteria, for example, the Map Location option displays all of your Saved Locations. Date, File Type and Camera are other popular options, but there's a wide range to suit most scenarios. **(Figure 10.12)**

Let's try a complex search. We'll search for all the photos shot in 2014 at the Sports Center, using an iPhone, and containing the keyword *Charlie*. **(Figure 10.13)**

1. In the first column, which is set to *Date—Hierarchical*, click on *2014* to highlight it. The photos from other years disappear from the grid below.

2. In the second column, which is set to *Camera*, click on iPhone. Photos shot on other cameras also disappear from the grid view.

3. Select *Map Location* in the third column pop-up, and select *Sports Center* below. At this point it only shows photos shot in 2014 at the Sports Center on an iPhone. Just Charlie left to find!

4. Select *Keyword* from the fourth column pop-up, and then select *Charlie* from the list below.

How do I use Text Filters?

There are certain types of metadata that you can't search using the Metadata filters, for example, the filename or the caption. The Text filter option allows you to search based on the text contents of these fields.

The first pop-up determines which metadata fields are searched. You can leave it set to *All Searchable Field*, or narrow it down to *Filename*,

Library Filter:	Text	Attribute	Metadata	None		Custom...	🔒

Date		Camera		Map Location		Keyword	
▶ 2011	786	iPhone	23	Shanklin Chine	0	All (3 Keywords)	135
▶ 2012	2568	iPhone 4S	598	Southampton...	0	$_Copyrighted	135
▶ 2013	4082	iPhone 6	134	Sports Centre	135	Charlie	1
▶ 2014	4787	iPhone 6 Plus	41	The Caledon B&B	0	William	2
▶ 2015	56	Nexus 4	1	The Lizard	0		

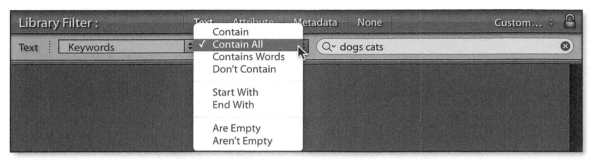

Copy Name, Title, Caption, Keywords, Searchable Metadata, Searchable IPTC, Searchable EXIF or Any Searchable Plug-in Field.

The next pop-up determines whether it has be an exact or partial match, and of course the text field contains the text you're looking for.

▲ **Figure 10.14** The pop-up in the Text Filters controls whether it runs an AND, OR or NOT filter.

How can I use the Text filters to do AND or OR filters?

By default, the second pop-up (**Figure 10.14**) is set to *Contains All*, which means that only photos matching all the words (or part words) you type are included, but there are a few other options:

- **Contains** runs an OR filter, such as photos with either *dogs* or *cats* keywords, including partial matches such as *hotdogs* or *tomcats*.

- **Contains All** runs an AND filter, such as photos with both *dogs* and *cats* keywords, including partial matches such as *hotdogs* and *tomcats*..

- **Contains Words** runs an AND filter, such as photos with both *dogs* and *cats* keywords, but only including whole matching words.

- **Doesn't Contain** runs a NOT filter, such as photos without the keyword *dogs* or partial matches such as *hotdogs*.

- **Starts With** runs an OR filter with photos starting with your chosen letters, for example, *dogs* would show photos with *dogs* or *dogsledding*, but not *hotdogs*.

- **Ends With** runs an OR filter with photos ending with your chosen letters, for example, *dogs* would show photos with *dogs* or *hotdogs*, but not *dogsledding*.

To combine search types, you can add some special characters. A space is *AND*, ! is *NOT*, a leading + means *Starts With*, and a trailing + means *Ends With*. They only affect the adjacent word, so you can use *dogs !cats !mice* to find images with dogs but not cats or mice. (**Figure 10.15**)

SPACES IN KEYWORDS

Text searches don't allow you to use quotes to search for whole phrases, so when you search for a keyword with a space in it, such as *John Jack*, it sees them as individual words. It would return photos tagged with *John Jack*, *Jack John* or with both *John* and *Jack*. If you regularly use the Text Filters or Smart Collections to search for keywords, you could use an underscore instead of a space, such as *John_Jack*. Alternatively, using Metadata Filters allows you to select the complete keyword from a list, so spaces aren't an issue.

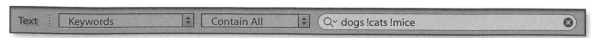

Figure 10.15 Special characters can be used to create complex Text Filters.

Quotation marks don't work, so you can't search for "John Jack" to exclude photos of another man called "Jack John."

How do I search for a specific filename?

Let's try an example: you know the filename (e.g. IMG_2938.dng) but you don't know where the photo's stored.

1. Select *All Photographs* in the Catalog panel to search the whole catalog.

2. Select *Any Searchable Field* or *Filename* options in the pop-up menu.

3. Leave the next pop-up on *Contains All* to include partial matches, or *Contains Words* to match the entire filename.

4. Type the filename into the text field and press Enter to leave the field. If you've selected *Contains All*, you can just enter part of the filename (e.g. 2938) but if you've selected *Contains Words*, you'll need the entire filename including the extension (e.g. IMG_2938. dng). **(Figure 10.16)**

If you want to search for a series of filenames, enter them all into the search field with spaces or commas between the filenames, and change *Contains All* to *Contains.*

Can I combine Text filters, Attribute filters, and Metadata filters?

As with most tasks in Lightroom, there are multiple ways of combining features, and the filters are no exception. For example, if you want to find all the photos with the word 'dogs' somewhere in the metadata, with a red color label, shot in 2014, on a Canon 600D, with 18-200mm lens, and rated above 3 stars, you could combine all 3 filter types. **(Figure 10.17)**

To open multiple filter bars, simply enter your criteria in one filter before clicking on the next filter name. If you want to open all of the empty filters in one go, hold the Shift key while clicking on the filter names.

The criteria filters down in order, from top to bottom and from left to right, and it can be narrowed down further by first selecting a specific folder or collection view.

Figure 10.16 Text Filters allow you to choose which metadata fields to search.

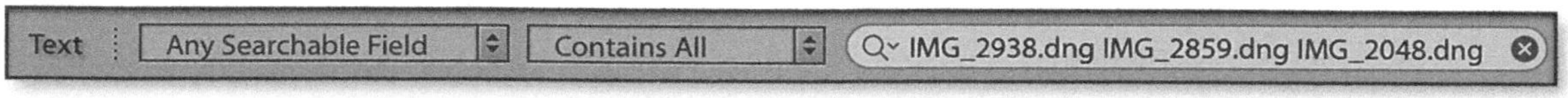

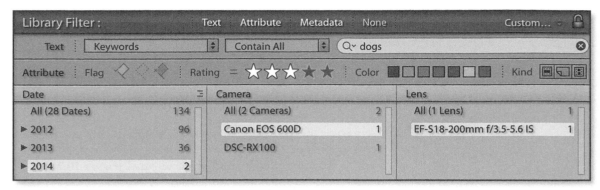

More complex filtering is available via smart collections, which we'll cover in the next section, starting on page 190.

▲ **Figure 10.17** Combining multiple filters allows you to drill down to specific photos.

How do I lock filters, so they don't disappear when I switch to another folder?

When you switch to another folder or collection, any filters are automatically disabled.

In most cases, that's useful behavior, but there may be occasions when you want your filter to remain enabled, for example, browsing all of the 5 star photos across different folders.

To the right of the Filter bar is a small **Filter Lock** icon. **(Figure 10.18)** By default, it's unlocked but if you click to lock it, the current filter remains enabled as you browse different folders or collections.

If the Filter Lock remains unlocked, you can enable the previous filter by pressing Ctrl-L (Windows) / Cmd-L (Mac), or using the switch at the end of the Filmstrip Filters.

This only turns back on the last filter that you used, not the last filter used on that specific folder. If you prefer to remember the filter settings used on each individual folder/collection, rather than a single global filter, go to *File menu > Library Filters* and select *Lock Filters*, and then return to that same menu and select **Remember Each Source's Filters Separately**.

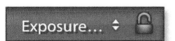

▲ **Figure 10.18** The Filter Lock keeps the filter enabled when you switch folders. The pop-up contains Filter Presets.

Can I save the filters I use regularly as presets?

The pop-up on the right of the Filter bar holds filter presets with different combinations of criteria. The same pop-up appears in the Quick Filters on the Filmstrip, which makes your presets accessible from any module.

There are a few presets built in, but you can also save your own

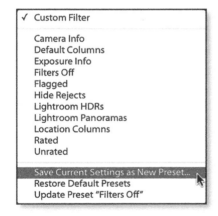

▲ **Figure 10.19** Select your filter criteria and then select *Save Current Settings as New Preset* to save them for quick access in future.

frequently used filters for easy access. Select your filter options and then select *Save Current Settings as New Preset* from the preset pop-up. **(Figure 10.19)**

USING SMART COLLECTIONS

As well as filter presets, you can use Smart Collections to save filter criteria. They're like saved searches, smart folders or rules in other programs, and they live in the Collections panel. **(Figure 10.20)**

Photos automatically appear in the Smart Collection when they meet the criteria you choose, and they disappear again when they stop meeting that criteria. For example, you can create a Smart Collection to show your 3+ star photos, so you can quickly view your best work without having to go to *All Photographs* and set up a filter. Smart Collections automatically search your entire catalog unless you specify a folder or collection as part of the criteria.

Smart Collections also allow you to do more extensive filtering than the Filter bar, as some criteria is only available for Smart Collections.

Let's try a simple example:

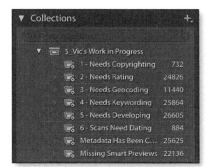

Figure 10.20 Smart Collections are stored in the Collections panel.

1. Press the + button on the Collections panel and select **Create Smart Collection**.

2. Enter a name for your Smart Collection at the top of the dialog.

3. Enter one or more rows, selecting the metadata type in the pop-up and the criteria to the right. The + button at the end of the row creates an additional row. Our earlier example of photos with the word 'dog' somewhere in the metadata, with a red color label, shot in 2014, on a Canon 600D, with 18-200mm lens, and rated above 3 stars, is shown in **Figure 10.21**.

4. Press *Create* to finalize your smart collection. Your new Smart Collection appears in the Collections panel and you can click to view it again at any time, or double-click to edit the criteria.

CONTINUES ON PAGE 193

Smart Collections are far more powerful than they look at first glance though, so let's learn some power-user tricks...

How do I create complex smart collections?

There are additional conditions you can apply to your smart collections to make them even smarter.

Above the rows of search criteria, you can choose whether to include photos that **Match All** of the criteria (AND query), **Any** of the criteria (OR query) or **None** of the criteria (NOT query).

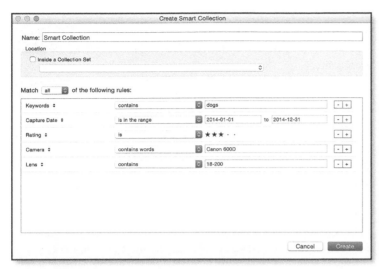

Figure 10.21 Smart Collections are like Saved Searches, automatically updating as photos meet, or stop meeting, the criteria you choose.

If you hold down Alt (Windows) / Opt (Mac) while clicking on the + button at the end of a row, you can fine tune your criteria further with conditional rules, which show as indented rows. Each of those conditional rules has its own *All/Any/None* pop-up, so the combinations are endless.

Smart collections, particularly with conditional rules, are ideal for workflow collections. For example, I have an 'Unfinished' smart collection **(Figure 10.22)**, in case I don't get to finish adding metadata when selecting my favorite photos. It contains any photos that are either rated, labelled or flagged, but are either missing keywords or are missing my copyright information.

How do I find empty metadata fields which don't have an *is empty* option?

There are many occasions where you want to search for missing metadata—for example, 'Title is empty'—but many of the smart collection fields are missing *Is Empty*. You can work around that, however, by using *doesn't contain a e i o u*, with spaces between each letter, as most words include one of those letters. If there's a chance you may have used words that wouldn't include those letters, or

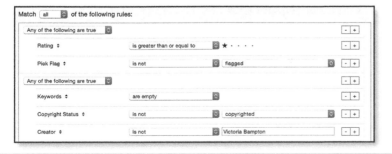

STANDARD VS. SMART COLLECTIONS

Standard collections, which we discussed in the Selecting & Grouping your Photos chapter (page 107), require you to manually add or remove photos from the collection or select filter criteria. Smart collections update themselves without any user-intervention.

Figure 10.22 Criteria can be nested to create complex searches.

VIRTUAL COPIES

Virtual Copies are an unexpected omission in the smart collection criteria, but you can work around the missing option by selecting *File Name / Type > Copy Name* and setting it to *isn't empty*.

you're using a field that may have had a code such as y-1, you can take it one stage further and type *a b c d e f g h i j k l m n o p q r s t u v w x y z 0 1 2 3 4 5 6 7 8 9* with spaces between, to catch every almost eventuality.

How do I duplicate a smart collection?

If you're creating a set of smart collections with similar criteria, for example, 5 star photos taken in 2012 and tagged with names of family members, you may want to set up the first person's smart collection, duplicate it and edit the duplicates. To do so, hold down the Alt key (Windows) / Opt key (Mac) and drag the smart collection to a new location in the Collections panel. You can either drag onto a collection set, in which case a + icon appears, or you can drag between existing root-level collections, so that a line appears.

How do I transfer smart collection criteria between catalogs?

Smart collections, like other collections, are stored within the catalog, so if you want to use them in other catalogs, you need to create them in each catalog. If they use complicated criteria, that could take a while. Instead, right-click on the smart collection and select *Export Smart Collection Settings* to export them to individual template files.

If you have many smart collections, even importing and exporting them individually can take a long time. The quickest solution is to select a single photo, go to *File menu > Export as Catalog* to create a catalog of the single photo, switch to the target catalog, go to *File menu > Import from Another Catalog* to pull that tiny catalog into your open catalog. All of your smart collections are automatically imported at the same time, and then you can remove the temporary photo. We'll go into importing and exporting catalogs in more detail in the Multi-computer chapter starting on page 481.

WORKFLOW SMART COLLECTIONS

As an excellent example of the workflow benefits of Smart Collections, download John Beardworth's complete set of workflow smart collections from http://www.Lrq.me/beardsworth-workflowsc

FILTER & SMART COLLECTION SHORTCUTS

Enable/Disable Filters	Ctrl L / Cmd L
Show Filter Bar	\
Select Text Filter	Ctrl F/ Cmd F
Add nested smart collection line	Alt / Opt click on + button

DEVELOP BASIC EDITING

One of the first things most photographers want to do is edit their photos, and Lightroom excels in this area. Most of your image adjustments will be performed using the Basic panel on the right side of the Develop module. Just because there are a lot of sliders in the Develop module doesn't mean you have to adjust every single one!

First, we'll consider basic tutorials to help you get started, then we'll investigate the Basic panel **(Figure 11.1)** in more detail. In the following chapters, we'll explore selective or local edits, more advanced adjustments and finally Develop module tools that make your life easier.

Introduction to Editing

Let's start with the basic workflow, and then we'll work on some examples before going into detail.

1. It sounds obvious, but look at the photo carefully first and decide what you want to change. Is it too dark? Too light? Perhaps it's

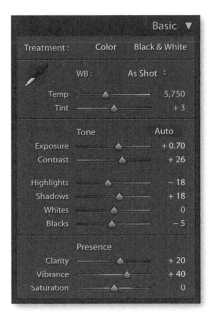

▲ **Figure 11.1** You'll make most of your image adjustments using the Basic panel in the Develop module.

> ### MONITOR CALIBRATION
>
> Calibrating your monitor with a hardware calibration tool such as Spyder, Eye One Pro or Colormunki is essential. If your monitor's not calibrated, you have no way of knowing whether your photo will look right on other people's screens, or whether it will print correctly.

▶ **Figure 11.2** Start by analyzing the photo. This one's too dark and too blue. We want to bring out the blue sky, the detail in the bushes and the colors of the flowers.

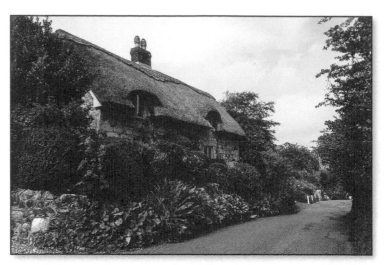

DEVELOP SHORTCUTS

Go to Develop	D
Toggle B&W	V

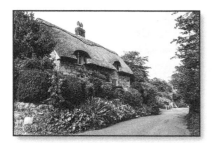

▲ **Figure 11.3** Fix the biggest problem first, so you can identify other issues. In this case, we've roughly fixed the exposure first but the photo is still too blue and we've lost the fluffy clouds.

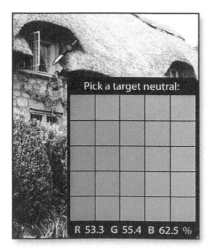

▲ **Figure 11.4** Select the White Balance Eyedropper from the Basic panel and click on something that should be neutral to correct the color cast.

a little too yellow from indoor lighting? Has it lost detail in the highlights? Is it a bit flat and lacking contrast? Is there lens distortion? Is there noise that needs attention? Was your sensor dusty? Does the blue of the sky need enhancing slightly? Would it look better cropped? Would it be a stronger photo in black & white?

If you jump straight in without analyzing the photo, you can spend a lot of time making adjustments and going in circles.

2. Roughly fix the biggest problem first. In most cases, this is the exposure or the white balance (color) of the photo. This makes it easier to see what else needs to be done. **(Figure 11.2)**

If the photo's very under or over exposed (too dark or too light), adjust the *Exposure* slider to get the overall exposure in the right ballpark, but don't worry about fine tuning yet. **(Figure 11.3)**

(Optional) You could try pressing the **Auto** button in the Basic panel. Sometimes it does a great job and other times it's wildly wrong. If you don't like the result, press Ctrl-Z (Windows) / Cmd-Z (Mac) to undo, or use it as a starting point for further adjustments.

3. If the photo's the wrong color, adjust the **White Balance** sliders. This compensates for the color of the light in which the photo was taken. For example, a photo taken indoors without flash may be too yellow.

The quickest way to set the white balance is to select the White Balance Selector tool (it looks like an eyedropper) and click on something that should be light gray. **(Figure 11.4)**

You can then go back and fine tune the white balance by adjusting the **Temperature** and **Tint** sliders. Move the *Temperature* slide left to make the photo cooler or to the right to make it warmer. If the photo's too pink or green, adjust the *Tint* slider too.

4. Adjust the **Exposure** slider to set the overall brightness of the photo, moving to the right to brighten the photo or to the left to darken it. The easiest way to decide the correct exposure is to look at the little Navigator preview in the top left corner while you move the slider, so you're not distracted by the content of the photo. **(Figure 11.5)**

5. The **Contrast** slider is next. Does the photo look a little flat and muddy? Try increasing the contrast by moving the slider to the right.

6. The **Highlights** and **Shadows** sliders affect the light and dark areas of the photos. If the light areas are lacking detail, try moving the *Highlights* slider to the left to darken them slightly. If the dark areas and shadows are lacking detail, try moving the *Shadows* slider to the right to lighten them slightly. **(Figure 11.6)**

7. The **Whites** and **Blacks** sliders affect the clipping of the lightest and darkest tones. Hold down the Shift key and double-click on the words *Whites* and *Blacks*. This auto setting often does a good job with these sliders.

8. **Clarity** adds 'punch' to the photos. Architecture and landscapes can benefit from higher values, but avoid using it on portraits, as it accentuates lines and wrinkles.

9. If the colors in your photo are a little dull, try increasing the **Vibrance** slider. It adjusts how saturated or colorful your photo appear, and it's more intelligent than the **Saturation** slider. **(Figure 11.7)**

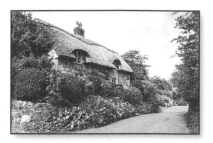

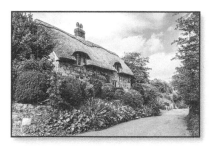

▲ **Figure 11.5** Once you've fixed the white balance, you can fine tune the exposure and contrast.

▲ **Figure 11.6** Use the *Highlights* slider to pull back the fluffy clouds and the *Shadows* slider to bring detail in the bushes.

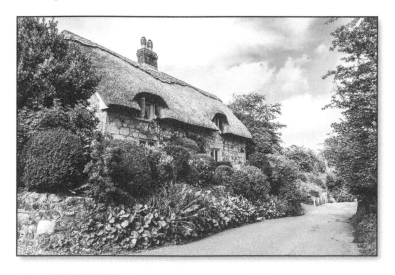

◄ ▲ **Figure 11.7** The finished result is a matter of personal taste. You can adjust it to the way you like it. These are the settings I used.

NON-DESTRUCTIVE EDITING

You can move the sliders as many times as you like. It doesn't degrade the image quality because the adjustments are saved as text instructions and only applied to the on-screen preview until you export the finished photo.

10. If you want to try the photo in B&W, select *B&W* at the top of the Basic panel or press the V key.

You might also want to crop/straighten the photo, remove red eye and sensor dust spots or apply adjustments to specific areas of the photo—we'll come back to these adjustments in the Selective Editing chapter starting on page 227. You may then want to apply sharpening, noise reduction and lens corrections to your photo—we'll come back to these adjustments in the Advanced Editing chapter starting on page 257. And finally, you can also copy your settings to other photos and apply special effect presets to your photos—we'll come back to these tools in the Develop Tools starting on page 297.

Before we go into more detail, let's try another example... **(Figure 11.8)**

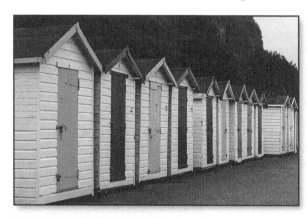

Figure **11.8** The picture's too dark, so we'll increase the exposure by 2/3 stop.

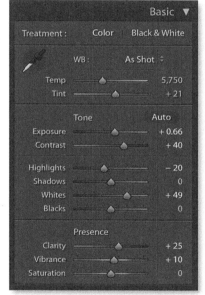

It's still too flat, so we increase the contrast.

The overall brightness looks better but the whites are dull. Shift double-click on the *Whites* slider and then pull back the highlight detail.

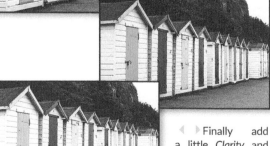

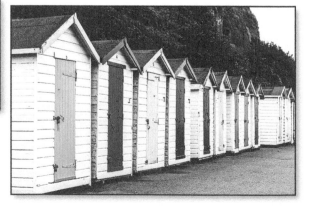

Finally add a little *Clarity* and *Vibrance* to make the colors pop.

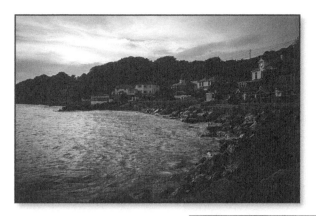

Figure 11.9 The coastline's too dark, but if we just increase *Exposure*, we'd blow out the sky. Instead, we're going to decrease the *Highlights* and increase the *Shadows* to pull back the details.

▸ The resulting picture holds both the highlight and shadow detail, but it's lost the midtone contrast, so we'll increase the *Contrast* slider.

TRY IT WITH ME

If you've registered your paperback book or bought it direct from my website, you can download these photos from the Members Area and follow along using your own copy of Lightroom.

◀ The contrast is now much better, but it doesn't reflect the late evening warmth, so we'll adjust the *White Balance*.

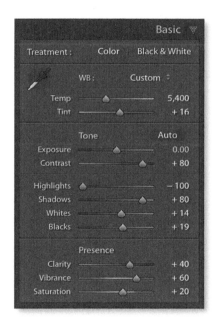

Basic ▾		
Treatment :	Color	Black & White
WB :	Custom ◆	
Temp		5,400
Tint		+ 16
Tone		Auto
Exposure		0.00
Contrast		+ 80
Highlights		− 100
Shadows		+ 80
Whites		+ 14
Blacks		+ 19
Presence		
Clarity		+ 40
Vibrance		+ 60
Saturation		+ 20

▸ Finally, we'll increase the *Vibrance, Saturation* and punch up the *Clarity*. For a final tweak, hold Shift double click on the *Whites* and *Blacks* sliders.

◀ The resulting photo more accurately reflects the warm low light just before the sun disappeared.

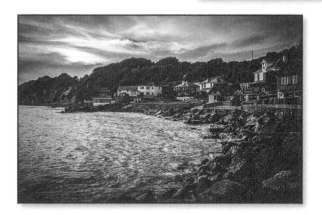

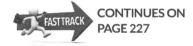
FASTTRACK CONTINUES ON PAGE 227

Workflow—Editing Your Photos

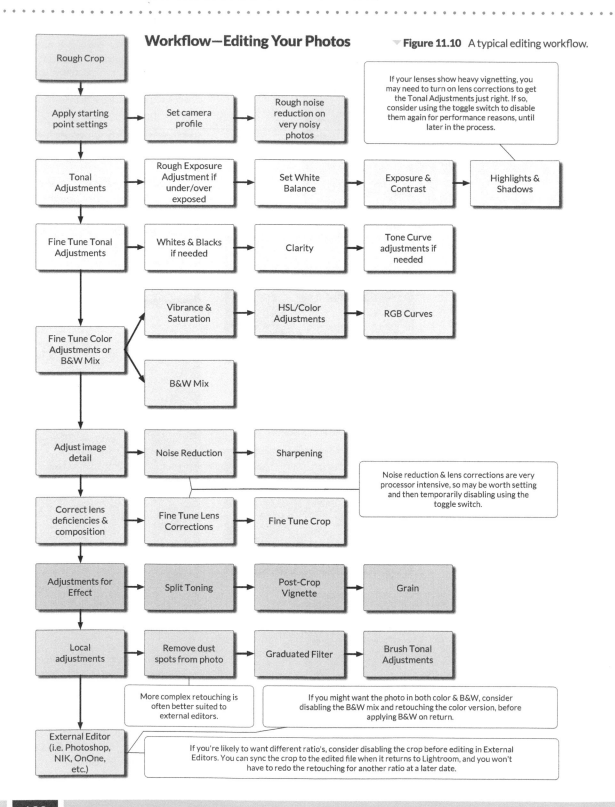

▼ **Figure 11.10** A typical editing workflow.

SHOOTING RAW, SRAW OR JPEG

Let's start right at the beginning of your workflow. Some of the camera settings at the time of capture can affect your options when you later come to edit the photos. These include the file format, picture style, crop ratio and high dynamic range camera settings. Most other camera settings are ignored by raw editors such as Lightroom.

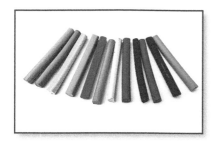

Should I shoot raw or JPEG?

The most important camera setting is the file format. Shooting in your camera's raw file format offers a lot more flexibility than JPEG, especially if your exposure or white balance aren't perfect, or if you're shooting at high ISO or in a high contrast situation.

Lightroom's Develop tools are primarily designed for raw image processing, giving you the greatest latitude, but Lightroom also works with rendered files (JPEG, TIFF, PSD, PNG), giving you an easy way to edit batches of photos. So if you can use Lightroom with JPEGs, which take up less hard drive space, why would you want to consider shooting raw? Well, think of it this way... did you ever play with colored modeling clay when you were a child? **(Figure 11.11)**

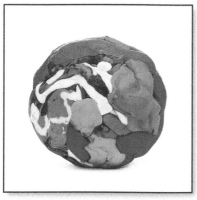

Figure 11.11 When using modeling clay, you get a better result starting from the raw material than trying to reuse an existing model. In the same way, you'll have more flexibility when working with raw files than you will with ready-made JPEGs.

Imagine you have a ready-made model made of a mixture of different colors, and you also have separate pots of the different colors that have never been used. You can push the ready-made model around a bit and make something different, but the colors smudge into each other and it's never quite as good as it would have been if you'd used the individual colors and started from scratch.

A JPEG is like that ready-made model: it's already been made into a photo by the camera before you start editing it. You can change its appearance, but if you try to change it too much, it's going to end up a distorted mess. Your raw file is like having the separate pots of clay—you're starting off with the raw material, and you choose what to make with it.

When you come to edit JPEG photos in the Develop module, you'll notice that some of Lightroom's controls are more limited when working with rendered files (JPEG, TIFF, PSD, PNG). They include:

- **White Balance**—White Balance sliders change from Kelvin values to fixed values, as you're adjusting from a fixed color rather than adjusting white balance. Incorrect white balance is much harder to fix on rendered files.

- **Exposure Latitude**—If photos are under or over exposed or very high contrast, there's a lot more information to work with in a

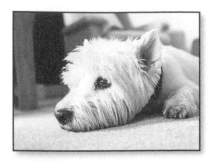

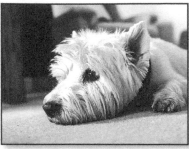

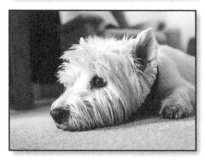

⌃ **Figure 11.12** If your file is overexposed or has the wrong white balance (top), the detail is much more recoverable from a raw (bottom) file than a JPEG (center). The highlight detail on William's nose is missing on the JPEG and it's very difficult to adjust the white balance.

raw file. JPEGs start to fall apart a lot more quickly than raw files. **(Figure 11.12)**

• **Camera Profiles**—Camera profiles are only available for raw files as they emulate the look of the camera's picture styles.

• **Lens Profiles**—Most lens correction profiles are built for raw files as the camera may have already applied additional processing (e.g. vignette correction) to JPEGs.

• **Sharpening and Noise Reduction** - Sharpening and noise reduction are turned off by default as these may have already been applied by the camera. Lightroom's sharpening and noise reduction controls work better on raw files, as they have more information to work with.

Which file format you choose is your decision. If you shoot raw, there are a couple of additional settings to watch out for...

Why doesn't the photo look the same as it did on the camera?

When you shoot in your camera's raw file format, the data isn't fully processed by the camera. The mosaic sensor data is recorded in the raw file, and this sensor data must be converted into an image using raw processing software.

Each raw processor interprets the raw data in a slightly different way. As a result, the photo won't look exactly the same in Lightroom as it did on the back of the camera. There isn't a right or wrong rendering—they're just different.

Adobe could use the camera manufacturer's SDKs (Software Development Kits) to convert the raw data and the rendering would be the same as the camera JPEG, but then they couldn't improve the processing or add additional features to Lightroom, such as local adjustments. It's all or nothing. One of the major benefits of the raw file format is the ability to tweak the photo to your own taste rather than being tied to the manufacturer's rendering.

The initial preview you see in Lightroom is the JPEG preview embedded by the camera, so it has the manufacturer's own processing applied. Lightroom then renders its own preview, ready for you to start editing. This is why it looks like Lightroom is changing the image.

I shot in B&W—why is Lightroom changing the photos back to color?

The same principles apply to the camera's B&W or monotone setting. The sensor data in the raw file remains in color, and Lightroom doesn't know that you were shooting B&W, so it displays the full color photo. You can then use Lightroom to convert the photo to B&W, with full control over the color mix used to convert the file.

If you want to remember which ones you shot in B&W (or any other picture style), enable RAW + JPEG in the camera and import both files into Lightroom. The JPEG will remind you of what you were thinking at the time of shooting, so you can select the matching raw files and convert them all to B&W or a matching picture style in one go.

Can I emulate the camera's own color?

If you prefer the camera's manufacturer's rendering, there are special camera profiles which emulate the camera style settings for the most popular cameras. These are found in the **Profile** pop-up in the Camera Calibration panel. **(Figure 11.13)**

- **Adobe Standard** is Adobe's default profile for your camera, and it's available for all camera raw files. It's designed to be as consistent as possible across a range of different cameras.

- **Camera Standard** emulates the camera's default style.

- **Camera Portrait, Camera Neutral, Camera Landscape** and others with similar names emulate other camera styles offered by your camera.

- **Embedded** is a profile embedded/applied by the camera. This is the only option for rendered files (JPEG, TIFF, PSD, PNG) but can also be found on DNG files, which can contain embedded custom profiles.

Although the profiles have generic names in the pop-up, they intelligently select the correct profile for your camera model behind the scenes. For example, the *Adobe Standard* profile applied to a Canon EOS 5D Mark III is not the same profile as the one applied to a Nikon D810. They use these standard names so that you can save them in presets to apply to multiple different camera models.

If you're going to use a non-default profile, select it before making your Basic panel adjustments, as the profiles significantly change the appearance of the photos. Lightroom doesn't automatically select the correct profile based on your camera settings, and it doesn't know

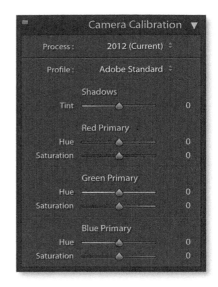

▲ **Figure 11.13** The *Profile* pop-up is found in the Camera Calibration panel.

DNG PROFILE EDITOR

In addition to the included camera profiles, you can build your own profiles using the free DNG Profile Editor. This is particularly useful for extreme white balances, infrared photography and tweaking existing profiles. You can learn more in the Appendix on starting on page A-16.

about any other customizations applied in the camera, such as added contrast or sharpening.

If you use a camera emulation profile on most photos, for example, *Camera Standard*, you can set it as the default setting so it's automatically selected for new imports. We'll discuss custom defaults in the Develop Tools chapter starting on page 297.

Why are my photos so dark?

Certain camera settings can affect the exposure of your raw file directly or indirectly. Most of the settings you can change on your camera only apply to the manufacturer's own JPEG processing. For example, contrast, sharpening, picture styles and color space don't affect the raw data, however these settings do affect the JPEG preview you see on the back of the camera and the resulting histogram and clipping warnings, which can cause you to change your exposure. There are some specific ones to look out for...

Canon's Highlight Tone Priority automatically underexposes the raw data by one stop to ensure you retain the highlights, leaves a tag in the file noting that this setting was applied, and applies its own special processing to the JPEG preview that you see on the back of the camera. Lightroom also understands this tag and increases the exposure by one stop behind the scenes to compensate, but if you accidentally underexpose the image with HTP turned on too, you can end up with a very noisy file. When shooting raw for use in Lightroom, there's no advantage to using this setting instead of changing the exposure compensation yourself, so you may wish to turn off HTP and set your exposure to retain the highlights manually.

Canon's Auto Lighting Optimizer and Nikon's Active D-Lighting don't affect the raw data itself, but Lightroom has no idea that you've used these settings, and even if it did, the processing applied by the camera is variable. When ALO or ADL are turned on, that special processing is applied to the JPEG preview that you see on the back of the camera, as well as to the resulting histogram. Seeing this false brighter preview could cause you to unknowingly underexpose the image. You'd then be disappointed to find it's underexposed when you view the unedited photo in Lightroom, so it's a good idea to turn these settings off unless you're shooting JPEG or only using the manufacturer's own software.

Other camera manufacturers have similar settings, so check your camera manual for similar highlight priority and high dynamic range settings. They include Dynamic Range Optimization (Sony), Shadow Adjustment Technology (Olympus) and Intelligent Exposure (Panasonic).

Are there any other camera settings that Lightroom understands?

There are a couple of other settings that Lightroom does understand. The White Balance setting is understood by most raw converters. For example, if you set your camera to *Cloudy* and Lightroom is set to *As Shot*, Lightroom uses the white balance values set by the camera (although it's still an interpretation by the software programmers). The Kelvin numbers may not match as the values are stored differently in a different format behind the scenes.

Lightroom also respects the in-camera crop ratio, for example, if you have your camera set to a 1:1 (square) crop, it's also 1:1 in Lightroom. For cameras produced since the end of 2012, you can access the full sensor data using the pop-up in the Crop Options panel in Develop, but older cameras must use the DNG Recover Edges plug-in to access the extra data.

If I shoot sRAW format, can Lightroom apply all the usual adjustments?

While we're talking about raw files, there's also a hybrid file type to consider. Canon and Nikon's reduced resolution formats work slightly differently to standard raw formats. Full raw files are demosaiced by the raw processor, whereas sRAW/mRAW files are demosaiced by the camera and some of the data is discarded to create a lower resolution file. (The demosaic is the process of turning the raw sensor data into image data.)

You still have access to all the controls that are available for raw files, however there are a few things which are usually part of the demosaic processing which are not applied to your sRAW files. Artifacts may also be present, for example, Lightroom maps out hot pixels (bright pixels that appear on long exposures) on full raw files, but can't do so on sRAW files. On some cameras, for example, the Canon 7D, the highlight recovery potential is reduced when shooting in sRAW. Other settings may also behave differently, for example, the sharpening and noise reduction may need slightly different settings.

If you convert to DNG (except Lossy DNG), you'll notice that Canon's sRAW files get bigger instead of smaller because the way the sRAW data is stored is specific to the manufacturer and not covered by the DNG specification.

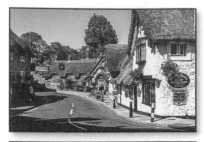

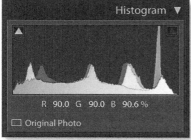

Figure 11.14 A photo with a wide range of tones is spread across the whole histogram.

HISTOGRAM AND RGB VALUES

Before we look at the individual sliders in more detail, it helps to understand how to read a histogram.

A Histogram is a bar graph showing the distribution of tonal values. It runs from the blackest shadow on the left to the brightest highlight on the right, and vertically it shows the number of pixels with that specific tonal value.

There's no such thing as a 'correct' histogram, but an average photo with a wide range of tones usually fills the whole width, so understanding how to read it can help you set the exposure on the camera and in Lightroom. **(Figure 11.14)**

A photo that is primarily light, for example, William in the snow, has most of the data on the right-hand side of the histogram. That's entirely normal, just as a photo taken in fog is unlikely to have any dark black pixels. **(Figure 11.15)**

On the other hand, if you have an average photo, where you'd expect to have tones running from pure white to pure black, and you find the histogram stops half way across, then you know the photo is underexposed and lacking in contrast. **(Figure 11.16)**

You'll find the Lightroom's Histogram panel in the top right corner in the Library and Develop modules. As you hover over the *Exposure*, *Highlights*, *Shadows*, *Whites* or *Blacks* slider in the Basic panel, the approximate range affected by slider is highlighted on the histogram.

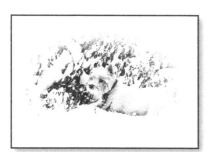

Figure 11.15 A light photo has most of its pixels at the right-hand side of the histogram.

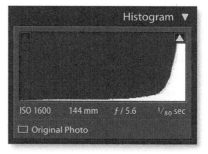

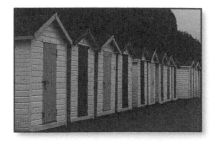

Figure 11.16 An underexposed photo has most of its pixels at the left-hand side of the histogram.

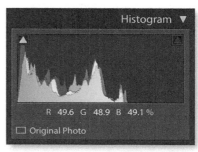

In addition to the information the Histogram provides, you can also use it to adjust the photo. You can click and drag directly on the Histogram to lighten or darken the affected tones, and the highlighted slider moves as you do so. **(Figure 11.17)**

If the last pixel on the left or the right spikes, it means that some of pixels in your photo are solid white or black without any detail. These are called clipped highlights or shadows, or you may hear them referred to as blown highlights and blocked shadows.

If the clipping's in an area of the photo where you're not expecting to see detail, for example, a window in the background of an indoor shot, then it's not necessarily a problem, but if it's on someone's skin, you'll need to recover the detail if possible. **(Figure 11.18)** So how do you know whether the clipped pixels are in an important area of the photo?

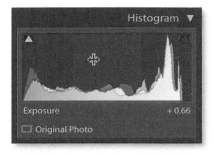

Figure 11.17 You can adjust the Basic tone sliders by dragging on the histogram itself.

How do I see which pixels are clipping? Or, why are there red and blue areas on my photos?

If you need to check where the clipped pixels are on the photo, turn on the clipping warnings by clicking the triangles in the top left and right corners of the histogram or by pressing the J key. Clipped blacks display in blue and clipped whites display in red. The triangles also change color when a channel is clipped, showing which of the channels has lost detail. **(Figure 11.19)**

It can be useful to briefly see the clipping warnings which adjusting a slider, to decide how far you can push the adjustment. Hold down the Alt (Windows) / Opt (Mac) key while dragging the *Exposure, Highlights, Shadows, Whites* or *Blacks* sliders for PV2012 (or *Exposure, Recovery* or *Blacks* sliders in PV2010... we'll come back to process versions at the end of this chapter on page 222).

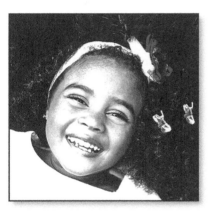

Figure 11.18 Clipped pixels aren't always a problem if they're in an unimportant area of the photo, but skin should never be clipped.

Can I view RGB values using a normal 0-255 scale?

As you hover the cursor over the photo, Lightroom displays the RGB values for the selected pixels underneath the Histogram.

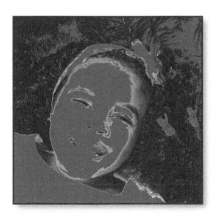

Figure 11.19 Clipping warnings show as red for clipped whites and blue for clipped blacks.

CLIPPING SHORTCUTS	
Show Clipping Warnings	J
Temporarily Show Clipping	Hold Alt/Opt while moving slider

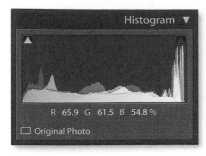

Figure 11.20 Lightroom displays the RGB values of the selected pixel as you float over the photo.

L*A*B*

You can also display L*a*b* values under the Histogram, as an alternative to the normal RGB values. To switch from RGB to L*a*b*, right-click on the Histogram and select *Show Lab Color Values.*

They're primarily used in scientific and reproduction environments, but they can also be useful for correcting skintones. For 'average' skintones, if there is any such thing, keep the a* and b* values close, often with the b* value slightly higher.

CAMERA SETTINGS

Just under the Histogram is basic information about your camera settings, which are visible any time that your mouse isn't hovering over the photo itself. You can also toggle the Info Overlay using the I key.

(Figure 11.20) 0 0 0 % is pure black and 100 100 100 % is pure white. Matching numbers in between are neutral, for example, 50 50 50% is mid gray.

If you've used Photoshop or other photographic software, you might be used to seeing the RGB values displayed using a 0-255 scale, for example, 128 128 128. In Lightroom, the RGB values are shown in percentages (0-100%) because 0-255 is an 8-bit scale and Lightroom works in 16-bit. When you turn on Soft Proofing, the RGB values switch to the 0-255 scale, as you're simulating an 8-bit output color space. We'll come back to soft proofing in the Develop Tools chapter starting on page 314, and bit depth in the External Editors chapter on page 328.

Having learned the basics, you can start editing your photos. As you become more familiar with editing in Lightroom, it helps to understand what's going on behind the scenes, so let's take a closer look at the inner workings.

WHITE BALANCE

In the Introduction to Editing, we said that the White Balance sliders at the top of the Basic panel compensate for the color of the light in which the photo was taken. Our eyes automatically adapt to the changing light, but cameras don't, which can result in a color cast on your photos.

You don't necessarily want to neutralize the white balance on every photo though. If you look outside on a cold winters day, the light is cool and blue, but during a beautiful sunset, it may be warm and orange. If you neutralize these photos, you lose the atmosphere.

How do I fix the white balance?

White balance adjustments are made using the *Temperature* and *Tint* sliders, but there are a few ways of deciding on the best values. (Figure 11.21)

In the **WB** pop-up, there are a number of presets like those found on your camera, which set the *Temperature* and *Tint* sliders to preset values. They include *As Shot, Daylight, Cloudy, Shade,* and *Tungsten, Fluorescent* and *Flash* settings. These are only available for raw files, as the white balance compensation is applied to the image when it's converted to a rendered file such as a JPEG.

In this pop-up, you'll also find the **Auto** white balance setting, which aims to neutralize the photo, just like the auto white balance setting on your camera.

If you want a little more control, the White Balance Eyedropper (White Balance Selector/White Balance Picker) allows you to click on a neutral point in the photo to automatically neutralize any color cast, and you can tweak the sliders to taste from this starting point. As you float over the photo with the Eyedropper selected, watch the Navigator panel. The preview automatically updates to display a preview of your white balance adjustment. When you click, the pop-up changes to *Custom* and the sliders automatically adjust.

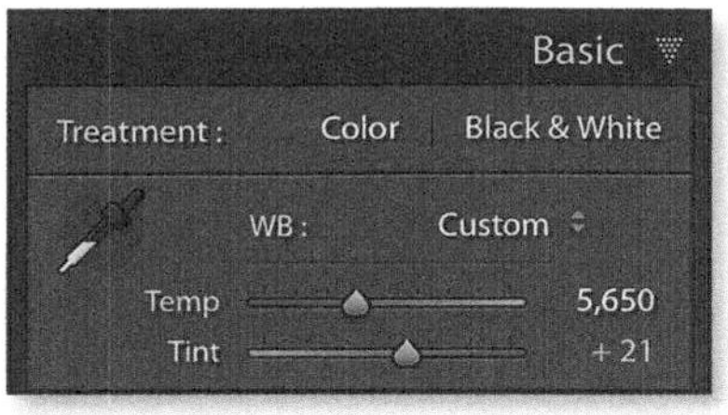

Figure 11.21 The White Balance Eyedropper and sliders are at the top of the Basic panel.

Where should I click with the White Balance Eyedropper?

To set the white balance using the Eyedropper, ideally you want to click on something that should be light neutral. While the white balance is incorrect, it may have a color cast.

You need to choose a light gray for the best accuracy, but don't choose something so bright that any of the channels are clipped. Specular highlights (highlights with no detail) are no good either, however nice and white they look! If any channels are clipped (or maxed out), you'll get a weird result, if it works at all.

Something like the shadows on a man's white shirt usually work well. You need to be careful about the color that you choose. Remember that white objects take on a color cast if they get reflected light from

WHIBAL & GRAY CARDS

If you regularly shoot in difficult lighting, a WhiBal or other calibrated neutral light gray card is an easy way to guarantee correct white balance. You shoot a photo of the card in the lighting conditions and click the Eyedropper on that photo to get an accurate white balance setting, which you can then copy to other photos shot in the same conditions. Note that Kodak 18% Gray Cards are designed for setting exposure, not white balance, and so they're not necessarily neutral.

WHITE BALANCE SHORTCUTS

Select White Balance Tool	W
Auto White Balance	Ctrl Shift U / Cmd Shift U

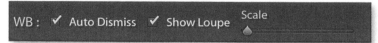

> **Figure 11.22** The White Balance Eyedropper options are on the Toolbar.

another object—so a glossy white hat outdoors under a clear blue sky should look slightly blue, not white. Inside, paintwork that should be white often goes slightly yellow over time, so making that neutral may make the rest of the photo a little too blue.

The White Balance Eyedropper disappears every time I click anything—how do I keep it turned on?

While you have the White Balance Eyedropper active, there's an **Auto Dismiss** checkbox in the Toolbar. **(Figure 11.22)** With this checkbox unchecked, the Eyedropper remains on screen until you intentionally dismiss it by pressing W, clicking the *Done* button in the Toolbar or returning the Eyedropper to its base. This can be useful if you're trying a number of different areas of the photo to find the best click white balance. If you can't see the Toolbar beneath the photo, press T.

Can I change the eyedropper averaging?

When the Eyedropper is selected, the White Balance Loupe appears next to it. It displays an enlarged view of the area you're sampling, so you can make sure you're selecting the best set of pixels without any other colored areas that might influence the white balance calculation.

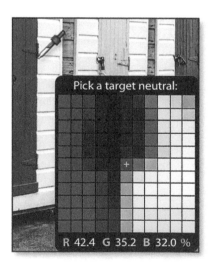

The Eyedropper averages the pixel values you can see in its loupe, so there are two ways you can affect the sampling area. **(Figure 11.23)** When you zoom out, you're sampling a larger area than when you're zoomed in, which is particularly useful for noisy photos. Also, you can change the loupe scale using the **Scale** slider on the Toolbar, to change from a 5x5 pixel area up to a 17x17 pixel area, so it averages over a smaller or larger number of pixels.

If you find the Loupe distracting, you can disable it using the **Show Loupe** checkbox on the Toolbar.

▲ **Figure 11.23** The White Balance Loupe shows a zoomed view of the area under the Eyedropper, so you can check that you're not polluting your selection with pixels that aren't meant to be neutral, like this red door.

How do I adjust the white balance sliders?

Having set the white balance in the right ballpark using the eyedropper or presets, you may then need to tweak it further using the **Temperature** and **Tint** sliders. If the photo's too yellow or warm, move the *Temperature* slider to the left to compensate, and if it's too blue or cold, move the slider to the right. The *Tint* slider adjusts from green on the left to magenta on the right.

For example, to retain the atmosphere in an indoor photo, neutralize it but then add 200-400K on the *Temperature* slider to bring back the warmth you expect to see.

Why don't the Temp and Tint sliders have the proper white balance scale when I'm working on JPEGs?

When working on rendered files, such as JPEGs or TIFFs, you'll notice that the *Temperature* slider no longer shows Kelvin values, but switches to a -100 to 100 scale. Raw files use a Kelvin scale because you're actually shifting the white balance compensation that is being applied to the raw data, whereas on rendered files, Lightroom is just shifting colors from a fixed point. **(Figures 11.24 & 11.25)**

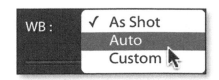

Figure 11.24 Rendered files (JPEG, TIFF, PSD, PNG) only have three white balance presets.

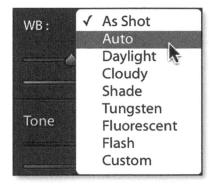

Figure 11.25 Raw files have multiple white balance presets.

TONE & PRESENCE

In the Fast Track, we learned roughly how to use the Basic sliders, but now let's take a closer look at how each slider affects the tones of the photo and how they interact.

As everyone learns differently, we're going to demonstrate the effect of the sliders in four ways: **(Figure 11.26)**

- A raw photo.

- A gray 21 step wedge.

- The histogram showing the effect of the sliders on the 21 step wedge.

  Each spike on the histogram is one of the gray squares on the step wedge.

  As the spikes move to the left, the tones are getting darker. As they move to the right, the tones are getting lighter.

  As the spikes move further apart, there's greater contrast in that range of tones, and as they move closer together, the contrast is reduced.

- A curve based on sRGB measurements from the 21 step wedge.

  If you're comfortable reading curves, it makes it easy to see the amount of contrast introduced to different tones. (If you've never used curves, we'll discuss them in more detail in the Advanced Editing chapter starting on page 257)

Bear in mind that the histogram and curve are only guides showing the effect of each slider. The actual measurements and slider values

LIGHTROOM 3 UPGRADERS

If you're upgrading from Lightroom 3 or earlier, you'll find that the Basic panel sliders are completely different. This change is called PV2012, and we'll come back to the difference in Process Versions at the end of this chapter on page 222.

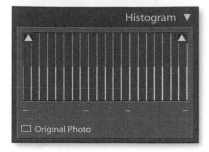

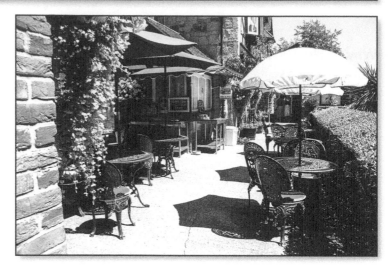

▲ **Figure 11.26** As a baseline for comparison, these are the images with everything set to 0.

vary depending on the content of each photo, as the processing is image-adaptive.

What does the *Exposure* slider do?

The **Exposure** slider sets the overall image brightness, and it uses the same f-stop increments as your camera, so +2.0 of *Exposure* is the equivalent of opening the aperture on your camera by 2 stops. **(Figure 11.27)**

The *Exposure* slider knows where the highlights of your image are, and it rolls off the highlights smoothly in a film-like fashion, to avoid harsh digital zclipping.

It's important to get the *Exposure* setting right before moving on to the other sliders, as the range of other sliders are affected and they won't work as well if your *Exposure* is set incorrectly.

So how do you know where to set the *Exposure* slider? Try these tips:

- **Focus on the midtones**—Pretend it's the only control you have available. If there weren't any other sliders, how bright would you make the photo?

- **Ignore clipping**—Turn off the highlight clipping warnings by clicking the triangles in the corners of the Histogram panel. Ignore any clipped highlights or shadows at this stage (white/black areas with no detail), as you'll pull them back later.

PRINTING PRESS LIMITATIONS

The limitations of printing presses affects the reproduction in printed form, so if you're reading this in paperback book, do check the examples in the complimentary PDF version on a calibrated monitor. Better still, if you'd like to try some of these tests for yourself, you can download these files from http://www.Lrq.me/stepwedge

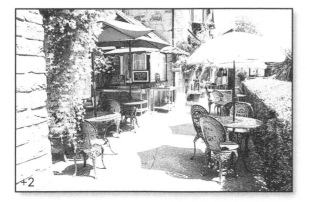

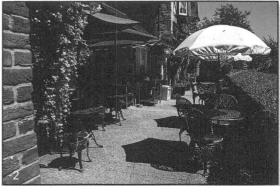

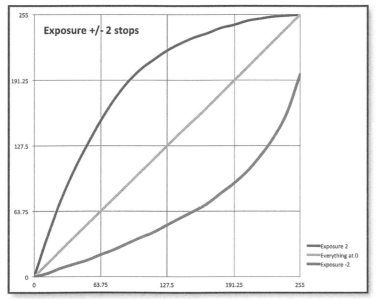

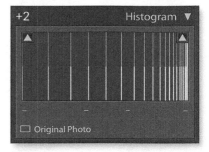

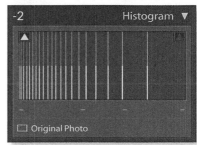

- **Use the Navigator**—Use the preview in the Navigator panel while setting the *Exposure*. It's far easier to judge the overall brightness when you're looking at a small preview, as you won't get distracted by the details.

- **Confuse your brain**—Your eyes adjust to the original camera exposure, making it difficult to judge the correct exposure. It can help to confuse your brain by swinging the Exposure slider to the left and right (darker and lighter) and then settle somewhere in the middle, wherever it looks right.

▲ **Figure 11.27** *Exposure +/- 2 stops.*

The *Exposure* slider brightens or darkens the photo overall. The histogram is moved to the left when the photo is brightened, and to the right when it's darkened. On the stepwedge and curve, the contrast between highlight steps is reduced when the exposure is increased, and the same happens to the shadows when the exposure is decreased.

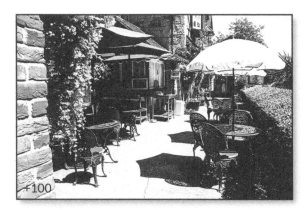

▼**Figure 11.28** *Contrast +/- 100.*

The *Contrast* slider increases or decreases the amount of midtone contrast in the photo. The histogram spikes are moved apart when the contrast is increased, and closer together where the contrast is decreased. As the contrast is increased in the midtones, it's decreased in the highlights and shadows, and vice versa.

What does the *Contrast* slider do?

The ***Contrast*** slider is a standard S-curve which lightens the highlights and darkens the shadows to increase midtone contrast, or vice versa. **(Figure 11.28)**

So how do you decide how much contrast to add to your photo (or remove from your photo)? This's largely a question of personal choice, as some photographers prefer much higher contrast than others. When adjusting the *Contrast* slider, focus on the midtones and don't worry too much about losing detail in the highlight and shadow

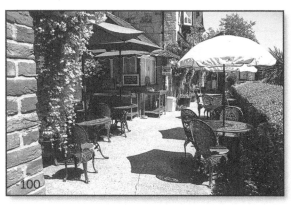

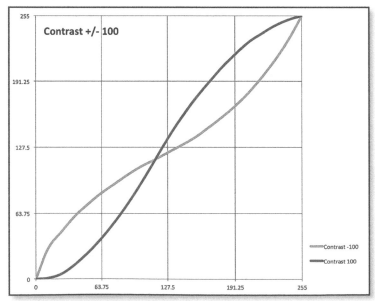

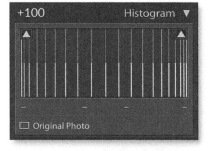

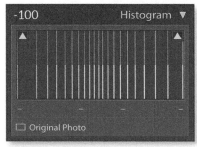

TONE CURVES FOR CONTRAST

Some prefer to use the Tone Curve panel to add contrast to a photo, as it offers greater control over which tones gain and lose contrast. We'll come back to Tone Curves in the Advanced Editing chapter starting on page 257. As a general rule, the image-adaptive controls in the Basic panel are designed to do the 'heavy lifting' or major adjustments, followed by the Tone Curve for fine-tuning (if needed).

tones, because you'll pull back that detail using the *Highlights* and *Shadows* sliders.

What do the *Highlights* and *Shadows* sliders do?

The **Highlights** and **Shadows** sliders obviously affect the light and dark tones in the photo, but they're smarter than basic highlight and shadow adjustments. They build a mask to limit their effect to specific tones in each individual photo.

You can see from the examples that the *Highlights* slider is masked to adjust only the brighter tones in the photos and barely touches the darker tones. It's generally intended to be used as a minus figure, dragged to the left to pull back highlight details.

What does that mean in practice? Having used the *Exposure* slider to set the overall image brightness, you can selectively pull back highlight detail without impacting the shadows or destroying the midtone contrast.

In the case of our sample photo, it means that we can pull back the detail in the white parasol and concrete floor. **(Figure 11.29)** In other photos, *Highlights* would affect fluffy clouds in the sky, detail on a bride's dress, and other highlight areas.

The *Shadows* slider is the opposite of the *Highlights* slider. You can see from the examples, especially the curve, that the *Shadows* slider adjusts only the darker tones in the photos and barely touches the lighter tones. It's generally intended to be used as a plus figure, moved to the right to pull back shadow details.

In the case of our sample photo, it means that we can pull back the detail in the shaded area to the left and in the bushes. **(Figure 11.30)** In other photos, *Shadows* would affect shadowed areas on people's faces, detail in a groom's suit, and other darker areas.

You can move *Highlights* or *Shadows* to around 50 in either direction and still have a fairly natural looking result, whereas beyond 50 starts to get an HDR look.

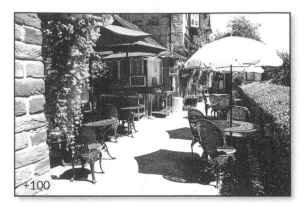

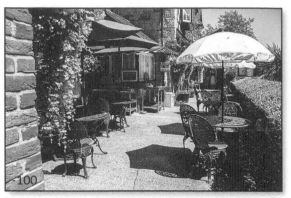

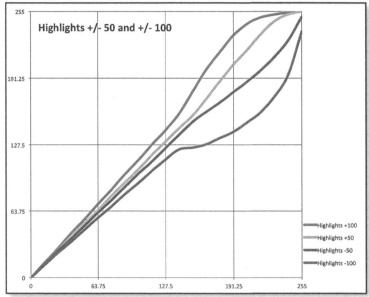

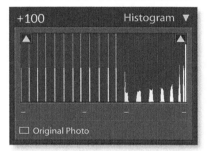

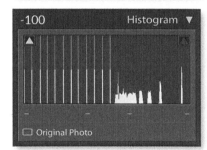

▲ **Figure 11.29** *Highlights +/- 100.*

The *Highlights* slider lightens or darkens the highlight tones. The histogram spikes are merge as they move closer together. The histogram, curve and stepwedge show that the shadow tones are barely affected when adjusting *Highlights*. The slider is usually pulled to the left, bringing back highlight detail such as the ground and umbrella in the photo.

Why don't the *Highlights* or *Shadows* sliders seem to do much?

We said earlier that the *Exposure* slider needs to be about right, as it affects the range of the other sliders. Let's illustrate that using *Highlights*, and setting the *Exposure* 2 stops higher than it should be. **(Figure 11.31)** You can see from the curve that the range of the *Highlights* slider is much more limited than it is when the midtones are set correctly. (This doesn't mean that *Exposure* at 0 is necessarily

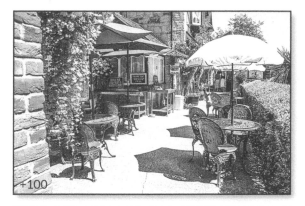

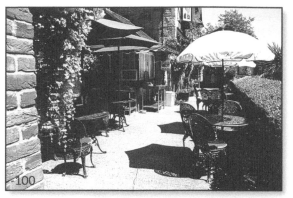

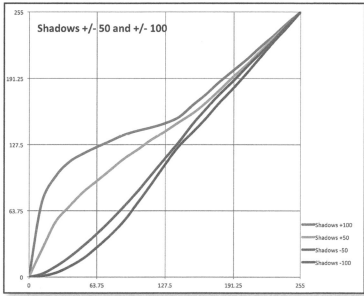

Shadows +/- 50 and +/- 100

Shadows +100
Shadows +50
Shadows -50
Shadows -100

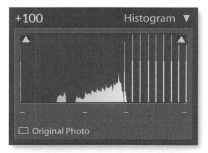

+100   Histogram ▼

☐ Original Photo

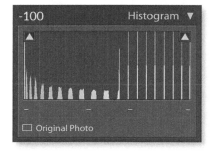

-100   Histogram ▼

☐ Original Photo

+100

-100

the 'correct' value for your photo. If your photo is underexposed, +2 *Exposure* might be just right, and +4 would be too high.)

As a guide, if *Highlights* doesn't seem to be doing much, *Exposure* is probably too high, and if *Shadows* doesn't seem to be doing much, *Exposure* is probably too low.

▲ **Figure 11.30** *Shadows +/- 100.*

The *Shadows* slider lightens or darkens the shadow tones. The histogram spikes are merge as they move closer together. The histogram, curve and stepwedge show that the highlight tones are barely affected when adjusting *Shadows*. The slider is usually pulled to the right, bringing back shadow detail such as the building and bushes in the photo.

▶ **Figure 11.31** If the *Exposure* setting is incorrect, the *Highlights* and *Shadows* sliders won't have as great a range of movement..

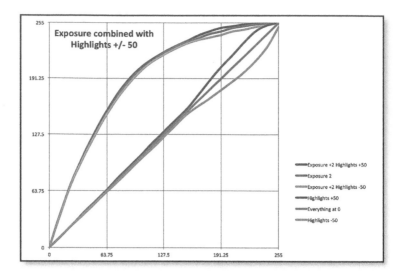

WHITE STUDIO BACKGROUNDS

Although highlight recovery is invoked automatically, you can still blow out intentional white backgrounds by dragging the *Whites* slider to the right. If the photo was correctly exposed, with the whites close to clipping, a small value such as 15-25 is enough to blow the white background without having a noticeable impact on the overall exposure. Studio photographers can apply this as a preset while importing to save time.

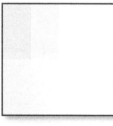

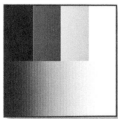

▲ **Figure 11.32** The sliders adapt to the range of the photo, so even a foggy white photo (top) can be stretched to fill the entire tonal range (bottom).

What do the *Whites* and *Blacks* sliders do?

The **Whites** and **Blacks** sliders affect the clipping point and roll off at the extreme ends of the tonal range. They're not intended to make major tonal adjustments, but just for fine-tuning the effect of the earlier adjustments (although, as always, rules are made to be broken!).

Unlike the masked *Highlights* and *Shadows* sliders, they affect the full range of tones. If you've used other image editing software, they're similar to the black and white points in Levels. Brightening the whitest point by moving the *Whites* slider to the right allows you to clip highlights that would otherwise be protected by the *Exposure* slider's gentle roll off, whereas moving to the left brings a little more contrast into the brightest highlights **(Figure 11.33)**, and the opposite obviously applies the *Blacks* slider. For example, the *Blacks* slider is ideal for adding contrast when you've made a large *Shadows* adjustment. **(Figure 11.34)**

You'll notice a slight difference between raw and rendered photos, as the raw photos have additional data available at either end of the tonal range, whereas clipped blacks and whites on rendered photos remain pure black or white.

What are image adaptive sliders?

You may have heard the terms *image adaptive, intelligent, tone-mapped* and *masked* when talking about the PV2012 Basic sliders. We've used some of these terms in this chapter. So what does that actually mean?

- **Smart Highlights**—The *Exposure* slider (PV2012) calculates where

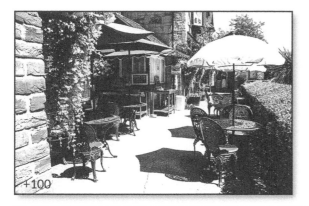
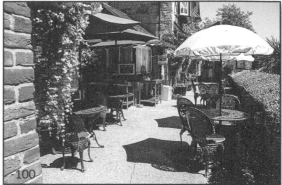

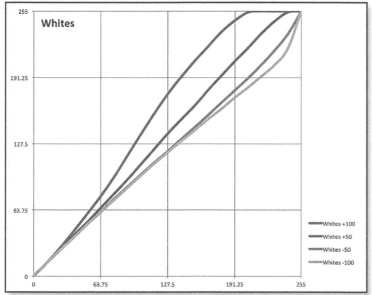

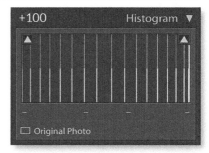

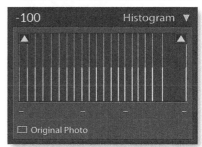

the highlights of your image are, and intelligently protects them. (The *Exposure* slider in Lightroom 3 and earlier (PV2003/2010) clipped overexposed highlights, resulting in a harsh digital look.)

- **Masked Tones**—Other controls, like *Highlights*, *Shadows* and *Clarity* do their calculations using masks computed from the image itself. This limits the range of the adjustments to particular tones in a photo, for example, *Highlights* barely affects the lower 50% of tones.

- **Adapted Range**—*Whites* and *Blacks* are also aware of the content

▲ **Figure 11.33** *Whites +/- 100.*

The *Whites* slider lightens or darkens the lightest tones. This allows you to clip the whites.

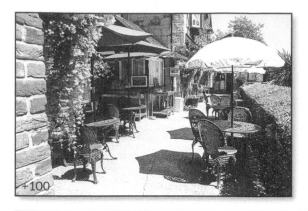

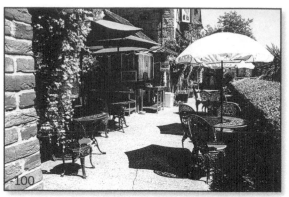

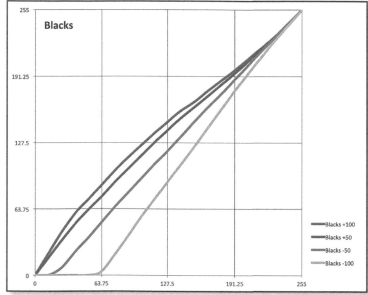

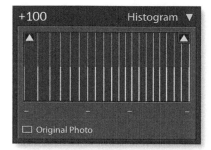

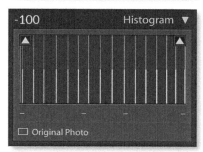

Figure 11.34 *Blacks* +/- 100.

The *Blacks* slider lightens or darkens the darkest tones. This allows you to clip the shadows to bring back contrast.

of the photo, and the range of these sliders adapt accordingly. For example, a foggy scene may only contain data in the very lightest tones of a photo. The *Blacks* slider knows that, mapping −100 to pure black and stretching the range of the tones. This becomes even more useful when working with scans of old faded photos, as it allows you to create a bright white and deep black point in even the lowest contrast photos if you need to do so. **(Figure 11.32)**

This means that the values you use for each photo will vary. +50 on a slider has a different effect on different photos, depending on the image content and the other settings, so don't focus too much on the numerical values—focus on the photo itself.

What does the *Clarity* slider do?

The **Clarity** slider adds local area contrast, concentrating primarily on the midtones, which helps to lift the photo off the page or screen. **(Figure 11.35)**

As a general rule, it's best to use a very low setting for portraits, if you use it at all, as it can accentuate lines and wrinkles. Slightly higher values are brilliant on architecture and landscapes, adding a distinctive crisp feel, and it can also look great on a high contrast B&W photo. Although the slider goes to 100, that's almost always too strong.

Set to a negative amount, it adds a gentle softening effect, which is particularly effective on close-up portraits. It gives a gentle glow to the photo, so it can look good on vintage style or infrared photos too.

Clarity doesn't increase saturation, so if you use high *Clarity* values,

▼ **Figure 11.35** *Clarity* set to positive values (left) works well for architecture but not for faces.

Clarity set to negative values (right) softens faces, but -100 is generally too strong. Try *Clarity* in the adjustment brush for a more natural effect.

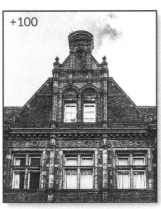
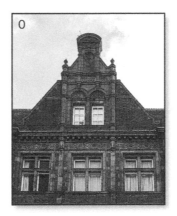
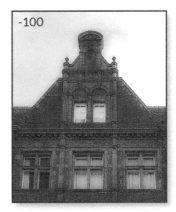
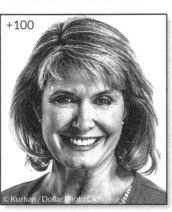
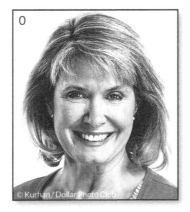
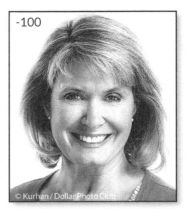

GADGETS!

For speed, I use a Wacom Graphics Pen in one hand to float over the sliders, and a Contour Shuttle Pro 2 dial programmed to up/down keys when I turn the dial, with the buttons programmed to other useful shortcuts.

There are also specialist devices such as RPG Keys, Motibodo, and similar gadgets. There are links to these devices at http://www.Lrq.me/links/lr-keyboards

you may find that the colors start to look a little muted. Adding a little *Vibrance* or *Saturation* can make the effect look more natural.

What's the difference between *Vibrance* and *Saturation*?

The *Vibrance* and *Saturation* sliders make the photo look more or less colorful.

Saturation is quite a blunt instrument which adjusts the saturation of all colors equally. This can result in some colors clipping as they reach full saturation.

Vibrance is far more useful as it adjusts the saturation on a non-linear scale, increasing the saturation of lower-saturated colors more than higher-saturated colors. This especially helps to protect skin tones from becoming over saturated.

SLIDER SHORTCUTS

Auto White Balance	Ctrl Shift U / Cmd Shift U
Auto Tone	Ctrl U / Cmd U
Select next Basic panel slider	. (period/full stop)
Select previous Basic panel slider	, (comma)
Increase slider value	= (or +)
Decrease slider value	-
Reset slider	; (semi-colon)
Move slider value by larger increment	Shift while using = (or +) or -
Move slider value by smaller increment	Opt while using = (or +) or—(Mac only)
Reset Slider	Double-click on slider label
Reset Group of Sliders	Double-click on group name
Reset All Settings	Ctrl Shift R / Cmd Shift R

WORKING WITH SLIDERS

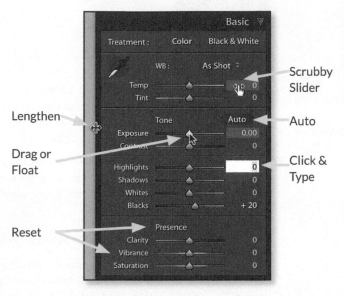

- **Drag**—The obvious thing to do with a slider is to grab the marker and move it, and of course that works, but there are also other options which may suit your workflow better.

- **Lengthen**—If you like dragging sliders, but find it difficult to make fine adjustments, drag the edge of the panel to make the panel wider. It makes the sliders longer and easier to adjust.

- **Float**—If you hover over the slider without clicking, you can use the up and down keys to move the slider. Adding Shift moves in larger increments or Alt (Windows) / Opt (Mac) decreases the increments.

- **Scrubby Sliders**—Scrubby sliders, such as those used in Photoshop, also work in Lightroom. As you float over the numeric value field at the end of the slider, the cursor changes to a hand with a double arrow, and clicking and dragging to the left or right moves the slider.

- **Click & Type**—While we're looking at the numeric value fields, you can click directly in one of these fields and either type the number that you're aiming for, or use the up/down arrow keys to move in smaller increments. If you've activated a field to type directly, don't forget to hit Enter or click elsewhere to complete your adjustment.

- **Shortcuts**—If you click on a slider label, that slider becomes highlighted, and using the + / – keys on the numberpad adjusts that slider. Adding modifier keys changes the increments, so adding Shift again moves in larger increments, and Opt (Mac only) moves in smaller increments. The ; key highlights the Exposure slider, and the , and . keys move up and down through the sliders, selecting each in turn.

- **Reset**—To reset a single slider, you can double-click on the slider label. Within many panels, you'll also find a panel label, such as *Tone* in the screenshot, and double-clicking or Alt-clicking (Windows) / Opt-clicking (Mac) on that label resets that whole panel section.

- **Auto**—Holding down Shift and double-clicking on the slider label sets the slider to its Auto position without adjusting the other sliders. Unlike the main Auto button, the slide's Auto setting is based on the existing slider settings, including the crop.

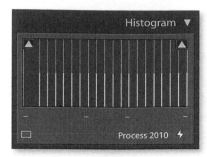

Figure 11.36 A lightning bolt appears under the Histogram if your photo uses an older process version.

PROCESS VERSIONS

Over the last few years, there have been significant changes in Lightroom's processing algorithms to improve the image quality that it can produce.

As Lightroom's edits are stored nondestructively as text instructions, simply removing the old sliders or changing the effect of existing sliders would change the appearance of existing photos, as the interpretation of the stored values they represent would change. All of your photos would need editing again whenever major changes were made to Lightroom.

To avoid this situation of significantly different rendering, Lightroom uses a concept called Process Versions. This tells Lightroom which set of algorithms to use when rendering a photo.

Which process version should I use?

New photos default to PV2012 (unless you apply an old Develop preset), which offers the best image quality. Existing photos can be upgraded to PV2012 when you have time to tweak their settings, or you can leave them with their current PV2003 or PV2010 settings.

If a photo displays the old Basic panel sliders (**Figure 11.37**) and a lightning bolt icon in the Histogram panel (**Figure 11.36**), the photo is still set to PV2003 or PV2010. This means that you're not using the latest technology, but the photos retain their existing appearance. You can choose whether you want to update their processing or edit them again or not.

Why are my new imports set to PV2003 or PV2010 instead of the most recent process version?

If the newly imported files already have settings—for example, as a result of XMP sidecar files with settings from a previous Lightroom or ACR version, or a preset with the process version checked being applied—then the photos are set to that process version instead of the current PV2012.

How do I switch between process versions?

To switch process versions, select your chosen version from the **Process** popup in the Calibration panel or via *Settings menu > Process*. (Figure 11.38)

To update to the latest process version, you can also click on

PV'S OVER THE YEARS

- PV2003 is the original rendering from ACR 1 (new sliders were added over time, but existing ones remained constant).

- PV2010 was added in Lightroom 3. It changed *Sharpening, Noise Reduction* and *Fill Light*.

- PV2012 was added in Lightroom 4. It changed most of the Basic panel sliders, resulting in a completely different rendering, as well as adding RGB point curves and new local adjustment sliders.

Lightroom CC/6 continues to default to PV2012.

the lightning bolt in the Histogram panel. In the resulting dialog **(Figure 11.39)**, choose:

- ***Review Changes via Before/After*** displays the before/after side-by-side so you can decide whether to go ahead. If you decide not to update, use Ctrl-Z (Windows) / Cmd-Z (Mac) or select the previous state in the History panel to revert to the earlier setting.

- ***Update*** just updates the selected photo. If you're going to select this option, it's quicker to hold down the Alt (Windows) / Opt (Mac) while clicking on the lightning bolt, as this skips the dialog.

- ***Update All Filmstrip Photos*** updates all of the photos in the current view. Be careful, as you'll likely have to edit all of these photos again using the new sliders.

Should I update all of my old photos to PV2012? Or, why has updating my photos to PV2012 spoiled their appearance?

Lightroom attempts to preserve the appearance of photos when updating to PV2012, but it's such a significant change in processing that it's only a rough estimate—and sometimes it's a very rough estimate! Any photos that you update from a previous version are likely to need editing again using the new controls.

If you're happy to edit all the photos again, or you haven't edited them yet, you can update multiple photos in one go by selecting them in Grid view and then go to *Photo menu > Develop Settings > Update to Current Process (2012)*. If you're unsure, update them one at a time or leave them set to their existing Process Version. You can come back and update them later.

How do I find photos set to older process versions?

To find photos that are still set to PV2003 or PV2010, go to *Library menu > Find Previous Process Photos*, and Lightroom creates a

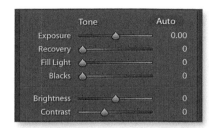

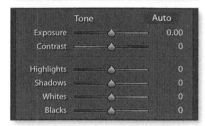

▲ **Figure 11.37** The sliders vary depending on whether you've selected PV2003/2010 (top) or PV2012 (bottom).

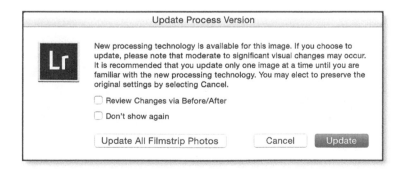

▲ **Figure 11.38** The Camera Calibration panel holds the *Process* and *Profile* pop-ups. The other sliders are legacy sliders.

◀ **Figure 11.39** When you click on the lightning bolt, Lightroom asks whether you'd like to update just that photo or multiple photos.

CALIBRATION SLIDERS

The rest of the sliders (**Shadows, Red Primary, Green Primary** and **Blue Primary**) in the Camera Calibration panel are primarily legacy sliders. They were used for adjusting camera calibration before the detailed camera profiles were invented, so they're rarely needed now. That said, they can be useful for creative effects.

VIDEO EDITING SOFTWARE

Lightroom doesn't make it easy to open your videos into editing software such as Adobe Premiere, but you can right-click and choose *Show in Explorer* (Windows) / *Show in Finder* (Mac) and then open into the editor of your choice.

Alternatively, John Beardsworth's Open Directly plug-in allows you to open the original video into the software of your choice, including video editing software. http://www.Lrq.me/beardsworth-opendirectly

temporary collection in the Catalog panel. It won't update live, but you can force the collection to update at any time by selecting that menu command again, or you can clear it by right-clicking on the collection.

EDITING VIDEOS

Many digital cameras now produce, not only still photographs, but also video. We've already used the Loupe view to play your videos, so before we move on to more advanced stills editing, let's take a quick look at Lightroom's basic video editing tools.

How do I trim videos?

In the Loupe view, click on the cog button on the video overlay to show the individual video frames. If the overlay isn't wide enough to accurately scrub through the video, you can drag both ends to enlarge it.

The trim handles are shown at the left and right ends of the overlay, and dragging these toward the center trims the ends from the video. The easiest way to select the best trim position is to drag the position marker or pause the video in the right spot. When you drag the trim handles, they snap to the selected frame.

The trimmed sections of video aren't removed from the original file, but they're hidden when playing the video in Lightroom, and are excluded when you export the video to a new file.

You can't clip sections out of the middle of the video, as it only allows you to trim the ends, however you could create virtual copies of your video, allowing you to trim a different section from each.

Can I join videos together?

There isn't officially a way of merging video clips together into a single video within Lightroom, but there is a workaround... Add the videos to the Slideshow module, remove the extraneous overlays and background and then go to *Slideshow menu > Export Video Slideshow* to create a merged video.

What do *Capture Frame* and *Set Poster Frame* do?

Under the rectangular thumbnail button on the video overlay (**Figure 11.40**) are two additional options.

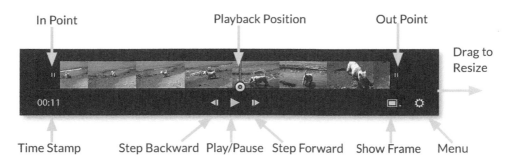

In Point   Playback Position   Out Point

Drag to Resize

00:11

Time Stamp   Step Backward   Play/Pause   Step Forward   Show Frame   Menu

- **Capture Frame** extracts the current frame as a JPEG and automatically adds it to the folder. If you're viewing a folder or standard collection, the captured frame should appear next to the video, but it may be hidden if you're working in *Previous Import, Quick Collection* or you a filter or smart collection set to only show videos.

- **Set Poster Frame** allows you to select which frame is shown as the video thumbnail in the Grid view, and as the preview in other modules.

If you're trying to select a specific frame for the Capture Frame or Poster Frame, it can be difficult to drag the position marker to exactly the right spot. If you drag it to approximately the right spot, you can use the arrow buttons either side of the play button to step through one frame at a time.

Can I view video metadata such as *Frame Rate*?

If you select the *Video* preset at the top of the Metadata panel, you'll be able to see additional video metadata, such as the *Frame Rate, Dimensions* and *Audio Sample Rate.* **(Figure 11.41)**

You will note that there's limited metadata included in most video files. Details that we're used to seeing in digital image EXIF data, such as the camera and lens used, are not usually present. If this data is important to you, consider taking a photo just before recording, so that you have a permanent record.

You can add or edit the capture time for videos, just as you can for photos, which can help if the capture time wasn't initially recorded with the video.

Can I edit the color and exposure of my videos in the Develop module?

Video isn't supported in the Develop module, however you can make Develop changes using the Quick Develop panel or Develop presets.

Figure 11.40 Video playback and editing options

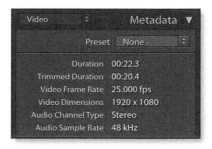

Video	Metadata	▼

Preset   None

Duration	00:22.3
Trimmed Duration	00:20.4
Video Frame Rate	25.000 fps
Video Dimensions	1920 x 1080
Audio Channel Type	Stereo
Audio Sample Rate	48 kHz

Figure 11.41 The Video preset in the Metadata panel shows additional information such as Frame Rate.

VIDEO CACHE

If you regularly work with video, you can enlarge the **Video Cache Settings** in the *Preferences dialog > File Handling tab,* so that more of your video footage is cached for faster previews.

▶ **Figure 11.42** Only some Develop settings can be synchronized when working with videos. The other checkboxes are disabled.

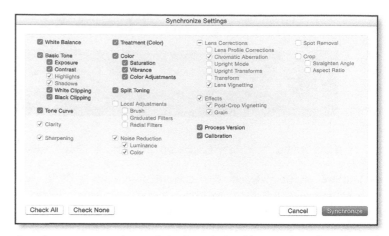

Any changes you make apply to the whole video, not just the selected frame.

The Quick Develop panel in the Library module gives you quick access to basic Develop controls—*Treatment (Color or B&W), White Balance, Auto Tone, Exposure, Contrast, White Clipping, Black Clipping, Vibrance*, and also *Saturation* when holding down the Alt (Windows) / Opt (Mac) key.

Additional adjustments can be made to Tone Curve, Split Toning, Process Version & Camera Calibration by including them in a Develop preset. This enables you to make your videos sepia or apply other effects, in addition to basic exposure and white balance corrections.

The easiest way to make the adjustments is to use *Capture Frame* to create a JPEG from the video. You can edit this JPEG in the Develop module and then save it as a preset or sync the changes to the video. It allows you to preview your adjustments before applying them to the whole video, rather than using trial and error. When syncing the settings, you'll note that only settings that can be applied to videos are available in the Sync dialog. **(Figure 11.42)** (We'll come back to creating presets and synchronizing settings in the Develop Tools chapter starting on page 297.)

VIDEO SHORTCUTS	
Set In Point	Shift I
Set Out Point	Shift O
Toggle Play/Pause	Space

DEVELOP SELECTIVE EDITING

Once you've made basic tonal adjustments to your photos, you can make more selective adjustments. These include cropping the photo, removing dust spots, fixing red eye and applying tonal adjustments to specific areas of the photo using gradients and brush masks. These tools are found in the Tool Strip directly beneath the Histogram panel. We'll investigate each in turn. **(Figure 12.1)**

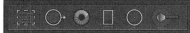

▲ **Figure 12.1** The Tool Strip.

CROPPING & STRAIGHTENING

In an ideal world, you would have the time to make sure a photo was perfectly composed in the camera at the time of shooting. Unfortunately, few of us live in an ideal world, and by the time you've perfected the shot, you've missed the moment.

Most photos benefit from cropping, whether to remove distracting objects, straighten horizons, for artistic effect, or simply to fit your chosen ratio.

1. To open the Crop tool, select the first icon in the Develop Tool Strip below the Histogram or press the R key. The Crop Options display below. **(Figure 12.2)**

2. First, straighten your horizon by pressing the **Auto** button. If that doesn't work well, select the Straighten tool in the Crop Options panel, and click and drag a line along the horizon. Lightroom automatically rotates the photo to make it horizontal. **(Figure 12.3)**

3. Select your crop ratio in the *Aspect* pop-up. (You don't choose the size until you export the photo.) To switch the crop orientation,

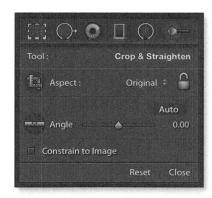

▲ **Figure 12.2** To open the Crop tool, select the first icon in the Tool Strip. The options appear below.

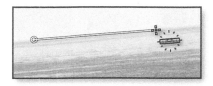

▲ **Figure 12.3** Straighten the photo by selecting the Straighten tool and dragging a line along the horizon.

FREEFORM CROP

For a free form or non-standard crop ratio, unlock the Lock icon and click and drag a rectangle on the photo or drag the edges of the bounding box.

FASTTRACK

CONTINUES ON PAGE 234

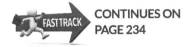

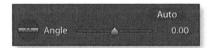

▲ **Figure 12.4** The Straighten tool is stored in the Crop Options panel, next to the *Angle* slider.

▲ **Figure 12.5** To rotate a crop, float the mouse around the outside of the crop area until the double-headed arrow appears.

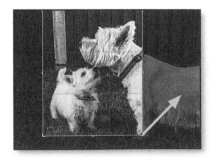

▲ **Figure 12.6** Reverse the crop orientation by dragging a corner at a 45 degree angle or pressing the X key.

for example, to make a vertical crop from a horizontal photo, press the X key.

4. Adjust the crop by dragging the corners or the edges of the bounding box.

5. Move the photo around under the crop overlay by clicking within the bounding box and dragging the photo into position. Rotate the photo by clicking and dragging around the outside of the bounding box. Think of it as moving the photo underneath the crop overlay, rather than moving the crop.

6. Once you've finished cropping, press the Enter key or the *Done* button on the Toolbar.

That's the basics, but now let's do a deeper dive into the crop options.

How do I straighten or rotate a photo?

As well as clicking on the Straighten tool icon in the Crop Options panel, you can quickly access the tool by holding down the Ctrl key (Windows) / Cmd key (Mac) while you drag along the horizon line on the photo. **(Figure 12.4)**

If you prefer to straighten by eye, hover outside of the crop boundary, so that the cursor changes to a double-headed arrow **(Figure 12.5)**, then click and drag to rotate the photo up to 45 degrees in either direction. Or you can manually adjust the degree of rotation using the **Angle** slider.

As you rotate the crop, the photo remains level so you don't have to turn your head to see how the photo will look once it's cropped. **(Figure 12.6)**

How do I resize the crop?

To resize the crop, drag the edges of the photo. If you drag the corners, you can adjust two sides in one go.

You can also move the photo around under the crop overlay by dragging the center of the photo.

How do I crop a vertical portion from a horizontal photo?

To change the crop orientation, drag the corner of the crop diagonally until the long edge becomes shorter than the short edge and the grid flips over (it gets easier with practice!), or just press the X key to flip the crop overlay.

Alternatively, unlock the ratio lock in the Crop options panel and adjust to the crop of your choice. You can also drag a crop freehand, by dragging a rectangle on the photo, but if you already have a crop applied, you have to press the *Reset* button in the Crop Options panel first.

How do I change the crop ratio?

If you're planning on printing the photo, you may want to restrict your crop to a standard ratio. As Lightroom never throws away pixels, it doesn't crop to a specific size—just a ratio. This enables you to reuse the same crop for multiple different sizes, for example, a 4x5 ratio crop can be output as 800x1000 pixels, 4"x5", 8"x10", etc.

By default, the crop ratio is set to *Original* (or *As Shot* for photos that have an in-camera crop). If you'd prefer a different ratio, select it from the **Aspect** pop-up.

How do I set a custom crop aspect ratio?

The standard ratios are: *As Shot, Original, Custom, 1x1, 4x5/8x10, 8.5x11, 5x7, 2x3/4x6, 4x3, 16x9* and *16x10.* **(Figure 12.7 & 12.8)** If your chosen crop ratio isn't on this list, you can create your own custom crop ratio.

In the *Aspect* pop-up, select *Enter Custom* and type your own crop ratio. **(Figure 12.9)** It'll automatically be added to the bottom of the list. You can't delete custom crop ratios manually, but they work on a

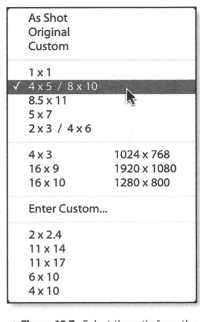

Figure 12.7 Select the ratio from the list or create a custom one.

Figure 12.8 The standard aspect ratios vary from square to long and thin.

Figure 12.9 Create your own custom ratios by selecting *Enter Custom* from the *Aspect* pop-up.

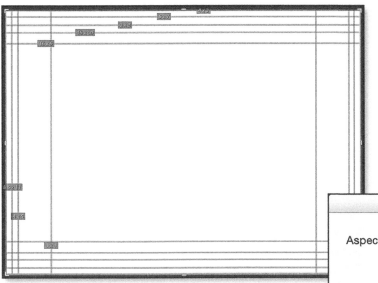

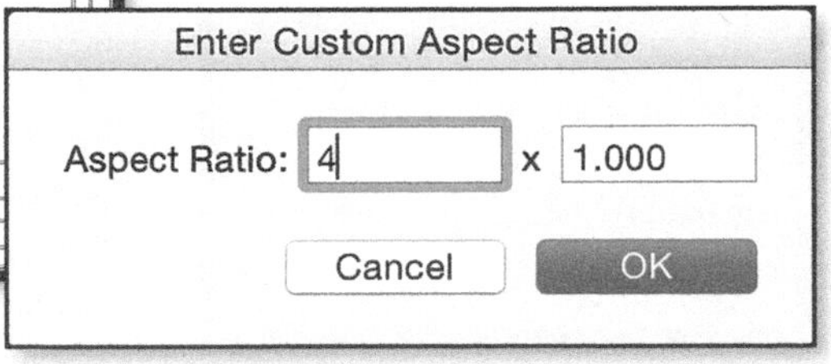

Figure 12.10 The lock icon fixes your crop to your chosen aspect ratio.

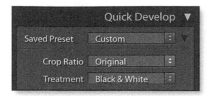

Figure 12.11 Crop ratios can also be accessed from the Quick Develop panel in the Library module.

rolling list of 5, so only your most recent custom ratios remain in the list. As you add a new one, the oldest one is removed from the list.

How do I lock my crop ratio?

When you select a crop ratio from the pop-up, the lock icon to the right automatically locks. **(Figure 12.10)** As you drag the edges of the crop bounding box, the nearest three edges move, retaining your chosen crop ratio. To allow the crop edges to move freely, one at a time, click the crop ratio lock icon to unlock it.

Can I set a default crop ratio?

If you always crop your photos to a specific ratio, for example, 8x10, you may want to apply this ratio automatically instead of selecting 8x10 from the *Aspect* pop-up on each photo. You can't change the default crop ratio, but there are two easy workarounds.

- Return to the Grid view and select all of the photos. In the Quick Develop panel **(Figure 12.11)**, click the disclosure triangle to the right of the *Saved Preset* pop-up to show the *Crop Ratio* pop-up, then select your chosen ratio.

- Alternatively, crop the first photo in the normal Crop mode, and synchronize or copy/paste that crop to all the other photos. (We'll come to Synchronize in the Develop Module Tools chapter on page 297.)

Once you've done this, your chosen ratio will already be selected in the Crop options panel and you can go through the photos and adjust the crop to taste.

Either way, it's intelligent enough to rotate the crop for the opposite orientation photos, but beware, it also resets any existing crops.

SETTING THE SIZE

When you're cropping in Lightroom, you're deciding which bits of the photo will be cropped, rather than setting a fixed size. When you come to export, you then define the size of the exported photo, either as pixel dimensions or as inches/cm combined with a resolution setting.

How do I view or clear my in-camera crop?

Some cameras allow you to crop the photos to a specific ratio at the time of shooting, or display crop lines on the screen. Some photographers want their in-camera crop (i.e. 3:2, 16:9, 1:1) applied in Lightroom and others want the full raw file. Adobe chose to respect the in-camera crop, but in response to user feedback, a new feature was added in Lightroom 4.2, allowing you to recover the additional image data.

In new cameras added to Lightroom 4.2 or later, the *As Shot* crop ratio displays the photo with the in-camera crop applied, but changing to *Original* in the *Aspect* pop-up displays all the available sensor data.

For older cameras (those released before mid-2012), you'll need to use the free DNG Recover Edges plug-in, which is available for download from Adobe Labs. http://www.Lrq.me/adobe-recoveredges

To install the plug-in, download and unzip it, and then go to Lightroom's *File menu > Plug-in Manager*. Click *Install* and navigate to your downloaded plug-in. (For additional install instructions, turn back to the Plug-ins section starting on page 19.)

To run the plug-in, your raw photo needs to be in the DNG format, so select the file then go to *Library menu > Convert Photo to DNG* **(Figure 12.12)**. If you want to keep the proprietary raw format in addition to the new DNG file, uncheck *Delete originals after successful conversion*. You can learn more about the DNG format in Appendix B starting on page A-1.

Select the resulting DNG file and go to *Library menu > Plug-in Extras > DNG Recover Edges – Apply*. An additional DNG file appears stacked with the original photo. The duplicate DNG file includes all the sensor data that was recorded by the camera. (You could then delete the first DNG file.)

When you view the photo in Develop's Crop mode, the crop is set to the *As Shot* ratio by default, but the rest of the image data is available for an alternative crop.

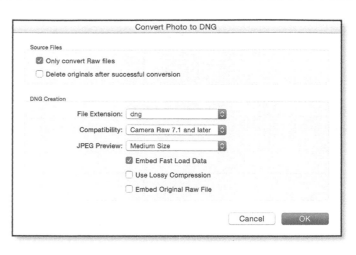

Figure 12.12 If you selected an in-camera crop on an older camera, you must convert to DNG format to access extra pixels.

How do I change the Crop Overlay?

When you first enter the Crop mode, gray grid lines are overlaid over the photo. This is called the Crop Overlay and it's useful as a composition guide. It's set to *Thirds* by default, named after the Rule of Thirds, but there's a variety of different overlays to choose from: *Grid, Thirds, Diagonal, Triangle, Golden Ratio, Golden Spiral* and *Aspect Ratio*.

Press the O key to cycle through a variety of overlays **(Figure 12.13)**, and Shift-O changes the orientation of these overlays. You may only use some of the overlays so you can hide the others by selecting *Tools menu > Crop Guide Overlay > Choose Overlays to Cycle*. **(Figure 12.14)**

The *Aspect Ratio* overlay displays a number of different ratio lines to help envisage how it'll look at different ratios. You can choose which ratios to display using the *Tools menu > Crop Guide Overlay > Choose Aspect Ratios* dialog. **(Figure 12.15)**

ZOOM WHILE CROPPING

You can't zoom while in Crop mode, but if you need a larger preview, select the Crop tool and then press Shift-Tab to hide all the side panels. It's particularly useful when straightening a photo.

If you need even more space, Shift-F hides the window title bar and T hides the Toolbar.

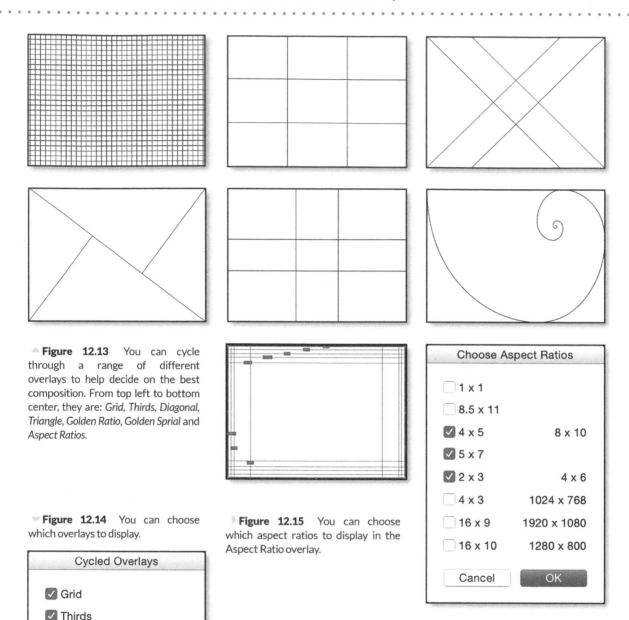

Figure 12.13 You can cycle through a range of different overlays to help decide on the best composition. From top left to bottom center, they are: *Grid, Thirds, Diagonal, Triangle, Golden Ratio, Golden Sprial* and *Aspect Ratios.*

Figure 12.14 You can choose which overlays to display.

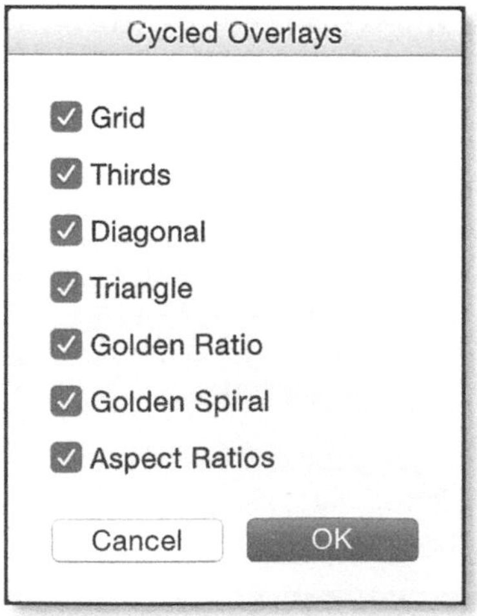

Figure 12.15 You can choose which aspect ratios to display in the Aspect Ratio overlay.

You can't change the Crop Overlay color but if you find the overlays distracting, press the H key to hide them, or select *Never* from the pop-up on the Toolbar. If the pop-up's set to *Auto*, the Grid overlay only displays when you're rotating the photo.

Is there a way to see what the new pixel dimensions will be without interpolation?

If you go to *View menu > View Options*, you can set the Info Overlay to show *Cropped Dimensions*, which is the cropped pixel dimensions without any resampling. Every time you let go of the edge of the bounding box, these dimensions update. You'll also find the original and cropped dimensions in the Metadata panel in the Library module.

Should I check *Constrain to Image*?

Finally, there's a **Constrain to Image** checkbox in the Crop Options panel. It prevents you from including blank white pixels in your crop, which may be caused by lens corrections. It means that you can crop your photo without having to be too careful to avoid including blank areas, so it's usually worth leaving checked. There's a *Constrain Crop* checkbox in Lens Corrections which does the same thing.

How do I reset the crop?

If you change your mind about the crop setting, you can cancel it at any time by pressing the **Reset** button at the bottom of the Crop Options panel.

CHANGING RATIO ON EXISTING CROPS

When you change the crop ratio on an existing crop in the Develop module (not Quick Develop), Lightroom applies the new ratio to the existing crop instead of resetting the crop to maximum size. If you'd like it to reset the crop to the largest possible size, hold down the Alt (Windows) / Opt (Mac) key while selecting a ratio.

CROPPING SHORTCUTS

Go to Crop Tool	R
Reset Crop	Ctrl Alt R / Cmd Opt R
Crop As Shot	Ctrl Alt Shift R / Cmd Opt Shift R
Constrain Aspect Ratio	A
Crop to Same Aspect Ratio	Shift A
Rotate Crop Aspect	X
Reset Crop to Maximum for new Aspect Ratio	Hold Alt / Opt while changing aspect ratio
Crop from Center of Photo	Hold Alt/Opt while dragging
Rotation Angle Ruler	Ctrl-click / Cmd-click on start and end points
Cycle Guide Overlay	O
Cycle Guide Overlay Orientation	Shift O
Rotate photo 90 degrees left	Ctrl [/ Cmd [
Rotate photo 90 degrees right	Ctrl] / Cmd]

SPOT REMOVAL—CLONE & HEAL TOOLS

The second icon in the Tool Strip beneath the Histogram is the Spot Removal tool, also known as the Advanced Healing Brush. **(Figure 12.16)** It's not intended to replace Photoshop or other pixel editors, but it allows you to quickly remove dust spots and other small distractions.

Let's try removing a small spot **(Figure 12.17)** before we go into more detail.

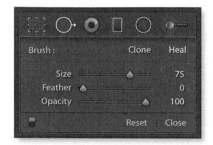

Figure 12.16 Select the Spot Removal tool from the Tool Strip under the histogram.

1. Select the second icon in the Tool Strip, beneath the Histogram, or press the Q key.

2. Adjust the brush size using the slider in the Options panel and then click on the spot in the photo, or click and drag to remove a line or non-circular shape. **(Figure 12.18)**

3. The spot overlay appears on the screen, showing the outline of the retouched area and the source of the new pixels. The circular black and white pin allows you to move or reselect the spot overlay. Lightroom automatically tries to find a good source, but you can click and drag the circular pins to fine tune the correction. **(Figure 12.19)**

4. To delete a spot correction, hold down the Alt key (Windows) / Opt key (Mac) to change the cursor into a pair of scissors, and then click on the spot again.

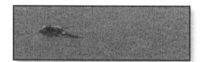

Figure 12.17 Find a spot or distraction in the photo, such as this piece of seaweed on the sand.

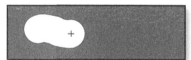

Figure 12.18 Click and drag to paint over the distraction.

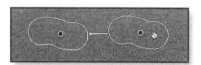

Figure 12.19 Lightroom finds some new pixels to cover the distraction, but you can click and drag the overlay to choose a different source.

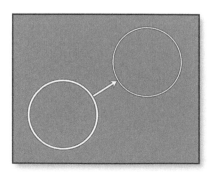

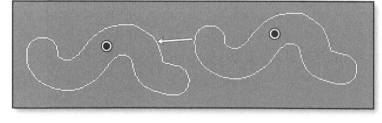

Figure 12.20 Click on the dust spot to create a circle spot.

Figure 12.21 Click and drag over a non-circular shape to create a brush spot.

What's the difference between clicking and dragging?

There are two kinds of spot—circle spots and brush spots (non-circular healing).

- **Circle spots** are created by a single click. They display as single round spots and they can be moved and resized. **(Figure 12.20)**

- **Brush spots** are created by clicking and dragging. As you paint across the photo, a white brush stroke appears, and it's then replaced by two white outlines showing the source and target. Brush spots can have an arbitrary shape but they can't be resized later. **(Figure 12.21)**

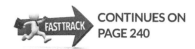

CONTINUES ON PAGE 240

How do I move or delete an existing spot?

Spots have circular pins in the center, which mark their location and allow you to reselect or move the spot correction. The pins have two states—selected or not selected, or active and inactive. Not selected is shown by a white pin, and clicking on the pin selects that spot, turning the pin black.

When you hover over the center of an existing selected (black) spot, the cursor changes to a hand, and you can then drag to move the spot to a new location. **(Figure 12.22)**

To delete a spot, click on it to make it active, and then press the Delete key on your keyboard. Alternatively, if you hold down the Alt key (Windows) / Opt key (Mac), the cursor changes to a pair of scissors, and then clicking on the individual spots or dragging a rectangular marquee selection around the spots deletes them. **(Figure 12.23)** To remove all spots, press the **Reset** button.

Spot Removal is the one tool in Lightroom that's sensitive to the order in which the corrections are applied. The target for one spot can become the source for another spot, and if you then delete the first spot, the latter spot is affected too.

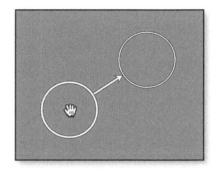

▲ **Figure 12.22** To move a spot, click and drag the center of the spot.

How do I choose the source of the replacement pixels?

When you create a circle or brush spot, Lightroom intelligently searches for the most suitable source of replacement pixels, even if that's outside of the current crop boundary. You can then pick up the source spot's pin, and drag it to a better source.

If you're creating a circle spot, you can select the source while you're creating it. Hold down the Ctrl (Windows) / Cmd (Mac) key while clicking on the spot and drag to your chosen source without letting go of the mouse button.

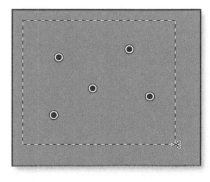

▲ **Figure 12.23** To delete spots, hold down the Alt (Windows) / Opt (Mac) key and click on the spots or drag a marquee around them.

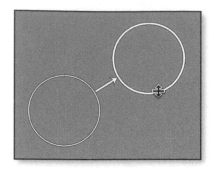

Figure 12.24 To resize a circle spot, drag the edge of the spot.

Figure 12.25 The difference between feathering on circle spots and brush spots. From left to right:

1. Circle spot size 80, feather 0, results in hard edges.

2. Circle spot size 80, feather 100, results in soft edges.

3. Spot removal cursor, size 80. Note the inner and outer circles showing the range of the feathering.

4. Brush spot size 80, feather 100, results in soft edges. The edges are much softer than the second circle spot of the same size, as brush spots have greater feathering range.

5. Brush spot drawn with a small size 75 brush has minimal feathering as the feathering is relative to the size of the brush tip.

6. Brush spot drawn with a larger size 90 brush has much greater feather as it's relative to the size of the brush tip and this brush is much larger.

This does have implications when copying/synchronizing the spot removal to other photos. If Lightroom automatically finds the source, and then you copy the spot removal to other photos, Lightroom will check for the best source on each of the photos. If you select a source manually, Lightroom copies from the same location on each of the photos. This is particularly useful when using the spot tools to remove sensor dust in a clear area of sky, as it's intelligent enough to adjust for orientation.

How do I adjust the brush size or the size of an existing spot?

In the Spot Removal Options panel under the Tool Strip is a brush **Size** slider, which affects the size of the circle spot or brush stroke. You can also use the [and] keyboard shortcuts or your mouse scroll wheel to adjust the size. Holding down the Ctrl+Alt keys (Windows) / Cmd+Opt keys (Mac) while clicking and dragging on a spot, sets the spot size on-the-fly, overriding the Size slider.

You can readjust an existing circle spot by clicking on the pin to make it active and then adjusting these same controls. Alternatively, if you hover over the edge of an existing circle spot, the cursor changes and you can then drag the edge to adjust the size. **(Figure 12.24)** You can't resize brush spots, which are the non-circular strokes.

What's the difference between *Clone* mode and *Heal* mode?

While you're in the Spot Removal Options panel, you'll note that you have a choice of *Clone* or *Heal*.

- **Heal** works like the Healing Brush in Photoshop, intelligently blending the edge pixels.

- **Clone** works like Photoshop's Clone tool, picking up the pixels and dropping them in another location.

For most spots, the *Heal* option works best, particularly in clean areas such as sky. If you're trying to retouch a spot along an edge in the photo, for example, a roofline against the sky, the *Heal* tool can smudge, in which case the *Clone* option may work better. We'll come back to some tricky retouching examples later in this section.

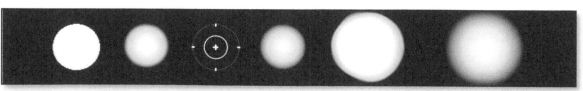

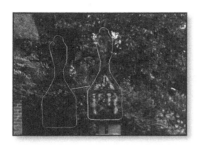

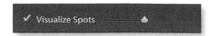

Figure 12.26 Avoid using the *Feathering* slider with *Heal* mode, because you may end up with transparent patches, such as the red triangular sign which is still visible in this photo.

Figure 12.27 The *Visualize Spots* checkbox shows in the Toolbar when Spot Removal is selected.

The **Feather** slider is particularly useful when combined with the *Clone* mode. The *Heal* mode works best with *Feathering* set to 0 as it automatically attempts to blend the edges. *Clone* mode stands out if it has hard edges, so a higher value, such as 90, works better. **(Figure 12.25 & 12.26)**

The **Opacity** slider allows you to fade the retouching, for example, you may not want to completely remove the lines on a person's face, but just fade them slightly. If you want to remove the blemish completely, leave it set to 100.

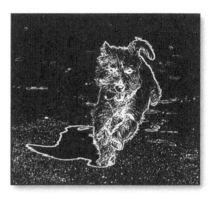

Figure 12.28 *Visualize Spots* makes it easier to spot distractions, such as the stones and seaweed in the sand.

How do I use *Visualize Spots* to quickly find dust spots?

When the Spot Removal tool is selected, there's a checkbox and slider in the Toolbar (below the photo) marked **Visualize Spots**. **(Figure 12.27)** When you check its checkbox or press the A key, Lightroom displays a black and white mask of your photo. **(Figure 12.28)** If you drag the slider to the right, more dust spots are revealed, and dragging it to the left hides them. It's similar to the mask used for the sharpening *Masking* slider, which we'll come to on page 268. You can retouch the spots with the mask active, or you can turn it off again once you've found them.

STRAIGHT LINES

Holding down the Shift key while you're drawing a brush spot constrains it to a horizontal or vertical line, which is rarely helpful. However the Shift key can be used to create straight lines at other angles, which is particularly use for power or telephone lines. Click at the beginning of the line to create a circle spot, and then hold down the Shift key and click at the end of the line. Lightroom joins the spots using a straight brush spot.

YOU MISSED A SPOT!

If you zoom into 1:1 view to retouch dust spots, start in the top left corner and then press the Page Down key to work through the photo. It divides the photo up into an imaginary grid, so when you reach the bottom of the first column, it automatically returns to the top of the photo and starts on the next column. By the time you reach the bottom right corner, you'll have retouched the entire photo without missing any spots.

HOT PIXELS

If you're wondering where your hot pixels on your camera's sensor have gone, Lightroom automatically maps out hot pixels, as does ACR, but it only works on standard raw or mosaic DNG files, not sRAW.

What are the limitations of the Lightroom's Spot Removal tools?

It's possible to do fairly complex retouching using Lightroom's Spot Removal tools, however, as Lightroom is a metadata editor, it has to constantly re-run text instructions, so it gets slower with the more adjustments that you add.

The tools are ideal for removing distractions such as sensor dust, power cables in the sky, leaves on the grass, etc., but detailed retouching is still quicker and easier in a pixel editing program, such as Photoshop or Photoshop Elements. The point where a pixel editor becomes more efficient than Lightroom depends on your computer hardware, as well as the retouching you're trying to do. When it gets frustrating, stop and switch to Photoshop!

SPOT REMOVAL SHORTCUTS

Go to Spot Removal	Q
Create New Circle Spot with auto source	Click
Create New Circle Spot (scale from center)	Ctrl Alt / Cmd Opt while clicking
Create New Circle Spot (scale from starting point)	Ctrl Shift / Cmd Shift while clicking
Create New Circle Spot with manual source	Ctrl / Cmd while click spot and drag to chosen source
Create New Brush Spot	Click and drag
Create New Brush Spot (constrain to horizontal/vertical axis)	Shift and drag
Edit Existing (connect existing circle spot to new spot, changing to brush spot)	Select existing circle spot then hold down Shift and click
Toggle Clone/Heal	Shift Q
Select new auto source	/
Increase circle spot size	]
Decrease circle spot size	[
Increase Feather	Shift-]
Decrease Feather	Shift-[
Visualize Spots	A
Hide Spot Overlays	H
Delete Spot	Select Spot then Delete or hold Alt / Opt while clicking
Delete Multiple Spots	Hold Alt/ Opt and drag marquee to surround spots

Let's try a couple more examples...

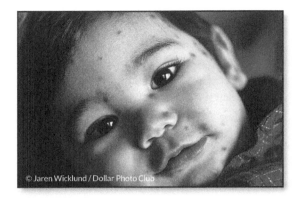

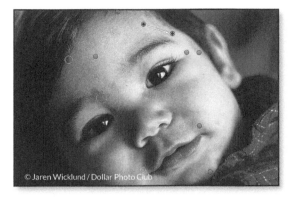

Figure 12.29 Chickenpox spots or acne can easily be removed using Circle Spots.

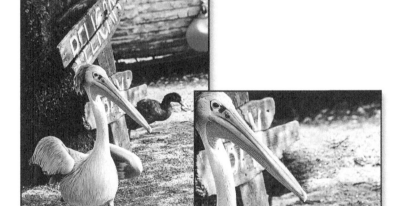

Figure 12.30 The duck photobombed this photo (left), so we want to remove him, but if we just paint up to the edge of the beak and sign in *Heal* mode, it leaves a dark smudge (right), and *Clone* mode leaves harsh edges.

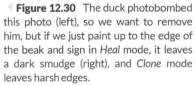

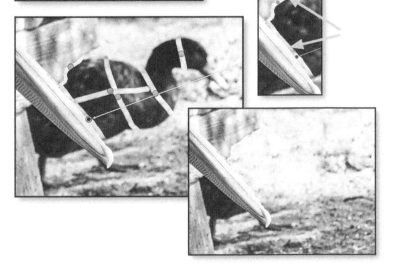

Figure 12.31 Instead, we use two thin *Clone* lines along the edge of the beak and sign (top right). When we then paint a large *Heal* stroke over the duck's head and body, and slightly overlap the earlier *Clone* strokes, we can get a much cleaner result. In this case, there's only one suitable small clone source to the right of the duck's head, which isn't big enough to clone over his whole head and body. To solve this, we divide him up using additional *Clone* strokes (left), and add multiple smaller heal chunks, slightly overlapping the clone dividers to clone over the duck (right). Additional strokes could be used to heal any leftover artifacts.

RED EYE & PET EYE CORRECTION TOOLS

Red eye in photography—or green eye, in the case of pets—is caused by light from a flash bouncing off the inside of a person's eye. Although many cameras now come with red eye reduction, their pre-flashes tend to warn people that you're about to take a photograph, and can lose any spontaneity. If you turn it off, you can use Lightroom's Red Eye tool to fix red eye in post-processing.

To remove red eye or pet's green eye:

1. Select the third icon in the Tool Strip beneath the Histogram. **(Figure 12.32)**

2. Select **Red Eye** or **Pet Eye** from the Options panel below.

3. Drag from the centre of the eye, to encompass the whole eye. Lightroom automatically searches for the red/green eye within the selected area, and then makes the other options available in the Options panel. **(Figure 12.33)**

4. Once it locks, you'll see a dark gray spot which replaces the red eye. **(Figure 12.34)** Using the **Pupil Size** slider, adjust the size of the spot to cover the pupil, then adjust the **Darken** slider to darken or lighten the pupil. **(Figure 12.35)** If you're adjusting a pet eye, check the **Add Catchlight** checkbox to add a small white catchlight spot on the pupil. **(Figure 12.36)**

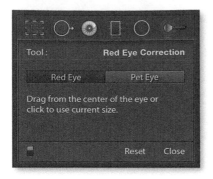

Figure 12.32 The Red Eye Correction tool is the third tool in the Tool Strip.

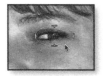

Figure 12.33 (left) Drag from the center of the eye.

Figure 12.34 (right) Once the pupil has been detected, adjust the size and darkness of the pupil.

Lightroom's Red Eye Correction tool can't lock on to the red eye—is there anything I can do to help it?

If the Red Eye Correction tool can't lock on to the red eye, scroll down to the HSL panel, select the *Saturation* tab and increase the *Red* slider, then try again. Once it locks, you can set the HSL panel back to its previous settings (0 by default).

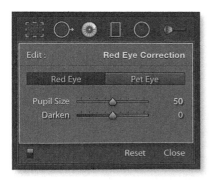

Figure 12.35 Once the circles are in place, edit the *Pupil Size* and *Darken* settings.

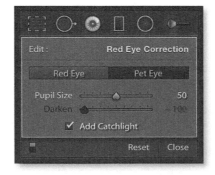

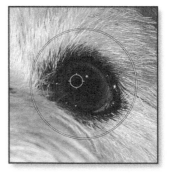

Figure 12.36 Using the Pet Eye Correction, you can add a white catchlight by clicking the *Add Catchlight* checkbox. Adjust the catchlight position by moving the inner circle.

LOCAL ADJUSTMENTS— GRADIENTS & BRUSHES

Most of Lightroom's sliders apply to the whole photo, but the local adjustment tools allow you to apply settings to specific areas, either using a gradient or a brush.

The linear (or straight) Graduated Filter is particularly useful for darkening the sky in a sunset photo, but it can also be useful if the lighting on one side of the photo is different to the other side. Let's try it...

1. Select the Linear Graduated Filter—the fourth icon—in the Tool Strip, just below the Histogram. **(Figure 12.37)**

2. In the Options section below **(Figure 12.38)**, select the settings that you want to apply selectively. It can help to select more extreme settings when creating the gradient, for example, *Exposure −1*, so you can easily see the effect. You can go back and change the settings later.

3. Click on the photo and drag to create your gradient, for example, drag from the top down to darken the sky.

4. Lines appear on screen, showing the limits of the gradient. The outer lines show where the gradient starts and stops. **(Figure 12.39)** Drag the lines to increase or decrease the range. The center line rotates the gradient.

5. Once you're happy with the gradient, you can fine tune the sliders in the Options panel to get the effect you desire.

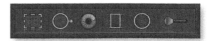

▲ **Figure 12.37** The Graduated Filter, Radial Filter and Adjustment Brush are the fourth, fifth and sixth tools in the Tool Strip under the histogram.

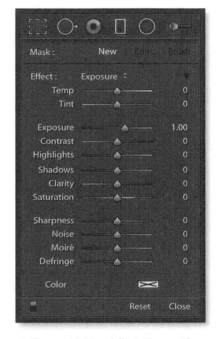

▲ **Figure 12.38** Adjust the settings using the Graduated Filter Options panel.

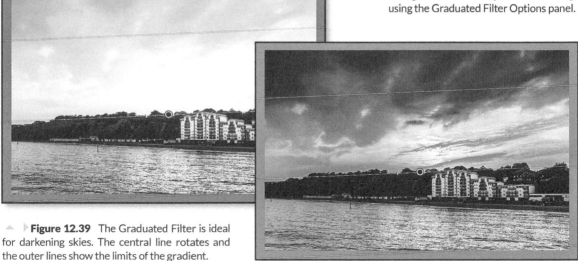

▲ ▶ **Figure 12.39** The Graduated Filter is ideal for darkening skies. The central line rotates and the outer lines show the limits of the gradient.

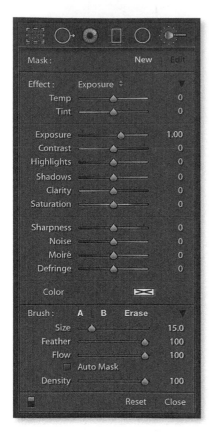

Figure 12.40 Adjust the brush settings using the Adjustment Brush Options panel.

MISSING TOOLBAR

If you can't find certain controls, such as the *Done* button for Develop tools, your Toolbar may be missing. Press the T key to make it reappear.

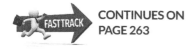

CONTINUES ON PAGE 263

The same principle applies for the Radial Graduated Filter—the fifth icon—except the Radial Filter creates a circular or oval gradient, so you drag out from the center of the photo towards the edges. It's particularly useful for off-center vignettes, but it can also be used to lighten faces in photos and blur backgrounds, amongst other things.

The Adjustment Brush allows you to paint on the photo, perhaps to lighten dark shadows, sharpen eyes, or apply a different white balance to a specific area of the photo.

1. Select the Adjustment Brush—the sixth icon—in the Tool Strip.

2. Select your chosen slider values in the Options panel below. **(Figure 12.40)** As with the Graduated and Radial Filters, you can go back and fine tune these settings later.

   There's a selection of presets in the *Effects* pop-up to help you get started. They include basic presets for each of the sliders, plus presets for *Burn (darken)*, *Dodge (lighten)*, *Iris Enhance*, *Soften Skin* and *Teeth Whitening*.

   The presets just move the sliders to specific values, but they can be helpful if you're not sure which sliders to adjust. For example, the *Teeth Whitening* preset increases the exposure to lighten the teeth and reduces saturation to desaturate the yellow.

3. Select your brush size at the bottom of the Options panel.

4. Click and drag on the photo to paint your brush strokes. If you make a mistake, hold down the Alt key (Windows) / Opt key (Mac) to turn the brush into an eraser, and click and drag over the mistake to remove the brush stroke.

In the Options panel, you can select a mixture of slider settings to apply to your masked area. For example, the *Exposure* adjustment is similar to dodging and burning in Photoshop or in a traditional darkroom. Settings such as *Sharpness*, *Clarity* and *Noise Reduction* can be used for softening skin on portraits. *White Balance* or *Color* are useful when adjusting for mixed lighting situations. Settings can be combined, so a combination of perhaps *Exposure*, *Highlights*, *Saturation*, *Clarity* and a blue tint can make a dull sky much more interesting.

When you've finished making local adjustments, press the *Done* button on the Toolbar or click the icon in the Tool Strip to close the tool.

We'll work on some more examples at the end of this chapter, but first, let's explore the tools in more detail, starting with the different types of gradient, then the brush, then questions that apply to editing both types of local adjustments.

How do I create a new Graduated or Radial Filter mask?

When you select the Graduated or Radial Filter tool, it's automatically ready to start a new mask. The word *New* is highlighted at the top of the Options panel.

Click at your gradient starting point, and drag to your gradient end point before releasing the mouse button. **(Figure 12.41)** If you prefer to work from a central point, rather than selecting your gradient start and end points, hold down the Alt (Windows) / Opt (Mac) key while dragging. The gradient then expands equally from both sides of your starting point. You can hold down the Shift key while creating the gradient to constrain it to a 90 degree angle.

For a radial filter, click in the center of your new circle/oval, and drag out towards the edge of the photo before releasing the mouse button. **(Figure 12.42)** Holding down the Shift key constrains it to a circle instead of an oval. There's a multitude of other shortcuts and modifier keys for the Radial Filter, which are listed in the Keyboard Shortcuts box page 255.

How do I edit an existing Graduated/Radial Filter?

The local adjustments are marked with small gray circles called Pins. To select an existing local adjustment, click on the pin. The center of the pin turns black, the word **Edit** is highlighted at the top of the Options panel, and the overlay lines for this adjustment appear on the screen.

A **Graduated Filter** mask is controlled by three lines, which allow you to adjust the size, rotation and position of the gradient.

- **Feather/stretch the gradient**—When you float over the outer lines—the ones without the pin—the cursor changes to a hand tool, enabling you to adjust how far the gradient stretches. Moving the outside lines further apart increases the feathering, and moving them closer together reduces the feathering.

- **Rotate the gradient**—When you float over the central line—the one with the pin—the cursor changes to a double-headed arrow, enabling you to adjust the rotation of the gradient. You'll have more control if you drag the outer ends of the lines. **(Figure 12.43)**

- **Invert the gradient**—If the gradient is the wrong way round, you could drag both outer lines, swapping their positions, but it's quicker to simply press the ' key to invert it.

- **Move the gradient**—If you need to move the whole mask, click and drag the central pin itself. **(Figure 12.44)**

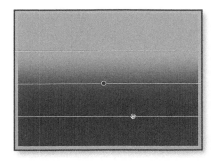

Figure 12.41 Graduated Filters use three lines to control the distance and rotation of the gradient.

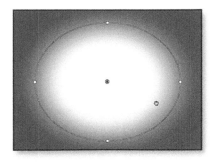

Figure 12.42 The Radial Filter has a single circle/oval overlay which controls the size, shape and rotation of the gradient.

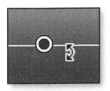

Figure 12.43 Rotate the gradient using the double-headed arrow which appears when you float over the central line.

Figure 12.44 Drag the pin to move the gradient.

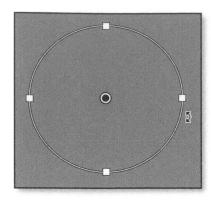

Figure 12.45 Rotate the Radial Filter using the double-headed arrow, and change the shape by dragging the squares on the overlay.

A **Radial Filter** is controlled by the circular bounding box and the 4 square markers.

- **Resize the radial filter**—When you float over the square markers, the cursor changes to a straight double-headed arrow, enabling you to adjust how far the gradient stretches. To automatically expand the mask to the edges of the photo, double-click inside the oval bounding box.

- **Feather the radial filter**—The feathering on the Radial Filter is controlled using the **Feather** slider in the Options panel.

- **Rotate the radial filter**—When you float over the line itself, the cursor changes to a curved double-headed arrow, enabling you to click and drag to adjust the rotation of the gradient. **(Figure 12.45)**

- **Invert the radial filter**—If the gradient is the wrong way round, you can press the **Invert Mask** checkbox in the Options panel, but it's quicker to simply press the ' key to invert it. **(Figure 12.46)**

- **Move the radial filter**—If you need to move the whole mask, click and drag the central pin itself.

To start a new gradient, in order to apply different adjustments to another area of the photo, press the **New** button at the top of the Options panel and start painting. You can have multiple adjustments (pins), on an image, and they can overlap.

To delete a gradient, select the pin then press the Delete key or right-click on the pin and select **Delete**. To delete all gradients, press the **Reset** button.

How do I brush away part of the gradient?

At times you may want to prevent parts of the photo being affected by a gradient. For example, if you're darkening the sky, you may not

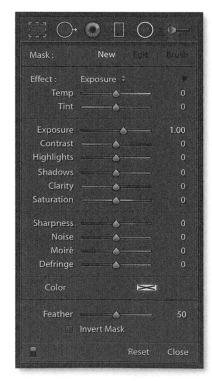

Figure 12.46 Adjust the settings using the Radial Filter Options panel.

RADIAL FILTER REVERSED

The Radial Filter was primarily designed in response to requests for off-center vignettes, so by default it affects the outside of the circle. If that's not the way you expect it to behave though, it's simple to change the default behavior. To do so, select the Radial Filter and make sure the Options panel is set to *New* rather than *Edit*. Check the *Invert Mask* checkbox, and that, along with any other slider settings in the Options panel, is set as the new defaults.

---

want to darken the building on the horizon at the same time. In this case, you can brush away part of the gradient.

To do so, select the **Brush** option at the top of the Graduated Filter or Radial Filter Options panel and set the brush options to *Erase* at the bottom of the panel. **(Figure 12.47)** Select the **Size** and **Feather** (softness) for the brush and click and drag across the photo to remove areas of the gradient. To delete the brush strokes, press the **Reset Brushes** button.

The Brush options in the Graduated Filter or Radial Filter work like the main Adjustment Brush tool, so let's investigate these next.

Why would I use the Adjustment Brush rather than editing a photo in Photoshop?

The Adjustment Brush tool allows you to paint local adjustments onto the photo, so you can easily lighten shadow areas, pull back highlight detail in other areas, and selectively soften skin on faces.

Photoshop's traditionally been used for localized adjustments, so why would you use Lightroom's Adjustment Brush? Two simple reasons—non-destructive editing and raw data.

When you edit a photo in Photoshop, you have yet another large photo file to store, and if you want to edit it without degrading the original image data, you have to retain multiple layers, which increases the file size further. Lightroom's Local Adjustments store the local adjustment information as metadata in the catalog, so you can safely go back and change your adjustments repeatedly.

Also, when you're using the adjustment brush in Lightroom, you have access to the full raw data, whereas Photoshop uses rendered data (unless you use the raw file as a smart object). For example, if you're using a masked area to lighten shadow areas, there's a much wider range of data available in the raw file, so you can pull back greater detail.

This doesn't mean that Lightroom entirely replaces Photoshop. There are still many pixel based adjustments that require Photoshop, and sometimes it's simply more efficient to use Photoshop for localized adjustments. Because Lightroom has to constantly re-run text instructions, rather than immediately applying them to the original pixels, it can become quite slow when there are lots of local adjustments, so the practicality depends largely on your computer hardware.

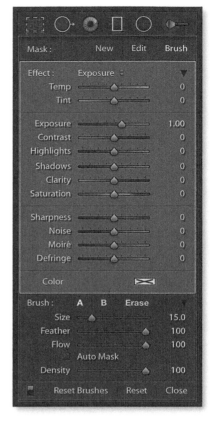

Figure 12.47 You can remove parts of a gradient using a brush.

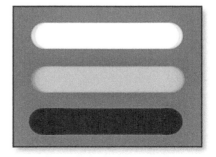

Figure 12.48 *Exposure.* +4.0 brightens the exposure by +4.0 (top), +1.0 brightens the exposure by +1.0 (center), and -4.0 darkens the exposure by -4.0 (bottom).

How do I create a new brush mask?

When you select the Adjustment Brush, it's automatically ready to start a new mask. The word *New* is highlighted at the top of the Options panel. Select the size and feathering of the brush using the controls at the bottom of the Options panel, and select the effect you're going to apply. **(Figure 12.48)**

When you're ready to start painting on the photo, hold down the mouse button and drag the cursor across the photo. Holding down the Shift key while you paint draws the stroke in a straight vertical or horizontal line. In some cases, you may find it helpful to paint with the effects sliders turned up higher than your intended result, or with the mask overlay turned on (press O), in order to clearly see where you're painting. You can then adjust the sliders again when you've finished painting.

Like the gradients, your brush masks are marked with small gray circles called Pins. To select an existing adjustment, click on the pin. The center of the pin turns black, the word *Edit* is highlighted at the top of the Options panel, and you can continue painting on the same brush mask, or switch to the eraser to remove some of the mask.

To start a new brush mask, in order to apply different adjustments to another area of the photo, press the *New* button at the top of the Adjustment Brush Options panel and start painting. You can have multiple adjustments (pins) on an image, and they can overlap.

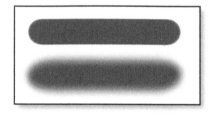

Figure 12.49 *Feathering* set to 0 (top) and 100 (bottom).

How do I choose the size and softness of my brush?

At bottom of the Adjustment Brush Options panel are the brush settings. The **Size** slider runs from 0.1, which is a tiny brush, to a maximum size of 100. **Feather** runs from 1, which is a hard edged brush, to 100 which is soft. **(Figure 12.49)**

You can also use the [and] keys or scroll the mouse wheel to increase and decrease the size of the brush, and Shift-[and Shift-] keys or Shift/scroll to increase and decrease the feathering.

There are two brushes, plus an eraser, all accessed from this panel. This allows you to quickly switch between a hard and soft brush or a large and small brush, without having to constantly adjust the sliders.

To store the settings for each brush, click on **A**, adjust your brush settings for your A brush, and then click on **B** and adjust your settings for that brush too. You can quickly switch between them by clicking on the A or B button, or by using the / key.

You set the size and softness of the **Erase** brush in the same way,

WACOM TABLET

The only control designed specifically for graphics tablets is the flow/opacity of the Adjustment Brush stroke, which is controlled by the pressure sensitivity of your pen. Everything else behaves like a mouse.

except Lightroom won't allow you to select the eraser brush until you've added a brush stroke to the photo.

What's the difference between Flow & Density?

The **Flow** slider controls the rate at which the adjustment is applied.

With *Flow* at 100, the brush behaves like a paintbrush, laying down the maximum effect with each stroke. In **Figure 12.50** you can see that the effect is applied equally with each stroke.

▲ **Figure 12.50** *Flow* at 100 creates solid lines.

With *Flow* at a lower value such as 25, the brush behaves more like an airbrush, building up the effect gradually. Each stroke adds to the effect of the previous strokes, giving the effect shown in **Figure 12.51**, where areas that have multiple brushstrokes are stronger than those with a single stroke.

Density limits the maximum strength of the stroke. Regardless of how many times you paint using those brush settings, the mask can never be stronger than the maximum density setting. Unless you need the Density control for a specific purpose, I would suggest leaving it set at 100. **(Figure 12.52)**

To fully understand the difference, try creating a single 50% gray file and testing different combinations of sliders. It's easier to see the differences when you're not distracted by an image.

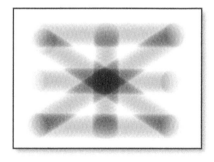

▲ **Figure 12.51** *Flow* at 25 builds up the effect gradually.

How do I erase brush strokes?

If you make a mistake when brushing, it's not a problem. Simply select the *Eraser* in the Adjustment Brush Options panel or hold down the Alt (Windows) / Opt (Mac) key to select it temporarily, and then you can erase all or part of the existing stroke. Of course, if you've just painted a stroke, Ctrl-Z (Windows) / Cmd-Z (Mac) will also undo your last action.

To delete the whole brush stroke, select the pin then press the Delete key or right-click on the pin and select **Delete**. To delete all brush strokes, press the **Reset** button.

How do I move brush strokes?

New in Lightroom CC/6, you can now move Adjustment Brush strokes by dragging the pin, just like the Graduated and Radial Filter pins.

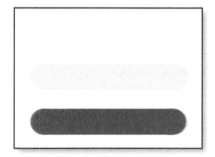

▲ **Figure 12.52** *Density* 0 (top), 25 (center) and 100 (bottom). The *Density* slider prevents the brush strokes getting any stronger than the maximum setting, regardless of how many times you paint over it.

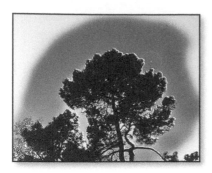

Figure 12.53 *Auto Mask* may leave a halo if you don't use it carefully.

SPECKLES

If you find speckles or dots in the brushed area, turn off *Auto Mask* and paint the area again. It can miss some odd pixels due to noise in the photo, leaving a speckled appearance.

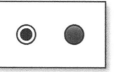

Figure 12.54 The pins have a black center when the mask is selected (left) and a gray center when the mask is not selected (right).

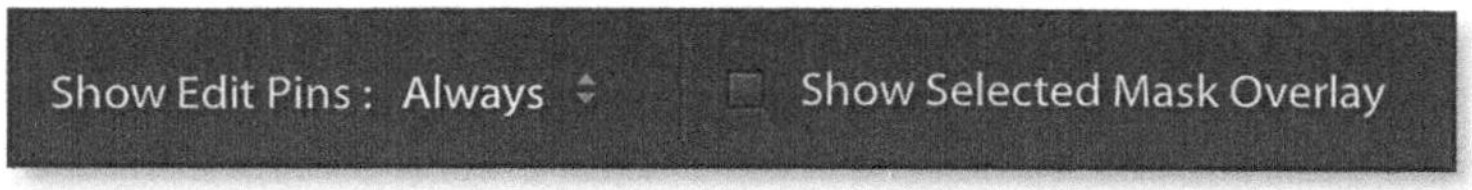

Figure 12.55 The pins and mask overlay can be turned on and off using the controls in the Toolbar.

Can I invert the mask?

You can't invert a brush mask, however you can use a large brush to paint over everything, and then use a small brush to erase from that mask. For example, you can paint the entire photo using a -100 Saturation brush to make it Black & White and then erase to show a small amount of the original color photo below.

What does Auto Mask do?

The **Auto Mask** checkbox confines your brush strokes to areas of similar color, based on the tones that the center of the brush passes over, helping to prevent your mask spilling over into other areas of the photo. For example, you can paint over a child's shirt to selectively adjust the color, without having to carefully brush around the edges.

It's very performance intensive so it may slow Lightroom down, and it can also result in some halos, for example, trying to darken a bright sky with a silhouette of a tree in the foreground may leave a halo around the edge of the tree. **(Figure 12.53)**

Auto Mask actually works better in reverse—use a large brush without Auto Mask to paint a large area first, and then enable Auto Mask while erasing areas of your mask.

Why is nothing happening when I brush over the photo?

If you're brushing over the photo and nothing seems to be happening, it's usually because either the *Flow* or *Density* sliders are set too low. If those are both set to 100, try turning on the mask overlay by pressing the O key, or move one of the sliders to an extreme value such as *Exposure +4* so you can see where you're brushing.

How do I use the pins?

Earlier in the chapter, we mentioned that your gradient or brush masks are each marked with small circles called Pins. The mask pins have two states—selected or not selected, or active and inactive. Not selected is shown by a gray pin, and clicking on the pin selects that mask, turning the pins black with a white border. **(Figure 12.54)** Once your existing mask is reselected, you can adjust the sliders to change the effect, or go back and edit the mask itself.

If you find the pins and the gradient lines distracting, you can change

Show Edit Pins : Always ◆   ☐ Show Selected Mask Overlay

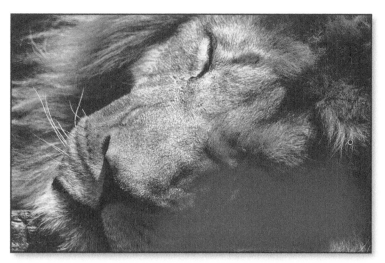

Figure 12.56 The red Mask Overlay highlights the masked area.

their view options. Under *Tools menu > Tool Overlay*, you have the option to *Auto Show* which only shows the pin when you float the mouse nearby, as well as *Always Show, Show Selected* and *Never Show*. You'll also find those options in the **Show Edit Pins** pop-up on the Toolbar while the local adjustment tools are active. **(Figure 12.55)**

How do I use the mask overlay?

The adjustment mask overlay is a colored mask that shows the location and opacity of your brush strokes or gradient.

To show the mask, check the **Show Selected Mask Overlay** checkbox on the Toolbar (or under *Tools menu > Adjustment Mask Overlay*) or press the O key to toggle it on and off. If the pin's deselected (gray), you can just hover the cursor over the pin to view the mask. **(Figure 12.56)**

By default, it's a red mask, but you can select red, green, lighten or darken using the *Tools menu > Adjustment Mask Overlay* or by pressing Shift-O to cycle through the options. There's a choice because some colors are more visible on specific photos than others. For example, the lighten mode isn't much help on a snow scene!

How do I fade the effect of an existing mask?

When you come to edit a mask, you may want to increase or fade the effect of your adjustments. You can adjust each of the individual sliders separately, but if you've applied a lot of different adjustments, you may prefer to use the *Amount* slider to adjust them all in one go.

Click the disclosure triangle to the right of the *Presets* pop-up menu to switch between a combined **Amount** slider and the more advanced

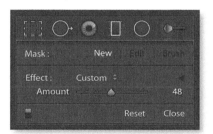

Figure 12.57 The disclosure triangle hides the individual sliders and shows a single *Amount* slider.

Figure 12.58 Hold down the Alt or Opt key and drag over the mask pin to change the *Amount* without visiting the Options panel.

slider mode. The *Amount* slider increases or decreases the strength of all the adjustments on the selected mask, with all the sliders being adjusted by the same percentage of change. **(Figure 12.57)**

You can access the same *Amount* control without having to click on the disclosure triangle, by holding down the Alt (Windows) / Opt (Mac) key while floating over the active pin. The cursor changes to a double headed arrow, and clicking and dragging left and right increases and decreases the *Amount* slider. **(Figure 12.58)**

Hold down the Alt/Opt key while floating over the pin to adjust all of the slider amounts in one go.

Can I duplicate the masks? And layer the effect of multiple masks?

If you've reached the limit of a slider, you may want to duplicate the mask. To do so, right-click on the pin and select **Duplicate**. You can then edit the new pin's settings separately.

You can create as many different masks as you like, and they can be overlapped and layered, with the effect being cumulative.

How do I set default slider settings?

If you're editing a set of photos that need the same adjustments, it can be irritating to have to reselect the slider values for each new photo and pin, but to save time, you can save the settings as new defaults. To do so, select one of the local adjustment tools, make sure the Options panel is set to *New* rather than *Edit* mode, and adjust the sliders to your new chosen defaults. Lightroom remembers these settings and uses them for any new Graduated Filters, Radial Filters or Adjustment Brush strokes, until you next repeat the process.

How do I save sets of slider settings as a preset?

In the Fast Track, we also mentioned local adjustment presets, which simply move the sliders to preset positions. Lightroom ships with some built in presets. If the default presets disappear, select *Restore Default Presets* from the **Effect** pop-up.

You can also save your own presets of settings you use regularly. To do so, set your chosen slider settings, and then select *Save Current Settings as New Preset* from the *Effect* pop-up menu. Your new preset appears in the pop-up, ready to select. Like the other pop-up menus through the program, you have to select the preset in the pop-up to show the *Rename*, *Update* and *Delete* options.

LOCAL ADJUSTMENT SLIDERS

The Local Adjustments can make localized changes to *Temperature, Tint, Exposure, Contrast, Highlights, Shadows, Clarity, Saturation, Sharpness, Noise Reduction, Moiré Reduction, Defringe* and apply a *Color Tint* for PV2012 photos.

Older PV2010 photos only have access to *Exposure, Brightness, Contrast, Saturation, Clarity, Sharpness* or *Color Tint*, but updating them to PV2012 allows access to all the sliders.

Can I save brush strokes or gradients as presets?

If you've created your ideal off-center vignette, or another Graduated or Radial Filter, you can save it as a Develop Preset for use on other photos. To do so, click on the + button on the Presets panel and press *Check None* to clear the checkboxes. Check the *Graduated Filter* and/or *Radial Filter* checkboxes and give the preset a name, then press *Create*. Your preset appears in the Presets panel. We'll come back to Presets in more detail in the Develop Module Tools chapter on page 301.

Lightroom doesn't allow you to save brush strokes in a preset, although you can sync or copy/paste the masks across multiple photos.

Let's explore the sliders and some practical applications...

Iris Enhance

To brighten the eyes, select the *Iris Enhance* preset from the *Effect* pop-up and brush over the iris of the eye. **(Figure 12.59)**

Soften Skin

The *Soften Skin* preset allows you to soften the skin without affecting the rest of the photo. Brush it over the face, avoiding the eyes, eyebrows, nose, mouth, hair and clothing. **(Figure 12.60)**

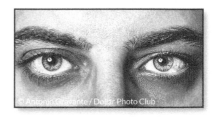

Figure 12.59 The *Iris Enhance* preset brightens the iris of the eye. The blood shot look can be reduced using the adjustment brush set to positive *Exposure*, positive *Shadows* and negative *Saturation*.

Figure 12.60 The *Soften Skin* preset allows you to soften the skin without affecting the eyes, nose, mouth, hair or clothing.

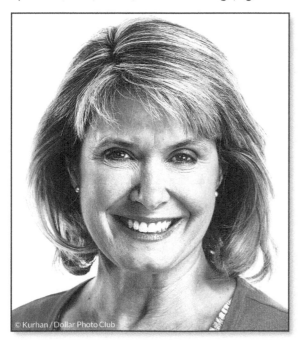

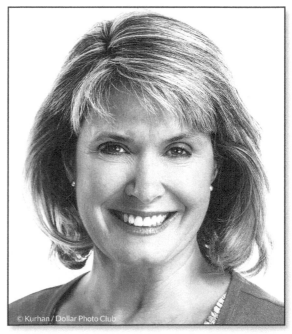

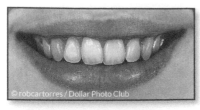

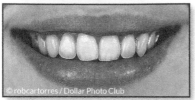

▲ **Figure 12.61** Clean up yellowing teeth using the *Teeth Whitening* preset.

Teeth Whitening

The *Teeth Whitening* preset in the *Effect* pop-up whitens yellowing teeth, although you may need to increase or decrease the *Exposure* slider to suit the photo. **(Figure 12.61)**

White Balance Adjustments

The *Temp* and *Tint* sliders allow you to apply different white balance settings to different areas of the photo. This is particularly useful when correcting photos shot in mixed lighting.

Tone Adjustments

One of the most logical uses for local adjustments are tonal changes—*Exposure, Contrast, Highlights* and *Shadows*. They can use for darkening skies, off center vignettes, brightening shadows, reducing bright highlights and many other adjustments. **(Figure 12.62 & 12.63)**

Vibrance vs. Saturation

The *Saturation* slider is a cross between intelligent *Vibrance* and linear *Saturation*. Positive values behave like + *Vibrance* in the Basic panel, but negative values behave like - *Saturation*, completely desaturating the photo. Negative *Saturation* is useful for creating B&W photos with spot color.

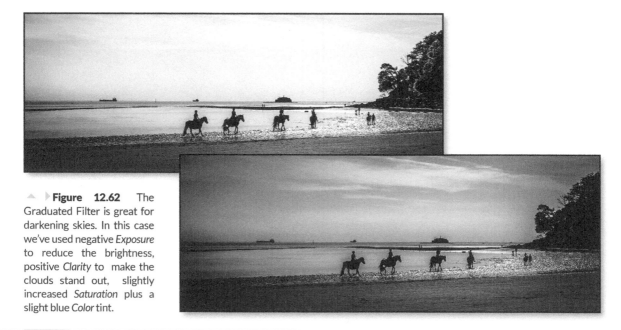

▲ ▶ **Figure 12.62** The Graduated Filter is great for darkening skies. In this case we've used negative *Exposure* to reduce the brightness, positive *Clarity* to make the clouds stand out, slightly increased *Saturation* plus a slight blue *Color* tint.

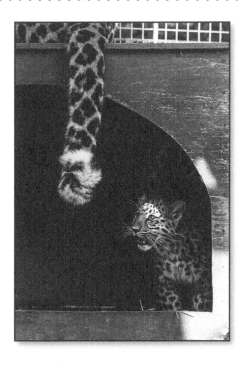

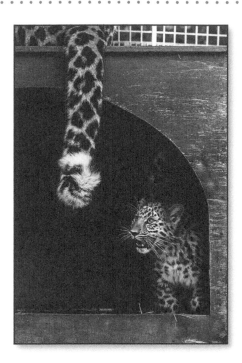

◁ ▷ **F i g u r e 12.63** The light falling through the trees is distracting on the kennel walls. An adjustment brush set to negative *Exposure* helps to remove the distraction.

The light on the leopard cub's face is also uneven. A mixture of *Exposure*, *Highlights* and *Saturation* pulls back the light and dark areas to even it out.

Selective Sharpening & Clarity

The Sharpening slider can be used to selecting increase or decrease the sharpening applied to specific areas of the photo, for example, the eyes of a portrait often benefit from a little extra sharpening.

The local adjustments only affect the *Amount* of sharpening, and the *Radius*, *Detail* and *Masking* settings remain identical across the photo, using the settings selected in the Detail panel.

The *Clarity* slider allows you to add local midtone contrast, which is particularly useful for the clouds in the sky.

Add Lens Blur

If you set the *Sharpening* slider to between -50 and -100, it applies a blur similar to a lens blur, allowing you to blur the background of a photo. It's very processor intensive, so it can be slow. Negative *Clarity* gives a slightly different softening effect.

Selective Noise Reduction

The *Noise* slider in the Local Adjustments panels should be called Noise Reduction, but there's not enough space, particularly in some languages. When you paint with a negative noise value, it doesn't

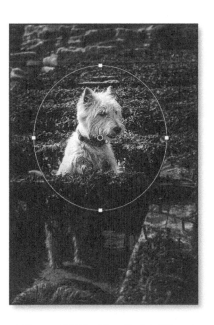

△ **Figure 12.64** The Radial Filter is ideal for off-center vignettes. In this case we've used negative *Exposure*, negative *Highlights* and negative *Sharpening*.

add noise, but it reduces or removes any global noise reduction that you've applied or other noise reduction brushstrokes.

Reduce Moiré

Moiré is a rainbow-like pattern which is often seen when photographing fabrics. It's caused by two patterns combining—in this case, the weave in fabric and the grid of the camera sensor—which creates a new pattern.

The *Moiré* removal slider in the Adjustment Brush allows you to paint the moiré rainbow away. It can only usually remove the color rainbow, not any luminosity changes, but it works very well. It works on both raw and rendered photos, although the additional data in a raw file means that it is far more effective on raw files.

To use it, select a plus value on the *Moiré* slider, ensure that you've turned off *Auto Mask*, and brush over the pattern. If you cross a boundary of another color in the photo, it can blur or smudge, so it's best to use a hard edged brush (*Feather*=0) and be careful where you brush. **(Figure 12.65)** This gives the cleanest result without any side effects. If you set the *Moiré* slider to a negative value, it won't do anything—it's only used to reduce the effect of another brush stroke which already has positive moiré removal applied.

Defringe

The *Defringe* sliders remove color fringing. We'll come back to these in the Lens Corrections section starting on page 273.

Add a Color Tint

To select a color tint from the photo, first click on the *Color* icon to bring up the Color Picker. Select your chosen color from the gradient.

To select a color from the photo, click in the Color Picker and while holding the mouse button down, drag the cursor onto the photo. As you drag across the photo, the Color Picker updates live to reflect the color beneath your cursor. When you release the mouse button, the color under the cursor is selected in the Color Picker.

To clear the tint, double-click on the *Color* label and the *Color* box changes to a white box with a cross in it to show it's disabled.

Black and white aren't available in the color tint section, but you can set the *Exposure* to +4 for white or −4 for *Black*. If the effect isn't strong enough, you can duplicate the mask by right-clicking on the pin.

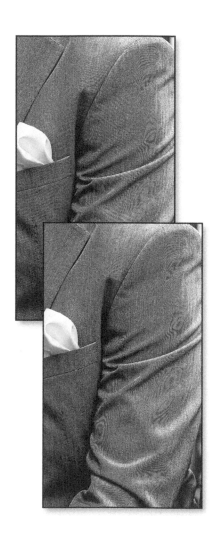

Figure 12.65 Moiré causes a colored pattern on the image (left) but it can be fixed using the *Moiré* slider and the Adjustment Brush (right).

LOCAL ADJUSTMENT SHORTCUTS

Show Overlay	O
Cycle Overlay Color	Shift O
Hide Pins and Bounding Boxes/Lines (Toggle Auto Show/Never Show	H
Delete Pin	Select pin then Delete
Increase or decrease Amount slider	Alt / Opt click and drag horizontally on pin
Apply & dismiss Radial Filter tool	Double-click

GRADUATED FILTER SHORTCUTS

Go to Graduated Filter	M
Create New	Click and drag
Duplicate Graduated Filter Pin	Hold Ctrl Alt / Cmd Opt while dragging pin
Edit Existing (extend/contract)	Click and drag outer lines
Edit Existing (rotate)	Click and drag center line
Edit Existing (move)	Click and drag pin
Constrain Gradient to 90 degrees	Shift while dragging
Invert Graduated Filter Mask	' (apostrophe)

RADIAL FILTER SHORTCUTS

Go to Radial Filter	Shift M
Create New (scaled from center)	Click and drag
Create New (scale from starting point)	Alt / Opt while dragging
Create New (constrain to circle)	Shift while dragging
Create New (scale from starting point and constrain to circle)	Alt Shift / Opt Shift while dragging
Create New (constrain to crop bounds)	Ctrl / Cmd double-click
Duplicate Radial Filter Pin	Hold Ctrl Alt / Cmd Opt while dragging pin
Edit Existing (opposite sides move)	Click and drag edge
Edit Existing (selected side moves)	Alt / Opt while dragging edge
Edit Existing (constrain to existing aspect ratio)	Shift while dragging edge
Edit Existing (expands 3 nearest sides)	Alt Shift / Opt Shift while dragging edge
Edit Existing (maximize to crop bounds)	Ctrl / Cmd double-click within ellipsis
Edit Existing (move)	Click and drag pin

Invert Radial Filter Mask	' (apostrophe)

ADJUSTMENT BRUSH SHORTCUTS

Go to Adjustment Brush	K
Paint brush stroke	Click and drag
Switch brush A / B	/
Temporary Eraser	Hold Alt / Opt
Increase brush size	]
Decrease brush size	[
Increase brush feathering	Shift]
Decrease brush feathering	Shift [
Toggle Auto Mask	A
Set Flow value	0-9
Constrain Brush to Straight Line	Shift while clicking or dragging
Duplicate Brush Pin	Hold Ctrl Alt / Cmd Opt and click on the pin
Confirm brush stroke	Enter/Return

DEVELOP ADVANCED EDITING

We've explored the Basic panel and selective adjustments, but there are plenty of extra panels with advanced controls yet to investigate. They include selective color and contrast adjustments, advanced sharpening and noise reduction, lens and perspective corrections, and special effects.

TONE CURVES

Below the Basic panel is the Tone Curve panel. Like the Basic panel, it allows you to lighten or darken the tones in your photo. The sliders even have similar names: *Highlights, Lights, Darks* and *Shadows*. That's where the similarities end, as the behavior can be quite different.

How do I read a tone curve?

The first thing you'll see when you look at the Tone Curve panel is the 4x4 grid which holds the tone curve.

Along the horizontal (x/input) axis are all the possible tones, with black (0%) on the left and white (100%) on the right. You'll spot the histogram showing faintly in the background.

The vertical (y/output) axis represents the adjustments you make using the Tone Curve.

The tone curve starts as a straight diagonal line, with no changes being applied to the photo. **(Figure 13.1)** Moving the line up makes the tones lighter, and moving down makes the tones darker.

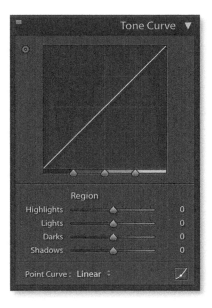

Figure 13.1 Before adjustment, the Tone Curve is a straight line.

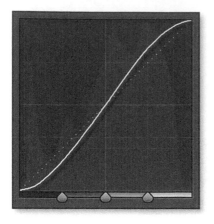

Figure 13.2 A typical S shaped tone curve adds contrast.

Why use curves?

Tone Curves are primarily used for controlling brightness and contrast in specific tonal ranges. The steeper the angle of the curve, the higher the contrast becomes. When the curve gets steeper, increasing the contrast in one range of tones (e.g. the shadows), it gets shallower in another range of tones (e.g. the highlights), decreasing the contrast in that range. It allows you to control where you're willing to sacrifice contrast to gain it in other areas.

The most frequently used curve is an S shape, which increases midtone contrast by lightening the highlights and darkening the shadows. **(Figure 13.2)** The middle of the curve becomes steeper, giving the midtones greater contrast, while the highlights and shadows become shallower with less contrast. **(Figure 13.3)**

How are Tone Curves different to the Basic panel?

So you might be wondering how that's different to the Basic panel. After all, you can lighten the highlights using the *Highlights* sliders and darken the shadows using the *Shadows* slider.

Remember we said that the *Highlights* and *Shadows* sliders in the Basic panel build a mask to limit the effect of the slider to part of the tonal range. This means that brightening the shadows has the greatest effect on the darkest shadows, tapering off to a minimal effect on the highlights and vice versa. **(Figure 13.5)**

The tone curve doesn't build a mask. There's always a trade-off. If you increase the shadows to see more detail, you also brighten the highlights. If you then pull the the highlights back down, you flatten the

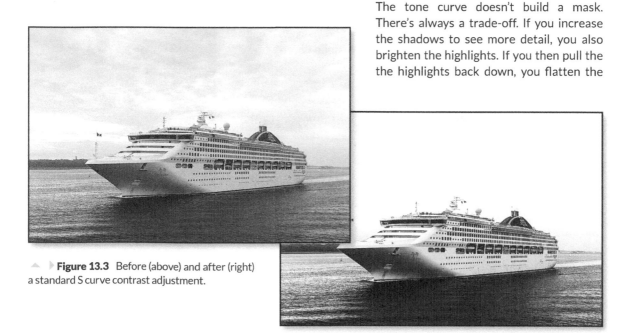

Figure 13.3 Before (above) and after (right) a standard S curve contrast adjustment.

contrast in the midtones. **(Figure 13.4)** This doesn't mean it's a bad tool to use, but it's different.

You might also compare the tone curve to the *Contrast* slider in the Basic panel, which creates a simple S curve behind the scenes. You can create an identical S curve using the Tone Curve panel, but the tone curve gives you much greater control. Depending on the content of the photo, you can decide which range of tones need more contrast and which tones can be safely compressed.

As a rule of thumb, the Basic panel does the heavy-lifting—the major adjustments—and the Tone Curve is usually used for fine tuning. (Rules are, of course, made to be broken, so feel free to experiment!)

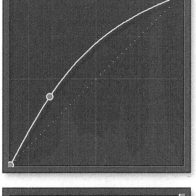

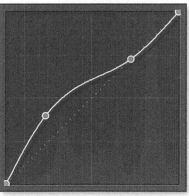

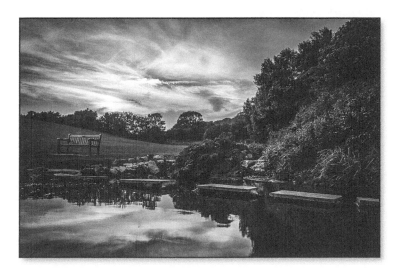

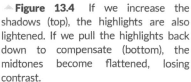
Figure 13.4 If we increase the shadows (top), the highlights are also lightened. If we pull the highlights back down to compensate (bottom), the midtones become flattened, losing contrast.

Figure 13.5 Using the Tone Curve to pull back highlight and shadow detail reduces the midtone contrast (top), whereas the Highlights and Shadows sliders retain the contrast (bottom).

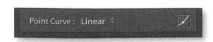

Figure 13.6 The point curve is accessed using the button in the bottom right corner of the Tone Curve panel.

MISSING SLIDERS

If you're missing the Tone Curve sliders, you're viewing the point curve interface, so press the point curve button to return to the parametric curves.

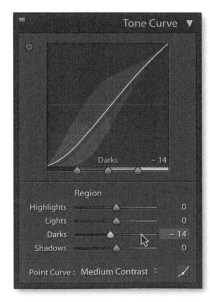

Figure 13.7 When you float over a slider, the maximum adjustment limits are highlighted on the curve.

What's the difference between the parametric curve and the point curve?

Lightroom offers two different tone curves: a parametric curve and a point curve.

The parametric tone curve is the default view, and it allows you to adjust sections of the curve rather than individual points. It protects the photo from extreme adjustments, so it's generally considered the easier option.

The point curve interface is usually used by advanced users, or those familiar with Photoshop's curves dialog. It gives you full control over the curve, including the individual RGB channels. **(Figure 13.6)**

Point curves aren't necessarily an alternative to the parametric curves. You may be more comfortable with one or the other, but both curves are active at the same time and the effect is cumulative.

How do I adjust the standard parametric tone curve?

To adjust the parametric tone curve, click and drag up and down on the curve itself or adjust the sliders below. For example, to darken the darker midtones tones in a photo, you'd click between the 25% and 50% gridlines and drag downwards. You could also drag the *Darks* slider to the left to get the same result. The gray highlighted section shows the maximum range of movement for that slider.

How do I use the Targeted Adjustment Tool?

The easiest and most intuitive option is to use the TAT tool, which stands for Targeted Adjustment Tool. It's available for both the parametric and point curve.

1. Click the circle icon in the top left corner of the panel to select it.

2. Float the cursor over the photo. As you float, a small circle displays on the curve, showing which section of the curve you'll be adjusting, but you don't need to take too much notice of the curve. Just focus on the photo itself. **(Figure 13.7)**

3. Click on the image and drag up to make the tones lighter or down to make the tones darker. For example, to darken the shadows, click and drag downwards on a shadowy area of the photo until you're happy with the result.

    Alternatively, you can hover the TAT cursor over the shadows in the photo and press the Up/Down keys on your keyboard to adjust it.

TAT, OR TARGETED ADJUSTMENT TOOL

Appearing in the Tone Curve, Hue, Saturation, Luminance and B&W panels, the Targeted Adjustment tool, or TAT for short, allows you to directly control the sliders by dragging on the photo itself. It means you can concentrate on the actual photo rather than the sliders, and saves you having to work out which sliders you need to adjust for a specific color or tone. This rather unobtrusive little tool is a real gem! **(Figure 13.8)**

Figure 13.8 The TAT, or Targeted Adjustment tool, appears in the top left corner of the Tone Curve, HSL, Color & B&W panels.

4. Repeat on other tones in the image, for example, drag upwards on a light area to make the highlights lighter.

5. Once you've finished, just press Escape or return the tool to its base in the corner of the panel

What are the triangles at the bottom of the parametric tone curve?

At the bottom of the parametric tone curve are three triangles called split points. **(Figure 13.9)** They define the tonal range for each of the sliders. For example, if you've used the *Lights* and *Darks* sliders to create strong midtone contrast, you may move the 25% and 75% split points out to restrict the flattened contrast to the lightest highlights and the deepest shadows. Double-clicking on any of those triangles resets it to the default position.

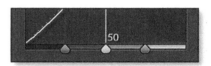

Figure 13.9 The split point triangles at the bottom of the curve control how much of the tonal range is affected by each slider.

TARGETED ADJUSTMENT TOOL SHORTCUTS

Deselect TAT	Ctrl Alt Shift N / Cmd Opt Shift N
Tone Curve	Ctrl Alt Shift T / Cmd Opt Shift T
Hue	Ctrl Alt Shift H / Cmd Opt Shift H
Saturation	Ctrl Alt Shift S / Cmd Opt Shift S
Luminance	Ctrl Alt Shift L / Cmd Opt Shift L
Black & White Mix	Ctrl Alt Shift G / Cmd Opt Shift G

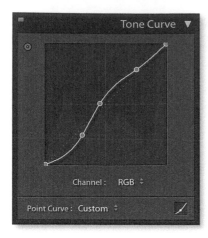

▲ **Figure 13.10** The point curve allows you to create a freeform curve.

How do I use the point curve?

To adjust the point curve, click the small button to the right of the *Point Curve* pop-up menu to switch to the point curve interface. The sliders disappear and you're left with a basic curve.

Click anywhere on the curve line to add a control point, and then drag it up or down to adjust the photo.

Like the parametric curve, the TAT tool makes it easy to work out where on the curve to place an additional point. Be careful not to place too many points as extreme twists and turns in the curve can create posterization (banding) in the photo. **(Figure 13.10)**

Unlike Photoshop, you can't use the keyboard to adjust the points, but holding down the Alt (Windows) / Opt (Mac) key while dragging slows the movement.

To remove a point, drag it off the left or right edge of the grid or right-click and choose *Delete Control Point*. To reset the entire curve, remove all of the individual points or right-click and select *Flatten Curve*.

You can also access RGB curves in the same point curve interface (PV2012 photos only) using **Channel** pop-up. The individual red, green and blue curves are particularly useful for adjusting colors in rendered files such as scans. Where color casts differ between the highlights and shadows—perhaps where the overall color is correct but the shadows have a magenta tinge—normal white balance adjustments would be unable to fix it, but RGB curves allow you detailed control over each channel.

The **Point Curve** pop-up holds point curve presets which are shared with Camera Raw (ACR) in Photoshop. *Linear* is the default for PV2012 photos, but two more legacy presets—*Medium Contrast* and *Strong Contrast*—also add a slight S curve. To save your own point curve as a preset, select *Save* from the pop-up. (You can also save it as a normal Develop preset.) Unlike most of the preset pop-ups, you can't update, rename or delete the point curve presets from within Lightroom. Instead, you must find them in the Camera Raw user folder (page 550) using Explorer (Windows) / Finder (Mac) and delete them manually.

INVERT NEGATIVE

To invert the photo, select the point curve and drag the left point to the top left corner and the right point to the bottom right corner. It's handy for negative scans as well as special effects. Don't forget to save it as a preset, as it's tricky to get the points in the right place.

B&W & SPLIT TONES

Black and white photography is an art in its own right, and Lightroom offers great control, not only over the contrast of the B&W photo, but also the way the colors are mixed. Even if you've never tried B&W photography, now's the time to start. Some photos look far better in black & white than they do in color, and it can also help rescue photos that are very underexposed or overexposed.

Converting your photo to black and white is very simple—just press the V key or select **Treatment: Black & White** at the top of the Basic panel. **(Figure 13.11)** Lightroom creates a basic black & white photo, which you can then fine tune by adjusting the way the colors are mixed and tweaking the contrast.

CONTINUES ON PAGE 268

How do I the change the color mix for a black & white photo?

Go to the B&W panel **(Figure 13.12)** and click on the Targeted Adjustment Tool in the top left corner to select it. The TAT tool allows you to adjust the B&W mix visually by dragging directly on the photo, while it figures out which sliders to move.

Find an area of the photo that you'd like to be darker—perhaps the blue sky—and click and drag down on that area. As you drag, the blue tones get darker and the sliders in the B&W panel move. Find another color in the photo that you'd like to be lighter—perhaps something red—and as you click and drag up the red tones lighten.

You may also want to adjust the contrast to better suit the B&W version of the photo using the Basic or Tone Curve panel.

By default, the B&W slider mix is set automatically, depending on the content of the photo, and these settings are often a great starting point. If you'd prefer to start from 0 for each new B&W conversion, go to *Preferences > Presets tab* and uncheck **Apply auto mix when first converting to black and white**. To quickly reset the auto settings on existing photos, double-click or Alt-click (Windows) / Opt-click (Mac) on the **Black & White Mix** label.

The auto mix varies depending on your current white balance, so you can create some interesting variations by adjusting the white balance and then pressing the **Auto** button in the B&W panel.

How do I create a sepia photo?

To create a great sepia or softly-toned black and white photo, first convert the photo to B&W. In the Split Toning panel set the *Hue*

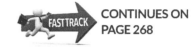

Figure 13.11 Convert to B&W using the button at the top of the Basic panel.

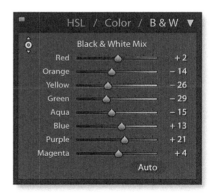

Figure 13.12 Fine tune the B&W channel mix using the B&W panel.

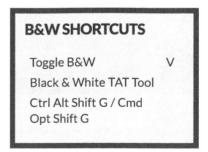

B&W SHORTCUTS

Toggle B&W   V

Black & White TAT Tool

Ctrl Alt Shift G / Cmd Opt Shift G

INFRARED

If you don't own an infrared-converted camera, you can create some infrared-style effects using Lightroom. There are many styles of infrared photography, but the most popular has three main traits: blue sky is very dark, green foliage is white, and it has a slight glow.

To create something similar in Lightroom, try this:

1. Switch to *B&W* at the top of the Basic panel.

2. In the B&W panel, increase *Yellow* and *Green* to +100 and reduce *Blue* to -100.

3. In the Basic panel, move the *Temp* and *Tint* sliders to the left. The exact value depends on each individual photo.

4. Set *Clarity* to a negative value to create the glow, for example, -40.

5. Save it as a preset for use on other photos. (But note that they're extreme adjustments, so they work better on raw files than JPEGs).

If you do own an infrared-converted camera, Lightroom's white balance sliders can't handle the extreme values by default. To solve this, open an infrared DNG file using the DNG Profile Editor and on the *Color Matrices* tab, move the *Temp* slider to around -75 to -100, making the foliage as neutral as possible. Export the profile, then restart Lightroom and select the new profile in the Camera Calibration panel. Use the white balance eyedropper to click on green foliage (or something else that should be white), then edit as usual. You can learn more about the DNG Profile Editor in the Appendix starting on page A-16.

sliders to around 40 to 50, and then adjust the *Saturation* sliders to increase or decrease the strength of the effect.

To get you started, there's a *Sepia Tone* preset in the *Lightroom B&W Toned Presets* folder in the Presets panel, but let's take a closer look at the Split Toning panel.

How do I use the Split Toning panel?

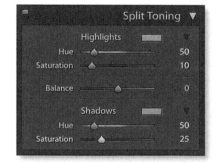

▲ **Figure 13.13** The Split Toning panel creates sepia or other toned photos, or even cross-processed effects.

The Split Toning panel is primarily designed for effects such as toned black & whites and cross-processed color. **(Figure 13.13)** There are two pairs of **Hue** and **Saturation** sliders. The first pair affect the color of the highlights in the photo and the second pair affect the shadows. The **Balance** slider in the center balances the effect between the highlights and the shadows

You can manually adjust the *Hue* and *Saturation* sliders to choose the tone, but it's easier to click on the color swatch rectangle and select your chosen color using the Color Picker. **(Figure 13.14)**

As you tweak the *Hue* slider, holding down the Alt key (Windows) / Opt key (Mac) displays a heavily saturated version to help you decide on the perfect color. Holding it down while moving the *Balance* slider

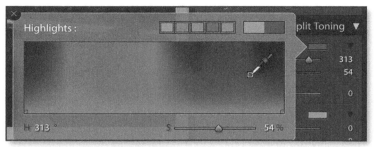

Figure 13.14 Click on the color rectangle for *Highlights* or *Shadows* to access the Color Picker.

displays a red and green mix, so you can see which areas of the photo are affected by the *Highlights* sliders and which are affected by the *Shadows* sliders.

The number of combinations are almost endless, although some look better than others! If you're just starting to experiment with cross-processing and toned black & whites, there are many free presets to give you ideas. **(Figure 13.15)** There are some built in to Lightroom, for example, those in the Lightroom B&W Toned Presets and Lightroom Color Presets sets in the Presets panel.

How do I create a B&W photo with some areas in color?

There's a technique which is often called B&W with Spot Color. It's a B&W photo with a small area of the photo in its original color. It's possible to reproduce this in Lightroom using the Adjustment Brush, although you have little control over the B&W conversion. First, make Develop adjustments to create a good color version. Then select a large adjustment brush set to −100 *Saturation*, and paint over the entire photo to make it all B&W. Finally, switch the brush to a smaller eraser and erase the B&W brush stroke to bring back the spot color.

THE COLOR PICKER

The Color Picker is used throughout Lightroom. The main gradient shows a full range of colors, and the eye-dropper selects your chosen color. You can also select a color from the photo or any-where else on the screen by clicking in the gradient and dragging the eyedropper onto the photo. Along the top of the Color Picker are swatch-es or presets. When you find a color you like, you can save it as a swatch by Alt-click-ing (Windows) / Opt-clicking (Mac) on one of the swatches.

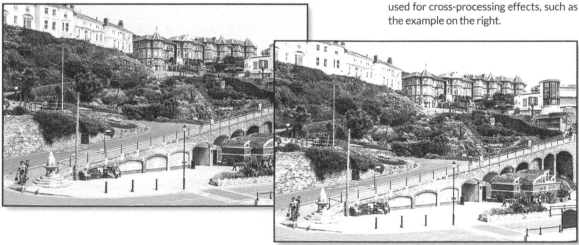

Figure 13.15 The Split Toning panel is used for cross-processing effects, such as the example on the right.

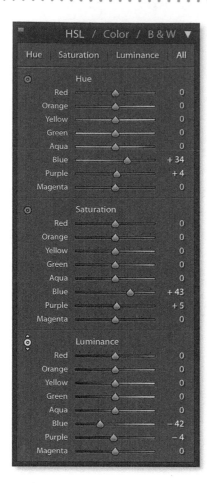

Figure 13.16 HSL adjustments target specific colors.

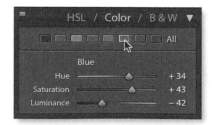

Figure 13.17 The Color panel shows the HSL sliders in a different format.

HSL & COLOR

The HSL and Color panels can look slightly daunting to start with, as there is a multitude of sliders divided into separate tabs. They allow for much finer adjustments of specific colors in your photos.

What are the HSL and Color panels used for?

They allow you to adjust the colors in your photo.

- H stands for **Hue**, which is the color.

- S stands for **Saturation**, which is the purity or intensity of the color.

- L stands for **Luminance**, which is the brightness of the color.

The tabs at the top of the HSL panel change the view, displaying the *Hue* sliders, *Saturation* sliders, *Luminance* sliders or all of the sliders in a single view. **(Figure 13.16)**

The sliders are tinted to help you remember how the color will change, for example, moving the *Red Saturation* slider to the left reduces the saturation of the reds in the photo.

In the top left corner of the panel is the TAT tool, like the one used in the Tone Curve panel. It's particularly useful when working with HSL, as color in your photo is usually affected by more than one slider. The grass may not be green, but a mix of green and yellow.

The Color panel works in exactly the same way. **(Figure 13.17)** They're the same tools laid out differently. The *Hue*, *Saturation* and *Luminance* sliders are grouped for each color, with the color options along the top.

When would I use HSL and Color?

HSL is particularly useful when your white balance is perfect but you want to enhance particular colors. For example, if you have some grass in your photo, moving the *Green* slider to the left makes that grass more yellow, without affecting the reds significantly. If someone's skin is too pink, you may need to adjust a few of these sliders, including the *Magenta* and *Red* sliders.

Rather than having to work out which combination of sliders to adjust, the TAT tool allows you to drag directly on the photo and it calculates which sliders need to be adjusted. **(Figure 13.18)** The **Target Group** pop-up in the Toolbar controls whether the TAT tool affects the hue, saturation or luminance slider for that color. **(Figure 13.19)**

My favorite use of the TAT tool and the HSL panel is for a quick blue sky fix. When brightening a photo causes those beautiful blue skies and white fluffy clouds to become too light, select the TAT tool, set it to *Luminance* in the pop-up (or select the *Luminance* tab in the HSL panel), and click on the blue sky and drag downwards to darken the sky. You may want to switch to *Saturation* and drag upwards to increase the blue too. Don't go too far, as you'll start to introduce noise, but it's a quick fix. **(Figure 13.20)**

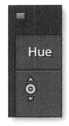

Figure 13.18 The HSL TAT tool is the easiest way to select the right mix of sliders.

HSL SHORTCUTS

Deselect TAT	Ctrl Alt Shift N / Cmd Opt Shift N
Hue	Ctrl Alt Shift H / Cmd Opt Shift H
Saturation	Ctrl Alt Shift S / Cmd Opt Shift S
Luminance	Ctrl Alt Shift L / Cmd Opt Shift L

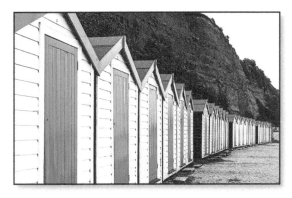

Figure 13.19 HSL *Hue* adjustments can be used to change colors, such as the blue/purple color in these beach huts.

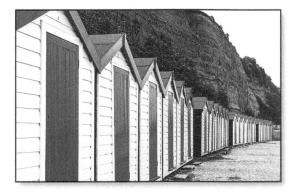

Figure 13.20 HSL adjustments are a quick way to create deeper blue skies.

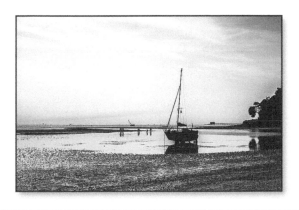

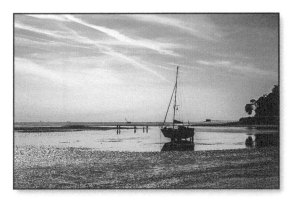

DETAIL—SHARPENING & NOISE REDUCTION

Most digital photographs require some degree of sharpening, and although camera sensors are improving, most high ISO photos also benefit from noise reduction. Some even say that the quality of the sharpening can make or break an image. Lightroom's Detail panel contains advanced tools to improve your photos. **(Figure 13.21)**

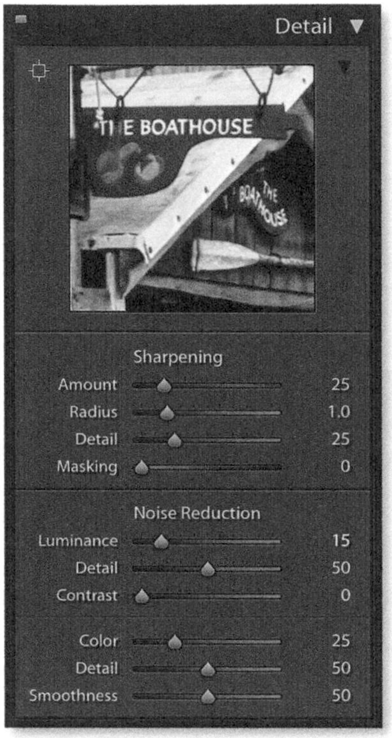

Fixing Noisy or Soft Photos

In the *Sharpening* section of the Detail panel, the *Amount* slider controls the amount of sharpening applied. The default settings are an excellent starting point and you may be satisfied with these settings. If you want to experiment further, try the sharpening presets found in the Presets panel. We'll come back to the other sliders in more detail shortly.

Noise in your photos can be distracting. You'll particularly notice it in photos shot at high ISO, for example, shot without flash in a darkened room. If you've increased the exposure considerably within Lightroom, it can also increase the appearance of noise. Fortunately, Lightroom's Noise Reduction tools are excellent.

If you're working on raw files, try a setting of around 15-20 *Luminance* as a starting point. This reduces the noise without losing too much image detail. The aim is to reduce the noise, rather than making the subject look like plastic, so don't push it too far. JPEGs may have already had some noise reduction applied by the camera, so you'll need a lower value for these.

Figure 13.21 Sharpening and Noise Reduction are applied using the Detail panel.

ZOOM TO 100%

When adjusting the sharpening or noise reduction on your photos, it's important to zoom into 1:1 view by clicking the 1:1 icon on the top of the Navigator panel. Other zoom ratios aren't as accurate.

The Detail Preview, which can be hidden using the disclosure triangle to its right, always displays a 1:1 view. If you select on the square spiky icon to the left of the preview and then click on the photo, you can choose which section of the photo to preview.

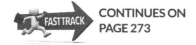

CONTINUES ON PAGE 273

What is multiple pass sharpening?

Lightroom's sharpening is based on Bruce Fraser's multiple pass sharpening techniques. The sharpening is done in stages:

- **Capture sharpening** is intended to offset the inherent softness caused by digital capture and the demosaicing that's done by the raw converter, and it's done using the sliders in the Detail panel.

- **Creative sharpening** is usually applied to specific parts of the photo, for example, the eyes in a portrait. Clarity and the sharpening in the Local Adjustments would be classed as creative sharpening.

- **Output sharpening** is the last stage, depending on whether the photos are viewed on screen, inkjet print, photographic print or a variety of other presentation options. The sharpening applied in the Export dialog or Print module would be classed as output sharpening, as it's calculated based on the output size and type.

How do the sharpening sliders interact?

Let's take a closer look at the individual sharpening sliders and how they interact...

Digital image sharpening works in two ways.

- **USM**, or unsharp mask, works by creating small halos along edges to make them appear sharper. On the dark side of an edge it creates a darker halo, and on the light side of an edge it makes a lighter halo.

- **Deconvolution** sharpening attempts to calculate and reverse the cause of the blurring.

Lightroom uses both kinds of sharpening, balanced using the *Detail* slider.

- *Amount* works like a volume control. It runs from 0-150, with a default of 25 for raw files or 0 for JPEGs, as the JPEGs may have been sharpened in the camera. The higher the value, the more sharpening applied. You won't usually want to use it at 150 unless you're combining it with the masking or detail sliders which suppress the sharpening.

- *Radius* affects the width of the sharpening halo. It runs from 0.5-3, with a default of 1.0. Photos with fine detail need a smaller radius, as do landscapes, but a slightly higher radius can look good on portraits.

Detail and *Masking* are dampening controls, allowing you to control

---

ZERO IS REALLY ZERO

When Lightroom's sharpening and noise reduction sliders are at 0, these tools are disabled, whereas many other programs apply additional sharpening and noise reduction behind the scenes, even with their tools set to 0.

X-TRANS SHARPENING

Fuji X-Trans sensors benefit from a much higher *Detail* setting than conventional sensors, even going as high as 80-100 in some cases.

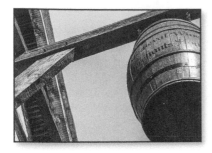

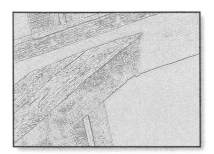

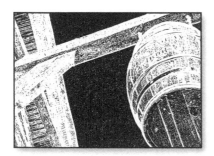

▲ **Figure 13.22** Holding down the Alt (Windows) key / Opt key (Mac) while moving a slider shows a mask to make it easier to select the right slider value. *Amount* mask (first), *Radius* mask (second), *Detail* mask (third), *Masking* mask (fourth).

which areas get the most sharpening applied and which areas are protected, but there's a difference in the way they behave.

- **Detail** is very good at controlling sharpening of textures. Low values use the USM sharpening methods, and as you increase the slider, it gradually switches to deconvolution methods. The default of 25 is a good general sharpening setting. A low setting is ideal for large smooth areas, such as portraits or sky. Try a high setting for landscapes or other shots with lots of fine detail, where you want to sharpen details like the leaves on the trees. As you increase *Detail*, it also starts to amplify the noise in the image, so you may need to reduce the *Amount* slider and increase the *Masking* and *Luminance* noise reduction to compensate.

- **Masking** creates a soft edge mask from the image, protecting pixels from sharpening. It runs from 0-100, with a default of 0 (no masking). Higher values are particularly good for close-up portraits, allowing higher sharpening settings for the eyes, but still protecting the skin from over-sharpening.

Holding down the Alt key (Windows) / Opt key (Mac) while moving the sharpening sliders shows a grayscale mask of the effect, which can help you determine the best value for each slider individually, for example, when using the *Masking* slider, the white areas of the mask are sharpened and the black areas aren't. **(Figure 13.22)**

So how do you know where to set the sliders to get a crisp result, without over sharpening? Try this:

1. Zoom out to Fit view so you see the entire photo.

2. Hold down the Alt key (Windows) / Opt key (Mac) and drag the *Masking* slider to the right. You're aiming to make areas of low detail, such as the sky, turn black so that that'll be protected from sharpening.

3. Zoom into 1:1 view to accurately preview your further adjustments.

4. Increase the *Amount* slider to easily preview the effect of your adjustments. Try around 75-100 temporarily.

5. Hold down the Alt key (Windows) / Opt key (Mac) and drag the *Detail* slider slightly to the left for portraits or slightly to the right for detailed shots such as landscapes. The aim is to enhance the detail, shown in white, without sharpening the noise, protected in gray.

6. Hold down the Alt key (Windows) / Opt key (Mac) and drag the *Radius* slider slightly to the left for detailed shots such as landscapes or slightly to the right for portraits. Watch the width of the black and white halos you're creating along the edges,

and note where these halos are most visible. A value around 1 is usually perfect.

7. Hold down the Alt key (Windows) / Opt key (Mac) and drag the *Amount* slider to the left until the halos almost disappear.

8. Check over the photo for any areas that appear over sharpened. Select the Adjustment Brush, set to *Sharpening* 0 to -50 (no further, as that starts to blur) and brush over the over sharpened areas to reduce the sharpening. Don't remove it entirely, as it may look too smooth in comparison with the rest of the photos.

9. Finally, you may want to go back to the Basic panel and adjust the *Clarity* slider to increase midtone contrast slightly.

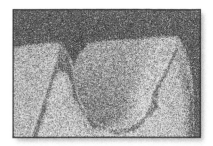

Figure 13.23 An ISO 25600 photo shows a lot of luminance and color noise.

How do the noise reduction sliders interact?

There's also an array of noise reduction sliders, but just because they exist doesn't mean you need to use them on every photo. Most photos only require the *Luminance* and *Color* sliders. **(Figure 13.23)** The other sliders are there for more extreme cases, and can be left at their default settings most of the time.

*   The **Luminance** slider controls the amount of luminance noise reduction applied, moving from 0, which doesn't apply any noise reduction, through to 100 where the photo has an almost painted effect. **(Figure 13.25)**

*   The **Color** slider tries to suppress single pixels of random noise without losing the edge detail. **(Figure 13.24)** By default, it's set to 25 for raw files, which is usually plenty. It's set to 0 for JPEGs, but if there's still colored noise in your photo, particularly in the dark shadows, try increasing it slightly.

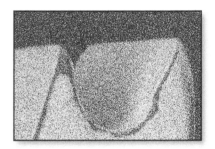

Figure 13.24 Color Noise Reduction set to the default of 25 minimizes the colored speckles.

The other sliders only make a noticeable difference to extremely noisy images, such as those produced by the highest ISO rating that your camera offers, or where a high ISO file is extremely underexposed. You're unlikely to see a difference at lower ISO ratings, for better or for worse, so in most cases you won't need to change these settings from their defaults.

*   The **Luminance Detail** slider sets the noise threshold, so higher values preserve more detail but some noise may incorrectly be identified as detail.

*   The **Luminance Contrast** slider at 0 is a much finer grain than 100. Higher values help to preserve texture, but can introduce a mottling effect, so lower values are usually a better choice.

*   The **Color Detail** slider refines any fine color edges. At low values it reduces the number of color speckles in these edges but may

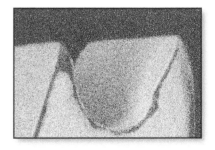

Figure 13.25 Luminance Noise Reduction at 35 reduces the noise further, but without turning it to smooth plastic.

slightly desaturate them, whereas at high values, it tries to retain the color detail but may introduce color speckles in the process.

- The **Color Smoothness** slider is similar to the *Color* slider, but it aims to remove larger areas of color mottling or splotchiness. You're most likely to see this on very underexposed images, where you've brightened an area considerably, or extreme contrast images that you're tone-mapping. The default is 50, which works very well on most images. Moving the slider to the right increases the smoothing at the cost of performance.

Can I apply or remove sharpening or noise reduction selectively?

The sliders in the Detail panel apply to the whole photo, but the Adjustment Brush allows you to apply or remove sharpening and noise reduction in specific areas of the photo. You can 'paint in' increased sharpening over a selected area, such as the eyes in a portrait, or selectively reduce global sharpening on large smooth areas of sky. Local noise reduction allows you to selectively increase or decrease the global noise reduction, perhaps because the noise is more noticeable where you've lightened the shadows. (Turn back to the Local Adjustments section on starting on page 241 for more information on using the Adjustment Brush.)

The Local Adjustment Sharpening is directly tied to the sharpening sliders in the Detail panel, so the *Radius*, *Detail* and *Masking* settings from the Detail panel are combined with the amount set in the Brush options panel. This also gives you the ability to remove sharpening that's been applied by the main sharpening *Amount* slider in the Detail panel.

0 to -50 on the Local Adjustment sharpening reduces the amount of sharpening applied by that global sharpening. Beyond -50 starts blurring the photo with an effect similar to a lens blur, but that's very processor intensive, so don't be surprised if Lightroom starts to slow down.

The Local Adjustment noise reduction applies luminance noise reduction only. You'll need to use the global *Color* noise slider in the Detail panel to reduce color noise.

SHARPENING & NOISE REDUCTION SHORTCUTS

| Show Mask | Hold Alt / Opt while dragging slider |

LENS & PERSPECTIVE CORRECTIONS

You may notice some distortion in your photos, either because of defects in the lens itself or because of the shooting angle. Fixing these issues is as simple as checking the checkboxes in the **Basic** tab of the Lens Corrections panel. **(Figure 13.26)**

1. First, check the **Enable Profile Corrections** checkbox to apply the default lens profile. If the photo doesn't change, switch to the *Profile* tab and select the correct lens profile from the pop-ups (if it's available). We'll come back to the other options later in this section.

2. If you're using a raw file from a recent camera (except SLR's), a lens profile may have already been applied behind the scenes. If so, it'll say *Built-in Lens Profile applied* at the bottom of the *Profile* tab.

3. Next, check the **Remove Chromatic Aberration** checkbox. It removes specific types of fringing in the photo, particularly around high-contrast edges or in the corners of the photo.

4. **Constrain Crop** crops the photo to remove any gaps around the edge, which can be caused by lens or perspective corrections.

5. Finally, you can press the **Upright Auto** button to apply automatic perspective adjustments. Most of the time, *Auto* is the best choice, but you can try the other *Upright* buttons to see if you prefer the result.

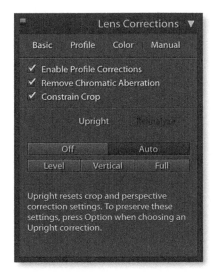

Figure 13.26 The *Basic* tab of the Lens Corrections panel contains the main lens and perspective correction controls.

These settings are all grouped together on the *Basic* tab because their corrections interact. Upright, particularly, works much better when a Lens Profile has been applied first.

There are additional controls on the other tabs in the Lens Corrections panel, so let's take a closer look at the options. Since the Lens Correction controls jump between different tabs, we'll cover them in the order you're likely to need them.

CONTINUES ON PAGE 288

How do I know whether my lens profile's built in?

Many recent cameras have lens profile information embedded in the raw file and applied automatically by Lightroom. These include many compact cameras and newer mirrorless cameras, and they usually have the same lens corrections applied to JPEGs by the camera.

To check whether your camera is affected, switch to the *Profile* tab and check for the information at the bottom of the panel. **(Figure 13.27)** If it says *Built-in Lens Profile applied*, click on the *i* button to view additional information about the automatic

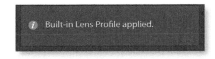

Figure 13.27 Many recent cameras have the lens profile information built-in and applied automatically.

▶ **Figure 13.28** If a built-in profile has been applied, click on the *i* icon to see which corrections are included.

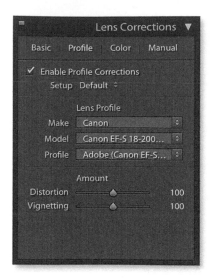

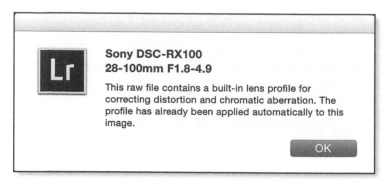

Figure 13.29 Check the correct profile is selected in the *Profile* tab.

fixes. **(Figure 13.28)** The built-in profile can apply corrections for distortion, chromatic aberration and/or vignetting. For example, the Sony RX100 applies corrections for distortion and chromatic aberration behind the scenes, but you might still want to check *Enable Profile Corrections* to remove the vignetting.

How do I select the correct profile for my lens?

When you check the **Enable Profile Corrections** checkbox in the *Basic* or **Profile** tab of the Lens Corrections panel, Lightroom checks the EXIF data in the file to identify the lens. If it finds a matching profile, the pop-up menus below automatically populate, and you're done. If Lightroom can't find the correct profile, then you can help by selecting the correct lens profile in the **Make, Model** and **Profile** pop-up menus in the *Profile* tab. (If there isn't a suitable profile listed, we'll come back to your options shortly.) **(Figure 13.29)**

How do I set a default lens profile?

If your lens isn't automatically recognized by Lightroom, you can set a default lens profile to save manually selecting it each time. This default includes the lens details selected in the pop-up menus and the *Amount* sliders below.

1. Open a photo taken with the camera/lens combination.

2. Go to the Lens Correction panel and check the *Enable Profile Corrections* checkbox.

3. Select the lens make, model and profile from the pop-up menus.

4. (Optional) Adjust the *Amount* sliders. (We'll come back to these shortly).

5. Go to the *Setup* pop-up menu and select *Save New Lens Profile Defaults.* **(Figure 13.30)**

WHY IS THE LENS PROFILE NOT SELECTED AUTOMATICALLY?

The EXIF 2.3 official standard for recording lens information in the metadata is only just starting to come into effect, and therefore it isn't always clear which lens was used. Lightroom uses all the information available to make an educated guess, but if it's not sure, it leaves you to select the profile. Once you've chosen the lens, you can set this as a default for that camera/lens combination, so you don't have to select it on every photo in future.

In the *Setup* pop-up menu, what's the difference between *Default, Auto & Custom*?

In the *Setup* pop-up, you'll note three other options:

- **Auto** leaves Lightroom to search for a matching profile automatically. If it can't find a matching profile, either because the profile doesn't exist yet, or because it doesn't have enough information in the photo's EXIF data, the pop-ups remain blank.

- **Default** does the same, but also allows you to customize the settings for specific lenses. For example, if *Auto* can't find a lens because it doesn't have enough information, you can select the correct profile from the pop-up menus below and save it as a default for the future. From then on, whenever you select *Default* for a photo with that camera/lens combination, it applies your new default lens setting. It's also useful if you have multiple profiles for a lens—perhaps one provided by Adobe and one you've created yourself—and you want to automatically select one of these profiles.

- **Custom** means that you've manually changed the profile or one of the *Amount* sliders.

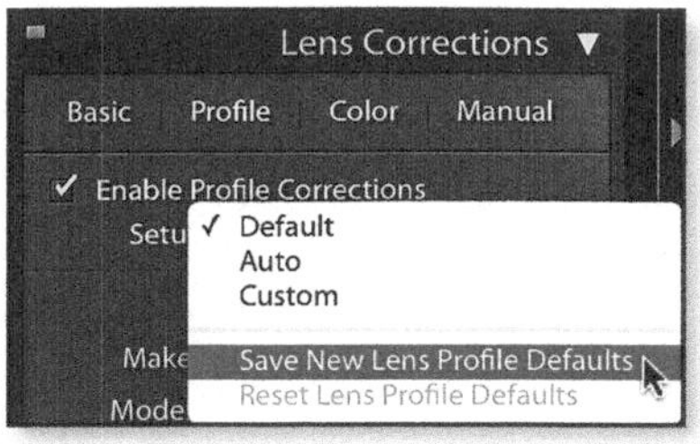

Why is the lens profile available for some photos and not others, using the same lens?

Many of the lens profiles are for raw files only, so if a profile goes missing, check the format of your selected photo.

The processing applied by the camera to non-raw formats can affect the corrections needed, for example, some cameras apply distortion correction and many apply processing that reduces the lens vignetting and chromatic aberration.

If you apply a raw profile to a rendered file (i.e. a JPEG), you may get an unexpected result as it tries to correct for a defect which has already been corrected. There are unofficial ways of making a raw profile available for use with JPEGs by editing the profile with a text editor, but creating your own profile or downloading one created using JPEGs gives a more accurate result.

What are my options if my lens profile isn't available?

If your lens doesn't appear in the Lens Profile pop-up menus, you have a number of different options:

- Switch to the *Manual* tab and adjust the sliders manually. (We'll come back these at the end of the section.)

Figure 13.30 If Lightroom doesn't recognize your lens correctly, you can update the default settings.

APPLY BY DEFAULT

To automatically enable lens corrections for all new imports, first set your photo to its normal default settings (e.g. press *Reset*), and then check the *Enable Profile Corrections* checkbox and make sure the *Setup* pop-up menu is set to *Default* (this is crucial). Finally, go to *Develop menu > Set Default Settings* to set the default for that camera. We'll come back to setting defaults in the Develop Module Tools section on page 305.

- Wait for Adobe to create a profile for that lens. Lens profiles are being added gradually in each dot release.

- Build your own profiles using the free Adobe Lens Profile Creator tool. You can learn more in the Appendix starting on page A-16.

- Search the community-created profiles using the free Adobe Lens Profile Downloader tool.

How do I use the Lens Profile Downloader?

The Lens Profile Downloader is included with the Lens Profile Creator, which you can download from http://www.Lrq.me/lensprofilecreator It allows you to browse profiles created by other users, and then download these profiles to your computer to use with Lightroom, ACR and Photoshop. You'll need the free Adobe AIR app installed to run the Lens Profile Downloader.

When you first open the Lens Profile Downloader, the grid is blank. Select your brand of camera from the first pop-up menu, and it then contacts the web server to download a list of available user profiles. **(Figure 13.31)**

You can browse the full list of profiles for your camera brand, or you can select the lens model from the next pop-up menu to filter the list. If you type in the *Lens Model* field, it becomes a text search, for example, typing 17 would find lenses including 17-40, 17-55, and 10-17. As some of the lens naming is slightly inconsistent, this can help to find your specific lens.

The Lens Profile Downloader also allows you to filter the list by camera model, but this information is the lowest priority. The crop factor, on the other hand, is crucial. You need to select a profile that was created on a sensor with the same crop factor or larger, so selecting the crop factor of your camera shows any profiles that are suitable. If a profile is created using a camera with a 1.6 crop factor, then only the central portion of the lens, marked by the inner rectangle, will have been profiled. **(Figure 13.32)** Using that profile with another 1.6 crop camera works well, but the rest of the lens information outside of that line will be missing, so you wouldn't be able to use it with a full frame camera. Adobe's own profiles are created on a full frame camera, because smaller crop factors are simply using a smaller portion of the lens and the corrections can therefore be calculated accurately.

You'll also note that the profiles specify Raw or JPEG, which refers to the file format used when creating the profiles. You'll need to select the file format you shoot, as Lightroom won't apply raw profiles to rendered photos, or vice versa.

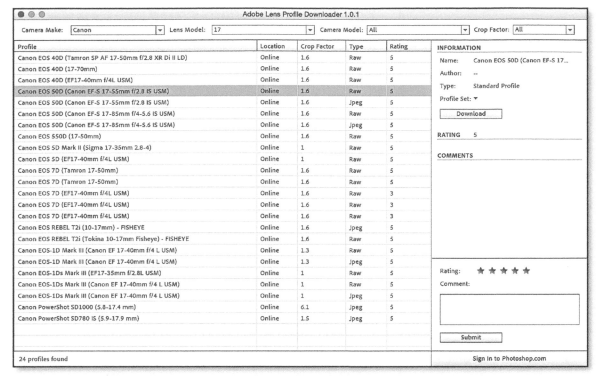

As time goes by, and more user profiles are added to the database, the list of available profiles for each lens will increase. There is a rating system, which allows users to mark the quality of these profiles, which helps you to select the best user profile available. If you click on the *Rating* column header, the profiles sort in ascending order.

Once you select a profile from the list, the metadata about that profile shows in the panel on the right. The *Profile Set* pop-up menu allows you to see the sets of images used when creating the profile. You'll also see notes that other users have left regarding that particular profile, which can help you to decide whether you wish to try it yourself. If you sign in using your Adobe ID, you can add ratings or comments on the profiles that you've tried.

When you press the *Download* button, it automatically downloads the profile directly to the correct location with your computer's user files, and the Lens Profile Downloader updates to show that you have installed that profile. The *Download* button changes to *Delete*, so if you find that the profile isn't suitable, you can easily remove it again. If Lightroom's open while you're downloading, your new profile won't be available for use until you close and reopen Lightroom, but then it appears in the *Lens Corrections* pop-up menus like any other profile.

▲ **Figure 13.31** The Lens Profile Downloader gives you access to lens profiles created by other users.

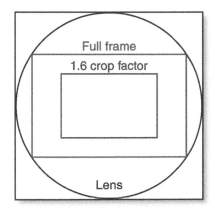

▲ **Figure 13.32** Profiles created using full frame cameras can be used for photos shot on crop sensors, but profiles created on crop sensors won't include enough information for full frame photos.

> ## EXISTING LENS CORRECTIONS
>
> Photos edited in much earlier versions of Lightroom may have distortion or vignetting adjustments applied in the *Manual* tab. Applying a profiled lens correction doesn't reset any existing manual settings, so switch to the *Manual* tab and reset these settings.

How do the Amount sliders interact with the profile?

There are some situations where you might want to use some of the profiled correction, but not all of it. The **Amount** sliders at the bottom of the *Profile* tab act as a volume control, increasing or decreasing the amount of profiled correction that's being applied. 0 doesn't apply the correction at all, 100 applies the profile as it was created, and higher values increase the effect of the correction. For example, with a fisheye lens, you might want to remove the vignette automatically, but keep the fisheye effect. To do so, reduce the **Distortion Amount** slider to 0 but leave the **Vignetting Amount** slider at 100.

How do I fix Chromatic Aberration or colored fringes?

Chromatic aberration, or CA, refers to the little fringes of color that can appear along high contrast edges, where the red, green and blue light wavelengths are unable to focus at the same point. There are two different kinds of chromatic aberration, which require different treatment.

Type 1—Lateral/Transverse Chromatic Aberration

Lateral or transverse chromatic aberration results from color wavelengths hitting the focal plane next to each other. **(Figure 13.33)** It's most noticeable around the corners of photos taken with a lower quality wide angle lens, and doesn't appear in the center of the image. You'll recognize the two different colored fringes appearing on opposite sides of your image details.

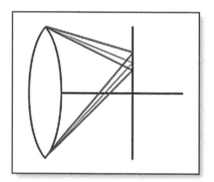

▲ **Figure 13.33** Lateral/Transverse Chromatic Aberration.

This type of chromatic aberration is fixed using the **Remove Chromatic Aberration** checkbox in the *Color* tab of the Lens Corrections panel (and duplicated in the Basic tab). It's disabled by default as it can slow Lightroom down slightly, and in rare cases may introduce new fringing.

Type 2 – Axial/Longitudinal Chromatic Aberration

The second type of chromatic aberration is called axial or longitudinal chromatic aberration, which results from the color wavelengths focusing at different lengths. **(Figure 13.34)** Unlike lateral CA, with its pairs of opposing colors, axial CA causes a halo of a single color – purple in front of the focal plane or green behind it—which can be present anywhere on the image.

Axial CA isn't the only cause of purple fringing. Flare and sensor issues can also cause it, usually along high contrast backlit edges, but the treatment of these purple fringes is the same regardless of the cause.

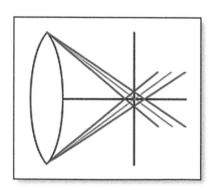

▲ **Figure 13.34** Axial/Longitudinal Chromatic Aberration

This type of chromatic aberration is fixed using the **Defringe** sliders and eyedropper in the *Color* tab. **(Figure 13.35)** These allow you to target specific hues to remove the fringing.

To demonstrate how to use these tools, let's correct this example image **(Figure 13.36)**, which exhibits both types of chromatic aberration.

1. Develop the image, working from the top down as normal.

2. Correct lens distortion using the *Profile* tab of the Lens Corrections panel (if the profile isn't automatically applied), as the distortion corrections can affect the chromatic aberration. **(Figure 13.37)**

3. Go to the **Color** tab of the Lens Corrections panel and enable the **Remove Chromatic Aberration** checkbox. This removes the lateral chromatic aberration causing the green and magenta fringes. **(Figure 13.38)**

4. After removing the lateral chromatic aberration, this photo still exhibits purple fringing along the backlit edges. Zoom in to 1:1 or greater magnification in order to clearly see the fringe pixels.

If the leftover chromatic aberration is limited to a small area, and your photo is set to the newest Process Version (PV2012), it's

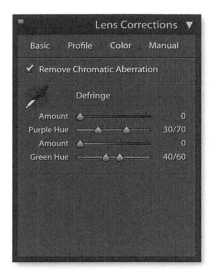

Figure 13.35 Fringing controls are in the *Color* tab.

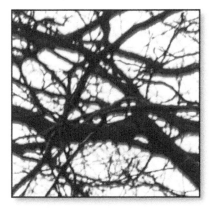
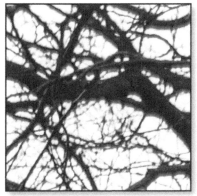

Figure 13.36 (left) Chromatic aberration refers to little fringes of color.

Figure 13.37 (right) With the lens profile applied, the purple and green fringes are still visible.

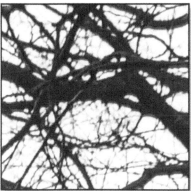
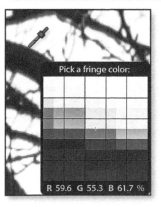

Figure 13.38 (left) After checking the *Remove Chromatic Aberration* checkbox, the photo still shows some purple fringing.

Figure 13.39 (right) The tip of the Fringe Color Selector changes color based on the color of the pixels.

quicker and safer to use the local brush or gradient rather than the global lens corrections, so skip the next 2 steps. Otherwise continue to the next step to apply global corrections.

5. Select the eyedropper tool from the *Color* tab of the Lens Corrections panel and float over the fringes. The end of the eyedropper becomes purple or green, depending on the color of the fringe you're sampling. **(Figure 13.39)** If the end is white, it won't work. Click on the purple fringe to automatically remove it. If there's any green fringing, click to sample the green fringe too.

For many photos, that's all you need to do. When you sample the fringe using the eyedropper, the *Defringe* sliders in the *Color* tab of the Lens Corrections panel are automatically adjusted.

6. If you need to fine tune the corrections further, you can adjust the **Defringe** sliders manually.

There are two pairs of sliders for correcting purple and green fringes. The **Amount** sliders affects the strength of the adjustment, and the **Hue** sliders affects the range of colors being corrected. As you move the *Hue* sliders further apart, the fringe removal affects a wider range of colors.

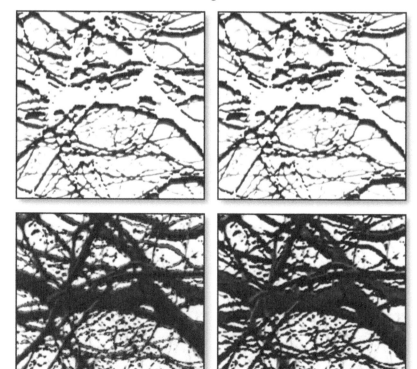

▷**Figure 13.40** When you hold down the Alt (Windows) / Opt (Mac) key and drag the *Amount* slider, the photo shows a B&W mask with your fringe highlighted (left). Drag the slider until the fringe disappears (right).

▷**Figure 13.41** The same Alt/ Opt mask applies with the *Hue* slider, with the colored fringes (left) turning black (right) as you move the slider, showing that you've captured all the stray colored pixels.

At first glance, it may appear easiest to set the amount to 20 with the widest hue range possible, but doing so would also desaturate the edges of other objects in your image. To avoid this, use the lowest amount and narrowest hue range possible, while still removing the fringing.

The easiest way to check that you've captured all the fringe pixels is to hold down the Alt key (Windows) / Opt key (Mac) while dragging the slider.

For the *Amount* sliders, only the affected area is shown, with the rest of the image being masked in white. This enables you to check that the fringe pixels have been completely desaturated. **(Figure 13.40)**

Used with the *Hue* sliders, the affected fringes turn black, allowing you to check that there are no stray colored fringe pixels. **(Figure 13.41)**

7. Finally, once you've removed the fringing using the global controls, you may want to increase or decrease the fringe removal in some areas.

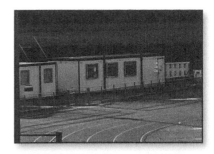

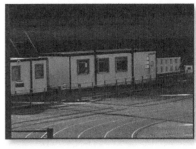

Figure 13.42 The global defringe may affect other edges in the photo (top) but setting the Adjustment Brush to -100 *Defringe* and painting over the area brings back the color (bottom).

How do I remove localized fringing?

As long as your photo is set to PV2012, you can use the adjustment brush or gradient tool to apply defringe to specific areas, or to protect objects from the global fringe removal.

For example, you may find that global defringe adjustments have unavoidably affected the edges of other objects, such as this building. **(Figure 13.42)**

Select the adjustment brush, set the *Defringe* slider in the adjustment brush settings to a negative slider value (i.e., -100) and brush over the areas you want to protect from the global adjustment. (Turn back to page 241 for general information on the local adjustments)

You can also use a positive *Defringe* value (i.e., +100) on the adjustment brush to remove any leftover fringing that wasn't removed by the global adjustment, or to apply small amounts of fringe removal on photos that don't require a global adjustment.

The positive values on the local adjustment *Defringe* slider are not tied to the global sliders, so it removes fringing of any color, such as the red fringe shown in **Figure 13.43**.

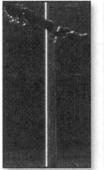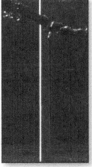

Figure 13.43 The Adjustment Brush *Defringe* slider set to positive values removes fringing of any color, such as the red fringe in this photo.

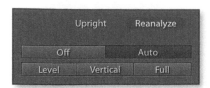

Figure 13.44 The *Upright* buttons are found in the *Basic* tab of the Lens Corrections panel.

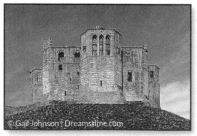

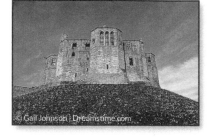

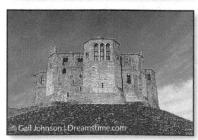

Figure 13.45 *Upright* corrects perspective distortion, but a full correction may look unnatural. *Original* (first), *Full* (second), *Auto* (third).

How do I fix the perspective?

Moving back to the *Basic* tab, the **Upright** tool can fix perspective automatically by analyzing the straight edges in your photo. **(Figure 13.44)** For example, it attempts to automatically to fix tilted horizons and straighten buildings. The results depend on the subject matter, but even on images that aren't quite right, it usually provides a good starting point. You can tweak the results using the sliders on the *Manual* tab to get the exact correction you desire.

What do the different Upright buttons do? Which one should I use?

- The **Off** button is simple—Upright is disabled, so no adjustments are made.

- The **Auto** button is the most intelligent option. It not only tries to level the photo and correct converging horizontal and vertical lines, but it also takes into account the amount of distortion that's created by the correction. It aims to get the best visual result, even if that's not perfectly straight.

- The **Full** button is the most extreme option. It levels the photos and fixes converging horizontal and vertical lines, even if that means using very strong 3D corrections which distort image features.

- The **Level** button only tries to level the photo, fixing tilted horizons and verticals. It's similar to straightening the photo when cropping. It doesn't try to adjust for converging lines.

- The **Vertical** button levels the photo, like the *Level* button, but also fixes converging verticals.

There's a little bit of trial and error involved in picking the right one for each photo, but more often than not, the *Auto* button gives the best result. **(Figure 13.45)**

When do I need to press *Reanalyze*?

The **Reanalyze** button is only available when the adjustments need to recalculated, perhaps because you've checked or unchecked the *Enable Profile Corrections* checkbox.

How do I stop Upright clearing my crop?

By default, Lightroom clears existing manual perspective corrections and rotations when you press an Upright button, otherwise the result

SYNCING UPRIGHT MODE VS. TRANSFORMS

We'll come back to synchronizing settings in the next chapter on page 297, but it's worth noting that the wording on some of the Upright Sync options isn't entirely clear. **Transform** refers to the *Manual* sliders (*Vertical, Horizontal,* etc). **Upright Mode** uses the same Upright button (*Auto, Level,* etc.) but analyzes each photo individually, whereas **Upright Transforms** uses exactly the same settings behind the scenes, without adjusting for each photo. In most cases, *Upright Mode* is the option you'll choose. If you're syncing across photos that are almost identical, then *Upright Transforms* gives a more consistent result. **(Figure 13.46)**

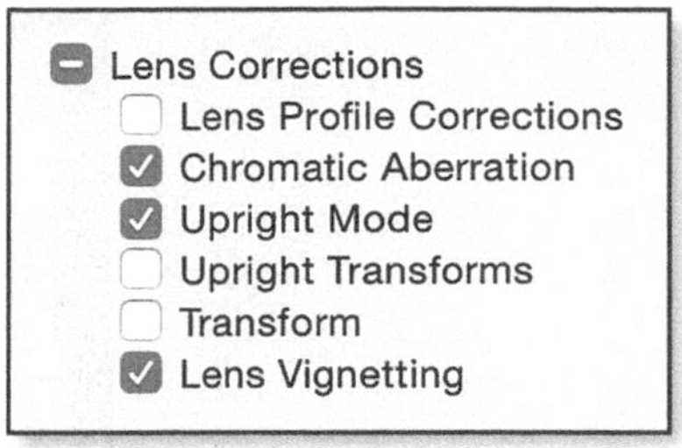

Figure 13.46 Note the difference betwee *Upright Mode* and *Upright Transforms* when syncing settings to other photos.

can look more distorted. It also clears the whole crop at the same time, as the cropped area changes with the perspective adjustments.

If you hold down Alt (Windows) / Opt (Mac) while pressing an *Upright* button, it doesn't clear any existing settings, but you'll need to tweak the crop and clear any existing corrections in the *Manual* tab yourself.

How do I reduce the effect of the Upright correction?

You'll notice that the sliders on the *Manual* tab aren't adjusted automatically when using Upright. This is because the complex calculations would require numerous extra sliders, so it's all done behind the scenes. The *Manual* sliders are still useful for reducing the effect of the Upright corrections.

We're used to seeing converging verticals in everyday life, so full correction can look unnatural. If you switch to the *Manual* tab, you can adjust individual axes of rotation, reducing their effect. For example, setting the *Vertical* slider to +10 reintroduces some converging verticals, giving a more natural appearance.

What do the Manual Transform Lens Corrections sliders do?

The final tab in the Lens Corrections panel is the **Manual** tab. **(Figure 13.47)** It allows you to manually correct distortion if you don't have a lens profile, but it's most useful for reducing the effect of Upright, slimming people, and recovering pixels pushed out of the frame by other lens corrections.

The **Distortion** slider corrects for barrel or pincushion distortion if you don't have a profile for that lens. **(Figure 13.48)**

LENS CORRECTION SHORTCUTS

Cycle Upright Modes

Ctrl Tab

Cycle Upright while preserving crop

Ctrl Alt Tab / Ctrl Opt Tab

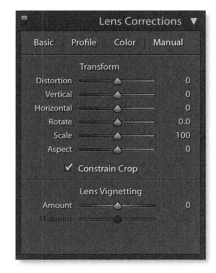

Figure 13.47 Transform sliders are in the *Manual* tab of the Lens Corrections panel.

Figure 13.48 *Distortion* +100 (left) and -100 (right).

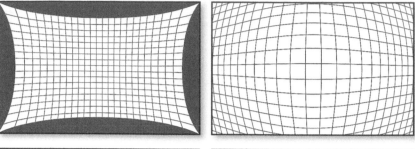

Figure 13.49 *Vertical* -100 (left) and *Horizontal* +100 (right).

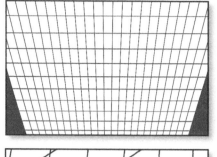
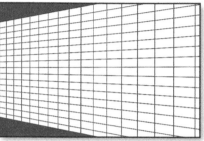

Figure 13.50 The same grid was rotated using the *Crop Angle* slider (left) and the *Rotate* slider (right) followed by an identical -100 *Vertical* transform. This small crop was taken from the corner of each photo, so you can see there's a difference in the slider behavior.

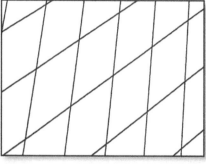
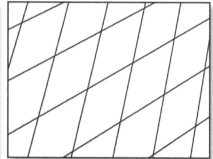

Figure 13.51 With *Scale* at 0 (left), some of the image is being lost from the corners, whereas *Scale* -50 (right) shows the extra image data.

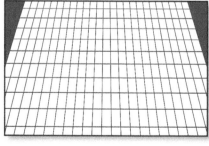
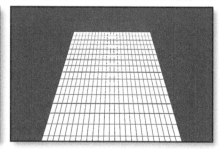

Figure 13.52 *Aspect* set to +100 (left) and- 100 (right).

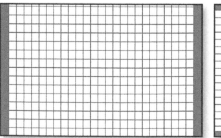
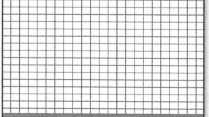

The **Vertical** and **Horizontal** sliders adjust for perspective. It's most useful for reducing the effect of Upright corrections. **(Figure 13.49)**

The **Rotate** slider adjusts for camera tilt. It's applied at a much earlier stage in the processing than the crop, with a different result. *Rotate* pivots on the center of the uncropped photo instead of the center of the crop.

If you're using the Manual Lens Corrections to correct perspective, and your camera wasn't level, it's better to use the *Upright* buttons or the *Rotate* slider in the Manual Lens Corrections to level the camera, rather than *Angle* in the Crop tool. **(Figure 13.50)**

The **Scale** slider interpolates the data to pull back pixels which have been pushed out of the frame by other lens or perspective corrections, which the Crop tool can't do.

Scale can also remove blank areas of the photo caused by the lens and perspective corrections, but it interpolates the data (creates new pixels) in the process, so cropping these blank areas is usually a better choice. **(Figure 13.51)**

The **Aspect** slider squashes or stretches the photo to improve the appearance. Strong keystone corrections can make a photo look unnatural, especially when they include people. The slider direction is sensitive to the image rotation, but in most cases, dragging the slider to the left makes things look wider, and dragging the slider to the right makes them look taller and thinner. **(Figure 13.52)**

Even if you haven't used the other perspective corrections,

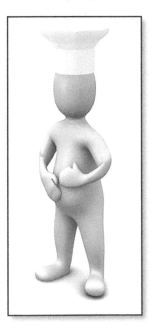

> ## HIDE THE GRID
>
> You can't turn the lens correction grid off, but it only appears when you float over the Manual Lens Corrections sliders. If you want a permanent grid, go to *View menu > Loupe Overlay > Grid*.

◀ **Figure 13.53** The *Aspect* slider can make anyone look slimmer!

moving the *Aspect* slider slightly (usually to the right) slims down the subject, reversing "the camera adds 10lbs!" **(Figure 13.53)**

The **Lens Vignetting Amount** and **Midpoint** sliders correct lens vignetting if you don't have a lens profile. Unlike the Post-Crop Vignette in the Effects panel, the *Lens Vignetting* sliders are not affected by the cropping.

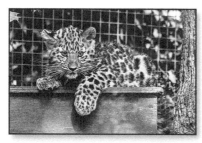

EFFECTS—POST-CROP VIGNETTE & GRAIN

Vignetting is the darkening or lightening of the corners of a photo. **(Figure 13.55)** Although traditionally it's caused by the camera lens, it's become popular as a photographic effect, so the controls are found in the Effects panel. **(Figure 13.54)** There's also a grain effect, designed to simulate traditional film grain, which feels more natural than digital noise.

▲ **Figure 13.54** The Effects panel contains the *Post-Crop Vignetting* and *Grain* controls.

What's the difference between Highlight Priority, Color Priority and Paint Overlay?

The **Style** pop-up in the Effects panel gives a choice of three different post-crop vignettes, which all fit within the crop boundary, rather than the original lens correction vignette which is designed for correcting lens problems.

- **Highlight Priority** is the default and imitates a traditional lens vignette with the colors remaining heavily saturated throughout.

- **Color Priority** retains more natural colors into the vignette, with smoother shadow transitions.

- **Paint Overlay** adds a plain black or white overlay.

How do the Post-Crop Vignette sliders interact?

- **Amount** logically affects the amount, with -100 being dark and +100 being light. It helps to use a more extreme setting while you adjust the other sliders, and then reduce it.

- **Midpoint** controls how close to the center of the photo the vignette affects, ranging from 0 affecting the center and 100 barely touching the sides. It's easier to judge the correct midpoint once you've set the feathering.

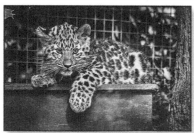

- **Roundness** runs from -100 which is almost rectangular, to +100 which is circular.

▲ **Figure 13.55** A vignette can help to draw your eye into a photo and focus on the main subject.

OFF-CENTER VIGNETTE

The Post-Crop Vignette is always centered within the Crop boundaries, but the Radial Filter allows you to create your own off-center vignettes. Turn back to page 241 to learn how.

Figure 13.56 Test the *Vignetting* controls on a plain grey image to see the difference between the sliders.

- **Feather** runs from 0 to 100, with 0 showing a hard edge, and 100 being soft.

- **Highlights** runs from 0, which has no effect, to 100, which makes the highlights under a dark vignette brighter, allowing you to darken the edges without the photo becoming too flat and lacking in contrast.

To easily see the effect of each slider, try applying them to a plain gray image file, or set the *Feather* slider to 0 to preview the other sliders. **(Figure 13.56)**

How do the Grain sliders interact?

We spend a lot of time trying to reduce the noise in our photos... and then put grain back! However, some photos look great with a little extra grain, particularly if they're B&W or sepia. **(Figure 13.57)** It can also help to hide the plasticky look that results from high noise reduction. Lightroom's **Grain** sliders aim to emulate a traditional film grain, which looks a little different to digital noise. **(Figure 13.58)**

- **Amount** obviously affects the amount of grain applied. The noise is applied equally across the photo, giving a much more film-like quality than digital noise, which tends to be heavier in the shadows.

- **Size** affects the size of the grain, just as grain on film came in different sizes, and it gets softer as it gets larger.

- **Roughness** affects the consistency of the grain, so 0 is uniform across the photo, whereas higher values become rougher.

Like sharpening and noise reduction, you'll need to zoom into 1:1 view to get an accurate preview. Grain is very sensitive to resizing, sharpening and compression, so if you're going to downsize the photo when exporting, you'll need stronger grain. It won't reproduce well in this book, so I'll leave you to try the *Size* and *Roughness* sliders .

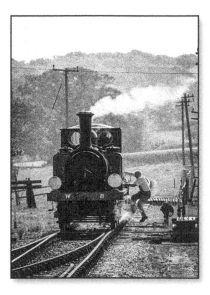

Figure 13.57 Some photos benefit from added grain for effect.

Figure 13.58 The *Grain* sliders add grain with a film-like quality.

PHOTO MERGE

Until now, if you wanted to merge multiple photos, you had to use other software such as Photoshop. Lightroom CC/6 introduces a new Photo Merge feature, which allows you to stitch together multiple photos into a panorama or create a high dynamic range (HDR) file from multiple images.

Stitch a panorama

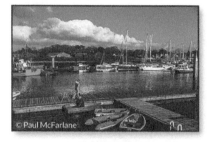

1. Select a series of photos. The order of the photos in the Filmstrip doesn't matter, as Lightroom matches the photos visually. This means you can even stitch multi-row panoramas. **(Figure 13.59)**

2. Go to *Photo menu > Photo Merge > Panorama.* **(Figure 13.60)**

3. Check the *Auto Select Projection* checkbox or manually select a projection button.

4. Check the *Auto Crop* checkbox to remove the blank white space.

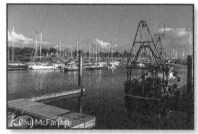

5. Press *Merge.* **(Figure 13.61)**

6. The resulting photo is automatically imported into Lightroom, where you can edit it in Develop as a normal photo.

Figure 13.59 Select multiple photos to merge into a panorama.

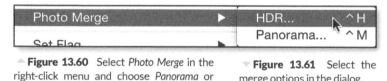

Figure 13.60 Select *Photo Merge* in the right-click menu and choose *Panorama* or *HDR.*

Figure 13.61 Select the merge options in the dialog.

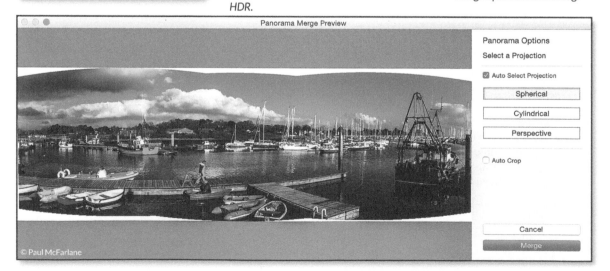

Create an HDR file

1. Select a series of bracketed photos. In most cases, select just two photos—one for the highlights and one for the shadows. **(Figure 13.62)**

2. Go to *Photo menu > Photo Merge > HDR*.

3. Check the *Auto Align* and *Auto Tone* checkboxes.

4. If there's movement in the photo (e.g. water), try the *Deghost* options until you find the one that gets the best result. If there's no movement, leave it set to *None*.

5. Press *Merge*. **(Figure 13.63)**

6. The resulting HDR photo is automatically imported into Lightroom, where you can edit it in the Develop module. You'll note that the *Exposure* slider now runs from -10 to +10 instead of -5 to +5.

The Photo Merge options also appear in the right-click menu in the Grid and Filmstrip, which is useful when you're working in the Develop module. They're only available when you have two or more photos or a collapsed stack selected. If you want to use the same settings as your last merge, hold down the Shift key while selecting the Merge option to bypass the dialog.

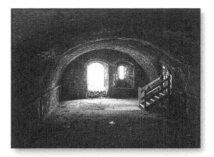
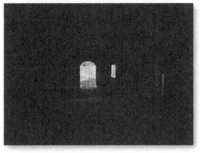

▲ **Figure 13.62** Select two photos to merge into an HDR file.

▼ **Figure 13.63** Select the merge ooptions in the dialog.

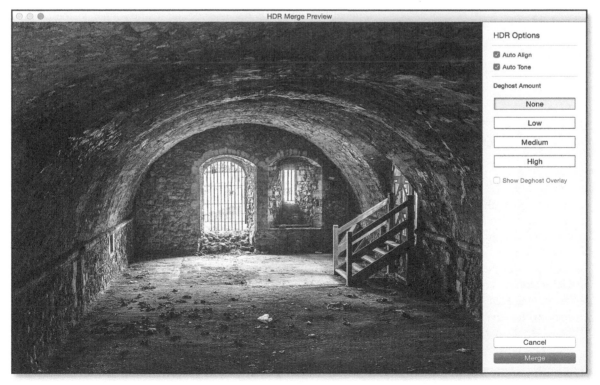

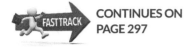

CONTINUES ON PAGE 297

The Merge preview is low resolution for speed, so you can resize the dialog or zoom in slightly, but you can't zoom in to a full 1:1 view.

When you press **Merge**, the merge happens in the background so you can continue working on other photos. If your computer is a high enough specification, you can run multiple merges at the same time, however it's very memory intensive. The **Cancel** button cancels without merging, of course.

Why use Lightroom for merging instead of Photoshop or other software?

In External Editors, we'll briefly discuss the Edit In > Merge to HDR Pro and Merge to Panorama using Photoshop, which was Adobe's older merge method. Photoshop's Merge to Panorama is still useful for merging rendered files (e.g. JPEGs) as it gives you greater control over the blending, but Lightroom's new merge has a distinct advantage when working with raw files.

Photoshop and other software have to partially convert the raw data before merging, reducing the possible dynamic range and applying the white balance. This affects the image quality.

When the merge is performed on the raw image data, as Lightroom now offers, the resulting file has all the editing flexibility of the original raw files. It is demosaiced, so it's no longer in the original sensor format, but it's still scene-referred data so you have full control over the white balance as well as a much wider dynamic range.

What type of files do I need for merging?

There are a few requirements for the source files. The files must be:

- All the same file type (raw or rendered). Raw files get significantly better results.
- All original files—smart previews won't work.
- All shot on the same camera (required for HDR, but best for panoramas too).
- All the same size and orientation (vertical or horizontal).
- All shot using the same focal length.
- Metadata containing at least the exposure time for HDR.

USING OTHER SOFTWARE

There are still some cases where you might want to use other software. For example, for tricky panoramas, dedicated software such as Hugin may get a better result. Also, Lightroom creates fairly natural looking HDR files, but you may prefer the surreal HDR style that dedicated HDR software produces.

What format are the merged files?

The merged files are stored as 16-bit DNG files. Lightroom automatically names the merged file using the name of the active photo and it adds -Pano or -HDR to the end of the filename to help identify them. (Make sure you keep this Pano/HDR ending, as it's currently the only way to filter for these files.)

In the case of HDR images, the files don't need the full 32-bit depth used for Photoshop HDR merges as the pixel data is stored as floating-point data. This makes it possible to store the image values accurately across a huge contrast range without such a huge file size.

Panoramic images have to be no more than 65000 pixels along the longest edge or 512 megapixels (whichever is smaller) to fit within ACR/Lightroom's maximum, so Lightroom automatically downsizes any panoramas that would fall outside these limits when creating them.

Should I edit the photos before I merge them?

There's no need to edit the photos before you merge them as the data remains scene-referred (assuming it's a raw file in the first place). This means you can edit the file after it's merged without any loss of quality.

There is one thing to look out for, and that's lens corrections on panoramas. Lightroom applies the default lens profile and chromatic aberration correction to the raw data before merging the panorama to get the best result, whether you've enabled it for the selected files or not. If Lightroom doesn't automatically select the right profile for your lens, turn back to page 274 and save a default profile before merging.

If you do choose to edit the photos before merging, Lightroom automatically copies some of the Develop settings from the active photo onto the merged photo. It skips things like the crop, lens corrections and local adjustments as they may not end up in the right place on the merged photo.

Let's take a closer look at some of the merge options.

What's the difference between the Panorama projection options?

Auto Select Projection usually selects *Spherical*. **(Figure 13.64 & 13.65)**

- **Spherical** aligns and transforms the photos as if they were

---

CAMERA SETTINGS

Merge works so much better on raw files, don't even consider shooting JPEG if you have a choice. For the best results, use a tripod to ensure the photos are correctly aligned, especially when shooting HDR sets. Overlap panorama sections by around 30% so they blend smoothly, and shoot panoramas with a 20mm-50mm lens in Manual mode to avoid significant lens distortion and exposure differences (although Lightroom does attempt to normalize the exposure for raw files).

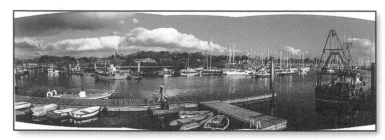

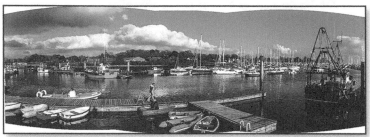

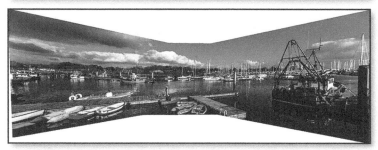

▶ **Figure 13.64** There are three projection options—*Spherical* (top), *Cyclindrical* (center) and *Perspective* (bottom).

mapping the inside of a sphere. If you've taken a 360° panorama, this is usually the best choice.

- **Cylindrical** displays the images as if they're on an unfolded cylinder, using the middle image as the reference point and transforming the photos where they overlap. It reduces the bow-tie type distortion you can get with Perspective. It works well on wide panoramas.

- **Perspective** uses the middle image as the reference point and transforms the other images where they overlap, but it can result in a bow-tie type distortion.

Should I enable *Auto Crop*?

The **Auto Crop** checkbox automatically crops the panorama to remove the blank areas and maximize the image area. If you check it, all of the pixel detail is retained and you can use the Crop tool to reset or edit the crop later in the Develop module.

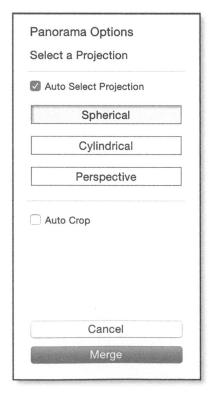

▲ **Figure 13.65** Panorama options

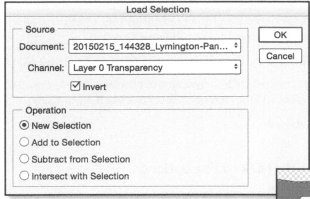

Figure 13.66 Load the transparent area as a selection.

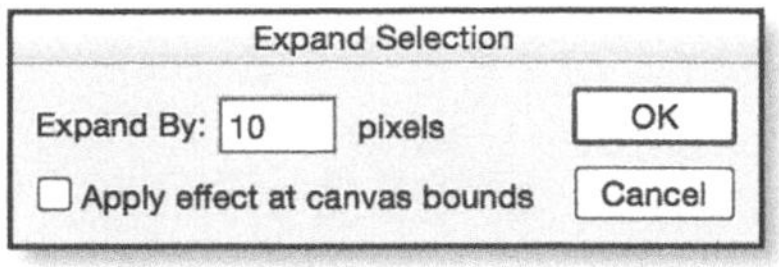

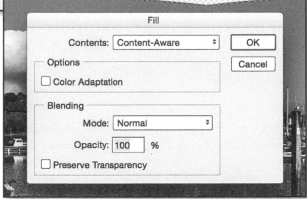

Figure 13.67 Expand the selection to include extra pixels.

How do I fill in the gaps around the edges? Is there Content Aware Fill?

Lightroom doesn't currently offer a way to fill in the gaps, so shooting wide enough to crop off the gaps around the edges is the simplest option.

If you have Photoshop, you can use Content Aware Fill to rebuild the edges, although doing so will create an additional rendered file. This is making up new pixels with varying results, but it often works well on areas of low detail such as sky.

1. Edit the photo in the Develop module to adjust the tone and color.

2. Go to *Photo menu > Edit in Photoshop*.

3. *Select menu > Load Selection*, select the Layer 0 Transparency channel and check *Invert*. **(Figure 13.66)**

Figure 13.68 Add Content Aware Fill to fill in the gaps.

Figure 13.69 The resulting photo may need additional retouching.

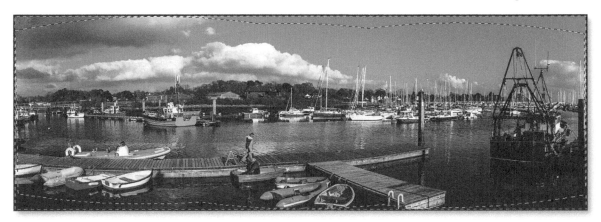

4. Go to *Select menu > Modify > Expand* and choose 2px to 10px, depending on the size of the photo. This tells Photoshop which pixels to base the new ones on. **(Figure 13.67)**

5. Go to *Edit menu > Fill* and select *Content Aware.* **(Figure 13.68)**

6. Once it's complete, click anywhere to deselect. You may need to tidy it up with a little cloning or spot removal. **(Figure 13.69)**

7. Save and close

Where are the HDR editing options?

Many photographers use the term HDR to describe a specific surreal style of editing, but think about the letters HDR... they stand for high dynamic range.

There are two stages to the process:

1. Merging multiple source files to create a single image with a much higher dynamic range. The result is an HDR file.

2. Manipulating the high dynamic range data to compress it into a lower dynamic range suitable for viewing on a screen or print. The result is a normal photo with a specific style of editing applied.

Most HDR software combines these two steps, allowing you to merge the files into an HDR image, apply your chosen style and output that photo with a low dynamic range.

Lightroom splits this process into its separate stages, first merging the photos into an HDR image, and then tone-mapping this image in the Develop module before outputting the photo. This allows you to go back and change the look of the photo non-destructively at a later date without having to merge the original images all over again.

How many photos should I select for an HDR file?

Unlike most HDR software, Lightroom works best with as few source images as possible. In most cases, this is only two raw files—one correctly exposed for the highlights and one correctly exposed for the shadows. As Lightroom's working with the raw data, it doesn't need the images in between, and additional images actually increase the risk of misalignment and ghosting.

If the images are more than 3 stops apart, add one or more additional images in between to reduce noise, ideally shot on a tripod to avoid introducing ghosting.

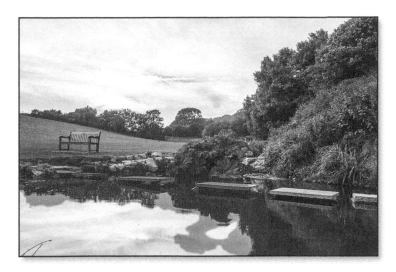

Figure 13.70 Check the *Deghost Overlay* to see which areas are being taken from a single photo to minimize ghosting.

There's no point trying to do a 'fake HDR' using a single file, because you won't gain any additional dynamic range.

Should I check *Auto Align* and enable *Deghost*?

There are a couple of options available in the HDR Preview dialog. **(Figure 13.71)**

Auto Align is worth checking if the photos were shot handheld and may not be perfectly aligned. If the photos were shot using a tripod and remote release, with no risk of movement, you can leave it unchecked.

The **Deghost** options are needed if there's a moving subject in the photo, for example, water or trees, as these can creates ghosts when photos are merged. There are three levels to choose from—*Low*, *Medium* or *High*—and they control how sensitive Lightroom is to movement in the photo. The *High* setting is much more aggressive, whereas *Low* just picks up significant ghosting.

Check the **Show Deghost Overlay** checkbox to see which areas are affected by the deghosting, and remember to check them in the finished photo to ensure the deghosting hasn't introduced additional noise or sharp edges. **(Figure 13.70)**

How do I edit the HDR file after merging?

Auto Tone is applied to the preview to give you an idea of the tonal range before merging. Once the photo's merged, you can edit it in the Develop module. The resulting file has a much greater range of data with more highlight headroom and shadows with less

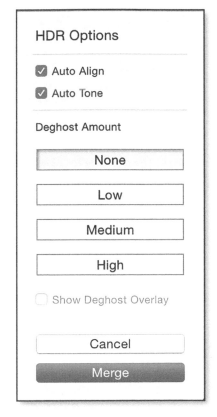

Figure 13.71 HDR options

Figure 13.72 The resulting HDR file has detail in the brightest highlights and the darkest shadows, so you can edit to your own taste.

Figure 13.73 Use the Develop module to edit the HDR file. The *Exposure* slider changes to a +10/-10 range.

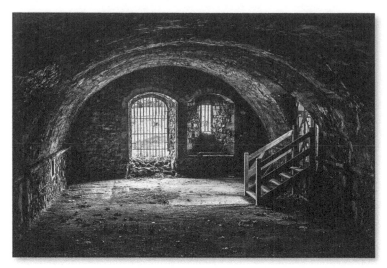

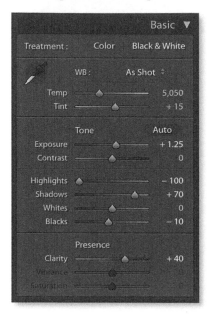

noise. **(Figure 13.72)** The *Exposure* slider runs to +10/-10 instead of +5/-5, and the *Highlights* and *Shadows* sliders have a greater range. **(Figure 13.73)** If you need to push the *Highlights* or *Shadows* further than +/- 100, you can paint on greater values using the local adjustments such as the Adjustment Brush or Graduated Filter.

PHOTO MERGE SHORTCUTS

HDR Merge	Ctrl-H / Cmd-H
HDR Merge (bypass dialog)	Ctrl-Shift-H / Cmd-Shift-H
Panorama Merge	Ctrl-M / Cmd-M
Panorama Merge (bypass dialog)	Ctrl-Shift-M / Cmd-Shift-M
In HDR dialog, Show Overlay	O
In HDR dialog, Cycle Overlay Colors	Shift O

DEVELOP MODULE TOOLS

In the previous chapters, we've covered the types of changes you can make to your photos, but the Develop module also includes a range of tools to make your editing quicker and easier. For example, you can sync your settings across multiple photos, save settings as presets to apply to other photos, update the default settings that are applied to new imports, undo changes that you've made and compare your edits against other versions of the photo.

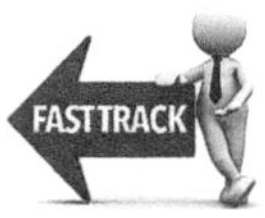

COPYING SETTINGS TO SIMILAR PHOTOS

Lightroom is a workflow tool, so it's designed to work with multiple photos. If you shoot a series of photos in similar light, you may want to copy settings from one photo to the other similar photos. There are multiple ways to do that...

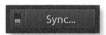

Figure 14.1 The *Sync* button is at the bottom of the right panel group.

Sync

Sync uses the data from the active (lightest gray) photo, and pastes it onto all the other selected (mid-gray) photos. That's why there are three different levels of selection.

1. Adjust the first photo, which is the source of the settings.

2. Keeping this photo active, also select the other photos by holding down Ctrl (Windows) / Cmd (Mac) or Shift key while clicking directly on their thumbnails, rather than the cell borders.

3. Click the **Sync** button in the Develop module **(Figure 14.1)**, or

---

SKIP THE DIALOG

Holding down the Alt (Windows) / Opt (Mac) button while pressing the *Sync* button synchronizes the settings but bypasses the dialog. It remembers which checkboxes were checked last time you accessed the dialog.

Sync Settings in the Library module, to show the Sync Develop Settings dialog.

4. Select the checkboxes for the slider settings that you want to copy to the other selected photos, and then press *Synchronize* to transfer the settings.

Copy and Paste

The Copy and Paste buttons allow you to copy settings into memory, and then paste them onto individual photos.

1. Adjust the first photo, which is the source of your settings.

2. Click the **Copy** button in the Develop module. **(Figure 14.2)**

3. Select the checkboxes for the slider settings that you want to copy.

4. Press the arrow key on your keyboard to move to the next photo, or select a different photo in the Filmstrip.

5. Click the **Paste** button to paste the settings onto the selected photo.

You don't have to copy all the settings. *Sync* and *Copy/Paste* both have dialogs allowing you to choose specific settings to transfer, so you may just sync *Noise Reduction* or *White Balance*, for example, without copying the *Exposure* settings. You may want to exclude things like Crop, Red Eye and Spot Removal that are specific to the photo.

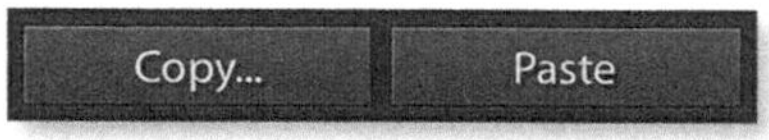

▲ **Figure 14.2** The *Copy* and *Paste* buttons are at the bottom of the left panel group.

FASTTRACK CONTINUES ON PAGE 301

Previous

The Previous option copies all the settings from the most recently selected photo to the next photo you select.

1. Adjust the first photo.

2. Press the arrow key on your keyboard to move to the next photo, or select a different photo in the Filmstrip. (Don't view any photos in between, as it takes the settings from the previously selected photo).

3. Press the **Previous** button to paste the settings onto the selected photo. **(Figure 14.3)**

There's one exception—if you're moving from a photo with no crop, to a photo with an existing crop, the crop is not reset.

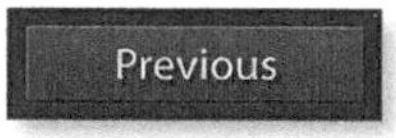

▲ **Figure 14.3** The *Previous* button only shows at the bottom of the right panel group when a single photo is selected.

Auto Sync

When you have multiple photos selected, any slider adjustments are applied to all the selected photos. (This matches the behavior of ACR in Photoshop/Bridge.) It can be slow for large numbers of photos, particularly when used with the crop or local adjustment tools.

1. Select multiple photos.

2. Toggle the switch next to the Sync button so that the label changes to **Auto Sync**. **(Figure 14.4)**

3. As you adjust the photos, all the selected photos update with any slider adjustment at the same time.

Auto Sync is powerful but dangerous, as it's easy to accidentally apply a setting to multiple photos without realizing that they're all selected. It gets particularly confusing if you often switch between standard Sync and Auto Sync, so you may find it easiest to leave it turned on at all times, or at least leave the Filmstrip visible so you can see the number of photos that are selected.

When you have Auto Sync turned on, you can still use the keyboard shortcuts for the other sync options such as Previous, Paste or standard Sync, but they apply to ALL selected photos, not just active (most-selected) photo, as Auto Sync is still active.

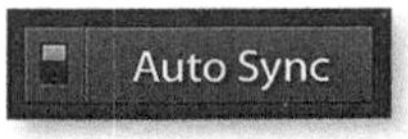

Why won't my white balance sync?

There's one quirk that trips everybody up when syncing settings. Your white balance is perfect on photo A, so you sync the settings to photo B... but it doesn't change. So you try it again... and it still doesn't change. Why?

As Shot is the key. If photo A is set to *As Shot* white balance, photo B

Figure 14.4 *Auto Sync* can be enabled by clicking the switch to the left of the Sync button.

MIXING PROCESS VERSIONS

If you mix PV2003/2010 photos with PV2012 photos when synchronizing settings, be aware that there may be unexpected results because they include different sliders. If you're synchronizing all the sliders, checking the Process Version checkbox in the Copy or Sync dialog ensures that the correct settings are applied. If you're only synchronizing specific sliders, the result depends on which sliders are selected and whether they have the same effect in both process versions.

COPY, PASTE & SYNC SHORTCUTS

Copy Settings	Ctrl Shift C / Cmd Shift C
Paste Settings	Ctrl Shift V / Cmd Shift V
Paste Settings from Previous	Ctrl Alt V / Cmd Opt V
Sync Settings	Ctrl Shift S / Cmd Shift S
Sync Settings (bypass dialog)	Ctrl Alt S / Cmd Opt S
Toggle Develop Auto Sync	Ctrl Alt Shift A / Cmd Opt Shift A
Match Total Exposures	Ctrl Alt Shift M / Cmd Opt Shift M

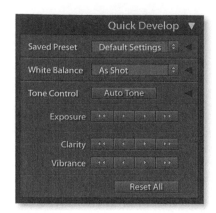

Figure 14.5 The Quick Develop panel is collapsed by default.

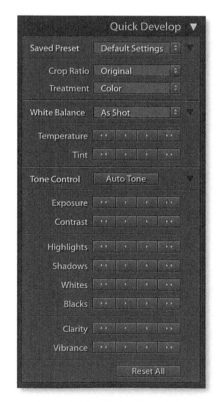

Figure 14.6 Click the disclosure triangles to view additional buttons.

is also then set to As Shot, not the same numerical values. To solve it, select *Custom* from the white balance pop-up, or shift the values slightly, and then sync with photo B, and your numerical values will be copied.

Can I make relative adjustments, for example, brighten all selected photos by 1 stop?

Imagine you've processed a series of photos, each with different settings, and then you decide you would like them all 1 stop brighter than their current settings. The first photo is set to -0.5 exposure, the next is 0 exposure, and the third is +1 exposure.

You could use Synchronize Settings, but that would move the sliders of the selected photos to the same fixed value as the active (most-selected) photo. Instead, you need relative adjustments, relative to their current settings.

You can't make relative adjustments directly within the Develop module, but you can do so using the Quick Develop panel in the Library module.

Select the photos and make sure you're viewing the Grid view, so that your changes apply to all selected photos.

By default, the Quick Develop is collapsed, so only a few of the buttons are available. Click the disclosure triangles to expand the full panel, then press the buttons to adjust the sliders. **(Figure 14.5 & 14.6)**

The double-arrow buttons move in large increments, and the single-arrow buttons move in smaller increments. For even smaller adjustments, hold the Shift key while pressing the single-arrow buttons. *Sharpening* and *Saturation* don't have buttons of their own, but they appear when you hold down the Alt key (Windows) / Opt key (Mac).

If some of the buttons are unavailable, your selected photos include a video or a mix of process versions.

What does *Match Total Exposures* in the Settings menu do?

While we're on the subject of synchronizing settings, let me introduce you to **Match Total Exposures**. It's a little known command found under the *Settings menu* in Develop, and it's very useful. It intelligently adjusts the exposure value to compensate for variations in camera settings.

Where photos are shot in the same lighting, but on Aperture Priority/

AV, Shutter Priority/TV or Program, it results in varying exposure values. This clever command calculates and adjusts the exposure on all selected photos to end up with the same overall exposure. It doesn't adjust for the sun going behind a cloud though!

To use it, correct the exposure on a single photo, then select other photos taken at the same time in the same light. In the Develop module, go to *Settings menu > Match Total Exposures*. The photos are automatically adjusted to match the overall exposure of the active photo, taking into account the variation in camera settings. You'll also find it in the Library module under *Photo menu > Develop Settings*, so you can apply it from Grid view.

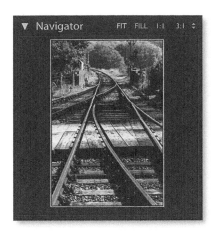

▲ **Figure 14.7** When you float the cursor over a preset name, it's previewed in the Navigator panel.

PRESETS—SAVING SETTINGS TO APPLY TO OTHER PHOTOS

Presets save sets of settings to apply to other photos over and over again. They simply move sliders to preset positions.

Some presets ship with Lightroom, so you can experiment with them before creating your own presets.

To apply a preset:

1. Go to Presets panel on the left in Develop **(Figure 14.8)**. As you float over the preset names, it displays a preview in Navigator panel above. **(Figure 14.7)**

2. To apply the preset to your photo, simply click on the preset name.

To create your own preset:

1. Adjust a photo to the settings that you want to save as your preset.

2. Press the + button on the Presets panel to show the New Develop Preset dialog. **(Figure 14.9)**

3. Check or uncheck the sliders you want to save in your preset. If a checkbox is unchecked, that slider won't be adjusted when you apply your preset to another photo. For example, if your preset is just for Sharpening settings, uncheck the other checkboxes and only leave the *Sharpening* checkbox checked.

4. Give your new preset a name, and you can also create folders to group similar presets together.

5. Press the *Create* button. Your preset now appears in the Presets panel for use on any photos.

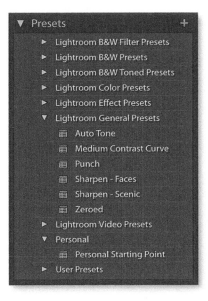

▲ **Figure 14.8** Develop presets are stored in the Presets panel.

▶**Figure 14.9** Create a new preset by pressing the + button on the Presets panel and checking the sliders you want to include in the preset.

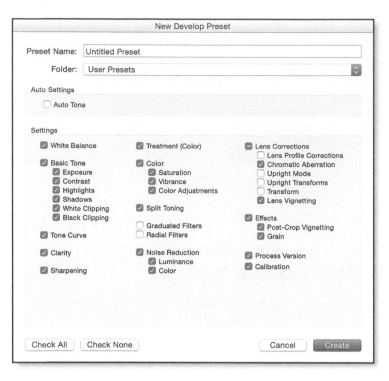

How do I install downloaded Develop presets?

If you're installing presets from a single folder, the automatic method is quick and easy. If you're installing lots of presets in one go, perhaps because you've bought a whole set, and they're organized into multiple folders, then the manual installation may be quicker.

Automatic installation

1. Unzip the presets if they're zipped.

2. Go to Develop module Presets panel, right-click the *User Presets* folder and choose *Import*.

3. Navigate to the folder of presets, select them and press the *Import* button.

Manual installation

1. Unzip the presets if they're zipped.

2. Find the Develop Presets folder in Explorer (Windows) / Finder (Mac) by going to *Preferences > Presets tab* and pressing the ***Show Lightroom Presets Folder*** button.

3. Drag (or copy/paste) the presets into that folder, still in their folders if you'd like to keep them organized in the same way.

4. Restart Lightroom.

DOWNLOAD PRESETS

A whole community has sprung up, sharing and selling Lightroom Develop presets. They can offer a good starting point for your post-processing, or more often, some weird and wonderful effects. I keep a list of the most popular Develop preset websites at http://www.Lrq.me/links/develop-presets for your easy access.

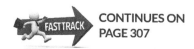

CONTINUES ON PAGE 307

How can I organize my presets into folders or groups?

Many users are now overflowing with presets that they've created or downloaded, and it can be difficult to find the one you're looking for. You can create folders for the presets by right-clicking on any existing user preset or preset folder and choosing **New Folder**. Once you've created folders, you can drag and drop the presets into logical groups. If you have hundreds of presets, you might find it useful to group your most often used presets in a single folder, rather than having to scroll through them all.

How do I apply presets to multiple photos?

To apply your preset in the Develop module to the currently selected photo, you can just click on the preset in the Presets panel.

To apply it to multiple photos, it's easiest to select all the photos in Grid view and choose your preset from the pop-up in the Quick Develop panel or from the right-click > *Develop Settings menu*. Anything you do in Grid view applies to all the selected photos. If you want to stay in Develop module, you can apply the preset with Auto Sync enabled, or you can apply to one photo and then use Sync to copy the settings to the rest of the photos.

Can I apply multiple presets to the same photo, layering the effects?

Presets only move a slider to a new position. They don't calculate new settings relative to the current slider settings.

If Preset A only adjusts, for example, the Exposure and Contrast sliders, and Preset B only adjusts the Vibrance slider, all of the settings are applied to the photo.

If the presets change the same sliders, for example, Preset A sets

---

PRESET SHORTCUTS

New Preset	Ctrl Shift N / Cmd Shift N
New Preset Folder	Ctrl Alt N / Cmd Opt N

You can't apply presets using a built in keyboard shortcut. Some commercial hardware devices, such as custom keyboards designed specifically for Lightroom, can apply presets using a button. The most popular options are listed at http://www.Lrq.me/links/lr-keyboards

the Exposure to -1 and then Preset B sets the Exposure to 0, then the changes made by the first preset are overwritten by the second preset.

How do I update, rename or delete Develop Presets?

To edit or update a preset, set the photo to the settings of your choice (as you did when creating it) and then right-click on a preset in the Presets panel and choose **Update with Current Settings**. Check or uncheck the sliders you want to save in your updated preset. If a checkbox is unchecked, the slider value isn't saved with the preset.

To rename a preset, right-click on it and select **Rename**. Renaming the preset file manually in Explorer (Windows) / Finder (Mac) doesn't work because the preset name is embedded in the file itself. It's possible to edit the preset with a text editor, but a minor error could corrupt the preset, so be careful!

To delete a preset, right-click on the preset and choose *Delete*. You can also navigate directly to the Develop Presets folder via the *Show Lightroom Presets Folder* button in the *Preferences dialog > Presets tab*, and delete/move multiple presets in one go, and then restart Lightroom. I keep a 'Spare Develop Presets' folder next to the main Develop Presets folder for the presets I uninstall but may want to reinstall in future, which helps to reduce the clutter.

How do I share my presets?

If you've created a really good Develop preset, you may want to share it with other Lightroom users. To do so, right-click on the preset and select **Export**, then select a folder on your hard drive. Alternatively, you can right-click on a preset and select *Show in Explorer* (Windows) / *Show in Finder* (Mac). That takes you directly to the current template location, ready to copy to another computer. Showing the whole folder is particularly useful when copying a larger number of templates.

Where have my presets gone?

If your presets suddenly disappear, go to *Preferences dialog > Presets tab* and try toggling the *Store presets with this catalog* checkbox to see if they reappear. You can learn more about this checkbox in the Multi-Computer catalog on page 514. In most cases, it's best to leave it unchecked.

DEFAULTS

Default settings are automatically applied whenever you import photos. Adobe sets the original default settings, but you can change them to suit your own taste. The defaults you set in Lightroom are also used by ACR (Camera Raw) in Photoshop/Bridge, and vice versa.

Why would I change the default settings instead of using a preset?

You could apply a Develop preset in the Import dialog instead of changing the defaults, but the defaults have a couple of additional benefits:

* The default settings only apply to newly imported photos that don't have existing settings stored in XMP, whereas a preset would override these existing settings.

* The default settings also apply any time you press the *Reset* button, whereas the resetting a photo imported with a preset resets to Adobe's defaults.

* The defaults can be set for specific camera models or ISO values, whereas presets apply to all of the photos in the import.

Why would I want different defaults for each ISO and serial number combination?

The default settings only apply to the specific camera model and file type combination used to create the default. For example, your Canon 5D Mk2 raw photos may require a little more contrast than your Nikon D800 JPEG files.

In the *Preferences dialog > Presets tab*, there are additional checkboxes to apply the defaults to specific files. **(Figure 14.10)**

* ***Make defaults specific to camera serial number*** is useful if you have multiple camera bodies of the same model, for example, with

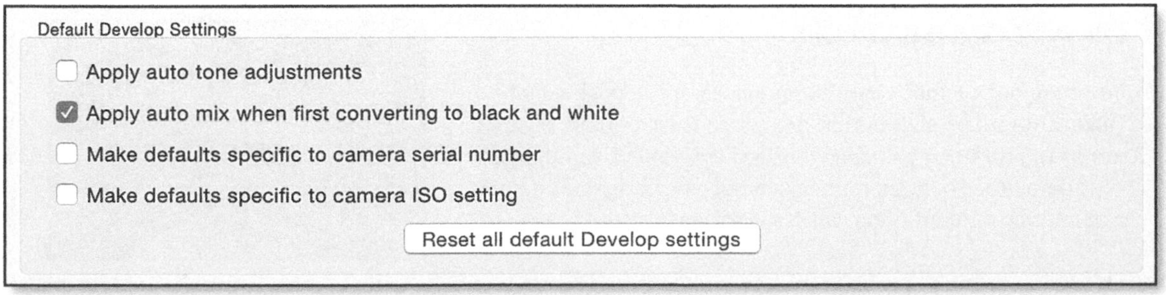

▼**Figure 14.10** In the Preferences dialog, you can choose whether the defaults should be specific to a camera body or ISO rating.

Default Develop Settings

☐ Apply auto tone adjustments

☑ Apply auto mix when first converting to black and white

☐ Make defaults specific to camera serial number

☐ Make defaults specific to camera ISO setting

Reset all default Develop settings

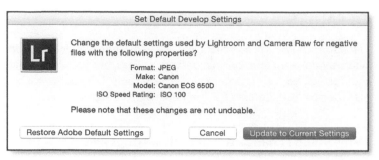

one set up for infrared photography requiring a different camera profile.

• **Make defaults specific to camera ISO setting** is useful for applying additional noise reduction at high ISO ratings.

Which settings should I use as the defaults?

Your default settings are a matter of personal taste, but Adobe's own defaults are a good starting point for most people. You might prefer a different camera profile, slightly more clarity or vibrance, or a higher contrast or sharpening setting. It's up to you, and if you change your mind, you can change your defaults again.

How do I change the default settings?

First go to *Preferences dialog > Presets tab* and decide whether you want *Make defaults specific to camera serial number* and *Make defaults specific to camera ISO setting* turned on or off. Then you're ready to change your default settings:

1. Open a photo in the Develop module and set your new settings. It's a good idea to press *Reset* first, to ensure that you only change the defaults that you intend to change.

2. Go to *Develop menu > Set Default Settings*.

3. Press *Update to Current Settings*. Although the dialog gives the

DIMMED SLIDER VALUES

You may notice that some slider values are a brighter white than others. The sliders that are set to their default settings are gray, and once you change the slider value from the current default setting, then the value becomes bright white. It's a quick way of identifying which sliders you've used.

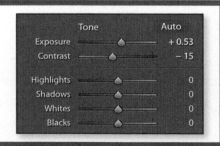

warning that the changes aren't undoable, you can return to the dialog at any time to restore the Adobe's own default settings or set new ones. **(Figure 14.11)**

4. Repeat with a sample photo from each camera, and each combination of ISO/Serial Number if these options were selected in Preferences.

Your new default settings apply to new imports, and any photos that you reset. To apply your new defaults to a group of existing photos, select them in Grid view and press *Reset* in the Quick Develop panel or in the right-click context-sensitive menu.

HISTORY & RESET

Because Lightroom's edits are stored as metadata, you can easily undo any of the adjustments.

As in most programs, Ctrl-Z (Windows) / Cmd-Z (Mac) is the Undo command. When pressed repeatedly, it steps back through your recent actions, whether that's slider movements, star ratings, or simply switching between modules. There are a few actions that can't be undone using these shortcuts, such as deleting photos from the hard drive, but the dialogs always warn if an action is not undoable using this shortcut.

Lightroom also keeps a record of all the Develop changes made to each photo. You can see this list in the History panel on the left in Develop module. You can try different settings without worrying, and then return to your earlier state if you don't like the result of your experiment.

To go back to an earlier version, click on an earlier history state in the History panel. **(Figure 14.12)** If you make further changes, a new history is written from that point on, replacing the steps that followed.

Finally, if you don't like the results of your edits and want to start again, press the *Reset* button at the bottom of the right-hand panel group to reset the photo's settings back to their defaults. There are reset options for individual panels and sliders too. Let's explore further...

How long do the adjustments stay in the History panel?

Thanks to its database, Lightroom keep a per-photo list of the Develop steps you've taken to get to the current settings. Unlike Photoshop, the history remains in the catalog indefinitely, even if

History		
Temperature	-50	5.3K
Black Clipping	+10	-10
Temperature	-200	5.3K
White Balance: Custom		
Tint	+45	4
Tint	-65	-41
Tint	+20	24
Temperature	-1.8K	5.1K
Temperature	+1.8K	6.9K
Post-Crop Vignette Hig...	+100	100
Post-Crop Vignette Am...	-15	-15
Clarity	-40	10
Contrast	+20	90
Shadows	0	40
Shadows	+20	40
Contrast	+20	70
Exposure	-0.10	0.43
Exposure	+0.40	0.53
Exposure	-0.20	0.13
Shadows	+20	20
Contrast	+20	50
Highlights	-20	-40

Figure 14.12 The History panel keeps track of the Develop changes you make, as well as any exports.

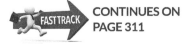

CONTINUES ON PAGE 311

> **LINEAR HISTORY**
>
> The Develop History is linear, so you can't remove an earlier history state. If you look at the numbers to the right, it tells you how far you moved the slider, and you can manually move the slider back by the same amount.

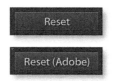

Figure 14.13 The *Reset* button sets the sliders back to your current default settings, which may be different to Adobe's default settings.

you close Lightroom. As long as you don't remove the photo from the catalog, you can come back months later and pick up where you left off, or go back to an earlier history state and carry on processing from there.

The **X button** at the top of the History panel clears the list of History states from the list, but it doesn't reset the Develop settings for the photo. It's useful if you've used a large number brush strokes, which are taking up a huge amount of space in the catalog and can increase RAM usage, but it's not usually necessary.

To clear the history states for multiple photos, select the photos and then go to *Develop menu > Clear History*. If more than one photo is selected, Lightroom asks whether to clear the history for the active photo or all of the selected photos.

How do I reset Develop settings?

To reset a photo back to default, press the **Reset** button at the bottom of the right-hand panel in the Develop module. If you've changed the default settings, you can reset the photo to Adobe's default settings by holding down the Shift key. This changes the *Reset* button to **Reset (Adobe)**. **(Figure 14.13)**

To reset multiple photos back to your default settings, it's easier to switch to the Grid view in the Library module and press the *Reset All* button in the Quick Develop panel (or select it in the right-click menu > *Develop Settings*).

To reset a single slider to its default setting, double-click on the slider label. To reset a whole section within a panel, hold down Alt (Windows) / Opt (Mac) and the panel label changes to a *Reset* button for that section (e.g. *Reset Tone*), or double-clicking on that same panel label without holding down the Alt (Windows) / Opt (Mac) buttons does the same.

BEFORE / AFTER PREVIEW

Once you've edited your photos, you'll want to see the results of your hard work. The Before/After Preview allows you to compare your current Develop settings with an earlier version, using your current crop settings. **(Figure 14.14)**

Press the \ key to toggle back and forth between before/after, or the Y key to see them side-by-side. The Y button on the Toolbar offers further options.

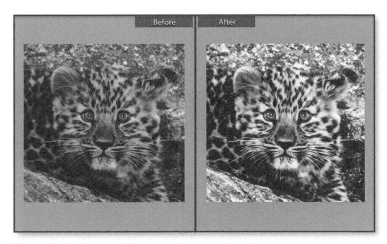

Figure 14.14 The Before and After views allow you to compare the results of your Develop adjustments.

How do I change the preview options?

By default, the Before/After preview displays side-by-side, but if you click the *Before / After Previews* button in the Toolbar (the one with Y's on it)—you'll see other options, such as side-by-side, top-and-bottom and split-view previews.

When would you use each option? Vertical side by side is useful for vertical photos, but hopeless for viewing wide panoramas, so click on the arrow to the left of the *YY* button and select *Before/After Top/ Bottom* instead. **(Figure 14.15)** If you're comparing something like noise reduction or sharpening, one of the split options is more useful, as it splits the photo down the middle.

How do I select a different history state for the Before view?

By default, the *Before* view is the last time you read settings from the file's metadata state which is usually when the photo was imported.

You can choose any history step or snapshot to be the Before view. To do so, right-click on the history step or snapshot, and choose **Copy History Step Settings to Before** or **Copy Snapshot Settings to Before**. **(Figure 14.16)**

If you have the *Before* view on screen, you can also drag a history state or snapshot from the History or Snapshot panel directly onto the *Before* preview, rather than going through the right-click menu. The key is dragging, rather than just clicking on the history or snapshot state, as clicking would change the *After* view instead of the

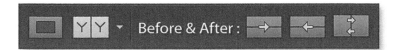

Before & After :

Figure 14.15 The *YY* button on the Toolbar allows you to change the display layout of the Before/After views.

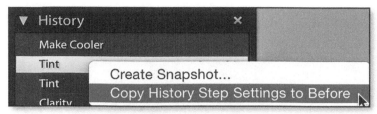

Figure 14.16 Select a different Before view by right-clicking in the History or Snapshot panel.

Before view. The arrowed buttons on the Toolbar allow you to swap the views currently on screen.

- To revert the photo's settings to the *Before* state, because you liked the old settings better, click the first arrow icon.

- To update the *Before* state to match the current *After* state, perhaps because you want to make further adjustments to the photo and compare them against the current state, click the second arrow icon.

- To swap the *Before* state and the *After* state, click the icon with two arrows.

CROP NOT INCLUDED

The Before/After preview excludes the crop settings, as different crops make it difficult to compare the other Develop adjustments.

Can I turn off the effect of a whole panel's settings, to see the preview with and without these settings?

On the end of most panel headers in the Develop module, such as the Tone Curve panel, there's a toggle switch. **(Figure 14.17)** This switch temporarily enables or disables the sliders in the section, so you can preview the photo with and without the effect of panel's sliders. It not only affects the preview but also any photos you export. This also applies to the selective editing tools in the Tool Strip, which have a switch at the bottom left of their Options panel.

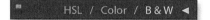

Figure 14.17 Use the toggle switch on panel headers to preview the image with and without that panel's adjustments.

PREVIEW SHORTCUTS

Toggle Before/After	\
Split Left / Right	Y
Split Top / Bottom	Alt Y / Opt Y
Split Screen	Shift Y / Shift Y
Copy After's Settings to Before	Ctrl Alt Shift left arrow / Cmd Opt Shift left arrow
Copy Before's Settings to After	Ctrl Alt Shift right arrow / Cmd Opt Shift right arrow
Swap Before and After Settings	Ctrl Alt Shift up arrow / Cmd Opt Shift up arrow

VERSIONS—SNAPSHOTS & VIRTUAL COPIES

The before/after preview is great if you only want to compare two history states, but what do you do when you want to compare multiple versions of a photo? You could keep switching between history states, but there's an easier option... snapshots and virtual copies.

If you want to experiment with different settings without overwriting your current version, you can create a virtual copy. Virtual copies show up in Lightroom as duplicate photos, and they have their own metadata and settings. They don't take up much more space on your hard drive as Lightroom doesn't need to duplicate the original image file.

To create a virtual copy, right-click and choose **Create Virtual Copy** or use the shortcut Ctrl-' (Windows) / Cmd-' (Mac). An additional copy appears next to the Master (the original file), and it has a small triangle in the corner of the thumbnail indicating that it's a virtual copy. It's automatically stacked with the original in the folder view. **(Figure 14.18)**

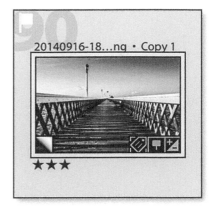

Figure 14.18 Virtual Copies can be identified by the triangular page turn icon in the corner of the thumbnail.

If you no longer want a virtual copy, you can delete it like any other photo. Deleting a virtual copy won't remove the original photo from the hard drive—only a Master can do that. It just removes that version of the metadata.

A snapshot is a special history state, which captures the slider settings at the moment of its creation. You can make changes to your photo, save it as a snapshot, make more adjustments, and then easily go back to the earlier snapshot state, even if you clear the History panel.

To create a snapshot, click the + button on the Snapshots panel. **(Figure 14.19)** By default, it names the snapshot using the current date/time, but you might prefer to give it a more useful name such as "4x5 crop." To update, rename or delete it, right-click on it. To reselect a snapshot, just click on its name (but remember that any Develop changes will overwrite your history).

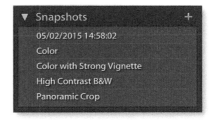

Figure 14.19 Snapshots capture the slider settings at the time of creation.

Virtual copies and snapshots are particularly useful for keeping different versions of your photos, for example, a color version, a black & white version, a special effect version, and different crops.

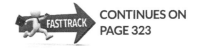

CONTINUES ON PAGE 323

How do I choose whether to use a virtual copy or a snapshot?

There's a crossover in the two concepts, so you can decide which works best for you.

Both options are virtual, so they don't take up additional space on the hard drive, with the exception of the metadata, and also the preview for a virtual copy.

A virtual copy is treated like a separate photo, so they show in Grid view alongside the master and any other virtual copies. This means you can compare the different versions side by side in the Compare or Survey views.

You can do almost anything to a virtual copy that you can do to a master photo. For example, you can give it a different star rating, label, keywords, or other metadata. A new virtual copy starts off with a copy of most of the metadata and Develop settings from the original photo, but the History panel only shows a single History state. (Just remember that if you edit the original image file in other software, such as Photoshop, your edits apply to all versions of the photo.)

A snapshot is more like a bookmarked history state. A photo can only be in a single snapshot state at any one time. A photo with multiple snapshots only appears as one photo in Grid view, and there's no way of telling that there are multiple versions from the Grid view.

If you write metadata to the files, as well as the catalog (we'll come back to this in the XMP section on page 343), there's one more deciding factor: information about virtual copies is only stored in the catalog and can't be written to the files, whereas snapshot information can be written back to the files.

Can I rename virtual copies?

If you rename a virtual copy, the name of the master photo changes too—after all, it's virtual. When you export the virtual copies, they can have different names from the originals as if they're individual photos, and you have some control over this naming while still in the Library module.

In the Metadata panel of a virtual copy is a *Copy Name* field which defaults to Copy 1. You can change it to an alternative name of your choice, for example, Sepia. **(Figure 14.20)**

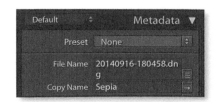

▲ **Figure 14.20** Set the *Copy Name* of virtual copies in the Metadata panel.

You can display the copy name on the thumbnails or Info Overlay using the *View menu > View Options* dialog. For example, *File Name and Copy Name* displays both the master file name and the copy name, whereas *Copy Name or File Base Name* displays the copy name unless it's blank, in which case it displays the existing filename.

You can also use the copy name to rename the photos when you export them, by selecting the *Copy Name* token in the Filename Template Editor. For example, if you've set the copy name to

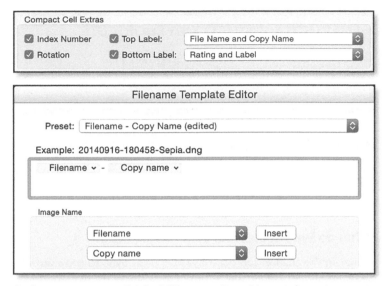

◀ **Figure 14.21** In the View Options dialog, you can set the thumbnail cell options to include the *Copy Name*.

◀ **Figure 14.22** Rename the photos when exporting, using their *Copy Name* as part of the new filename.

Sepia, you can use *Original Filename_Copy Name* tokens to create IMG_003_Sepia.jpg. **(Figure 14.21 & 14.22)**

Can I convert snapshots to virtual copies and vice versa?

If you're viewing a snapshot when you create a virtual copy, the virtual copy uses the current settings, and if you're viewing a virtual copy when you create a snapshot, the snapshots use the current settings.

Snapshots are available to all of the virtual copies, which is a really handy feature. It means you can use virtual copies when you're experimenting with different versions, and then save the final state of each virtual copy as a snapshot. You can then delete the virtual copies to clear the clutter when you've finished comparing them, without losing your Develop adjustments.

Can I promote virtual copies and delete the master?

If you need to swap a virtual copy for its master, perhaps because you want to keep the virtual copy's settings and delete the other, select the virtual copy and then select **Set Copy as Master** from the *Library menu*. If you want to do a whole batch of photos, it's not quite so simple. There are two options.

• Export the virtual copies to another folder, with the file format set to *Original*, and then import the new files into your catalog. You'd only have data that's stored in XMP, but it may be a good compromise in some circumstances.

BATCH SNAPSHOT CREATION

If you need to create snapshots for lots of photos, Matt Dawson's Snapshotter plug-in can automate the process.

http://www.Lrq.me/photogeek-snapshotter

SNAPSHOT & VIRTUAL COPY SHORTCUTS

Create Snapshot	Ctrl N / Cmd N
Create Virtual Copy	Ctrl ' / Cmd '

- Use the Syncomatic plug-in to sync settings from virtual copies to their master photos. It can sync flags, star ratings, labels, keywords and most Develop settings, but the crop is not copied. http://www.Lrq.me/beardsworth-syncomatic

What do Sync Copies and Sync Snapshots do?

Earlier in the chapter (on page 297) we used Sync to copy settings between photos. Under the *Settings menu*, there are two additional sync options which apply to virtual copies and snapshots. **Sync Copies** and **Sync Snapshots** allow you to sync settings from your current rendering to all of that photo's virtual copies or snapshots in one go. For example, if you've created different versions for different crop ratios, and then you brighten the photos or change the sharpening, you might want to update all of your other versions of that photo too.

COLOR MANAGEMENT & SOFT PROOFING

When it comes to color management, there's lots of confusion. Should you choose sRGB because it's commonly used? But you've heard ProPhoto RGB is better because it's bigger, so maybe you should choose this one?

Lightroom is internally color-managed, so as long as your monitor is properly calibrated, the only time you need to worry about color spaces is when you're outputting the photos. This may be passing the data to Photoshop or other software for further editing, passing the data to a printer driver for printing, or exporting the photos for other purposes, such as email or web.

LEARN MORE

If you'd like to learn more about color management, Jeffrey Friedl wrote an excellent article on color spaces at: http://www.Lrq.me/friedl-colorspace

So why are we talking about color management in Develop? There's a tool in Develop called Soft Proofing, which helps you to visualize the limitations of the output color spaces. Before we can dive into that though, we need a basic understanding of color management. Color management is a huge subject that could fill a separate book, so we'll just cover the bits you need to know.

Which color space should I use?

In the Histogram section on page 204, we said that photos are made up of pixels, and each pixel has a number value for each of the color channels (red, green and blue). For example, 0-0-0 is pure black. 255-255-255 is pure white. The numbers in between are open to interpretation. Who decides exactly which shade of green 10-190-10 equates to? That's where color profiles come into play: they define how these numbers should translate to colors.

There are two main groups of profiles—working profiles and output profiles—and they each cover different ranges of colors. Some color spaces contain a larger number of colors than others, so we refer to the 'size' of the color space.

Working profiles are standardized, so they can be used in a wide range of situations, whereas output profiles are designed for specific outputs, for example, a particular printer/paper/ink combination.

The most popular working spaces are:

- **sRGB** is a small color space, but fairly universal. It can't contain all the colors that your camera can capture, which results in some clipping, so it's not great as a working space. However, as it's a common color space, it's a good choice for photos that you're outputting for screen use (web, slideshow, digital photo frame), and many non-pro digital print labs expect sRGB files too.

- **Adobe RGB** is a slightly bigger color space, which contains more of the colors that your camera can capture, but still can't contain the full range. Many pro digital print labs accept Adobe RGB files. It's also a good choice for setting on your camera if you choose to shoot JPEG rather than the raw file format, if your camera can't capture in ProPhoto RGB.

- **ProPhoto RGB** is the largest color space that Lightroom offers, and it's designed for digital photographers. It can contain all the colors that today's cameras can capture, with room to spare. The disadvantage is that putting an Adobe RGB or ProPhoto RGB file in a non-color-managed program, such as most web browsers, give a flat desaturated result. This makes it an excellent choice for editing and archiving 16-bit photos, but a poor choice when sending photos to anyone else.

Output profiles are specific to the device, whether they're inkjet printers or huge photo labs.

So the right color space depends on the situation. You don't need to worry while the photo stays in Lightroom, as all the internal editing is done in a large color space which Lightroom manages. When the photo leaves Lightroom, then you need to make a choice. When you

EMBED PROFILES

Whichever color space you choose to use, always embed the profile. A digital photo is just a collection of numbers, and the profile defines how the numbers should be displayed. If there's no profile, the program has to guess—and often guesses incorrectly. Lightroom always embeds the profile, but Photoshop offers a checkbox in the Save As dialog, which you must leave checked.

edit in an External Editor such as Photoshop, you'll want to stick with a large working space. Once you've finished your editing, and you want to export the finished photo for a specific purpose, then you can choose a smaller color space which defines the characteristics of your output device (i.e. printer).

We'll discuss color spaces for editing in the External Editors chapter starting on page 327, and output profiles for editing in the Export and Print chapters (page 355 and page 424), but for now let's focus on soft proofing the finished result.

What is soft proofing?

Soft proofing attempts to simulate, on your calibrated monitor, how the photo will look with your chosen printer/paper/ink combination. You can then adjust the photo for that specific output without creating numerous test prints.

If you don't print to a locally attached printer, such as an inkjet printer, soft proofing can still be useful. If you send prints to an offsite lab, they may be able to provide their printer profile for soft proofing purposes.

Even if you only ever show your photos on a screen—perhaps on the web—soft proofing can show how your photos will look when exported to the smaller sRGB color space. Colors that are within

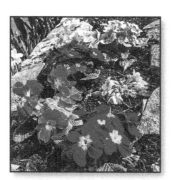

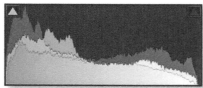

Figure 14.23 Lightroom's working space can contain the full range of colors that the camera captured.

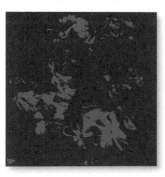

Figure 14.24 In sRGB, the highly saturated colors clip (shown as red highlights) because they fall outside of the small sRGB gamut.

Lightroom's working space may clip when converting to sRGB, for example, highly saturated reds become much less colorful when exported as sRGB. Soft proofing allows you to preview that effect and compensate if needed.

Let's illustrate with these flowers... the saturated colors make it clear to see the difference. We'll look at the histogram and clipping, in addition to the photo.

In the first photo **(Figure 14.23)**, the histogram doesn't spike at either end and the clipping warnings aren't showing, which means that all of of the colors can be contained in Lightroom's working color space.

And then we have the sRGB version **(Figure 14.24)**, with clipping warnings turned on, and it's clear to see, both from the clipping warning and the histogram, that the red channel is clipped in the smaller color space.

How do I enable soft proofing?

To turn on soft proofing, check the **Soft Proofing** checkbox in the Toolbar. **(Figure 14.25)** The Histogram panel changes to a Soft Proofing panel with additional options, and the background surrounding the photo changes from mid-gray to paper white. **(Figure 14.26)**

Select your output profile from the **Profile** pop-up menu. If your profile doesn't appear in the pop-up, select *Other* at the bottom of the *Profile* pop-up and put a checkmark next to your output profile in the Choose Profiles dialog. It then appears in the *Profile* pop-up, ready for selection. **(Figure 14.27)**

Should I select *Perceptual* or *Relative Colorimetric*?

When you've selected your profile, the **Intent** options become available. The rendering intent options only apply to output spaces such as printer profiles, not working spaces like sRGB, Adobe RGB and ProPhoto RGB.

Perceptual squeezes all the colors into the smaller color space while trying to retain their relationship to each other. That means that all the color values shift but it should still look natural. Perceptual rendering intent is good for highly saturated photos with a lot of out-of-gamut colors.

Relative Colorimetric leaves most of the colors alone, and just clips the out-of-gamut colors to the closest reproducible colors. It's usually a better choice if a photo is mostly within gamut, as it only shifts the out-of-gamut colors.

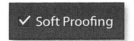

Figure 14.25 Soft Proofing is enabled using the checkbox on the Toolbar.

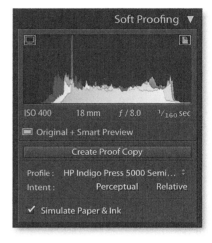

Figure 14.26 The Histogram panel changes to a Soft Proofing panel.

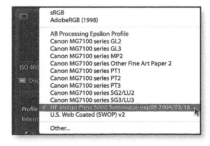

Figure 14.27 Select the profile you want to use for soft proofing.

UNSUPPORTED PROFILES

If your profile is correctly installed, but it still doesn't appear in the Choose Profiles dialog, then it may be an unsupported profile. Lightroom's limited to RGB or CMYK* profiles only, so it won't work with grayscale profiles, or some other non-standard profiles designed for Printer RIPs (Raster Image Processor).

Some RGB or CMYK profiles don't conform to the ICC Specification, and they're ignored too. Running *Profile First Aid* in ColorSync Utility on a Mac can often repair these profiles, making them available in Lightroom. I'm not aware of any free Windows software that can run an ICC profile repair.

* CMYK soft proof support was added in Lightroom CC/6, however you can't export to CMYK.

So which should you choose? If you're exporting the photo using the Export dialog, use *Relative Colorimetric*, as the Export dialog doesn't give you a choice of rendering intent. If you're printing through Lightroom, the Print module does give you a choice. In this case, it depends on the photo, so try both and see which looks best.

Should I check *Simulate Paper & Ink* when viewing my soft proof?

Simulate Paper & Ink simulates the reduction in contrast caused by dull white paper and dark gray black ink, so it's also known as the *Make the Photo Look Rubbish* checkbox. Your eyes adapt to the color and brightness of the whitest object in your view, making the soft proof look dark and flat.

To solve this, remove all other white/light reference points from your view and switch to Lights Out mode by pressing the L key. Your eyes then adjust to the soft proof version and you can adjust the photo accordingly.

With Lights Out, however, it's obviously impossible to adjust the photo, so when you're ready to start making adjustments, you'll need to disable Lights Out by pressing the L key again.

The 1:8 and 1:16 zoom ratios on top of the Navigator panel allow you to zoom out further, surrounding the photo with a larger area of paper white, while still being able to adjust the photo using the Develop controls.

Can I change the background color surrounding the photo while soft proofing?

By default, the background surrounding the photo shows a paper white, but the accuracy of that paper white depends on the quality of the profile. Some profiles show a bright yellow background which looks nothing like the paper. If it's wrong, you can switch to an alternative background by right-clicking in the background area. There's a range of shades of white and gray available, so you can select one which more closely matches the paper. Your chosen color is also used for the background when using Lights Out mode.

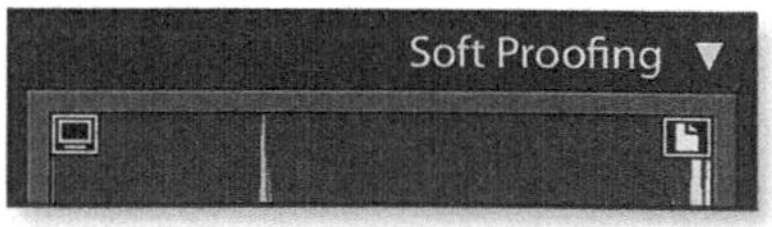

What's the difference between the Monitor Gamut and Destination Gamut warnings?

In the top corners of the histogram, the clipping warning buttons are replaced by gamut warning buttons. **(Figure 14.28)** (The gamut

Figure 14.28 The Monitor Gamut (left) and Destination Gamut (right) triangles take the place of the clipping warning buttons in the corner of the histogram.

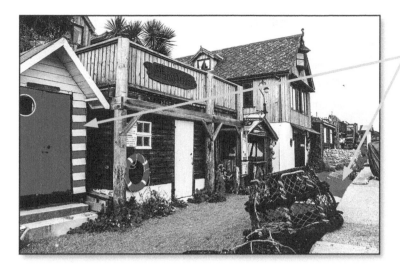

Figure 14.29 Colors that are out of gamut are highlighted to warn you that they may not print as expected.

is the complete subset of colors that can be reproduced in your chosen color space or by a specific device.) When you click to enable them, out of gamut areas of your photo are highlighted in blue, red or purple. If either out of gamut warning is showing, it's simply telling you that you're not seeing an accurate preview of those colors. **(Figure 14.29)**

- **Blue** indicates that a color is outside of the monitor gamut, which means that even if the color is printable, you won't get a good print-to-screen match because the monitor can't display that particular color accurately.

- **Red** means that a color is outside of the destination gamut, which means that it's not printable and will be remapped by the output profile.

- **Purple** is out of both gamuts.

What should I do if some colors are out of gamut?

If the colors are showing as out of gamut, it doesn't necessarily mean that you need to do anything about it. It's simply information. It tells you that the final print won't exactly match the screen preview in those areas.

Desaturating the photo, or locally desaturating the out-of-gamut colors, is traditionally suggested as a solution, however a good quality profile usually does a far better job of pulling these colors back into gamut without you having to adjust anything.

How should I adjust the photo while viewing the soft proof?

So if you're not going to reduce the saturation of the out of gamut colors, what's the point of soft proofing?

The main aim is to compensate for the losses in printing, to make the print look closer to the original. Often that's a difference in contrast and brightness, rather than color.

We discussed the Before/After views earlier in the chapter (starting on page 308), but they become particularly useful when soft proofing, as they allow you to compare your original intended rendering with the soft proofed copy. To turn it on, press the *Before/After Preview* button (the one with the Y's on it) in the Toolbar. Other views are also available when you click on the arrow next to the *Before/After Preview* button.

With the original photo on screen next to the soft proof preview, adjust the sliders to make the soft proof more closely match the original. You're simply trying to make the soft proof—and therefore the finished print—look better. **(Figure 14.30)**

How do I compare my proof adjusted photo with the original?

There's an additional **Before** pop-up in the Toolbar which allows you to select which version of the photo you want to compare against.

- **Current State** shows the current settings for the photo, without the soft proof applied. This allows you to see the effect that the output profile is having on the photo.

- **Before State** shows the normal 'before' state of the photo, without the soft proof applied. You can update this Before State by right-clicking on your chosen History state and selecting *Copy History*

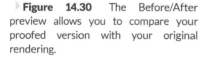
Figure 14.30 The Before/After preview allows you to compare your proofed version with your original rendering.

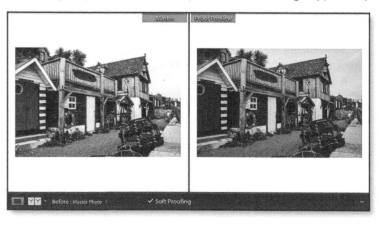

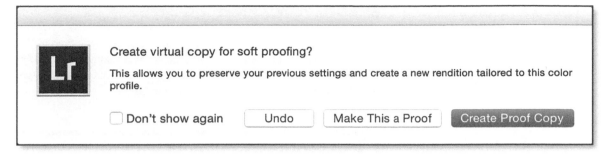

Step Settings to Before or by dragging the History state onto the Before view.

- **Master State** shows the current settings of the Master photo, without the soft proof applied. This allows you to see how well your profile-specific adjustments on the virtual copy match the general edits for that photo. You also have the option to compare with other virtual copies of the photo.

How do I save my photo after adjusting it for a specific profile?

Just below the histogram, there's a **Create Proof Copy** button, which creates a virtual copy of your photo for soft proofing. It means that your original settings, which were suitable for any kind of output, remain untouched, and your profile-specific adjustments are stored separately in a virtual copy.

If you start editing a photo without first creating a proof copy, Lightroom asks if you want to create a virtual copy for the soft proof, or whether you want to edit the original photo. **(Figure 14.31)**

If you select *Make This a Proof*, your current photo is marked as a proof under the *Settings menu*, and your adjustments apply to the master photo. It's not a bad choice if you're editing for sRGB use, but if you're adjusting for an output profile, it's better to select *Create Proof Copy*.

How can I tell which profile I used for a particular photo?

If you allow Lightroom to create a virtual copy for the soft proof, it enters the name of the profile in the *Copy Name* metadata field, and it updates if you switch to a different profile. You can view the Copy Name in the Metadata panel, the Grid view thumbnails, the Info Overlay or along the top of the Filmstrip. **(Figure 14.32)**

Any snapshots you create in Soft Proof mode also automatically include the profile in the Snapshot name.

Figure 14.31 When you edit a photo with soft proofing enabled, Lightroom offers to create a virtual copy.

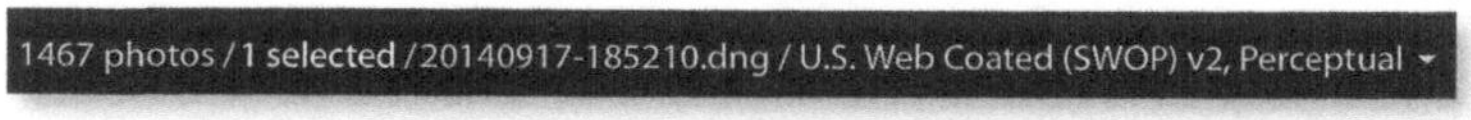

▶ **Figure 14.32** If you create a virtual copy for the soft proof, the name of the profile appears in the breadcrumb bar.

1467 photos / **1 selected** / 20140917-185210.dng / U.S. Web Coated (SWOP) v2, Perceptual ▾

When exporting the file, you can include the *Copy Name* field in the new filename for reference. *Filename-CopyName* tokens will result in a filename such as IMG_003-sRGB.jpg. Remember that Export always uses Relative Colorimetric as the rendering intent.

SOFT PROOFING SHORTCUTS

Show/Hide Soft Proof	S
Destination Gamut Warning	Shift S

FURTHER EDITING IN OTHER PROGRAMS

Lightroom is a brilliant workflow tool but there are still some tasks, such as detailed retouching, that require a pixel editor such as Photoshop. Lightroom can pass your edited photo over to your pixel editor and automatically add the resulting photo back into the catalog.

Integration with Photoshop

If a full version of Photoshop is installed on your computer, it appears in *Photo menu > Edit In* or the right-click menu. **(Figure 15.1)** You can also press Ctrl-E (Windows) / Cmd-E (Mac) to open the photo into Photoshop.

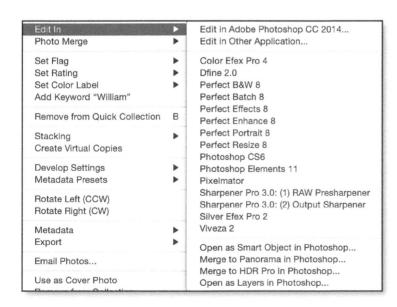

Figure 15.1 Lightroom can pass your photos to Photoshop and other external pixel editors.

If the photo is a raw file and you're using ACR 9 in CS6 or CC, Lightroom opens the photo directly into Photoshop. Older ACR versions ask how to handle the file, so press *Render Using Lightroom* in order to ensure the file renders correctly.

If you're working with a JPEG, TIFF, PSD or PNG file, a dialog asks how to handle the file. Select *Edit a Copy with Lightroom Adjustments* to open your photo with your Develop adjustments applied.

Once you've finished editing the photo in Photoshop, go to *File menu > Save* and then close the photo and switch back to Lightroom. Your edited photo is updated in your catalog automatically.

Integration with Photoshop Elements

Not everyone needs the power of full Photoshop. Elements can do many of the tasks photographers require. Like Photoshop, Lightroom recognizes when a recent version of Elements is installed, and *Photo menu > Edit In > Edit in Photoshop Elements* or Ctrl-E (Windows) / Cmd-E (Mac) opens the photo into Photoshop Elements. Once you've finished editing the photo, save (don't change the filename or file type) and close the file before returning to Lightroom.

Opening Photos in Other Editors

Lightroom can also send files to other external editors, such as OnOne software, Nik software, Pixelmator or PaintShop Pro.

Some of these editors come with their own Lightroom plug-ins and presets which are installed automatically. If your editor doesn't install its own connection, you can set it up manually. We'll come back to that a little later on page 341.

Why might I use an external editor?

But can't you do everything in Lightroom? Lightroom does offer a wide range of tools to cater for most of your editing needs, but that doesn't always make it the best tool for the job.

It's a parametric editor, which means that it runs text instructions rather than directly editing the pixels.

The benefit is it's non-destructive, so you don't need to save multiple versions of the file, taking up masses of hard drive space, and you can go back and change your edits again later.

The downside is that running text instructions over and over again is slower than making a single change to the pixels themselves. For global edits, that's barely noticeable, but Lightroom can start to drag

EXTERNAL EDITOR SHORTCUTS

Edit in Photoshop	Ctrl E / Cmd E
Edit in Other Application	Ctrl Alt E / Cmd Opt E

when using multiple local adjustments and retouching multiple spots. For this reason, pixel editors such as Photoshop and Elements are still better suited to more detailed retouching.

There may also be times when you want to do more specialized edits. For example, Lightroom can do great B&W conversions but Nik Silver Efex is designed purely for that purpose.

When in my workflow should I use Edit in Photoshop or other External Editors?

You may be wondering when to use your external editor. Is it better to edit your photo in the Develop module first, or wait until you've finished the retouching in the external editor?

Lightroom's Develop adjustments work best on raw files, because they have the largest amount of data available. For this reason, it's usually best to do most, if not all, of your Lightroom adjustments in Lightroom before using Edit in Photoshop to do your retouching. The same would apply to most other External Editors.

There are a couple of exceptions:

- You may prefer to leave cropping until after your external edits, leaving you the flexibility to non-destructively crop to multiple different ratios without having to repeat your retouching and other edits.

- If the photo is going to be in both B&W and color, you may also want to retouch the color version and then convert the resulting photo to B&W so that you only have to do the retouching once.

- If your photo was shot in JPEG, or it's a scan, the workflow order isn't as important. For example, you may decide to retouch dust on negative scans in Photoshop before editing them in Lightroom.

Having covered the basics, let's do a deeper dive into the settings.

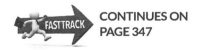

CONTINUES ON PAGE 347

SETTING EXTERNAL EDITOR PREFERENCES

We'll go into more detail on specific programs, but first, let's consider the settings that apply to all external editors. The file type, color space, bit depth, resolution and compression are all set in *Preferences > External Editing.* The top half of the dialog sets the primary editor's settings—the most recent version of Photoshop or Photoshop Elements—and the lower half creates presets for all other external editors. **(Figure 15.2)**

Figure 15.2 Set the default settings for Photoshop and other external editors using the Preferences dialog.

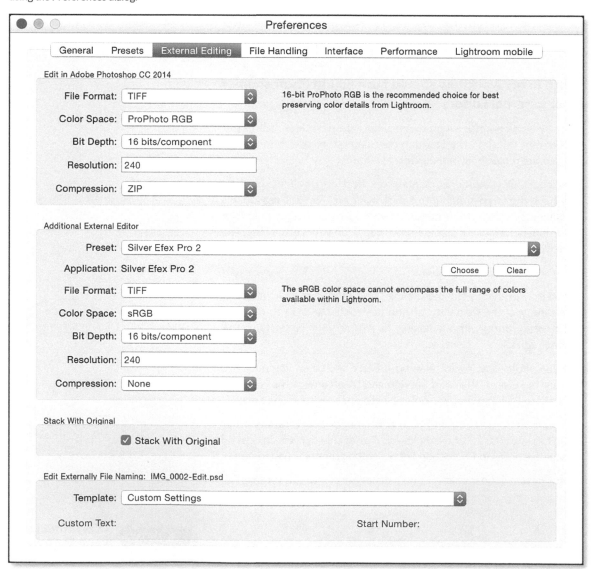

Which file format should I use?

The first pop-up, *File Format*, determines the file type that's passed to the external editor.

- **TIFF** is publicly documented, more efficient when updating metadata, compatible with a wide range of software, and can contain almost everything that PSD's do. It's generally considered the best choice for external edits. We'll come back to the various **compression** options in the Export chapter on page 353, but ZIP compression is a good choice for most external editors.

- **PSD** is Adobe's proprietary format. It's well supported by other applications, as long as you check *Maximize Compatibility* but it's generally considered an older format now, so even Adobe are recommending TIFFs instead of PSD files now. Some plug-ins, such as OnOne software, prefer PSD format.

- **JPEG** is only available for secondary external editors, as some (rare!) editing programs are unable to work with TIFF or PSD files. It's a lossy format, so it's not a great choice for external edits.

Which color space should I select?

Files are automatically color managed in Lightroom, but when you pass them to another editor, you'll need to choose a working space using the *Color Space* pop-up. We've already discussed color spaces in the previous chapter (starting on page 314), but as a reminder:

- **ProPhoto RGB** is the best choice if your external editor is color managed, as it preserves the widest range of color information. ProPhoto RGB doesn't play well with 8-bit though, because you'd be trying to jam a large gamut into a small bit depth, which can lead to banding, so stick with 16-bit while using ProPhoto RGB.

- **Adobe RGB** is a smaller color space, but it's a good choice if your external editor can only handle 8-bit files (or you're saving as JPEG).

- **sRGB** is the smallest color space available, so it's not ideal for external editors.

Why use a big color space when nothing can print that wide a range?

Now it's true, not all of these possible ProPhoto RGB colors can be reproduced on screen or print at this point in time, but that's not a good reason for throwing data away and using a smaller space. Even

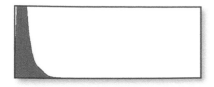

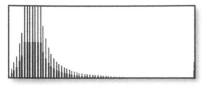

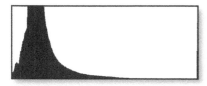

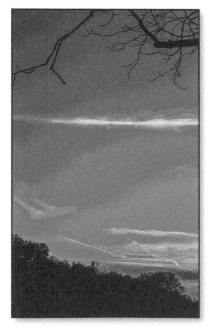

▲ **Figure 15.3** If you take an underexposed photo (top) and stretch the 8-bit data, you'll get gaps in the histogram (center) whereas 16-bit has more data to stretch (bottom).

▲ **Figure 15.4** This 8-bit image shows significant banding in the sky.

now, some printers can print some colors that can't currently be displayed on the best screens.

Remember when computer monitors were only B&W or 256 colors? Photographers still created full color images even though they couldn't see the full range of colors. If they'd limited themselves to what they could see, they'd have kicked themselves when the current monitors became available. So in the future, when even more advanced monitors are released, you'll be able to see your full range of image data.

There can be a little bit of guesswork involved when working with extremely saturated colors, but that's where the gamut warnings on the soft proof start to help. These give you information, telling you which colors may not match what you're seeing on screen. Unless you're pushing the saturation/vibrance really high, you won't run into issues on most images, and even when you do, profiles do an excellent job of pulling colors back into gamut without you having to change anything. But it helps to understand what's happening.

Whichever color space you choose, it's important that it's selected in both programs. We'll come back to settings the color space in Photoshop and Photoshop Elements in the next section (starting on page 331).

Should I choose 8-bit or 16-bit?

The next pop-up is **_Bit Depth_**. To the right, you'll notice a note that says 16-bit ProPhoto RGB is the officially recommended choice for best preserving color details from Lightroom, but what does that actually mean?

Every photo is made up of pixels. In an RGB photo, each pixel has a Red, a Green and a Blue channel, and in an 8-bit photo, each of those channels has a value from 0-255.

If you need to make any significant tonal changes, you only have a maximum of 256 levels per channel to play with. For example, if you've significantly underexposed the photo, all the detail may be in the first 128 levels (on the left of the histogram). As you correct the exposure, you stretch the detail out to fill the full 0-255 range, but you can't create new data. The missing data displays as gaps in the histogram. **(Figure 15.3)**

The gaps may not be visible on an average photo, but they display as banding (or steps) on photos with smooth gradients, such as a sky at sunset. **(Figure 15.4)** A 16-bit photo, on the other hand, has 65,536 levels per channel, so you can manipulate and stretch it without worrying about losing too much data.

The downside to 16-bit is that all that extra data takes up more space on your hard drive, so in the real world, it's not always quite so clear cut. 16-bit files can only be saved as TIFF or PSD, not JPEG, and the file sizes are much bigger than an 8-bit high quality JPEG, often with very little, if any, visible difference to the untrained eye on a small print. A Canon 5D Mk2 file is around 126 MB for a 16-bit TIFF, 63 MB for an 8-bit TIFF, but less than 15 MB for a maximum quality 8-bit JPEG. That's a big difference on a large volume of files!

So the reality is you may want to weigh it up on a case-by-case basis. If you're producing a fine art print, 16-bit would be an excellent choice to preserve as much detail as possible. Or if you're going to take a file into Photoshop and make massive tonal changes, 16-bit would be an excellent choice, giving greater latitude for adjustments. But if you're just doing light retouching on a large volume of files, 8-bit JPEG could be a far more efficient choice. You can always re-export from Lightroom as a 16-bit file if you find a photo which would benefit, such as a photo exhibiting banding in the sky, or suchlike.

Which resolution should I select?

We'll come back to the concept of **Resolution** in the Export chapter (page 358). While editing the photos in external editors, your choice of resolution doesn't really matter, as all of the pixels (less any cropped pixels) are passed to the external editor. There are a few cases where you might want to select a specific resolution, for example, when you're running a Photoshop action that uses specific measurements.

How do I change the file name and location?

At the bottom of the dialog, select the file naming template of your choice. By default, Lightroom simply adds *-Edit* to the end of the filename to show that it's a derivative file, and in most cases that's an excellent choice.

By default, the edited files are saved in the same folder as the original photo and automatically imported into your Lightroom catalog, but there are a few scenarios that can affect this:

Created by External Editor

- The file isn't saved until you select *File menu > Save* or Ctrl-S (Windows) / Cmd-S (Mac) in your external editor. It's automatically saved in the same folder as the original photo and automatically imported into your Lightroom catalog.

- If you select *Save As* and change the filename, file type or location,

---

8-BIT JPEG RETOUCHING FOR HIGH VOLUME PHOTOGRAPHERS

Everything's a trade-off. 16-bit ProPhoto RGB lossless TIFFs and PSDs result in the best quality, but they also take up a huge amount of hard drive space and time. High volume photographers doing a single pass of minor retouching and creating small prints, such as wedding photographers, may find an Adobe RGB or sRGB 8-bit JPEG workflow a more efficient and cost-effective solution for most photos. There is no right or wrong—weigh up the pros and cons and make an informed decision.

Lightroom loses track of the file, preventing it from being automatically imported.

- This applies to:
  - Primary external editor (Photoshop or Elements) with a matching ACR version.
  - Primary external editor with a mismatched ACR version but pressing *Open Anyway*.

Created by Lightroom

- The file is created by Lightroom, added to the catalog and passed to the external editor. When you select *File menu > Save* or Ctrl-S (Windows) / Cmd-S (Mac) in your external editor, the Lightroom preview is updated to include your edits.

- If you select *Save As* and change the filename, file type or location, Lightroom loses track of the new file, preventing it from being automatically imported. The unedited file that Lightroom created remains on the hard drive and in the catalog.

- This applies to:
  - Primary external editor with a mismatched ACR version but pressing *Render Using Lightroom*.
  - Secondary external editor

Other variations

- The other Photoshop options, such as *Open as Smart Object in Photoshop* and *Merge to Panorama* default to the last folder you used in Photoshop.

- If you're using Elements, you may also want to change Elements *Preferences dialog > Saving Files section > On First Save* pop-up to *Save Over Current File*, otherwise it asks you for a new filename each time you edit a file. Alternatively, simply ensure that you don't change the filename or file type when saving, otherwise the resulting file won't appear in Lightroom.

Can I automatically stack the files?

The final option in preferences is a ***Stack with Original*** checkbox that stacks the edited photo with the original, putting the edited version on top. Some photographers like to apply a color label to their finished photos to help quickly identify them.

SORT ORDER

If your sort order is set to *User Order, Edit Time,* etc., Lightroom puts the edited file at the end of the series of photos, and if you have it set to *Stack with Original* in Preferences, it also moves the original photo to the end. If you don't want to have to keep scrolling back again, use a sort order such as *Capture Time* or *Filename* that won't automatically be updated.

> ## EDITOR-SPECIFIC FILENAMES AND CUSTOM FOLDERS
>
> The single filename template in the External Editor preferences applies to all external editors, so you can't apply a different filename to each editor (e.g. 201503092100-NikSilverEfex.tiff). The edited photos are also saved in the same folder as the original, rather than a folder you specify.
>
> You can work around this limitation by using Export presets instead. We'll come back to the options in more detail in the Export chapter (starting on page 347), but in short, go to the Export dialog and select the options of your choice, for example:
>
> - *Export Location*—Set to the location of your choice, for example, *Same folder as original photo* and select *Put in Subfolder* called *Edited*. Check *Add to this Catalog* if you want the resulting photo imported automatically, as it would be with standard External Editors.
>
> - *Rename to*—Set to *Filename-Custom Text* with the custom text set to *NikSilverEfex* (or your editor's name)
>
> - *Image Format*—TIFF 16-bit or another rendered file format of your choice.
>
> - *Post-Processing*—Set it to *After Export: Open in Other Application* and navigate to the program. Select the exe file (Windows) / application (Mac).
>
> Finally, save your settings as a preset and cancel out of the Export dialog. To use the preset, right-click on a photo, scroll down to *Export* and click on your preset.

EDITING IN PHOTOSHOP OR PHOTOSHOP ELEMENTS

As you'd expect, Lightroom has greater interaction with Adobe software than it does with other pixel editors. In the case of Photoshop CS6 or CC, this includes the ability to pass the raw data, without first needing to create a TIFF/PSD file. It uses Adobe Camera Raw (ACR) to render the file, which we'll discuss in more detail in the next section, starting on page 337.

Why isn't Lightroom opening my photo as a TIFF or PSD file according to my preferences?

If Photoshop is set as the Primary External Editor (the first choice), the photo is opened directly into Photoshop and rendered using Adobe Camera Raw (ACR), so it's not saved as a TIFF or PSD until you choose to save it.

When you press Ctrl-S (Windows) / Cmd-S (Mac) in Photoshop, or go to *File menu > Save*, Photoshop creates the TIFF or PSD file according to your Lightroom preferences. You don't need to use *Save As* to create the TIFF/PSD file (in fact, it causes more complications if you do use *Save As!*)

DON'T FLATTEN MY LAYERS!

Lightroom doesn't understand layers—it's a different tool for a different job. This means that when you apply Develop changes to a layered photo, the layered photo must be flattened to apply the changes, losing your layers in the process. Of course, this doesn't have to be done until the final export.

That's a great feature, as if you're just experimenting and you decide not to keep your edited file, you can just close without saving and don't have to worry about going back to delete the TIFF or PSD. (Note that this only works with matching ACR versions, or when you select *Open Anyway* in the ACR mismatch dialog. We'll come back to ACR mismatches in the next section on page 337.)

What's the difference between Edit Original, Edit a Copy, or Edit a Copy with Lightroom Adjustments?

If you're passing a rendered file to Photoshop or Elements—a TIFF, a PSD, or a JPEG—then Lightroom first asks how you want to handle the file. **(Figure 15.5)** (It doesn't ask for raw files.)

- **Edit a Copy with Lightroom Adjustments** passes the image data and the settings to ACR to open directly into Photoshop, or creates a TIFF/PSD if you're using Elements. Any layers are flattened in the process. If there's a mismatch in ACR versions, it displays the same ACR Mismatch dialog as a raw file, with the same results.

- **Edit a Copy** creates a copy of the original file, in the same format, and opens this into Photoshop without any of your Lightroom edits. It allows you to edit the photo without overwriting your previous file, and also retains any layers in the file.

- **Edit Original** opens the original file into Photoshop without any of your Lightroom edits. It's useful if you want to continue editing a photo that you've previously edited in Photoshop, as it retains any layers in the file.

▶ **Figure 15.5** When you send rendered files to Photoshop, it asks you how to handle the file. This dialog is skipped for raw files.

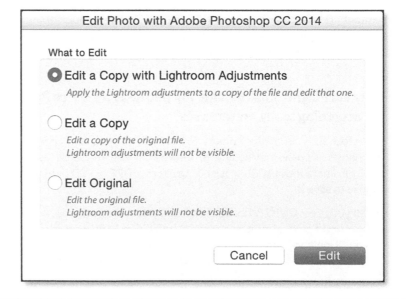

If you need to open the photo back into Photoshop to make further adjustments to the layers, perhaps for additional retouching, choose the *Edit Original* or *Edit a Copy* options, rather than *Edit a Copy with Lightroom Adjustments*. This opens the layered file into Photoshop without your Develop adjustments, and when you bring the file back into Lightroom, your Develop adjustments are still laid non-destructively over the top.

What do the other options in the Edit In menu do?

Using Edit in Photoshop as the primary External Editor, you can open the file or multiple files directly into Photoshop CS3 10.0.1 or later without first saving an interim TIFF or PSD file **(Figure 15.6)**, although you may get unexpected results if you're not using a fully compatible version of ACR. The older the Photoshop version, the more unexpected the results will be.

Open as Smart Object in Photoshop allows you to edit the Develop settings in the ACR dialog while in Photoshop, although these Develop settings won't then be updated on the original file in your Lightroom catalog, but remain with the edited copy.

Merge to Panorama, *Merge to HDR Pro* and *Open as Layers in Photoshop* only become available when you have multiple photos selected.

Merge to Panorama in Photoshop opens the files directly into the Photomerge dialog in Photoshop, allowing you to create panoramic photos with more control over the layout and blending than Lightroom's own *Photo Merge > Panorama* tool.

Merge to HDR Pro in Photoshop opens the files directly into the Merge to HDR Pro dialog in Photoshop to create HDR photos. Lightroom's own *Photo Merge > HDR* is a better choice as it works on the unprocessed raw data.

Using *Merge to Panorama* or *HDR Pro* automatically adds the resulting photos to your Lightroom catalog when you save them.

Open as Layers in Photoshop opens the files directly into Photoshop and places the photos into a single document as multiple layers, which is particularly useful if you need to merge multiple photos in Photoshop.

EXTENDING ELEMENTS

If you're using Photoshop Elements, these additional direct integration options are unavailable, but Matt Dawson's Elemental plug-in adds similar functionality for Elements 10 or later, and is available from: http://www.Lrq.me/photogeek-elemental

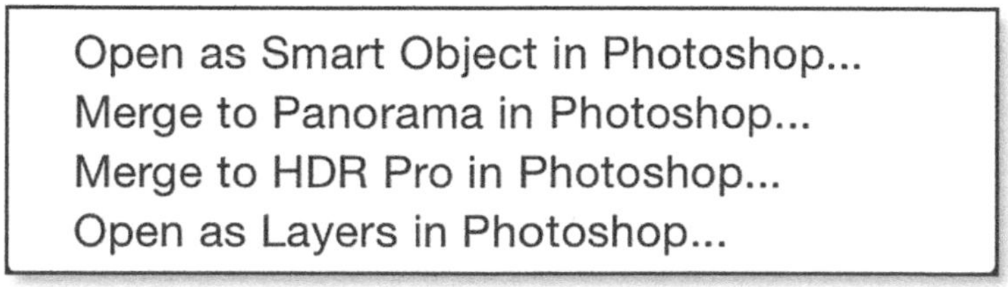

Open as Smart Object in Photoshop...
Merge to Panorama in Photoshop...
Merge to HDR Pro in Photoshop...
Open as Layers in Photoshop...

◀ **Figure 15.6** If you're using a recent full version of Photoshop, additional options will be available, such as *Merge to Panorama* and *Merge to HDR Pro*.

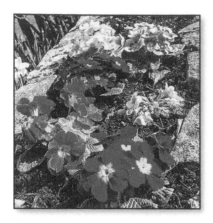

▲ **Figure 15.7** ProPhoto RGB displayed correctly in color managed software looks bright and colorful.

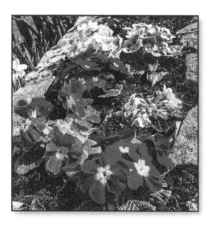

▲ **Figure 15.8** A ProPhoto RGB photo incorrectly displayed as sRGB is flat and desaturated.

Edit in Adobe Photoshop CC 2014

File Format:	TIFF
Color Space:	ProPhoto RGB
Bit Depth:	16 bits/component
Resolution:	240
Compression:	ZIP

▲ **Figure 15.9** Lightroom's External Editor Settings need to match Photoshop's Color Settings.

Should I still use Merge to HDR Pro or Merge to Panorama in Photoshop?

Lightroom now has its own HDR and Panorama merge tools, but there are occasions when you might want to use Photoshop's version of these tools.

If Lightroom has trouble with ghosting in an HDR file, Photoshop can occasionally do a better job. To try it, select the files, right-click and choose *Edit In > Merge to HDR Pro in Photoshop*. In the HDR Pro dialog, select 32-bit mode and press *OK*. The White Point Preview slider only affects the preview. When you save the resulting photo as a 32-bit floating-point TIFF, Lightroom allows you to import and edit the photo with an extended slider range.

If you're merging photos into a panorama and you want to control the blending yourself, or you want another perspective that Lightroom doesn't offer, you can use Photoshop instead.

When creating a panoramic photo using Photoshop, first edit your photos in the Develop module. Make sure they match, otherwise you'll find join lines in the finished panorama. Pay particular attention to the exposure, especially if you weren't shooting in Manual mode. It's also a good time to apply lens corrections, noise reduction, etc. The photo that comes back from Photoshop will be a rendered file (TIFF or PSD) with less editing flexibility, unlike Lightroom's own panorama merge.

Select the files, right-click and choose *Edit In > Merge to Panorama in Photoshop*. Select the merge options in Photoshop's Photomerge dialog and press *OK*.

Why do my photos look different in Photoshop?

If you open your files into Photoshop and they're a different color, it's usually due to incorrect color space settings. For example, a ProPhoto RGB photo **(Figure 15.7)** mistakenly rendered as sRGB displays as desaturated and flat. **(Figure 15.8)**

1. In Lightroom, go to the *Preferences dialog > External Editing tab*.

2. Make a note of the *Color Space* setting for Photoshop. **(Figure 15.9)**

3. Switch to Photoshop or Elements and go to *Edit menu > Color Settings* to view the Color Settings dialog.

4. In Photoshop:

   • Set the **RGB Working Space** to the same color space that

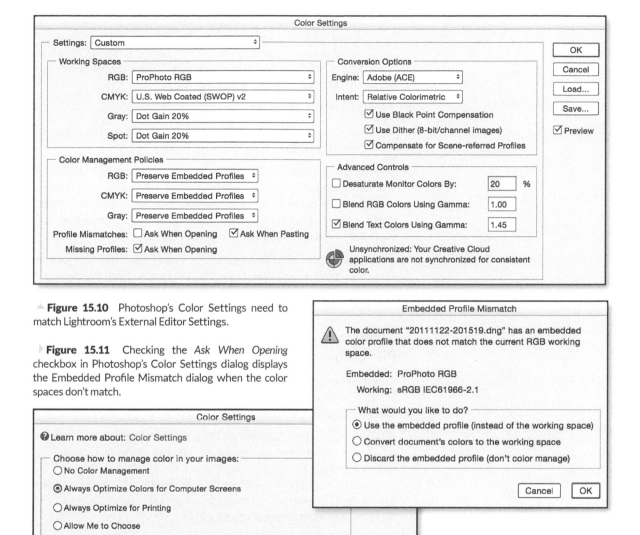

Figure 15.10 Photoshop's Color Settings need to match Lightroom's External Editor Settings.

Figure 15.11 Checking the *Ask When Opening* checkbox in Photoshop's Color Settings dialog displays the Embedded Profile Mismatch dialog when the color spaces don't match.

Figure 15.12 Photoshop Elements respects embedded profiles as long as it's not set to *No Color Management*.

you selected in Lightroom's External Editor preferences. **(Figure 15.10)**

- Selecting *Preserve Embedded Profiles* and/or checking the *Ask When Opening for Profile Mismatches* in that same dialog helps to prevent any profile mismatches.

- **Preserve Embedded Profiles** tells Photoshop to use the profile embedded in the file regardless of whether it matches your usual working space.

- *Ask When Opening for Profile Mismatches* displays a warning dialog when the embedded profile doesn't match your usual working space, and asks you what to do. If *Preserve Embedded Profile* is selected, you can safely leave the profile mismatch checkboxes unchecked. **(Figure 15.11)**

In Elements:

- Select any of the options except *No Color Management*. **(Figure 15.12)**

As long as your Photoshop and Lightroom color settings match, or you have Photoshop set to use the embedded profile, your photos should match between both programs. The same principles also apply to opening photos in other software, or when opening photos exported from Lightroom using the Export dialog.

If your color space settings are correct, a color mismatch can also be caused by a corrupted monitor profile. That's easy to check using the instructions on page 538 of the Troubleshooting chapter.

Lightroom can't find Photoshop to use Edit in Photoshop—how do I fix it?

When Lightroom starts up, it checks to see whether Photoshop or Photoshop Elements are installed, and if it can't find them, then the *Edit in Photoshop* menu command is disabled.

If you install a new version of Photoshop, and then uninstall an earlier version, the link can get broken by the uninstall. Uninstalling and reinstalling Photoshop usually solves it, or you can fix it by editing the registry key (Windows) or deleting Photoshop's plist file (Mac). There's more information on the official Adobe tech note at: http://www.Lrq.me/fixphotoshoplink

Of course, you may be able to take the easy course and add it as an *Additional External Editor*, however you would be missing out on some of the direct integration which comes with matching ACR versions.

Lightroom can't find Photoshop Elements to use Edit in Photoshop—how do I fix it?

If Photoshop Elements isn't automatically selected as the primary external editor, you can try to fix the link using the instructions in the previous question. Alternatively you can set it up as an *Additional External Editor* (page 341).

On Windows, you have to find the PhotoshopElementsEditor.exe file. This is the standard path for PSE13:

C:\Program   Files\Adobe\Photoshop   Elements   13\
PhotoshopElementsEditor.exe

On a Mac, the trick is to find the Editor itself, rather than the separate
Organizer app. In PSE 13, that's tucked away inside a *Support Files*
folder:

Macintosh HD/Applications/Adobe Photoshop Elements 13/Support
Files/Adobe Photoshop Elements Editor.app

ADOBE CAMERA RAW COMPATIBILITY FOR PHOTOSHOP

ACR, or Adobe Camera Raw, is the processing engine which allows
Adobe programs to read raw file formats and convert them into
image files. It's available as a plug-in for Adobe Bridge, Photoshop
and Elements, and the same engine is built directly into Lightroom
itself.

Updates are released every 3-4 months to add new camera and lens
support and bug fixes.

Lightroom runs as a standalone program, without any need for
Photoshop. If you do want to use the two together, it's important to
update both at the same time to make sure the ACR versions are fully
compatible, or at least ensure that you understand the implications
of a mismatch.

If you're using Photoshop CC, use the Adobe Creative Cloud app to
install the updates. If you're using Photoshop CS6 or Elements 13,
go to *Help menu > Updates* to launch the Adobe Application Manager
instead.

If you're using the most recent version of Lightroom and the most
recent ACR plug-in in Photoshop CC, everything's perfectly matched.

If you're using the most recent version of Lightroom and the most
recent ACR plug-in in Photoshop CS6 or Elements 13, Edit in
Photoshop works correctly, but some of the controls are missing
from the ACR dialog if you edit a raw file directly in CS6/Elements.

What happens if I'm still using an older version of ACR and Photoshop?

With older versions of ACR or Photoshop, it gets a little more
complicated.

Usually, when you open a photo into Photoshop from Lightroom,

Lightroom passes the original raw data and instructions over to the ACR plug-in hosted by Photoshop, and ACR performs the conversion and opens the image into Photoshop. **(Figures 15.14 & 15.15)**

If you're using an older version of ACR, it may not understand all of Lightroom's instructions, resulting in a completely different rendering. When the ACR version doesn't match, Lightroom displays the ACR Mismatch dialog mentioned on page 337. This allows you to choose how to handle the file.

What's the difference between *Render Using Lightroom* and *Open Anyway* in the ACR mismatch dialog?

The ACR Mismatch dialog **(Figure 15.13)** gives you two choices:

- *Render using Lightroom* uses Lightroom's own processing engine to render the TIFF or PSD file, which is then automatically opened into Photoshop. All of your Lightroom adjustments are applied correctly.

- *Open Anyway* ignores the mismatch and passes the image data and settings to Photoshop for ACR to process, which may produce something close to the correct rendering or may be completely different. It doesn't save the TIFF/PSD until you choose to save the changes.

  If you try to open a proprietary raw file from a camera that wasn't supported by your old ACR version, the file won't even open as ACR won't know what to do with it.

If your ACR version is recent, for example, you've just upgraded to Lightroom 6.3 but ACR is still on the previous version (i.e. 9.2), *Open Anyway* is a fairly safe choice. If your ACR version is older, select *Render using Lightroom* to ensure it renders correctly.

▼ **Figure 15.13** If your ACR version isn't fully compatible, Lightroom will ask whether to Render Using Lightroom, creating a TIFF/PSD and passing that to Photoshop, or Open Anyway, taking a chance that the rendering may be different.

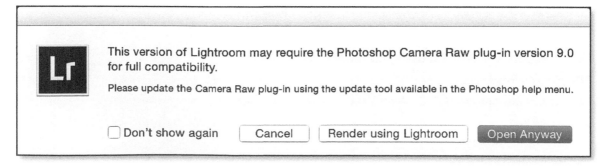

Rendered Files

▼ **Figure 15.14** Edit in Photoshop handling for rendered files.

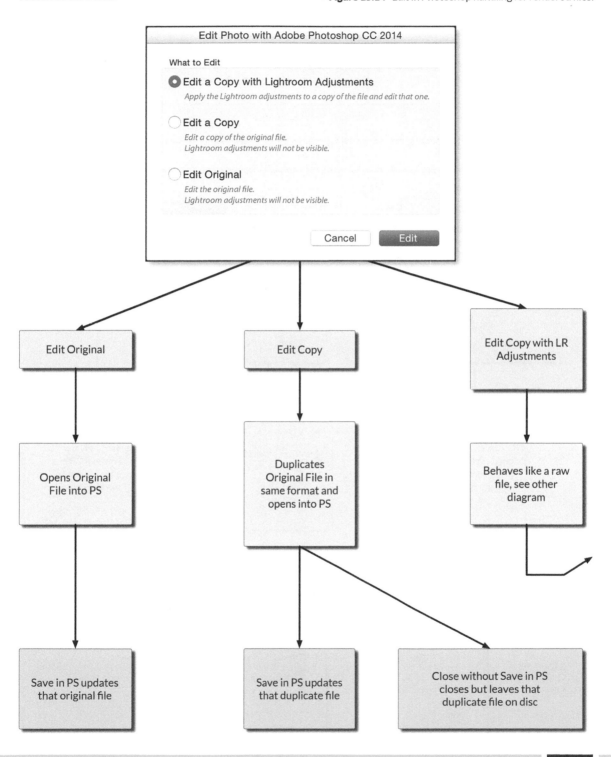

Raw Files

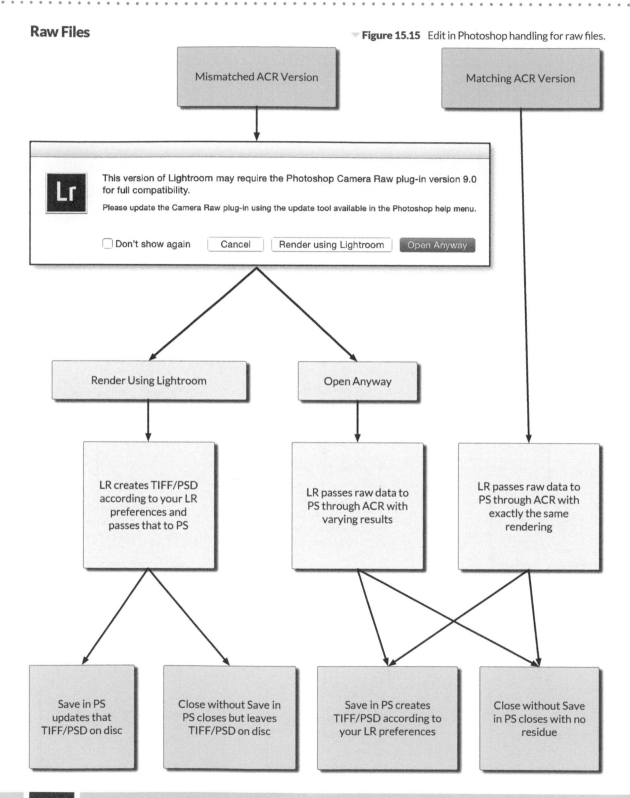

▼ **Figure 15.15** Edit in Photoshop handling for raw files.

SETTING UP ADDITIONAL EXTERNAL EDITORS

Although Photoshop or Elements are the obvious choice for use with Lightroom, they're not the only choice. Many photographers use Nik Software or OnOne software with Lightroom, among others.

Some programs automatically install plug-ins, external editor settings or export presets, which you can access from the *File menu > Plug-in Extras*, *Photo menu > Edit in* or *File menu > Export as Preset* respectively. You'll also find those options in the right-click menu. Check with the developer for each individual program.

How do I create my own external editor preset?

If you have a program that doesn't automatically link with Lightroom, you can create your own external editor preset.

1. Go to Lightroom's Preferences dialog, under the *Edit menu* (Windows) / *Lightroom menu* (Mac) and select the *External Editors tab*.

2. In the bottom half of the dialog, press *Choose* and navigate to the program's exe file (Windows) / app (Mac). **(Figure 15.16)**

3. Select other preferences below—TIFF is a good choice for file format, and 8-bit vs. 16-bit depends on your specific editor.

4. In the Preset pop-up, select *Save Settings as New Preset* and give your editor a name.

    You can use the same steps to create as many external editors presets as you like.

    When you close the dialog, the preset selected in the Preset pop-up becomes the main Additional External Editor shown

▼ **Figure 15.16** You can set up multiple additional external editors using the External Editing tab in the Preferences dialog.

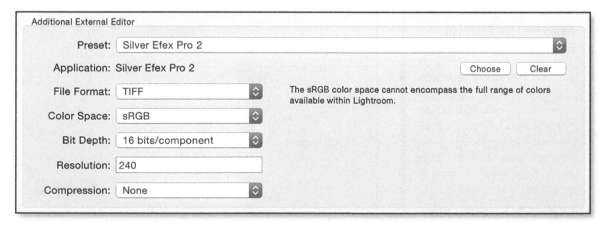

at the top of the list, and it's assigned the secondary keyboard shortcut, which is Ctrl-Alt-E (Windows) / Cmd-Opt-E (Mac).

5. To open a photo into your external editor, go to *Photo menu > Edit In* or access it from the right-click menu. **(Figure 15.17)**

How do I edit an external editor preset?

If you need to change one of your External Editors, return to the *Preferences dialog > External Editing tab* and select the preset from the pop-up menu. You can then edit the settings, perhaps changing the file format or color space, and go back to the pop-up and select *Update Preset* from the listed options. To rename or delete a preset, select it in the pop-up and then select *Rename preset* or *Delete preset*.

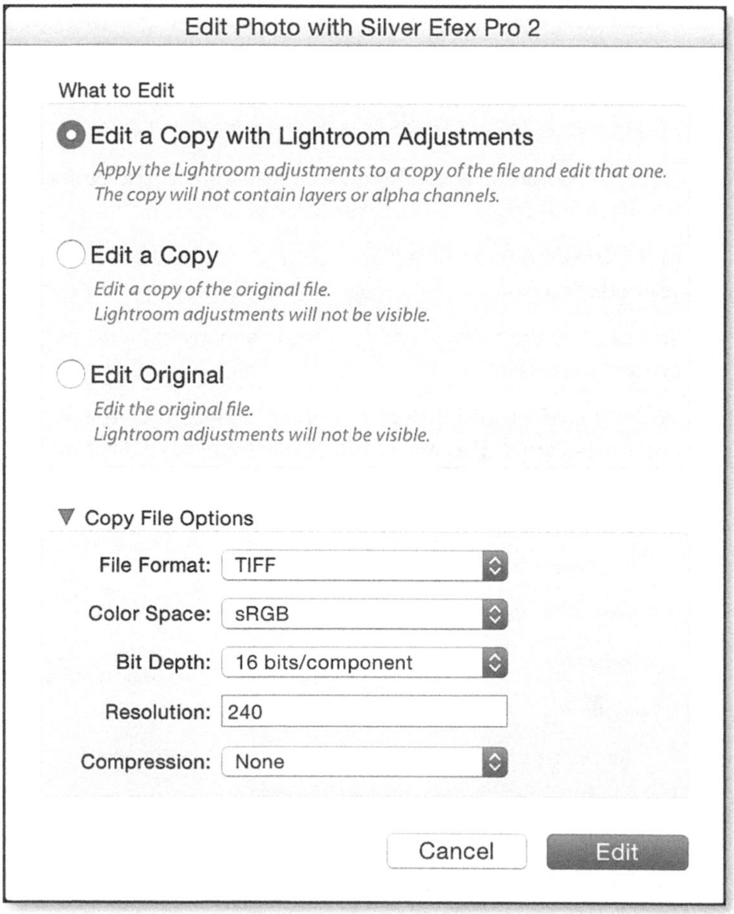

Figure 15.17 If you open a file into a secondary external editor, it allows you to change the file preferences on-the-fly.

Edit Photo with Silver Efex Pro 2

What to Edit

● Edit a Copy with Lightroom Adjustments
Apply the Lightroom adjustments to a copy of the file and edit that one. The copy will not contain layers or alpha channels.

○ Edit a Copy
Edit a copy of the original file. Lightroom adjustments will not be visible.

○ Edit Original
Edit the original file. Lightroom adjustments will not be visible.

▼ Copy File Options

File Format:	TIFF
Color Space:	sRGB
Bit Depth:	16 bits/component
Resolution:	240
Compression:	None

Cancel   Edit

MISSING EXTERNAL EDITORS

If some external editor presets go missing, toggle the *Store presets with this catalog* checkbox in Lightroom's Preferences > Presets tab to see if they reappear. To learn more about this checkbox, turn to page 514.

Can I open the raw file into another raw processor?

Lightroom sends TIFF/PSD files to its Additional External Editors, rather than the raw data, which is ideal for most pixel editing software, but there may be occasions when you want to open a photo into another raw processor (or a video into video editing software). On these occasions, right-click on the photo, choose *Show in Explorer* (Windows) / *Show in Finder* (Mac) and then open into your raw processor.

OPEN DIRECTLY

John Beardsworth's Open Directly plug-in takes the original file and passes it to the software of your choice. http://www.Lrq.me/beardsworth-opendirectly

SAVING METADATA TO THE FILES

While we're on the subject of editing photos in other programs, let's also talk about sharing metadata with other programs.

Because Lightroom is designed around a database, any changes you make in Lightroom are stored within Lightroom's catalog. This means that the changes aren't available to other programs such as Bridge. To make the metadata available to other programs, you need to store it in/with the files using a format called XMP.

XMP stands for Extensible Metadata Platform. It's simply a way of storing text metadata, such as Develop settings, star ratings, color labels and keywords, among other things, with the photos themselves. XMP is based on open standards and the SDK is freely available, which means that other companies can also write and understand that same format, making your metadata available to other image management software.

The XMP for most file types (e.g. JPEG, TIFF, PSD, DNG) is written to a section in the header of the file. These changes don't affect the image data, and therefore never degrade the quality of the photo. The metadata's written to a sidecar file for proprietary raw files because writing back to these file formats can prevent some other software from reading them.

Should I write to XMP?

Writing the metadata back to the files has pros and cons:

- **Sharing metadata**—To edit or view metadata using other software, it has to be written to the files.

- **Belt-and-braces backup**—Many use XMP data as an additional backup of settings in case their Lightroom catalog and backups become corrupted or they remove photos from the catalog by accident.

WRITE THE CAPTURE TIME

There's an exception to the sidecar rule for proprietary raw files. If you edit the capture time, the new capture time can be updated in the original file. It's written to a documented portion of the metadata file header, so it's relatively safe. Some people feel that their raw files should never be touched in any way, so there's a *Write date or time changes into proprietary raw files* checkbox in *Catalog Settings > Metadata tab* which allows you to choose whether the updated date/time is stored only in the catalog, exported files and XMP sidecar files, or whether it can be updated in the original raw files too.

- **Transferring between catalogs**—Some use XMP to transfer photos between catalogs (but only some of the metadata can be stored in XMP so Import from Catalog is a better choice... we'll come back to that in the Multi-Computer chapter starting on page 492).

- **Corruption**—On the downside, writing changes back to the original files does slightly increase the risk of file corruption for JPEG, TIFF, PSD and DNG files, even though it's only updating the header of the file.

- **Big backups**—Updating the metadata in the original JPEG, TIFF, PSD or DNG files means they're seen as changed by your backup software. If you use online backups, that could mean all the adjusted photos being re-uploaded each time you make a change.

- **Lots of little files**—If you write metadata to proprietary raw files, it's written to sidecar files. You may like or dislike all those extra little files!

- **Limited data**—Only some of your Lightroom settings can be written to the files, due to limits in the XMP specification. It's not a complete backup.

Which of Lightroom's data isn't stored in XMP?

Flags, virtual copies, collection membership, uncommitted location data, Develop history, stacks, Develop module panel switches and zoomed image pan positions are currently only stored in the catalog itself, and not the XMP sections of the files.

How do I write settings to XMP?

To write settings to XMP, select the files in Grid view and press Ctrl-S (Windows) / Cmd-S (Mac) or go to *Metadata menu > Save Metadata to Files*.

You can also turn on *Automatically write changes into XMP* in *Catalog Settings > Metadata tab* **(Figure 15.18)**, which updates the XMP every time a change is made to the photo (although it's smart enough to wait a few seconds for you to stop editing).

If you're considering enabling automatic writing, there are a few points to be aware of:

- Think about how it will affect your backups—XMP sidecars for proprietary raw files are tiny to back up, but updating XMP embedded in DNG, JPEG, PSD, TIFF or PNG files may trigger your backup system to back up the whole file again. Even something as simple as correcting the spelling of a keyword triggers an update.

- Making changes to large numbers of photos (i.e., thousands) may be noticeably slower with auto-write turned on, due to the sheer volume of individual files that need to be written. This is especially noticeable when reorganizing your keyword list.

- When you first turn auto-write on, performance may drop considerably while it writes to XMP for all the photos in the catalog. Once it's finished doing so, performance improves, so you're best just to leave it to work for a while.

- Avoid turning auto-write off and on again too often, as every time you turn it on, it has to update the files with all the changes.

Should I check or uncheck *Include Develop settings in metadata inside JPEG, TIFF, PNG and PSD files*?

There's an extra option in *Catalog Settings > Metadata tab* with regard to XMP, marked **Include Develop settings in metadata inside JPEG, TIFF, PNG and PSD files**. It controls whether Lightroom includes your Develop settings when it writes the other metadata. Personally, I leave it checked to include Develop settings when I write to XMP, but these text instructions can increase the file size if you've used lots of local adjustments or spot removal.

How do I read the metadata from the files?

Having written the metadata to the files, Lightroom essentially ignores it. The adjustments you make in Lightroom are still stored in the catalog, and that database is always assumed to be correct, whether XMP metadata exists or not.

The external metadata is only read at the time of import, or when you choose to read the metadata using *Metadata menu > Read Metadata*

> **UPDATE DNG PREVIEW & METADATA**
>
> When you're manually writing metadata to DNG files, you'll note that the Metadata menu offers two options:
>
> - *Save Metadata to File* just updates the XMP metadata, as it would with any other kind of file.
>
> - *Update DNG Preview & Metadata* does the same, but it also updates the embedded preview in any DNG files to include your Develop edits.

▼ **Figure 15.18** *Automatically write changes into XMP saves the metadata with the files as well as in the catalog.*

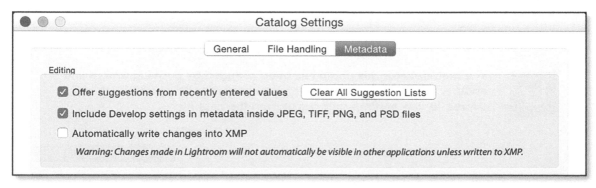

USING OTHER SOFTWARE

If you're going to make changes to the metadata in another program, save Lightroom's settings out to the files before editing in the other software. When you read the metadata again later, Lightroom's Develop settings are simply read back again, along with your new metadata edits, rather than being reset to default.

from Files. If you read the metadata from the files, it overwrites the information stored in the catalog for that photo.

Lightroom uses the metadata icons to show whether Lightroom's metadata or the external metadata was most recently updated (although it can take a few minutes before Lightroom notices an external change). **(Figures 15.19, 15.20 & 15.21)**

Clicking on this icon requests confirmation: **(Figure 15.22)**

- **Import Settings from Disk**—If you've intentionally changed the metadata using another program, this reads the metadata from the file and replacing the information in the catalog.

- **Cancel**—don't do anything.

- **Overwrite Settings**—If you're comfortable that everything looks correct in Lightroom, this replaces the external XMP metadata with Lightroom's data, clearing the warning icon.

◀ **Figure 15.19** The metadata in the catalog is newer than the metadata in the file.

◀ **Figure 15.20** The metadata in the file is newer than in Lightroom.

◀ **Figure 15.21** The metadata has changed both in Lightroom and externally, resulting in a conflict.

When resolving metadata conflicts, is there a way to preview what will happen?

If Lightroom tells you there's a metadata conflict, you have to decide which set of data to keep. The problem is, it doesn't tell you which data is different in each version, so you have to either remember which you last updated, or take a guess. The good news is there's a workaround, although it would be time-consuming if you have a large number of conflicts.

If you create a virtual copy before reading the metadata, the virtual copy retains the Lightroom metadata and the master is updated with the external metadata. You can then flick back and forth, comparing metadata and Develop settings, and decide which to keep. If you want to keep the data on the virtual copy, select *Photo menu > Set Copy as Master* before removing the other copy.

▼ **Figure 15.22** If there's a metadata conflict, clicking on the icon will ask how to handle it.

If the conflicted file is raw file, you can also open the XMP file using a XML or text editor to manually compare the contents with the information in the catalog.

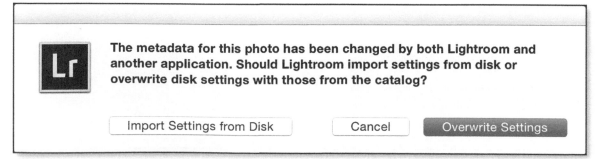

EXPORT, EMAIL & PUBLISH

Lightroom is non-destructive, which means that it doesn't save over your original image data. To apply your settings to your photos, you use **Export**, which is like a **Save As** in other programs.

When you export photos, it's usually for a specific purpose, such as posting on the web, giving them to someone else, or sending them away to be printed. Most exports can be deleted after use, as the photos can be exported again in future using the original image data and the settings saved in the catalog.

You can also email photos from within Lightroom, and publish photos to social media websites, but we'll come back to these a little later in the chapter (page 370 and page 375). First, let's cover the basics of export.

'SAVE AS' A COPY ON THE HARD DRIVE USING EXPORT

To export your finished photos, select them and then go to *File menu > Export* or press the *Export* button at the bottom of the left panel group in Library module.

These are the main settings you'll need to check: **(Figure 16.1)**

- **Export Location**—decide where on the hard drive to save the exported photos.

- **File Name**—you can rename on export, for example, creating a template for Sequence #(001)-Filename puts a sequence number before your existing filename to ensure that they sort correctly in other software. It doesn't affect the names of the original files.

EXPORT SHORTCUTS	
Export	Ctrl Shift E / Cmd Shift E
Export with Previous	Ctrl Alt Shift E / Cmd Opt Shift E
Email	Cmd Shift E (Mac only)

347

- **File Format**—JPEG is an excellent choice for web, email, etc. TIFF is best for pixel editors such as Photoshop.

- **Color Space**—select sRGB for screen/web use or ProPhoto RGB for color managed pixel editors such as Photoshop.

▼ **Figure 16.1** Use Export to create copies of your photos with your adjustments applied.

- **Size**—refers to the pixel dimensions of the photo. There are some sample sizes in the sidebar.

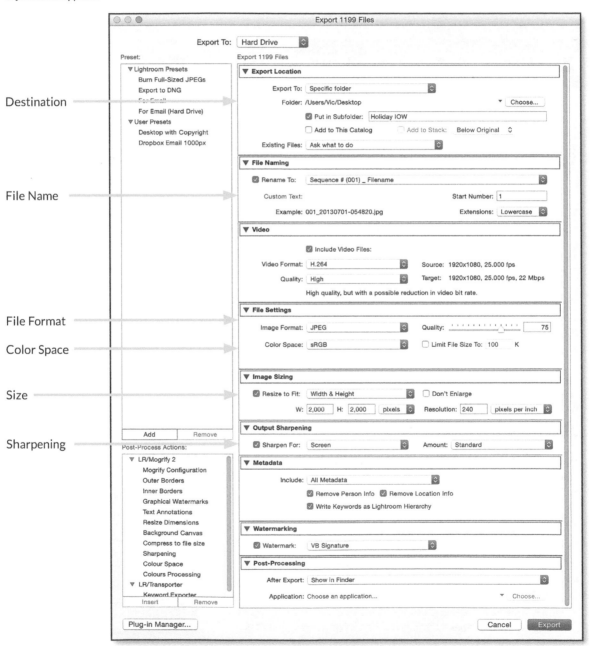

EXPORT SIZES

If you're just starting out, here are some sample export settings for different uses:

Email or small web photo—*Longest Edge* 800px, and you can ignore the resolution as we're specifying the size in pixels. Format JPEG, quality 60. sRGB.

4" x 6" digital print—*Dimensions* 4" x 6" at 300ppi. Format JPEG, quality 70. sRGB.

8" x 10" digital print—*Dimensions* 8" x 10" at 300ppi. Format JPEG, quality 80. sRGB (unless your lab requests another profile).

Full resolution file—uncheck the *Resize to Fit* checkbox. Format JPEG, quality 90-100. (There's a signifi-cant reduction in file size by dropping from 100 to 90, with minimal visible changes). sRGB.

Edit in another color managed program—uncheck the *Resize to Fit* checkbox. Format TIFF, no compres-sion, 16-bit, ProPhoto RGB.

- **Output Sharpening**—select *Screen* for screen/web use, and the type of paper for prints.

Now let's start exploring these settings in more detail, starting at the top of the Export dialog and working down.

At the top of the Export dialog is the ***Export To*** menu that's usually set to *Hard Drive* for normal exports. The other options include writing the exported files to *CD/DVD*, *emailing* photos, or exporting to specific plug-ins. **(Figure 16.2)**

On the left of the dialog are Export Presets and then space for plug-in options. We'll come back to these later (page 368). The right-hand side of the Export dialog is made up of a series of collapsible sections which hold all the export options, so we'll start exploring these.

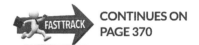

CONTINUES ON PAGE 370

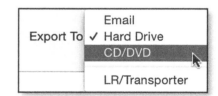

▲ **Figure 16.2** Set the export type in the *Export To* pop-up.

BURNING OPTICAL MEDIA

To burn exported photos to optical media directly from Light-room, change the pop-up menu at the top of the Export dialog to *CD/DVD*. When you press the *Export* button, it prompts you to insert a disc. If there's too much data for a single disc, Light-room calculates how many discs are needed and spans the data without splitting any individual files. Alternatively, you can export to the hard drive and use specialized software to burn instead.

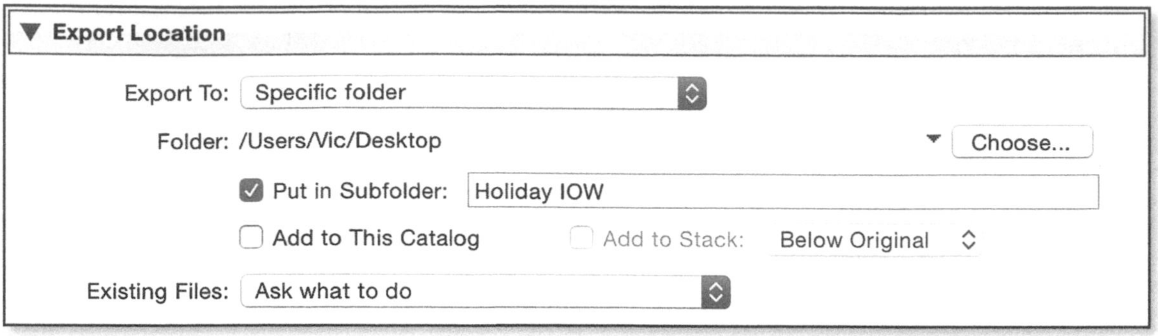

▼ **Export Location**

Export To: Specific folder ⬍

Folder: /Users/Vic/Desktop ▾ Choose...

☑ Put in Subfolder: Holiday IOW

☐ Add to This Catalog ☐ Add to Stack: Below Original ⬍

Existing Files: Ask what to do ⬍

Figure 16.3 In the *Export Location* section, select the Destination folder for the exported photos.

EXPORTING HIERARCHIES

If you need to replicate your folder structure during an export, for example, a wedding that's grouped into folders for each stage of the day, LR/TreeExporter plug-in can save you doing so manually.

http://www.Lrq.me/armes-lrtreeexporter

You can do the same using Publish Services (we'll come back to these on page 375) for both folder hierarchies and collection hierarchies, using Jeffrey Friedl's Folder Manager and Collection Manager plug-ins.

http://www.Lrq.me/friedl-folpub

http://www.Lrq.me/friedl-colpub

EXPORT LOCATION & FILE NAMING

The first pop-up in the **Export Location** section (Figure 16.3) determines the destination folder for the exported files. You have three choices:

- **Specific folder** groups all the exported photos in a single folder. Select the location by pressing the *Choose* button and navigating to a folder. The chosen folder path then displays below the pop-up. Clicking on the arrow to the right displays the other folders you've recently used for exports.

- **Select folder later** also groups all the exported photos in a single folder, but it pops up asking for a folder location just before the export begins. It's useful if you're creating a preset that will export to a different location each time you use it.

- **Same folder as original photo** stores the exported photos with their original files, so they may be spread across a variety of different locations. It's particularly useful when combined with the *Put in Subfolder* checkbox.

The **Put in Subfolder** checkbox creates a new subfolder inside your chosen destination folder, using the name you enter in the field. For example, you might select an *Exported Photos* folder on your desktop, inside which you create a named subfolder for each export you run, or you might want to create *Finished JPEGs* folders inside the original image folders.

Can Lightroom automatically re-import the exported files?

In most cases, you won't need to import the exported photos into your catalog, as they're exported for a specific purpose and can then be deleted. If, however, you're exporting photos ready to be retouched in an external editor, you may want these retouched versions to be catalogued along with the originals.

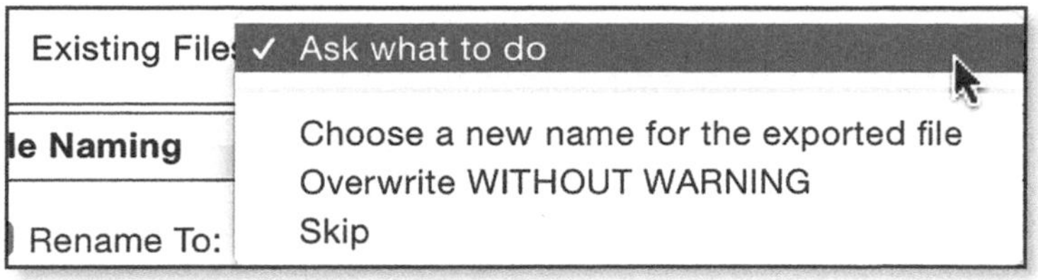

Existing File:	✓ Ask what to do
le Naming	Choose a new name for the exported file Overwrite WITHOUT WARNING
Rename To:	Skip

Figure 16.4 If files with the same name exist in the Destination folder, Lightroom asks you what to do. You can pre-empt the decision using the pop-up in the Export dialog.

You could use the Import dialog to manually import the exported photos into the catalog, but it's quicker to check the **Add to This Catalog** checkbox to add them automatically.

At the same time, the exported photos can be automatically stacked above or below the original photos using the **Add to Stack** checkbox. Remember, stacking is a way of grouping photos in the grid so they appear as a single photo. To make this option available, you must have the *Export To* pop-up set to *Same folder as original photo* (because stacked photos have to be in the same folder) and *Put in Subfolder* must be unchecked.

Of course, to add the exported photos to the same folder in order to stack them, they must have different filenames or file formats, otherwise they could overwrite the originals. The simplest solution is to add an additional word such as -Edit to the end of the filename. You can rename the photos while exporting—we'll come to that in a moment (page 351).

How do I handle existing photos with the same names?

If there are already photos with the same names in your destination folder, perhaps because you forgot to rename while exporting, Lightroom needs to know how to handle them. It can skip exporting these photos, overwrite them (only if they're not the original photos you're exporting) or automatically use unique names. Unique names just adds a -2 (or similar) to the end of the filename. You can select the default behavior in the Export dialog, or you can leave the **Existing Files** pop-up set to *Ask what to do* so it gives you the choice when those circumstances arise. **(Figure 16.4)**

How do I change the filename while exporting?

Beneath the Export Locations section is **File Naming**. Photos are only renamed if the **Rename To** checkbox is checked. The options should be familiar by now, as they're the same options used in the Import dialog (page 37) and Rename Photo dialog (page 130). To create a filename template, select *Edit* from the pop-up, add your chosen tokens and save it using the pop-up at the top of the Filename Template Editor dialog.

OVERWRITING ORIGINALS

Lightroom won't allow you to save over the original file that you're exporting, as it goes against its philosophy of non-destructive editing. Overwriting the originals is like throwing away the negatives once you've made a print that you like!

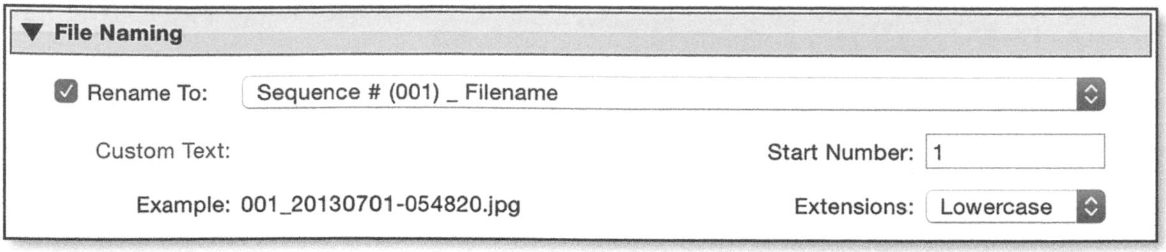

Figure 16.5 Set the filename in the *File Naming* section. If the *Rename* checkbox is unchecked, the files retain their existing names.

The *File Naming* section in the Export dialog **(Figure 16.5)** renames the exported photos, but it doesn't affect the original photos in your catalog, so there are a number of situations where it's helpful.

We've already mentioned the example of adding a word such as -Edit to the end of a filename, to distinguish a retouched photo from the original. To create this template, insert a filename token, then click in the white field and type -Edit (or use a custom text field if you want to change it regularly). **(Figure 16.6)**

If the photos you're exporting are to be viewed in other software, adding a sequence number with leading zeros to the beginning (i.e. 003-myfile.jpg) forces them to sort in the same order as the Grid view. Remember, in the *Sequence* pop-up, there's a variety of different sequence numbers, with varying numbers of leading zeros. If you're exporting 100 to 999 photos, you'll need 3 digits. **(Figure 16.7)**

When renaming exported photos, consider whether you'll later need to match them up with their originals. For example, if you export as wedding001.jpg to wedding300.jpg (custom name—sequence template), but your originals in Lightroom are still called IMG_3948 to IMG_8574, how are you going to match them up when the client brings back a list of orders?

VIDEO & FILE SETTINGS

The next sections in the Export dialog are *Video* and *File Settings*, where you select the file format, quality and color space.

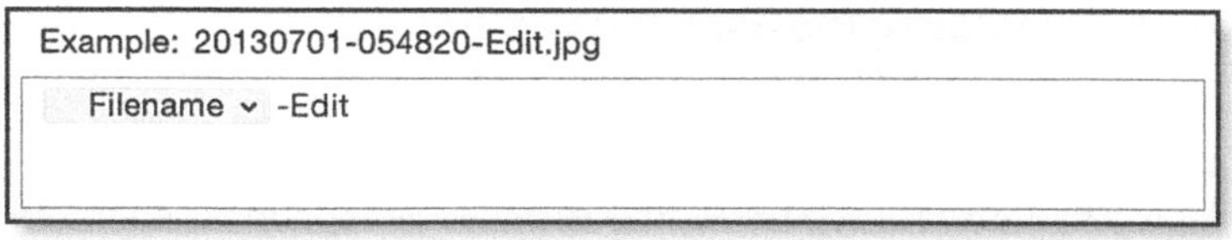

Figure 16.6 You can automatically add -*Edit* to the end of filenames.

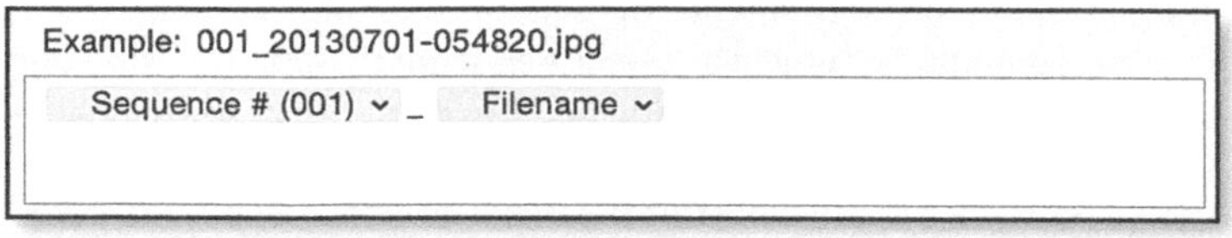

Figure 16.7 Use a *Sequence # (001)* token, then a hyphen (-) and then a *Filename* token, to ensure that photos sort correctly in other software.

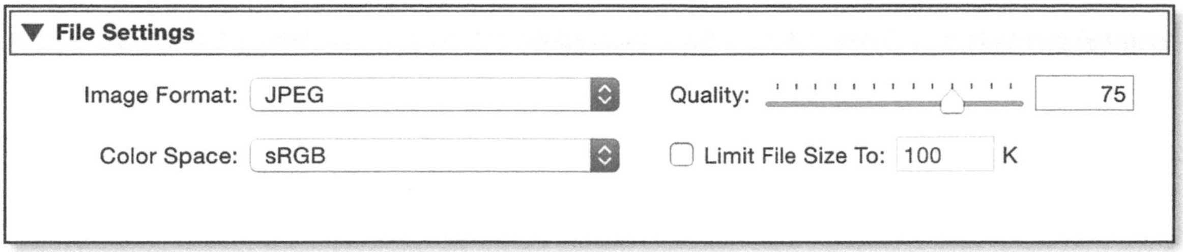

▼ **File Settings**

Image Format: | JPEG | ⬍ | Quality: |————————————| 75

Color Space: | sRGB | ⬍ | ☐ Limit File Size To: 100 K

The file format you select depends on the purpose of the photo or video. **(Figure 16.8)** We'll come back to video formats in a moment (page 356), but for photos you have four **Image Format** choices:

Figure 16.8 Set the image format and color space in the *File Settings* section.

- **JPEG** is an excellent choice for emailing photos or posting them on the web. It's a lossy format so there is a trade-off between smaller file sizes and artifacts, but these artifacts are often invisible at medium-high quality settings. JPEGs can only hold 8 bits of data per channel, so stick with smaller color spaces such as Adobe RGB and sRGB.

- **TIFF** is a lossless format, so it's great for storing working files and high-value edited photos. TIFFs can hold 16 bits of data (or even 32 bits for HDR photos) as well as Photoshop layers and transparency. Compression usually reduces the file size, although it takes a little longer to save.

- **PSD** is also lossless and allows you to save less frequently used Photoshop color modes such as duotone, but TIFF is more widely supported.

- **DNG** is the digital negative format. It wraps the raw data in a standardized format, along with the metadata. It's a good choice when sending raw data along with your Lightroom settings to another Lightroom or Photoshop user. You can learn more about DNG in the Appendix page A-1.

- **Original** exports in the original format, creating a duplicate of the original file but with updated metadata. Your Develop edits are not applied to the image data when selecting *Original* format, but may be visible if the photo's imported into Lightroom or opened in Bridge/Photoshop.

Should I apply compression to the photos?

There are two main kinds of compression: lossless and lossy.

- **Lossless compression**, as the name suggests, compresses the files, but they can be put back together perfectly, without any loss of quality.

- **Lossy compression** works by throwing away some of the data.

It can significantly reduce file size but at the expense of image quality and detail.

Because compressed files require more processing to open and close them, they can be a little slower to work with, but the space saving can be substantial.

The PSD format automatically compresses the files using lossless compression.

The TIFF format gives you a choice of compression, between *None*, *LZW* and *ZIP*.

- **None** applies no compression, so the file sizes are large.

- **ZIP** applies ZIP compression. It's a good all-round choice.

- **LZW** is only available for 8-bit files, because LZW compression doesn't work well with 16-bit files and often makes them larger. It's still available for compatibility with some programs that don't understand ZIP compression, although such programs are rare now.

The JPEG format has a **Quality** slider, which controls the amount of compression applied to the photo. The resulting file sizes vary depending on the content of the photo, and therefore how much they can be compressed. Photos with large flat areas of color compress much more than detailed or noisy photos.

As a rule of thumb, Lightroom's default setting of 75 is a good all-round choice. 60 creates smaller for photos for the web/email, without significant loss of quality. For 'master' images that aren't important enough to require lossless compression, try using 90 instead of 100. There's a substantial reduction in file size without visible degradation.

Can I export to a specific file size?

If you're uploading the JPEGs to a website with a specific file size limit (e.g. 70 KB), it can be time-consuming to repeatedly export the photos, changing the quality setting until the file falls inside the limit. If you check the **Limit File Size To** checkbox and enter a limit, Lightroom does that for you, however the export can take longer than a standard export. It also removes the embedded thumbnail to improve the reliability and reduce the file size.

Lightroom only adjusts the JPEG quality setting automatically, and not the pixel dimensions, so you'll need to select reasonable pixel dimensions for the file size. It's only intended to work for small web-size photos, so if you enter 8000K (i.e. just under 8 MB), it may well fall over.

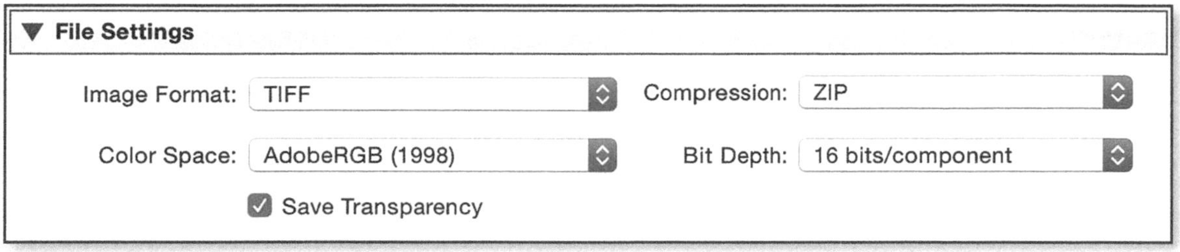

▼ **File Settings**

Image Format:	TIFF ⌄	Compression:	ZIP ⌄
Color Space:	AdobeRGB (1998) ⌄	Bit Depth:	16 bits/component ⌄
	☑ Save Transparency		

Which bit depth should I select?

We also discussed the subject of **Bit Depth** in the Edit in External Editors chapter on page 328. As a reminder:

- **8-bit**—saves hard drive space but may introduce banding in smooth gradients. It's a reasonable compromise for most finished files.

- **16-bit** retains a larger amount of image data, so it's a better choice for working files (e.g., to send to external editors) and important master images.

JPEGs are always 8-bit. PSD and TIFF files give you the choice.

What is *Save Transparency*?

There's one final option in the TIFF settings, marked **Save Transparency**. TIFF's the only format that offers the choice as PSD and DNG include transparency automatically, and JPG can't contain transparency. **(Figure 16.9)**

A PNG, TIFF or PSD file may have already included transparent areas before the photo was imported, Lightroom's manual lens corrections can create transparent areas where you've corrected for distortion or rotation, or a panorama may have transparent areas around the edge. In most cases, you'll want to save the transparency.

Which color space should I select?

While you're working in Lightroom, it manages the colors for you, however when you take the photos outside of Lightroom (such as when you're exporting), you're in charge of selecting the best color space using the **Color Space** pop-up. We discussed the pros and cons of different color spaces in the Soft Proofing section starting on page 314, but as a quick reminder, here are your options.

- **ProPhoto RGB** retains the most data, so it's the best choice when transferring photos to Photoshop or other external editors. ProPhoto RGB photos look odd in programs that aren't color

Figure 16.9 The TIFF format also allows you to select the *Bit Depth* and *Save Transparency*

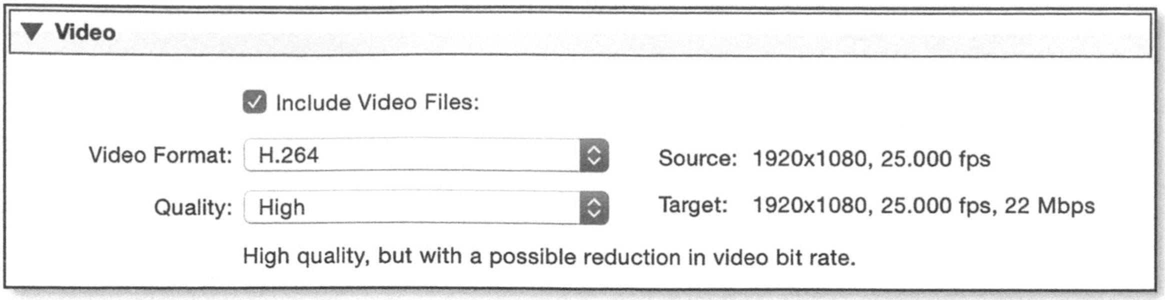

▼ **Video**

☑ Include Video Files:

Video Format: [H.264 ⌄]   Source: 1920x1080, 25.000 fps

Quality: [High ⌄]   Target: 1920x1080, 25.000 fps, 22 Mbps

High quality, but with a possible reduction in video bit rate.

Figure 16.10 Set the file format and quality in the *Video* section.

managed, such as web browsers. Because the space is so wide, it's not appropriate for 8-bit images.

- **Adobe RGB** is a good all-round choice, as long as you're working in a fully color-managed environment (for example, you're sending the files to a print lab that accepts Adobe RGB files).

- **sRGB** is a smaller color space, but it's the most widely used. It's a great choice for screen output, emailing or uploading to the web. It's also the safest choice if you don't know where the photos will end up.

- **Other** allows you to select other RGB ICC profiles installed on your system. For example, some professional labs may request that you convert the photos to their own custom ICC profile. To do so, select *Other* from the *Color Space* pop-up, add a checkmark next to your custom profile and then press OK. Your custom profile is automatically selected in the pop-up.

VIDEO SIZES

As a guide, a 10 second clip from a Canon 600d resulted in the following file sizes:

Original file: 155 MB for 27 seconds, so around 51 MB for 10 seconds

DPX—2.07 GB

H264   Max—29.7   MB, 1920x1080, 22 Mbps approx.

H264   High—29.7   MB, 1920x1080, 22 Mbps approx. (in this case it didn't make a difference)

H264   Medium—11.3   MB, 1280x720, 8 Mbps approx.

H264 Low—1.5 MB, 480x270, 1 Mbps approx.

How do I export or save my edited videos?

If you've edited a video, you likely want to apply the changes before sending it to someone else, just as you would for an image file. Using Export, you can create a duplicate of the original unedited video, or output to DPX or H.264 mp4 format. The options in the *Video Format* pop-up **(Figure 16.10)** are:

- **DPX** is a lossless format used for editing in some professional video editing programs, such as Adobe Premiere.

- **H.264** is the best option for compressing your final videos, and it offers multiple quality settings.

  - *Maximum* quality uses a bit rate as close to the source file as possible, to prevent any loss of quality.

  - *High* quality retains the resolution but may reduce the file size slightly.

  - *Medium* quality is useful for sharing on the web, as it's a lower resolution and bit rate.

- *Low* quality is intended for mobile devices such as mobile phones, with a much lower resolution and bit rate resulting in a much smaller file size.

- **Original**, as with photos, is a duplicate of the original file.

IMAGE SIZING & RESOLUTION

While you're exporting the photos, you can also resize them to the right size for your intended purpose. Remember, Lightroom doesn't resize the original photos while cropping, as this would go against it's non-destructive design. After all, there's nothing more destructive than deleting original pixels! Instead, you crop to a specific ratio in the Develop module and then set the size (or number of pixels) you require in the Export dialog. **(Figure 16.11)**

If you leave the **Resize to Fit** checkbox unchecked in the Image Sizing panel, the photos remain at their native resolution, (less any cropped pixels). If you check it, the photo's resized according to the dimensions you specify.

When digital photographers speak of image size, they're usually referring to the pixel dimensions—the total number of pixels along a photo's width and height.

Pixels don't have a fixed physical size. They expand or contract to fill the space available. If you expand them too far, the photo appears blurry and pixelated (you can see the squares), so the aim is to keep the pixels smaller than or equal to the monitor pixels or printer dots.

Let's illustrate this with smiley faces **(Figure 16.12)**. Imagine we start off with a large smiley face, and we export it at different sizes.

If we resize to 150 x 150 pixels, and we print it as 0.5" x 0.5", it's a tiny photo but it still looks sharp. This is because there are 300 pixels per inch (150px divided by 0.5" = 300 ppi)

If we try to stretch that same 150px file to print at 2" x 2", there are only 75 pixels per inch (150px divided by 2" = 75ppi). The pixels get too big and you can start to see the individual pixels.

So to print a 2" x 2" smiley face, we need more pixels. We've already seen that 300ppi is great for printing, so 2" multiplied by 300ppi =

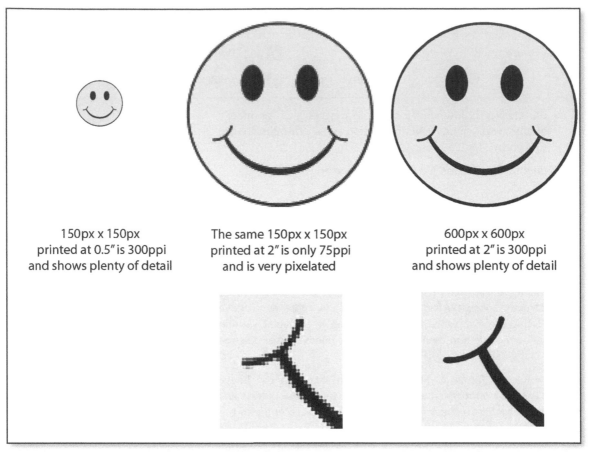

150px x 150px
printed at 0.5" is 300ppi
and shows plenty of detail

The same 150px x 150px
printed at 2" is only 75ppi
and is very pixelated

600px x 600px
printed at 2" is 300ppi
and shows plenty of detail

Figure 16.12 The *PPI* setting only matters when it's combined with a physical size. The overall pixel dimensions are important.

600px along each edge. That's the size we'd select in the Export dialog. (Some printers can produce a good print with less pixels, but 300ppi is a good ballpark.)

How do I work out what size I need?

So how do you work out the right size for your intended purpose?

An uncropped file from an 18 megapixel camera may be 5184 x 3456 pixels, which would comfortably create a high quality 18" x 12" print. (To check my math, divide the pixel dimensions by 18" and 12" and you'll get 288ppi, which is close enough to 300ppi to get a good result.)

But what if you want to print it as a huge poster that fills the wall? Then you'll need to create extra pixels.

And what if you want to email the file to a friend to view on their computer? It would fill nine average size computer monitors, so there's no point sending a file that big. You can throw away unnecessary pixels.

This process of creating new pixels or selectively throwing away pixels is called resampling.

The good news is Lightroom can do most of the math for you. You just have to enter the **Size** and **Resolution**.

Screen sizes are usually defined in pixels, so they're easy. You just enter the pixel dimensions you require and select *pixels* in the pop-up, for example, you may email a file that is 800px along the longest edge. When you're defining the image size in pixels, the *Resolution* setting is irrelevant.

Print sizes are usually defined in inches or cm, so enter your print size and select *inches* or *cm* from the pop-up, for example, 4" x 6". We said the *Resolution* setting is only useful when combined with units of measurements. If you enter the PPI required by your print lab (usually between 250ppi and 300ppi), Lightroom automatically calculates the right number of pixels for that size print.

> ## DPI VS PPI
>
> Many people mix up PPI and DPI. DPI refers to Dots Per Inch. It doesn't apply to digital images until they're dots on a piece of paper. While they remain as pixels, the resolution is measured in PPI, or pixels per inch.
>
> Pixels per cm is also available in the Export dialog, but it's rarely used, even if the print dimensions are measured in cm.

What's the difference between *Width & Height, Dimensions, Longest Edge, Shortest Edge, Megapixels & Percentage?*

The differences between the *Width & Height, Dimensions, Longest Edge* and *Shortest Edge* options are more easily illustrated using diagrams. **(Figures 16.13-16.16)** The red lines mark the dimensions entered

▼ **Figure 16.14** *Dimensions* fits your photo within a bounding box, but it's a little more intelligent than *Width & Height*. It takes into account the rotation of the photo, and it makes the photo as big as it can within your bounding box, even if it has to turn the bounding box round to do so. The *Dimensions* setting isn't width/height sensitive, so settings of 400 wide by 600 high produces a 400×600 or 600x400 photo, if the photo has a 4x6 ratio.

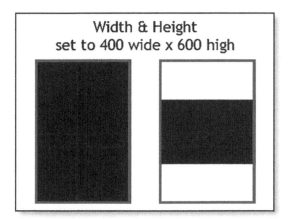

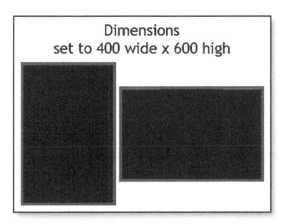

▲ **Figure 16.13** *Width & Height* fits the photos within a bounding box in their current orientation. This setting is width/height sensitive—settings of 400 wide by 600 high produces a 400×600 vertical photo, but only a 400×267 horizontal photo, assuming it's a 4x6 ratio.

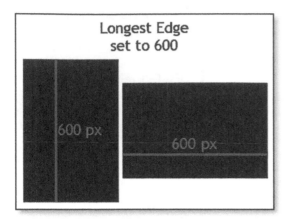

Longest Edge
set to 600

600 px

600 px

◀ **Figure 16.15** *Longest Edge* sets the length of the longest edge, as the name suggests. A setting of 10 inches long would give photos of varying sizes such as 3"×10", 5"×10", 7"×10", 8"×10", 10"×10", depending on the ratio of the photo.

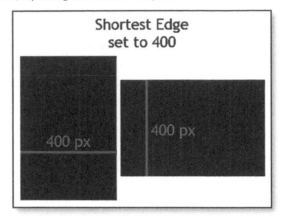

Shortest Edge
set to 400

400 px

400 px

▶ **Figure 16.16** *Shortest Edge* sets the length of the shortest edge, again as the name suggests. A setting of 5 inches along the shortest edge would give varying sizes such as 5"×5", 5"×8", 5"×10", 5"×12", depending on the ratio of the photo.

into Lightroom's Export dialog, and the black rectangle shows the resulting photo size and orientation.

Megapixels sets the dimensions automatically, based on your chosen pixel count. For example, selecting 24MP (24,000,000 pixels) would result in files of 4000x6000 and panoramas of 2400x10000, depending on their crop ratio. (Note that megapixels aren't the same as megabytes, so a 24MP file won't be 24 MB when saved.)

These measurements must still fall within the ACR limits of 65,000 pixels along the longest edge and 512MP, so if your photo falls outside of this range according to the measurements you've set, Lightroom simply makes the photo as big as it can.

New to Lightroom CC/6, there's also a *Percentage* option, so you can create files that are 50% of the original pixel dimensions, and so forth.

What does the *Don't Enlarge* checkbox do?

The *Don't Enlarge* checkbox prevents small photos from being upsized to meet the dimensions you've set, while still downsizing photos which are too large to fit your chosen dimensions.

Is it better to upsize in Lightroom or in Photoshop?

When Lightroom resizes, you don't have a choice of interpolation method, unlike Photoshop which offers *Nearest Neighbor, Bilinear, Bicubic, Bicubic Smoother* and *Bicubic Sharper*. Instead, Lightroom uses an intelligent adaptive bicubic algorithm which automatically adjusts for the increase or decrease in size. In theory, because Lightroom is working with the raw data and isn't limited to one specific resizing algorithm, it should give the best results. Either program can do a good job though.

OUTPUT SHARPENING

Once you've set the sizing, the **Sharpening** option are is next in line. The output sharpening may only have two pop-up menus, but it's far more powerful than it looks. **(Figure 16.17)**

The complex output sharpening algorithms were created by the team at Pixel Genius, who also created the well-known Photoshop plug-in PhotoKit Sharpener. Based on the size of the original file, the output size and resolution, the type of paper, and the strength of sharpening you prefer, it automatically adjusts the sharpening to create the optimal result.

Which Export Sharpening setting applies more sharpening—*screen, matte* or *glossy*?

The difference between *Matte* and *Glossy* is barely noticeable on screen, but there is a difference between each of the settings. At a glance, you'll see that the *Screen* setting sharpens the high-frequency details less than the *Matte* or *Glossy* settings, but there are a lot more technicalities behind that.

As a general rule, pick the right paper type, and you'll be about right. Sending matte sharpening to a glossy paper looks worse than sending glossy sharpening to matte paper, because the matte sharpening is compensating for the softer appearance of matte paper. Screen sharpening may look a little soft on old CRT monitors as it's optimized for LCD screens.

The **Amount** pop-up controls the amount of sharpening applied to the photo, and this decision is a question of personal taste. To get the best out of the automated output sharpening, you do need a properly capture-sharpened photo, so the sharpening settings in the Develop module are still essential. Avoid over-sharpening in the Develop module though, as the Export Sharpening makes it look a lot worse.

If you have no idea how the photos will be used, perhaps because

Figure 16.17 Output Sharpening complements the Capture Sharpening applied in the Develop module.

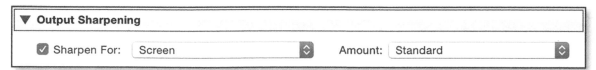

▼ Output Sharpening			
☑ Sharpen For:	Screen ⬍	Amount:	Standard ⬍

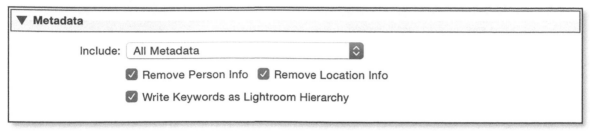

Figure 16.18 You can remove specific metadata from exported photos using the *Metadata* section.

you're giving them to a friend or client, *Glossy Standard* is a reasonable default.

METADATA & WATERMARKING

As soon as you release your photos, whether on the web or in printed form, they're at risk of being stolen. While you can't control that, ensuring that you have copyright metadata stored in the files, and possibly adding a watermark, can help to deter would-be thieves. On the other hand, you might want to strip some metadata from your files to protect your privacy.

How do I select which metadata to include in my files?

The ***Metadata*** section of the Export dialog **(Figure 16.18)** allows you to decide how much of the photo's metadata to ***include*** in the exported file. The basic options are self-explanatory. From the most retained metadata to the least, they are: *All, All Except Camera & Camera Raw Info, Copyright & Contact Info Only* or *Copyright Only*.

If you've added Map locations to your photos, you may want to strip the location data to protect your privacy. The ***Remove Location Info*** checkbox removes both the GPS coordinates and the IPTC Location data. You can also selectively remove specific locations, for example, your home address, by encircling these locations in a Saved Location using the Map module and marking it as private.

For the same privacy reasons, you may want to check the ***Remove Person Info*** to automatically exclude people's names from the exported keywords. Like the location data, you can right-click on the individual keywords in the Keyword List panel, select *Edit Keyword Tag* and uncheck *Include in Export* to only exclude specific people.

There's also a ***Write Keywords as Lightroom Hierarchy*** checkbox in the *Metadata* section. When it's checked, Lightroom uses the pipe character (|) to show parent/child relationships for your keywords, for example, *Animals | Pets | William*. It's useful if you'll be importing the photos back into the catalog, or into other software that

STRIP SPECIFIC METADATA

If you want to be even more selective, Jeffrey Friedl's Metadata Wrangler Export Plug-in allows you to choose which metadata to remove and which to keep. You can download it from: http://www.Lrq.me/friedl-metadatawrangler

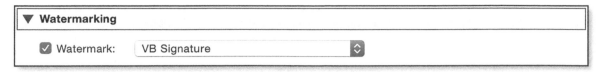

understands keyword hierarchies. If you uncheck it, the keywords assigned to the photo are only recorded individually, resulting in separate keywords for *Animals*, *Pets*, and *William*.

Figure 16.19 Select your watermark in the *Watermarking* section.

How do I add a watermark to my photos?

In the **Watermarking** section **(Figure 16.19)**, you can select a watermark to apply to your photos.

Check the **Watermark** checkbox and then select your watermark from the pop-up.

The most basic form of watermark is a small text watermark in the lower right corner of the photo, aptly named the *Simple Copyright Watermark*. It takes its text from the Copyright metadata field in the Metadata panel, and it's so simple you can't even change the font or size.

If you'd like something a little more decorative, select *Edit Watermarks*

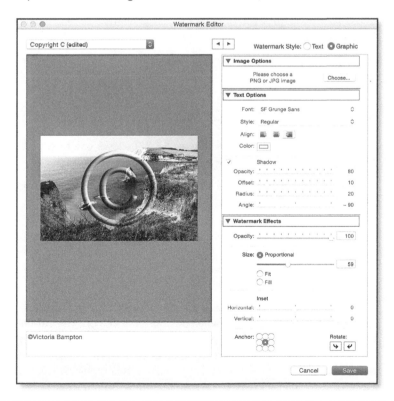

Figure 16.20 In the Watermark Editor dialog, you can design your own watermarks.

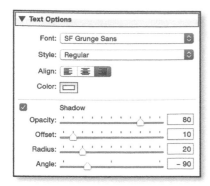

▲ **Figure 16.21** Set the options for your text watermark.

to design your own text or graphical watermark using the Watermark Editor dialog. **(Figure 16.20)**

How do I create a text watermark?

Let's first create a text watermark. Select the *Text Style* option at the top of the dialog, and then enter your text in the text field beneath the preview image. To add a © copyright symbol, hold down Alt while typing 0169 on the number pad (Windows) or type Opt-G (Mac).

Using the options in the **Text Options** section **(Figure 16.21)**, choose the **Font**, **Style** and **Color** of your watermark text. The **alignment** buttons apply to the text alignment within the bounding box and they only come into effect when you have multiple lines of copyright text. You can also add a **Shadow** behind the text.

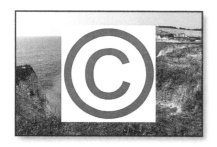

▲ **Figure 16.22** A graphical watermark without transparency won't work!

How do I create a graphical watermark?

If you'd prefer a graphical watermark, press the *Choose* button in the **Image Options** section and navigate to the PNG or JPEG file of your choice.

The PNG format has the advantage of allowing transparency, or semi-transparency—for example, you may want a large © symbol across your photo, but you don't want a large white square showing. **(Figure 16.22)**

You can download some of my favorite watermarks from: http://www.Lrq.me/resources

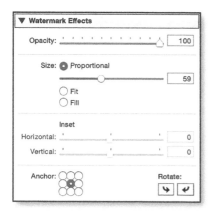

▲ **Figure 16.23** Set the position and size of the watermark using the *Watermark Effects* section.

How do I set the size and placement on the photo?

The **Watermark Effects** section **(Figure 16.23)** allows you to set the size and placement of the watermark.

The **Size** is proportional to the size and orientation of the exported photo, and you can decide whether to *Fit* the watermark within the short edge, *Fill* the long edge, or keep it *Proportional* to the current orientation. If it's set to *Proportional*, you can adjust the size using the slider or the small square in the corner of the bounding box on the preview. **(Figure 16.31)** Remember to consider how it'll look on horizontal, vertical, square and panoramic photos.

To move the watermark around on the image, you can't drag it, but you can use the 9-way **Anchor** buttons to lock it to the center, a corner, or an edge of the photo. Once it's anchored, you add additional spacing to distance it from the edge of the photo using the **Inset** sliders. If, for some reason, you've saved the graphic the wrong way round, you can also use the arrows to **rotate** the watermark.

CREATE A WATERMARK PNG

To create a transparent PNG, you'll need pixel editing software such as Photoshop. We'll create a simple embossed © watermark:

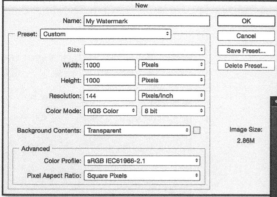

Figure 16.24 Go to *File menu > New* and create a new document. The document size depends on whether you'll use the watermark on high or low resolution photos, but enter 1000 px x 1000px for this example. Ensure the *Background Contents* pop-up is set to Transparent.

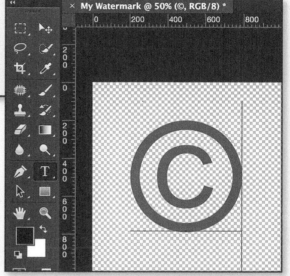

Figure 16.25 Click on the Type tool (T in the Toolbar on the left) and click in the center of the document to place the cursor. Type your copyright symbol using Ctrl-Alt-C (Windows) / Opt-G (Mac).

Figure 16.26 Press Escape to deselect the text, then change the formatting using the Options bar at the top of the screen. Select the font of your choice, and make the font size large enough to fill the document (you can type directly in the font size field).

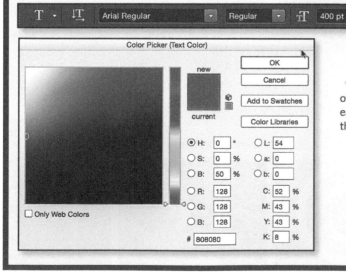

Figure 16.27 Click the color block to the right of the Options bar and select a mid-gray (the easiest way is to enter 808080 in the # field) and then click OK to confirm.

CREATE A WATERMARK PNG CONTINUED

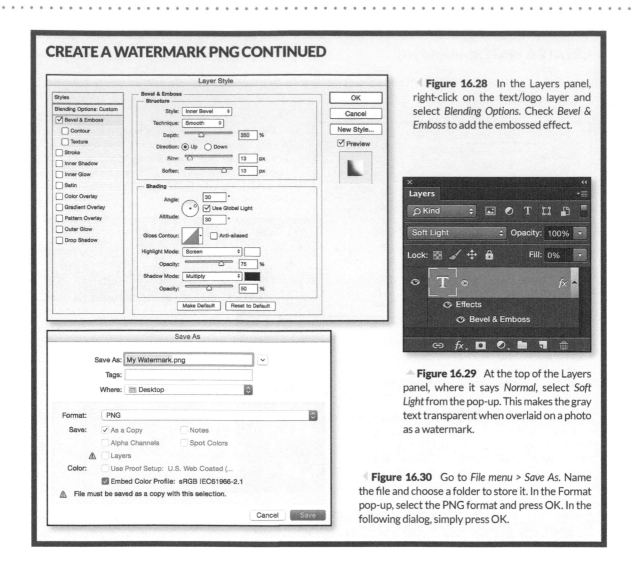

Figure 16.28 In the Layers panel, right-click on the text/logo layer and select *Blending Options*. Check *Bevel & Emboss* to add the embossed effect.

Figure 16.29 At the top of the Layers panel, where it says *Normal*, select *Soft Light* from the pop-up. This makes the gray text transparent when overlaid on a photo as a watermark.

Figure 16.30 Go to *File menu > Save As*. Name the file and choose a folder to store it. In the Format pop-up, select the PNG format and press OK. In the following dialog, simply press OK.

Figure 16.31 The size of the watermark is always relative to the size of the photo.

Fill setting.   *Fit* setting.   *Proportional* setting.

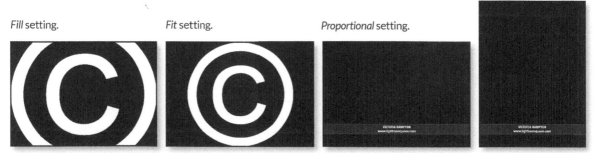

IMAGE-SPECIFIC PLACEMENT

The Watermark tool's purpose is to apply a watermark to large numbers of photos in the same size and position, so there isn't an interface for moving the watermark on individual photos, unless you want to keep returning to the Edit Watermark dialog every time you export. You could save multiple versions of a watermark preset, with the watermark in different positions, however you'd still have to select the photos to use with each preset. Using the Identity Plate and Print to JPEG, which we'll cover in the Print module, is a partial workaround if you need to carefully position a watermark on each individual photo.

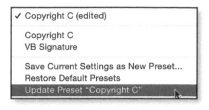

Figure 16.32 To overwrite an existing Watermark preset, select it, make your changes, and then *Update* appears in the pop-up.

If you haven't adjusted the opacity of the graphic, or you're using text, use the **Opacity** slider to reduce the opacity of the watermark, fading it into the photo.

How do I save my watermarks?

Once you're happy with your watermark, use the pop-up menu at the top of the dialog to *Save Current Settings as New Preset* ready for use on your photos. **(Figure 16.32)**

To edit a preset you've already saved, first select the preset in the pop-up, edit it, and then return to the pop-up and select *Update Preset*. To rename or delete, first select the preset in the pop-up and then the *Delete Preset* and *Rename Preset* options become available.

POST-PROCESSING & OTHER EXPORT QUESTIONS

The final **Post-Processing** section **(Figure 16.33)** of the export dialog focuses on what happens to the photos after they're exported.

The **After Export** pop-up is set to *Do Nothing* by default, but *Show in Explorer* (Windows) / *Show in Finder* (Mac) is a useful alternative, taking you directly to the exported photos.

COMPLEX OR METADATA-BASED WATERMARKS

Using Lightroom's watermark feature, you can add either a text or a graphical watermark, but not both. If you want greater control over the watermarking and you're willing to experiment to get your ideal result, the LR/Mogrify plug-in offers extensive options for adding multiple lines of text, metadata, multiple graphics and borders. You can download it as donationware from: http://www.Lrq.me/armes-lrmogrify2

Figure 16.33 In the *Post-Processing* section, seleet the action to take once the export has completed.

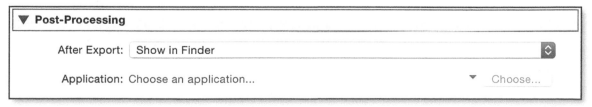

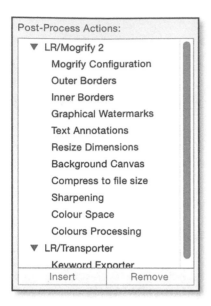

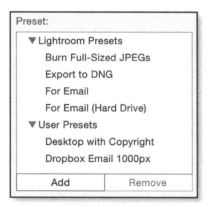

If you're exporting photos for editing in another program, select the *Open in Other Application* option and press the *Choose* button below to select the program.

If you choose the *Go to Export Actions Folder Now* option, it opens an Explorer (Windows) / Finder (Mac) window. Placing shortcuts/aliases to applications or even Photoshop Droplets in this folder adds them to the main *After Export* pop-up for easy access.

What are Post-Process Actions?

If you've installed certain plug-ins, such as LR/Mogrify 2, there may be an additional section in the Export dialog marked **Post-Process Actions**. (**Figure 16.34**) To use one of these actions, select it and press the *Insert* button. The action options become available as another panel on the right of the Export dialog.

◄ **Figure 16.34** The *Post-Process Actions* section may be added by a plug-in.

OTHER EXPORT QUESTIONS

Before we move on to email and Publish Services, there are a few other questions that often arise when exporting photos.

Can I save my Export settings as a preset?

Having chosen all of your settings in the Export dialog, you can save them as a preset for easy access next time. A few Export presets are already included by default, but it's useful to save your own settings too. You might choose to create presets for regular exports, such as email, blog, printing at a lab, archiving full resolution, and so forth.

To create an Export preset, set your Export options, and then press the *Add* button in the **Presets** panel of the Export dialog. (**Figure 16.35**)

Your presets are stored in the User Presets folder by default, but

◄ **Figure 16.35** Export presets show on the left hand side of the Export dialog, and you can group them into folders to keep them organized.

▸ **Figure 16.36** Export presets can be accessed from the right-click menu, in addition to the Export dialog.

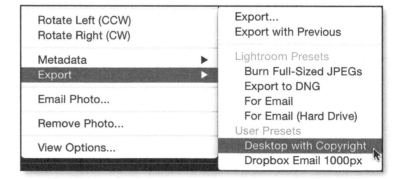

you can organize them into folders by right-clicking in the Presets panel and choosing *New Folder*, and then dragging the presets into your folders. To rename, delete or update them when your settings change, right-click on the preset. To share the presets with others, use the *Import* and *Export* options in that same right-click menu.

Having set up Export presets, you can easily access these through *File menu > Export with Preset*, or through the right-click context-sensitive menu for any photo. **(Figure 16.36)** This is particularly useful if you're using the Export preset to open the files in an external editor.

Why are my adjustments not being applied to my exported file?

If you choose *Original* as the File Format in the Export dialog, you'll create a duplicate of the original file, without your Develop settings applied. The file size may be slightly different as Lightroom updates the metadata, unlike an operating system duplication, but it won't re-compress the image data, so the quality won't be reduced.

It gives an error message—*Some export operations were not performed. The file could not be written.* or *The file could not be found.* What went wrong?

If Lightroom says it couldn't export the files **(Figure 16.37)**, press the *Show in Library* button to view an *Error Photos* temporary collection, so you can see the photos in question.

If the error says *The file could not be found*, then some of the selected photos are missing because you've moved or renamed them with other software, or the drive is offline. Click on the exclamation mark on the thumbnail and locate the original file, and run the export again. We'll come back to locating missing files in more detail in the Troubleshooting chapter starting on page 525.

If the error says *The file could not be written*, check the permissions on

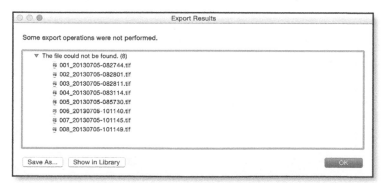

◀ **Figure 16.37** If an export fails, Lightroom displays an error dialog listing which photos failed and the reason for the failure.

the export folder or parents of that folder, because they're probably read-only, or you're running out of disc space on that drive.

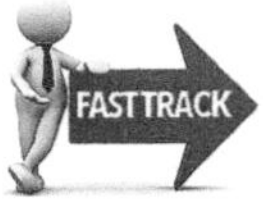

EMAILING YOUR PHOTOS

You could export your photos to a folder on your hard drive and then attach them to an email, but Lightroom makes even easier to email the photos direct.

Select the photos (no more than 100) and then go to *File menu > Email Photos*.

If your default email client is supported, such as Outlook or Apple Mail...

1. Lightroom displays the Email dialog. **(Figure 16.38)** (See the Supported Mail Clients sidebar.) Your email software is automatically selected in the *From* pop-up.

2. Select the photo size using the ***Preset*** pop-up in the bottom left corner.

3. Leave the address and the rest of the email blank and press ***Send***. It'll open the email message into your email software, where you can type your message and access your address book.

4. Alternatively, you can type the recipient's email address and your message into the Email dialog and send it directly.

If you use webmail or an unsupported email client...

1. Lightroom first asks you for your email account SMTP settings. **(Figure 16.39)** (These are the settings you'd use to set up your

SUPPORTED MAIL CLIENTS

On Windows, most email clients are supported, using standard Windows APIs to pass the images. This includes Windows Live Mail, Thunderbird, Eudora, Microsoft Outlook, etc.

On Mac, only Apple Mail, Microsoft Outlook, Microsoft Entourage and Eudora are supported, as each is coded separately.

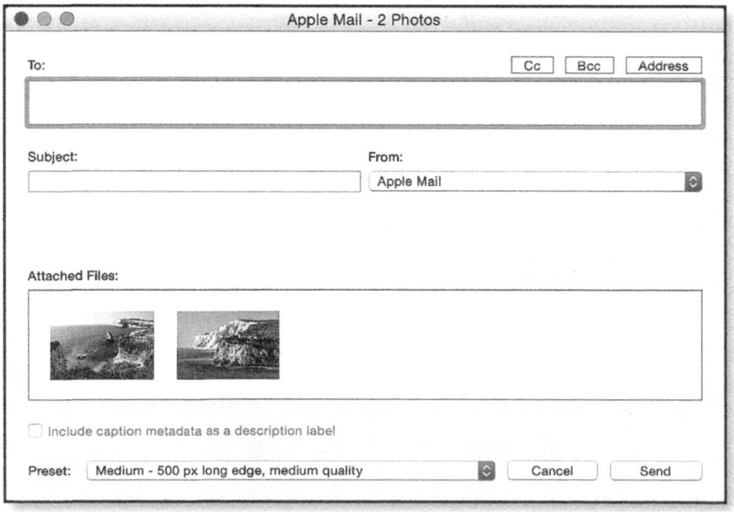

Figure 16.38 If your email client is supported, you can select it in the *From* pop-up.

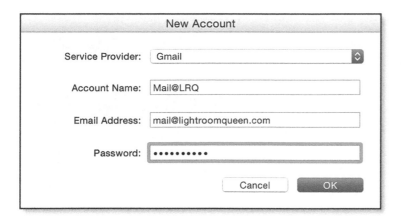

◀ **Figure 16.39** If your default email client isn't supported, Lightroom asks for your server details.

SMTP SETTINGS

If you're not sure of your SMTP details, google the name of the provider and SMTP (e.g. "iCloud SMTP") or ask your email provider. When the Port is 465, the Security setting is usually SSL/TLS. When the port is 587, it's usually STARTTLS.

email in a desktop email program.) You'll only need to add them once, as they're stored for future emails.

2. In the New Account dialog, select your email *Service Provider—AOL, Gmail, Windows Live Hotmail* or *Yahoo Mail*. Enter a name for the account to help you identify it, and enter your email address and password, and press *OK*.

3. If you use another email host, select *Other* from the *Service Provider* pop-up, enter the basic account details and press *OK*.

▼ **Figure 16.40** If your email client isn't supported, enter your email server SMTP details into the Email Account Manager dialog.

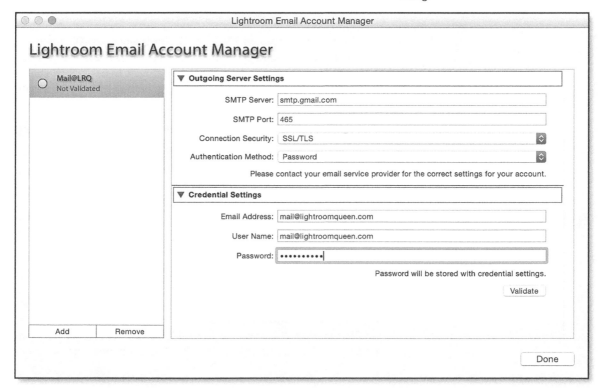

▶ **Figure 16.41** Enter the recipient's email address in the *To* field and your email message below. Set the image size using the pop-up in the bottom left corner.

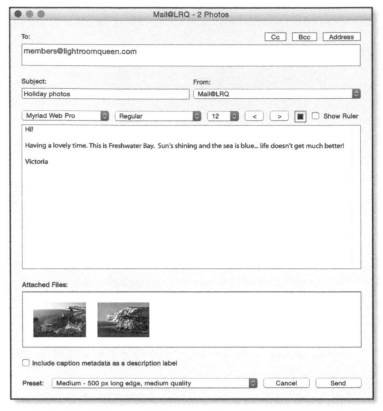

In the Email Account Manager dialog **(Figure 16.40)**, enter the rest of your email SMTP server settings. (If you're not sure which details to enter, check the SMTP Settings sidebar.) Once you've finished entering the details, press *Validate* to confirm that you've set up the account correctly, and press *Done* to confirm.

4. Select your new account in the **From** pop-up in the Email dialog **(Figure 16.41)**, and you'll be ready to send your first email.

5. Enter the address of the recipient, a subject for your email, and the message to include with your photos. Select the size of photos from the *Preset* pop-up in the lower left corner of the dialog, and finally press *Send*. To send an email to multiple email addresses, separate them with a ; and a space.

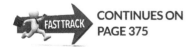

CONTINUES ON PAGE 375

Can I have multiple accounts?

If you're manually setting up email accounts using the Email Account Manager dialog, you can store settings for multiple accounts. To add additional accounts, select *Go to Email Account Manager* in the *From* pop-up, and click the *Add* button to add accounts. The accounts

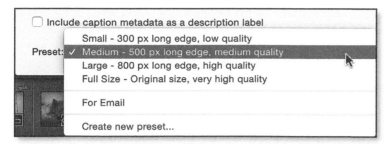

are then listed in the *From* pop-up as presets. (You can also delete accounts using the *Remove* button in the same dialog.)

How do I set the size of the photos I want to email?

In the bottom left corner of the Email dialog is the *Preset* pop-up. **(Figure 16.42)** Lightroom comes with 4 email presets by default, with different sizes and JPEG quality settings. They are: 300px low quality, 500px medium quality, 800px high quality, and full resolution very high quality.

Bear in mind the overall email size if you're sending lots of photos, or you're sending a few full resolution photos. Many email accounts have a 10mb-per-email limit, both for sending and receiving email, although Gmail/Yahoo have increased this to 25mb. A few full resolution photos can quickly reach this limit and cause the email to bounce.

If you need to send many photos to the same person, consider creating a web gallery or uploading them to a photo sharing website instead of attaching them to an email. Lightroom web is ideal for sharing galleries of photos and it's included in any Adobe Creative Cloud subscription.

If the recipients need to download a large number of photos, export them to a Dropbox folder (http://www.Lrq.me/dropbox) and email the download link, or use WeTransfer (http://www.Lrq.me/wetransfer) to send the files. It's more efficient for both you and the email recipient, and avoids clogging their email inbox.

Can I save a custom email preset including extra settings, such as a watermark or a different file format?

If you'd like to specify your own export settings for the photos, perhaps to include a watermark, or a different sharpening setting, you can create your own preset using the Export dialog.

If you're viewing the Email dialog, select *Create New Preset* from the *Preset* pop-up in the bottom left corner to open the Export dialog. If

> ### WRONG SIZE
>
> If your emailed photos don't match the size you've selected in the Email dialog, check that your email software isn't downsizing the photos further. For example, Apple Mail has an *Image Size* pop-up that must be set to *Original Size*.

you're already viewing the Export dialog, select *Email* at the top of the dialog to save an email Export preset. When you've selected your export settings, don't forget to save it as a preset. Turn back to Saving Presets (page 368) for a quick reminder.

How do I use Lightroom's address book?

If you use a supported desktop mail client, Lightroom passes the photos over to the mail client, so you can use your standard email address book.

If you send emails direct from Lightroom, you won't have access to your main address book. Instead, Lightroom allows you to save email addresses in a Lightroom address book. **(Figure 16.43)** To access Lightroom's address book, press the **Address** button in the Email dialog.

To save a new address, press the *New Address* button and enter the details. The new address is listed in the main Address Book.

If you regularly send emails to the same group of people—perhaps family members—you may want to create a group of their email addresses for easy access. In the Address Book dialog, press *New Group* and click to put a checkmark against their email addresses in the left column. **(Figure 16.44)** Press the >> button to send them to the group, shown in the right column. Give your group a name and press *OK*. Your group is then listed in the Address Book dialog.

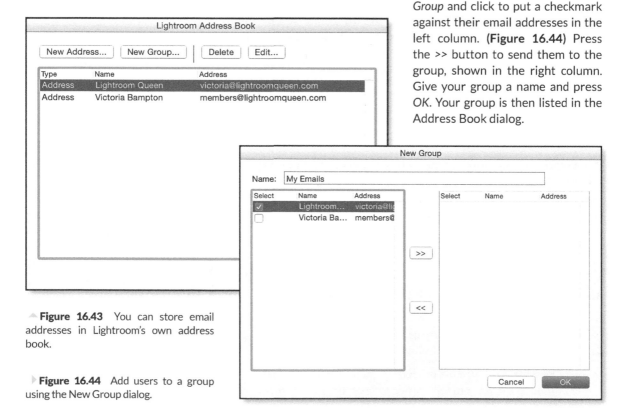

Figure 16.43 You can store email addresses in Lightroom's own address book.

Figure 16.44 Add users to a group using the New Group dialog.

To use saved addresses in your email, press the *Address* button to return to the Address Book dialog and put a checkmark next to the individual or group, and their email addresses is automatically added to the *To* field. For individuals, rather than returning to the Address Book dialog, you can simply start to type the name of the recipient or the beginning of the email address in the *To, CC* or *BCC* fields, and it autofills. The autofill doesn't work for group names.

How do I keep a copy of my sent email?

If you send through your default email client, the sent email storage depends on the preferences for that software—if it usually saves your sent emails, it continues to do so for emails initiated by Lightroom.

If you send through Lightroom directly, saving the sent email depends on the email host. Some, for example, Gmail/Google Apps, automatically keep all outgoing as well as incoming emails, whether they're sent via SMTP or directly through webmail. Most other hosts do not keep all email, but pressing the *BCC* button in the Email dialog and typing your own email address would send the email to your own inbox, as well as the primary recipient's inbox.

PUBLISH SERVICES

Publish Services is another way of sharing your photos. You could consider it a 'managed export' as it keeps tracks of the photos exported to specific locations, and when you update the photos within Lightroom, it offers you the opportunity to update them at their exported location too. Depending on the service used, some updates such as comments made on websites can also be transferred back to your catalog.

How do I set up a Publish Services account?

We'll use Facebook for the step-by-step instructions, and then go into more detail.

1. Go to the Publish Services panel (**Figure 16.45**), on the left in the Library module. By default, you'll see four Publish Services— Hard Drive, Behance, Facebook and Flickr. There may also be others, depending on the plug-ins you've installed, but these four plug-ins ship with Lightroom.

2. Click on the **Facebook Set Up** button to show the Lightroom Publishing Manager dialog. (**Figure 16.46**)

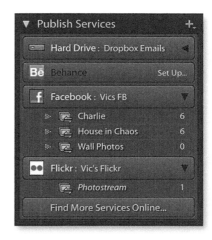

Figure 16.45 Publish Services have their own panel in the left panel group in the Library module.

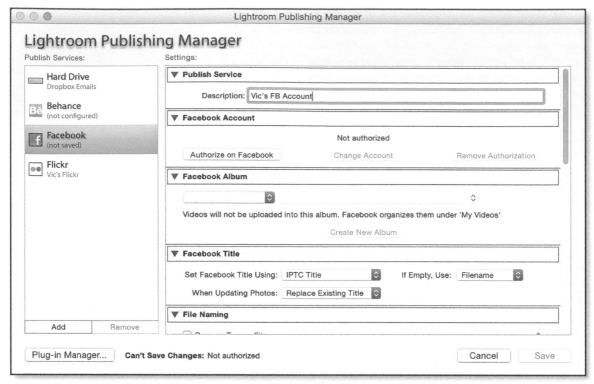

Figure 16.46 Authorize your account in the Publishing Manager dialog.

3. At the top of the dialog, give your account a name and then press the **Authorize on Facebook** button. Lightroom asks for confirmation and then opens Facebook's website.

4. Log in using your normal account details and confirm that you want to allow Lightroom access to your Facebook account. If you've previously authorized Lightroom access, it may skip the authorization page.

5. Switch back to Lightroom. In the **Facebook Album** section, use the pop-up to select a default album to hold the photos, or create a new album. **(Figure 16.47)**

6. In the **Facebook Title** section, select the title/caption to display with the photo.

7. Set your normal export preferences below, for example, file name, size, sharpening and watermark. The options should be familiar from the standard Export dialog, which we discussed earlier in the chapter.

8. Press *Save* to store the settings. The dialog closes and in the Publish Services panel, you'll see your new Facebook connection, with your chosen album displayed underneath.

9. Drag photos from the grid to the Facebook album/collection.

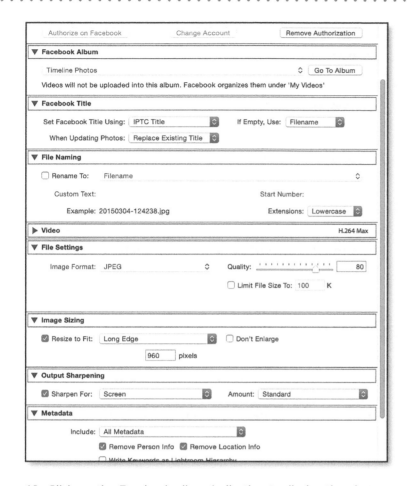

Figure 16.47 Once the connection is authorized, set your image export preferences.

10. Click on the Facebook album/collection to display the photos. The grid is divided into sections, showing the current status of the photos.

11. Click on the **Publish** button at the bottom of the left panel group, or right-click on the Facebook album and select *Publish Now*.

12. Go to the Facebook website to view your uploaded photos.

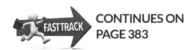

CONTINUES ON PAGE 383

Other Publish Services

The basic principles of Publish Services setup are the same regardless of which service you're using. Some just offer additional features.

For example, you can organize your photos into collections, creating photosets for Flickr, albums for Facebook, or a hierarchy of folders and subfolders for the Hard Drive.

Let's take a look at some of these differences...

▶**Figure 16.48** Create additional collections by right-clicking on the existing collection, selecting *Create Collection*, and then deciding whether to create a new album at Facebook or photoset at Flickr, or whether to link your new Lightroom collection to an existing album/photoset.

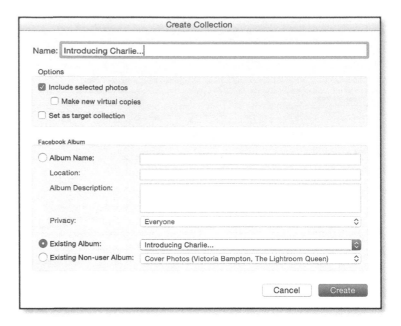

Facebook

There's one primary difference to note with Facebook. Most Publish Services can update existing photos when you make changes in Lightroom, but the Facebook Publish Service can't do that due to Facebook's API. If you republish photos to Facebook, it simply uploads a new one and leaves you to delete the old one in your web browser. Comments and likes aren't transferred to the updated photo either.

You can have multiple Facebook albums under a single Facebook connection. To create additional collections, right-click on a collection within your Facebook Publish Service in Lightroom and choose *Create Collection* from the context-sensitive menu. **(Figure 16.48)** This dialog gives you the option of creating a new album, or using an album which already exists at Facebook. If you're using an existing album, I'd recommend using the same name within Lightroom, otherwise it can easily get confusing. You only need to create separate Facebook connections if you want to change the size of the images, or other settings such as the watermark.

What size photos should I send to Facebook?

Facebook recommend uploading photos that are 720, 960 or 2048 pixels along the longest edge. Lightroom automatically converts the photos to sRGB. Facebook recompresses the photo and strips the metadata too.

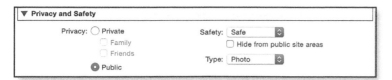

Figure 16.49 Flickr's *Privacy and Safety* settings control who can view the photos.

Flickr

The Flickr Photostream automatically appears in the Flickr section of the Publish Services panel when you create a Flickr connection. You can add photos to that collection as if it was a standard collection, or you can right-click to create another collection (except here they're called photosets to match with Flickr's name). To add additional photos to existing photosets, create a collection with precisely the same name.

Unlike Facebook, when you republish updated photos, the existing photo is updated.

The Flickr Publish Service also offers additional privacy settings at the bottom of the setup dialog. **(Figure 16.49)** These settings control who can view your photos, so they can be set to *Public* to be visible to everyone or limited to your friends and family. *Safety* controls Flickr's own content filters, rating the photos as safe for anyone to view through to restricted which are unsuitable for some age groups, like movie parental guidance ratings.

What can I use the Hard Drive option for?

One of the most useful Publish Services is the Hard Drive service, as it manages photos exported to a folder on your computer. If you create additional collections, they become subfolders.

Any changes you make to these photos within your catalog after the initial export are tracked, allowing you to selectively export only the photos that have changed or are not yet published, without re-exporting the whole set.

For example, maybe you like to keep photos on your iPad, so you could have an iPad collection which updates the photos in a folder ready to be transferred by iTunes next time you sync your iPad.

Perhaps you like to have your screensaver showing your latest photos, so a smart collection sending your last month's photos to your screensaver folder would be useful.

If you're using album design software, it's also a convenient way of making changes to the individual photos in Lightroom, and then being able to keep the exported versions updated in the album design.

If you need to export different sizes of photos, you'll need to set

THIRD PARTY PLUG-INS

The built-in plug-ins are just a starting point—a sample to show what can be done with Publish Services. Third-party developers use Adobe's SDK (software development kit) to build Publish Service plug-ins to add additional photo sharing websites.

If you're using the built-in Flickr and Facebook plug-ins, consider upgrading to Jeffrey's more advanced and more regularly updated versions which can be downloaded as donationware from http://www.Lrq.me/friedl-plugins

Third-party developers have also created Publish Service plug-ins for many other popular photo sharing websites, including Zenfolio, SmugMug and Picasa. Each of the services have slightly different limitations, dependent on the photo sharing website facilities and API, but the basic setup is the same. There's a list of the most popular Publish Service plug-ins at http://www.Lrq.me/links/plugins

LIGHTROOM MOBILE

Lightroom mobile isn't technically a Publish Service, but there are similarities. It allows you to select collections to sync to the cloud, and these web galleries can then be shared publicly. Any likes or comments that friends or family add to the photos are automatically synced back to your catalog. As you edit the photos in Lightroom, your changes are updated on the web and mobile devices, and when you edit the photos on your mobile device, they're updated in your desktop catalog.

up two separate Publish Services connections as the settings are per-connection.

There are a couple of things to be aware of. If you move to a new computer, you can't change the location of the folder. Also, if you rename the files in Lightroom after the initial export, the exported photos aren't renamed to match. For a more advanced plug-in, try Jeffrey's Collection Publisher http://www.Lrq.me/friedl-colpub

What is Behance?

The remaining built in option is Behance. It's an online portfolio website owned by Adobe, and it's designed for creative professionals to show off their creative work, and businesses to find talented creative professionals for hire. You can create a free account at http://www.behance.net

The Behance plug-in only interacts with the Work in Progress (WIP) section of the website, which is used for feedback on your current work. As a result, there are a couple of differences in the way the Behance plug-in works, compared to other Publish Services:

- You can only have a single collection. The *Work in Progress* collection is automatically created for you.

- It asks for additional information for each photo you upload, to encourage you to use the Behance workflow.

You may have also heard of Behance ProSite, which is included in the full Creative Cloud subscriptions (but not the Photographer's Plan). ProSite is a premium service which publishes your finished work from Behance as a customizable portfolio website.

SYNCHRONIZING CHANGES

Once you've set up your Publish Service, chosen your photos, and grouped them, you're then ready to synchronize it with the other service, whether that's a website or a hard drive location.

How do I publish my photos?

We've already used the **Publish** button to publish a single collection. To publish multiple collections in one go, Ctrl-click (Windows) / Cmd-click (Mac) or Shift-click on the collections to select them all before pressing *Publish*. The photos start to upload which, depending on the dimensions chosen and your internet connection upload speed, could take a while!

To temporarily limit your upload to specific photos, hold down the Alt (Windows) / Opt (Mac) key. The *Publish* button at the bottom of the left-hand panel changes into a *Publish Selected* button which only uploads the selected photos.

Does it automatically publish changes I make to my photos?

Publish Services tracks the changes you make to the photos, but it doesn't upload the updated photos automatically. Lightroom waits for you to click on the collection and choose *Publish*, otherwise it would be constantly uploading every time you made a change to a photo and you could end up accidentally publishing photos that you're part-way through editing.

How do I update my service with the changes I've made to my photos?

Lightroom divides the Grid view into different sections— **New Photos to Publish, Deleted Photos to Remove, Modified Photos to Republish** and **Published Photos**. (Figure 16.50) To update your service with your changes, right-click on the collection and choose *Publish Now* or press the *Publish* button below. To update multiple collections in one go, select them all before pressing the *Publish* button.

If photos are in the *Deleted Photos to Remove* section, they're removed from most services. Facebook is the main exception, as Facebook's API doesn't allow you to remove photos using other programs. To remove a photo from Facebook, delete it on the Facebook website (and from Lightroom's published collection, if you don't want to republish it).

How do I mark photos as already published, so they don't upload again?

If you make a change to a photo, such as changing some metadata, it moves to the *Modified Photos to Re-Publish* section. If you don't want to republish it, perhaps because the change was minor or you don't want to upload it as a new photo on Facebook, right-click on the photo and

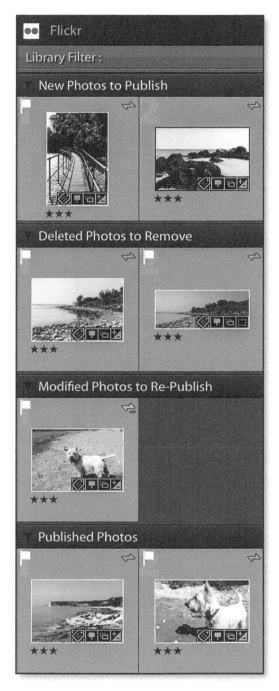

▲ **Figure 16.50** Lightroom keeps track of the changes you make and groups the photos into *New Photos to Publish*, *Deleted Photos to Remove*, *Modified Photos to Re-Publish* and *Published Photos*.

COMMENTS

The Comments panel is designed to work with Publish Services and Lightroom mobile, synchronizing comments with supported photo sharing services, so it's only available when you have a Publish collection or Synced collection selected. If someone comments on one of your photos on the website, their comments are retrieved when you next publish/sync that collection. **(Figure 16.51)**

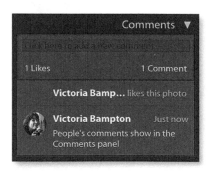

▲ Figure 16.51 People's comments show in the Comments panel

choose **Mark as Up-To-Date** to move it back into the *Published Photos* section.

I didn't mean to remove a photo from a collection—how do I restore it?

If you accidentally remove a photo from a collection, just drag it back again. If you pressed *Publish*, nothing will have changed on the service (Flickr/Facebook, etc.) and it moves straight back into the *Published Photos* section. If the photo has been deleted from the service, it's uploaded again.

I accidentally revoked the authorization on the website—how do I fix it?

While we're on the subject of accidents, you may accidentally revoke the authorization on the website (e.g. Facebook), preventing Lightroom from publishing your photos. To fix it, right-click on the Publish Service in Lightroom and choose *Edit Settings* to access the Publishing Manager dialog. There you can log in again and re-authorize Lightroom's access.

Can I have the same account connected to multiple catalogs?

The same Flickr or Facebook account can be connected to multiple catalogs, but there are limitations. You can't easily transfer your collections/photosets between catalogs, even using Export as Catalog, and Lightroom won't know about anything that's already on the website or in your other catalog. Some advanced plug-ins, such as those created by Jeffrey Friedl, attempt to match up photos in your catalog against existing photos on the website, but it's a situation best avoided.

EXPORT AS CATALOG

Publish collections are tied to one specific catalog, and aren't carried over when using Export as Catalog, unlike normal collections, so be careful to set it up in your master catalog rather than a temporary catalog.

There is a plug-in which can transfer Publish Services information between catalogs, although it does have some limitations. You can find more information about the Lightroom Voyager plug-in at http://www.Lrq.me/alloy-lrvoyager

SLIDESHOW MODULE

Lightroom's Slideshow module **(Figure 17.1)** isn't designed to replace specialized software, but it's an easy way to create a simple slideshow. You can design the slides yourself, add branding and text overlays to personalize your slideshow, and add audio backing tracks. The finished slideshow can be played in Lightroom, or it can be exported as video, PDF or JPEG format.

SLIDESHOW BASICS

Before we dive into the details, let's just run through the basics and create your first slideshow.

1. In Library module's Grid view, decide which photos you want to include in your slideshow. This might be a folder or a collection

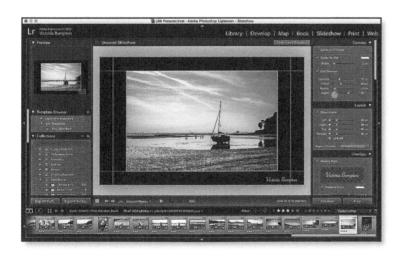

Figure 17.1 The Slideshow module.

of photos. If the photos are spread across multiple folders or collections, use the Quick Collection to group them together.

2. Switch to the Slideshow module by selecting it in the Module Picker.

3. At the top of the Preview Area, press the *Create Saved Slideshow* button and give your slideshow a name. Saving the slideshow at the beginning means you won't accidentally lose your work. The saved slideshow appears in the Collections panel, and it remembers the photos you're using as well as the slideshow settings.

4. In the Template Browser panel on the left, click on the different templates to apply them to your slideshow until you find a design that you like.

5. You can adjust the colors and design of the slides, as well as the text overlays, using the panels on the right. We'll come back to these settings in the following pages.

6. (Optional) Add a musical backing track by going to the Music panel and press the + button. Navigate to your music on the hard drive, and choose a DRM-free MP3 or AAC music file.

7. (Optional) Check the *Sync Slides to Music* checkbox in the Playback panel to align the slide timings with the music tracks.

8. Preview your slideshow in the Preview Area by pressing the *Preview* button at the bottom of the right panel group. Press the Escape key or the square stop button on the Toolbar to stop the slideshow and adjust settings, and then preview again until you're happy.

9. Finally, you're ready to play your slideshow full screen. Press the *Play* button, which is next to the *Preview* button. It's worth doing a dry run before showing it to someone else, as Lightroom builds slide previews before playing the first time.

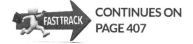

CONTINUES ON PAGE 407

SLIDE LAYOUT & DESIGN

Having learned the basics of the Slideshow module, you can start customizing the design to suit your own taste.

One of the first choices to make when building a slideshow is the design of the slides. Do you want a fine art look with wide borders, or full screen photos? With a neutral background or a patterned backdrop? Let's explore the possibilities.

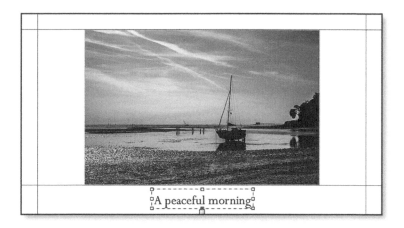

Figure 17.2 The grey lines are Guides. These mark the margins, showing the maximum image area on the slide. Unlinking the bottom slider allows you to have a wider bottom margin to hold your caption.

How do I adjust the size of the photo?

When you look at the slide in the Preview Area, you'll see horizontal and vertical gray lines. Those lines are called Guides. **(Figure 17.2)** They mark the maximum image area, or cell, to help you set the width of your margins and the size of the photos.

The maximum image area is adjusted either by dragging the gray guides or moving the **Left, Right, Top** and **Bottom** sliders in the Layout panel. **(Figure 17.3)** I say maximum image area, because the photo may not fill the entire cell, depending on whether the ratio of the photo and the cell match. We'll look at how to fill the cell in a moment, but let's experiment further with the margins first.

When you click and drag a guide or slider for the first time, they'll all move at the same time. That's because the sliders are linked by default. In the Layout panel, you'll see small white squares next to the sliders, indicating their linked state.

If you click on one of these squares, turning it gray, the slider is no longer linked to the others and moves independently. For example, you may want the top, left and right margins to be identical, and a wider margin at the bottom to hold your photo caption. The square below the sliders, marked **Link All**, toggles all the link squares at once.

If you find the guides distracting, you can hide them by unchecking the **Show Guides** checkbox in the Layout panel.

How do I set the aspect ratio of the slides?

The slide layout automatically adapts to the screen ratio, allowing you to display the finished slideshow on a variety of different screens. This also means that if you're preparing the slideshow on a screen with a 4:3 ratio (i.e. 1024x768) and then later play it on a widescreen

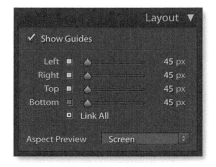

Figure 17.3 The sliders in the Layout panel adjust the margins, and therefore the maximum image area. The squares next to the sliders indicate whether the sliders are linked or move independently.

MOVING MARGINS

If the sliders are unlinked, the guides move independently—but if you drag the corner of the cell, where the guides intersect, both guides move at once.

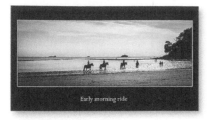

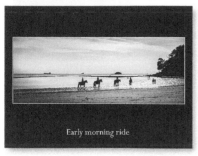

Figure 17.4 Use the *Aspect Preview* pop-up to check how your slide layout will look on different shape screens.

TV (or export to a widescreen video format), your slide layout can appear quite different.

To overcome this, you can set the aspect ratio of the slide in the preview area using the **Aspect Preview** pop-up in the Layout panel. *Screen* uses the aspect ratio of the current screen. *16:9* is a widescreen option and *4:3* is a more traditional screen ratio. As you select each option, the slide in the preview area updates. **(Figure 17.4)**

If you know which screen ratio will be used to play your finished slideshow, you can select the correct ratio from the outset. Otherwise, test the other ratios before exporting, to check you're happy with the result. (The size options in the Export Slideshow dialogs control the ratio of the exported slideshow.)

Why doesn't the photo fill the photo cell?

Having set the maximum image area using the guides, you may find that the photos don't fill the cell. This is because Lightroom fits the photo within the cell boundary without distorting or rotating it.

For example, to display a vertical photo within a horizontal cell, there are two options: you can either show the whole photo, leaving additional space down the sides, or you can fill the cell, cropping some of the photo. **(Figures 17.5-17.7)**

To automatically crop the photo and fill the cell, check **Zoom to Fill Frame** in the Options panel. Lightroom centers the photos by default, but you can manually position each photo within its cell by clicking and dragging it. The positioning is stored with the rest of the saved slideshow settings. To retain your existing crop, leave *Zoom to Fill Frame* unchecked.

Figure 17.5 With *Zoom to Fill Frame* unchecked, your photo is fitted into the cell without cropping, leaving additional space around the photo.

Figure 17.6 When you check *Zoom to Fill Frame*, Lightroom expands the photo to fill the entire cell, cropping off part of the photo.

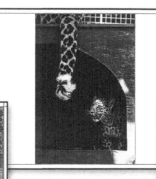

Figure 17.7 The only other way to fit a vertical photo into a horizontal cell is to squash the photo. Since that rarely looks good, Lightroom doesn't offer this option.

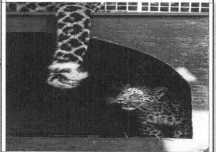

How do I change the background of the slides?

The space surrounding the photo is called the background or backdrop. When you first open the Slideshow module, the background is set to 70% gray, with a darker gray color wash or gradient. Let's be honest, it's a bit boring!

You can change the background to settings of your choice using the Backdrop panel. **(Figure 17.8)** The background color, wash (gradient) and image can be used separately or together to change the effect. You can also add a stroke or keyline around the photo, and a shadow behind it, using the settings in the Options panel. Let's investigate these options.

How do I set the background color?

To select a different color for the background, check the **Background Color** checkbox in the Backdrop panel and click the rectangle to the right. The Color Picker shows a range of neutral colors, to avoid distracting from your photos. However it's possible to access other colors by clicking on the bar on the right side of the Color Picker. As you click in the Color Picker to select different colors, the slide preview updates. Unchecking the checkbox reverts to a simple black background.

How do I add a border around the photo?

A border or keyline can help to separate the photo from the background, making it stand out. You can turn the border on and off using the **Stroke Border** checkbox in the Options panel. The width of the border is measured in pixels and adjusted using the **Width** slider below.

The border defaults to a light gray, but you can select a different shade to complement your background. **(Figure 17.9)** A white narrow keyline stands out against a black background, whereas it would obviously disappear on a white background. More colorful shades can distract from the photo. To adjust the color, click the rectangle

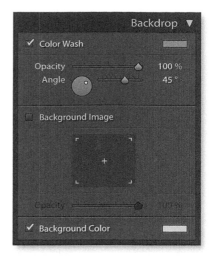

Figure 17.8 The Backdrop panel holds the settings for the background of the slide.

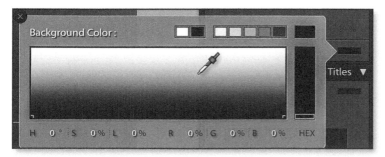

Figure 17.9 Click in the Color Picker to select a color. To access a wider range of colors, click the bar on the right. The rectangles at the top are presets, or you can type HSL or RGB values at the bottom to access specific colors. To select a color from the image, click in the Color Picker and drag onto the photo.

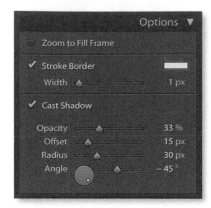

Figure 17.10 The photo-specific settings—*Zoom to Fill Frame, Stroke Border* and *Cast Shadow*—are all found in the Options panel.

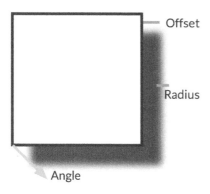

Figure 17.11 *Cast Shadow* adds a shadow behind the photo.

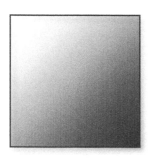

Figure 17.12 The *Angle* slider affects the direction of the color wash gradient. Setting a black wash to around -30 shows the blackest corner in the bottom right.

to the right of the *Stroke Border* checkbox to display the Color Picker and then click on your chosen shade using the Eyedropper.

How do I add a drop shadow?

In addition to the border, you can a drop shadow beneath the photo. The shadow is enabled and disabled using the **Cast Shadow** checkbox in the Options panel. **(Figure 17.10)** The additional sliders allow you to control the look of the shadow. **Opacity** affects the brightness (or darkness!) of the shadow. **Offset** controls the distance from the photo, and **Radius** is the feathering of the shadow. The **Angle** wheel and slider allow you to control the direction the light is coming from, so a value of -35 to -45 usually looks good. **(Figure 17.11)**

The easiest way to set the angle is to drag the small dot inside the circle. If you drag the dot to the bottom right corner of the wheel, the shadow appears around the bottom right corner of the photo.

Shadows are, of course, dark, so they won't be visible if your background color is set to black.

How do I add or remove a gradient or color wash on the background of the slide?

The controls marked **Color Wash** in the Backdrop panel control any gradient you choose to add to the background. The checkbox obviously turns it on and off, and **Opacity** affects the strength of the gradient. The color is selected using the rectangle on the right.

The **Angle** slider affects the direction of the gradient. The easiest way to set this is to look at the wheel and drag the small circle to the corner where you want your chosen gradient color to be strongest. For example, dragging the wheel up to approximately 140 starts the gradient in the top left corner of the slide, depending on the ratio of your screen. **(Figure 17.12)**

How do I add a background image to my slides?

In addition to plain backgrounds and gradients, you can also add images to the backgrounds of the slides. The background image doesn't need to be a photo. It could be a texture, a pattern such as a map, or even something like a photo of an empty frame or window which would appear to surround your slideshow photos. **(Figure 17.13)**

To add your background image, first make sure that your background photo has been imported into Lightroom, and then drag it from the

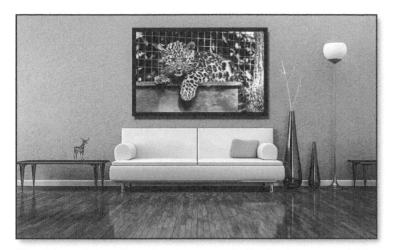

Figure 17.13 Using a photo of your lounge as the background image can even help you decide which photos to hang on the wall! Adjust the Guides to the inner edges of the frame, so that the photo appears to fill the frame

Filmstrip and drop it on the drop zone in the Backdrop panel. The **Background Image** checkbox is automatically checked. **(Figure 17.14)**

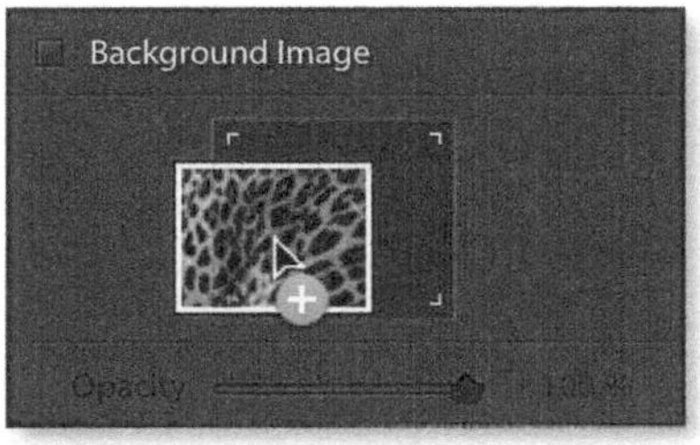

If you're using a pattern or photo as the background, it may compete for your attention, distracting you from the slides in the slideshow. Reduce the strength of the background image using the **Opacity** slider, and combine it with a black background color for a dark background or white for a light background.

To use a background image to frame the photos, drop the frame background image on the drop zone, then check the *Zoom to Fill Frame* checkbox in the Options panel. Finally, adjust the guides to the inner edges of the frame, so that the photo appears to fill the frame.

Figure 17.14 To add a background image, drag a photo from the Filmstrip and release it over the drop zone.

TEXT CAPTIONS & OTHER OVERLAYS

Having created your basic slide layout, you can then add your branding to the slides, as well as captions for each individual photo.

How do I add branding to my slideshow?

You may have seen slideshows where the photographer displays their logo in the top left corner **(Figure 17.15)** or at the bottom, below the photo. In Lightroom, that's added using the Identity Plate. You can also use the Identity Plate to add your signature to the photos, perhaps in the lower right corner.

To add your Identity Plate to the slide, check the **Identity Plate** checkbox in the Overlays panel **(Figure 17.16)**, and then click the preview field below to select your Identity Plate. You can return to this preview field to change the Identity Plate again later.

Figure 17.15 You can set your logo to appear on every slide.

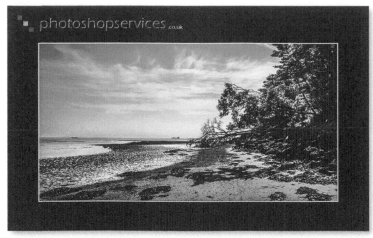

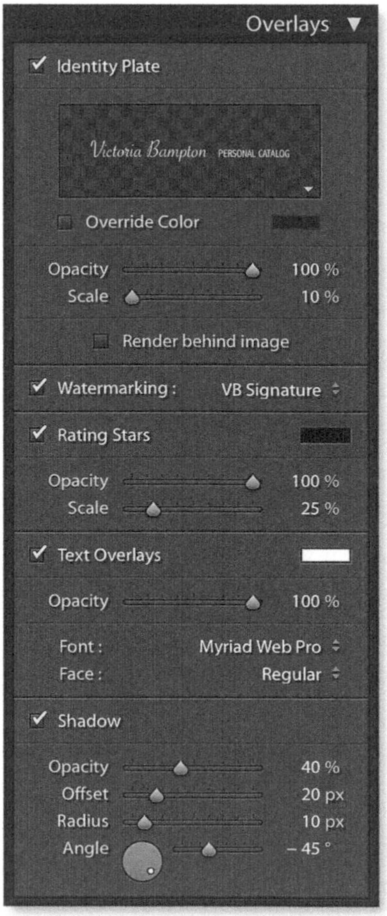

If you haven't created one yet, select *Edit* to show the Identity Plate dialog. We've already explored this dialog in detail in the Workspace chapter (page 77), but if you're not familiar with it, feel free to turn back to these instructions and then continue.

Once your standard Identity Plate is enabled, you can apply further customization. For example, if your Identity Plate uses white text and your slide background is also white, you can check the **Override Color** checkbox and select another color using the Color Picker. If your Identity Plate is a brightly colored logo, it may be distracting at full opacity, so you can reduce the strength using the **Opacity** slider, fading it into the background. On some slides, your Identity Plate might overlap the photo, but checking the **Render behind image** checkbox tucks it behind the photo, avoiding distraction (but hiding part of the Identity Plate).

You can also change the size and location of the Identity Plate. By default, it's small and tucked away in the top left-hand corner of the slide. When you click on the Identity Plate, a bounding box appears with white squares in the corners and along the edges. To change the size, you can either drag those white squares or adjust the **Scale** slider in the Overlays panel.

To move the Identity Plate, click on the center of it, avoiding the white squares, and drag it around the slide. This is easier to do once you've enlarged it. As you move the Identity Plate around the slide, you'll notice a larger white square attached to the Identity Plate with a thin white line. This is called an Anchor Point.

How do I use Anchor Points?

Figure 17.16 In the Overlays Panel, select the *Identity Plate* (e.g. logo) that will appear on the slides

Anchor Points determine the position of the Identity Plate or text field on the slide. They lock to one of 16 different points—the corners

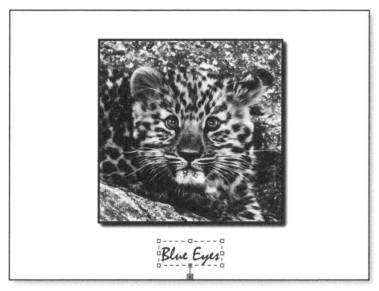

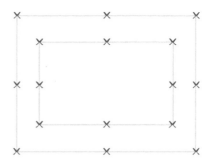

Figure 17.17 There are 16 anchor points on each slide, marked with an X.

Figure 17.18 Regardless of the changes to the photos, the Identity Plate remains static when it's locked to the edge of the slide.

of the photos, the corners of the slides, the center of the edge of the photos, or the center of the edge of the slides. (Figure 17.17)

The Identity Plate and the text fields are positioned relative to the anchor points. When you select an anchor point on the edge of the slide, the Identity Plate or text field remains in the same place on each slide regardless of the photo orientation. This is useful for branding the slide with your logo or displaying your photo caption in a fixed position. (Figure 17.18)

If, however, you lock the anchor point to the corner of the photo, it automatically adjusts the position for vertical and horizontal photos. For example, if you lock it to the bottom right corner, the Identity Plate or text field always remains in the lower right corner of the photo where you might expect to see a signature. (Figure 17.19)

When the Anchor Point is white, moving the Identity Plate/text field causes the anchor point to change too, anchoring itself to the nearest of the 16 points.

If you click on the Anchor Point, the square changes from white to yellow, showing that it's anchored in position. If you then click and drag the Identity Plate/text field, the anchor stays locked in place, although you can still move the yellow anchor point separately by dragging it. (Figure 17.20)

Once you're happy with the rough position of the Identity Plate/text field, you can fine tune the position using the arrow keys on the keyboard.

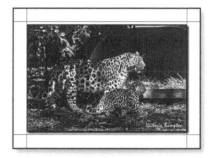

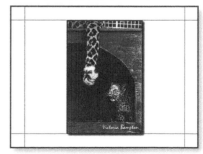

Figure 17.19 If the Identity Plate is anchored to the corner of the photo, it adjusts for differing orientations and crop ratios, making it useful for signing your photos.

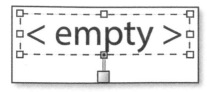

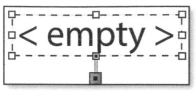

Figure 17.20 A white anchor point moves when you move the overlay, whereas a yellow anchor point remains fixed.

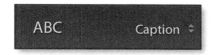

Figure 17.21 To add a text field to the slide layout, press the ABC button in the Toolbar.

How do I add a watermark to my photos?

In addition to the Identity Plate overlay, you can also add a watermark to your photos. For example, you may want to watermark the slides if you're sending a PDF slideshow to a client, exporting the bordered slides as JPEGs to upload to the web, or putting a video of the slideshow online.

To do so, check the **Watermarking** checkbox in the Overlays panel and select your watermark from the pop-up. If you haven't created any watermarks yet, turn back to the Export chapter (page 362), where we discussed it in detail.

How do I add a text caption?

In addition to branding your slides with an Identity Plate, you can also add additional text fields that update for each photo.

For example, your camera club may appreciate your EXIF data under each photo. If your slideshow is for your clients, you may prefer to add the filename and star rating, or for your friends, the captions that you've added to your vacation photos.

To create a text field, press the **ABC** button on the Toolbar. **(Figure 17.21)** If the Toolbar's missing, press the T key to show it again.

Each time you press the ABC button, a new text field is created, and they can each have different settings.

How do I reselect or delete a text field?

If you accidentally create too many text fields, click on the text field to select it (shown by the bounding box surrounding it), and then press the Delete key on your keyboard to delete it.

If you find that the text overlays become too distracting, but you don't want to delete them, you can disable them using the **Text Overlays** checkbox in the Overlays panel. This just hides them, so you check it to show them again later.

What is *Custom Text*?

The default setting for the text field is *Custom Text*, which you type into the field on the Toolbar. *Custom Text* is a static line of text, so it's the same on each slide. In most cases, it's not very helpful!

OVERLAY SHORTCUTS

Move up	Up key
Move down	Down key
Move left	Ctrl left arrow / Cmd left arrow
Move right	Ctrl right arrow / Cmd left arrow
Move in larger increments	Shift up/down/left/right arrows

How do I make the caption different for each photo?

To have the text field automatically update for each photo, it needs to use the photo's metadata instead of static text.

In the pop-up next to the *ABC* button, there are a variety of presets built into the program, including title, caption, capture time or filename. They use the metadata that was embedded by the camera (EXIF) or that you've entered in the Metadata panel in the Library module (IPTC) for each photo. You can select one of these ready-made presets or you can create your own.

How do I create my own metadata-based preset?

If you select *Edit* from the bottom of the pop-up, you'll be taken to the Text Template Editor. **(Figure 17.22)** This dialog allows you to create your own text presets from a wider variety of metadata using tokens. Tokens are text in curly brackets on Windows, or blue lozenges on Mac, and they're replaced with metadata from the file.

To create your own template, click in the white token field and delete any existing tokens. Select your chosen tokens from the pop-ups below, for example, title, then a line break, then caption below. On a Mac, you can create a line break by pressing Opt-return. You can also type directly into the white field, but that text is the same on each slide. An example appears above the white field, based on the metadata of the selected photo, so you can preview the result.

Figure 17.22 You can create your own metadata-based caption using the Text Template Editor.

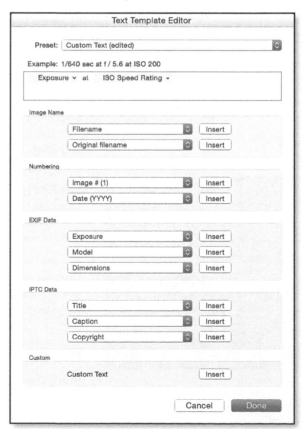

CAPTION IN QUOTES

The built in *Caption & Rating* template includes quotation marks around the caption. When the Caption field is empty, it simply shows "", which looks odd. You can edit this caption to remove the quotation marks using the Text Template Editor, as if you were editing one of your own text presets, and then save a new Slideshow Template.

To save it as a preset for use with other slideshows (and other modules that use text templates), select the *Preset* pop-up at the top of the dialog and choose *Save Current Settings as New Preset*. Give the preset a name and close the dialog using the *Done* button. To rename or delete a preset, first select the preset in the pop-up and then return to the pop-up to select *Rename Preset* or *Delete Preset*. To edit a saved preset, select the preset, change it, and then return to the pop-up and select *Update Preset*.

Why does the text field say *<empty>*?

Returning to the slide preview, you may find that your text field says *<empty>* for some photos. That's because you've selected a metadata-based text field, such as *Title* or *Caption*, and the selected photo doesn't currently have anything in this metadata field. To fix it, switch back to the Library module and enter the missing data in the Metadata panel. For example, if you're using *Title*, you'll need to enter a title into the *Title* field for each photo. If you choose to leave it empty, the *<empty>* text disappears when you play the slideshow.

How do I change the font for my captions?

You're not limited to updating the content of the text fields. Each of the text fields can have its own custom styling, for example, the date may be a small sans-serif font in the corner, while the photo title has a larger fancier font in the center.

Select the text field that you want to adjust by clicking on it. The font size is set by dragging the white squares on the edges of the bounding box, and the rest of the settings are found in the Overlays panel. **(Figure 17.23)**

The **Font** pop-up lists the fonts installed on your computer, and the **Face** pop-up selects the style of the font, for example, bold, italic, etc. The **Opacity** slider allows you to fade the text into the background, and of course the Color Picker allows you to select the color.

The text alignment is set automatically based on the anchor point for that text overlay. Text fields anchored on the left of the slide or photo are left aligned, those anchored on the right are right aligned, and those anchored in the center are center aligned.

How do I add shadows behind my overlays?

In addition to changing the type style for the captions, you can also add shadows behind the Identity Plate and other overlays. Like the text fields, the shadow settings apply only to the selected field, so

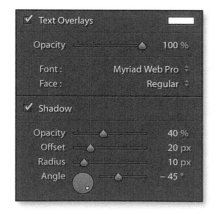

▲ **Figure 17.23** The Text formatting options are at the bottom of the Overlays panel.

it can be enabled for some fields and not for others. The **Shadow** checkbox is in the Overlays panel, and the **Opacity, Offset, Radius** and **Angle** sliders behave in the same way as the photo shadow options in the Options panel we discussed earlier.

How do I display my star ratings?

We also mentioned star ratings at the beginning of this section, which may be useful when displaying a slideshow for clients. There's a text token to show the number of stars as text in a caption (i.e. *5 Stars*), but in the Overlays panel there's also a checkbox for **Rating Stars**. When it's checked, the little star icons appear in the top left corner of the photo and you can drag them to a location of your choice. Like the other overlays, you can change the transparency and the size of the stars using the **Opacity** and **Scale** sliders, and the color using the Color Picker to the right.

On the Toolbar beneath the preview area, there are two bent arrows which rotate the selected overlay in 90 degree increments. Unless you enjoy reading captions with your head tilted to the side, these buttons are more useful for rotating the star ratings than they are for text!

Can I rate the photos while the slideshow's running?

You can use the 0-5, 6-9 and P, U, X shortcut keys to mark the photos with star ratings, color labels or flags while the slideshow is playing. Even if you don't have these markers showing as captions on your slideshow, the new rating appears briefly in the lower left corner of the screen so you can see the rating you've just applied.

PLAYBACK SETTINGS

Having designed the slides, you'll need to double check that the layout works on a range of photos with different orientations and crops. The arrow buttons on the Toolbar or keyboard step through the photos, so you can check that the text doesn't unexpectedly overlap the photos.

Preview the slideshow in the Preview Area, complete with music and transitions, by pressing the triangular Play button in the Toolbar. **(Figure 17.24)** It turns into a Pause button to pause playback. When

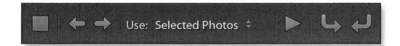

Figure 17.24 The arrows on the Toolbar step through each slide in turn.

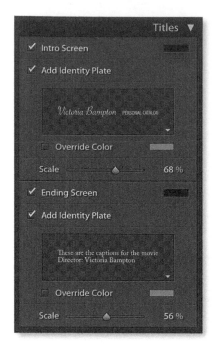

Figure 17.25 Add Intro and Ending screens using the Titles panel.

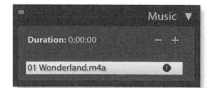

Figure 17.26 Add a background music track to your slideshow using the Music panel.

you've finished, press the square Stop button. When a slideshow's not running, that square button moves the selection to the first photo in the set instead.

How do I add blank slides at the beginning and end of the slideshow?

If you're going to show your slideshow to other people, you may want to add Title Screens. The Intro Screen appears before the first photo in the slideshow, so you can start the slideshow and immediately press the Spacebar key to pause it while the Intro Screen is still visible. That hides the first photo in the slideshow, building anticipation. At the end of the slideshow, you might also want to include an Ending Screen, like the credits of a movie.

To turn them on, check the **Intro/Ending Screen** checkboxes in the Titles panel **(Figure 17.25)**, and use the Color Picker to select the background color. Whenever you make an adjustment, the preview stays on screen for a few seconds and then fades back to the normal slide view.

In addition to the basic plain background color, you can check **Add Identity Plate** to make your Intro Screen a little more interesting. It could simply be your name or logo, or you could create a custom Identity Plate as a title page, perhaps including the name of the client, or the topic of the slideshow. Like the main Identity Plate, you can override the color and change the size.

To use multiple lines in your Identity Plate, it's easiest to type them in other software and copy/paste them into the Identity Plate dialog.

If you'd like to add more complex title/end pages, create them in Photoshop or another image editor, save them as an image file and import them into Lightroom. You can then add them them to your slideshow as normal photos. The same idea works if you want to add additional title slides in the middle of your slideshow, for example, introducing different places you visited on vacation.

How do I add a music track to my slideshow?

To add to the professional appearance, you can add a musical backing track to accompany your slideshow.

Lightroom doesn't integrate with iTunes, Windows Media Player, or similar software, so it won't offer you a list of your playlists. Instead, press the + button in the Music panel and navigate to a music track on your hard drive. **(Figure 17.26)** Lightroom can play any MP3 or

AAC music files, as long as they're DRM free. When you press *Choose*, the track name and length appears next to the button.

Can I add multiple music tracks?

In previous Lightroom versions, slideshows were limited to a single music track, but I have good news for you... in Lightroom CC/6, one of the new features is the ability to use up to 10 different tracks!

When you press the + button, you can select multiple tracks by holding down the Ctrl key (Windows) / Cmd key (Mac) and clicking on each of your chosen tracks, or you can click on the first and hold down Shift while clicking on the last in a series of tracks.

If the tracks are in different folders, pick the tracks from the first folder, press *Choose*, then press the + button again to navigate to another folder to add additional tracks.

Once you've added your tracks, you can drag and drop them into the order of your choice.

How do I remove a music track?

If you change your mind about a music track, click to select it and then press the—button above to remove it.

To temporarily prevent any music tracks playing, without removing them completely, toggle the switch on the Music panel header.

Why is there an exclamation mark next to the track name?

If Lightroom can't play the track, it displays an exclamation mark next to the track name. This means that the music file can no longer be found, or it's not a format that Lightroom is able to play, perhaps due to DRM.

How do I fade the music track when I'm playing a video?

If you're including videos in your slideshow, the video soundtrack could conflict with the music track. Using the **Audio Balance** slider in the Playback panel **(Figure 17.27)**, you can choose soundtrack which takes precedence. When the slider is on the left, the video soundtrack plays instead of the music. On the right, the music plays and the video soundtrack is muted. When the slider is in the middle, both soundtracks are played at once, with the balance determined by the position of the slider.

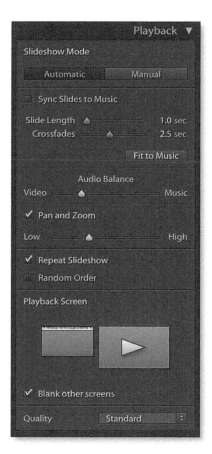

▲ **Figure 17.27** Set the slide length and transitions using the Playback panel.

INDIVIDUAL TIMINGS

Lightroom doesn't offer individual manual slide timings, which is a feature often associated with dedicated slideshow software. If you have particular photos you want to leave on screen for longer, you can work around that limitation by creating additional virtual copies of the photos. For example, three copies of the same photo would keep it on screen three times as long as the other photos.

How do I set the timings for the slideshow?

In the Fast Track, we used the **Sync Slides to Music** checkbox in the Playback panel to set the slide timings. It's smarter than it sounds— it not only adjusts the slide and fade length to fit the length of the tracks, but also based on the rhythm of the music. The fade is quick if the music has a fast beat, and it fades more slowly with gentler music.

If you'd like a little more control, you can adjust the timings manually. The **Slide Length** slider controls how long the slide remains on screen, and the **Crossfades** slider sets the length of time it takes to fade from one photo into the next. The aim is to balance the timings, as you don't want the slides constantly fading from one to the next.

If you're using a music backing track, but setting the slide timings manually, Lightroom can calculate the best slide length for you. Otherwise, the slideshow and the music end at different times. First, select a *Crossfades* time that seems reasonable, for example, 4 seconds. Then press the **Fit to Music** button and the *Slide Length* slider automatically adjusts. Preview the slideshow to check the timings look right. If they don't, increase or decrease the *Crossfades* slider, and try the *Fit to Music* button again until you're happy with the balance. You can see the total length of the slideshow on the Toolbar.

Can I change the style of transitions?

By default, the photos fade from one to the next, but you can add an effect called **Pan and Zoom**. It's also known as a Ken Burns effect, after the well-known director and producer who popularized the pan and zoom style. The amount of panning and zooming is controlled slider below, with *Low* being a gentle movement. If you select *High*, combine it with a longer slide length for best effect.

Can I advance the slideshow manually?

If you don't want the slideshow to advance automatically, perhaps because you'll be giving a commentary while it plays, you can change the **Slideshow mode** at the top of the Playback panel from **Automatic** to **Manual**. Most of the music, timing and transition settings disappear, and you can then move through the slideshow manually using the left and right arrow keys on your keyboard, or a programmed remote control. The slides don't fade in Manual Slideshow mode.

How do I set the order of the slides?

The slideshow always plays in the selected sort order of the folder or collection, unless you check the **Random Order** checkbox in the Playback panel.

If you want to change the sort order, switch back to the Grid view and select an alternative sort order using the sort order pop-up in the Toolbar. If you're in a view that supports custom user orders, for example, you've saved your slideshow and it's selected in the Collections panel, then you can also drag and drop the photos in the Grid view or in the Filmstrip to rearrange them.

When the slideshow reaches the end of the photos, it stops playing by default, but checking the **Repeat Slideshow** checkbox runs it on a loop, starting back at the beginning automatically.

How do I select which monitor to use?

Ready to play your slideshow? There's one more decision to make. If you have multiple monitors attached to your computer, or your laptop is plugged into your tv, an icon appears in the Playback panel for each screen. The icon with the triangular Play icon indicates which screen will display the slideshow. To change it to a different screen, click on your chosen screen icon.

The **Blank other screens** checkbox turns the other screens black while the slideshow's playing, to avoid distractions.

How do I play the slideshow?

Having tweaked the settings to your heart's content, it's finally time to play your slideshow. Press the *Play* button at the bottom of the right panel group. Lightroom builds the previews then it's ready to start playing. The **Quality** pop-up controls the length of time it takes to build the previews, with *Draft* or *Standard* previews being much quicker than *High* quality previews.

If you have a large number of photos, or a slow computer, you may wish to press *Play* well ahead of time and then press Spacebar to pause the slideshow at the beginning, otherwise your viewers could be waiting a while for the previews to build. To stop a slideshow at any time, Spacebar pauses and Escape returns to Lightroom.

NO PICTURES

When you press *Play*, the slideshow should obviously start playing. If the screen turns gray or black instead of showing the photos, it's usually a sign of a problem with the video card driver, so it's worth checking for updates from the manufacturer. (Windows Update rarely has the most recent drivers.) It can also be caused by an underpowered graphics card, in which case a lower screen resolution can help.

How do I play a subset of my slideshow without creating a new one?

Finally, if you just want to play part of the slideshow, perhaps to show a specific location you visited on vacation, select only those photos in the Grid view or Filmstrip. In the Toolbar, change the **Use** pop-up from *All Filmstrip Photos* to *Selected Photos* and press Play. (You can also select *Flagged Photos* in that same pop-up to play only the flagged ones.)

SAVING SLIDESHOWS & TEMPLATES

Having crafted your ideal slideshow, the last thing you want to do is lose your hard work, so it's important to know how to save it. Lightroom allows you to save in two different ways: as a slideshow containing the photos, or only the settings as a template to apply to other photos.

If you followed the Fast Track instructions at the beginning of the chapter (page 383), your slideshow settings will already be saved in the catalog, and the name of the slideshow is displayed at the top of the Preview Area and in the Collections panel. If you continue working in Lightroom and later come back to show the slideshow to a friend, you can simply double-click on the saved slideshow to get back to your current state.

How do I save my slideshow to edit or play again later?

If you haven't saved your slideshow yet, press the **Create Saved Slideshow** button at the top of the Preview Area, or press the + button on the Collections panel and select *Create Slideshow*. **(Figure 17.28)**

Lightroom asks for a name for your new slideshow. You also have a choice of where to file it in the Collections panel. It can be stored within a Collection Set, within a standard collection or as flat list of Collections. If you can't remember the difference, turn back to the Collections section in the Library chapter (page 115) for a refresher.

If the slideshow *Use* pop-up is currently set to *Flagged photos* or *Selected photos* in the pop-up on the Toolbar, there's an additional checkbox marked *Include only used photos*. As the name suggests, only the photos currently included in the slideshow are included in the saved slideshow if it's checked.

The final checkbox allows you to create new virtual copies of the included photos. That can be helpful if you might accidentally edit one of the photos that you've previously included in this

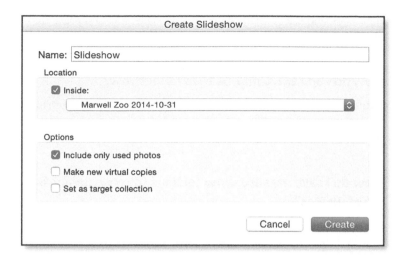

Figure 17.28 Save your slideshow to play or export again later.

slideshow—perhaps converting it to B&W—resulting in it looking out of place next time you play the slideshow.

If you check the *Make new virtual copies* checkbox, consider adding a color label to help identify their purpose, so you don't later delete them, wondering where all these excess virtual copies have come from. The purple label is ideal as it doesn't have a keyboard shortcut. To do so, select all the photos included in the slideshow, right-click on a thumbnail in the Filmstrip and select Set Color Label > Purple.

How do I open my saved slideshow again later?

Later, having saved your slideshow in the Collections panel, you can easily open it again to play or even edit. You'll note that your slideshow collection has its own icon in the Collections panel, identifying it as a slideshow. **(Figure 17.29)** If you're already in the Slideshow module, a single-click on the slideshow in the Collections panel opens it. If you're viewing another module, you need to double-click on it.

Figure 17.29 In the Collections panel, Slideshows have an icon to identify them.

How do I edit or delete my saved slideshow?

As you make changes to your reopened slideshow, the changes are saved automatically. If you want to try some different settings without overwriting your saved slideshow, right-click on it in the Collections panel and select *Duplicate Slideshow*. You can also hold down the Alt (Windows) / Opt (Mac) key while dragging the slideshow to a Collection Set or between two other top-level collections in the Collections panel.

If you later change your mind and want to delete the slideshow, right-click and select *Delete* or select the slideshow and press the— button at the top of the Collections panel.

How do I add extra photos to my slideshow?

To include additional photos in a saved slideshow, simply switch back to Grid view and drag the extra photo thumbnails from the grid onto the slideshow in the Collections panel.

How do I save my slideshow settings to reuse on another set of photos?

If you've created a slideshow design that you love, you may want to save it to reuse on other photos. Unlike slideshows saved in the Collections panel, templates only save the settings without the photos, ready to apply to other collections of photos.

To save your settings as a template, click the + button on the Template Browser panel. Give your new template a descriptive name and select a folder to store it in. By default, it saves it in the User Templates folder, but if you have a lot of templates, you can organize them into folders.

To create a new folder, open the pop-up menu in the New Template dialog, and select *New Folder* or right-click on any existing template and select *New Folder*, then enter the folder name. You can drag and drop the templates into different folders later, if you don't want to organize them at this stage.

If you later tweak the settings, you can update the template by right-clicking on the template and choosing *Update with Current Settings*. You can also rename and delete any templates that you create, using the *Rename* and *Delete* options in the right-click menu. The built-in templates can't be updated, renamed or deleted.

As you float the cursor over the templates in the Templates panel, the Preview panel above displays a preview of each template, enabling you to quickly identify the template you want to use. To apply a different template to your slideshow, click on it. **(Figure 17.30)**

Finally, if you've created the perfect slideshow template, you may want to share it with other Lightroom users or transfer it to a different computer. To do so, right-click on the template and select *Export*, then select a folder on your hard drive. The template files have a *.lrtemplate extension. Alternatively, you can right-click on a user template and select *Show in Explorer* (Windows) / *Show in Finder* (Mac). That takes you directly to the current template location, ready

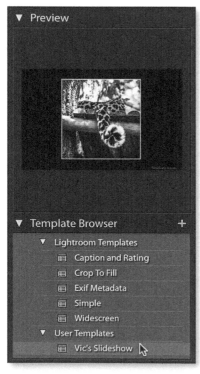

Figure 17.30 When you float over a template in the Template Browser panel, it's previewed in the Preview panel above.

to copy to another computer. Showing the whole folder is particularly useful when copying a larger number of templates.

To install the templates on another machine, right-click on an existing template and select *Import*, then navigate to the slideshow template on your hard drive. Alternatively, right-click on a user template and select *Show in Explorer* (Windows) / *Show in Finder* (Mac). Place the templates in this folder and restart Lightroom.

EXPORTING SLIDESHOWS FOR USE OUTSIDE OF LIGHTROOM

Playing the slideshow within Lightroom is easy, but what if your friend or client isn't sat next to you? Lightroom offers three different export formats to allow you to play your slideshows outside of Lightroom.

Which format should I use?

Each of the export formats has strengths and weaknesses, so the format you choose will depend on your usage.

- **Video format** is the closest to the slideshow you'll see in Lightroom, complete with the music and slide transitions. Videos can be hosted on websites such as YouTube and embedded in your own website, as well as sharing on Flickr, Facebook or Dropbox. The files can be quite large, so they're not great for email.

- **PDF format** creates a smaller file, better suited to email, and it can run as a slideshow in free Adobe Reader software on any computer, however the slide timings are fixed and the music track isn't included. Adobe Reader is a free download from http://www.Lrq.me/adobereader, so many people have it installed. This makes PDF an excellent choice for sharing a selection of photos by email or download link (e.g. via Dropbox).

- **JPEG format** allows you to design your slides within Lightroom, and then export the complete slides as JPEGs for use in other slideshow software. Some DVD players can also play JPEGs as a slideshow on your television without any additional software.

Let's explore these export options in more detail...

How do I export my slideshow as a video?

To export your slideshow as an MP4 format video, go to *Slideshow menu > Export as Video*, or press the **Export as Video** button at

---

IMPROMPTU SLIDESHOW

The Impromptu Slideshow runs from any module using the shortcut Ctrl-Enter (Windows) / Cmd-Return (Mac) or *Window menu > Impromptu Slideshow*. It plays all the photos in the selected folder or collection unless you select specific photos. Like the main Slideshow module, the Spacebar pauses and resumes the slideshow and Escape ends it.

You can choose which template it uses by right-clicking on your chosen template and selecting *Use for Impromptu Slideshow*. That template is marked with a + sign to show it's selected.

▶**Figure 17.31** Set the exported video size using the Export Slideshow to Video dialog.

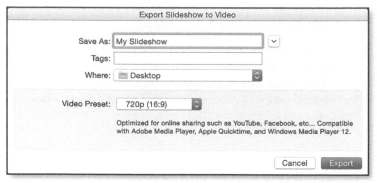

the bottom of the left panel group. The Export as Video dialog **(Figure 17.31)** asks for three details: where you want to save the exported video, the name of the new video file, and the size of the video.

The size of the video depends on its purpose. If you're going to show the video on your mobile phone, you'll need a much smaller file than a 1080p television. Adobe offer recommendations in the Export as Video dialog itself, but for reference, here are their recommendations:

- **320 x 240**—smallest file size, suited to email, compatible with Quicktime, iTunes, Adobe Media Player, Windows Media Player 12, etc.

- **480 x 320**—ideal for mobile devices such as iPhone, iPod Touch, Android, etc.

- **720 x 480**—small handheld devices, email, web

- **960 x 540**—home media display i.e. AppleTV

- **720p**—medium size HD for online sharing, YouTube, Facebook, blip.tv, and for home media/entertainment such as iPad, AppleTV or Windows Media Center

- **1080p**—high quality HD video

How do I export my slideshow as a PDF?

To create a PDF of your slideshow, go to *Slideshow menu > Export as PDF* or press the ***Export to PDF*** button at the bottom of the left panel group. Like the video export, Lightroom asks where to save the file, the new file name, and the size. **(Figure 17.32)** It also asks how much JPEG compression to apply, which affects the file size of the resulting PDF.

As with video, the size you choose depends on the purpose. For a high quality slideshow, setting the slideshow to screen resolution is a good

MUSIC COPYRIGHT

If you're going to upload your slideshow to a website such as YouTube or play it in public, take care not to include any commercial music tracks that would infringe copyright. There's some excellent royalty-free music available for photographers to use in slideshows such as Triple Scoop Music http://www.triple-scoopmusic.com

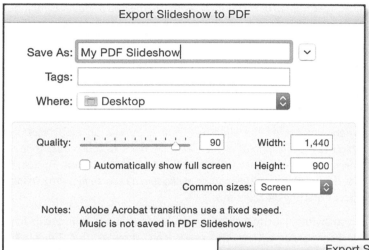

Figure 17.32 Set the size and quality of the PDF file in the Export Slideshow to PDF dialog.

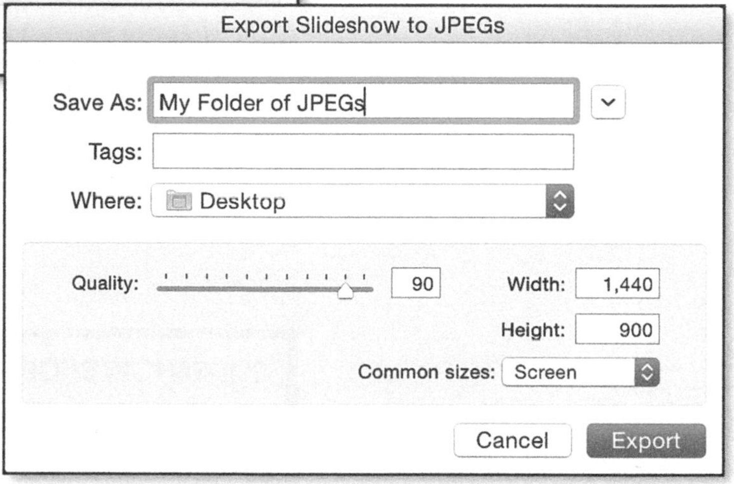

Figure 17.33 Export a folder of JPEGs to use in alternative slideshow software using the Export Slideshow to JPEGs dialog.

choice. If you don't know the size of the screen that will be used to view it, 1920x1080 is large enough to display well in most circumstances.

There's no additional security applied to the PDF, so if you're sending the slideshow to a client to choose their photos, you may decide to use a smaller size, for example, 1024x768 and add a watermark to help protect your photographs from unauthorised use.

Finally, you'll need to set the JPEG compression or quality. Turn back to the Export chapter (page 353) for a more detailed discussion of JPEG compression rates. As a rule of thumb, a setting of 60-75 is a good trade-off between file size and quality for many slideshows.

How do I export my slideshow as a folder of JPEGs?

The Export as JPEG option can also be found under the *Slideshow menu*. If you prefer buttons, the **Export to JPEG** button is hidden under the *Export to PDF* button, so you need to hold down the Alt (Windows) / Opt key to access it.

As with the other export options, Lightroom asks where to save the exported slideshow and a name for it. **(Figure 17.33)** When you export, it creates a folder with your chosen name, and each of the

TIMELAPSE PHOTOGRAPHY

If you're interested in Timelapse Photography, there's an advanced Lightroom plug-in at http://www. Lrq.me/timelapse and Jeffrey's Timelapse plug-in helps to adjust the Develop settings at http://www.Lrq.me/ friedl-timelapse

JPEGs are named using your slideshow name and a sequence number to keep them in order.

Like the PDF, you'll need to select a size and JPEG compression rate, depending on the intended use of the JPEG slides.

Why are my photos missing?

When you export the slideshow, you may see an error message which says *Some photos in the slideshow point to source files that are current unavailable. They will be omitted from the slideshow. To create a slideshow without omitted photos, make sure all source files are available before exporting the slideshow.*

If you switch back to Grid view, you'll see that the thumbnails have the rectangular exclamation mark icon, showing that the photos can't be found at their last known location. Turn to the Missing Files section in the Troubleshooting chapter (starting on page 525) for more information on how to fix that error, and then you'll be able to export your slideshow successfully.

SLIDESHOW SHORTCUTS

Run Slideshow	Enter / Return
Run Impromptu Slideshow	Ctrl Enter / Cmd Return
Pause Slideshow	Spacebar
Go to Next Slide	Right arrow
Go to Previous Slide	Left arrow
End Slideshow	Escape
Show Header Bar	\
Show / Hide Guides	Ctrl Shift H / Cmd Shift H
New Template	Ctrl N / Cmd N
New Template Folder	Ctrl Shift N / Cmd Shift N
Create Saved Slideshow	Ctrl S / Cmd S
Export PDF Slideshow	Ctrl J / Cmd J
Export JPEG Slideshow	Ctrl Shift J / Cmd Shift J
Export Video Slideshow	Ctrl Alt J / Cmd Opt J

PRINT MODULE

Although most photos today start out as digital files, at some stage you may to want to print them. Exporting the photos and sending them to an online lab is an easy option but Lightroom also includes a Print module. **(Figure 18.1)** You can print single prints on a local printer, or build contact sheets and lay out multiple photos on a page to print on a local printer or send away.

PRINT BASICS

Lightroom offers three different layout options for printing, which you select in the Layout Style panel. **(Figure 18.2)**

- ***Single Image/Contact Sheet*** is a single photo on a page, or different photos all the same size, laid out as a contact sheet grid.

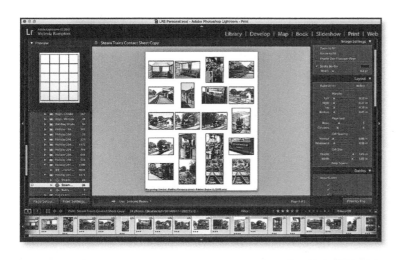

EXPORT FOR STANDARD LAB PRINTS

If you're using a printer attached to your computer, or you want to include multiple photos in a single print, use Lightroom's Print module. If you're just sending individual photos to an online or local lab to be printed, it's quicker to turn back to the Export chapter (starting on page 347) and export JPEGs instead.

◄ **Figure 18.1** The Print module

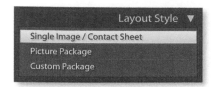

Figure 18.2 The Layout Style panel allows you to choose whether to create a print with single or multiple photos.

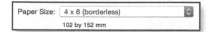

Figure 18.3 Set the paper size to 4" x 6" borderless in the Page Setup dialog.

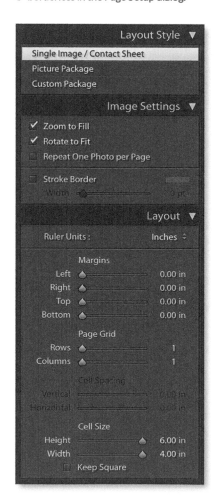

Figure 18.4 These are layout settings you'll need to create a 4"x6" borderless print.

- **Picture Package** is the same photo in different sizes, laid out free-form on the page.

- **Custom Package** is different photos in different sizes, laid out free-form on the page.

We'll run through the basics of setting up each style of print and how to print your design, before we then go back and investigate the options in detail.

How to... create a 4" x 6" borderless print

First, let's create a simple 4"x6" borderless print (assuming your printer can print borderless!):

1. Select the photo or photos you want to print, and then switch to the Print module using the Module Picker at the top of the screen.

2. At the bottom of the left panel group, click the *Page Setup* button to display your printer's dialog. (The options vary depending on the operating system and printer.)

3. Select your paper size, for example, if you're using 4x6 borderless paper, you'll need to select the 4" x 6" borderless setting. Close the *Page* Setup dialog. **(Figure 18.3)**

4. In the Layout Style panel at the top of the right panel group, select *Single Image/Contact Sheet*.

5. In the Image Settings panel, check *Zoom to Fill* and *Rotate to Fit*. This fills the cell with the photo.

6. In the Layout panel, set all the margins to 0 for borderless printing. If they won't go down to 0, the Page Setup isn't set to borderless or your printer can't print borderless, in which case you'll need to use a larger piece of paper and cut it down after printing.

7. Still in the Layout panel, set the *Rows* and *Columns* sliders to 1 to place a single photo on the page, and set the *Cell Size* to 6x4 for a 6" x 4" print. **(Figure 18.4)**

8. In the Toolbar underneath the preview, choose *Selected Photos* from the *Use* pop-up to print the selected photo(s) or *All Filmstrip Photos* to print all of them. Try a single print to double check your settings before printing a large number of photos.

How to... print it

Once you've finished designing your layout, whether that's a single print or a complex design, it's time to print.

1. Scroll down to the Print Job panel. **(Figure 18.5)** As a default, set the *Print Resolution* field to 360ppi for Epson or 300ppi for Canon/HP.

2. Enable the *Print Sharpening* checkbox, selecting the amount in the first pop-up (*Low*, *Standard* or *High*) and the paper type (*Glossy/Matte*) in the second pop-up. If in doubt, select *Standard Glossy*.

3. If you have a profile for your printer, select *Other* from the *Color Management Profile* pop-up and choose the profile. Press *OK* and select the profile in the pop-up. If you don't have a profile, select *Managed by Printer* so that the printer cares for the color management.

4. Press the *Printer* button to view the Print dialog. Like the Page Setup dialog, this dialog varies depending on the operating system and printer driver. If you're using a Mac, you may need to press the *Show Details* button to access the printer driver options. **(Figure 18.6)**

   Select your paper type, quality settings and any other settings specific to your printer driver. (If these options aren't available, ensure that you've installed the printer driver direct from the manufacturer rather than the default driver provided by the operating system.) If you've selected a profile in the *Color*

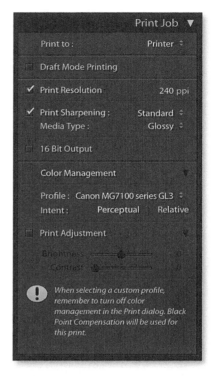

▲ **Figure 18.5** Select the *Resolution*, *Sharpening* and *Color Profile* for the print in the Print Job panel.

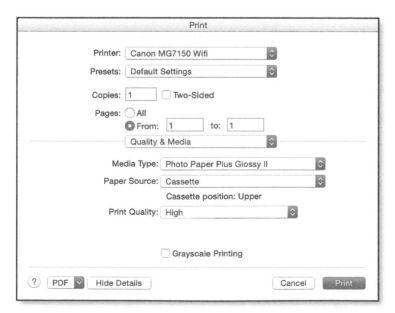

◀ **Figure 18.6** After setting up the print layout in Lightroom, press the *Printer* button and select the correct paper and quality settings.

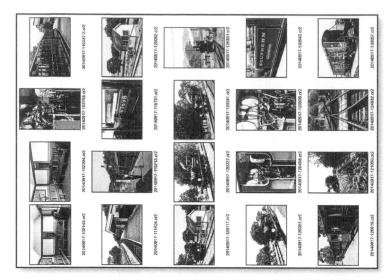

▶ **Figure 18.7** Contact sheets were traditionally used for selecting the best photos, but are still useful for test prints today.

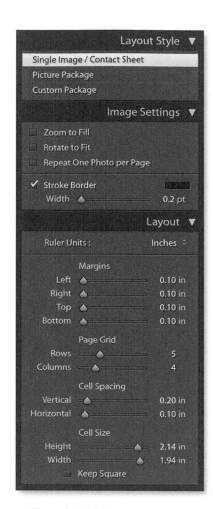

▲ **Figure 18.8** Select your page layout settings in the right panel group in the Print module. These are settings for a contact sheet.

Management Profile pop-up, select *No Color Adjustment* or *ColorSync* in the printer dialog.

5. Finally, press *Print* and wait with bated breath!

How to... create a contact sheet

A contact sheet is a selection of photos laid out as a grid, often with a filename underneath. **(Figure 18.7)** They're often used by photographers to help clients select their photos or as an index page in an album. Others use contact sheets to check their prints will turn out as expected, without wasting ink on full size test prints.

1. In Library module's Grid view, decide which photos you want to include in your contact sheet. This might be a folder or a collection of photos. If the photos are spread across multiple folders or collections, use the Quick Collection to group them.

2. Switch to the Print module using the Module Picker at the top of the screen.

3. In the Toolbar underneath the preview, choose *All Filmstrip Photos* from the *Use* pop-up.

4. At the bottom of the left panel group, press the *Page Setup* button and select your paper size (e.g. Letter or A4 size) in the printer dialog before returning to Lightroom.

5. In the Layout Style panel at the top of the right panel group, select *Single Image/Contact Sheet*.

6. In the Layout panel, choose the numbers of rows and columns

for your contact sheet using the *Page Grid* sliders, and adjust the spacing between the cells using the *Cell Spacing* sliders. As you adjust the slider, the preview updates live. **(Figure 18.8)**

7. If you have a mixture of horizontal and vertical photos, toggle the *Rotate to Fit* checkbox in the Image Settings panel to enable or disable rotation.

8. To display the filename beneath each photo thumbnail, check *Photo Info* in the Page panel and select *Filename* in the pop-up to the right.

9. Then turn back to page 409 to send it to your printer.

How to... create a picture package

The Picture Package enables you to print multiple versions of the same photo in varying sizes on the same piece of paper, for example, printing two small copies for your wallet, and a larger copy for a frame.

1. Select the photo, and then switch to the Print module using the Module Picker at the top of the screen.

2. In the Toolbar underneath the preview, choose *Selected Photos* from the *Use* pop-up.

3. At the bottom of the left panel group, press the *Page Setup* button and select your paper size (e.g. Letter or A4 size) in the printer dialog before returning to Lightroom.

4. In the Layout Style panel, select *Picture Package*.

5. In the Ruler, Grid & Guides panel, select cm or inches from the *Ruler Units* pop-up, depending on your preference.

6. Click a button in the Cells panel to add a cell of that size, for example, press the 4x6 button to add a 4" x 6" cell to the page. Repeat to add additional photo cells. To delete a cell, click on it and then press the Delete key. Press *Clear Layout* if you want to start again. **(Figure 18.9)**

7. Once you've added the cells, click the *Auto Layout* button to automatically arrange the cells on the page or drag and drop them into a layout that you like.

8. In the Image Settings panel, check the *Zoom to Fill* and *Rotate to Fit* checkboxes to fill the cells you've created.

9. Turn back to page 409 to send your design to your printer.

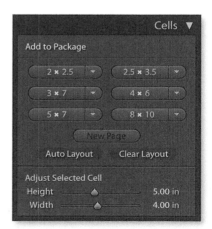

Figure 18.9 Add cells to the page using the Cells panel.

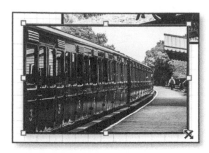

Figure 18.10 Drag the bounding box handles to resize the cells and drag the center of the cell to arrange the cells on the page.

How to... create a custom package

The Custom Package enables you to print any photos in a mixture of sizes to avoid wasting paper, so you have two choices: either you place the cells first and then drop the photos into those cells, or you drop the photos directly onto the page and their cells are automatically created, ready for you to resize. In this example, we'll drop the photos onto the page.

1. In Library module's Grid view, decide which photos you want to include in your design. This might be a folder or a collection of photos. If the photos are spread across multiple folders or collections, use the Quick Collection to group them for easy access.

2. Switch to the Print module using the Module Picker at the top of the screen.

3. In the Layout Style panel, select *Custom Package.*

4. Select a photo in the Filmstrip, drag it to the page and drop it.

5. Using the squares in the corners of the bounding box, adjust the size of the cell. To move it, click in the center of the cell and drag it. **(Figure 18.10)**

6. To add an additional photo, drag it from the Filmstrip and drop it on a blank area of the page. If you drop a new photo on an existing cell, the photo is replaced. To delete a cell, click to select it (shown by the bounding box) and press the Delete key.

7. Turn back to page 409 to send your design to your printer.

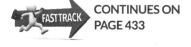

CONTINUES ON PAGE 433

PRINT LAYOUT

Having learned the basics of printing, let's do a deeper dive into some of the layout options and controls. The options vary depending on the selected layout style.

How do I change the page size and paper orientation?

The first thing to decide when designing a print is the paper size. The printer driver sets the paper size, orientation and maximum printable area, so you must click the **Page Setup** button to change these settings. The dialog varies depending on the operating system. **(Figure 18.11)**

Although the Print module is primarily designed for printing to a locally attached printer, you can also save your print creations as

ROLL PAPER

If your printer is using roll paper, create a custom paper size using the roll width and your chosen length.

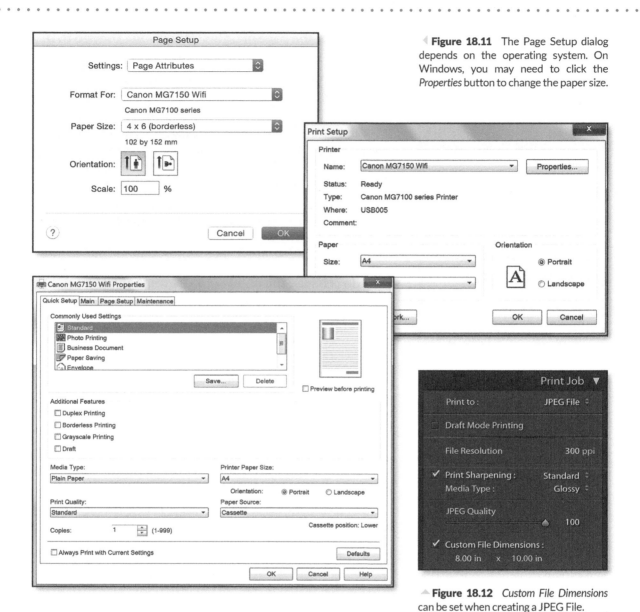

Figure 18.11 The Page Setup dialog depends on the operating system. On Windows, you may need to click the *Properties* button to change the paper size.

Figure 18.12 *Custom File Dimensions* can be set when creating a JPEG File.

JPEGs to send to an offsite lab. To do so, go to the Print Job panel and set the *Print to* pop-up to *JPEG* instead of *Printer*. When you're creating a JPEG, it's easier to override your local printer's paper sizes and set a custom print size, for example, 8" x 10". Check the **Custom File Dimensions** checkbox and enter your chosen size. For example, 8" x 10" creates a vertical page and 10" x 8" creates a horizontal page. Don't forget to enter your lab's preferred **File Resolution**, for example, 300 ppi. **(Figure 18.12)**

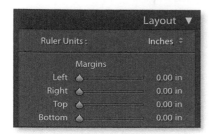

Figure 18.13 *Margins* are set in the Layout Panel. These can only be set to zero if the paper size is borderless.

POINTS AND PICAS

I'm sure we all know what inches, centimeters and millimeters are, but points and picas are a little more unusual. They're units used in typography. 1 point is 1/72 inch and 1 pica is 12 points, or 1/6 inch.

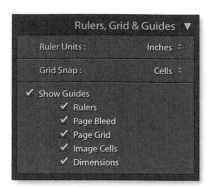

Figure 18.14 Options to show different guides are controlled using the Guides/Rulers, Grids & Guides Panel.

Figure 18.15 The *Rulers*, *Page Bleed*, *Page Grid* and *Image Cell* visibility are all set in the Guides/Ruler, Gride & Guides panel.

How do I set the page margins? Why won't they go to 0?

After setting the paper size, you can then adjust the margins for Single Prints/Contact Sheets. All of the photo cells fit within these margins. (The limits are set automatically for Picture/Custom Packages.)

The **Margins** sliders are found in the Layout panel **(Figure 18.13)**, and as you move them, the preview in the center updates. If you have *Margins & Gutters* checked in the Guides panel, you can also drag the gray guides directly on the page preview to adjust them visually.

The maximum printable area (or page bleed) is set by the printer driver, so to set the margins to 0, you first have to select a borderless paper size in the printer settings.

How do I change the units of measurement?

The units of measurement are set using the **Ruler Units** pop-up in the Layout panel for *Single Print/Contact Sheet* or the Ruler, Grid & Guides panel for the *Picture Package* or *Custom Package* style. You have a choice of inches, centimeters, millimeters, points and picas.

There isn't a pixels option, which seems like a strange oversight. If you need to set the file dimensions in pixels, especially for web use, simply divide your pixel dimensions by your *File Resolution* setting. For example, to create a file with dimensions of 2400 x 3000, you could set 24" x 30" at 100ppi for a quick calculation.

How do I change the guides displayed on the page?

There's a selection of guides that can help when laying out your print. They're found in the Guides panel (Single Image/Contact Sheet) or Ruler, Grid & Guides panel (Picture Package/Custom Package). **(Figure 18.14 & 18.15)**

- **Rulers** display on the top and left edges of the Preview Area. If you right-click on the rulers, you can quickly change the units of measurement.

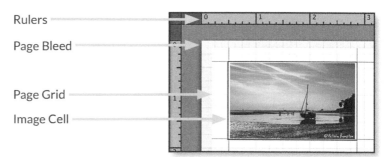

Rulers

Page Bleed

Page Grid

Image Cell

PRINT GUIDE SHORTCUTS

Show / Hide Guides	Ctrl Shift H / Cmd Shift H
Show / Hide Page Bleed	Ctrl Shift J / Cmd Shift J
Show / Hide Margins and Gutters	Ctrl Shift M / Cmd Shift M
Show / Hide Image Cells	Ctrl Shift K / Cmd Shift K
Show / Hide Dimensions	Ctrl Shift U / Cmd Shift U
Show / Hide Rulers	Ctrl R / Cmd R

- **Page Bleed** helps you to visualize the maximum printable area. The unprintable area displays as a light gray border around the page and everything must fit within this border.

- **Margins & Gutters** displays the margins on the page as gray lines, and dragging the lines adjusts the margins. It only applies to the Single Print/Contact Sheet style.

- **Page Grid** displays a light blue grid on the page in the Picture Package or Custom Package styles. It's useful for lining up photos on the page, especially when combined with *Grid Snap*. We'll come back to *Grid Snap* a little later in the chapter (page 417).

- **Image Cells** displays the edges of the image cells using thin black lines. The lines don't appear in the finished prints.

- **Dimensions** displays the size of the photo in the top left corner of each photo, and it updates live as you resize the cells. If you select a cell, you can also check the dimensions by looking at the *Width* & *Height* sliders in the Layout panel (Single Image/Contact Sheet) / Cells panel (Picture Package/Custom Package).

The **Show Guides** checkbox turns all of the guides on and off in one go.

How do I adjust the contact sheet layout?

If you're printing a contact sheet with multiple photos, you not only have to set the margins, but also the number of photos and spacing between them. This is done using the Layout panel. **(Figure 18.16)**

The **Page Grid Rows & Columns** sliders control how many columns of photos run across the page and how many rows run down the page. For a single photo on the page, both sliders obviously need to be set to *1*.

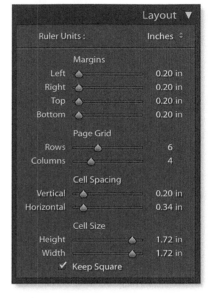

▲ **Figure 18.16** Set the contact sheet layout in the Layout panel.

SORT ORDER

The contact sheet photos display in the current sort order, so if you rearrange the sort order in Grid view or Filmstrip, the contact sheet automatically updates to show your new sort order.

If you're going to need to re-print the contact sheet again later, you may decide to save the photos in a Print collection, as the collection retains the sort order as well as your Print module settings.

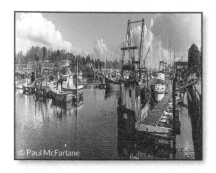

Figure 18.17   To force a panoramic photo to fit a fixed size, you'd need to squash it. This looks odd, so Lightroom doesn't let you do that.

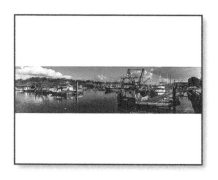

Figure 18.18   If you uncheck *Zoom to Fill*, it fits your photo onto the paper without cropping.

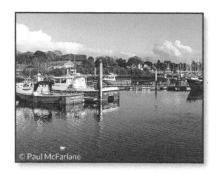

Figure 18.19   If you check *Zoom to Fill*, it fills the paper with your photo, but crops some of the photo in the process.

The **Cell Spacing Vertical & Horizontal** sliders control the space between the image cells, while the **Cell Size Height & Width** sliders define the size of the image cells themselves. Photos may not fill the entire cell if the aspect ratio differs... we'll come back to this in a moment.

The **Keep Square** checkbox links the *Cell Size* sliders so they both move at the same time. Square cells are particularly useful if you have a mix of horizontal and vertical photos.

All of the sliders in the Layout panel interact, so as you adjust the cell spacing, the cell size automatically updates accordingly, and vice versa.

Why won't my photo print without adding white borders along two edges or cutting off some of the photo?

If the aspect ratio of the photo and the cell (or sheet of paper for a single print) differ, you have two choices: you can crop the photo to fit the cell or you can leave white borders.

Let's use an extreme example to illustrate these aspect ratios—a panoramic photo and a 8" x 10" borderless print.

If you forced the panoramic photo to fit within the cell, you'd have to squash it, which would look odd. You can't squash a photo in Lightroom to this extreme, so I've done it in Photoshop. **(Figure 18.17)**

By default, Lightroom fits the photo within the cell, printing it as 10" along the long edge, but that leaves white borders along the other 2 edges. **(Figure 18.18)**

If you go to the Image Settings panel and check **Zoom to Fill**, the photo is automatically cropped to fill the cell. **(Figure 18.19)** To reposition the photo within the cell in a Single Photo layout, click and drag. When using a Package layout, hold down the Ctrl key (Windows) / Cmd key (Mac) while dragging. To have more control over which areas are cropped, switch back to the Develop module Crop tool.

While you're in the Image Settings panel, there are a couple of additional checkboxes:

- **Rotate to Fit** automatically rotates the photo within the cell to make it as large as possible. This is particularly useful for contact sheets and can usually be left enabled.

- **Repeat One Photo per Page** is only available when using a Contact Sheet layout. It repeats the same photo in all cells of the contact sheet page, creating a new contact sheet page for each additional photo.

How do I lay out a Picture or Custom Package or collage?

Unlike the Single Print/Contact Sheet mode, the Picture and Custom Packages are laid out freeform on the page using individual cells. Remember, in the Picture Package, each page contains multiple versions of the same photo, whereas the Custom Package can include different photos. The cells can be a mix of different shapes and sizes, and they can even overlap to create simple composite photos.

Most of the layout controls are found in the Cells panel **(Figure 18.20 & 18.21)**, so let's summarize the main things you'll need to do:

- To **add a cell** to the page, press one of the numbered buttons in the Cells panel. A cell of the specified size is added to the page and Lightroom optimizes its placement on the page for the fewest cuts.

- To create a button for a **custom size cell**, click the arrow to the right of a numbered button, select *Edit* and then enter your size.

- To **reselect a cell**, click on it. A bounding box appears with resize handles on the corners and edges.

- To **resize the selected cell**, drag the *Height* and *Width* sliders in the Cells panel or drag the handles (squares) on the bounding box of the cell. Hold down Shift when dragging the handles to retain the existing aspect ratio, and hold down Alt (Windows) / Opt (Mac) while dragging the handles to resize from the center instead of the edge.

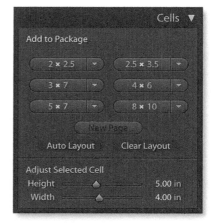

Figure 18.20 The Cells panel options for Picture Package.

- To **set the aspect ratio of the cell to match the photo** (Custom Package only), right-click on the photo and select *Match Aspect Ratio*. This is a one-time resize which only affects the selected cell, so any further resizing could alter the ratio again.

  The **Lock to Photo Aspect Ratio** checkbox forces all the cells on the page to match the aspect ratio of the photos they contain.

- To **move the selected cell**, click inside the bounding box and drag it to a new location.

Lightroom can snap to the grid or other cells to assist line up the cells. This is controlled using the **Grid Snap** pop-up in the Ruler, Grids & Guides panel:

- **Off** leaves the movements completely flexible.

- **Cells** snaps the cell to the edge of other cells on the page.

- **Grid** snaps the cell to the light blue grid.

In Picture Package layout, click the **Auto Layout** button in the

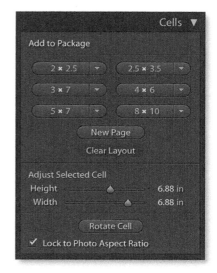

Figure 18.21 The Cells panel options for Custom Package.

Cells panel to automatically rearrange all of the cells into the easiest layout for cutting the prints.

- To **change the layer order** of overlapping cells, right-click on the cell and choose *Send to Back, Send Backwards, Send Forwards* or *Send to Front* (Custom Package only).

- To **duplicate the selected cell**, hold down Alt (Windows) / Opt (Mac) while dragging the cell.

- To **rotate the selected cell**, right-click and select *Rotate Cell*. To rotate a cell in Custom Package, you can also press the ***Rotate Cell*** button in the Cells panel.

- To **pin or anchor a cell** on a page, so that the cell and its contents appear on every page in exactly the same place, right-click and choose *Anchor Cell* (Custom Package only). It's particularly useful for adding a logo to each page.

- To **delete the selected cell**, press the Delete key on your keyboard, or right-click and select *Delete Cell*.

To remove all of the cells from the layout, press the ***Clear Layout*** button in the Cells panel.

You can also edit the photos themselves within the cells:

- To **replace a photo**, just drag another photo from the Filmstrip onto the existing cell.

- To **move a photo** within a cell (e.g. a panoramic ratio photo in a 4x6 cell), hold down the Ctrl (Windows) / Cmd (Mac) key while dragging the photo (Custom Package only). The movement is limited to the short edge of the cell, so if you need a specific crop, it's better do the cropping first in the Develop module.

- To **rotate a photo** is a little more tricky. You can't rotate a photo within a cell, but you can change the orientation of the cell itself. If *Rotate to Fit* is checked in the Image Settings panel, the photo automatically rotates within the cell.

Your layout isn't limited to a single page.

PRINT PAGE SHORTCUTS

Go to First Page	Ctrl Shift / Cmd Shift left arrow
Go to Previous Page	Ctrl / Cmd left arrow
Go to Next Page	Ctrl / Cmd right arrow
Go to Last Page	Ctrl Shift / Cmd Shift right arrow

- To **add a new** page, click the **New Page** button in the Cells panel.

- To **select a page**, just click on it.

- The pages display up to 6 in one go. If your design has multiple pages, click the **Zoom Page** button on the Navigator panel to **zoom into single page view**. (You can't zoom in any closer, so fine tuning arrangements isn't perfect.)

- To **scroll through** the sets of pages, or single pages in zoom view, click the arrow buttons on Toolbar. The square button returns to page 1.

- To **delete a page**, click the black X button in the upper-left corner of the page. At least one page must remain.

- If there's an **exclamation mark** in the top right corner of a Picture Package page, it means the photos are overlapping. It doesn't display on a Custom Package page, as overlapping is more frequently intentionally used to create a montage.

PRINT DESIGN & OVERLAYS

Having laid your photos out on the page, you may want to add additional details to the page, such as borders around the photos, filenames in the case of a contact sheet, or your logo or other personalization. These controls are found in the Page panel. **(Figure 18.22)**

How do I set the background color?

First, there's the background color. By default, there is no background color, so the paper color shows in areas not covered by the photo. Whether you're creating a contact sheet or composite photo, or you're printing a single print with a wide border, you can set the background color of the page. **(Figure 18.23)**

To change it, check the **Page Background Color** checkbox in the Page panel, then click the rectangle to the right to show the Color Picker and select a color. The Color Picker shows a range of neutral colors to avoid distracting from your photos, however it's possible to access other colors by clicking on the bar on the right side of the Color Picker. To select an accent color from the photo, click on the Color Picker and drag the eyedropper onto the photo, releasing the mouse on your chosen color.

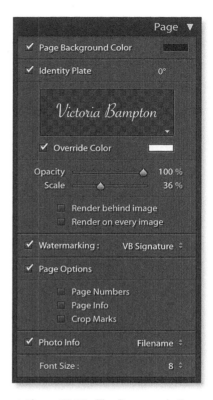

Figure 18.22 The Page panel allows you to customize the page design.

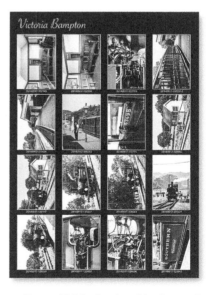

Figure 18.23 A colored background makes a contact sheet more striking.

▷**Figure 18.24** A wide border and Identity Plate caption enhances the photo.

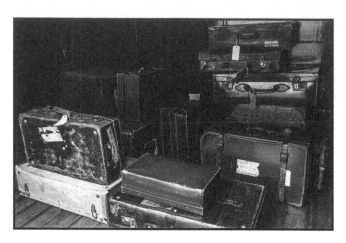

Isle of Wight Railway

How do I add a border?

Using the controls in the Image Settings panel, you can add a border directly around the photos to help to separate them from the background. **(Figure 18.24)**

For a single print or contact sheet, there's a single ***Stroke Border*** checkbox, which adds a stroke or keyline along the edge of the photo. Like the page background, the rectangle on the right opens the Color Picker. The ***Width*** slider controls the width of the stroke border.

The Picture Package and Custom Package offer an additional border option. The *Stroke Border* has been renamed ***Inner Border*** so it clings to the edge of the photo. The ***Photo Border*** adds extra padding to the cell, moving the photo and its border away from the cell boundary. **(Figure 18.25)**

Photo Border is only available when using the Picture Page or Custom Package layout. It adds an outer border of the specified width to the photo.

When you're setting the borders, go to the Guides panel or Ruler, Grid & Guides panel and uncheck the *Show Guides* checkbox. The guides aren't printed, and they can make the printable borders more difficult to see.

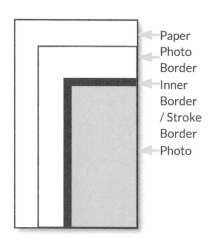

◄ Paper

◄ Photo Border

◄ Inner Border / Stroke Border

◄ Photo

▲**Figure 18.25** Borders are added around the photo.

How do I add my logo or Identity Plate to the page?

While you're personalizing your contact sheet or print, you can also add your logo using the Identity Plate, also found in the Page panel. You may need to change the page margins to leave space for your Identity Plate, using the sliders in the Layout panel.

To add your Identity Plate to the page, check the **Identity Plate** checkbox in the Page panel, and then click the preview field below to select your Identity Plate. You can return to this preview field to change the Identity Plate again later.

If you haven't created one yet, select *Edit* to show the Identity Plate dialog. We've already explored this dialog in detail in the Workspace chapter (page 77), but if you're not familiar with it, turn back to the instructions and then continue.

Once your Identity Plate is enabled, you can apply further customization. For example, if your Identity Plate uses white text and your page background is also white, check the **Override Color** checkbox and select another color using the Color Picker. If your Identity Plate is a brightly colored logo, it may be distracting at full opacity, so you can reduce the strength using the **Opacity** slider, fading it into the background.

You can also change the size and location of the Identity Plate. When you click on the Identity Plate, a bounding box appears with white squares (handles) in the corners and along the edges. **(Figure 18.26)** To change the size, you can either drag these white squares or adjust the **Scale** slider in the Page panel.

To move the Identity Plate, click on the center of it (avoiding the handles on the edge) and drag it around the page. This is easier to do once you've enlarged it. If you're working on a multi-page package, the Identity Plate only appears once, but you can choose which page to put it on.

Depending on the orientation of your print, you might also need to select an alternative rotation for the Identity Plate using the **0°** button to the right of the Identity Plate checkbox.

Your Identity Plate might overlap the photo, so checking the **Render behind image** checkbox tucks it behind the photo, avoiding distraction (but hiding part of the Identity Plate).

To show the Identity Plate on every photo, check the **Render on every image** checkbox. It's placed centrally on every photo, which means it's not much use as a signature, however you could use it as a proof watermark and then use the Watermarking tool to add your signature to each photo.

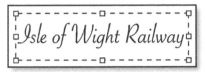

▲ **Figure 18.26** Drag the center of the bounding box to move it, or use the handles along the edges to resize it.

CUSTOM WATERMARK

If you're creating single prints and you need to apply a watermark in a different location on each photo, depending on the photo's content, it's quicker to manually position an Identity Plate in the Print module and then Print to JPEG than using the Watermark tool in the Export dialog. The downside is the resulting JPEG has no metadata embedded.

How do I add a watermark to my photos?

To add a watermark to each photo, check the **Watermarking** checkbox and select your watermark from the pop-up. Turn back to the Export chapter for more information on designing your watermarks (starting on page 362). Watermarks are particularly useful if you're printing proofs for a client or you're exporting a composite JPEG for your blog, as they appear on every photo.

How do I add text to my page?

If you're working in Single Image/Contact Sheet layout, you can add additional text to the page. (If you're using Picture Package/Custom Package, using the Identity Plate is your only option for adding text.)

To add text below each photo, select a template from the **Photo Info** pop-up. This pulls information from the photo's metadata, which you can view and edit using the Metadata panel in the Library module. Some Photo Info templates are built into Lightroom, for example, the filename or capture date. If the options you want aren't available by default, select *Edit* and create your own template using tokens like those used in the renaming dialog. The **Font Size** pop-up selects the font size for the photo info, but there's no further control over the styling, so you can't select a custom font or typeface.

How do I display page numbers or crop marks?

In the Page panel for Single Image/Contact Sheet layout, the **Page Numbers** checkbox prints a page number on the lower-right corner of each page, which is useful for organizing multi-page contact sheets. The **Page Info** checkbox prints the Print Sharpening setting, Profile setting, and the printer name at the bottom of each page. This is particularly useful when doing test prints, or if you may need to recreate a print again in future. The **Page Options** checkbox enables/disables all three checkboxes in one go.

The **Crop Marks** checkbox prints small crop marks around the corners of each photo to use as cutting guides after printing. (Figure 18.27) These come into their own when your photos have white edges, allowing you to see where the edge of the photo should

▶ **Figure 18.27** The *Crop Marks* show where to cut the prints, and the *Page Info* displays your print settings along the bottom of the print.

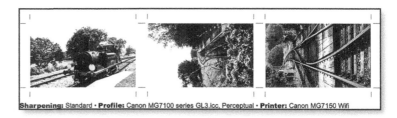

Sharpening: Standard • Profile: Canon MG7100 series GL3.icc, Perceptual • Printer: Canon MG7150 Wifi

be. There's a similar setting—**Cut Guides**—for Picture Packages and Custom Packages. This gives you a choice of *Crop Marks* or entire *Lines*.

PRINTING & EXPORTING

Once you've finished setting up your layout, it's finally time to print. We should say from the outset that printing is rarely an exact science. Lightroom's settings are only one part of the puzzle. There are other variables that can change and affect the finished print, including variations between batches of inks and paper and the viewing conditions for the finished print.

How do I print my layout?

Using the **Print To** pop-up at the top of the Print Job panel, select *Printer* to print to a locally attached printer (i.e. USB/Wifi). We'll come back to the *JPEG* option later in this section (page 429). The other checkboxes and sliders displayed in the Print Job panel are based on this choice, so we'll examine them each in turn.

What is Draft Mode Printing?

Draft Mode Printing uses Lightroom's ready-built previews for speed, however if the previews are missing or out of date, the printed result may be low quality. When *Draft Mode* is enabled, most of the other settings are disabled. It can be useful for quick contact sheets or checking the position of the photo on the page, but you'll need to disable it for finished prints.

How high should I set the resolution?

The **Print Resolution** checkbox determines the amount of data sent to the printer. If it's unchecked, Lightroom sends the original data and leaves the resampling to happen somewhere in the print pipeline. That could be anything from 72ppi-1440ppi. For a quick print, that may be fine, but if you're doing a high quality print and want to get the best results, a little more attention to detail is worthwhile. Lightroom can do a better job of resampling your image data than the unknown print pipeline.

First, check the printer's dpi. Epson use 360 dpi (or 720 dpi with *Finest Detail* selected in the printer driver), and Canon & HP use 300 dpi (or 600 dpi with *Highest Quality* selected in the printer driver).

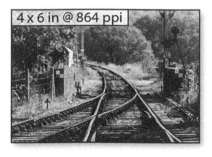

▲ **Figure 18.28** Unchecking *Print Resolution* checkbox displays the native resolution.

JEFF SCHEWE

Credit goes to Jeff Schewe for extensive testing of print resolution in Lightroom. For a deeper dive into the science behind photo printing technology, see Jeff's book *The Digital Print* http://www.Lrq.me/schewe-digitalprint

Other printers may vary. The specifications on the manufacturer's website usually include this information.

Next, check the native resolution of your image at the selected print size. To do so, go to the Guides panel and check *Dimensions*, and also uncheck the *Print Resolution* checkbox in the Print Job panel. The native resolution displays in a small overlay on each photo, for example, 4" x 6" @ 864ppi. **(Figure 18.28)**

If the native resolution of the image is **under** 360 ppi for Epson, or 300 ppi for Canon/HP, type 360 (Epson) or 300 (Canon/HP) in the *Print Resolution* field.

If the native resolution of the photo is **over** 360 ppi for Epson, or over 300 ppi for Canon/HP, type 720 (Epson) or 600 (Canon/HP) in the *Print Resolution* field (and select *Finest Detail/Highest Quality* in the printer driver, when we come to that dialog).

When should I turn on 16-bit printing?

The **16 Bit Output** checkbox in the Print Job panel sends 16-bit data to the printer driver, which can help prevent banding in gentle gradients. It requires 16-bit printer drivers provided by your printer manufacturer, which are currently limited to high end printers on Mac OS X. If you send 16-bit data to a printer that doesn't support it, printing is slower than normal.

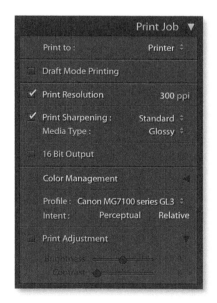

Figure 18.29 If Lightroom is set to manage the colors, set the printer driver to *No Color Adjustment*.

Which Print Sharpening option do I choose?

Print Sharpening applies output sharpening to your print or JPEG file. Like the Export output sharpening, you can choose *Low*, *Standard* or *High* and set the paper type—*Matte* or *Glossy*—using the **Media Type** pop-up. Lightroom calculates the sharpening automatically based on the size of the original file, the output size and resolution, and the type of paper.

How do I set up my printer to match the preview I see on screen?

Finally, it's time to set the color management options. You can either allow Lightroom to manage the color, which is usually the best option, or you can give the printer driver control. It's important to pick one option or the other. If you allow both Lightroom and the printer to manage the color, the result will be unexpected at best, often creating dark magenta (pink) prints. **(Figure 18.29)**

INSTALL CUSTOM PROFILE

If your paper manufacturer or digital lab provides custom printer profiles, you'll need to install them on your computer so that Lightroom can access them, and then restart Lightroom.

Windows

Right-click on the profile in Explorer and select Install Profile from the context-sensitive menu. If this doesn't work, you can install them manually by placing the profile in C:\Windows\system32\spool\drivers\color, which may be a hidden folder.

Mac

Place the profile in Macintosh HD/Users/[your username]/Library/ColorSync/Profiles, or the global ColorSync folder if multiple users need access to it. The user folder is a hidden folder by default.

Once the profiles are installed and you've restarted Lightroom, you can select the *Profile* pop-up menu and choose *Other* to view a list of all available profiles. Putting a checkmark next to a profile adds it to the main *Profile* pop-up menu, allowing you to select it as your output profile.

To remove an ICC profile, simply retrace your steps and uncheck the profile.

Option 1—Lightroom manages color

1. In the Color Management **Profile** pop-up, select the correct ICC profile for your printer/ink/paper combination. If your printer profile doesn't appear in the pop-up, select *Other* and check it

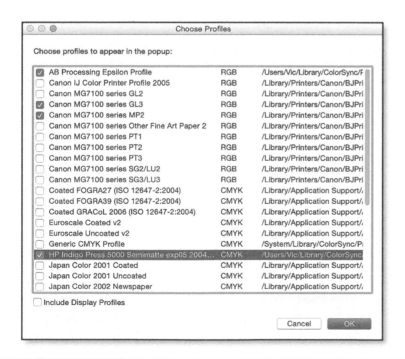

◀ **Figure 18.30** When you select *Other* from the *Profile* pop-up, Lightroom displays a list of available output profiles.

Figure 18.31 With the color profile set in Lightroom, the printer driver may automatically prevent you from applying double color management.

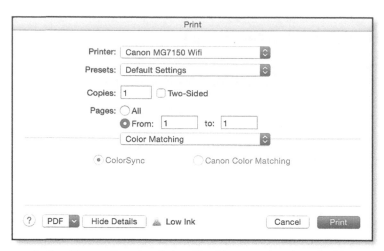

in the Choose Profiles dialog. (Profiles are often installed by the manufacturer's printer driver but may also be downloaded from the paper/ink manufacturer's websites. See the Install Custom Profiles sidebar for more information.) **(Figure 18.30)**

2. If you used soft proofing to preview and adjust the photo for this profile, using the **Intent** options to select your preferred rendering intent. If haven't used soft proofing to preview the photo, select *Relative* to use Relative Colorimetric rendering. (Turn back to page 314 for more information on soft proofing.)

3. Click **Print Settings** button to display the printer driver dialog. On OS X, you may need to press the *Show Details* button to access the controls. **(Figure 18.31)**

4. Select the correct paper type and quality settings, and set the Color Management section to *No Color Adjustment*, *ColorSync* or another similar option. The aim is to prevent the printer driver adjusting the photo.

5. While you have the printer driver open, you may also select the print quality and media type.

6. Press *Save* to save the printer driver settings.

7. When you're ready to print, press the *Print* or *Printer* button to send the image to the printer.

Option 2—Printer manages color

1. If you'd prefer the printer to manage the colors, perhaps because you don't have an ICC profile for your printer/ink/paper combination, select *Managed by Printer* from the *Profile* pop-up menu. **(Figure 18.32)**

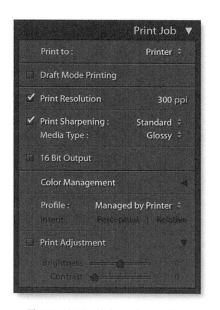

Figure 18.32 If the printer driver is set to manage the colors, set Lightroom to *Managed by Printer*.

2. Click **Print Settings** button to display the printer driver dialog. On

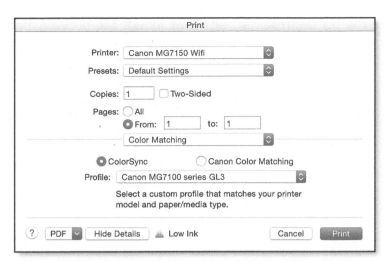

Figure 18.33 Printer settings when Lightroom is set to let the printer control the color management.

PRINTER DRIVERS

Each printer offers different options, depending on the operating system and the driver installed, so your printer dialogs might not look exactly the same as these screenshots. The basic principles apply to all printers, but you may need to adapt them to your specific printer. If your printer driver has very limited options available, check the manufacturer's website for an updated driver.

OS X, you may need to press the *Show Details* button to access the controls. **(Figure 18.33)**

3. Select the correct paper type and quality settings and select the correct profile in the Color Management section if it offers that choice.

4. When you're ready to print, press the *Print* or *Printer* button to send the image to the printer.

Why do Page Setup, Print Settings and Printer buttons show the same dialog?

Some driver/operating system combinations show the same dialog when you press the *Page Setup*, *Print Settings*, and/or *Printer* buttons, while other combinations show different dialogs. **(Figure 18.34)** This means that none of the buttons can be removed, even though they may not be needed for your setup.

Where different dialogs are shown for the different buttons, the **Page Setup** dialog generally sets the paper size, orientation and maximum printable area, whereas **Print Settings** sets up paper type, quality, color management and other printer-specific settings. This means you can set up and save your settings as part of a template without actually printing. The **Print** button sends the print directly to the printer, bypassing the printer dialog, whereas the **Printer** button displays the printer dialog before printing.

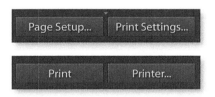

Figure 18.34 The *Page Setup*, *Print Settings* and *Printer* buttons may show different dialogs, depending on your printer driver and operating system.

Why do Lightroom's prints not match the preview on screen?

We said earlier that printing isn't an exact science, as there are so many variables. The same settings that print correctly in one program, can react differently in another program, simply as a result of using a newer print path which links the software to the operating system. There are a few things to double check if you're having problems getting your prints to look like the photo on screen.

- **Monitor Calibration**—Calibrate your monitor using a hardware calibration device, otherwise you have no way of telling whether you're seeing an accurate preview on screen. Most monitors are too bright straight out of the box. They're set up to be bright and punchy, which is great for movies, but that doesn't match printed output. Ideally you want to calibrate your monitor using a hardware calibration device and adjust the luminance to about 110-120 cd/m2, depending on your viewing conditions. (You may need it a little brighter in a bright room, or darker in a dark room.) This may be under the Advanced section of your calibration software. If your software doesn't offer this option, try reducing the brightness to approximately match a print before running the calibration software.

- **Printer Profiles**—Use the correct ICC profile for your printer/ink/paper combination, because printer profiles aren't one-size-fits-all. If you're not using the manufacturer's own ink and paper, or other properly profiled combinations, there will be some trial and error to create prints vaguely matching your screen.

- **Printer Drivers**—Make sure you have the latest printer drivers direct from the manufacturer. If it worked previously, try rolling back to an earlier driver.

- **Double Color Management**—Check your print settings in Lightroom. You either want Lightroom to manage the colors, or your printer to do so, but not both.

If you're still having trouble getting your prints to match, there's a "quick and dirty" method for print matching. If your inkjet prints are always a little light, a bit dark, or a bit flat compared to your screen, even though your screen is properly calibrated, you can use the **_Print Adjustment_** sliders to compensate. They're not intended to be a replacement for proper color management, but as we've seen, even with the best color management in the world, printing isn't always 100% accurate.

To set the best values for the **_Brightness_** and **_Contrast_** sliders, do a test print, tweak these sliders, do another test print, tweak again, and repeat until you get a good visual match between the print and the screen. The adjustments aren't previewed on screen because it's compensating for something that only happens when printing, just like the output sharpening. Once you've found the right values for your printer, you shouldn't need to change them again.

How do I create a JPEG of my print layout?

If you don't own a large photo printer, or you want to remove a few of the variables and let a photographic lab handle the printing for you, you can save your layout as a JPEG format. (Remember, if you're just sending individual prints, rather than contact sheets or composite layouts, it's quicker to use the standard Export dialog instead.)

To print to JPEG, select *JPEG* in the *Print To* pop-up at the top of the Print panel. **(Figure 18.35)** The export options should be familiar, as they're also used in the Export dialog. (Turn back to the Export chapter, page 347, for more detail on each of the options.)

File Resolution controls the resolution of the JPEG, combined with either the paper size set in Page Setup or the custom file dimensions specified below. Most labs request 240ppi to 300ppi.

The **Custom File Dimensions** allows you to override the paper size for the print preview as well as the exported file. If it's unchecked, Lightroom uses the paper size set in the Page Setup dialog. If you remember, we set the paper size earlier in the Print Layout section (page 412), before we started laying out your print.

The **JPEG Quality** slider sets the amount of compression applied to the file. 75-90 is ideal for most prints, and lower values can be used if the composite will be displayed on the web rather than printed.

Finally, select your lab's requested color space using the **Profile** pop-up. Some pro labs request Adobe RGB or their own custom ICC profile, but most labs require sRGB files. The rendering intent depends on your preference and only applies to custom ICC profiles, not sRGB/Adobe RGB/Pro Photo RGB. Turn back to Soft Proofing (page 314) to learn more about rendering intents.

To save the file, press the **Print to File** button, navigate to a location for the finished files and enter a filename. If you're just printing a single page, Lightroom uses your chosen filename and location. If you're printing multiple pages, Lightroom creates a folder using that name, and adds a sequence number on the end of your chosen filename. For example, if you give it the name *Test*, it creates a *Test* folder and create files called *Test-1.jpg*, *Test-2.jpg*, etc. Lightroom doesn't automatically use the name of the photo that you're printing, as you may be printing more than one photo per page.

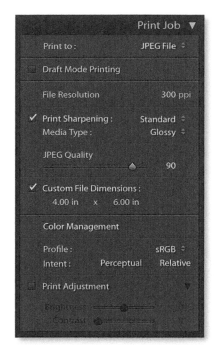

Figure 18.35 To create a JPEG rather than printing to an inkjet printer, select *JPEG File* at the top of the Print Job panel.

PRINT TO PDF

Lightroom doesn't offer a Print to PDF option in the Print module. Mac users can select *Save as PDF* from the PDF pop-up in the bottom left corner of the main print dialog. Windows users must use a PDF printer driver, such as Bullzip Free PDF Printer. http://www.Lrq.me/bullzip

SAVING PRINTS & TEMPLATES

Having designed a complex custom print, the last thing you want to do is lose your hard work, so it's important to know how to save it. Lightroom allows you to save in two different ways: as a print containing the photos, or only the settings as a template to apply to other photos.

How do I save my design to edit or print later?

To save your print, press the **Create Saved Print** button at the top of the Preview Area, or press the + button on the Collections panel and select *Create Print*. **(Figure 18.36 & 18.37)**

Lightroom asks for a name for your print, and you have a choice of where to file it in the Collections panel. It can be stored within a Collection Set, within a standard collection or as flat list of Collections. If you can't remember the difference, turn back to the Collections section in the Library chapter (page 115) for a refresher.

If the *Use* pop-up in the Toolbar is currently set to *Flagged photos* or *Selected photos*, there's an additional checkbox marked *Include only used photos*. As the name suggests, only the photos currently included in the design are included in the saved print if it's checked.

The final checkbox allows you to create new virtual copies of the included photos. This can be helpful if you might accidentally edit one of the photos that you've previously included in this print.

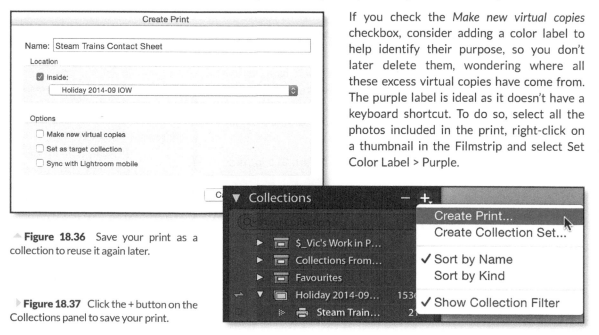

If you check the *Make new virtual copies* checkbox, consider adding a color label to help identify their purpose, so you don't later delete them, wondering where all these excess virtual copies have come from. The purple label is ideal as it doesn't have a keyboard shortcut. To do so, select all the photos included in the print, right-click on a thumbnail in the Filmstrip and select Set Color Label > Purple.

Figure 18.36 Save your print as a collection to reuse it again later.

Figure 18.37 Click the + button on the Collections panel to save your print.

How do I edit or delete my saved print?

Later, having saved your print in the Collections panel, you can easily open it again to edit or reprint. You'll note that your print collection has its own icon in the Collections panel, identifying it as a print. If you're already in the Print module, a single-click on the print in the Collections panel opens it. If you're viewing another module, you need to double-click on it.

As you make changes to your saved print, the changes are saved automatically. If you want to try some different settings without overwriting your saved print, right-click on it in the Collections panel and select *Duplicate Print*. You can also hold down the Alt (Windows) / Opt (Mac) key while dragging the print to another Collection Set or between two top-level collections in the Collections panel.

To include additional photos in a saved print (e.g. in a contact sheet), simply switch back to Grid view and drag the extra photo thumbnails from the grid onto the print in the Collections panel.

If you later change your mind and want to delete the saved print, right-click and select *Delete* or select the print and press the—button at the top of the Collections panel.

How do I save my print layout to reuse on another set of photos?

Once you've set up the layout, you can save it as a template to apply to other photos. This is not only useful for packages, but also for single print sizes that you use regularly. Unlike prints saved in the Collections panel, templates only save the settings without the photos, ready to apply to other photos. The printer settings from the Page Setup and Print Settings dialogs are also included in the template.

To save your settings as a template, click the + button on the Template Browser panel. Give your new template a descriptive name and select a folder to store it in. By default, it saves it in the User Templates folder, but if you have a lot of templates, you can organize them into folders. **(Figure 18.38)**

To create a new folder, open the pop-up menu in the New Template dialog, and select *New Folder* or right-click on any existing template and select *New Folder*, then enter the folder name. You can drag and drop the templates into different folders later, if you don't want to organize them at this stage.

If you later tweak the settings, you can update the template by right-clicking on the template and choosing *Update with Current Settings*.

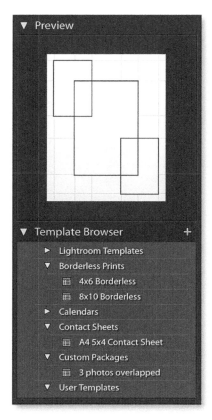

Figure 18.38 You can also save your settings as a template for use with other photos. As you float over the template, the layout displays in the Preview panel above.

You can also rename and delete any templates that you create, using the *Rename* and *Delete* options in the right-click menu. The built-in templates can't be updated, renamed or deleted.

As you float the cursor over the templates in the Templates panel, the Preview panel above displays a preview of each template, enabling you to quickly identify the template you want to use. To apply a different template to your print, click on it.

Finally, you may want to share your template with other Lightroom users or transfer it to a different computer. To do so, right-click on the template and select *Export*, then select a folder on your hard drive. The template files have a *.lrtemplate extension. Alternatively, you can right-click on a user template and select *Show in Explorer* (Windows) / *Show in Finder* (Mac). This takes you directly to the current template location, ready to copy to another computer. Showing the whole folder is particularly useful when copying a larger number of templates, as you can copy/paste them in one go.

To install the templates on another machine, right-click on an existing template and select *Import*, then navigate to the print template on your hard drive. Alternatively, right-click on a user template and select *Show in Explorer* (Windows) / *Show in Finder* (Mac). Place the templates in that folder and restart Lightroom.

PRINT SHORTCUTS

New Template	Ctrl N / Cmd N
New Template Folder	Ctrl Shift N / Cmd Shift N
Show Header Bar	\
Create Saved Print	Ctrl S / Cmd S
Page Setup	Ctrl Shift P / Cmd Shift P
Print Settings	Ctrl Alt Shift P / Cmd Opt Shift P
Print	Ctrl P / Cmd P
Print One	Ctrl Alt P / Cmd Opt P

WEB MODULE

Some Lightroom books skim quickly over the Web module **(Figure 19.1)**, and others skip it altogether, considering static galleries obsolete in this fast-moving day and age. So does it still have a place in a photographer's toolkit? Yes, but before we start diving into how to use the Web module, let's consider your options for displaying your photos on the web.

Lightroom offers multiple ways of publishing your photos online, and it can be difficult to figure out which is best suited to your needs. There are, of course, a huge number of alternative photo sharing websites, so we're just going to compare the most popular options in each category. **(Figure 19.2)**

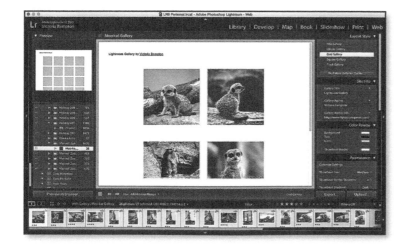

Figure 19.1 The Web module.

▼ **Figure 19.2**   There are numerous ways of publishing your photos on the web. These are a few of the pros and cons.

	Facebook	Flickr	SmugMug/Zenfolio
Type of Gallery	Social media website	Dynamic—updates when you Publish	Dynamic—updates when you Publish
Lightroom Integration	Publish Services (upload only)	Publish Services	Publish Services
One-off cost of plug-ins plus web hosting	Free	Free (ad-supported) or Paid (ad-free)	Monthly fee
Stored On	Facebook's Servers	Flickr's Servers	SmugMug/Zenfolio's Servers
Include video	Yes	Yes	Yes
Customization	None	None	Control page styles from the website
Viewer Comments	Yes	Yes	Yes
Security	Limited security controls	Limited security controls	Password protect galleries
eCommerce Features	n/a	n/a	Sell or print your photos directly from the website
Mobile offline use (e.g. portfolio app)	No	Yes (third party mobile apps)	Yes (own mobile app)
Own domain name	No	No (except redirection)	Some levels
Use as entire website with home page	No	No	Yes
Minimum web design experience needed	None	None	None
Intended volume	Low volume	Medium-high volume	Medium-high volume
Website	http://www.facebook.com	http://www.flickr.com	http://www.smugmug.com or http://www.zenfolio.com

	LR Mobile	Web Module	The Turning Gate
Type of Gallery	Dynamic—updates when you sync	Static galleries (not easily updated)	Can be updated using Publish Services plug-in
Lightroom Integration	Mobile Sync	Web module (initial design only)	Web module (initial design) & Publish Services (updates)
One-off cost of plug-ins plus web hosting	Varies by membership level	Incl. in CC Photographer's Bundle at $9.99 a month	Cost of web hosting
Stored On	Adobe's Servers	Your own web space—you're in control	Your own web space—you're in control
Include video	No	No	With some components
Customization	None	Design in Web module	Design in Web module
Viewer Comments	Yes	No	With some components
Security	Secret gallery links	None	Password protect galleries
eCommerce Features	n/a	n/a	Sell your photos from your website
Mobile offline use (e.g. portfolio app)	Yes (own mobile app) including editing	No	No
Own domain name	No (except redirection)	Yes	Yes
Use as entire website with home page	No	Not built in, but some third-party galleries	Yes
Minimum web design experience needed	None	Basic understanding of web hosting	Some web design experience helps
Intended volume	Regular use	Small galleries that don't need updating	As many as you like
Website	http://lightroom.adobe.com	n/a	http://theturninggate.net

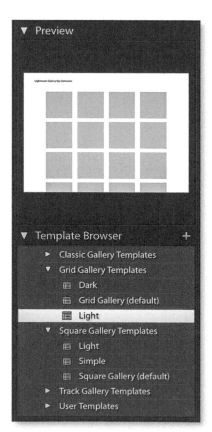

▲ **Figure 19.3** Float the cursor over templates in the Template Browser to preview them in the Preview panel above.

The Web module has it's place. It makes it easy to create static galleries, and if you do need to be able to easily update your galleries, third-party designs (such as those by The Turning Gate) offer additional flexibility. The photos are hosted on your server, so they remain in your control (without having to figure out complicated T&C's!).

WEB GALLERY BASICS

Before we dive into the details, let's just run through the basics and create your first web gallery.

1. In Library module's Grid view, decide which photos you want to include in your web gallery. This might be a folder or a collection of photos. If the photos are spread across multiple folders or collections, use the Quick Collection to group them together.

2. Switch to the Web module by selecting it in the Module Picker.

3. At the top of the Preview Area, press the *Create Saved Web Gallery* button and give your gallery a name. Saving the web gallery at the beginning means you won't accidentally lose your work. The saved web gallery appears in the Collections panel, and it remembers the photos you're using as well as the gallery settings.

4. In the Template Browser panel on the left, click on the different templates to select a design (or float over them to preview in the Preview panel above). For this example, we'll select *Grid Gallery Templates > Light*. **(Figure 19.3)**

5. (Optional) You can adjust the colors and design of the gallery, as well as the text overlays, using the panels on the right. We'll come back to these settings in the following pages.

   If you customize any of the settings, click + button on Template Browser to save your design as a new template. This allows you to apply the same settings to other groups of photos.

6. Once you're happy with the preview in the Web module, click *Preview in Browser* at the bottom of the left panel group to open it in your default web browser.

7. Finally, to export your web gallery, click the *Export* button at the bottom of the right panel group. This saves the web gallery on your hard drive, ready to upload to your website using FTP software (such as FileZilla).

   It's also possible to upload the gallery directly from Lightroom by entering the FTP server details in the Upload Settings panel, however the built-in FTP is not as robust as dedicated FTP software.

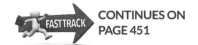

CONTINUES ON PAGE 451

WEB GALLERY LAYOUT & DESIGN

Having learned the basics of the Web module, you can start customizing the design to suit your own taste using the panels on the right.

How do I select the layout?

One of the first choices to make when building a web gallery is the basic layout, which is selected using the Layout Style panel. **(Figure 19.4)**

Lightroom ships with four different web gallery styles: **(Figure 19.5)**

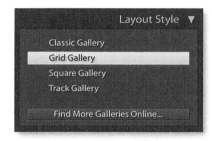

Figure 19.4 Select your chosen layout in the Layout Style panel. If you download third-galleries, they're also added to this list.

- **Classic Gallery** is the traditional HTML gallery from earlier Lightroom versions. (As it's a legacy gallery, and it's not responsive for mobile devices, we're not going to explore its settings in too much detail.)

- **Grid Gallery** is a responsive HTML gallery, displaying a mix of vertical and horizontal photos without cropping.

- **Square Gallery** is a responsive HTML gallery, displaying all of the thumbnails cropped square (although the full size version is uncropped).

- **Track Gallery** is a responsive HTML gallery, displaying all of the photos at the same height regardless of whether they're vertical or horizontal.

You'll note that the gallery names are familiar from the built-in templates in the Template Browser panel, because the templates store the Layout Style as well as color and text settings.

You can also download additional third-party web galleries and, once installed, they appear as additional options in the Layout Style panel.

Some third-party galleries are available from the Adobe Add Ons website, which is accessed via the **Find More Galleries Online** button. Many of the better-known developers have chosen not to use the Adobe Add Ons site, but they're listed in the Third Party Galleries section later in this chapter, starting on page 447.

FLASH IS DEAD

Flash galleries are no longer supported by Lightroom CC/6. They've been replaced by responsive HTML5 galleries which work well on desktop computers and mobile devices.

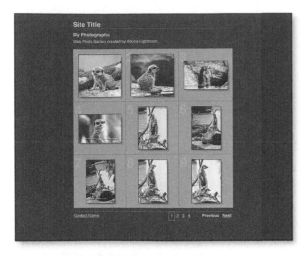

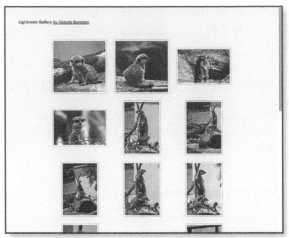

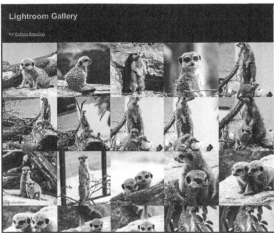

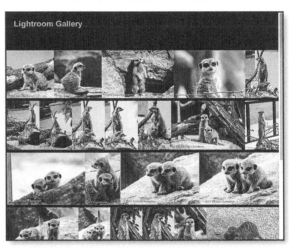

Figure 19.5 There are four default layouts: *Classic* (top left), *Grid* (top right), *Square* (bottom left) and *Track* (bottom right).

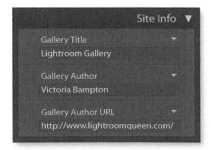

Figure 19.6 With Site Info include your name and URL.

How do I personalize my gallery?

The subsequent panels on the right allow you to customize your gallery. The panel options vary slightly depending on the selected gallery layout, so we'll continuing primarily using the Grid Gallery layout for now.

First, the Site Info panel holds information specific to that gallery. **(Figure 19.6)** This includes the **Gallery Title**, which appears in the top left corner of the galleries. The **Gallery Author**—that's your name—comes next, followed by the **Gallery Author URL**, which turns your name into a hyperlink to your website or about page. When entering the URL, include the http:// before your web address or start with mailto: before your email address to ensure that the links work correctly. The arrow to the right of each field displays a pop-up menu of your recent entries.

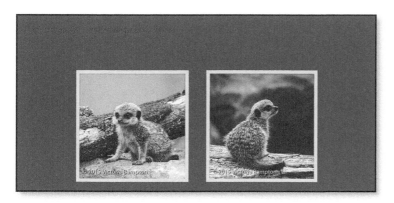

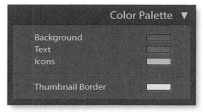

Figure 19.7 The Color Palette panel is used to customize the page colors.

Figure 19.8 Temporarily using bright colors makes it easy to see which settings affect which sections.

How do I change the gallery colors?

The color options are found in the Color Palette panel. **(Figure 19.7)** The ***Background*** obviously applies to the page background. The ***Text*** applies to the text, such as the Gallery title and the Title/Caption on the main photo. The ***Icons*** applies to the buttons on the page and ***Thumbnail Border*** applies to the border around the thumbnails, of course!

Click on the rectangle to the right of each label to display the Color Picker. By default, it shows a range of neutral colors to avoid distracting from your photos. It's possible to access other colors by clicking on the bar on the right side of the Color Picker. As you click in the Color Picker to select different colors, the gallery preview updates.

Different galleries may use other options. To quickly identify which areas of the web page each control affects, temporarily assign them bright colors. This makes them very easy to spot. **(Figure 19.8)**

How do I change the thumbnail page layout?

You can fine tune the layout of the thumbnail page using the Appearance panel. **(Figure 19.9)** Again, the options vary for each gallery, but the same principles apply.

The thumbnail settings ***Thumbnail Size***, ***Thumbnail Border Thickness*** and ***Thumbnail Shadows*** affect the style of the thumbnails on the main page. The Track Gallery uses a ***Row Height*** and ***Row Spacing*** setting to control the thumbnail size.

Pagination Style keeps all of the thumbnails on a single page or splits them across multiple pages. Single page is less frustrating for viewers, but the page can take longer to load if you have hundreds of photos in a gallery. If you select multiple pages, the ***Items per page***

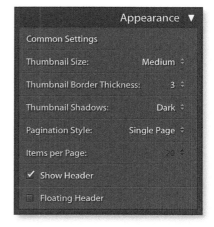

Figure 19.9 The Appearance Panel adjusts the design of the thumbnails..

pop-up becomes available, allowing you to decide whether to show 5, 10, 15, 20, 25 or 30 thumbnails per page.

The Square Gallery and Track Gallery swaps these settings for a **Thumbnail Loading** pop-up, which displays all of the photos on the same page but can load them all at once or gradually as you scroll down the page.

Show Header displays the header at the top of the page. If you've left the Site Info panel blank, or you're embedding the gallery in another page using an iFrame, you might want to uncheck this. **Floating Header** means that the header remains visible at the top of the page even when you scroll down.

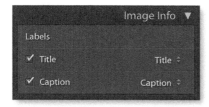

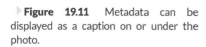

▲ **Figure 19.10** The Image Info panel sets the metadata displayed in the large photo view.

How do I choose which metadata to display on the main image page?

When your viewer clicks on a thumbnail, they're presented with a larger view of the selected photo. The arrows on the left and right or below the photo move to the next and previous photos, and the X in the corner returns to the thumbnail view.

There are two text fields you can fill with metadata from the photo using the Image Info panel. **(Figure 19.10)** The **Title** field appears on the photo itself, so you have to pick a text color (in the Color Palette field) that will show on both light and dark photos. The **Caption** field displays below the photo, so it's easier to read.

Although they're called *Title* and *Caption*, they can be filled with your choice of metadata. This might be the file name, the EXIF Metadata or even your keywords. The metadata for each photo is drawn from the Metadata panel in the Library module. **(Figure 19.11)**

▷ **Figure 19.11** Metadata can be displayed as a caption on or under the photo.

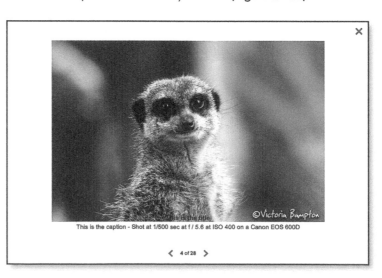

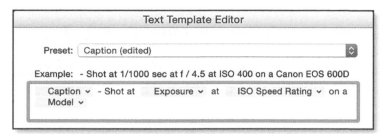

If you select Edit from the pop-up menu, you can create your own caption using multiple metadata tokens. (Figure 19.12)

Figure 19.12 Build your caption using metadata tokens, for example, *"Caption—Shot at Exposure at ISO Rating on a Model"*

How do I select the quality of the main photos?

The Output Settings panel controls the settings for the main photos. **(Figure 19.13)**

The JPEG **Quality** setting is a balance between file size (and therefore page load speed) and visible artifacts. Values in the range of 62-69 are generally ideal for web use. 70-76 can be used if you can see visible banding or artifacts, but 77 onwards makes the file sizes balloon without a visible increase in quality.

The **Metadata** pop-up gives a choice of *Copyright Only* or *All* metadata, and how much metadata to include is personal choice.

If you're putting the photos online, you may want to add your watermark using the **Watermarking** checkbox and pop-up. We discussed designing watermarks in the Export chapter, starting on page 362. If you're using the Square gallery, you may want to center your watermark on the photo, as it may be partially or entirely clipped by the square thumbnails.

The final setting is **Sharpening**, with a choice of *Low*, *Standard* or *High*,

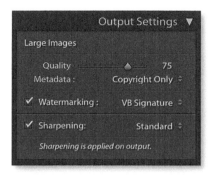

Figure 19.13 The Output Settings panel sets the quality of the larger images.

SPEED TIP

On the Toolbar (press T), you'll find the **Use** pop-up, which controls which photos are included in your web gallery. You can choose from *All Filmstrip Photos*, *Selected Photos* or *Flagged Photos*.

If you're designing a large gallery, select a few photos in the Filmstrip and set the *Use* pop-up to *Selected Photos*. Adjusting settings in the Web module is much faster when it only has to build a few photos, and you can switch back to *All Filmstrip Photos* just before you export the finished gallery.

like those found in Export. The output sharpening is only applied to the exported/uploaded gallery, and isn't visible in the preview.

SAVING WEB GALLERIES & TEMPLATES

Having designed your ideal web gallery, the last thing you want to do is lose your hard work, so it's important to know how to save it. Lightroom allows you to save in two different ways: as a web gallery containing the photos, or only the settings as a template to apply to other photos.

If you followed the Fast Track instructions at the beginning of the chapter (page 433), your web gallery settings are already saved in the catalog, and the name of the web gallery is displayed at the top of the Preview Area and in the Collections panel. If you continue working in Lightroom and later come back to edit the design, you can simply double-click on the saved web gallery to get back to your current state.

How do I save my settings as a web gallery?

If you haven't saved your web gallery yet, press the **Create Saved Web Gallery** button at the top of the Preview Area, or press the + button on the Collections panel and select *Create Web Gallery*.

Lightroom asks for a name for your new gallery. You also have a choice of where to file it in the Collections panel. It can be stored within a Collection Set, within a standard collection or as a flat list of Collections. If you can't remember the difference, turn back to the Collections section in the Library chapter (page 115) for a refresher. **(Figure 19.14)**

Figure 19.14 Web Galleries can be identified in the Collections panel by the Web icon.

If the *Use* pop-up is currently set to *Flagged photos* or *Selected photos* in the pop-up on the Toolbar, there's an additional checkbox marked *Include only used photos*. As the name suggests, only the photos currently included in the web gallery are included in the saved gallery if it's checked.

The final checkbox allows you to create new virtual copies of the included photos. This can be helpful if you might accidentally edit one of the photos that you've previously included in this gallery. If you check the *Make new virtual copies* checkbox, consider adding a color label to help identify their purpose, so you don't later delete them, wondering where all these excess virtual copies have come from. The purple label is ideal as it doesn't have a keyboard shortcut. To do so, select all the photos included in the gallery, right-click on a thumbnail in the Filmstrip and select Set Color Label > Purple.

How do I edit or delete my saved web gallery?

Later, having saved your web gallery in the Collections panel, you can easily open it again to edit and export to again. You'll note that your collection has its own icon in the Collections panel, identifying it as a web gallery. If you're already in the Web module, a single-click on the gallery in the Collections panel opens it. If you're viewing another module, you need to double-click on it.

As you make changes to your reopened gallery, the changes are saved automatically. If you want to try some different settings without overwriting your saved web gallery, right-click on it in the Collections panel and select *Duplicate Web Gallery*. You can also hold down the Alt (Windows) / Opt (Mac) key while dragging the gallery to another set in the Collections panel.

If you later change your mind and want to delete the gallery, right-click and select *Delete* or select the gallery and press the—button at the top of the Collections panel.

How do I add extra photos to my web gallery?

To include additional photos in a saved gallery, simply switch back to Grid view and drag the extra photo thumbnails from the grid onto the collection in the Collections panel.

While you're in Grid view, you can also change the sort order of the photos to adjust the web gallery sequence.

How do I save my web gallery settings to reuse on another set of photos?

If you've created a web gallery design that you love, you may want to save it to reuse on other photos, particularly if they'll all be linked on the same website. Unlike web galleries saved in the Collections panel, templates only save the settings without the photos, ready to apply to other collections of photos.

To save your settings as a template, click the + button on the Template Browser panel and give your new template a descriptive name. By default, it's saved in the User Templates folder, but if you have a lot of templates, you can organize them into folders using the *Location: Inside* pop-up in the New Template dialog.

To create a new folder, open the pop-up menu, and select *New Folder* or right-click on any existing template and select *New Folder*, then enter the folder name. You can drag and drop the templates into different folders later, if you don't want to organize them at this stage.

FTP SETTINGS, TEMPLATES & GALLERIES

FTP Upload Settings are saved with web galleries (because you'll likely want to upload them to the same location). They're not stored with templates, as they're applied to new sets of photos, and you'll need to change the upload location for each new gallery.

If you later tweak the gallery, you can update the template by right-clicking on it and choosing *Update with Current Settings*. You can also rename and delete any templates that you create, using the *Rename* and *Delete* options in the right-click menu. The built-in templates can't be updated, renamed or deleted.

As you float the cursor over the templates in the Templates panel, the Preview panel above displays a preview of each template, enabling you to quickly identify the template you want to use. To apply a different template to your photos, click on it.

Finally, if you've created the perfect web gallery template, you may want to share it with other Lightroom users or transfer it to a different computer. To do so, right-click on the template and select *Export*, then select a folder on your hard drive. The template files have a *.lrtemplate extension. Alternatively, you can right-click on a user template and select *Show in Explorer* (Windows) / *Show in Finder* (Mac). That takes you directly to the current template location, ready to copy to another computer. Showing the whole folder is particularly useful when copying a larger number of templates.

To install the templates on another machine, right-click on an existing user template and select *Import*, then navigate to the web gallery template on your hard drive. Alternatively, right-click on a user template and select *Show in Explorer* (Windows) / *Show in Finder* (Mac). Place the templates in that folder and restart Lightroom.

EXPORT FOR WEB

Once you've finished creating your web gallery, it's time to upload it to your website. You can either let Lightroom upload the files using its built-in FTP client or export the gallery to your hard drive and use your own dedicated FTP software.

Should I let Lightroom upload the gallery or use dedicated FTP software?

The built-in FTP upload facility is convenient, but it has some limitations:

- It doesn't show the existing folder contents on the server, so you could easily overwrite existing files.

- If the connection drops, which is not unusual, Lightroom has to start all over again, whereas dedicated FTP software can resume from where it left off.

- Lightroom's error reporting is limited, so if you suffer connection errors, it can be hard to figure out what's wrong.

For larger galleries, it's better to use dedicated FTP software, but we'll learn how to set up the built-in FTP for the occasions when you need convenience.

How do I set up Lightroom's built-in FTP client?

Lightroom's FTP settings are entered using the Upload Settings panel. **(Figure 19.15)**

1. Select *Edit* from the **FTP Server** pop-up to display the Configure FTP File Transfer dialog. **(Figure 19.16)**

2. Enter the FTP account details provided by your web host. These include **Server, Username** and **Password**.

3. The default settings for **Protocol** (FTP), **Port** (21) and **Passive mode for data transfers** (Not Passive) are usually fine.

4. Click the *Browse* button to the right of the **Server Path** field. Lightroom connects to your web server and displays a full listing of the account contents.

5. Navigate to the folder that will hold your galleries and click *Select*. The full path is displayed in the *Server Path* field, and it may have an odd path such as */public_html/lightroomqueen.com/galleries* or */var/www/html/websites/lightroomqueen.com/galleries*

6. Using the pop-up at the top of the dialog, select *Save Current*

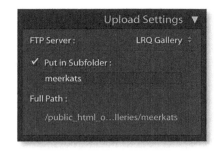

▲ **Figure 19.15** Save your FTP Server settings as a preset so you don't have to enter them each time you create a web gallery.

▼ **Figure 19.16** You may need to check with your web host to find out the FTP server details and path.

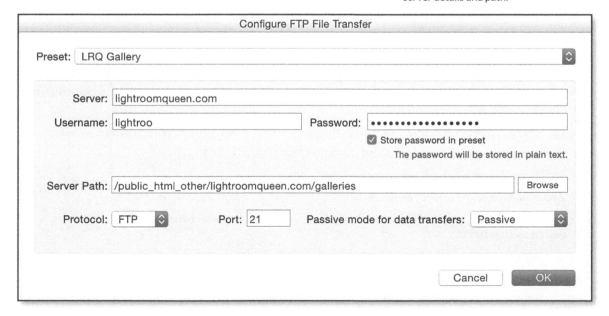

Settings as New Preset to save them for future reference. (As with most of these pop-ups, select the preset to access the rename/delete/update options.)

7. Click *OK* to close the dialog and return to Lightroom.

8. In the Upload Settings panel, check the **Put in Subfolder** checkbox and enter a name for this gallery's folder. You must change this for each new gallery, otherwise you'll overwrite your existing galleries. The resulting gallery path shows below for your reference.

9. Press the **Upload** button to begin the upload. You can carry on working in Lightroom while the upload runs in the background, and you can check the progress in the Activity Center in the top left-hand corner of the screen. Once Lightroom's created the gallery, the upload speed depends on your internet connection.

I changed an existing gallery—why hasn't it changed on the website?

If you change a web gallery within Lightroom, you have to delete and re-upload the gallery to the website, otherwise no one will see the changes. There is no link between the Web module and the uploaded gallery, so they don't automatically update. Some third-party galleries use Publish Services to populate the galleries, which allows greater flexibility.

FILE NAMING FOR THE WEB

File naming for Web is more restrictive than general DAM recommendations. If you regularly publish to the web, it's worth bearing this in mind when naming your files, so that the names on the website match those in your catalog.

-   Lightroom allows underscores (_) and hyphens (-) in file names but no other punctuation is allowed.
-   Lightroom automatically converts "bad characters" to underscores (_).
-   Spaces are not allowed and will be converted to underscores.
-   Accented characters are not allowed.
-   File names may be used to fill HTML id or class attributes, so they affect web validation. To comply with web standards:
    -   File names should not begin with numbers.
    -   File names must not begin with the number zero (0).

How do I export to the hard drive to upload using FTP software?

In order to upload the gallery using standalone FTP software, you'll need to export the gallery to your hard drive. To do so, simply click the **Export** button at the bottom of the right panel group, enter a name for the gallery folder and select a location on your hard drive. Once the export completes, upload the whole gallery folder to your web server using FTP software such as FileZilla https://filezilla-project.org

Can I have multiple galleries on my website?

To display multiple galleries on your website, simply place them in their own subfolders on your web server, and create an index page with a link to each gallery.

If you already have a website, creating a link to your galleries is the easiest way of integrating them. If you want to embed a gallery into an existing page, it is possible, but requires some web design skills.

Other third party web galleries can also create whole websites, linking multiple galleries together.

THIRD PARTY GALLERIES

Although Lightroom only ships with four gallery styles, many web designers have created additional web galleries for use in Lightroom. They offer a variety of different styles and functions, making it possible to create entire websites using Lightroom's Web module.

Where can I download third-party galleries?

We've already mentioned Adobe's official Add Ons site, which is accessed via the **Find More Galleries Online** button in the Layout Style panel. Some of the best galleries, however, are offered by other developers, including:

The Turning Gate (Matt Campagna & Ben Williams)—http://theturninggate.net/

Sean McCormack—http://www.photographers-toolbox.com/

Tim Armes—http://www.photographers-toolbox.com/

Juicebox—http://juicebox.net/

There's an index of web gallery designers on my website at http://www.Lrq.me/links/web-galleries

---

AUTO INDEX

To save you manually creating links to your galleries, TTG Auto Index plug-in can create automatic index pages, whether they're created using Lightroom's built in galleries or third-party galleries. http://www.Lrq.me/ttg-autoindex

---

What kind of features do third-party galleries offer?

While Lightroom's built-in galleries are smart but limited, developers have added a range of extra features to their galleries. Here's a few of the best features available in some of the third-party galleries:

A wide range of gallery styles

- Cell-based or Masonry thumbnail grids, slideshow and full-screen layouts.

- Lightbox-style large image presentations with slideshow-type playback.

- Responsive, touch-friendly galleries for desktop and mobile.

- Additional pages tie galleries together to become a full website.

- Organize galleries using "gallery index" pages.

Highly customizable

- Customization is not just limited to a couple of text fields and a few colors.

- No coding needed to customize them (unless you want to).

- Security—password protection for private galleries.

Use Publish Services to maintain galleries

- Create new galleries from the Library module.

- Add images to existing galleries without having to re-upload everything.

- Delete images from galleries without having to re-upload everything.

- Update previously published images with new Develop or Metadata changes without having to re-upload everything.

Shopping cart

- Order management including pricing for different product options, discounts, shipping, taxes, payment via PayPal, order confirmations.

- Fotomoto.com integration for selling prints and downloads automatically, without having to fulfill orders manually.

Direct links to other services

- Integrate into other websites such as Wordpress blogs.

- Social media integration.

- SEO optimized.

- Google Maps integration for photos with GPS metadata.

How do I install a third-party web gallery?

When you've purchased a third-party gallery, you'll need to add it to Lightroom. Check the developer's installation instructions, as the installation process may vary depending on the features offered.

WEB MODULE SHORTCUTS

Reload Preview	Ctrl R / Cmd R
Preview in Browser	Ctrl Alt P / Cmd Opt P
Use Advanced Settings	Ctrl Alt Shift / Cmd Opt Shift
Create Saved Web Gallery	Ctrl S / Cmd S
New Template	Ctrl N / Cmd N
New Template Folder	Ctrl Shift N / Cmd Shift N
Export Web Photo Gallery	Ctrl J / Cmd J

THE TURNING GATE

As an example, let's take a look at The Turning Gate's most robust and flexible gallery plug-in, CE4 Gallery. The CE4 Gallery is fully responsive, and touch and mobile-friendly. It features Lightbox-style image presentations, customizable layout, appearance, branding and navigation, social media integration, search engine optimization, password protection, Google Maps support, optional image downloads, Fotomoto e-commerce support, and more.

The Turning Gate's system is made up of components, so you can mix-and-match to build your ideal website. The initial setup is a little complex for beginners, and some basic web design experience would help, but with that complexity comes incredible flexibility.

You can combine it with their CE4 Publisher plug-in to offer Publish Services support, image search, navigation breadcrumbs and other advanced publishing features.

You can also combine it with CE4 Cart, which is a powerful shopping cart system. This allows to you to sell your photographs as digital downloads, prints, photo packages and other products. It includes higher-end eCommerce features such as automated digital delivery, international shipping options, and flexible tax customization to comply with local e-commerce regulations worldwide. It'll take automatic online payments via Paypal or send an invoice for you to follow up offline.

You can also use it with CE4 Auto Index, which automatically organizes your galleries into categories, which is invaluable as your galleries grow.

Other TTG Offerings include:

- TTG CE4 Client Response Gallery, which is an image gallery with client proofing features, for making image selects and gathering client feedback.

- TTG CE4 Theme for Wordpress allows you to customize a WordPress theme using Lightroom's Web module, perfectly matches the design of TTG image galleries, etc. This means that your blog can easily blend into your photo website.

- TTG CE4 Pages creates an HTML-based website/ portfolio with up to six pages, a gallery, a gallery index and an email contact form.

(To be clear, I receive no compensation for recommending them, but I believe it's a great system if you want to use self-hosted galleries.)

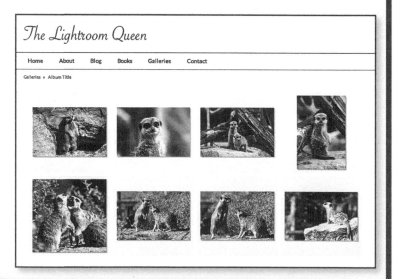

▶ The Turning Gate's popular CE4 Gallery grid.

BOOK MODULE

The Book module **(Figure 20.1)**, as its name suggests, assists you in creating photo books without the need for external software. Using a template-based system and drag-and-drop interface, you can create a beautiful book complete with text, and then easily upload it to Blurb for printing. Blurb are a well known photobook company who print and ship high quality books to photographers worldwide.

BOOK BASICS

Before we dive into the details, let's just run through the basics so you can start to create your first photo book.

1. In Library module's Grid view, decide which photos you want

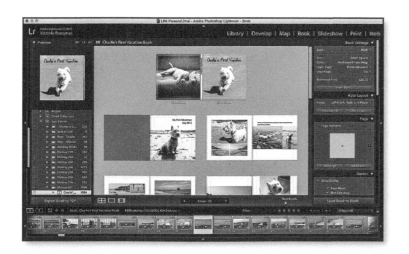

◁ **Figure 20.1** The Book module.

to include in your book. This might be a folder or a collection of photos. If the photos are spread across multiple folders or collections, use the Quick Collection to group them together.

2. Switch to the Book module by selecting it in the Module Picker.

3. The first time you switch to the Book module, Lightroom takes the photos from your current view and creates a book using Auto Layout. This gives you opportunity to explore before starting on your first book project.

4. There are three different view modes in the Book module, all accessed using the buttons on the Toolbar. **(Figure 20.2)** (If you can't see the Toolbar, press T.) Select each in turn, then return to the Multi-Page view. **(Figure 20.3)**

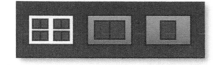

Figure 20.2 The view modes are found on the Toolbar—Multi-Page view (left), Spread view (center) and Single Page view (right).

- **Multi-Page view** is like the Library module Grid view, complete with the thumbnail size slider on the Toolbar.

- **Spread view** fills the preview area with facing pages and the buttons on the Toolbar move from one page to the next. **(Figure 20.4)**

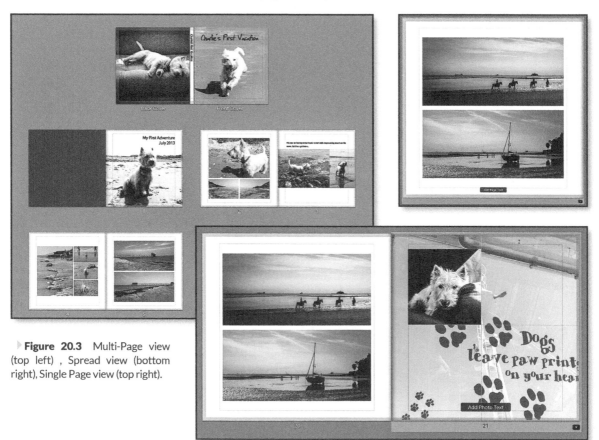

Figure 20.3 Multi-Page view (top left) , Spread view (bottom right), Single Page view (top right).

- **Single Page view** is particularly useful when working with text, as it allows you to zoom in closer. You'll find the zoom options on the top of the Preview panel, just as they'd be on the Navigator panel in Library module.

5. In the Auto Layout panel, press *Clear Layout* to start with a clean slate.

6. At the top of the Preview Area, press the *Create Saved Book* button and give your empty book a name. **(Figure 20.5)** Saving the book before you start means you won't accidentally lose your work. The saved book appears in the Collections panel, and it remembers the photos you're using as well as the book layout.

7. Select your book size and orientation using the *Size* pop-up in the Book Settings panel and ignore the other options for now. **(Figure 20.6)**

8. The first pair of pages in the book are the front and back cover. You can change the template and photos and add text, just as you would with a page inside the book. Let's work on the inside of the book first...

9. In the Page panel, click on the template preview to display the Page Template Picker. **(Figure 20.7)**

10. The templates are grouped into sets based on the number of photos or template style. Click on the set names at the top of the

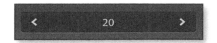

Figure 20.4 In Spread or Single Page view, you can move between photos using the arrows on the Toolbar.

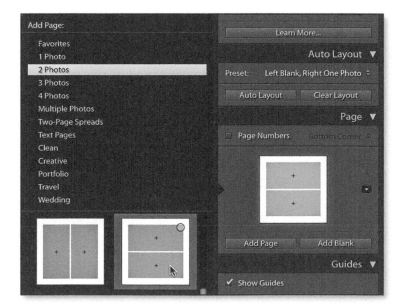

Figure 20.5 Save your book before you start on the design.

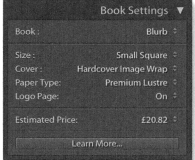

Figure 20.6 Select your book size and orientation.

Figure 20.7 Select a template for the page layout.

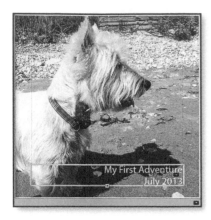

Figure 20.8 Select Single Page view before entering text.

Page Template Picker to view the templates below. The gray cells are photo cells and the lines are text cells.

When you find a template you like, click on it to add a new page.

11. Select a photo from the Filmstrip at the bottom of the screen, and drag its thumbnail onto a gray photo cell on the page in the main Preview Area. If you can't see the Filmstrip, click the black bar at the bottom of the screen.

12. Return to the Page panel and repeat the process to add additional pages and photos.

13. To change a page template, click on the page to select it, shown by a large orange border, then click on the template in the Page panel to display the Page Template Picker, and select a different template.

14. To move a photo to a different photo cell, click on it and drag to the new location.

15. Switch to Single Page view by clicking on the third icon in the Toolbar. Press T if the Toolbar is missing.

16. In the Text panel, check the *Page Text* checkbox and start typing in the text field that displays on the page. **(Figure 20.8)**

17. You can adjust the colors and design of the pages, as well as the

BOOK SHORTCUTS

Multi-Page View	Ctrl E / Cmd E
Spread View	Ctrl R / Cmd R
Single Page View	Ctrl T / Cmd T
Zoomed Page View	Ctrl U / Cmd U
Next View Mode	Ctrl = (or +) / Cmd = (or +) /
Previous View Mode	Ctrl - / Cmd -
Increase Grid Size	= or +
Decrease Grid Size	-
Go to Beginning	Ctrl Shift left arrow / Cmd Shift left arrow
Go to Previous Page	Ctrl/ Cmd left arrow
Go to Next Page	Ctrl / Cmd right arrow
Go to End	Ctrl Shift/ Cmd Shift right arrow
Save Book	Ctrl S / Cmd S

text overlays, using the panels on the right. We'll come back to these settings in more detail in the following pages.

18. Scroll back to the beginning and click on the words *Front Cover* to highlight the cover pages, then change the template, add photos and text.

19. At the bottom of the left panel group, press the *Export Book to PDF* button to create a PDF preview of your finished book. You can then upload the book to Blurb for printing using the *Send Book to Blurb* button at the bottom of the right panel group.

Having learned the basics, it's time to begin fine-tuning your book. We'll consider how to use the pages and templates first, before going on to add photos, text and decoration.

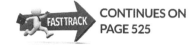

CONTINUES ON
PAGE 525

WORKING WITH PAGES & TEMPLATES

In the Book Settings panel **(Figure 20.9)**, you can choose to create a Blurb book, or a standard PDF or JPEG for other uses. The most important choice to make when beginning your book is the size. You can change this later, but Lightroom then has to reflow the photos and layout to fit, which can result in the design of your book changing.

The **Size** options are:

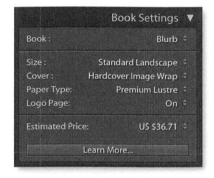

Figure 20.9 Select your book size in the Book Settings panel.

- **Small Square** is approximately 7" x 7" / 18cm x 18cm

- **Standard Portrait** is approximately 8" x 10" / 20cm x 25cm

- **Standard Landscape** is approximately 10" x 8" / 25cm x 20cm

- **Large Square** is approximately 12" x 12" / 30cm x 30cm

- **Large Landscape** is approximately 13" x 11" / 33cm x 28cm

The sizes aren't exact, as they're built for Blurb's book sizes. This means that an 8"x10" book won't create a PDF or JPEGs measuring exactly 8"x10".

The other options, such as the cover style and sharpening are dependent on whether you select Blurb, PDF or JPEG from the *Book* pop-up. We'll come back to these at the end of the chapter (page 477).

How do I select a page template and add new pages?

The Page panel controls the pages and page templates. **(Figure 20.10)** Click on the template preview, or the small arrow to the right, to view the Page Template Picker. The templates for your

MAXIMUM PAGES

Blurb books can have a maximum of 240 pages, with as many photos are you like on these pages. PDF and JPEG books don't have a limit.

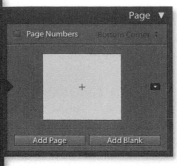

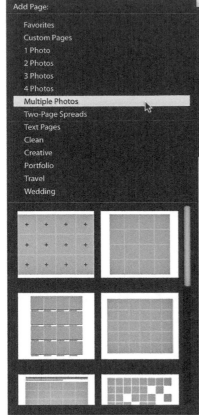

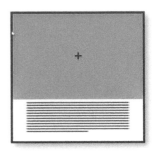

▲ **Figure 20.11** The gray cells are photo cells, and the cells with lines are text cells.

chosen book size are grouped into sets according to their style and number of photo cells.

Select a template set at the top and scroll through its templates in the lower half of the Page Template Picker.

The gray cells hold photos, whereas the white ones with gray lines are text cells. **(Figure 20.11)** There are templates with 1, 2, 3, 4, or even more photo cells per page. You'll also see some two-page spreads, allowing you to stretch a photo—perhaps a panoramic photo—across two facing pages. Some of the templates have straight edges and text, whereas others have textured borders around the photos. **(Figure 20.12)**

Once you've found a page template that you like, click on it to add the page to your book. If you already have a page selected, shown by a bright orange border, it replaces the template on that page instead of adding a new one. (The Page Template Picker says *Add Page* or *Modify Page* at the top to remind you.)

There are two additional buttons in the Page panel. ***Add Page*** adds a new page using the template shown in the template preview, so it's useful for adding multiple pages of the same template. ***Add Blank*** adds a blank page, so you can go back and apply your choice of template later.

▲ **Figure 20.10** Add a new page using the Page panel, and select different page templates using the Page Template Picker. The Page Template Picker is divided into different collections of templates, including templates with multiple photos and two-page spreads.

▸ **Figure 20.12** *Clean* templates (left) have straight edges whereas *Creative* templates (right) have textured borders. The *Clean, Creative, Portfolio, Travel* and *Wedding* sets of templates are simply slightly different themes.

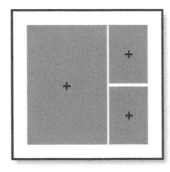

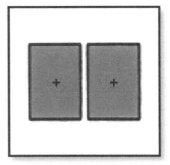

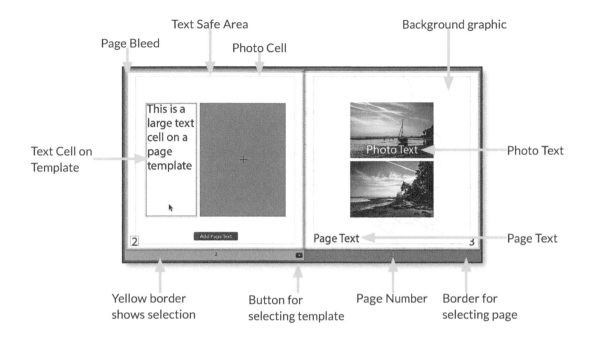

Page Bleed

Text Safe Area

Photo Cell

Background graphic

Text Cell on Template

This is a large text cell on a page template

Photo Text

Photo Text

Page Text

Page Text

Yellow border shows selection

Button for selecting template

Page Number

Border for selecting page

How do I select a page?

If you add a page, and later decide to change the template or move the page, you'll need to select it. If you click the wrong spot on the page, you can accidentally move a photo or text. The easiest way of accurately selecting the page is to select the border or number just below the page. Once the page is selected, it's surrounded by an orange border.

How do I change the template for an existing page?

Having selected the page, you'll see a small black arrow in the bottom right corner of the orange page border. **(Figure 20.13)** This displays the same Page Template Picker used in the Page panel. From there, or from the Page panel, you can select a new template for the page. Any photos on the page try to auto flow into the new design. If you pick a template with fewer photo cells, some of the photos are removed.

The template you choose is applied to all the selected pages, so you can update multiple pages in one go. Shift-clicking selects consecutive pages, or Ctrl-clicking (Windows) / Cmd-clicking (Mac) selects non-consecutive pages.

Figure 20.13 Elements of a book page.

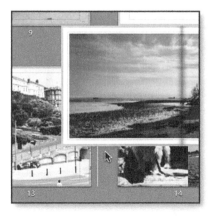

Figure 20.14 Reorder pages by dragging and dropping. A yellow line appears, showing where the page will drop.

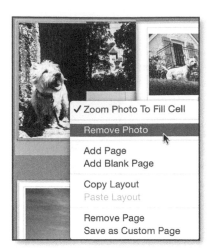

Figure 20.15 Remove pages using the right-click menu.

START AFRESH

To start afresh, you can either select the *Clear Book* button at the top of the preview area, or the *Clear Layout* button in the Auto Layout panel. It's quicker than deleting the pages individually.

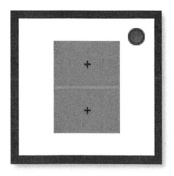

Figure 20.16 Favorite pages can be identified by the circle in the top right corner.

How do I rearrange the page order or insert a page?

To rearrange the page order, simply drag and drop in the Multi-Page view, just as you would rearrange thumbnails in the Library module Grid view. Select the page by clicking in the border and drag it to its new position. The pages separate slightly showing where you can drop the page and a vertical line appears showing where it will land. **(Figure 20.14)**

To insert a page between existing pages, the easiest option is to add a new page anywhere and drag it into position. Alternatively, you can select an existing page and then press the Add Page button to insert it to the right of the existing selected page.

How do I delete pages?

Deleting pages isn't quite so obvious, as the Delete key removes the photo from the page, not the page itself. If you right-click on the page or page border, however, there is a **Remove Page** option in the context-sensitive menu. **(Figure 20.15)** If multiple pages are selected, they'll all be deleted.

At the beginning and end of the book there are darker gray pages, which are the inside of the front and back covers. You can't delete these end pages or add photos or text to them.

How do I mark a template as a favorite?

You'll probably find that you use certain templates more frequently than others. Rather than having to scroll through all the templates to find them again, you can mark them as favorites to group them together.

In the Page Template Picker, right-click on the template and select *Add to Favorites* or click the small circle in the corner (like the Target Collection marker). **(Figure 20.16)** These favorites are then grouped together in the Favorites set at the top of the Page Template Picker. Two-page spreads (or double-page spreads) can't be added to favorites, but they're already separated into a small group of their own, so they're easy to find.

If you later change your mind, right-click and select *Remove from Favorites* or click the small circle again to remove them from the Favorites set.

If you've already used a template in your book, click on the arrow in the page border and you'll see that your page template is already selected in the Page Template Picker, so you don't have to search through all the templates to find it.

BOOK LAYOUT SHORTCUTS

Copy Layout	Ctrl Shift C / Cmd Shift C
Paste Layout	Ctrl Shift V / Cmd Shift V
Remove Photo from Page	Backspace / Delete
Remove Page	Ctrl Shift Backspace / Cmd Shift Delete
Select All Text Cells	Ctrl Alt A / Cmd Opt A
Select All Photo Cells	Ctrl Alt Shift A / Cmd Opt Shift A
Select Multiple Cells	Shift-click
Show Header Bar	\
Show Info Overlay	I

Can I build my own templates?

The Book module uses a template based system, so you can't enlarge or move the existing cells or build your own templates. You can, however, use cell padding to shrink the cells and then save your designs as custom pages. It offers more flexibility than it first appears. You can also leave some cells empty, as the cell borders won't appear in the finished book.

To alter an existing cell, select a template with a larger cell than you need, and then increase the **Padding** in the Cell panel to reduce the size of the photo within the cell. **(Figure 20.17)** The disclosure triangle hides additional sliders, which allow you to set the *left*, *right*, *top* and *bottom* to different values.

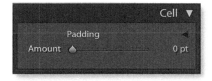

Figure 20.17 The Cell panel is collapsed by default. Click the disclosure triangle to the right to expand it.

The individual padding sliders have white squares next to them by default. When a square is white, it means the sliders are linked, and move at the same time. You can click on the squares to link or unlink sliders, so you may link the left and right sliders to move them in tandem, without moving the top and bottom sliders, or vice versa. **(Figure 20.18)** The **Link All** square links all of the slider movements.

You can then save the custom page design to reuse on other pages. To do so, right-click on the page and select *Save as Custom Page* from the context-sensitive menu. They'll appear in the *Custom Pages* set in the Page Template Picker. To delete a custom page, right-click on the template in the Page Template Picker and select *Remove from Custom Pages*.

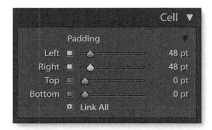

Figure 20.18 The white squares show that sliders are linked and will move at the same time.

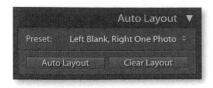

Figure 20.19 Auto Layout automatically creates a book from the photos in the Filmstrip.

Can I duplicate a page? Or can I copy the layout from a previous page?

If you just want to duplicate the page layout for use on another page, without saving it as custom page, you can use *Edit menu > Copy Layout*, then select another page and choose then *Edit menu > Paste Layout* to duplicate the layout. They're also found in the right-click context-sensitive menu. It includes any padding and text formatting but excludes the photos or text, so it's ready to reuse.

AUTO LAYOUT

Auto Layout is a quick way of placing your photos into a book, and it's often a great starting point for your design, rather than adding one page at a time. You can create a preset defining which page templates Auto Layout is allowed to use, and Lightroom takes all the photos from the Filmstrip and automatically builds a book using these templates.

Figure 20.20 The Auto Layout Preset Editor allows you to select specific templates for use with Auto Layout.

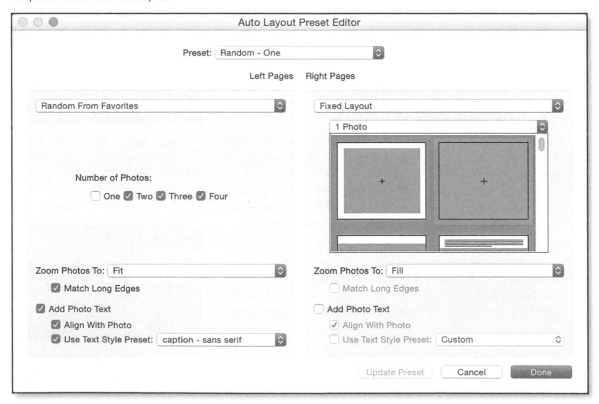

How do I use Auto Layout?

Using Auto Layout is simple—select a built-in preset in the Auto Layout panel (**Figure 20.19**), or select *Edit* to create your own. Once you're happy with your chosen preset, press the ***Auto Layout*** button. Lightroom uses the templates included in the preset to add pages and fill them with the photos in the Filmstrip. If you've already added empty pages with templates, Lightroom fills these empty cells with photos from the Filmstrip instead.

How do I create my own Auto Layout preset?

Lightroom ships with a few Auto Layout presets, however you can also create your own to suit your personal tastes. Go to the Auto Layout panel and select the ***Preset*** pop-up. At the bottom is an *Edit* option, which displays the Auto Layout Preset Editor dialog. (**Figure 20.20**) This is where you select your Auto Layout preferences.

The options are replicated for both sides, so you can apply one template to the left pages and a different template to the right pages. For example, you may choose to have a single large photo filling the right page, and a mix of different sized photos on the left pages.

Either side can be left blank, use a fixed template selected within the Auto Layout Preset Editor, or use random templates from your favorite templates.

There are further options for selecting default fit/fill zoom settings and adding text captions, which we'll explain further on the following pages.

Having chosen your Auto Layout options, you can save it as a preset using the pop-up at the top of the dialog, ready to run.

What does *Match Long Edges* do?

If you've selected *Zoom Photos to Fit* in the Auto Layout Preset Editor, the photos are placed in the cell without cropping, rather than filling the cell. That means you could end up with different aspect ratios on the same page, and that mixture of sizes can look untidy, so *Match Long Edges* sets the photo zoom to line up mixed ratio photos. (**Figure 20.21**)

How do I control which metadata is used for Photo Captions when using Auto Layout?

When you enable *Add Photo Captions* in the Auto Layout Preset Editor dialog, the content of the text captions is controlled by the

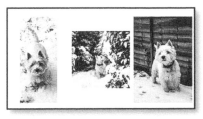

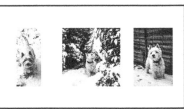

▲ **Figure 20.21** *Match Long Edges* turned off (top) and on (bottom).

NO FAVORITES

If you've selected *Random from Favorites* at the top of the Auto Layout Preset Editor, you need to have selected some favorite templates using the instructions in the previous section (page 458).

If, when you press the *Auto Layout* button, it displays an error saying it doesn't have any favorites, it's likely because the favorites you selected were not for the same size and shape book. Alternatively, you may have checked 1, 2, 3 and 4 photos in the Auto Layout Preset Editor dialog, but only have favorite templates with 1 and 4 photos, for example.

Book menu > Book Preferences > Fill text boxes with setting. If this is set to *Filler Text*, instead of *Title* or *Caption*, the text cells are added but left blank. If you want the metadata to be selected automatically, select *Title* or *Caption* in that preferences dialog.

Why isn't Auto Layout doing anything?

If all the photos in the Filmstrip already appear in your book, there's nothing for Auto Layout to do.

If you've manually filled your book, Auto Layout adds any leftover photos, filling any leftover cells with unused photos and adding additional pages at the end if needed.

WORKING WITH PHOTOS

While Auto Layout can place all your photos automatically in the book, you'll still need to manually add new photos and move them around, so let's explore the options.

How do I add or rearrange photo on a page?

Adding photos to your pages manually is a simple drag and drop operation. You must have a template on the page, ready to receive the photo. You can either drag the photo from the Filmstrip at the bottom of the screen or use the secondary window set to Grid view and drag from there, dropping it into a photo cell on a page.

You can replace photos by dragging other photos up from the Filmstrip, or you can drag the photos between cells in the book to swap the photos.

How do I zoom into a photo?

Having added a photo, you can zoom in and move it around within the cell. Click on a photo in a cell to display the zoom slider. **(Figure 20.22)** The zoom range goes from small enough to fit the photo entirely within the cell without cropping, to twice the length of the longest cell edge, which is enough for most situations. If you need to zoom in further, or you want a specific ratio for your photo, switch back to the Develop module to crop accurately and then adjust the photo on the page.

Once you've zoomed in on a photo (or if it's set to fill the cell automatically), you can click on the photo and drag it around within the cell to get the positioning just right.

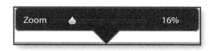

Figure 20.22 If you click on a photo in a cell, the *Zoom* slider appears.

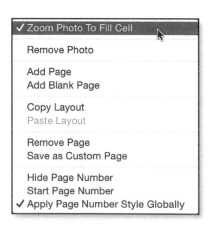

Figure 20.23 To automatically fill the cell, right-click and select *Zoom Photo To Fill Cell.*

GUIDES SHORTCUTS

Show Guides	Ctrl Shift G / Cmd Shift G
Page Bleed	Ctrl Shift J / Cmd Shift J
Text Safe Area	Ctrl Shift U / Cmd Shift U
Photo Cells	Ctrl Shift K / Cmd Shift K
Filler Text	Ctrl Shift H / Cmd Shift H

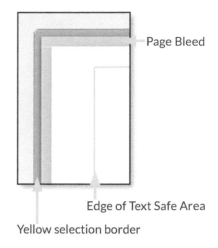

Page Bleed

Edge of Text Safe Area

Yellow selection border

Figure 20.24 Book page guides.

If you've been experimenting with the zoom slider, but want to automatically fill the cell, right-click on the photo and select *Zoom Photo To Fill Cell* from the context-sensitive menu. **(Figure 20.23)**

What is *Page Bleed*?

While you're adjusting the position of photos close to the edge of the page, look out for the page bleed. That's the part of the page that's supposed to be trimmed off when the book's printed, and it's shown as a transparent gray border when **Page Bleed** is checked in the Guides panel (Blurb only). **(Figure 20.24 & 20.25)**

If your photo is intended to stretch off the edge of the page (full bleed), make sure it also fills the bleed area in case the book isn't trimmed perfectly straight, but don't include any important elements of the photo in this area.

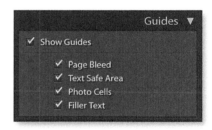

Figure 20.25 The Guides panel shows/ hides the book page guides.

Can I set it to automatically fit the photos to the cells without cropping, rather than filling the cell?

By default, the photos automatically fill the cell, which may crop part of your photo. If you find that you always zoom out to fit within the cell without cropping, you can change the default setting. If you look under the *Book menu > Book Preferences*, there are a few book specific options, including the *Default Photo Zoom* options. **(Figure 20.26)** When you use Auto Layout, there's a matching preference in the Auto Layout Preset Editor dialog.

What does the exclamation mark on the photo mean?

If you see a black exclamation mark on the photo, it's warning you that the photo will be low resolution at the selected zoom and cell size and therefore may not print well. **(Figure 20.27)** If you click on the exclamation mark, it displays the current resolution and holding

▶**Figure 20.26** Set defaults for new books and pages using the Book Preferences dialog.

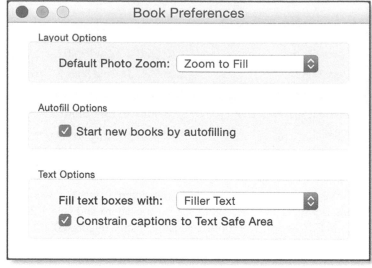

down the Alt key (Windows) / Opt key (Mac) switches to resolution (PPI) instead of the zoom percentage while adjusting the zoom slider.

If you can't replace the photo with a higher resolution version, zoom out, increase the cell padding to make photo smaller, or move the photo to a smaller cell to improve the print quality.

A red exclamation mark indicates that the photo is offline, and if you try to export the book to PDF, JPEG or Blurb, the photo will be missing.

▲**Figure 20.27** A black exclamation mark on the photo cell indicates that it will be low resolution at that size.

How do I remove a photo?

To remove a photo from a page, you can either drag it to another page, select it and press the Delete key on your keyboard, or right-click on the photo and select *Remove Photo* from the context-sensitive menu. You can select multiple cells by Ctrl-clicking (Windows) / Cmd-clicking on them, to delete the photos from multiple cells in one go.

How can I tell which photos I've used so far?

In the Filmstrip, each of the photos that you've used has a black marker with a number. **(Figure 20.28)** The number indicates the number of times you've used the photo within the book. If you've used photos as backgrounds or cover photos, as well as within the book pages, this also increases the use count.

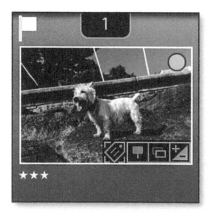

▲**Figure 20.28** The black marker and number show how many times the photo has been used in the book.

Can I filter to see which photos are currently used in my book?

To quickly find all of the photos you haven't used in your book design, select *Unused* from the Filmstrip Filters presets pop-up. That hides all of the photos you've already used, so it's useful for finding photos that you've missed. There's also an *Unused* preset to show just the photos that are already included in your book.

When I've finished designing the book, can I still edit the photos in Develop?

Having placed the photos on the pages, you may find that some photos need further adjustment to make them look their best on the page together. That's not a problem – just switch back to the Develop module and adjust the photos as normal, and the changes are reflected in your book.

PAGE STYLES

Once you've added photos to your book, it's time to start thinking about other page decoration. At the bottom of the right panel group is the Background panel, which allows you to change the background color or graphic, either on a single page or globally using the **Apply Background Globally** checkbox.

How do I change the background color of my pages?

To change the page background color, check the **Background Color** checkbox in the Background panel and click the box to its right to show the Color Picker. **(Figure 20.29)** By default, the Color Picker only displays shades of gray, but if you want a colored page background, click on the bar on the right of the Color Picker and the full range of colors becomes available. As in the Develop module, if you click on the Color Picker and drag the eyedropper onto the photo, it also selects colors from the photo.

Figure 20.29 Change the background color by clicking on the *Background Color* rectangle and selecting your chosen color in the Color Picker.

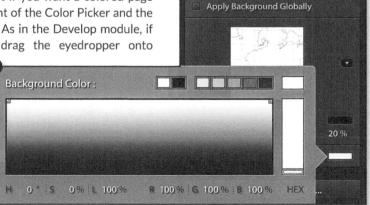

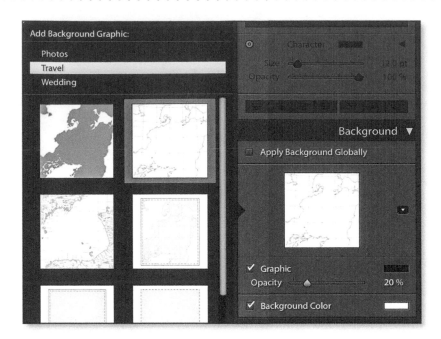

How do I add a graphic or photo as a page background?

You're not limited to only using plain colors as your page backgrounds. You can also use photos, textures or other graphics.

There are some graphics built into Lightroom, such as map images for travel photography and some gentle swirls intended for weddings. **(Figure 20.30)** To view and select these graphics, click on the background graphics preview or the arrow to the right. The *Graphic* checkbox

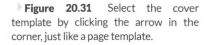 **Figure 20.30** The page background is set using the Background panel, and options include graphics, photos and plain colors.

is checked automatically. You can also adjust the color of the graphic by clicking the box to the right of the checkbox.

You can use your own photos by dragging and dropping them from the Filmstrip onto the background graphic preview in the Background panel and reducing the *opacity*. Textures downloaded from the web, for example paper textures, also work very well as backgrounds.

How do I change the cover or spine color?

We all tend to judge a book by its cover, so it's important to get the cover just right. Like the internal pages, there's a range of cover templates to choose from, for example, one of the available templates wraps a panoramic photo right around the cover, and it also has full

Figure 20.31 Select the cover template by clicking the arrow in the corner, just like a page template.

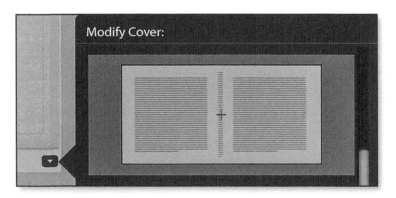

sized text fields which will allow you to place text anywhere on the front or back cover. **(Figure 20.31)**

You can adjust the cover background color using the controls in the Background panel. If the cover is set to the default template, which has photos covering the front and back covers, adjusting the background color only affects the spine color. We'll come back to adding text in the next section.

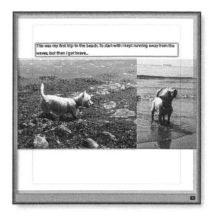

ADDING TEXT TO YOUR BOOK

Many photographers also like to add text captions to their books, describing the photos. You can go even further, adding lengths of text, telling a whole story. Lightroom offers three different options for adding text—photo text, page text and page template cells.

▲ **Figure 20.32** Some text cells are built in to the page.

How do I add text to a page?

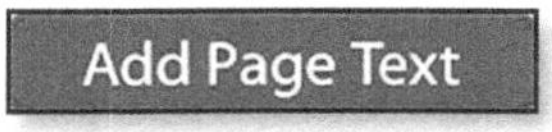

To add text to a page template with built in text cells (those are the cells that displayed as gray lines in the Page Template Editor), you can simply click in the text cell and start typing, or paste text from a text editor. **(Figure 20.32)**

By default, Lightroom shows *Photo Title* or *lorem ipsum* placeholder text until you click in the text cell. If you've hidden it by unchecking *Filler Text* in the Guides panel or by clicking in the cell, they can be difficult to spot. When you float the mouse over the page, the gray cell border appears.

If you're in Spread view or Single Page view, you'll also find a button on every page that either says *Add Page Text* or *Add Photo Text*, depending on whether you have the page or the photo selected. **(Figure 20.33)** Clicking on these buttons puts you straight into text entry mode. *Photo Text* and *Page Text* can also be enabled using the

Add Page Text

▲ **Figure 20.33** Text can also be added anywhere on the page.

ZOOM TEXT

It's easiest to enter text in Single Page view, which allows you to zoom in. Zoom ratios up to 4:1 are found on top of the Preview panel. The keyboard shortcut Ctrl-U (Windows) / Cmd-U (Mac) is the quickest way of switching to the Zoomed Page view (since the standard Z or spacebar shortcuts would interfere with text entry). **(Figure 20.34)**

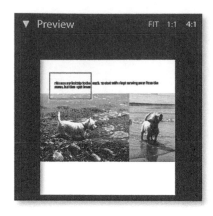

Figure 20.34 To zoom in on text, select the 1:1 or 4:1 zoom ratio on the Preview panel.

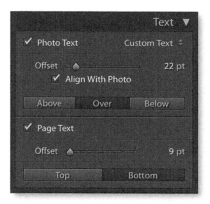

Figure 20.35 Select the Photo Text and Page Text position in the Text panel.

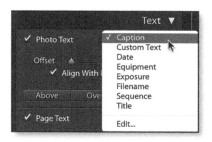

Figure 20.36 Photo Text can be automatically created from metadata.

Figure 20.37 Page Text and text cells that are part of the template can also use metadata, but they're limited to *Title*, *Caption* or *Filename*.

checkboxes in the Text panel, where you'll have access to additional options.

To move around the page when zoomed in, either drag the rectangle in the Preview panel or hold down the Spacebar (without a cursor in a text field) to access the hand tool to drag the page itself.

What's the difference between Page Text, Photo Text and text cells on page templates?

If there are three different types of text cell though, when would you use each kind?

- **Photo Text Cells** are aligned to the photo or photo cell. They can be above, below, or overlaid on top of the photo, and you can move them up and down using the **Offset** slider in the Text panel, or by dragging the edge of the cell. If the photo doesn't fill the cell, the **Align With Photo** checkbox offsets the text from the edge of the photo instead of the edge of the cell. *Photo Text Cells* also have more metadata available for Auto Text than the other types of text cells.

- **Page Text Cells** span the full width of the page, rather than being tied to a specific photo. Like the *Photo Text Cells*, you can move up and down using the **Offset** slider in the Text panel, or you can drag them around on the page. Combining a page text **(Figure 20.35)** with cell padding allows you to put text anywhere on the page.

- **Page Template Cells** are built into the templates in a fixed position, although you can use padding to position the text within the text cell. They're ideal for longer paragraphs of text, and there's a template which is purely for text.

What is *Custom Text*?

Text entered directly in the Book module is called *Custom Text*. It's only saved with that specific page, so it can be accidentally wiped by changing the photos or page templates. If the text relates to a specific photo, it's better to add it to that photo's metadata using the Metadata panel in the Library module, instead of typing it directly on the page. You can then use the Auto Text options to automatically add

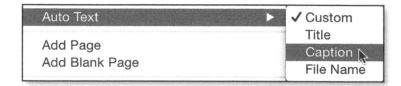

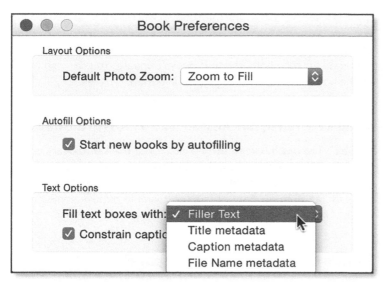

Figure 20.38 Select the default for text cells that are part of the templates using the Book Preferences dialog.

the text to the book pages, without worrying about it accidentally being deleted.

How do I automatically enter text based on metadata?

The metadata associated with your photos can be used to create captions automatically, whether that's metadata you've added yourself (Title, Caption, keywords, etc.) or metadata that was added by the camera (camera model, aperture, shutter speed, etc.). This is called Auto Text.

In the Text panel, you can choose from a variety of metadata presets for the **Photo Text** cells. Some presets are included, for example, *Title*, *Exposure* or *Equipment*. **(Figure 20.36)** If you select *Edit* in that pop-up menu, you can also use the Text Template Editor to create your own combination of metadata.

You don't have quite so much choice for the *Page Text* cells or page template text cells. If you right-click on these cells, you can select *Auto Text* from the context-sensitive menu, and choose from *Title*, *Caption* or *Filename*. **(Figure 20.37 & 20.38)**

I've changed the metadata—how do I update the text in the book to match?

If you use Auto Text and then later edit the metadata in the Metadata panel, Lightroom won't immediately update the book text captions to match, otherwise you could unintentionally change the content of your book. To update the book with the new metadata, go to *Book menu > Update Metadata Based Captions*.

SPELL CHECK

On the Mac version, there is a spellcheck available under the *Edit menu*, which utilizes the OS X built-in dictionary, however it doesn't work in the Book module. This feature is not available on Windows. If you're typing a long section of text, it's worth typing in a text editor and then pasting into Lightroom, to ensure that you make any needed spelling corrections before printing.

Figure 20.39 The Overset Text icon shows when there's too much text to fit in the cell.

If you've used Auto Text, and then you click in the cell, it automatically becomes a custom text cell, but leaves the previous text there ready for you to edit. If you then change the related photo or update the metadata for the photo, the text doesn't update. You can right-click on the text cell to reselect an Auto Text option.

What's the red square marker with a cross in the middle?

If there's too much text to fit in a cell, a red marker appears in the bottom right corner. **(Figure 20.39)** This is called an overset text warning. To solve the problem, you can reduce the font size, reduce the padding to make the cell larger, or simply remove some of the text.

How do I position the text on the page?

The Photo Text and Page Text cells can be moved up and down the page using the sliders in the Text panel or by dragging the yellow border of the cell.

You can also adjust the text position within the cell using the *Padding* sliders in the Cell panel, just like the photo cells. The individual *Padding* sliders are hidden by a disclosure triangle. When you click on the triangle to see the sliders, you'll note white squares to the left of the sliders. They indicate that the sliders are linked and all move by the same amount, but unchecking *Link All* below the sliders separates them.

What is the *Text Safe Area*?

The **Text Safe Area** is marked with a thin gray line when it's turned on in the Guides panel. It's possible to put text outside of these lines by going to *Book menu > Book Preferences* and unchecking **Constrain captions to Text Safe Area**, however your text may get cut off when

Figure 20.40 The spine of the book will only accept text if the book has enough pages.

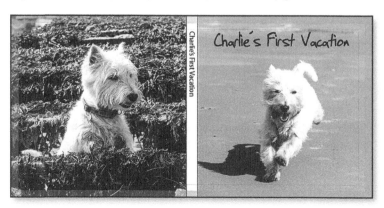

printing and trimming the book, so it's sensible to stay inside the lines.

How do I add automatic page numbers?

In addition to automatic photo captions, you can automatically add page numbers to your book using the *Page Numbers* checkbox in the Page panel. It places the page numbers in the bottom corners of the pages by default, but you can change the position to the top corner, bottom corner or the center of one of the outside edges using the pop-up.

Once the page numbers are enabled, you can select one of the numbers and change the text formatting using the Type panel, which we'll come to in the next section.

When you right-click on a page number, you'll find further options. By default, your text formatting applies to all the page numbers in your book, but you can uncheck *Apply Page Number Style Globally* to customize the format on each page. From this menu you can also *Hide Page Number* on specific pages, and choose to start numbering somewhere other than page 1 of the book (for example, if you have a title page inside the book).

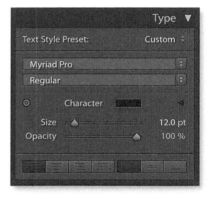

Figure 20.41 The Type panel holds all of the text formatting controls.

How do I add text to the cover and spine of the book?

All of the front and back cover templates include text cells to enter the title for your book, just like the pages in the book. Cover templates also include a spine text cell, which automatically rotates the text by 90 degrees along the spine, as long as the spine isn't too narrow. **(Figure 20.40)**

TEXT FORMATTING

Your text captions are not limited to the default sans-serif font. In the Type panel **(Figure 20.41)**, there are extensive text formatting tools taken from industry standard software, such as Photoshop, Illustrator and InDesign.

How do I change the font, size and color?

Having selected the text, or placed the cursor in an empty text cell, go to the Type panel. From here, you can choose from the **fonts** installed on your system, and adjust the font **size**, **opacity**, color and alignment of the text, as well as more advanced text formatting tools.

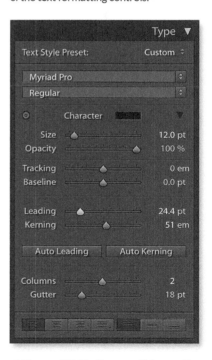

Figure 20.42 If you click on the disclosure triangle, there are additional options.

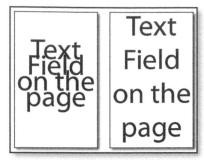

Figure 20.43 *Leading* is the space between the lines, or the line height. A low value will cramp the text (left) whereas a higher value will spread out the text (right).

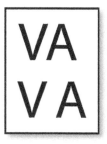

Figure 20.44 *Kerning* is the space between pairs of characters, for example, a large gap between V and A looks odd.

Next to the ***Character*** label is a Color Picker which allows you to select the color of the font. It defaults to shades of gray, however you can access the full range of colors by clicking on the bar on the right of the Color Picker.

What are *Tracking, Baseline, Leading* and *Kerning*?

Hiding behind the disclosure triangle in the Type panel **(Figure 20.42)** are more advanced text options:

- ***Tracking*** is the space between multiple characters (l i k e _ t h i s).

- ***Baseline shift*** moves characters off their normal baseline. The baseline is the line most letters sit on, although some letters such as 'y' hang below the baseline. You may use it for situations such as the 'TH' in 9TH March 2015.

- ***Leading***, which is pronounced like heading, is the space between lines. It's the equivalent of line height in programs such as Microsoft Word. If the text is bunched up because the leading value is too low, you can also use the **Auto Leading** button instead of adjusting it manually. **(Figure 20.43)**

- ***Kerning*** is the space between pairs of characters, for example, V and A are moved closed together as a standard gap would look unnaturally large. **(Figure 20.44)** Most fonts handle kerning automatically, so you don't usually need to worry about it, however important text (e.g. on a cover) may benefit from a manual kerning adjustment. To adjust the kerning, you place the cursor between two characters and adjust the slider. The **Auto Kerning** button sets the kerning automatically.

TEXT TARGETED ADJUSTMENT TOOL SHORTCUTS

Text Size	Drag horizontally / Drag horizontally
Leading/Line Height	Drag vertically / Drag vertically
Tracking	Ctrl-drag horizontally / Cmd-drag horizontally
Baseline Shift	Ctrl-drag vertically / Cmd-drag vertically
Kerning	Drag horizontally over cursor / insertion point
Temporarily deactivate TAT tool	Hold down Alt / Hold down Opt
Exit the TAT tool	Escape

How do I use the Text Targeted Adjustment Tool?

Like the Develop module, the Book module has a Targeted Adjustment Tool. It's an easy way of visually adjusting the text without having to understand or remember each of the slider names. The adjustments are relative to the existing settings, so if the selected text is two different sizes, it changes both by a relative amount. (Figure 20.45)

To use it, select the text you want to adjust. Select the TAT from the Type panel—it's the small circle with a dot in it—and then click on the text or cursor and drag in the following directions:

- Dragging horizontally over a selection adjusts text size.

- Dragging vertically over a selection adjusts leading or line height.

- Holding down Ctrl (Windows) / Cmd (Mac) while dragging horizontally over a selection adjusts tracking.

- Holding down Ctrl (Windows) / Cmd (Mac) while dragging vertically over a selection adjusts baseline shift.

- Dragging horizontally over the insertion cursor adjusts kerning.

- Holding down Alt (Windows) / Opt (Mac) temporarily deactivates the TAT tool so you can change your text selection. This only applies if you're trying to change a selection in an area that's already selected.

When you're finished, hit the Escape key to exit the TAT tool.

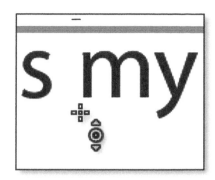

▲ **Figure 20.45** The Targeted Adjustment Tool allows you to visually adjust the text.

SELECT THE TEXT

If there's existing text in a cell, you need to select the text before adjusting the Type settings.

How do I adjust the horizontal and vertical alignment?

At the bottom of the Type panel are the text alignment buttons, for left, center, and right alignment, as well as various text justification options and vertical alignment too. They're a little easier to miss, as they're not as bright as most of Lightroom's other buttons. (Figure 20.46)

How to do I split text into columns and adjust the spacing?

You can split your text into columns using the **Columns** slider in the Type panel. The **Gutter** slider only comes into effect when you have more than one column of text, as the gutter is the space between the columns. (Figure 20.47)

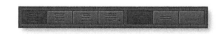

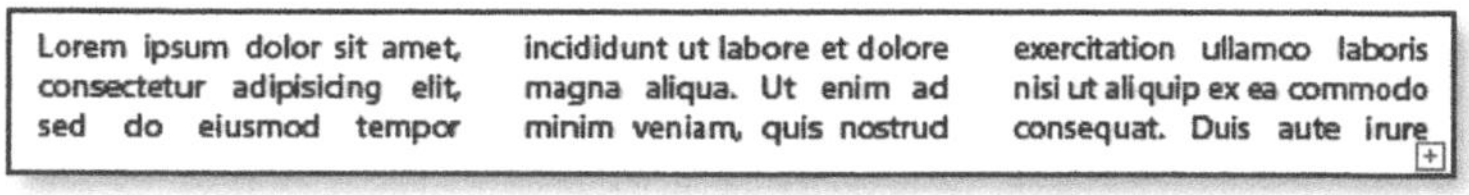

▲ **Figure 20.46** The horizontal and vertical alignment buttons are hard to see.

◀ **Figure 20.47** The gutter is the space between the columns of text.

| Lorem ipsum dolor sit amet, consectetur adipisicing elit, sed do eiusmod tempor | incididunt ut labore et dolore magna aliqua. Ut enim ad minim veniam, quis nostrud | exercitation ullamco laboris nisi ut aliquip ex ea commodo consequat. Duis aute irure |

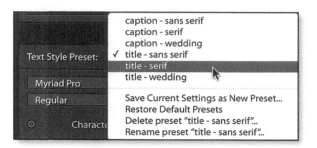

▶ **Figure 20.48** You can save text formatting as Text Style Presets, for use on other cells or books.

How do I change the text style on multiple text cells?

To change the text style on multiple cells at the same time, go to *Edit menu > Select All Text Cells*, or if you only want to change specific cells, hold down Ctrl (Windows) / Cmd (Mac) while clicking to select them. You can then apply a Text Style preset or adjust the settings in the Type panel, and all the selected cells update at the same time.

The settings are sticky, so any new cells you create inherit the settings of the previously selected cell.

Can I save my text style to apply to other cells?

At the top of the Type panel is a **Text Style Preset** pop-up. **(Figure 20.48)** This allows you to save your text settings as a preset for use on other cells or even other books. Set your text style settings and then select *Save Current Settings as New Preset* from the pop-up menu. When you select text in another cell, you can then select the preset to apply all of your text style settings without adjusting them individually.

SAVING BOOKS

Having spent time and effort on designing your book, you'll no doubt want to save it! Considering the amount of time involved in designing a book, I recommend saving your work before you start.

What's an unsaved book?

When you enter the Book module, unless you've selected an existing book from the Collections panel, you'll be viewing an unsaved book. You'll see the header bar above the preview area has *Unsaved Book* listed as the book name. This is like a scratchpad, where you can play around with things without saving them. The Filmstrip in *Unsaved Book* shows all photos used in the book so far, plus the photos from the currently selected folder or collection.

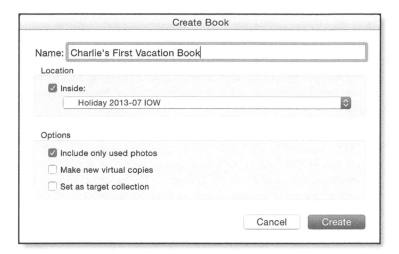

Figure 20.49 Save your book before you start working, so you don't lose the work you've done.

How do I save my book?

To save your work for the first time, either click the **Create Saved Book** button at the top of the preview area, or press the + button on the Collections panel and select *Create Book* from the panel menu. In the Create Book dialog **(Figure 20.49)**, you can choose to save the book within an existing collection or set, or at the top level of the Collections panel. Grouping your books within collections or sets keeps them organized so you can easily find them later. **(Figure 20.50)**

If you haven't used all the photos shown in the Filmstrip, it also gives you the option to *Include only used photos*. This removes the unused photos from the collection, although you can easily add them back into your book later.

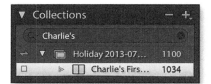

Figure 20.50 Your saved book is stored in the Collections panel.

If you're concerned that you may later edit one of the photos, making it look out of place in the book, you can also select *Make new virtual copies* instead of including the original photos in the book collection. If you do so, consider adding a color label to help identify their purpose, so you don't later delete them, wondering where all these excess virtual copies have come from. The purple label is ideal as it doesn't have a keyboard shortcut. To do so, select all the photos included in the book, right-click on a thumbnail in the Filmstrip and select *Set Color Label > Purple*.

Once you've saved your book, the name appears at the top of the preview area. Any changes you make to the book are automatically be saved in the background from that time on, so you don't need to worry about saving your work again.

How do I edit or add extra photos to my saved book?

Once you've given your book a name, you'll find it listed in the Collections panel. You can return to it at any time by double-clicking on the name if you're in the Library, Develop or Map modules, or by single-clicking on the name if you're in one of the other output modules.

If you haven't finished designing your book, you may want to add additional photos. To do so, switch to the Library module and find the photos in the Grid view. Select them, then drag them (holding them by their thumbnail, not the border) onto the saved book in the Collections panel. When you switch back to the Book module, they'll be waiting in the Filmstrip, ready to add to your book.

How do I create a snapshot of my book, in case I make changes and want to go back to a previous version?

Anything you do to a saved book is automatically saved within a few seconds. If you make a change and then decide you don't like it, Ctrl-Z (Windows) / Cmd-Z (Mac) undoes the change, however if you've closed Lightroom, the edit history will be gone.

If you want to try something different, right-click on the book in the Collections panel and select *Duplicate Book*. This new copy appears in the Collections panel as a separate book, so you can experiment with different variations. Once you've created a book version that you're happy with, you can delete the other versions of the book.

Once you've finished designing your book, you can export the book collection as its own catalog to make absolutely sure you never change it by accident. To do so, right-click on the saved book in the Collections panel, select *Export this Collection as a Catalog* and choose a location on your hard drive. You can include or exclude the previews and originals, depending on how much disc space you can afford to use on this backup. We'll come back to Export as Catalog in the next chapter, starting on page 481.

How do I save my book layout as a template for use on other photos?

Unlike the Slideshow, Print and Web Modules, the Book module doesn't have a concept of presets or templates for the entire book—only individual pages. In most cases, you'll add page templates from your favorites, selecting the best one for the photos. If, however, you do want to reuse an entire book design, it is possible. Go to the Collections panel and right-click on the book that you wish to use as a template. Select *Duplicate Book* from the context-sensitive menu and then, with your new book selected, go to *Edit menu > Select All Photo Cells* and then press Delete (or switch back to Grid mode and delete the photos from that collection). If you added text, go to *Edit menu > Select All Text Cells* to select all the text cells and then press the Delete key on your keyboard. All the photos and text are removed from the new book, leaving you with just the page layout, ready for you to insert other photos.

EXPORTING & PRINTING BOOKS

Having finished designing your perfect book, it's time for everyone else to see it. Your book can be exported as a PDF file, a folder of JPEGs, or uploaded directly to Blurb for printing as a high quality photo book.

Who are Blurb and why are other vendors not available for printing books?

Blurb are a well-known book printing company, who ship to countries all over the world. You can explore their website at http://www.blurb.com

Focusing on one supplier meant that Adobe could create a fully integrated system, complete with the ability to select papers and covers directly from Lightroom, and get the sizing and sharpening just right. Blurb are based in San Francisco, not far from Adobe's headquarters in San Jose, which meant that they could do extensive quality testing. Blurb already has an excellent reputation for creating high quality photo books for photographers worldwide.

Just because Blurb are currently the only integrated service, however, doesn't mean that they're the only company who can print your book. The PDF and JPEG output allows you to send your photo book to any other companies, although these options are a little limited as the page sizes are fixed to Blurb's dimensions.

Can I view a soft proof of my Blurb book?

Blurb provide a CMYK profile which Lightroom can use in the Develop module for soft-proofing. Select the Blurb profile and *Perceptual* rendering intent. Turn back to the Soft Proofing section on page 314 to learn more.

Note that Blurb use a number of different printers/presses and different papers, so ideally you'd have a profile for each combination.

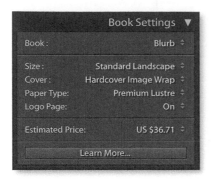

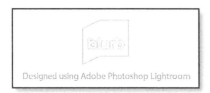

Figure 20.51 In the Book Settings panel, select your Blurb *Size, Cover* and *Paper Type.*

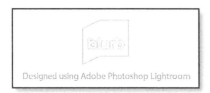

Figure 20.52 The Blurb logo at the end of the book reduces the cost.

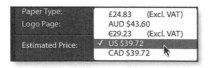

Figure 20.53 The *Estimated Price* displays in the Book Settings panel, and you can change the currency using the pop-up.

Blurb only provide a single generic profile, so the soft-proof preview will be in the right ballpark rather than being completely accurate.

Which cover style and paper should I select?

Using the Book Settings panel, you can select the book size, cover style and paper type for your Blurb book. **(Figure 20.51)**

You can see examples of the different cover styles and paper options by visiting http://www.Lrq.me/blurboptions, but here's a quick summary:

The ***cover*** options are:

- ***Softcover*** has a laminated glossy finish, like many paperback books, and is only available for the Small or Standard sized books.

- ***Hardcover, Dust Jacket*** has a plain black linen cover with a laminated glossy dust jacket and front and back flaps.

- ***Hardcover, Image Wrap*** has a durable matte printed hard cover sealed directly onto the book

There are 5 different grades of ***paper*** available from Blurb through Lightroom:

- ***Standard*** is 120gsm, so it's the thinnest paper, and has a semi-smooth matte finish. It's the budget option.

- ***Premium Lustre*** is 148gsm coated paper with a lustre finish, so it has a slight sheen without being high gloss.

- ***Premium Matte*** is also 148gsm with a matte finish.

- ***ProLine Pearl Photo*** is their heaviest paper, at 190gsm paper. It's similar to Premium Lustre, but has a slightly more glossy finish in addition to the thicker paper.

- ***ProLine Uncoated*** is 148gsm uncoated paper with an eggshell-textured finish.

How do I select quality, color profile, resolution and sharpening for a Blurb book?

If you're exporting a Blurb book, you don't need to worry about the quality, color profile, resolution or sharpening settings, as Adobe have done extensive testing and selected the best output settings for Blurb's presses. Sharpening is set to *Standard Glossy* behind-the-scenes.

What is the *Logo Page*?

When the logo page is enabled, a Blurb logo is added to the final page and the price is discounted. You can remove it by setting the **Logo Page** pop-up to *None*, but the price increases accordingly. **(Figure 20.52)**

How much will my Blurb book cost?

The **Estimated Price** is displayed in the Book Settings panel **(Figure 20.53)**, based on the size of book, number of pages, and cover/page/logo selected. The pop-up displays the price in a number of different currencies. The price shown doesn't include local sales taxes or shipping costs, but those are confirmed before you check out. You can also check Blurb's pricing by visiting their website pricing page at http://www.Lrq.me/blurbprice

How do I send my book to Blurb?

Once you've finished designing your book and you're ready to order, the first thing to do is export the book to PDF as a proof. You may spot a mistake! To do so, press the *Export Book to PDF* button at the bottom of the left panel group. Having confirmed that there aren't any mistakes, you can start the order process.

1. Press the *Send Book to Blurb* button at the bottom of the right panel group.

2. The Purchase Book dialog asks for your Blurb.com login details. If you don't already have an account, click the *Not a Member* link in the bottom left corner to sign up. Otherwise, go ahead and sign in to your account. **(Figure 20.54)**

3. The next dialog asks you to assign a *Title* and *Author* to the book, to help identify it.

4. Lightroom starts rendering the book before uploading. That process may take some time, depending on your computer speed and internet connection. You can watch the progress in the Activity Center.

5. Once the upload is complete, Lightroom opens your default web browser, where you can preview the book (check it again!), edit certain settings, and finalize your order.

How do I save my book as a PDF or JPEGs?

In addition to sending your book to be printed by Blurb, you can output it in a digital form, either as a PDF or a folder of JPEGs.

CHANGING OPTIONS AFTER UPLOAD

If you spot a mistake or change a setting (such as the paper type) after uploading the files to Blurb, you'll need to wait while it uploads the whole book again.

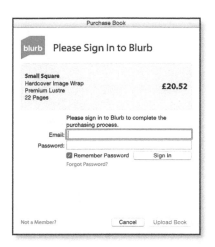

▲ **Figure 20.54** Sign into your Blurb account within Lightroom and enter the book details.

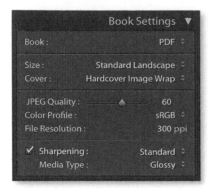

Figure 20.55 If you're saving the book as a PDF instead of sending it to Blurb, you'll need to select the *JPEG Quality, Color Profile, File Resolution* and *Sharpening*.

This allows you to show friends or family on your computer or tablet computer, send them a copy by email or web gallery, or even send the book to an alternative photo book printer.

To do so, change the book type to *PDF* or *JPEG* in the **Book** pop-up in the Book Settings panel, and select your **Quality**, **Color Profile**, **Resolution** and **Sharpening**. (Figure 20.55)

Your chosen settings will depend on whether the PDF is for screen or print use.

- **For screen use**—If you're planning to e-mail the PDF or view the JPEGs solely on a computer screen, you may use a lower quality setting (e.g. 65), sRGB color profile and 72 PPI resolution.

- **For print use**—If the book is going to be printed by another printer, check the settings for that specific company. As a guide, a high-quality setting (e.g. 90), sRGB profile and 200 to 300 PPI resolution are often used for print. Remember, the page sizes use Blurb's measurements, so an 8"x10" book won't create a PDF or JPEGs measuring exactly 8"x10".

Press the *Export Book to PDF* or *Export Book to JPEG* button at the bottom of the right panel group and select a folder to save the finished book.

EBOOKS

The PDF export saves the cover and interior as separate files. If you want to use the PDF as an eBook, ignore the cover pages and design your cover on page 1 of the book. You can then delete the separate cover PDF after export as your cover design is included in the interior file.

PDF VS. BLURB PDF

The main purpose of the Blurb PDF is to give you a proof copy of your book before you send it off, so it's exactly the same file that will be sent to Blurb (although Blurb won't allow you to upload it manually). The Blurb PDF includes the logo page if you have that turned on, and it uses the output settings, such as output sharpening, that are used when sending to Blurb. A standard PDF gives you additional control, such as the resolution and sharpening.

WORKING WITH MULTIPLE COMPUTERS OR CATALOGS

At the beginning of the book, we talked about creating a database called a catalog. The catalog contains records of all the photos you've imported, plus metadata and other settings you've applied to these photos in Lightroom.

First, we'll consider how to look after that catalog, then how to move your Lightroom files, whether that's on the same computer or to a new computer. We'll also explore the options for working on multiple computers, and the pros and cons of using more than one catalog.

Some people ask whether they have to use a catalog. Why not just browse the photos on the hard drive instead? Quite simply, many of Lightroom's features are dependent on its database backbone, and wouldn't be possible using a simple file browser. For example, Lightroom can create virtual copies, store extensive edit history for each image, and track information on settings for books, slideshows, prints and web galleries and their associated photos, all of which depend on the database. Searching image metadata (EXIF, keywords, etc.) is much faster as a result of the database, and Lightroom can also search for photos that are offline, as well as those currently accessible.

MANAGING CATALOGS

Let's start off with some catalog basics—finding, renaming and maintaining your catalog.

ADOBE BRIDGE

If you prefer a file browser instead of a database, consider using Adobe Bridge. It uses the same Adobe Camera Raw processing engine in a different interface. It's available as part of the Adobe Photographer's Bundle subscription, along with Photoshop CC and Lightroom.

SEARCHING FOR CATALOGS

If you can't open Lightroom, perhaps due to catalog corruption, then you'll need to use your operating system's search facility to search for files with a *.lrcat file extension (that's LRCAT).

How do I find my catalog on the hard drive?

When you opened Lightroom the very first time, using the information in the Before You Start section (page 15), Lightroom created a catalog to store the information about your photos.

By default, Lightroom places the catalog in your user account *Pictures* folder and calls it *Lightroom Catalog.lrcat*, but you may have chosen a different name or location.

If you don't remember where you stored your catalog, go to *Edit menu* (Windows) / *Lightroom menu* (Mac) > *Catalog Settings*. The name and location of your open catalog is displayed on the *General* tab of the Catalog Settings dialog. Press the *Show* button to open an Explorer (Windows) / Finder (Mac) window at that location.

What do the catalog files contain?

When you view the catalog location in your file browser, you'll note there are a variety of different Lightroom files. **(Figure 21.2)**

- ***.lrcat** is the catalog (SQLite database) which holds all of your settings. This stands for LightRoom CATalog. (Version 1.0 catalogs used *.lrdb and prerelease beta catalogs were *.aglib files.) **(Figure 21.1)**

The catalog contains a note of where the images are stored on the hard drive plus other metadata—that's information about the photos, including the EXIF data from the camera, any IPTC data, keywords and other metadata you add in Lightroom, any Develop changes you make in Lightroom, and any book, print, slideshow and web gallery settings, all of which are stored as text records.

- ***Previews.lrdata** and ***Smart Previews.lrdata** contain your standard and smart previews. On Windows, the individual previews are contained in a hierarchy of folders and subfolders, and on a Mac, they're wrapped up in a package file. The individual previews inside the lrdata folder/file are *.lrprev files for standard previews, and *.dng files for smart previews.

▼ **Figure 21.1** A Lightroom catalog is a SQLite database.

i...^	id_global	baseName	er...	er...	extension	externalMo...	fol...	idx_filename	importHash	lc...	lc_l...	md5	modTime	originalFilenamı
	12DC791B-7A0... ▼	19950402-132230 ▼			dng ▼	381096665	23	19950402-132230.dng ▼	-181478250:19... ▼	1...▼	dng ▼		381096665	19950402-1322... ▼
46	C0950B7D-505... ▼	19950402-132305 ▼	NUL	NUL	dng ▼	381096665	23	19950402-132305.dng ▼	-181478215:19... ▼	1...▼	dng ▼	NULL	381096665	19950402-1323... ▼
68	EAC9D561-3AE... ▼	19950402-132442 ▼	NUL	NUL	dng ▼	381096665	23	19950402-132442.dng ▼	-181478118:19... ▼	1...▼	dng ▼	NULL	381096665	19950402-1324... ▼
84	602962FD-EF7... ▼	19950402-132548 ▼	NUL	NUL	dng ▼	381096666	23	19950402-132548.dng ▼	-181478052:19... ▼	1...▼	dng ▼	NULL	381096666	19950402-1325... ▼
100	D5FA1D00-6DF... ▼	19950402-132636 ▼	NUL	NUL	dng ▼	381096666	23	19950402-132636.dng ▼	-181478004:19... ▼	1...▼	dng ▼	NULL	381096666	19950402-1326... ▼
126	138B78AF-E49... ▼	19950402-132726 ▼	NUL	NUL	dng ▼	381096666	23	19950402-132726.dng ▼	-181477954:19... ▼	1...▼	dng ▼	NULL	381096666	19950402-1327... ▼
142	66210F90-23E4... ▼	19950402-132800 ▼	NUL	NUL	dng ▼	381096666	23	19950402-132800.dng ▼	-181477920:19... ▼	1...▼	dng ▼	NULL	381096666	19950402-1328... ▼
158	50AF120B-844... ▼	20050801-211058 ▼	NUL	NUL	JPG ▼	381097437	23	20050801-211058.JPG ▼	144623458:200... ▼	2...▼	jpg ▼	NULL	381097437	20050801-2110... ▼
175	6B12EBBB-F1D... ▼	20050801-211127 ▼	NUL	NUL	JPG ▼	381097437	23	20050801-211127.JPG ▼	144623487:200... ▼	2...▼	jpg ▼	NULL	381097437	20050801-2111... ▼
191	9A4D9444-70D... ▼	20050801-211153 ▼	NUL	NUL	JPG ▼	381097437	23	20050801-211153.JPG ▼	144623513:200... ▼	2...▼	jpg ▼	NULL	381097437	20050801-2111... ▼
207	88E6DB99-A0C... ▼	20050801-211214 ▼	NUL	NUL	JPG ▼	381097438	23	20050801-211214.JPG ▼	144623534:200... ▼	2...▼	jpg ▼	NULL	381097438	20050801-2112... ▼
223	4B5A8DB8-687... ▼	20050801-211238 ▼	NUL	NUL	JPG ▼	381097438	23	20050801-211238.JPG ▼	144623558:200... ▼	2...▼	jpg ▼	NULL	381097438	20050801-2112... ▼
239	D96BA0C7-8D... ▼	20050801-211257 ▼	NUL	NUL	JPG ▼	381097438	23	20050801-211257.JPG ▼	144623577:200... ▼	2...▼	jpg ▼	NULL	381097438	20050801-2112... ▼
255	AFFA846D-C42... ▼	20050801-211314 ▼	NUL	NUL	JPG ▼	381097438	23	20050801-211314.JPG ▼	144623594:200... ▼	2...▼	jpg ▼	NULL	381097438	20050801-2113... ▼
271	89147D03-96A... ▼	20050801-211336 ▼	NUL	NUL	JPG ▼	381097438	23	20050801-211336.JPG ▼	144623616:200... ▼	2...▼	jpg ▼	NULL	381097438	20050801-2113... ▼

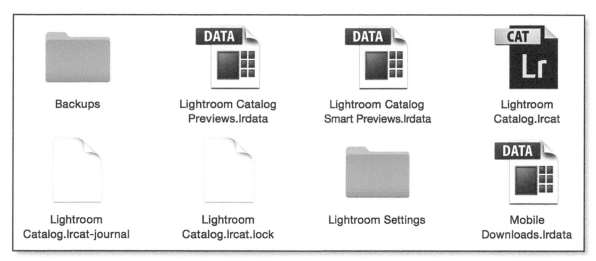

Backups

Lightroom Catalog Previews.lrdata

Lightroom Catalog Smart Previews.lrdata

Lightroom Catalog.lrcat

Lightroom Catalog.lrcat-journal

Lightroom Catalog.lrcat.lock

Lightroom Settings

Mobile Downloads.lrdata

If Lightroom is open, you may have a couple of additional files:

- ***.lrcat.lock** is a lock file that is created whenever you open the catalog. It protects the database from being corrupted by multiple users attempting to use it at the same time. If Lightroom is closed and the lock file remains, you can safely delete it. It can sometimes get left behind if Lightroom crashes, and may prevent you from opening the catalog again.

- ***.lrcat-journal** is a very important file that you never want to delete—it contains blocks of data that are in the middle of being rewritten. When Lightroom opens, it checks for a journal file to update any incomplete records.

- **Additional temporary files** may sometimes appear, such as Temporary Import Data.db-journal. If they're still there after closing Lightroom, and they're more than a few days old, you can safely delete them.

There may also be a few folders created by Lightroom with the catalog:

- **Images folders** may contain some or all of your photos. They're stored on your hard drives as normal image files, so they may be stored anywhere, but the default Destination folder selected in the Import dialog is an Images folder next to the catalog.

- **Backups folder** may contain catalog backups, if you haven't changed the default backup location.

- **Lightroom Settings folder** may contain some of your presets if you have *Store Presets with Catalog* checked in the Preferences dialog.

Figure 21.2 Lightroom uses a few different files and folders, in addition to the main catalog file.

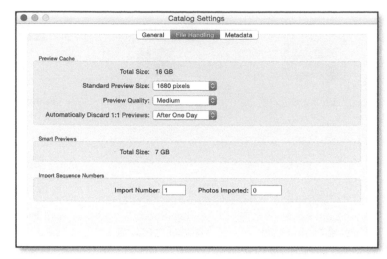

Figure 21.3 In the Catalog Settings dialog, you can check how much space your catalog and previews are using.

How much space does Lightroom's catalog take up on my hard drive?

That's a long list of files, so you may wonder how much space they take up on your hard drive. You can check this using the same Catalog Settings dialog. **(Figure 21.3)**

The catalog file size is listed under the *General* tab. The size depends on the number of photos and the amount of data stored for each photo. For example, local adjustments, spot healing and large numbers of history states increase the catalog size significantly.

Preview and Smart Preview cache sizes are noted under the *File Handling* tab.

Standard Preview size depends on the image content and your preview size and quality settings, as well as the presence of any 1:1 previews. Smart Previews also vary depending on the image content, averaging 0.5-1.5 MB each regardless of the original raw file size.

As a guide, a catalog that contains 25000 photos may be:

Catalog—1 GB (with zipped backups of around 250 MB)

Previews (1680px, medium quality, discard 1:1 after 1 day)—16 GB

Smart Previews—25 GB

Original Files—300 GB

How do I rename my catalog?

Lightroom doesn't offer a catalog renaming tool, but you can rename the catalog in Explorer (Windows) / Finder (Mac) as if you were renaming any other file. Just make sure you close Lightroom first.

When you rename the catalog file, you should also rename the preview folders/files to match. For example:

Lightroom Catalog.lrcat > New Name.lrcat

Lightroom Catalog Previews.lrdata > New Name Previews.lrdata

Lightroom Catalog Smart Previews.lrdata > New Name Smart Previews.lrdata

After renaming, double-click on the catalog file (*.lrcat) to open it into Lightroom.

If you don't rename the previews correctly, Lightroom simply recreates them all. There's no harm done except for the time involved. If you have offline files, previews for these photos won't be recreated until they're next online. If this happens, delete the old previews file to regain the drive space once your previews have been recreated.

Do I need to do any regular maintenance?

We've already discussed how important the catalog is, so how do you look after it? Under the *File menu*, the **Optimize Catalog** command checks through your catalog, reorganizing your database to make it run faster and more smoothly. **(Figure 21.4)**

It's worth running the catalog optimization whenever you've made significant database changes, such as removing or importing a large number of photos, or any time you feel that Lightroom has slowed down. There's also a checkbox in the Back Up Catalog dialog to automatically run the optimization each time you back up your catalog.

And most importantly, don't forget to back up regularly!

VACUUM CATALOG

For the more technically minded, over the course of time, with many imports and deletes, the data can become fragmented and spread across the whole database, making Lightroom jump around to find the information it needs. *Optimize Catalog* runs a SQLite VACUUM command to sort it all back into the correct order, bringing it back up to speed.

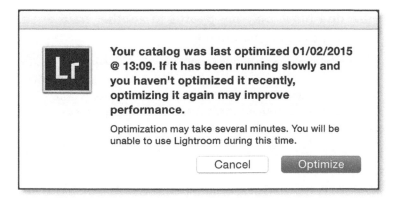

Figure 21.4 Catalog optimization 'tidies up' to make Lightroom run faster.

MOVING LIGHTROOM

The time may come when you run out of space on your hard drive and need to move Lightroom to a new home on a bigger hard drive, or you may need to move to a new computer or reinstall your operating system. Lightroom uses files in so many different locations, the move may look daunting at first, but it's surprisingly straightforward if you follow my step by step instructions carefully.

We'll cover four different scenarios:

- Moving just the catalog to a new location.

- Moving just the photos to a new location.

- Moving the catalog and the photos to a new location.

- Moving to a completely new computer or reinstalling the operating system.

How do I move only my catalog to another hard drive, leaving the photos where they are?

If only your catalog is moving, and the photos are remaining in their existing locations, the process is very simple:

1. Close Lightroom.

2. Move your catalog (and any extra files such as the previews) to the new location using Explorer (Windows) / Finder (Mac). It's usually easiest to move the entire folder containing your catalog and other related files.

3. Double click on the catalog (*.lrcat file) to open it.

As none of the photos moved, you can continue working without further issues. When the backup next runs, double check the location of the backups. (Instructions on page 62.)

How do I move only my photos to another hard drive, leaving the catalog where it is?

If you need to move photos to another hard drive, perhaps because you've outgrown your existing hard drive, there are two main options. As a rule of thumb, you can use option two for moving a few photos/folders, but option one is safer when moving larger numbers of photos.

Option One—move in Explorer/Finder and update Lightroom's links

1. Follow the instructions in the Library chapter (page 122) to show the folder hierarchy. This makes it easy to relink the folders/files that are marked as missing in the process.

2. Close Lightroom and use Explorer (Windows) / Finder (Mac) or file synchronization software to copy the folders/files to the new drive.

3. When the copy completes, rename the original folder (the one on the old hard drive) using Explorer (Windows) / Finder (Mac), or disconnect the old hard drive. This allows you to check everything is working correctly before deleting the files from the original location.

4. Open Lightroom and right-click on the parent folder. Select *Find Missing Folder* or *Update Folder Location* from the list, depending on which option is available. Navigate to the new location and press *Select Folder* (Windows) / *Choose* (Mac). The folder disappears from the old volume (drive) in the Folders panel and reappears under the new volume bar.

5. If you have more than one parent folder, repeat the process for any other parent folders until the question marks have disappeared from all the folders.

6. Once you've confirmed that all the photos are available for editing within Lightroom, you can safely detach the old hard drive or delete the files from their original location using Explorer (Windows) / Finder (Mac).

Option Two—move the photos using Lightroom's Folders panel

1. If you can't see the new folder in the Folders panel, go to *Library menu > New Folder*. Navigate to the new location and create a new folder, or select an existing folder where you plan to place the photos. (Existing folders can only be selected if they're empty, or by importing one of the photos in that folder.)

2. Within the Folders panel, drag the folders to their new location. One warning—don't press the X in the Activity Center to cancel this move. There have been (rare!) reports of problems caused by canceling the transfer, so it's best to let it complete uninterrupted.

3. Check that the entire folder contents have copied correctly before deleting the originals. If you drag individual photos to the new location, rather than whole folders, remember that files that aren't currently in the catalog (e.g. text files) won't be copied as Lightroom doesn't know that they exist.

DATA VERIFICATION

Most file corruption happens while moving/copying photos between hard drives. To ensure that the files gets to the new drive safely, I prefer to use file synchronization or other software with byte-for-byte/checksum verification. Consider using TeraCopy http://www.Lrq.me/teracopy or Vice Versa http://www.Lrq.me/viceversa on Windows or Chronosync http://www.Lrq.me/chronosync on Mac.

DON'T RE-IMPORT

Using these instructions to update the location in the catalog is essential. Don't import the photos at the new location, or use *Synchronize Folder* to update the folder references, as you'll lose all of the work you've done in Lightroom.

How do I archive photos to offline hard drives?

As your collection of photos grows, your working hard drives may eventually start to overflow, but Lightroom can continue to track photos held in offline storage. The easiest solutions for the working copy of your offline archives are external hard drives or NAS units, as they hold large amounts of data. Optical media (DVD/Blu-Ray) can be used, but they have a comparatively short lifespan and limited space.

If you move the photos to offline storage using the instructions in the previous question, the archived photos remain referenced in your main catalog. They are marked as missing when the drive is offline, but you can search through those offline photos along with the rest of your current photos, and Lightroom remembers where the photos are stored.

Ensure you have standard previews before you disconnect the hard drive, so you can still browse with the photos offline. To access the original file, perhaps to export a copy, plug that drive back into the computer and carry on working as normal.

How do I move my complete catalog & photos to another hard drive on the same computer?

If you need to move both the catalog and the photos to a new hard drive, use the same steps as moving each individually (instructions on page 486 and page 486).

There's another option which has been recommended in the past, which involves using Export as Catalog to create a new catalog and duplicate photos on the other hard drive, and then deleting the existing catalog and photos. There are, however, a few risks in using that option, as not all data is included when using Export as Catalog, so I can no longer recommend it.

Export as Catalog is better suited to exporting work temporarily to another computer and then importing back into the main catalog later, rather than moving whole catalogs. We'll come back to Export as Catalog in more detail later in the chapter on page page 507.

How do I move my catalog, photos and other Lightroom files to a new computer?

Moving Lightroom to a new computer can appear daunting at first, especially if you're moving cross-platform, but rest assured, it's straightforward as long as you follow these simple steps.

Note that these instructions are for a one-way move, for example,

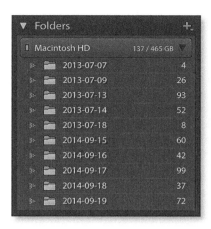

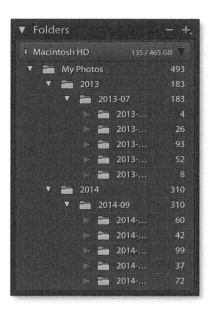

Figure 21.5 A flat folder list (left) is much harder to reconnect compared with a folder hierarchy (right).

moving from an old computer to a new one, or reinstalling the operating system. Working on multiple computers, for example, transferring between a desktop and a laptop, requires a slightly different process that we'll consider in the next section (page 492).

1. **Preparation – set up your folder hierarchy**

   It's a good idea to make sure that Lightroom's Folders panel shows a tidy hierarchy before you back up the catalog. You may need relink the files if the relative folder location, or the drive letter for an external drive, changes as a result of the move. Doing so using a hierarchy (right) is much easier than a flat list of folders (left). **(Figure 21.5)** There are instructions on setting up a folder hierarchy starting on page 121. It's especially important if you're moving to a different operating system.

2. **Check your backups**

   Next, you need to make sure that all the essentials are backed up—the catalogs, photos, preferences, presets, profiles, defaults, plug-ins and any other related files. Turn back to the backup chapter for a full list of all the Lightroom files you need to include in your backups (page 71). If you're wiping the hard drive in the process, rather than running both machines at the same time, it's even more important to make sure that you don't miss anything.

3. **Install Lightroom on the new machine**

   Once everything's safely backed up, we're ready to set Lightroom up on the new computer. Turn back to the installation instructions for more details (page 12).

   It's possible to upgrade Lightroom at the same time as transferring to a new computer, for example, from Lightroom 5 on the old computer to Lightroom CC/6 on the new one. I

XMP FOR SECURITY

For extra security, you can also write many of your settings to XMP, in addition to your catalog backups. To do so, select all the photos in Grid view and press Ctrl-S (Windows) / Cmd-S (Mac). This stores your most crucial settings with the files themselves, which can be useful if you make a mistake, but it doesn't include flags, collections, virtual copy data, stacks and a variety of other information which is only stored in the catalog, so you'll still need to follow the rest of the instructions to transfer your catalog. We discussed XMP in the External Editors chapter on page 343.

would, however, suggest that you do the upgrade and transfer as separate processes to minimize the risk of mistakes.

For example, either install Lightroom CC/6 on the old machine, allow it to upgrade the catalog, check everything's working as expected and then move to the new computer, or install Lightroom 5 on the new computer, follow all of the instructions to move to the new computer and check everything's working, and then install Lightroom CC/6 and allow it to upgrade the catalog.

4. **Transfer the files**

    Transfer the files to the new computer—the catalog, the photos, preferences and so forth—and place them in the same locations as they were on the old computer. Most people copy the files to an external hard drive for the transfer, or copy them over a wired network connection.

5. **Open the catalog on the new computer**

    Now it's time to open the catalog, which you've already transferred. Double-click on the *.lrcat catalog file to open it, or hold down Ctrl (Windows) / Opt (Mac) while launching

CROSS-PLATFORM MOVE

The process of moving your catalog cross-platform is exactly the same as moving to a new machine of the same platform. If you're transferring between platforms, it's even more important that you set Lightroom to show the folder hierarchy (step 1) to make it easy to relink missing files, as Windows works with drive letters and Mac OS X works with drive names.

If you're moving from Windows to Mac or vice versa, some of the file locations are different, especially for preferences and presets. The locations of those files on both platforms are listed in the Backup chapter on page 71.

The Lightroom license is cross-platform and the same license key and program DVD work on both Windows and Mac, although there are separate downloads for the Windows and Mac versions.

There's just one other main thing to look out for if you're moving cross-platform—the Mac OS can read Windows NTFS formatted drives, but can't write to them, and Windows can't read or write to Mac HFS formatted drives. If you're going to use your external drives with a different operating system, you may need to reformat them at some stage, after having copied the data off safely to another drive, of course.

If you're constantly moving between Mac and Windows, consider formatting transfer drives as FAT32, or using additional software such as NTFS for Mac (http://www.Lrq.me/ntfsmac) and HFS for Windows (http://www.Lrq.me/hfswin) that allow either operating system to have read/write access regardless of drive format, but be aware that it may be slower than using a native drive format.

Lightroom to show the Select Catalog dialog and navigate to the catalog.

6. **Relink any missing files**

You might find that there are question marks all over the folders **(Figure 21.6)** or there are rectangular icons containing exclamation marks in the corners of the thumbnails. These warnings appear if the original photos can no longer be found at the previous known location. STOP! Don't be tempted to remove the missing photos and re-import, or try to synchronize a folder, and don't try to relocate individual files by clicking on a thumbnail icon, as you'll create a bigger job.

Instead, right-click on the parent folder that we created in step 1, and choose *Find Missing Folder* from the context-sensitive menu, and navigate to the new location of that folder. Relocate any other top level folders (you should have one for each drive), until all the photos are online. There are more details on reconnecting missing files starting on page 525. If you get stuck at this stage, please ask and I'll be pleased to help.

7. **Check your preferences and presets**

Double check that all of your presets and templates appear correctly, for example, all of your Develop presets are available in the Develop module, to confirm that you copied all the files correctly.

8. **Reload any disabled plug-ins**

Finally, you might find your plug-ins need reloading as the locations may have changed in the move. Go to *File menu > Plug-in Manager* and check whether all the plug-ins have green circles. **(Figure 21.7)** If any plug-ins are incorrectly loaded or missing, add them again at their new locations. Turn back to the Before You Start chapter for a refresher (page 19).

That's it! It's as simple as that. The main things to remember are to transfer all the applicable files onto the new computer, don't try importing anything, don't use Synchronize Folder, and ideally don't wipe the old machine until you've checked that everything's up and running.

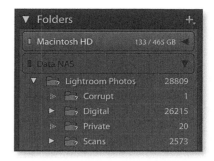

▲ **Figure 21.6** The hard drive or photos may be marked as missing.

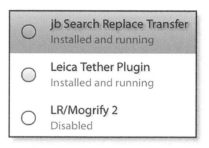

▲ **Figure 21.7** Plug-ins are marked with a green circle if they're enabled. Yellow, red or gray circles warn of problems with the plug-in.

LICENSING INFORMATION

You can have Lightroom activated on two computers at a time, for example, your desktop and your laptop. It can be installed on additional machines, but you would need to deactivate and reactivate when switching machines.

WORKING WITH MULTIPLE MACHINES

Many photographers today are working between multiple computers, for example, a laptop and a desktop.

Lightroom doesn't have network or multi-user capabilities, other than accessing photos that are stored on a network drive. The SQLite database format that Lightroom uses isn't well suited to being accessed across a network; the file would be too easily corrupted beyond repair by something as simple as the network connection dropping at the wrong moment. That's not just an oversight—SQLite was chosen for its other benefits, such as the simplicity for the user, cost, and most importantly, speed of access.

There are solutions, however. For example, Lightroom allows you to split and merge catalogs to move parts of catalogs easily between computers, and Lightroom can work with offline photos on the road too.

If you need to work on multiple machines or even with multiple users, there are many different options. We're going on concentrate on five primary options, each with their own variations. Whichever option you choose, you'll need to install the Lightroom software on each computer, as that's not portable. Later in the section, on page 514, we'll also look at ways of keeping your presets up to date on each computer.

CATALOG ON NAS

There are some 'solutions' posted on the web, suggesting that it's possible to trick Lightroom's network blocking by using a subst command on Windows or mounting a disc image stored on a network drive on a Mac. Take care! The network blocking is there for good reason. SQLite, which is the database used for Lightroom's catalog, depends on a guarantee from the operating system that what it thinks has been written to disk has actually been written to disk. Network volumes are notorious for lying about that to improve perceived performance. Adobe strongly discourages these workarounds because they can corrupt your catalog beyond repair, so I can't recommend it either. It's a risky hack.

You could, of course, store your catalog on a NAS and copy it to a local drive every time you want to work on it, and then copy it back again. The process can be automated using File Synchronization software, but it's still a lot of data to constantly move around the network. Alternatively, using software like Dropbox to keep the same catalog on multiple machines can work well, and although it's not supported by Adobe, it doesn't attempt to circumvent any of Lightroom's features, so the risks are limited.

The photos can be on your NAS or other network drive, but if you're putting the photos on your NAS, be aware that NAS file access can be slower than internal or even external drives, depending on the connection speed, so this may slow Lightroom down too.

The first three options give you access to your entire catalog on each machine, with or without the image files.

- **Self-Contained**—place your catalog and photos on an external hard drive, and plug it into whichever machine you're going to use at the time.

- **Semi-Portable**—place your catalog and previews on an external drive and plug it into whichever machine you're going to use at the time, but the photos remain on the main computer or on network accessible storage.

- **Copy/Sync (e.g. Dropbox)**—copy your catalog back and forth, using synchronization software such as Dropbox to keep both copies updated.

The final two options involve splitting and merging catalogs, so they're a little more complicated.

- **Import from a Temporary Catalog**—create a new catalog for the photos on the secondary machine and merge them back into the primary machine.

- **Split and Merge**—use one computer as a base (usually the desktop) and export chunks of work out as a smaller catalog out for use on the secondary computer (usually the laptop), then merge it back into the primary catalog on your return.

Self-Contained Catalog

Summary: The simplest solution is to place the entire catalog and all of your photos on a portable external hard drive, which you can then plug into whichever computer you want to use at the time.

For whom: You regularly work on different computers and your entire collection of photos is small enough to fit on a portable hard drive.

Difficulty Rating: 1/4

Pros:

- Your entire catalog is available.

- As the original photos are on the same drive, Lightroom's functionality is not limited.

Cons:

- External hard drive speeds are usually slower than internal drives, so you'd want to choose a fast connection such as a Thunderbolt, eSATA or USB 3.0 connection if possible.

MULTI-USER LIGHTROOM

Lightroom isn't designed for multi-user workflows, but some solutions are available. They include:

- Split and Merge workflow on page 502.

- Write the second user's settings to XMP and read them back into the main catalog (learn about XMP on page 343).

- Use Lightroom mobile to apply star ratings or flags on a mobile device such as a tablet.

- Slightly greater risk of corruption when the catalog is stored on an external drive, as they're more likely to become disconnected while you're working.

- Small external drives are at a higher risk of being lost, stolen, or dropped.

Storage—Catalog: Portable drive.

Storage—Photos: Portable drive.

Storage—Presets: Store Presets with Catalog or Dropbox Sync.

Other Considerations:

- Think about your backup strategy, as your portable drive may be excluded from your normal backups.

- If you work on multiple platforms, you may need to relink the files each time you switch computers, as Windows uses drive letters whereas Mac OS X uses drive names.

Setup Instructions:

1. Turn back to page 486 and follow the instructions for moving the photos to another drive.

2. Turn back to page 486 and follow the instructions for moving the catalog to another drive.

3. Turn to page 514 and follow the instructions for sharing your presets with both computers.

Switch Instructions:

1. Quit Lightroom on Computer A.

2. Safely disconnect the portable hard drive.

3. Plug portable the hard drive into Computer B.

4. Open Lightroom on Computer B. If the photos are marked as missing, perhaps because the drive letter has changed or you're moving cross-platform, turn to page 525 to fix the broken links.

Semi-Portable Catalog

Summary: Place the entire catalog on a portable external hard drive, which you can then plug into whichever computer you want to use at the time. Store most photos on one computer or network storage. Your current photos may fit on the portable drive with the catalog.

For whom: You regularly work on different computers but your entire collection of photos is too large to fit on an external drive.

Difficulty Rating: 2/4

Pros:

- Your entire catalog is available.

Cons:

- Access to the original files varies, depending on where they're stored.

- External hard drive speeds are usually slower than internal drives, so you'd want to choose a fast connection such as a Thunderbolt, eSATA or USB 3.0 connection if possible.

- Slightly greater risk of corruption when the catalog is stored on an external drive, as they're more likely to become disconnected while you're working.

- Small external drives are at a higher risk of being lost, stolen, or dropped.

Storage—Catalog: Portable drive.

Storage—Photos:

- Store photos on network storage (i.e. NAS) or shared drive. This allows you to access the photos from any computer on the network, but the data transfer rate may be slower.

- Store photos on main computer (internal/external drives). This has the benefit of faster data transfer on the main machine, with more limited edits from other computers.

- A mixture—store specific photos on the portable drive with the catalog (e.g. the ones you're currently working on), and store the rest on the main computer or NAS. This gives access to specific files from any computer, even when you're offline, with more limited access to the rest.

Variations:

When the original files are offline (e.g. you're not connected to

▼ **Figure 21.8** If you're using a Semi-Portable Catalog, the available Lightroom features depend on which previews or files you have available at the time.

Options	with standard previews	with 1:1 previews	with smart previews	with selected originals
Add new photos	Yes (move later)	Yes (move later)	Yes (move later)	Yes (move later)
View & search	Yes	Yes	Yes	Yes
View 1:1 (e.g. check focus)	No	Yes (if 1:1)	No	Yes (if original)
Edit in Develop	No	No	Yes (if smart)	Yes (if original)
Edit in PS	No	No	No	Yes (if original)
Rename/Delete Files	No	No	No	Yes (if original)
Export	No	No	Yes (up to 2560px)	Yes (if original)

the network storage), you can still work on those photos using Lightroom's previews. The kind of work you can do depends on the type of previews. **Figure 21.8** summarizes the main limitations. For the full list, turn to page 508.

Storage—Presets: Store Presets with Catalog or Dropbox Sync.

Other Considerations:

- Think about your backup strategy, as your portable drive may be excluded from your normal backups.

- If you work on multiple platforms, you may need to relink the files each time you switch computers, as Windows uses drive letters whereas Mac OS X uses drive names.

Setup Instructions:

5. Turn back to page 486 and follow the instructions for moving the catalog to another drive.

6. Turn to page 514 and follow the instructions for sharing your presets with both computers.

Switch Instructions:

1. Quit Lightroom on Computer A.

2. Safely disconnect the portable hard drive.

3. Plug the portable hard drive into Computer B.

4. Open Lightroom on Computer B.

5. (Optional) If the photos are available on network storage, but marked as missing, turn to page 525 to fix the broken links.

Portable Originals:

If you want to transfer some originals to your portable drive, or you shoot some new photos while you're away from your main storage and need to transfer them into your primary archives, turn back to page 127 and follow the instructions for safely moving those photos between hard drives.

Copy/Sync (e.g. Dropbox)

Summary: The catalog, the previews, smart previews and even the photos themselves can be automatically copied to multiple computers using Dropbox, or file synchronization software such as Vice Versa (Windows) / Chronosync (Mac). You can also copy the files manually, but that introduces more room for user error.

For whom: You regularly work on different computers but you don't like the idea of a portable hard drive.

Difficulty Rating: 3/4

Pros:

- Your entire catalog is available.

- The catalog is stored on internal hard drives, so it's not limited by portable hard drive speeds.

- There's no portable hard drive to drop or lose.

Cons:

- Access to the original files varies, depending on where they're stored.

- You have to be very careful to avoid creating conflicts when switching computers.

- Using Dropbox uses significant bandwidth as the previews are updated when you make Develop changes. File synchronization software uses the local network, but requires a little more tracking.

- Sync services such as Dropbox are not officially supported by Adobe. (I've used Dropbox for my own personal catalog for years, but I haven't tested other sync services.)

Storage—Catalog: Copied to both computers using Dropbox/file sync software.

Storage—Photos:

- Store photos on network storage (i.e. NAS) or shared drive. This allows you to access the photos from any computer on the network, but the data transfer rate may be slower.

- Store photos on portable drive. This allows you to access the photos from any computer, but only if the portable drive is plugged in.

- Store photos on main computer (internal/external drives). This has the benefit of faster data transfer on the main machine, with more limited edits from other computers.

- Sync photos to both computers (e.g. using Dropbox or file sync software). This allows you to access the photos from any computer, but may use lots of bandwidth and storage space.

- A mixture—sync specific photos to both computers (e.g. the ones you're currently working on, using Dropbox or file sync software), and store the rest on the main computer or NAS. This gives access to specific files from any computer, with more limited access to the rest.

Variations:

When the original files are offline (e.g. you're not connected to the network storage), you can still work on those photos using Lightroom's previews. The kind of work you can do depends on the type of previews. **Figure 21.9** summarizes the main limitations. For the full list, turn to page 508.

Storage—Presets: Store Presets with Catalog or Dropbox Sync.

Other Considerations:

- Make sure that the catalog isn't changed on both computers at once, as one of the catalogs would become a 'conflicted copy' in Dropbox. You must allow time for the catalog to be completely uploaded and downloaded before you open it on the other computer.

- There's more potential for things to go wrong when using File Sync software/services, whether due to bugs or user error, so make more frequent catalog backups (ideally every time you quit Lightroom).

- If you have performance problems with Dropbox running at the same time as Lightroom, pause Dropbox sync while you're working in Lightroom. If you don't, Dropbox runs constantly, trying to stay up to date with all the preview changes.

Setup Instructions:

1. Turn back to page 486 and follow the instructions for moving the catalog. Move it to your Dropbox folder (or other sync folder).

2. Turn to page 514 and follow the instructions for sharing your presets with both computers.

▼ **Figure 21.9** If you're copying your catalog back and forth, the available Lightroom features depend on which previews or files you have available at the time.

Options	with previews	with 1:1 previews	with smart previews	with some/all originals
Add new photos	Yes (move later)	Yes (move later)	Yes (move later)	Yes (move later)
View & search	Yes	Yes	Yes	Yes
View 1:1 (e.g. check focus)	No	Yes	No	Yes (if original)
Edit in Develop	No	No	Yes (if smart)	Yes (if original)
Edit in PS	No	No	No	Yes (if original)
Rename/Delete Files	No	No	No	Yes (if original)
Export	No	No	Yes (up to 2560px)	Yes (if original)

Switch Instructions:

1. Quit Lightroom on Computer A.

2. Wait for the sync to complete on Computer A and Computer B. This is VERY important.

3. Open Lightroom on Computer B.

4. (Optional) If the photos are marked as missing, turn to page 525 to fix the broken links.

Import from a Temporary Catalog

Summary: Create a new catalog for the shoot on the secondary machine (or a portable hard drive) and later merge it into the main catalog on the primary machine. **(Figure 21.10)**

For whom: You want to keep your new shoot separate (e.g. a location shoot or vacation photos) until you're ready to transfer it back to your main computer. You don't need access to your existing photos on the secondary machine.

Difficulty Rating: 3/4

Pros:

- It's relatively simple, especially if it's a one-off.

Cons:

- No access to existing photos.

- Keyword list isn't available in the new catalog, so you may end up with duplicates or different spellings.

- Face recognition data isn't available in the new catalog.

- Publish Services (e.g. Facebook, Flickr) and Lightroom mobile sync information isn't transferred between catalogs.

Storage—Catalog: Main catalog on main computer, new catalog on secondary computer.

Storage—Photos: Main photos on main computer, external hard drive or NAS. New photos on secondary computer or portable hard drive.

Storage—Presets: Leave on main machine or Dropbox Sync.

Other Considerations:

- Think about your backup strategy, as your secondary computer or portable drive may be excluded from your normal backups.

Workflow—Import from a Temporary Catalog

Figure 21.10 If you create a temporary catalog while travelling, you can merge it into your main catalog when you return.

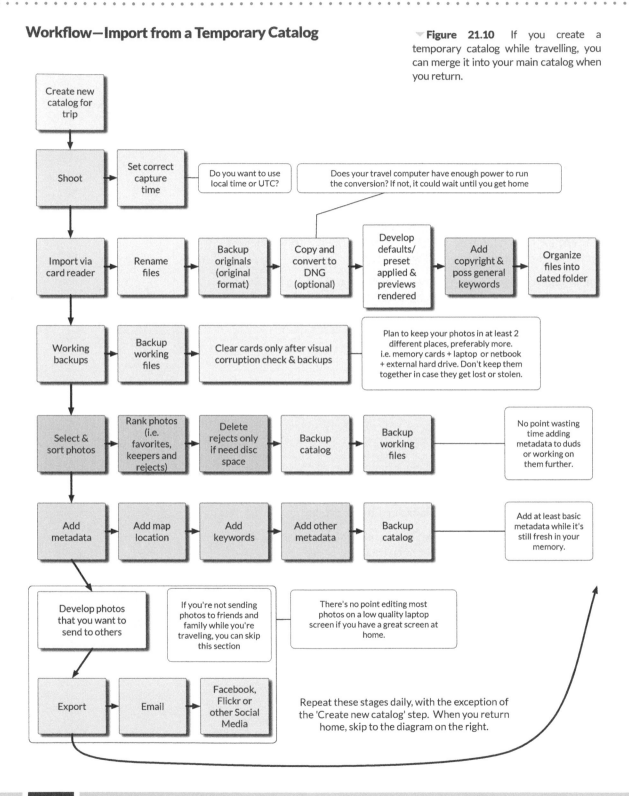

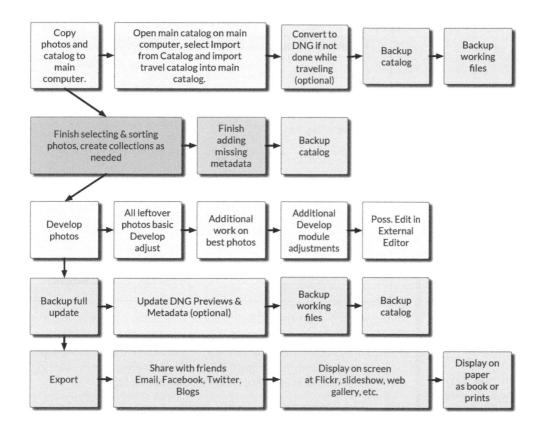

Setup Instructions:

1. On the secondary computer, go to *File menu > New Catalog* and create a catalog.

2. Import your photos as normal.

Switch Instructions:

1. Upon your return, copy the catalog and photos to the main computer, or transfer the portable hard drive.

2. Double-click on the temporary catalog to open it, then relink any files that are marked as missing, using the instructions on page 525.

3. Open the main catalog (*File menu > Open Recent*) and select *File menu > Import from Another Catalog.*

4. Navigate to the folder containing the temporary catalog, select the lrcat file and press *Choose*.

Figure 21.11 Use *Import from Another Catalog* to merge the travel catalog into your main catalog.

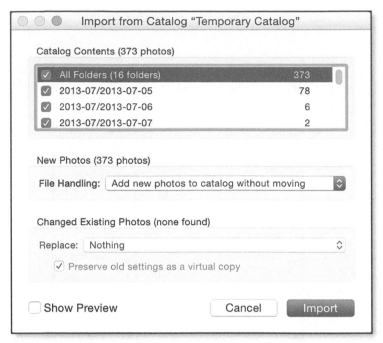

WRITE TO XMP

If your editing has been limited to ratings or other data stored in XMP, you might write the settings to XMP, copy just the photos to the main computer, and import the photos as usual, instead of using Import from Catalog. Learn the pros and cons of XMP starting on page 343.

5. In the Import from Catalog dialog, check the folders at the top. In the *File Handling* pop-up, decide whether to *Add new photos to catalog without moving* or *Copy new photos to a new location and import* as shown in **Figure 21.11**. Since this was a new catalog, the *Changed Existing Photos* section is unavailable.

6. Click *Import*.

7. When you're happy that everything's transferred correctly and backed up, delete the temporary catalog and photos from the secondary computer or portable drive.

Split and Merge

Summary: Use one computer as a base (your main workstation, often a desktop) and export chunks of work out as a smaller catalog out for use on the secondary computer, then merge it back into the primary catalog on your return. **(Figure 21.13)**

For whom: Someone else needs to work on some of the photos while you're working in the main catalog.

Difficulty Rating: 4/4

Pros:

- Multiple people can work on the photos.

- The photos are still primarily stored in a single searchable catalog.

Cons:

- You must keep track of who is working on each chunk of photos, as the latest edits win when merging catalogs.

- It can quickly become complicated if you're not careful.

- The exported catalog only has access to the selected photos.

- Face recognition data isn't available in the new catalog.

- Publish Services (e.g. Facebook, Flickr) and Lightroom mobile sync information isn't transferred between catalogs.

Storage—Catalog: Main catalog on main computer, exported chunks on other computers or portable drive.

Storage—Photos: Main photos on main computer, external hard drive or NAS. Selected photos on secondary computer or portable hard drive.

Variations:

When the original files are offline (e.g. you're not connected to the network storage), you can still work on the photos using Lightroom's previews. The kind of work you can do depends on the type of previews. **Figure 21.12** summarizes the main limitations. For the full list, turn to page 508.

Storage—Presets: None or Dropbox Sync.

Other Considerations:

- Think about how you'll track which photos you've exported, for example, add them to a special collection or apply a color label to remind you not to edit the photos in the main catalog while the exported catalog is 'checked out'.

▼ **Figure 21.12** If you're using *Export as Catalog* to take part of your catalog offsite, the available Lightroom features depend on which previews or files you include when creating the exported catalog.

Options	with selected previews	with selected 1:1 previews	with selected smart previews	with selected originals
Add new photos	Yes (move later)	Yes (move later)	Yes (move later)	Yes (move later)
View & search	Yes (only selected photos)	Yes (only selected photos)	Yes (only selected photos)	Yes (only selected photos)
View 1:1 (e.g. check focus)	No	Yes (if 1:1)	No	Yes (if original)
Edit in Develop	No	No	Yes (if smart)	Yes (if original)
Edit in PS	No	No	No	Yes (if original)
Rename/Delete Files	No	No	No	Yes (if original)
Export	No	No	Yes (up to 2560px)	Yes (if original)

Workflow—Split & Merge

▼ **Figure 21.13** Use *Export as Catalog* and *Import from Another Catalog* to take part of your catalog offsite.

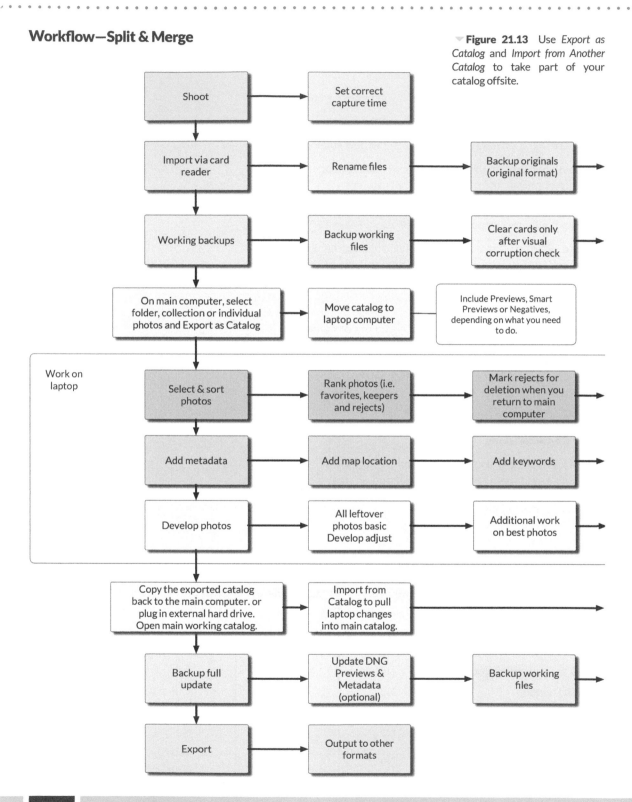

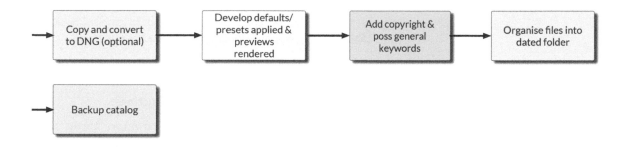

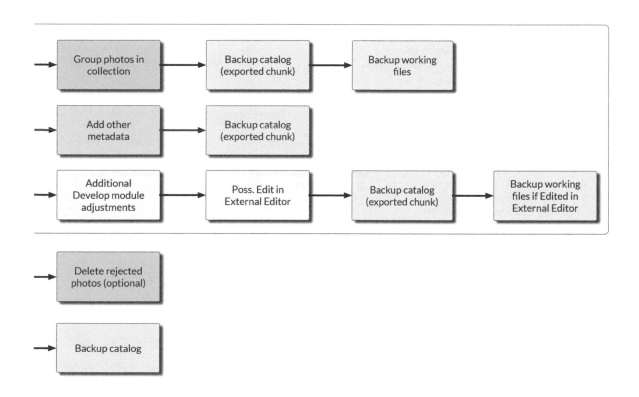

Setup Instructions:

1. In the main catalog, select the photos, folder or collections that you want to transfer.

2. Go to *File menu > Export as Catalog* and navigate to a location for the exported catalog (e.g. a portable hard drive). **(Figure 21.14)**

3. Depending on the kind of work you need to do, include only the previews and either the smart previews or originals. Check the table above to work out which you checkboxes you need.

4. On the secondary computer, double-click to open the exported catalog, and work as normal.

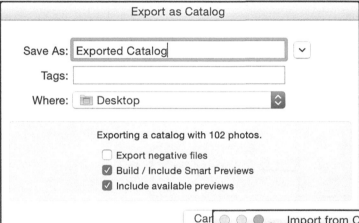

Switch Instructions:

1. When you return to the main computer, connect the portable hard drive or copy the catalog and any new/edited originals from the secondary computer (you don't need to copy the originals if you haven't changed them).

2. Select *File menu > Import from Another Catalog*. **(Figure 21.15)**

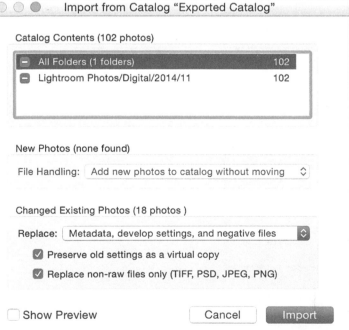

◂ **Figure 21.14** Use *Export as Catalog* to take a chunk of your catalog to another machine (or send it to another person). The checkbox settings depend on what you need to do with the files. See **Figure 21.12** to help you choose the right options.

▹ **Figure 21.15** Use *Import from Another Catalog* to merge the exported catalog back into your main catalog.

3. Navigate to the folder containing the exported catalog, select the lrcat file and press *Choose*.

4. As the photos are already in your main working catalog, the Import from Catalog dialog asks how to handle the new settings.

    In the *Changed Existing Photos* section, select *Metadata, develop settings and negative files* from the pop-up and check the *Replace non-raw files only (TIFF, PSD, JPEG, PNG)* checkbox below. (For more detail on the available options, turn to page 511.)

    If you've accidentally edited the photos in both catalogs, check the *Preserve old settings as a virtual copy* checkbox. To overwrite the main catalog with the settings from the exported catalog, leave it unchecked.

    Check the *All Folders* checkbox at the top of the dialog. If you've only edited some of the files, it displays a line instead of a checkmark.

5. Click *Import*.

6. When you're happy that everything's transferred correctly and backed up, delete the temporary catalog and photos from the secondary computer or portable drive.

How does Export as Catalog work?

We've used Export as Catalog and Import from Catalog in the last couple of multi-computer examples, but let's take a closer look at the options so you can apply it in a wider range of situations.

Export as Catalog allows you to take a subset of your catalog—perhaps a folder or collection—and create another catalog from these photos, complete with your metadata, the previews and smart previews, and the original files too if you wish. You can then take this catalog to another computer, and merge it back in to your main catalog later.

1. Decide which photos you want to include in the export. You can export any selected photos using *File menu > Export as Catalog*, or right-click on a folder or collection and select *Export Folder/ Collection as Catalog*.

2. Navigate to a folder that will hold your newly exported catalog, such as a portable hard drive. **(Figure 21.16)**

3. Decide which previews or files to include:

    • ***Include available previews*** exports the previews that have already been rendered. This is important if you're exporting a catalog subset to take to another computer and you won't be taking the original files with you, otherwise you'll just have a catalog full of gray thumbnails.

- **Build/Include Smart Previews** exports the smart previews, or builds them if they don't already exist. This allows you to edit your photos in the Develop module without the negative files (full size original images).

- **Export negative files** copies the original photos along with the catalog, you edit the photos in Photoshop or export full resolution photos.

The resulting catalog is a normal catalog, just like any other. If you've chosen to *Export negative files*, there are also one or more subfolders containing copies of your original files, in folders reflecting their original folder structure.

You can transfer this catalog to any computer with Lightroom CC/6 installed, and either double-click on it, hold down Ctrl (Windows) / Opt (Mac) on starting Lightroom, or use the *File menu > Open Catalog* command to open it.

Having finished working on that catalog, you can later use Import from Catalog to merge it back into your main catalog again. First, though, let's look at the limitations resulting for each checkbox setting in more detail.

What are the limitations of offline files, with standard or smart previews?

When the original files are offline, perhaps because you're working on another machine or the drive containing your original photos is disconnected, you'll still be able to do some work in Lightroom.

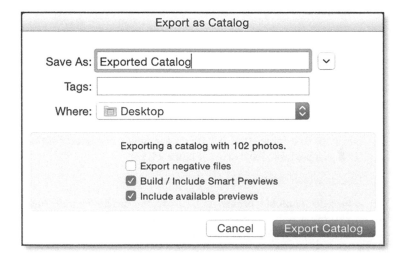

▶ **Figure 21.16** *Export as Catalog* allows you to take part of your catalog to another computer.

As long as you have standard-sized previews, you'll still be able to do Library tasks—labeling, rating, keywording, creating collections, etc. You can also view slideshows, design books, and export web galleries. If you've built 1:1 size previews, you'll also be able to zoom in to check focus in the Library Loupe view.

With Smart Previews, you can go one stage further—editing in the Develop module, and exporting medium resolution photos.

The Smart Previews have been designed to behave as much like the originals as possible, so Develop adjustments applied to the smart previews should look almost identical when applied to the original files. Noise reduction and sharpening know the size of the smart preview compared to the size of the original and scale the settings appropriately behind the scenes. You may choose to fine tune them later, but this won't be necessary in most cases.

The Smart Previews are only up to 2560px along the long edge, so if you zoom into 1:1 view when the originals are offline, it won't truly be a 1:1 view. (There's one exception—if you've created 1:1 standard previews and you have made any Develop changes, the Library Loupe 1:1 view is true 1:1.) They average around 1 MB each.

Of course with the originals offline, you can't do anything that requires the original files—moving files between folders, renaming, writing to XMP, deleting files, creating HDR or panoramic photos, editing the photos in Photoshop, and other similar tasks—until the original files are available again. **(Figure 21.17)**

	Standard Previews	Smart Previews	Original Files
Import			
Import from Catalog			✓
File Management			
Move			✓
Rename			✓
Remove from Catalog	✓	✓	✓
Delete from Hard Drive			✓
Metadata			
Add Stars, Labels, Flags	✓	✓	✓
Add Keywords	✓	✓	✓
Create Faces Index		✓	✓
Add Names to Faces	✓	✓	✓
Add Map Locations	✓	✓	✓

SMART PREVIEW ARTIFACTS

There are exceptional cases where you might see a difference between the Smart Previews and the original files. For example, if you make extreme adjustments, it may be possible to see artifacts in the smart previews, caused by the 8-bit lossy compression. The artifacts disappear when you reconnect the original raw files.

◀ **Figure 21.17** A quick summary of which previews you can use for each task

	Standard Previews	Smart Previews	Original Files
Add other Metadata	✓	✓	✓
Create Virtual Copies	✓	✓	✓
Work with Videos			✓
Create & Edit Collections	✓	✓	✓
Previews			
Build Standard Sized Previews		✓	✓
Build 1:1 Sized Previews			✓
Build Smart Previews			✓
Export as Catalog			
Export as Catalog with Standard Previews	✓	✓	✓
Export as Catalog with Smart Previews		✓	✓
Export as Catalog with Originals			✓
Import from Catalog with Standard Previews	✓	✓	✓
Import from Catalog with Smart Previews		✓	✓
Import from Catalog with Originals			✓
Develop			
Global Develop Adjustments		✓	✓
Local Develop Adjustments		✓	✓
Merge to Panorama			✓
Merge to HDR			✓
Soft-proof photos		✓	✓
Export			
Export best quality full resolution photos			✓
Export to any size photos		(larger than 2560px will be upsampled)	✓
Email photos		✓	✓
Publish Services			
Publish photos (as Export)		✓	✓
Book			
Design Book	✓	✓	✓
Export Book to PDF			✓
Export Book to JPEG			✓

	Standard Previews	Smart Previews	Original Files
Export Book to Blurb			✓
Slideshow			
Design Slideshow	✓	✓	✓
Preview Slideshow	✓	✓	✓
Play Slideshow on Computer	✓	✓	✓
Export Slideshow to PDF			✓
Export Slideshow to JPEG			✓
Export Slideshow to Video	✓	✓	✓
Print			
Set up Print	✓	✓	✓
Print to JPEG			✓
Print to Printer			✓
Web			
Design Web Gallery	✓	✓	✓
Export Web Gallery to Hard Drive	✓	✓	✓
Export Web Gallery to FTP	✓	✓	✓

How does Import from Catalog work?

Having finished working on the exported catalog, you can later use Import from Catalog to merge it back into your main catalog again. It can also be used to merge multiple catalogs into a single catalog, or transfer photos between catalogs without losing all the work you've done.

1. Open the target catalog that you want to merge into. If you're importing an exported catalog, you'll need to open your main catalog. If you're merging multiple catalogs into a single one, you might want to start with a new catalog.

2. Select *File menu > Import from Another Catalog*, and navigate to the source catalog, from which you want to pull the metadata.

3. Lightroom reads the source catalog and checks it against the target catalog, resulting in the Import from Catalog dialog. **(Figure 21.18)**

Depending on the choices you make, new photos are imported into the target catalog and existing photos are updated. The main options are:

- The **Catalog Contents** section lists all of the folders in the source catalog, and allows you to check the folders that you want to include in the import. It's particularly useful when you want to import selected folders.

- The **Show Preview** checkbox displays a thumbnail area to the right. Each thumbnail has a checkbox, allowing you to include or exclude specific photos. If you click on a folder in the *Catalog Contents* section, the thumbnail preview area updates to show only the photos in the selected folder. Dimmed photos are unavailable for import as they already exist in the target catalog with the same settings.

- **New Photos** controls how new photos are handled. These are photos that don't exist in the target catalog in a matching folder hierarchy.

  - **File Handling** offers a choice of *Add new photos to catalog without moving, Copy new photos to a new location and import* or *Don't import new photos.*

- **Changed Existing Photos** controls how photos that already exist in the target catalog are handled. Photos that are identical in both catalogs are skipped, as you won't need to update these.

  - The **Replace** pop-up offers a choice of *Metadata and develop settings only, Metadata, develop settings and negative files*

▼ **Figure 21.18** *Import from Catalog* allows you to merge catalogs together. You can select specific folders or photos to copy into the target catalog.

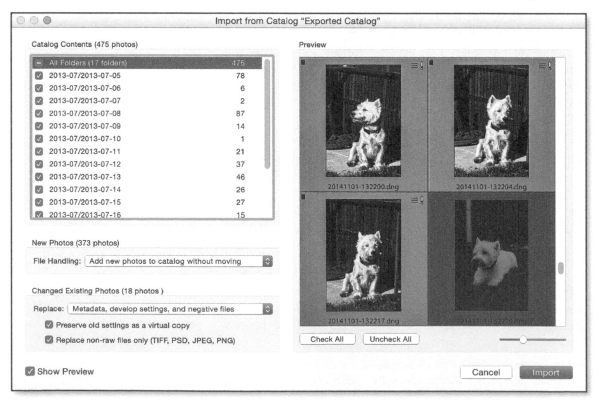

or *Nothing* from the pop-up. Unless you've edited the files themselves in another program, for example, retouching in Photoshop, then you can usually just copy the metadata and settings.

- If you select *Metadata, develop settings and negative files*, the **Replace non-raw files only (TIFF, PSD, JPEG, PNG)** checkbox becomes available. This saves time by only replacing files that may have been edited, for example, photos edited in Photoshop. Unless you've worked on the files themselves in another program, for example, retouching in Photoshop, then you can usually just copy the settings.

- **Preserve old settings as a virtual copy** is useful if you've accidentally edited the photos in both catalogs. It creates a virtual copy of the target catalog's settings and imports the source catalog's settings as the master photo. Once the import completes, you can check through the photos and determine which version to keep.

Are there any limitations when importing and exporting catalogs?

I should give one word of warning about the catalog import/export process: some data is excluded. This includes:

- **Extra Files**—Any files that are stored in the selected folders but aren't referenced in Lightroom's catalog, such as text documents, are not included in the exported catalog/folder.

- **Keywords**—Your keyword list in the exported catalog only includes keywords that have been applied to the selected photos. You can work around this by using *Metadata menu > Export Keywords* in the main catalog, and *Metadata menu > Import Keywords* in the exported catalog to add your full keyword list.

- **Publish Services**—Publish Services settings and collections are tied directly to their original catalog and are not transferred by Export as Catalog.

- **Lightroom mobile**—Lightroom mobile only syncs with a single catalog, and switching catalogs involves wiping all of the cloud data and re-uploading.

- **Plug-ins**—Some plug-ins store data in undefined areas of the catalog, which may not be transferred by Export as Catalog.

As with many things, it's simply a case of weighing the pros and cons.

It's also worth noting that Import from Catalog merges complete photo records, so if you've changed a photo's star rating in the source

---

IMPORTING OLDER CATALOGS

If you select an older catalog in the Import from Catalog dialog, Lightroom automatically upgrades the catalog before importing. You can save the upgraded catalog, as if you had opened the catalog normally and run the upgrade, or discard the upgraded catalog. Either way, the original catalog is left untouched.

LRVOYAGER

Although Publish Services data is excluded when using Import/Export Catalogs, it's possible to work around this limitation using the LRVoyager plug-in. http://www.Lrq.me/alloy-lrvoyager

catalog and Develop settings in the target catalog, the source catalog overwrites the target catalog. You can choose to create virtual copies, retaining both sets of settings at the expense of additional clutter in your catalog.

Can I share my catalog with multiple users on the same machine?

We've discussed using Lightroom on multiple computers, but what happens if you have multiple user accounts on the same computer and you want to share the same photos? All of the same options apply. Only one user can have the catalog open at a time, so if both users are logged in to the computer at the same time using Fast User Switching, the previous user needs to close Lightroom before the next user can open it.

How can I use my presets on both computers?

Your presets, by default, aren't stored with the catalog, but you can transfer them manually so that they appear on each machine.

If you only have a single catalog that you use on multiple machines, perhaps on an external hard drive, there's a **Store presets with this catalog** option in *Preferences > Presets tab.* **(Figure 21.19)** This option allows you to store the presets alongside the catalog itself, for use with that specific catalog on any machine. It does, however, mean that the presets are not available to other catalogs on either computer.

In most situations, it causes more confusion than it solves, so I'd recommend leaving it unchecked unless you have a specific reason for using it.

It's also worth noting that some settings are always stored in the global location, regardless of the *Store presets with this catalog* checkbox state. They include default Develop settings, custom point curves, lens and camera profiles, and email settings, which are always tied to that single machine.

▼ **Figure 21.19** If you work with a single catalog and use it on multiple computers, perhaps on an external drive or synced via Dropbox, consider checking *Store presets with this catalog*. Otherwise, it's best left unchecked.

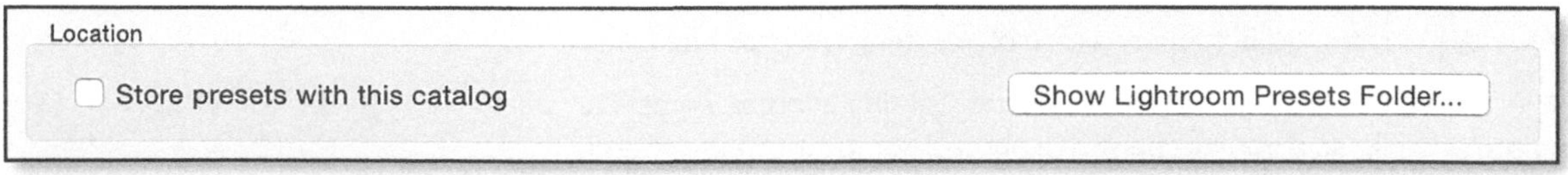

If you change the *Store presets with this catalog* setting, either turning it on or off, your presets may go missing. Don't panic; that's entirely normal. Changing this checkbox doesn't copy the existing presets to the new location—it only changes where Lightroom looks for them—so to access your presets, you need to copy them to the new location.

Location

☐ Store presets with this catalog   Show Lightroom Presets Folder...

1. Go to *Preferences > Presets tab* and uncheck *Store presets with this catalog* and press the **Show Lightroom Presets Folder** button.

2. An Explorer (Windows) / Finder (Mac) window opens, showing the presets in their global location. Keep it open in the background.

3. Check the *Store presets with this catalog* checkbox and press the *Show Lightroom Presets Folder* button again.

4. A second Explorer (Windows) / Finder (Mac) window opens, showing the catalog-specific Lightroom Settings folder.

5. Drag (or copy/paste) your presets from the global folder to the catalog-specific one.

If you have the opposite problem, and the presets are stored with the catalog, just swap the steps round. If you have multiple catalogs with multiples sets of presets, you can copy and paste them all into the global location to make them available to all catalogs.

It's easiest to allow file synchronization software to keep the entire Lightroom user settings folder synchronized between both computers, or in a network shared location.

How do I synchronize my presets using Dropbox?

The more technical (but more flexible) workaround for keeping presets updated on multiple computers involves using Dropbox (http://www.Lrq.me/dropbox) and junctions (Windows) / symlinks (Mac). It works well, particularly if the computers aren't on the same local network. You can also apply the same principle to the camera raw shared folders, such as camera and lens profiles, allowing these to be kept updated everywhere too. The computers can even run different platforms, for example, a Windows machine and a Mac.

Having installed Dropbox according to the instructions on their website, you first need to copy the presets and profiles into the Dropbox folder. Personally I keep a *Sync* subfolder in Dropbox, as I use this same principle for many different programs.

For both operating systems:

1. Close Lightroom.

2. Go to the application data folders at:

   Windows—C: \ Users \ [your username]\ AppData \ Roaming \ Adobe \

> **Figure 21.20** Symbolic Link Creator is an easy way to create symbolic links on Windows.

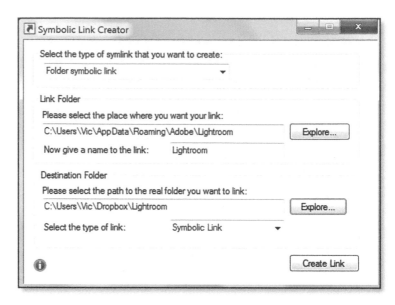

Mac—Macintosh HD / Users / [your username] / Application Support / Adobe /

(Note that these are hidden OS folders)

3. Copy both the CameraRaw folder and the Lightroom folder to your Dropbox folder.

4. Move, rename or delete the original folders in the Application Support folder.

Having copied the presets and other folders, it's time to create the symbolic links, so the instructions depend on your operating system...

Windows:

1. Download Symlink Creator (http://www.Lrq.me/winsymlink). It's a small free program which creates a symbolic link without needing to understand DOS and the mklink command.

2. There's no installation needed other than unzipping the download (or just selecting the .exe download in the first place). To avoid permissions issues, you'll need to right-click on the Symlink Creator.exe file and select *Run as Administrator*.

3. In the dialog, working from the top, select *Folder symbolic link* as the type of link. **(Figure 21.20)**

4. In the *Link Folder* section, browse for the C:\Users\[your username]\AppData\Roaming\Adobe\Lightroom folder (this may be a hidden folder) and call the link *Lightroom*.

5. In the Destination Folder section, browse to the Lightroom folder you created in your Dropbox folder.

6. Select *Symbolic Link* as the type of link, and press *Create Link*.

7. Repeat steps 3-6 using the Camera Raw folder instead of the Lightroom folder. Call the link *Camera Raw*.

8. Now restart Lightroom and check that it has found your presets and camera raw settings correctly.

9. Switch to the other computer and repeat steps 1-8. If you had different presets on the other computer, you may want to merge them into your Dropbox folders so that they're available on all computers.

Mac:

1. Download SymbolicLinker (http://www.Lrq.me/macsymlink). It's a small free program which creates a symbolic link without needing to visit Terminal.

2. Install it according to the instructions included with the app.

3. Right-click on the Lightroom folder in Dropbox and select *Make Symbolic Link*. **(Figure 21.21)**

4. The new symbolic link appears next to the Lightroom folder, and is called *Lightroom symlink*.

5. Drag the new Lightroom symlink to the Macintosh HD/Users/ [your username]/Application Support/Adobe/ folder, where the original folder was stored.

6. Rename the Lightroom symlink to remove the word symlink— you want to match the original name (Lightroom) so that Lightroom follows your link.

7. Repeat steps 3-6 using the Camera Raw folder instead of the Lightroom folder.

8. Now restart Lightroom and check that it has found your presets and camera raw settings correctly.

9. Switch to the other computer and repeat steps 1-8. If you had different presets on the other computer, you may want to merge them into your Dropbox folders so that they're available on all computers.

Once the setup is complete, Lightroom looks at the presets in the Dropbox folder, which should be updated whenever you add or edit a preset. If Lightroom is open on both computers at the same time,

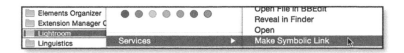

Figure 21.21 SymbolicLinker is an easy way to create symbolic links on Mac.

changes may not appear on the other computer until Lightroom is restarted.

SINGLE OR MULTIPLE CATALOGS

Until now, we've been working on the assumption that you have a single master catalog. Since version 1.1, Lightroom has made it easy to create and use multiple catalogs, but the question is, just because you can, should you? We'll consider some of the pros and cons, and how to make it work if you do decide that multiple catalogs are right for you.

Should I use one big catalog, or multiple smaller catalogs?

There's no 'right' number of catalogs. As with the rest of your Lightroom workflow, it depends on how you work. So should you use multiple catalogs for your main working catalog, or should you split your photos into multiple catalogs? We're not referring to temporary catalogs which are created for a purpose, for example, to take a subset of photos to another machine before later merging them back in, but more specifically your main working or master catalog.

The main benefit of keeping all of your photos in a DAM (Digital Asset Management) system is being able to easily search through them and find specific photos, but there are a few other pros and cons to consider:

Pros of Multiple Catalogs

- Smaller catalogs may be slightly faster on very low spec hardware. (Although even 50,000 photos counts as a small catalog!)

- Multiple catalogs give a clear distinction between types of photography, i.e., work vs home.

- You can't accidentally drag photos into the wrong folder (e.g. wedding photos can't end up with the wrong client).

- If your catalog becomes corrupted, you have less to lose (although frequent backups will avoid this issue).

- If multiple users need to be working on photos at the same time, it's easier to track individual catalogs.

Cons of Multiple Catalogs

- Can't search across multiple catalogs (e.g. to find the best photos from multiple shoots).

- Mobile sync only works with one catalog.

- You can end up with variations in metadata and keyword spellings.

- It's harder to keep track of backups.

- You have to keep switching catalogs.

- You can't switch catalogs while a process is running (e.g. if you're running an export in one catalog, you have to wait for it to complete before switching to another catalog).

- Some photos may be forgotten and not included in any catalog.

- You can end up with duplicate photos in multiple catalogs by accident.

There are few questions to ask yourself:

- How many photos are you working on at any one time? And how many do you have altogether?

- Do you want to be able to search through all of your photos to find a specific photo? Or do you have another DAM system that you prefer to use for cataloging your photos?

- If you decide to work across multiple catalogs, how are you going to make sure your keyword lists are the same in all of your catalogs?

- If you use multiple catalogs, is there going to be any crossover, with the same photos appearing in more than one catalog?

- How would you keep track of which photos are in which catalog?

- Do you want to keep the photos in your catalog indefinitely or just while you're working on them, treating Lightroom more like a basic raw processor?

- How will you keep track of catalogs and their backups?

Your answers likely depend on your reasons for using Lightroom. For some people, using multiple catalogs isn't a problem—they already have another system they use for DAM (digital asset management), and they want to use Lightroom for the other tools it offers. For example, some wedding photographers may decide to have a catalog for each wedding, and if they know that a photo from Mark & Kate's wedding is going to be in Mark & Kate's catalog, finding it really isn't a problem. But then, if you had to find a photo from a specific venue, or to use for publicity, you'd have to search through multiple catalogs.

Many high-volume photographers choose the best of both worlds: a small catalog for working on their current photos, and then transferring them into a large searchable archive catalog for storing completed photos. That's certainly another viable option, and a good compromise for many.

> **MULTI-CATALOG SEARCH**
>
> Lightroom doesn't allow you to search across multiple catalogs, or even have multiple catalogs open at the same time, so to find a specific photo, you have to open each catalog in turn. It's one of the biggest disadvantages. If you often need to search through different catalogs, consider merging them back into one larger catalog .

There are some easy distinctions, for example, you may also decide to keep personal photos entirely separate from work photos. These kind of clear-cut distinctions work well, as long as there's never any crossover between the two. Keeping the same photo in multiple catalogs is best avoided, as it becomes very confusing! The more catalogs you have, the harder they become to track.

As a simple rule of thumb, use the fewest catalogs you can and no fewer.

Is there a maximum number of photos a catalog can hold?

So you might be wondering, how big is too big? There's no known maximum number of photos you can store in a Lightroom catalog. Theoretically, your computer might run out of address space for your photos between 100,000 and 1,000,000 photos, although there are many users running catalogs of more than 100,000 photos, myself included. At the last count, the largest known catalog contained 1.9 million photos, and it's likely much larger now!

If your catalog's stored on a FAT32 formatted hard drive, 2 GB is the maximum file size allowable on that drive format, so your catalog could hit that limit, but then you could always move the catalog onto a drive formatted as NTFS on Windows or HFS on Mac.

Is there a maximum number of photos before Lightroom's performance starts to degrade?

There's no magic number of photos before performance declines either. Browsing, filtering or tagging faces in the All Photographs collection may be slightly slower as it's searching a larger number of photos, but general browsing and work shouldn't be badly affected by the larger catalog size, as long as it's optimized regularly. Opening the catalog may take a little longer while it checks all the folders are available, and backing up the catalog may also take longer due to the larger catalog file size.

These are minor inconveniences compared to repeatedly switching catalogs though! If the large catalog size causes a major problem for you, consider using a small working catalog of recent files plus a large searchable archive catalog.

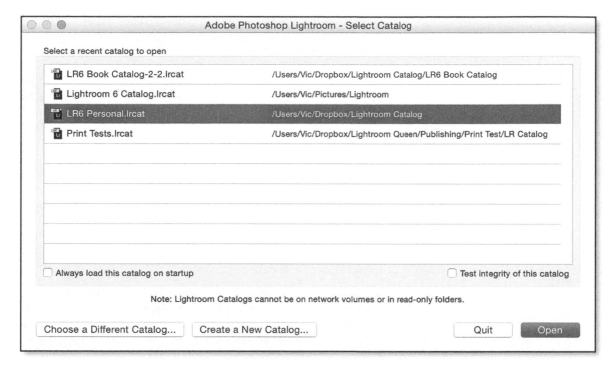

How do I create a new catalog and switch between catalogs?

Assuming you've decided to create a new catalog, you'll need to understand some basic catalog management, such as how to create new catalogs and switch between them.

If Lightroom's already running, you can create a new catalog using *File menu > New Catalog*, or open an existing catalog using *File menu > Open Catalog*.

If Lightroom's closed, hold down the Ctrl key (Windows) / Opt key (Mac) while opening Lightroom. In the Select Catalog dialog, it lists your recently used catalogs, or you can open another existing catalog or create a new catalog. **(Figure 21.22)**

Figure 21.22 If you hold down Ctrl (Windows) / Opt (Mac) while starting Lightroom, it asks which catalog to open.

How do I set or change my default catalog?

By default, Lightroom opens your last used catalog when it launches, however you can change this behavior in Lightroom's *Preferences >*

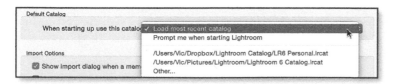

Figure 21.23 Set your default catalog in Lightroom's Preferences dialog.

General tab. **(Figure 21.23)** You can choose to open a specific catalog, open the most recent catalog, or be prompted each time Lightroom starts.

How do I set default Catalog Settings to use for all new catalogs?

Certain settings are catalog-specific, for example, anything set in the Catalog Settings dialog, Identity Plates, smart collections and keyword lists. Lightroom doesn't currently provide a way of making these settings available to new catalogs as templates, however there is a workaround. Set up a new empty catalog with the settings of your choice and save it somewhere safe. Whenever you need a new catalog with all of your favorite settings, simply duplicate the template catalog using Explorer (Windows) / Finder (Mac) instead of using *File menu > New Catalog.*

If you only need to import your smart collections into each new catalog, there's another handy trick. Export the existing smart collections (right-click > *Export Smart Collection Settings*) and change their file extension from ".lrmscol" to ".lrtemplate" Then go to *Preferences dialog > Presets tab* and press the *Show Lightroom Presets Folder* button. There you'll find a folder call *Smart Collection Templates.* If you add your renamed smart collections to that folder, they'll automatically be added to any new catalogs.

How do I delete a spare catalog?

If you've ended up with too many catalogs, you may want to delete any unused catalogs. It's probably a good idea to open it before you delete it, to check that you definitely don't want to keep it. To do so, either use *File menu > Open Catalog* or double-click on the catalog in Explorer (Windows) / Finder (Mac). You can safely delete the spare catalog and its previews files as long as you're sure there are no settings in it that catalog that you need. If in doubt, delete the previews (*.lrdata), zip the catalog (*.lrcat) and keep it somewhere safe.

How do I merge multiple catalogs into one larger catalog?

To merge your existing separate catalogs into one large catalog, it's simply a case of using Import from Catalog to pull the data into a new combined catalog. If you've accidentally ended up working in a backup catalog or created a new catalog by mistake, this process also allows you to fix your mistake without losing any data.

SPLITTING CATALOGS

To split an existing catalog into smaller catalogs, use the Export as Catalog command discussed on page 507. (There are few occasions when I'd recommend this, as using a single large catalog is usually a better choice. However there are occasions when it's useful, for example, you may need to take part of the catalog to another computer or have someone else work on part of the catalog.)

1. Open each individual catalog by double-clicking on it. If any folders or photos are marked as missing, turn to page 525 and fix the broken links before merging catalogs. You'll save a lot of time later.

2. Select *File menu > New Catalog* and create a clean catalog which will become your new master catalog.

3. Go to *File menu > Import from Another Catalog* and select one of the smaller catalogs (the *.lrcat file). Ideally you should work through in date order, from the oldest catalog to the newest. Note that we're importing the metadata from the existing catalog rather than importing the photos using the standard Import dialog. There's a big difference!

   Assuming that your photos are remaining in their current location, you'll need to select:

   • *New Photos > File Handling* set to *Add new photos to catalog without moving*.

   • *Changed Existing Photos > Replace* set to *Metadata and develop settings only*.

   • If photos appear in more than one catalog, and you're not sure which settings are the most recent, check *Preserve old settings as a virtual copy*. This creates virtual copies of each of the different sets of settings, so you can go back through later and decide which to keep.

   • For more information on the available options, turn back to page 511.

4. Repeat the Import from Catalog process for each of the other smaller catalogs until you've imported them all.

5. Keep the individual catalogs at least until you're sure that everything's transferred correctly and you have a current backup.

6. If some photos were duplicated in more than one catalog and you checked *Preserve old settings as a virtual copy*, sort through the photos and delete any virtual copies you don't need to keep. If the version you want to keep is a virtual copy, promote it to master status using *Photo menu > Set Copy As Master* and then delete the other version.

How do I transfer photos between catalogs?

If you do decide to use a small working catalog and a large archive catalog, you'll need to transfer photos between catalogs.

DUPLICATE PHOTOS

If you merge multiple catalogs, especially from multiple computers, you may end up with duplicate photos. The Duplicate Finder plug-in can help to identify them, although there's still some manual cleanup involved. http://www.Lrq.me/duplicatefinder

---

DON'T RE-IMPORT

Using Import from Another Catalog is essential when transferring photos between catalogs. Simply importing the photos instead of the catalog would lose all of the work you've previously done in Lightroom.

1. Open your Archive catalog, or create one if you haven't done so already.

2. Select *File menu > Import from Another Catalog*, and navigate to the Working catalog. In the Import from Catalog dialog that follows, select the folders that you want to transfer into your Archive catalog, deselecting the others.

    Assuming that your photos are remaining in their current location, you'll need to select:

    *   *New Photos > File Handling* set to *Add new photos to catalog without moving.*

    *   *Changed Existing Photos > Replace* set to *Metadata and develop settings only* if it's available.

    *   For more information on the available options, turn back to page 511.

3. Import these folders into your Archive catalog and check that they've imported as expected.

4. Close your Archive catalog and reopen your Working catalog.

5. Make sure you have a current backup, before you start removing photos from a catalog, just in case you make a mistake.

6. Select the photos that you've just transferred.

7. Press the Delete key to remove these files from the Working catalog, being careful to choose *Remove from the catalog* rather than *Delete from the hard drive.*

8. Repeat the process whenever you want to transfer more photos into the Archive catalog.

CATALOG SHORTCUTS

Open Catalog	Ctrl O / Cmd Shift O
Open Specific Catalog when opening Lightroom	Hold down Ctrl / Opt while opening Lightroom

TROUBLESHOOTING & PERFORMANCE

It's a computer—they don't always work the way you expect! Hiccups do occur, so let's explore some of the most frequent troubleshooting steps, as well as adjustments you can make to increase Lightroom's performance.

First, we'll look at the most frequent problems and their solutions, and then general troubleshooting steps you can try, if none of these fit. The most frequent problems are:

- Missing photos, marked with question marks or exclamation marks.

- Missing Toolbar.

- Missing panels and dialogs.

- Catalogs that won't open, perhaps due to corruption.

- Corrupted photos.

- Preview problems, including odd colors, gray thumbnails and corruption.

MISSING FILES

At some stage, most people run into worrying exclamation marks or question marks denoting missing files. Those warnings appear when Lightroom can no longer find the photos at their last known location.

Usually, it's because you've used other software such as Explorer (Windows) or Finder (Mac) to:

- Delete the photos or folders.

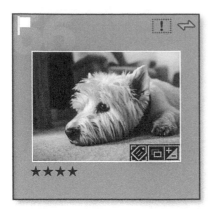

Figure 22.1 Missing photos have an exclamation mark icon.

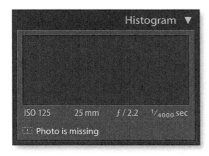

Figure 22.2 Missing Photo status also shows in the Histogram panel

- Move the photos or folders.

- Rename the photos or folders.

It can also happen when something's happened to the drive, such as:

- The external or network drive holding the photos is unplugged/disconnected.

- The drive letter has changed (Windows) or drive mount point has changed (Mac).

- You've moved to a new computer.

How do I know that Lightroom can't find my photos?

Missing files are identified by a rectangular icon in the corner of the Grid thumbnail, with or without an exclamation mark. **(Figure 22.1)** (In earlier versions, it displayed a question mark icon instead.)

If you've previously built Smart Previews, it says *Smart Preview* under the Histogram, to indicate that the original file is unavailable. You can continue working in Lightroom using those lower quality proxy files even though the original files are offline, with some limitations that we discussed in the Multi-computer chapter on page 508.

If there are no Smart Previews, the rectangular icon on the thumbnail contains an exclamation mark, and when you check the histogram, you'll find it's blank and says *Photo is missing*. **(Figure 22.2)** When you switch to the Develop module, the sliders are unavailable, as you can't edit a photo that's completely missing.

If the entire folder is missing, the folder name in the Folders panel goes gray with a question mark folder icon. **(Figure 22.3)**

If an entire drive is offline, the volume name in the Folders panel and the small rectangular icon on the left turn gray.

Lightroom thinks my photos are missing—how do I fix it?

If Lightroom tells you that files are missing, don't panic. First, stop and work out the extent of the problem, and if you can, why it's happened. Then fix it as soon as you can, using the instructions below, as problems tend to snowball if you ignore them.

The quickest way to fix the missing files is to follow these instructions in order. If you start relinking missing photos before you relink missing folders and drives, you can create a bigger job.

1. First, you must **find the files on your hard drive**. Lightroom can't tell you where you've put the files, if you've moved/renamed/

deleted them using other software, so you first need to locate the missing files on your hard drives.

Once you've found them on your hard drive using Explorer (Windows) / Finder (Mac), you can move on to step 2. If you get stuck, try using Windows Search or Mac Spotlight to search for one of the filenames.

2. Look in the Folders panel. **Is the whole drive offline**, shown by dark gray text and a gray rectangle on the left?

    If the answer's no, skip on to step 3.

    If the answer's yes, why is the drive offline? Is it disconnected? If you're on Windows, has the drive letter changed? If you're on a Mac, has the drive name changed?

    If the drive is disconnected, plug it back in or reconnect to the network storage.

    If the drive letter/name has changed, you can change it back (see the Windows Drive Letters box), or you can move on to step 3 and reconnect the individual folders.

3. Look in the Folders panel. **Are some of the folders marked as missing**, with gray text and a question mark on the folder icon?

    If the answer's no, skip on to step 4.

    If the answer's yes, why are the folders missing? Did you delete, rename or move a folder?

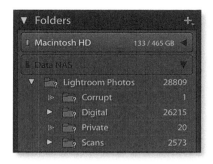

▲ **Figure 22.3** Missing folders have question mark icons. If the whole volume's offline, the drive goes gray.

WINDOWS DRIVE LETTERS

When using external drives, Lightroom doesn't change the drive letters, but Windows often does. That can confuse Lightroom, requiring you to relink missing files on a regular basis. Leaving the drives plugged in to your computer, or always reattaching them in the same order can help avoid the drive letter changing.

To set the drive letter a little more permanently, or reset them if they change, you can go into Windows Disk Management and assign a specific drive letter. You'll need to be logged in as an Administrator. On Windows 7, go to *Start menu > Control Panel > Administrative Tools > Computer Management* or use the Search charm on Windows 8. Disk Management is listed in the left-hand panel under *Storage*. Selecting this connects to the Virtual Disk Service and displays the drives seen in the main panel.

Find the relevant drive in the list, right-click and there's an option to *Change Drive Letter and Paths*. Be careful to ensure you have the correct drive! Selecting Change displays a list of available letters to select from. Selecting a letter outside the range Windows would usually assign automatically helps to reduce the possibility of it changing, so a letter from the latter half of the alphabet is a good choice. When you've finished, press *OK*, and select *Yes* when prompted to confirm the drive letter change.

If you deleted the folders, restore from the Recycle Bin/Trash or from a backup.

If you renamed or moved the folder, you could move/rename it back and then redo the move/rename within Lightroom.

If you can't put them back as they were, you can link Lightroom to the new name/location. That's the next step...

4. If you set up the folders as a hierarchy using the instructions earlier in the book, is a **whole folder hierarchy of parent/child folders** marked as missing? Or is it a single folder (or a few folders) that's marked as missing?

   If it's a whole folder hierarchy that's missing, right-click on the parent folder (rather than the individual subfolders) and select **Find Missing Folder** from the context-sensitive menu, then navigate to the new location of that parent folder. As long as the names and structure of the subfolders hasn't changed, all of the subfolders are fixed at the same time.

   If it's a single missing folder, right-click on the missing folder and select *Find Missing Folder* from the context-sensitive menu, then navigate to the new location of that single folder. Lightroom then updates its records to the new location and the question marks disappear.

   If there are multiple missing folders, that aren't in a folder hierarchy, do the same for each of these folders.

5. **Are individual photos still marked as missing**, with an exclamation mark inside a rectangle on each of the thumbnail borders?

   If the answer's no, your work is done. Go to *Library menu > Find Missing Photos*, just to double-check you haven't missed any photos.

   If the answer's yes, why are those photos missing? Do you remember moving or renaming them? Or deleting them?

   If you deleted them, you'll need to restore the photos to their previous location from the Recycle Bin/Trash or from a recent backup. Remember, the photos are never IN Lightroom, and most of Lightroom's tools won't work without the original photos. (We'll come back to worst case scenarios in a moment).

   If you moved the photos without renaming, you can either move them back, or you can link Lightroom's records to the new location of the photos.

   To link Lightroom to the new name/location, click on the rectangle in the corner of the thumbnail. Lightroom displays the

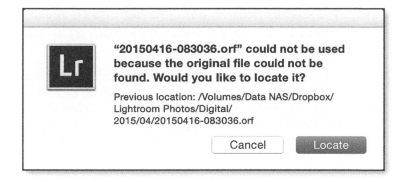

"20150416-083036.orf" could not be used because the original file could not be found. Would you like to locate it?

Previous location: /Volumes/Data NAS/Dropbox/
Lightroom Photos/Digital/
2015/04/20150416-083036.orf

Cancel   Locate

Figure 22.4 Click on the exclamation mark and navigate to the new location of the photo. Lightroom doesn't find them automatically, but it does display the last known location.

last known location of the photo. Click **Locate** and navigate to the new location of that photo. Check the **Find nearby missing photos** checkbox to allow Lightroom to try to automatically relink other files in the same folder. Lightroom updates its records to the new location and the rectangular icons disappear. **(Figure 22.4)**

If you renamed the photos outside of Lightroom, the quickest solution is to restore the photos with the old names from your backups and then redo the rename within Lightroom. If there are only a few photos, you can link Lightroom to the new name/location (using the previous instructions), however every renamed photo must be relinked individually.

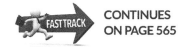

CONTINUES
ON PAGE 565

PREVENTING MISSING FILES

Prevention is better than cure, and preventing missing files will save you some additional work, so there are a few things to look out for...

- Don't delete the original files from your hard drive. Photos are not stored IN Lightroom.

- Move any files or folders within Lightroom's own interface, simply by dragging and dropping around the Folders panel. Don't "tidy up" using other software or the operating system (or if you do, fix Lightroom's links immediately).

- Rename any files before importing into Lightroom, or use Lightroom to rename them. Whatever you do, don't rename in other software once they're imported.

- Don't use *Synchronize Folder* to remove missing files and import them again at their new location as you'll lose all of your Lightroom settings.

- Set Lightroom's Folders panel to show the full folder hierarchy to a single root level folder. If a folder is moved from its previous location, or the drive letter changes, it can be fixed more easily than individual folders.

It says *The selected folder or one of its subfolders is already in Lightroom. Do you want to combine these folders?* Do I say yes or no?

If a folder has been marked as missing for a while, and you've since imported photos from the new location, when you select *Find Missing Folder*, it might say *The selected folder or one of its subfolders is already in Lightroom. Do you want to combine these folders?* If you're sure you've selected the correct folder, press the *Merge* button to combine them.

It says *The file is associated with another photo in the catalog.* How do I fix it?

There's another problem that can arise if you reimport the photos at their new location instead of fixing the broken links. This creates duplicate records, and prevents you from fixing the links.

How might you get into this state? Imagine your photos hard drive is originally called Drive D, and you import your photos and edit them. Then, at some point, Windows changes the drive letter to Drive F (or you rename a Mac drive). Later, you want to edit one of these old photos but it's marked as missing, so you import it again (big mistake!). Time passes, and you're reading this chapter, so you decide to relink all of the missing files. When you try to relink some of the files, Lightroom says "The file is associated with another photo in the catalog" and won't let you continue.

So how do you fix it? Let's work through it step by step:

1. Back up your catalog, just in case you make a mistake.

2. First, you have to determine which of the duplicates to keep. The original one that's marked as missing? Or the newer one? In most cases, you'll choose to keep the version that you've edited.

3. When you've decided which record you're going to remove from the catalog, make sure you have a folder selected (not a collection) then select the photo and press the Delete key. When Lightroom asks whether to *Remove* or *Delete*, make sure you select *Remove*.

4. Once that duplicate record has been removed from the catalog, check the photo you've decided to keep. If it was marked as missing, click the rectangle in the corner and navigate to the new location. Lightroom now allows you to select the photo.

5. Repeat for each of the photos with the same problem. If you have the same problem on a large number of photos, you may be able to check and delete a whole folder at a time, rather than fixing each photo individually.

It can be a time consuming job, so it's yet another good reason to fix missing photos at the earliest opportunity.

How do I check my catalog for missing files?

If you go to *Library menu* > *Find Missing Photos*, Lightroom creates a temporary collection of the missing photos so that you can relink them. It doesn't update live, so even after you've located the missing photo, it still appears in that collection. To remove this temporary collection from the Catalog panel, right-click on it and select *Delete this Temporary Collection*. **(Figure 22.5)**

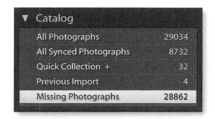

Figure 22.5 If you go to *Library menu* > *Find Missing Photos*, Lightroom creates a collection in the Catalog panel.

I accidentally deleted my photos from my hard drive and I don't have backups! Can I recover them using Lightroom's previews or smart previews?

If you've deleted your original files, you don't have backups, and they're not in the Recycle Bin (Windows) / Trash (Mac), the next thing to check is whether the photos are still on the memory card. If you haven't reshot the entire card, it may be possible to rescue some of the original photos using recovery software. You could also try recovery software on the hard drive, to see if they can be rescued from there.

If that's not possible, before you do anything else, close Lightroom, find the catalog on the hard drive, and duplicate the catalog and previews, just in case you make a mistake.

It's possible to convert Lightroom's previews into files. It's not ideal as the quality isn't as high as the original files, but they're not bad as a last-ditch rescue attempt.

First, check under the Histogram in the Library module to see whether you have Smart Previews for the missing photos. You're looking for the words *Smart Preview*. If there are Smart Previews, select the photos and go to *File menu* > *Export*. Choose *DNG* as the File Format (leave the checkboxes unchecked) and export them to a folder on the hard drive. They're only 2560px along the longest edge and they're lossy compressed, but they're better than nothing. (Turn back to the Export chapter starting on page 347 for more information on exporting).

Next, we'll save your standard previews as JPEGs. If you don't have smart previews, these standard previews are the only files you have left. Even if you did have smart previews, the standard previews may be larger (i.e. 1:1 size) so it's worth trying both options.

Adobe released a script that retrieves Lightroom's previews and saves them as image files, however there are also a couple of free plug-ins which make the process easier. The resulting JPEGs are only the size and quality of the previews, but they're better than nothing. In these instructions, we'll use a plug-in by Jeffrey Friedl.

1. Download Jeffrey's plug-in from http://www.Lrq.me/friedl-extractpreviews

2. Double click to unzip the plug-in.

3. Go to *File menu > Plug-in Manager* and press the *Add* button. Navigate to the plug-in you've just unzipped.

4. Back in Lightroom's Grid view, select the photos you need to rescue.

5. Go to *File menu > Plugin Extras > Extract Preview Images* to show the dialog.

6. Select the location for the extracted previews and press *Begin Extraction*.

7. In the results dialog, the plug-in reports on the size and quality of the extracted previews. **(Figure 22.6)**

Finally, import the new DNG files and/or JPEG files into your Lightroom catalog. You may need to reorganize them into folders while importing, and then sort them into collections again and reapply flags, but they're better than nothing. Once you're happy that your replacement files are sorted out, you can remove the old missing files from the catalog.

▼**Figure 22.6** Jeffrey's Extract Previews plug-in turns Lightroom's previews into normal JPEGs, if you've lost the originals.

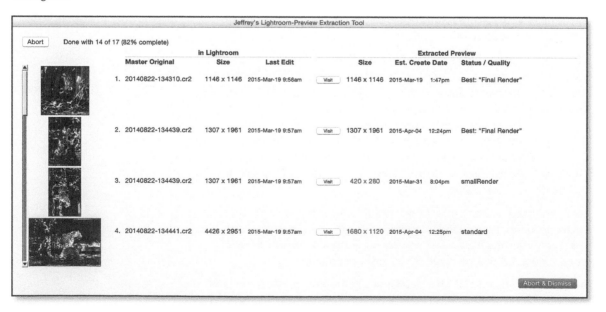

OTHER FREQUENT PROBLEMS

There are some other problems that frequently crop up on the forums, so here are the quick fixes for your reference...

My Toolbar's disappeared—where's it gone?

The Toolbar usually appears between the photos in the Preview Area and the Filmstrip. It holds buttons such as view options and the *Done* button in the Develop module. Flip back to the Workspace chapter on page 84 for more detail. If your Toolbar disappears, press T—you've hidden it!

Where have my panels gone?

If a panel goes missing, for example, the Basic panel in the Develop module, go to *Window menu > Panels* and click on the name of the panel to enable it. You can also right-click on a panel header (in the gray space next to the panel name) to show the context-sensitive menu and put a checkmark against the name of the missing panel. (Figure 22.7)

How do I show missing dialogs?

If you've hidden some of the dialogs by checking a *Don't Show Again* checkbox, you can bring them all back by pressing the *Reset all warning dialogs* button in the *Preferences dialog > General tab*.

Dialogs can also go missing if you use dual monitors. Lightroom remembers which monitor you last used to display each dialog. If you then unplug one of those monitors, Lightroom may still try to show the dialog on the detached monitor, resulting in an error beep when you try to press anything else. To solve it, press the Escape key to close the imaginary dialog, and either plug the second monitor back so you can see the dialog to move it back, or reset Lightroom's Preferences file. We'll come to these instructions a little later in the chapter on page 543.

CATALOG CORRUPTION

Lightroom's catalogs are basic databases, so it's possible for them to become corrupted, even though it's relatively rare. Don't worry, you have nothing to fear from keeping all of your work in a single catalog, as long as you take regular backups. But what do you do if you have problems with your catalog? Let's investigate.

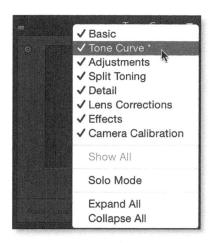

Figure 22.7 If a panel goes missing, right-click on one of the other panel headers and reselect it from the menu.

PREVENT CORRUPTION

A little bit of common sense goes a long way in protecting your work.

- Back up regularly, and keep older catalog backups.

- Always shut your computer down properly.

- Don't disconnect an external drive while Lightroom is open.

- Keep the catalog on an internal drive if possible.

- Turn on *Test integrity* and *Optimize catalog* in the Backup dialog to run each time you back up. If they have trouble running, it'll give you a clue that something's going wrong.

Why can't I open my catalog?

If you can't open your catalog, there are a few possible reasons, and the error message offers a few clues.

Lightroom may say: *The Lightroom catalog cannot be opened because another application already has it open. Quit the other copy of Lightroom before trying to relaunch.* If so, check the catalog's folder for a *.lrcat. lock file. If Lightroom's closed, it shouldn't be there, so you can safely delete it. They sometimes get left behind if Lightroom crashes. Remember, if there's a *.lrcat-journal file, don't delete this journal as it contains data that hasn't been written back to the catalog yet.

Lightroom requires read and write access to the catalog file, so it may show an error message that says: *The Lightroom catalog cannot be used because the parent folder ... does not allow files to be created within it* or *Lightroom cannot launch with this catalog. It is either on a network volume or on a volume on which Lightroom cannot save changes.*

If you see either of these errors, check your operating system's folder and file permissions as they're probably set to read-only. It may not be the catalog folder itself that has the wrong permissions, but perhaps a parent folder. On Windows, there are additional security layers which can cause similar issues. (You might need to Google how to do that, as these are operating system settings.)

Also check your catalog location—it can't stored be on a network drive, or on read-only media such as a DVD, or on an incorrectly formatted drive (e.g. an NTFS drive on a Mac).

Finally, Lightroom might give a warning about the catalog being corrupted. This can be more serious, so we'll cover it in more detail.

How do catalogs become corrupted?

In almost all cases, corruption results from a hardware problem. This can include the computer crashing due to a hardware fault, kernel panics, or power outages, any of which can prevent Lightroom from finishing writing to the catalog safely.

▸ **Figure 22.8** If Lightroom can't open the catalog, it warns you before quitting.

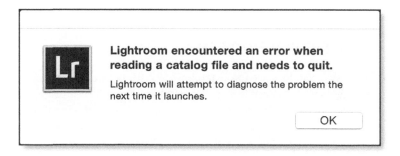

Lightroom encountered an error when reading a catalog file and needs to quit.

Lightroom will attempt to diagnose the problem the next time it launches.

OK

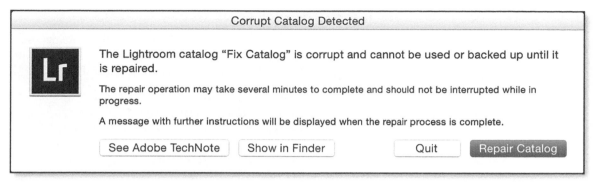

Catalogs also become corrupted if the connection to the drive cuts out while Lightroom is writing to the catalog, for example, as a result of an external drive being accidentally disconnected or the catalog being stored on a network drive (via an unsupported hack). Some external drives drop their connection intermittently for no known reason, so it's safest to keep your catalog on an internal drive if possible.

Figure 22.9 If Lightroom confirms that the catalog is corrupted, it offers to repair it.

Lightroom says that my catalog is corrupted—can I fix it?

If Lightroom warns you that your catalog is corrupted, it also offers to try to repair it for you. **(Figure 22.8)** In many cases, the corruption can be repaired automatically, but it depends on how it's happened. **(Figure 22.9)**

If the catalog repair fails, restoring a backup is your next step, which we covered in detail in the Backup chapter on page 67. **(Figure 22.10)** You can also try moving the catalog to a different drive, which can solve some false corruption warnings.

If you don't have a current backup catalog, there may be another way of rescuing your data. It involves using Import from Catalog to transfer the uncorrupted data into a new catalog. Usually the corruption is confined to one or two folders that were being accessed when the catalog became corrupted, so working through methodically can sometimes rescue almost all of your data. It's worth a shot!

Figure 22.10 If the catalog can't be repaired, you'll need to restore a backup.

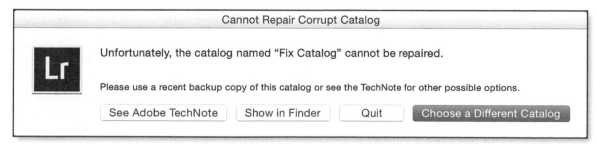

To attempt recovery:

1. Close Lightroom and duplicate the corrupted catalog using Explorer (Windows) / Finder (Mac) before you proceed with rescue attempts, just in case you make it worse.

2. Create a new catalog (by going to *File menu > New Catalog*) and then go to the Catalog Settings dialog and set the backup interval to *Every time Lightroom exits*. You can change this back again later, but it saves you starting this process again from the beginning if you pull some corrupted data into the new catalog.

3. Go to *File menu > Import from Another Catalog* and navigate to the corrupted catalog. If it gets as far as the Import from Catalog dialog box, select just a few folders in the *Catalog Contents* section. In the pop-ups below, select *File Handling > Add new photos to catalog without moving*.

4. Repeat the Import from Catalog, each time selecting a few folders to transfer. Between imports, close and reopen Lightroom, so that a new backup is created, and the integrity check runs to ensure that your new catalog hasn't become corrupted.

5. Keep repeating the process until all of the folders are imported from the corrupted catalog. If you hit another corruption warning, go back a step, restore the previous backup, and make a note of the folders you had just imported, skipping them. In the process, you may be able to narrow the corruption down to a single folder or even specific photos.

6. Once you've finished, and you have a working catalog again, select all the photos and go to *File menu > Export as Catalog*. Give the exported catalog a new name, and uncheck the checkboxes at the bottom. This extra step helps to remove any orphaned data.

7. Open the newly exported catalog. This now becomes your main working catalog.

8. After a significant corruption, it's also worth rebuilding the previews. To do so, select all the photos and go to *Library menu > Previews > Render Standard-Sized Previews*. This process takes a long time if you have a large number of photos, so you might choose to leave it running overnight.

9. Finally, if everything's working as expected, you can archive or delete the backups created in step 4, the temporary catalog created in step 2, and the corrupted catalog.

Of course, having current backups would have prevented all of this work, so you'll want to make sure that your backups are current in future!

IMAGE & PREVIEW PROBLEMS

Viewing accurate previews of your photos is essential. Problems do sometimes occur, so you'll need to know how to fix them, even if they're not Lightroom's fault.

Why do I just get gray boxes instead of previews?

If Lightroom's showing gray thumbnails **(Figure 22.11)** instead of image previews in the Grid view, there are a few possibilities...

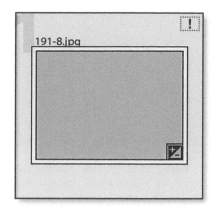

▲ **Figure 22.11** Gray thumbnails may be caused by a corrupted monitor profile, graphics card drivers, or missing files.

- **Previews don't exist**—If there's an exclamation mark in the corner of the thumbnail in Grid view as well as gray thumbnails, Lightroom simply hasn't been able to build the previews yet. The original file may have been renamed or moved outside of Lightroom, or the drive was disconnected before Lightroom was able to create the previews. If you reconnect the drive or find the missing files, the previews can be created. (Turn back to the Missing Files section starting on page 525 for more information.)

- **Previews can't display**—If there are no exclamation marks in the corner of the thumbnails in Grid view, a corrupted monitor profile is the most likely cause, or the graphics card driver may need updating. We'll discuss corrupted monitor profiles in more detail in the next question.

- **Corrupted preview cache**—It's also possible that the preview cache is corrupted, particularly if your catalog has been upgraded from an earlier version. We'll come back to that on page 538.

Everything in Lightroom is a funny color, but the original photos look perfect in other programs, and the exported photos don't look like they do in Lightroom either. What could be wrong?

In addition to previews that are completely missing, your previews may be displayed in the wrong color.

Strange colored previews that don't match the exported photos in color managed programs are usually caused by a corrupted monitor profile. Lightroom uses the profile differently to other programs (perceptual rendering rather than relative colorimetric), so corruption in that part of the profile shows up in Lightroom even though it appears correct in other programs. It often happens with the manufacturer's profiles that come with most monitors.

To confirm that the corrupted monitor profile is the mostly likely cause, select a B&W photo (or turn a photo B&W by pressing the

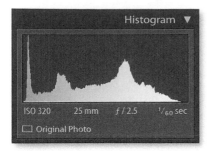

Figure 22.12 A color cast on the Histogram panel is a clear indication that the monitor profile is corrupted.

V key). The B&W photo and its histogram should be neutral shades of gray, but you may see a color cast (likely brown) if your profile's corrupted. **(Figure 22.12)**

Ideally you should recalibrate your monitor using a hardware calibration device, such as a Spyder, i1Display Pro or ColorMunki. If you don't have such a tool, put it on your shopping list, and in the meantime, remove the corrupted monitor profile as a temporary solution.

How do I remove my monitor profile to check whether it's corrupted?

Windows

1. Close Lightroom.

2. On Windows 7, go to *Start menu > Control Panel > Color Management* or type *color management* in the Start menu search box. On Windows 8, use the Search charm to search for 'color management' and then select *Settings > Color Management*.

3. Click the *Devices* tab if it's not already selected. **(Figure 22.13)**

4. From the *Device* pop-up, select your monitor. If you have more than 1 monitor connected, pressing the Identify monitors button displays a large number on screen for identification.

5. Check the *Use my settings for this device* checkbox.

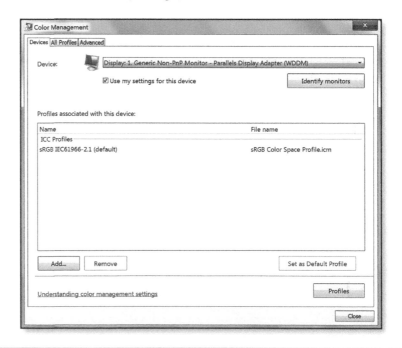

Figure 22.13 Setting the monitor profile to sRGB using the Windows Color Management dialog confirms or rules out a corrupted monitor profile.

6. Make a note of the currently selected profile, which is marked as (default). If there isn't an existing profile, you can skip this step.

7. Click the *Add* button.

8. In the Associate Color Profile dialog, select *sRGB IE61966-2.1* (sRGB Color Space Profile.icm) and press *OK*.

9. Back in the Color Management dialog, select the sRGB profile and click *Set as Default Profile*, and then close the dialog.

Mac OS X

1. Close Lightroom.

2. Go to *System Preferences > Displays*.

3. Select the *Color* tab.

4. Press the *Calibrate* button and follow the instructions. **(Figure 22.14)**

5. Turn on the *Expert Options* and calibrate to gamma 2.2.

Finally, restart Lightroom and check whether everything looks correct. If it does, you've confirmed that the previous monitor profile was the cause of the problem. You can temporarily leave sRGB as the monitor profile, as it's better than a corrupted one, but it would then be wise to calibrate your monitor accurately using a hardware calibration device.

MONITOR CALIBRATION

The only real way of calibrating a monitor is with a hardware calibration device. Software calibration is only ever as good as your eyes, and everyone sees color differently, but calibration hardware, such as the ColorMunki, i1 Display Pro or Spyder devices are now inexpensive, and an essential part of every keen digital photographer's toolkit.

Most calibration software offers an advanced setting, so if it gives you a choice, go for a brightness of around 100-120 cd/m2, 6500K or native white point for LCD monitor, and most importantly, an ICC2 Matrix profile rather than an ICC4 or LUT-based profile, as these more recent profiles aren't compatible with many programs yet.

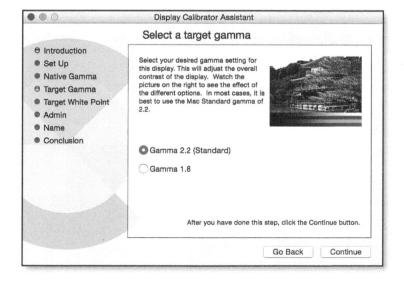

Figure 22.14 The basic Mac Calibration tool is ok for testing, but it's only as good as your eyes, so you'll still need calibration hardware.

Why is Lightroom changing the colors of my photos?

If Lightroom starts changing the appearance of the newly imported photos automatically, there are a few settings that you might have changed.

Are the photos raw? If so, the changes are likely just a difference in rendering, because raw data is just that—raw—and each raw processor has its own default style. Turn back to the Develop chapter on page 199 for a detailed discussion.

There are a few other possibilities, however, which would also apply to JPEG and other rendered formats:

- **Auto Tone**—If you go to Lightroom's *Preferences > Presets tab,* is *Apply auto tone adjustments* checked? If so, uncheck it to prevent future imports being automatically edited. **(Figure 22.15)**

- **Develop Preset**—You may have selected a Develop preset in the Import dialog. Set the *Develop Settings* pop-up to *None* in the Apply During Import panel and see if the problem recurs on future imports.

- **Default Settings**—You may have changed the Default settings. To check, open a newly imported photo in the Develop module and press the *Reset* button. If the photo doesn't change, hold down the Shift key to change the button to *Reset (Adobe)* and click again. If the photo now changes, go to *Preferences dialog > Presets tab* and press the *Reset all default Develop settings* button to reset the defaults back to Adobe's own settings.

- **Existing Edits**—Have the photos been edited in Lightroom or ACR previously? If so, they may have Develop settings recorded in the metadata.

For photos that are already imported, select them in Grid view and press the *Reset All* button in the Quick Develop panel to reset them all back to the default settings.

▼ **Figure 22.15** In Preferences dialog > Presets tab, turn off the *Apply auto tone adjustments* checkbox if you don't want auto settings applied when importing photos.

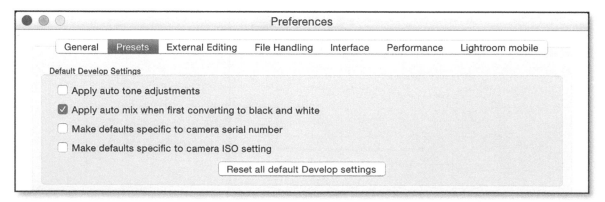

Lightroom says my preview cache is corrupted—how do I fix it?

There's one more problem that can occur with previews—a corrupted preview cache.

The most obvious clue is Lightroom showing an error message telling you that the preview cache is corrupted and then resets the preview cache automatically.

Alternatively you might find that Lightroom displays the wrong preview for some of your photos, some previews or thumbnails disappear when the photo is deselected, or the photo only shows in the Develop module.

If so, you can fix it by manually rebuilding the preview cache:

1. Find your catalog on the hard drive. If you can open Lightroom, go to *Edit menu* (Windows) / *Lightroom menu* (Mac) > *Catalog Settings > General tab* and press the Show button to open an Explorer (Windows) / Finder (Mac) window, then quit Lightroom. If you can't open Lightroom, and you don't know where to find your catalog, you'll need to search for *.LRCAT files.

2. Using Explorer (Windows) / Finder (Mac), move or rename the previews folder (*Previews.lrdata) and restart Lightroom.

3. Lightroom can now rebuild the previews from the original files. Select all the photos and go to *Library menu > Previews > Build Standard-Sized Previews* and leave it to work, perhaps overnight as it takes a long time. If any of the photos are offline (e.g. stored on disconnected external hard drives), these previews will remain blank until you reconnect the drive.

4. Once you're happy they've all rebuilt, you can delete the previous previews folder (*Previews.lrdata) if you haven't already done so. I don't usually recommend deleting the old previews before building new ones, just in case there are any missing original files, and the previews are the only copy you have left. If you're comfortable that you still have all of your original files available, then you can delete the old previews before building the new ones.

Lightroom appears to be corrupting my photos—how do I stop it?

In the Import chapter error messages starting on page 53, we briefly discussed the problem of images becoming corrupted, especially during import. It can happen to anyone.

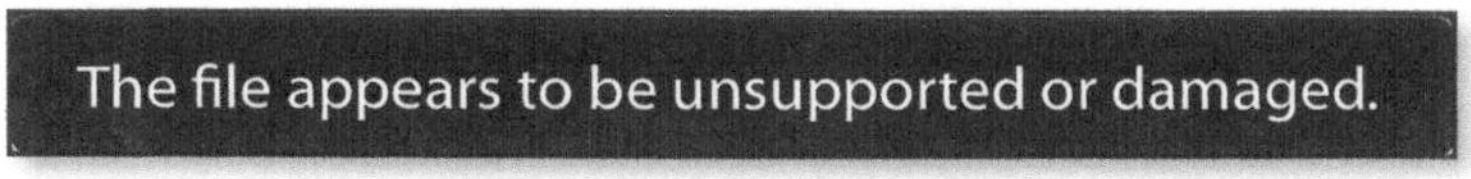

▶**Figure 22.16** When entering the Develop module, Lightroom may warn that a photo is unsupported or damaged, which usually indicates corruption.

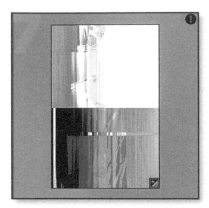

▲**Figure 22.17** A corrupted file may not import at all, may show a low resolution thumbnail with a black border, or may show very visible corruption.

The file appears to be unsupported or damaged.

Severe file corruption is often picked up at the Import stage, resulting in a *file is unsupported or damaged* error message **(Figure 22.16)**, but less serious corruption might not be discovered until you look at Lightroom's standard size previews.

Initially, Lightroom displays the embedded JPEG preview, which often escapes corruption because it's confined to a small area of the file. Lightroom then reads the whole file to create an accurate preview, at which point the corruption appears. That may lead you to believe that Lightroom's corrupting the files, but it's not.

If a file is corrupted **(Figure 22.17)**, Lightroom's unable turn the leftover data into an accurate image, which results in a distorted view and *There was an error working with the photo* error message in the Loupe view and Develop module.

Because most other image browsers only display the uncorrupted embedded JPEG, they often fail to detect the problem. It's therefore important to build standard or 1:1 previews and visually check them for corruption in Lightroom (or another full raw processor) before wiping your memory cards.

But if it's not Lightroom's fault, what causes corruption? Unfortunately the files are usually corrupted before they reach Lightroom, and it's almost always due to hardware problems.

Corrupted files are most frequently caused by a damaged card reader or cable. The good news is the file on the memory card is often uncorrupted, and can be safely imported without corruption by using another card reader.

Other regular suspects include damaged flash cards or problems with the camera initially writing the file, such as the battery dying or the card being removed while writing.

If a photo gets corrupted some time after the original import, your computer likely has a hardware problem. A dying hard drive or damaged connection (e.g. cable) or damaged RAM are frequent causes, but a variety of other hardware issues can also cause problems.

Whatever the cause, you'll need to re-download the file from the memory card or replace it with an uncorrupted backup.

JPEG FROM RAW

If you don't have an uncorrupted version, Instant JPEG from RAW may be able to extract a readable embedded JPEG preview. You can download it freely from http://www.Lrq.me/instantjpegfromraw

STANDARD TROUBLESHOOTING

If your issue isn't covered by the previous sections, or in the specific topic area of the book, there are some general troubleshooting steps you can try.

As always, make sure you have backups before you try any troubleshooting steps.

The magic reboot

If you're having odd problems with any computer program, the age-old wisdom "turn it off and turn it on again" still works wonders. First, try restarting the program, and if that doesn't solve it, reboot the computer.

Optimize the Catalog

Go to *File menu > Optimize Catalog* and wait for it to tell you it's completed before moving on.

Check for Updates

Next, check for updates, as the issue you're running into could be a bug that's been fixed in a later release. Make sure you're running the latest updates, both for Lightroom (by going to *Help menu > Check for Updates*) and also for your operating system. Also update drivers on your machine, particularly the graphics card drivers and any mouse or tablet drivers.

Reset Preferences

If you're still having problems, resetting Lightroom's Preferences file can solve all sorts of 'weirdness,' so it's a good early step in troubleshooting.

There's a simple automated way of doing it—just hold down Alt and Shift (Windows) / Opt and Shift (Mac) while opening Lightroom and it'll ask whether to reset the preferences. The timing is crucial—hold them down while clicking/double-clicking on the app/shortcut. **(Figure 22.18)**

Alternatively, you can reset the preferences manually. Moving or renaming the preferences file, rather than deleting it, means that you can put it back if it doesn't solve the problem, to save you manually recreating your preferences again.

Figure 22.18 Hold down Alt and Shift (Windows) / Opt and Shift (Mac) while opening Lightroom to reset the preferences.

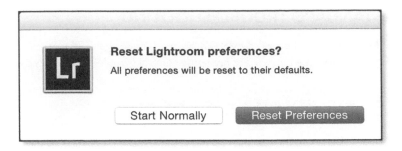

> **Reset Lightroom preferences?**
> All preferences will be reset to their defaults.
>
> Start Normally   Reset Preferences

Windows

1. Go to *Edit menu > Preferences > Presets tab.*

2. If *Store presets with this catalog* is unchecked, press the *Show Lightroom Presets Folder* button.

   If *Store presets with this catalog* is checked, uncheck it, press the *Show Lightroom Presets Folder* button. Don't forget to check the checkbox again after step 4, otherwise you'll wonder why your presets disappeared.

   Alternatively, you can navigate directly to C:\Users\[your username]\AppData\Roaming\Adobe\Lightroom\Preferences Note that this is a hidden folder, so the easiest way to do so is to open the Start menu search box (Windows 7) / Search charm (Windows 8) and type *%appdata%\Adobe\Lightroom\Preferences*

3. Whichever way you choose to find the folder, close Lightroom before going any further.

4. Rename, move or delete the Lightroom 6 Preferences.agprefs and any earlier versions (but leave the Lightroom 6 Startup Preferences there), then restart Lightroom.

Mac

1. Quit Lightroom.

2. Open Finder and select the *Go menu.*

3. Hold down the Opt key so *Library* appears in the menu, then click on *Library*.

4. In the Finder window, open the Preferences folder and scroll down to com.adobe.Lightroom6.plist

5. Move this file, plus any other Lightroom preference files (e.g. com.adobe.Lightroom6.LSSharedFileList.plist or older versions), to another folder or delete them.

6. Reboot your computer (because OS X caches some preference files), then restart Lightroom.

> ## WHAT'S STORED IN PREFERENCES?
>
> If you reset your Preferences file, the obvious settings that you lose are those in the Preferences dialog, but it also includes other details such as your View Options settings, last used settings, FTP server details, some plug-in settings, your country, etc.
>
> Your original photos, Develop settings, Develop defaults, collections, presets and other important settings aren't affected by deleting the Preferences file.
>
> The *Store presets with this catalog* setting also reverts to default (unchecked) if you reset the preferences file, but the presets themselves are perfectly safe, and checking the checkbox in Preferences causes the presets to reappear.
>
> There are also separate startup preferences which don't usually need resetting. These include the last used catalog path, the recent catalog list, which catalog to load on startup and the catalog upgrade history.

7. If your presets are missing, go to *Lightroom menu > Preferences > Presets tab*, check *Store presets with this catalog* and they should reappear.

Try a new catalog

If resetting the preferences doesn't help, create a new catalog to rule out minor catalog corruption. To do so:

1. Go to *File menu > New Catalog*.

2. If you can't open Lightroom to access the menu, hold down Ctrl (Windows) / Opt (Mac) while restarting Lightroom, then click the *Create New Catalog* button.

3. Choose a location for the temporary catalog such as the desktop. (Note that this is only a test to check whether the problem is catalog-specific. Don't delete your working catalog or start working in this temporary catalog!)

4. Import some photos into this new catalog to check everything is working as expected.

5. If this works, the problem is likely specific to your catalog. Don't panic, that can usually be fixed! Turn back to the Catalog Corruption section on page 533.

Rule out corrupted presets

The next thing to check for is corrupted presets, as they can cause strange problems like module hanging and performance problems. To do so:

Windows

1. Go to *Edit menu > Preferences > Presets tab*.

2. Press the *Show Lightroom Presets Folder* button.

   Alternatively, you can navigate directly to C:\Users\[your username]\AppData\Roaming\Adobe\Lightroom\ Note that this is a hidden folder, so the easiest way to do so is to open the Start menu search box (Windows 7) / Search charm (Windows 8) and type *%appdata%\Adobe\Lightroom*

3. Whichever way you choose to find this folder, close Lightroom before going any further.

4. Select the contents of the Lightroom folder, with the exception of the Preferences folder (as we've already ruled out preferences problems).

5. Move these subfolders (e.g. Develop Presets, Print Templates, etc.) to another location, such as the desktop.

6. Restart Lightroom.

Mac

1. Go to *Lightroom menu > Preferences > Presets tab*.

2. Press the *Show Lightroom Presets Folder* button.

   Alternatively, you can navigate directly to Macintosh HD / Users / [your username] / Library / Application Support / Adobe / Lightroom / Note that this is a hidden folder, so the easiest way to do so is to open Finder and select the *Go menu*. Hold down the Opt key so *Library* appears in the menu, then click on *Library*. Then navigate through *Application Support > Adobe > Lightroom*.

3. Whichever way you choose to find this folder, close Lightroom before going any further.

4. Select the Lightroom folder and move it to another location, such as the desktop.

5. Reboot your computer (because OS X caches some files), then restart Lightroom.

If the problem isn't solved, you can copy the preset folders back, overwriting the default preset folders that have been automatically created.

If it does solve the problem, copy the presets back a few at a time, to narrow down which specific preset (or group of presets) is causing the problem.

Corrupted fonts have also been known to cause problems, particularly in the Print and Book modules. Fonts aren't specific to Lightroom. If you're not familiar with managing your operating system's fonts, Google "uninstall font" and the name of your operating system for instructions on removing fonts.

Try a clean user account

Sometimes issues are specific to your computer's user account. Testing a clean user account can rule out a lot of potential problems in one go. If you're not sure how to create a clean user account, here are the official instructions:

http://www.Lrq.me/winuser (select your Windows version in the pop-up)

http://www.Lrq.me/macuser

Check for hardware and operating system problems

Lightroom taxes your computers hardware more than most of the programs you use, so it often finds hardware and operating system problems that don't show up in other software.

Damaged RAM can also cause some odd problems—Lightroom finds dodgy memory quicker than almost any other program. You can easily check that by running software such as Memtest.

Depending on the issues you're having, check other hardware for issues, for example, if Lightroom's running slowly, check the hard drives, particularly if it's an intermittent problem. They could be dying or just running low on space. If the screen is behaving oddly, check your graphics card, monitor and calibration. If you're having problems importing, check your card reader, USB ports and the destination hard drive.

Also check your boot drive to ensure it has plenty of space available, as a lack of space for operating system temp files can cause all sorts of problems.

Ask for help!

If none of those troubleshooting steps solve the problem, post a description at http://www.lightroomforums.net and we'll try to help you figure it out!

DEFAULT FILE & MENU LOCATIONS

If you need to find Lightroom's files at any time, you'll need to know where to look, so here are the most popular Lightroom file locations.

By default, the boot drive is C:\ on Windows and Macintosh HD on Mac. If your operating system is installed on a different drive, you may need to replace the drive letter/name on the file paths that are listed below.

[your username] refers to the name of your user account, for example, mine is called Vic.

The default location of the Lightroom catalog is...

Windows—C: \ Users \ [your username] \ My Pictures \ Lightroom \ Lightroom Catalog.lrcat

Mac—Macintosh HD / Users / [your username] / Pictures / Lightroom / Lightroom Catalog.lrcat

The default location of the Preferences is...

Windows—C: \ Users \ [your username] \ AppData \ Roaming \ Adobe \ Lightroom \ Preferences \ Lightroom 6 Preferences.agprefs

Mac—Macintosh HD / Users / [your username] / Library / Preferences / com.adobe.Lightroom6.plist

Preference files aren't cross-platform. By default, Preferences are a hidden file on Windows and Mac OS X.

There are also separate startup preferences. These include the last used catalog path, the recent catalog list, which catalog to load on startup and the catalog upgrade history.

Windows—C: \ Users \ [your username] \ AppData \ Roaming \ Adobe \ Lightroom \ Preferences \ Lightroom 6 Startup Preferences.agprefs

Mac—Macintosh HD / Users / [your username] / Library / Application Support / Adobe / Lightroom /Lightroom 6 Startup Preferences. agprefs

How do I show hidden files to find my preferences and presets?

On Windows, you can open the Start menu search box (Windows 7) / Search charm (Windows 8) and type *%appdata%\Adobe\Lightroom*, and you'll be taken directly to the Lightroom user folder.

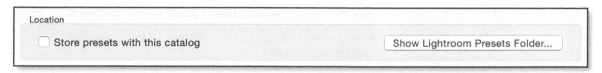

On OS X, the user Library folder is hidden by default. If you go to Finder, select the *Go menu*, and hold down the Opt key, you'll see Library appear in the menu, and then you can navigate to the Preferences or Application Support folder. Personally, I drag that Library folder to the sidebar so that it's always easily accessible.

The default location of the Presets is...

Windows—C: \ Users \ [your username] \ AppData \ Roaming \ Adobe \ Lightroom \

Mac—Macintosh HD / Users / [your username] / Library / Application Support / Adobe / Lightroom /

If you've checked the *Store presets with this catalog* checkbox in Preferences, they'll be stored next to your catalog file instead.

To find them easily on either platform, go to *Edit menu* (Windows) / *Lightroom menu* (Mac) > *Preferences* > *Presets tab* and press the *Show Lightroom Presets Folder* button. **(Figure 22.19)**

Each type of preset has its own folder, for example Develop Presets, Filename Templates and Metadata Presets. **(Figure 22.20)**

Presets are cross-platform and are saved in a Lightroom-only format (.lrtemplate). They're just text files with a different extension, so you can open them in any plain text editor.

Your Develop Defaults, Lens Defaults and Custom Point Curves are stored at...

Windows—C: \ Users \ [your username] \ AppData \ Roaming \ Adobe \ CameraRaw \

Mac—Macintosh HD / Users / [your username] / Library / Application Support / Adobe / CameraRaw /

Your Develop default settings, lens defaults and custom point curves are shared with ACR, so they're stored in the shared location, regardless of your *Store presets with this catalog* checkbox setting.

▲ **Figure 22.19** Press the *Show Lightroom Presets Folder* button in Preferences to easily find the presets.

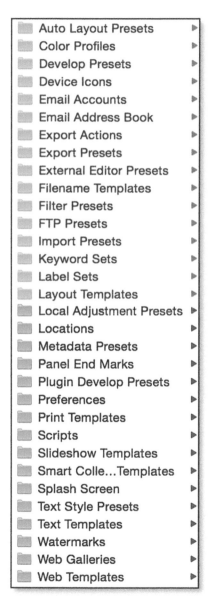

▲ **Figure 22.20** Presets are sorted into folders according to their type.

The default location of the Camera Raw Cache is...

Windows—C: \ Users \ [your username] \ AppData \ Local \ Adobe \ CameraRaw \ Cache \

Mac—Macintosh HD / Users / [your username] / Library / Caches / Adobe Camera Raw /

Your custom Camera & Lens Profiles should be installed to the User folders...

Lightroom no longer uses the shared ProgramData (Windows) / Application Support (Mac) folders for Camera or Lens Profiles. Instead, it stores the built-in profiles with its program files.

When you create camera or lens profiles, they must be stored in the user locations listed below. If you previously stored custom profiles in other locations, you'll need to move them to these user folders, otherwise Lightroom won't be able to find them.

Windows—C: \ Users \ [your username] \ AppData \ Roaming \ Adobe \ CameraRaw \ CameraProfiles \

Mac—Macintosh HD / Users / [your username] / Library / Application Support / Adobe / CameraRaw / CameraProfiles /

For the lens profiles, substitute the *LensProfiles* folder for the *CameraProfiles* folder in these paths.

The camera and lens profile file extensions are:

.dcpr—camera profile recipe file used for creating/editing a profile in the DNG Profile Editor

.dcp—camera profile

.lcp—lens profile

Preferences & Settings Menu Locations

A few of the menu commands are in different locations on Windows and Mac, depending on the operating system standard. Rather than repeating them every time I refer to Preferences or Catalog Settings, here's a quick reference:

Lightroom Preferences & Catalog Settings are...

Windows—under the *Edit menu*

Mac—under the *Lightroom menu*

PREFERENCES SHORTCUTS

Preferences	Ctrl , / Cmd ,
Catalog Settings	Ctrl Alt , / Cmd Opt ,

Photoshop Preferences are...

Windows—under the *Edit menu*

Mac—under the *Photoshop menu*

IMPROVING PERFORMANCE

Working with Lightroom isn't like working with Photoshop or Elements, and the hardware requirements are different. In Photoshop or Elements, you'll usually be working with one or a few photos at a time, whereas with Lightroom, you work with much larger numbers of photos. Besides buying a fast new computer, there are some speed tips which can help Lightroom run much more smoothly.

How can I get Lightroom to import faster?

Lightroom's import speed depends on three things:

- **Where the files are coming from**—Importing using a card reader is usually faster than importing directly from the camera, particularly if you buy a good quality card reader with a fast connection. Importing directly from the hard drive is obviously faster still.

- **The settings you choose in the Import dialog**—Setting the Import dialog to *Add photos to catalog without moving* is quicker than one of the *Copy* options, as Lightroom's not having to duplicate the files (but be careful to only use *Add* for files on your hard drive, and not those on memory cards).

- **The destination**—If you're copying or moving the files, sending them to a fast local drive is faster than copying them across a slow network, of course.

How can I speed up browsing in the Library module?

If you're browsing in the Library module, your choice of pre-rendered preview size can make major improvements in the speed. There's a

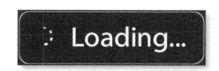

▲ **Figure 22.21** The Loading overlay can be very frustrating when you're in a hurry!

big difference between building previews that have never been built or that need updating, and loading ready-built previews from disk.

If the Loading overlay stays on the screen for a long time, Lightroom's likely building a preview for the first time, updating an old existing preview, or building a larger preview for your current zoom ratio—and you're having to wait for it! **(Figure 22.21)**

You can build the Library previews in advance in two ways:

- **Build on import**—Select Standard or 1:1 previews in the Build Previews pop-up in the File Handling panel of the Import dialog.

- **Build/Update for existing photos**—Switch to Grid view, select the photos and go to *Library menu > Previews > Build Standard-Sized Previews* or *Build 1:1 Previews*, and leave it until it's finished. This skips any photos that already have current previews, and you'll find browsing much quicker once it's finished rendering.

Remember to pick the best preview size for your needs:

- **Not Zooming**—If you're viewing at Fit/Fill size, build Standard Sized previews. Set the preview size to *Auto* in *Catalog Settings > File Handling tab* or turn back to the Previews section for a refresher.

- **Zooming In**—If you're zooming in the Library module (not Develop), you need 1:1 size previews. If you rarely zoom in the Library module, you're better off using Standard-Sized previews, as they'll take up less disc space and be slightly quicker to read from the preview cache.

Each time you make Develop changes, the rendered previews have to be updated. If you've made Develop changes to the photos, for example, by applying a preset, and you don't want to wait for the previews to update one at a time as you browse through them, use the same *Library menu > Previews > Build Standard-Sized Previews* command to update all the previews in one go. Once it's finished, Lightroom should run much more smoothly. You can see the full decision tree on **Figure 22.22**.

There's one other thing that can affect the speed of loading the previews, and that's the speed of the drive containing the catalog and previews. Storing these files on a SSD is significantly quicker than a 5400rpm drive.

How can I speed up opening photos in the Develop module?

Whereas the Library module displays lower quality rendered previews from the previews cache, the Develop module assumes you

Preview Loading Logic in the Library module

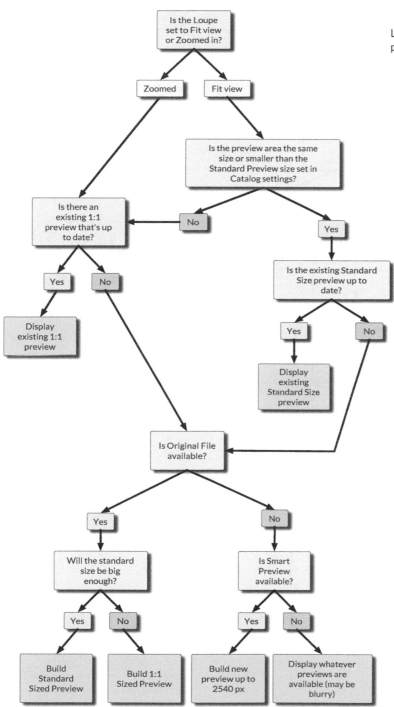

◀ **Figure 22.22** The decision tree Lightroom uses when deciding which preview to load in the Library module.

Preview Loading Logic in the Develop module

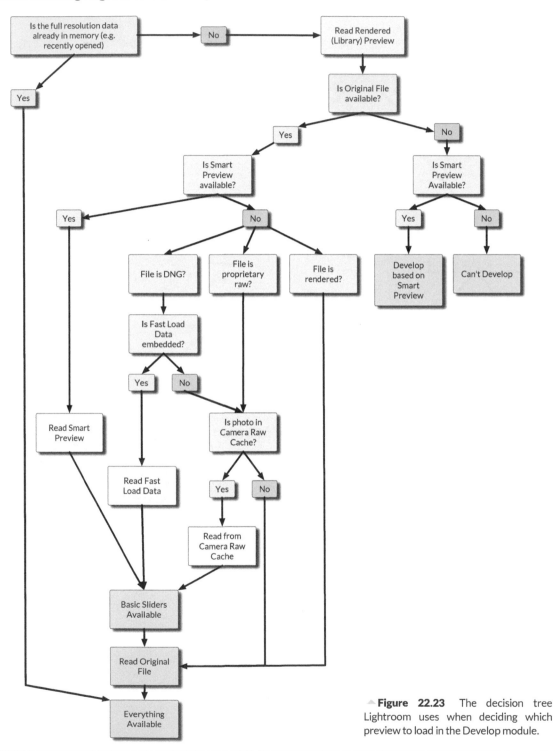

▲ **Figure 22.23** The decision tree Lightroom uses when deciding which preview to load in the Develop module.

need an accurate, rapidly changing view. It first displays the normal preview from Lightroom's main preview cache (if GPU is disabled), then it reads any existing cached data, makes the Basic sliders available for adjustment, and then finishes loading and processing the full resolution data. You can see the full decision process on **Figure 22.23**.

As a result, there are a few things that can affect the Develop loading speed:

- **Existing standard preview**—Having a current standard preview displays the photo slightly quicker, but only if the GPU is disabled.

- **Catalog drive speed**—The speed of the drive containing the catalog and previews can slightly affect loading speed in the Develop module.

- **Existing cached data**—Having partially processed data in the Camera Raw Cache, DNG Fast Load Data or Smart Previews makes it quicker to activate the sliders. We'll come back to these caches shortly.

- **Cache drive speed**—The speed of the drive containing the cached data affects how fast it can be read.

- **File drive speed**—The speed of the drive containing the images affects how fast that data can be read. There's a notable difference between files stored on an SSD or fast RAID vs. those stored on a network drive or slow external drive.

- **Computer processing power**—Once the data's been read from the disc, it still has to be processed, and this is primarily reliant on the speed of your CPU.

- **GPU Setting**—Enabling the GPU performance mode slows down the initial load time, as the data has to be passed from the CPU to GPU, although once it's there, the interactive performance is smoother.

You don't have to wait for the Loading overlay to disappear before starting work on the photo. If you find the overlay distracting, you can turn it off by going to the *View menu > View Options > Loupe tab* and turning off the ***Show message when loading or rendering photos*** checkbox.

There are so many different kinds of previews & caches— which ones do I need?

There are multiple kinds of previews and caches, and it can be difficult to track which ones are used in different areas of Lightroom.

Here's a quick summary of their main uses:

- **Standard-sized rendered previews** are used in all of Lightroom's modules to some degree. (The standard previews are actually a preview pyramid, with lots of different sized previews, from large ones right down to thumbnails.)

- **1:1 rendered previews** are primarily useful for zooming in to 1:1 (i.e. checking focus) in Library module or Draft Mode printing.

- **Smart Previews** (2560px long edge) are mainly used in place of original files when the originals are offline, but they can also help speed up Develop loading time.

- **ACR Cache**, or Camera Raw Cache, temporarily holds partially processed fast load data (1024px long edge) for the most recently accessed raw files, and is used in Develop to speed up loading times.

- **Fast Load DNG's** holds the same partially processed fast load data (1024px long edge) as the ACR Cache, but it's contained in DNG files permanently, whereas the ACR Cache is temporary. It's only available for DNG files, and you can learn more about these in the Appendix starting on page A-1.

In the Multi-Computer chapter on page 513, there's a table showing which previews are used for different tasks when the photos are offline, but let's consider their effect on performance too.

In Library module, your main decisions are the size of the Standard preview and whether you need to build 1:1 previews ready to zoom in the Library module.

In Develop module, you can also decide which kind of cached data suits your workflow.

Your cache options primarily depend on your file format:

- **Rendered files (JPEG, TIFF, PSD, PNG)**—Smart Previews only. In most cases, rendered files don't need caching, but it may be helpful for large TIFF's and PSD files.

- **Proprietary raw files**—Smart Previews vs. Camera Raw Cache

- **DNG files**—Smart Previews vs. Camera Raw Cache (for DNG's that don't include Fast Load Data) or DNG Fast Load Data (for DNG's that do contain it).

If you already use Smart Previews for an offline workflow, then Lightroom uses the smart preview automatically and you don't need to debate any further. If you don't use Smart Previews for offline use, then there are a couple of other factors to consider for raw/DNG files.

The speed of reading any of the cached data (Smart Previews, DNG Fast Load Data or Camera Raw Cache data) is very similar, depending primarily on the speed of the drive on which they're stored. For example, Smart Previews are stored with your catalog, which may be on a fast SSD drive, whereas your DNG files might be on a slower external drive.

Finally, there's the question of whether the photos are still in the cache when you next need them. Smart Previews are retained until you choose to discard them, and DNG Fast Load Data is stored indefinitely, whereas the Camera Raw Cache is a temporary cache. Only the most frequently viewed photos are stored in the Camera Raw Cache, although you can choose the size of the cache (and therefore the number of photos held in it).

As a rule of thumb, for most photographers the Camera Raw Cache is ideal, particularly if it's pre-loaded and enlarged to hold a larger number of photos. However, if you often go back to work on much older photos, which would no longer be held in that cache, or you work on multiple machines, consider using Smart Previews or DNG Fast Load Data instead.

How do I get the greatest benefit from the Camera Raw Cache, a.k.a. the ACR Cache?

When Lightroom reads the raw data, it adds it into the shared Camera Raw cache in a partially processed state, with the initial demosaic and other background work already done. They're stored as Cache*.dat files. When you load a raw photo into the Develop module, it first checks this cache to see if the data is already there to reuse, which is much quicker than reading and processing the original raw file data. The cache isn't used for rendered files (JPEG/TIFF/PSD) as they don't need this early stage processing. When you choose to store Fast Load Data with DNG files, it stores that same partially processed data, so they aren't added to the Camera Raw cache either, but these Fast Load DNG's show the same performance benefits as long as they're stored on a fast drive.

By default, the Camera Raw cache is only 1 GB in size, and when new data is added, the oldest data is removed. At 1 GB, it holds around 2000 photos of your most recently viewed photos, on average. If

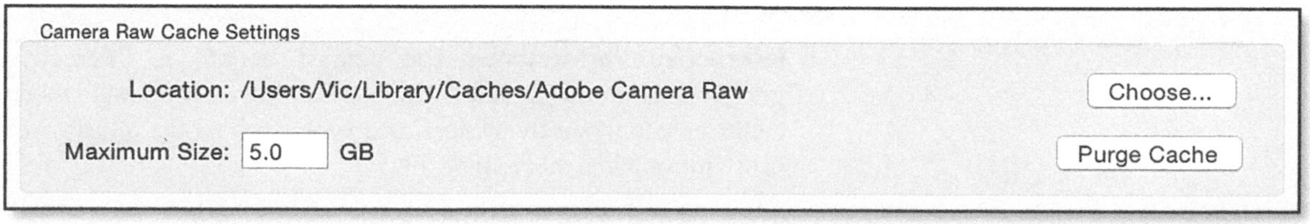

▼ **Figure 22.24** Set the *Camera Raw Cache* size in Lightroom's preferences.

Camera Raw Cache Settings

Location: /Users/Vic/Library/Caches/Adobe Camera Raw   Choose...

Maximum Size: [5.0] GB   Purge Cache

you go to Lightroom's *Preferences > File Handling tab* (**Figure 22.24**), you can change the cache size to suit—up to a maximum of 200 GB. In the past, bigger was better, however the cache format changed for Lightroom 3.6 and later (and ACR 6.6 and later), with JPEG compression being applied to the cached data. This means that the cache files are significantly smaller, now measuring hundreds of KB's instead of MB's. You can now fit a lot more cached images into the same amount of space, so it no longer needs to be as large. You can also change the location of this cache, but make sure it's on a fast hard drive. The Camera Raw cache settings that you change in Lightroom also apply to ACR in Bridge/Photoshop, and can be changed in the ACR Preferences dialog too.

Once this data's cached, it's a bit faster doing the initial load in the Develop module and the sliders freeing up so you can start working—almost instantaneous on high end machines if the GPU is disabled—although the Loading overlay may still show on screen while it does further processing. You'll notice the most significant difference on very large files, or those with significant amounts of initial processing. Of course, that's only helpful when Lightroom has recently read the raw file, and added it to the cache, and there isn't currently a menu command to pre-load the Camera Raw cache. All is not lost!

There's a trick to pre-loading the Camera Raw cache. In addition to actually viewing the photo in the Develop module, there's another time when Lightroom has to read, and therefore caches, the raw data—namely, when building previews. If you haven't already rendered previews for your photos, simply using the *Library menu > Build Standard-Sized Previews* command also pre-loads the photos into the Camera Raw cache. Leave it to finish, and by the time you come back, even the Develop module should be moving through the photos at a much more comfortable speed.

Should I enable the GPU to speed up interactive performance?

In Lightroom's Preferences dialog, there's a new *Performance* tab with a single checkbox—***Use Graphics Processor***. (**Figure 22.25**) Extra performance is always a good thing, so you should leave it turned on, right? It's not quite so clear cut as that. Using the graphics processor or GPU has pros and cons.

- **Interactive Performance**—The biggest benefit is interactive performance in the Develop module. The preview updates much faster as you move the sliders, and tools such as the adjustment brush move much more smoothly.

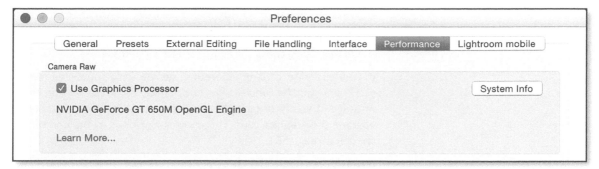

- **High resolution screens**—The higher the resolution of the screen, the greater the improvement, so it makes a world of difference on a 4K or 5K display.

- **Slower loading times**—The biggest downside is it takes a little extra time to pass the data from the CPU to the GPU, so there's a slight delay in initially the loading the photo.

- **Intermittent blurring**—When you zoom in, it briefly switches to a lower resolution preview before sharpening up again, which can be slightly off-putting.

- **Slower Detail adjustments**—The preview for sharpening, noise reduction and grain is slightly slower to update.

- **Second screen lag**—If you work with the Lightroom's secondary windows open, the lag in updating is more noticeable with the GPU enabled.

- **Buggy drivers**—Some graphics drivers are buggy and may even crash Lightroom with the GPU enabled, so it's important to check the manufacturer's website and install the latest drivers. Some graphics cards have the GPU setting disabled automatically as the drivers are too unstable.

You have to decide which trade-off you're willing to make—is load time or interactive performance more important to you? For most people, the improvement in interactive performance is too good to pass up.

There are some minimum specifications.

- You need to be running Windows 7 or later, or Mac OS 10.9 or later.

- The card needs to support Open GL 3.3 or later, which includes most cards from about 2010/2011 onwards.

- You need to be running recent drivers, especially if you have problems.

Figure 22.25 The *Use Graphics Processor* checkbox in Preferences has pros and cons.

Windows Update often suggests outdated drivers. Check the card manufacturer's website instead.

On Mac OS X, check the App Store for Updates.

If your graphics card or operating system isn't supported, when you check the *Use Graphics Processor* checkbox, it displays an error message. If you're using a Windows computer, you may be able to upgrade the graphics card. There are suggestions at the end of the chapter on page 561.

If you can't enable the GPU, try reducing the size of Lightroom's window, or making the side panels wider so that the image preview is smaller, as the size of the Develop preview has a significant effect on the speed at which the preview updates for each slider movement.

Which Develop slider order is best for performance?

The order of applying Develop adjustments doesn't impact the rendering, except for spot corrections placed on top of each other. However, the order of some adjustments can affect Lightroom's interactive performance.

The best order of operations for improving interactive Develop performance would be:

1. Tonal Adjustments.

2. Spot Healing.

3. Lens Corrections (Profile, Manual sliders, Upright, etc.).

4. Local Corrections (Adjustment Brush, Graduated Filter, Radial Filter).

Most sliders, for example, the Basic sliders, can be adjusted at any time without negatively affecting performance, although you may find that disabling noise reduction helps increase performance slightly.

Some operations are more processor intensive than others, for example, local adjustments, spot removal, lens corrections and noise reduction involve complex calculations. *Auto Mask* on the Adjustment Brushes is another heavily processor intensive task, which can bring even fast machines to a crawl if used extensively. If you're struggling for speed, local adjustments and retouching may be easier in a pixel editor such as Photoshop.

It's taking forever to delete photos—should it really take this long?

Deleting files within Lightroom can take a bit longer than deleting directly in Explorer (Windows) / Finder (Mac), while it finds and deletes previews and updates the catalog too, but it shouldn't be a vast difference. If you're finding it slow, there are a few things you can do to help.

Empty your Recycle Bin (Windows) / Trash (Mac) regularly, as that's been known to slow deletion significantly, particularly on Windows.

If you're trying to delete photos that you don't want to keep, rather than doing them one at a time, mark them with a reject flag instead, so you can delete them all in one go later without interrupting your workflow.

And finally, if it still doesn't work, rebooting solves most slow delete issues.

I'm buying a new computer—what should I look for?

I'm often asked which computer to buy for Lightroom, and trying to answer this is practically impossible as there are so many variations in components and budget. I can offer some general hardware tips, although they're likely to be out of date almost as soon as I write them.

There's no question, Lightroom loves good hardware. When deciding your budget, consider how many photos you'll be editing each week, and also the size of the files you'll be using.

It can still run on lower specification machines, but if you start trying to feed 20+ megapixel raw files into Lightroom on a minimum specification computer, don't expect it to be fast. If you're going to spend money on the latest cameras, bear in mind that your computer hardware may also require a helping hand to work with these new super-size files.

CPU

If you're looking for a new CPU, a recent generation Intel chip (Sandy Bridge, Haswell or later) is a great choice.

Lightroom does use multiple cores, especially for image processing tasks, so a quad core is a great choice if your budget will stretch. For a high end machine, a six core is currently in a sweet spot between price and performance.

If you're debating between an i5 or i7 chip, hyper threading helps a bit but it's not substantial.

Graphics Cards

On Windows, a mid-range card with 2 GB of RAM is a good choice for most Lightroom users. At the time of writing, these include the AMD R9 2xx series and the Nvidia Geforce GTX 700 or 900 series.

On Macs, the graphics card choices are more limited, but even the integrated IRIS graphics work well if you have enough RAM. If you're buying a new Mac, a discrete graphics card is a good idea for future-proofing, as further performance enhancement is likely in future Lightroom versions.

Memory/RAM

Although Lightroom CC/6's minimum requirements are set to 4 GB of RAM, I'd recommend no less than 8 GB of RAM. If you're buying a new machine and the budget will stretch, consider upgrading to 16 GB (or more for a high end machine).

Fast Drives

As we've seen in this section, drive speed can make a significant difference in Lightroom, but there are some places it's better value than others.

The program and catalog/previews get the most benefit from a fast drive such as an SSD. The program and catalog load faster, bulk metadata updates complete faster, and scrolling through previews is smoother.

Keeping your working photos on reasonably fast storage makes a difference too, especially when building previews, loading in Develop or exporting, among other tasks. As the original files are bigger, SSDs aren't usually cost-effective for holding a large number of files, but 7200rpm internal hard drives or external hard drives on a USB 3/Thunderbolt/eSata connection are faster than standard 5400rpm or network drives.

Screen

Monitor choices are also largely dependent on budget, but IPS screens are generally considered a good choice for photographers. For accurate color, NEC and EIZO are among the best. Don't forget you'll need calibration hardware too.

Is there anything I can do to make Lightroom perform better on my existing computer hardware?

If you can't afford a new computer, there's still plenty you can do to make the best of your current hardware. If your computer isn't too old, you may be able to upgrade specific components, but there are a few other things to try. In no particular order:

- **Optimize Regularly**—If you find Lightroom is feeling a little sluggish, select the *File menu > Optimize Catalog* command to perform database optimization. It's worth doing regularly, and any time you make significant database changes like importing or removing large numbers of photos.

- **Pause Lightroom's background tasks**—Lightroom may be running tasks in the background, such as indexing for face recognition or syncing photos. You can temporarily pause these tasks in the Activity Center, and enable them again when you won't be using the computer.

- **Close extra panels**—The more things that Lightroom has to update, the more work it has to do, and therefore the slower it becomes. Closing the Histogram and Navigator panels and the small preview in the Develop Detail panel can help a little if you're struggling for speed, as can turning off the badges in the Grid view under *View menu > View Options*.

- **Clear History**—If you have a photo with a huge number of steps in the History panel and a limited amount of RAM, clearing history can help.

- **Avoid Auto Sync**—On older machines particularly, tools such as *Auto Sync* force Lightroom to update all the selected thumbnails every time you make a change, whereas using *Sync* to apply all the changes in one pass only has to update the thumbnails once.

- **Don't automatically write to xmp**—Although it's improved greatly since the early Lightroom releases, *Automatically write changes into XMP* in *Catalog Settings > Metadata tab* can slow Lightroom down a little as it constantly writes to the external metadata. If you want to write to XMP but are concerned about a speed hit, wait until you've finished editing and then write to XMP manually.

- **Hard drive space**—Your computer gets slower as you start to run out of space, especially on the boot drive. Aim to keep 25% free if possible.

- **Empty the Recycle Bin/Trash**—While you're tidying up, make sure the Recycle Bin (Windows) / Trash (Mac) are emptied regularly as they can slow down some Lightroom functions even if they're not overflowing.

- **Defragment on Windows**—If you're on Windows, regularly defragment your hard drives.

- **Anti-Virus**—Virus protection constantly scanning the same files that Lightroom's trying to use can slow you down. Consider excluding the catalog (*.lrcat), the previews file (*.lrdata next to the catalog), and the ACR Cache (check the Lightroom Preferences dialog for the location) from the live scan, and perhaps the photos themselves too.

- **Stop background tasks**—The less you have running in the background, the better, particularly on older slower machines, and that includes those little system tray or menu bar programs that load on startup.

There's an official Adobe Tech Note, which may also be of interest, at http://www.Lrq.me/adobespecs

MOBILE SYNC

I n this increasingly connected world, photography is no longer confined to the desktop. Imagine having easy access to your photos everywhere...

You shoot an event with your DSLR, upload it to the desktop and walk away. Later, you're sat on the train and decide to start sorting through the photos using your tablet. You rate them, organize them into collections and even do some initial edits.

While traveling, you capture a photo with your phone, edit it using Lightroom right there on your phone, and post it to social media.

While you're out, you run into a friend or potential customer, and want to share some photos from your portfolio, so you open Lightroom on your tablet, navigate to the collection and start a slideshow. They want to see more, so you email them a link to view the entire collection in their web browser later.

When you return home, the photos taken with your phone have automatically been downloaded to your desktop, complete with your non-destructive edits and all of the other changes you made while you were out. **(Figure 23.1)**

Lightroom is the hub for all of your photos, whether they're shot

▼**Figure 23.1** Lightroom can sync your photos to mobile devices via the Lightroom Sync cloud.

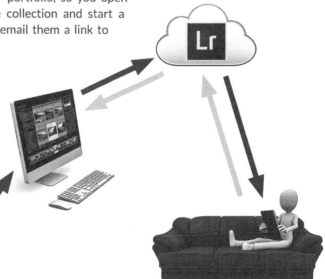

MULTIPLE CATALOGS

Lightroom only syncs a single catalog, so if you have more than one catalog, you'll need to decide which one you're going to use or merge them into a single catalog using the instructions on page 522.

with a traditional camera or with your mobile device. This is the future of photography.

THE CREATIVE CLOUD SUBSCRIPTION

Lightroom on the desktop, on mobile and on the web are all tied together through a Creative Cloud subscription. Unless you need the full range of Adobe Creative Cloud apps, the Photography Bundle is the best choice: http://www.adobe.com/go/photographyplan

At the time of writing, the Photography Bundle costs just $9.99 a month (plus local taxes—prices may vary by location), and it includes:

- The latest version of Lightroom CC, including any updates as they're released.
- The latest version of Photoshop CC, including any updates as they're released.
- 2 GB of Creative Cloud storage space.
- Unlimited Lightroom Sync space (which is the bit we're talking about in this chapter).
- The Lightroom mobile app for iOS and Android, including any updates as they're released.
- Hosted Lightroom Web Galleries.

If you have a perpetual license (serial number), you can use the Creative Cloud trial for 30 days to test sync and decide whether to upgrade to the subscription.

You also need a good web connection to use Lightroom mobile. Lightroom for desktop uploads around 2 MB of data per photo on average, because it's uploading the catalog metadata, a thumbnail, a standard JPEG preview, plus a Smart Preview for editing. That's worth remembering if your bandwidth is limited.

INTERNET SPEED TEST

If you're trying to figure out whether your connection is fast enough to be viable, you can estimate how long Lightroom will take to upload your photos by visiting http://www.speedtest.net Select a server on the US west coast, for example, San Jose. As a guide, a reported upload speed of 0.3 Mbps takes approximately 1 minute per photo.

SETTING UP SYNC

Let's get the desktop set up and syncing to the Lightroom Sync cloud. (We'll refer to a 'desktop' to differentiate between the desktop version of Lightroom and the mobile version, but that can be a desktop or a laptop, PC or Mac.)

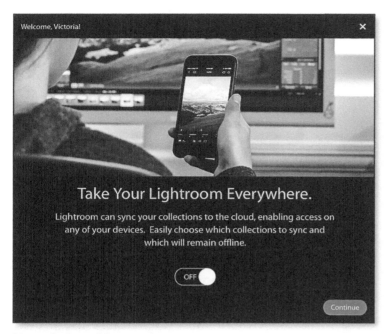

Welcome, Victoria!

Take Your Lightroom Everywhere.

Lightroom can sync your collections to the cloud, enabling access on any of your devices. Easily choose which collections to sync and which will remain offline.

OFF

Continue

Figure 23.2 When you open Lightroom CC/6 for the first time, it asks whether you'd like to enable Sync.

How do I enable sync?

Sync has three possible states:

- **On**—The Sync checkboxes show in the Collections panel and Create/Edit Collection dialogs. Lightroom automatically uploads the checked collections of photos and downloads changes made on mobile devices or the web interface.

- **Paused**—The Sync checkboxes show in the collection dialogs, but nothing is transferred to/from the cloud until sync is enabled. To pause or activate sync, click the pause button in the Activity Center.

- **Off**—The Sync checkboxes are hidden and nothing syncs. To enable it, select Start in the Activity Center.

The first time you open a catalog, Lightroom asks whether you want to enable sync for this catalog. **(Figure 23.2)**

If you select *On*, Sync is enabled but nothing starts happening until you select some collections to sync (unless you already have collections selected for sync in this catalog or you've already created a sync collection on a mobile device). If you've already been syncing another catalog, Lightroom asks whether you want to switch to syncing this catalog—we'll come back to that dialog at the end of the chapter. If in doubt, select *Don't Sync*.

If you select *Off*, Sync is either paused or turned off, depending on whether the catalog has previously been used for sync.

Figure 23.3 If Sync is enabled, the *Sync with Lightroom mobile* checkbox displays in the Create/Edit Collection dialog.

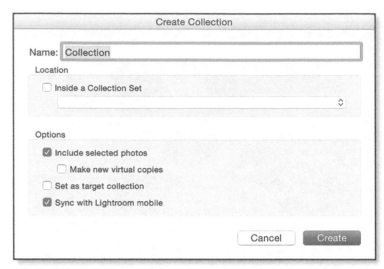

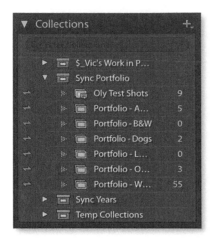

Figure 23.4 When Sync is enabled, the sync icons appear to the left of the collection names.

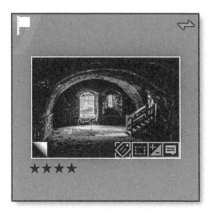

Figure 23.5 The Sync icon appears in the top right corner of the thumbnail if the photo's included in a Sync collection.

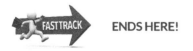 **ENDS HERE!**

How do I choose which photos to sync?

Once you've activated Lightroom Sync, either by selecting *On* in the initial dialog or by later selecting *Start* in the Activity Center, you can start choosing which photos to sync.

The sync is based around standard collections. If you need a refresher, turn back to the Library—Selecting and Grouping chapter starting on page 107 for more details on creating and managing collections.

When you're creating a new collection, check the **Sync with Lightroom mobile** checkbox in the New Collection dialog. **(Figure 23.3)**

If you have existing collections, there are checkboxes on the left in the Collections panel, which enable and disable sync. **(Figure 23.4)** To sync a collection, click in the checkbox and the sync icon appears. To remove the collection from the sync, click again to remove the sync icon. You'll also find a *Sync with Lightroom mobile* checkbox in the Edit Collection dialog.

When you add photos to a sync collection, additional icons appear on the thumbnails in Grid view. **(Figure 23.5)**

- The sync icon simply shows that it's included in a sync collection.

- Three dots below the sync icon means that something's happening to that photo—it's being synced, the metadata's being read or updated, or previews are being rendered.

Can I sync smart collections?

Smart Collections would be ideal for ensuring all of the photos shot in the last 60 days, for example, or all of your 5 star photos sync to

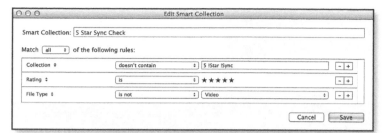

Figure 23.6 Although you can't sync smart collections, you can still use them to check you've included the right photos.

your iPad. Smart Collections can't be synced for numerous reasons, but there are two workarounds.

The simplest option is to create a smart collection alongside the sync collection, and manually drag the photos from the smart collection to the sync collection to add them to the sync.

The alternative is to use a smarter smart collection. Let's use the 5 star photos as an example. Create a collection called "5 Star Sync" and mark it to sync to your iPad. Then create a Smart Collection, set to *Rating equals 5 stars* and *File Type is not video* and *Collection doesn't include 5 !Star !Sync.* **(Figure 23.6)**

The Smart Collection checks for any photos that meet the criteria but aren't in your 5 star photos sync collection. If there are ever photos in that Smart Collection, drag them over to the 5 star photos collection to be included in the sync. If everything's synced, the Smart Collection should be set to 0.

In the Catalog panel, what is *All Synced Photographs*?

When you start syncing, a collection called **All Synced Photographs** is automatically created in the Catalog panel. **(Figure 23.7)** It works in exactly the same way as the *All Photographs* collection, but it only displays photos that are included in a sync collection. Note that deleting photos from this special collection doesn't only remove them from the sync collections, but it also deletes them from the catalog and/or hard drive, just like deleting from *All Photographs*.

How do I check the upload progress?

If you click on the Identity Plate, you can access the Activity Center, where it shows a countdown of the photos currently syncing. **(Figure 23.8)** If it can't connect to the Lightroom Sync cloud, it says *Waiting for Connection* instead.

If you right-click on the Identity Plate, you can choose whether to **Show Status and Activity** on the Identity Plate itself, in addition to the main Activity Center. The *Sync with Lightroom mobile* option is enabled by default. **(Figure 23.9)**

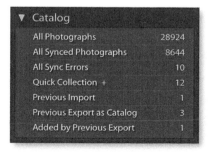

Figure 23.7 The *All Synced Photographs* and *All Sync Errors* collections appear in the Catalog panel.

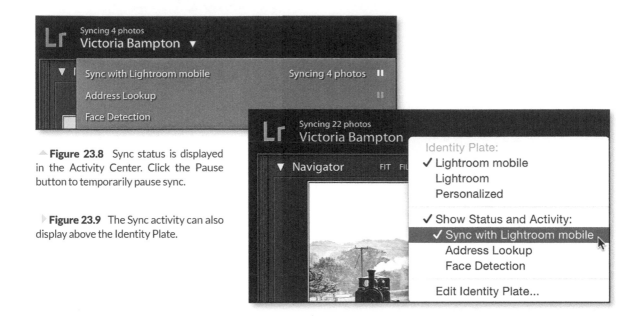

Figure 23.8 Sync status is displayed in the Activity Center. Click the Pause button to temporarily pause sync.

Figure 23.9 The Sync activity can also display above the Identity Plate.

Can I pause syncing?

If you need to pause the sync, perhaps because you need the bandwidth for a higher priority upload, you can pause the sync by clicking the *Sync with Lightroom mobile* pause button in the Activity Center. When you later click again to turn it back on, Lightroom continues uploading from where it left off.

If you close Lightroom while it's syncing, it automatically continues when you next relaunch Lightroom. It asks for confirmation before it quits, just in case you're unaware that the sync hasn't completed.

In the Catalog panel, what is *All Sync Errors* and how do I clear it?

If Lightroom runs into problems syncing, it creates a temporary collection in the Catalog panel called **All Sync Errors**. In many cases, there's a logical reason for the error, for example, if the original photos are offline and smart previews don't currently exist, Lightroom can't sync these photos. The errors usually clear automatically.

SYNC UPDATES

Once you've set up sync, you're ready to access the photos on your phone or tablet.

How do I access my photos on my mobile device?

There are separate apps for iOS and Android, each available for free download from their respective App Stores.

Once the app's installed, follow the instructions to sign in using your Adobe ID. The app automatically starts syncing with the cloud, downloading information about your collections.

The apps are being updated with new features regularly. At the time of writing, features include:

- Browse photos in Grid or Loupe views.

- Add flags and star ratings.

- Filter the photos.

- Apply Develop adjustments using sliders and presets, as well as crop.

- Auto import photos from the mobile device's camera.

- Share your collections

- View comments left by viewers

How do I access my photos in a web browser?

You can also access your photos through any web browser by visiting http://lightroom.adobe.com/ If you sign in using your Adobe ID, you can access all of your photos and even apply some edits such as star rating and flags. Like the mobile apps, new features are being added constantly, so the list of features would be out of date the day I wrote it!

How do I share my web galleries with others?

If you right-click on a collection on the desktop and choose **Lightroom mobile Links**, you can select **Make Collection Public**. This makes the collection accessible to other people, but only if they have the secret link. The link is displayed at the top of the Grid view, or you can select **Copy Public Link** in the same right-click menu to copy it to the clipboard. You can make a collection public from the mobile apps or the web browsers too.

When someone clicks on the secret link, they can view the photos in Grid or Loupe view and leave Likes and Comments on the photos, but they have much more limited access than your own gallery view.

MOBILE APP EBOOKS

The mobile apps are simple to use, but there are plenty of hidden features. You could discover many of them on your own, but allow me to save you some time and share some of the insider secrets and power user tips with you.

I've published separate books for iPhone/iPad and Android because the apps have operating system specific features, and new features are added at different times. They're available from http://www.lightroomqueen.com/shop

---

Figure 23.10 The collection icon adds a small speech bubble when there are comments, and it turns orange when the comments are new.

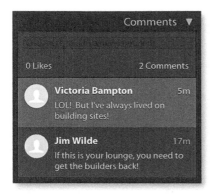

Figure 23.11 Comments made on the web interface are synced back to the Comments panel on the desktop.

How do I see my friends comments?

When someone comments on your photos, a little yellow icon appears on the collection on the desktop. The quickest way to find the latest comments is to select the *Last Comment Time* sort order from the *Sort By* pop-up on the Toolbar. The thumbnails themselves display a yellow comment badge, which turns gray when you've selected the photo. **(Figure 23.10)**

The comments are displayed in the Comments panel, at the bottom of the right panel group, and if you click in the field at the top, you can reply to the comments too. **(Figure 23.11)**

The comments are also accessible from the mobile apps and the web interface.

How do I access the changes I made on my mobile device or web galleries?

As you make changes on the mobile devices, they're synced back to the cloud, and when you next open your desktop, they're automatically synced back down to your desktop catalog.

Where are the photos I uploaded to my mobile device?

When you add photos to Lightroom using your mobile device or upload them using the website, they're uploaded to the Lightroom Sync server and then down to your desktop catalog, where it stores them in a special folder (Windows) /package file (Mac) on your computer. The full folder path is:

Windows—C: \ Users \ [your username] \ My Pictures \ Lightroom \ Mobile Downloads.lrdata

Mac—Macintosh HD / Users / [your username] / Pictures / Lightroom / Mobile Downloads.lrdata

This is a fixed location, regardless of where you store your catalog, and at the time of writing, you can't change this location.

How do I move my mobile photos into my normal folder structure?

When you get back to the desktop and the sync has completed successfully, it's worth moving the uploaded photos to your normal photo folders, as the default location may not be included in your photo backups.

1. Go to *Library menu > New Folder* and create a folder with the rest of your photos, called *My Mobile Photos* or suchlike.

2. In the Folders panel, find the mobile device volume. It might be the name of your phone, for example, mine is called *Victoria's iPhone*, or it might say *Other Lightroom mobile device*.

3. Click the disclosure triangle to view the contents if the volume is closed, and then click on the *Imported Photos* folder to view the photos.

4. Using Grid view, select the photos and drag them to your newly created *My Mobile Photos* folder in your normal photo folder. You'll need to drag them by their thumbnails, not the surrounding borders, otherwise they won't move.

You'll need to repeat the process whenever you add new photos on the mobile device, or plan to do it every week or two.

If you're comfortable moving photos around within Lightroom, they don't have to go into a folder called *My Mobile Photos*. You can filter the photos by date to drag them into your dated folder structure, or move them into any other folders of your choice. If you usually select *Make a Second Copy* in the Import dialog, don't forget that these photos won't be included in these temporary backups.

What happens if the same photo changes on the desktop and mobile device while they're offline, creating a conflict?

With many syncing situations, it's possible to end up with conflicts, where the same photo has changed in both locations at the same time, or while they're both offline.

Lightroom resolves these conflicts automatically. If a setting's changed on both the desktop and the mobile device while they're offline, the latest change wins. For example, if you change the flag status on one device, and Develop settings on the other device, both changes will be updated. If you change the flag status on both devices, whichever change was made last is the setting that sticks.

When Lightroom updates the Develop settings from the mobile sync, it adds a *From Lightroom mobile* history state to the History panel.

What happens with sync if I revert to a backup catalog?

If you need to revert to a backup catalog, but the backup is recent, Lightroom uses that same conflict resolution to update the settings

▸**Figure 23.12** If you restore a backup catalog, you may need to reset sync.

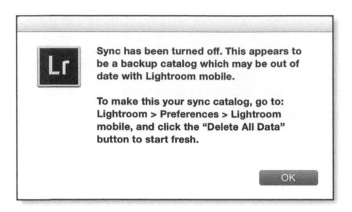

for the sync photos. Lightroom recognizes it as the same catalog and compares it against the cloud data.

If you've added or removed photos from sync collections since you created the backup, either on the desktop or on a mobile device, Lightroom warns that the backup is too old and it automatically disables sync. **(Figure 23.12)**

To enable sync again, go to Lightroom's Preferences dialog, which is under the *Edit menu* (Windows) / *Lightroom menu* (Mac). Select the Lightroom mobile panel and press the *Delete All Data* button. This resets the sync, deleting the sync information from your computer, the Lightroom Sync cloud, and later the mobile devices. It doesn't delete your catalog or photos from your computer, but it does mean you'll have to upload/download all of the data again. It's a good reason to back up regularly!

What happens if I want to sync a different catalog?

You can only have one Lightroom catalog syncing with your Lightroom Sync account at a time. If you enable sync in a different catalog, Lightroom asks whether you want to switch to syncing this new catalog.

If you select **Switch to Syncing This Catalog**, Lightroom removes the previous catalog from the cloud and uploads the new one. When you next open Lightroom on your mobile device, the old sync data is removed and the new catalog data is downloaded. Any data that hasn't finished syncing before switching is lost. **(Figure 23.13)**

If you select **Don't Sync** in this dialog, the sync on the new catalog is automatically disabled and your existing catalog carries on as normal.

While there's nothing to stop you repeatedly switching catalogs, repeatedly wiping data from the cloud and reuploading everything, it

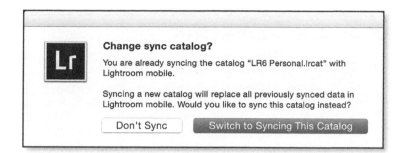

Figure 23.13 Lightroom can only sync one catalog at a time. If you need to sync another catalog, click *Switch to Syncing This Catalog*. This wipes any existing synced data.

takes a lot of time and bandwidth. Sticking to a single catalog is much, much simpler.

What happens to the sync data if I use Export as Catalog or Import from Another Catalog?

If you use Export as Catalog or Import from Another Catalog to transfer data between catalogs, the Sync Collection checkmarks are not transferred. All of the settings that have already been synced are, of course, transferred into the new catalog and the photos can then be added to sync collections.

How do I completely disable sync?

If you decide to stop syncing, click the pause button in the Activity Center, then go to Lightroom's Preferences and select the *Lightroom mobile tab*. Pressing the **Delete All Data** button clears all of the sync data from the catalog and Adobe's servers, and turns Lightroom Sync off.

REGISTER YOUR BOOK FOR ADDITIONAL BENEFITS

By registering your copy of this book, you gain access to additional benefits absolutely free—and who doesn't like free?!

The benefits include:

- **Premium Membership**, which gives you access to the book contents from any web browser, among other features.

- **Downloads**—access to the eBook downloads (PDF, ePub and Mobi/Kindle).

- **Updates** to your version of the book (LRCC 2015 / Lightroom 6) in the Members Area.

- **Discounts** on future book purchases.

- **Priority Email**—personal Lightroom support for your book's Lightroom version (CC 2015/ Lightroom 6) if you use the LRCC/6 Premium Email Support form in the Members Area at http://www.Lrq.me/lr6-contact.

To register your book, I need:

- **Proof of Purchase** – your confirmation email, shipping confirmation, a scan/photograph of the packing slip, or a screenshot of the order confirmation on Amazon's website – I need to be able to read the order number and order date.

- The **book reference** code: **LRCC6LGH29M**

If you purchased the book direct from http://www.lightroomqueen.com, you'll already be registered, and you should have received your Members Area login details by email shortly after ordering. If you haven't received your login details, just ask.

Send them via:

- Book Registration form at http://www.Lrq.me/newticket (that's LRQ.ME/NEWTICKET)

- or email them to members@lightroomqueen.com

What happens next:

I'll personally upgrade your Members Area account to Premium Membership and send you the login details, usually within 48 hours. You can then log into the Members Area at http://lightroomqueen.com/members to access the downloads, updates and priority email form.

INDEX

The index references starting with A or B refer to Appendix A or B, which are only available in the eBook formats.